Seeing More

Seeing More

Kant's Theory of Imagination

SAMANTHA MATHERNE

Great Clarendon Street, Oxford, OX2 6DP,
United Kingdom

Oxford University Press is a department of the University of Oxford.
It furthers the University's objective of excellence in research, scholarship,
and education by publishing worldwide. Oxford is a registered trade mark of
Oxford University Press in the UK and in certain other countries

© Samantha Matherne 2024

The moral rights of the author have been asserted

All rights reserved. No part of this publication may be reproduced, stored in
a retrieval system, or transmitted, in any form or by any means, without the
prior permission in writing of Oxford University Press, or as expressly permitted
by law, by licence or under terms agreed with the appropriate reprographics
rights organization. Enquiries concerning reproduction outside the scope of the
above should be sent to the Rights Department, Oxford University Press, at the
address above

You must not circulate this work in any other form
and you must impose this same condition on any acquirer

Published in the United States of America by Oxford University Press
198 Madison Avenue, New York, NY 10016, United States of America

British Library Cataloguing in Publication Data
Data available

Library of Congress Control Number: 2023948940

ISBN 9780198898283

DOI: 10.1093/9780191999291.001.0001

The manufacturer's authorised representative in the EU for product safety is
Oxford University Press España S.A., Parque Empresarial San Fernando de Henares,
Avenida de Castilla, 2 – 28830 Madrid (www.oup.es/en).

Links to third party websites are provided by Oxford in good faith and
for information only. Oxford disclaims any responsibility for the materials
contained in any third party website referenced in this work.

For my friends:
for "the comfort" of "having neither to weigh thoughts nor measure words"

Contents

Acknowledgments	ix
Citation Notes	xi
Abbreviations	xiii
Introduction	1

PART I IMAGINATION IN GENERAL

1. Imagination as a Cognitive Capacity	33
2. Imagination and the Two Stems of Cognition	50
3. Imagination Is Part of Sensibility	68
4. Three Definitions of Imagination	101

PART II IMAGINATION IN PERCEPTION AND EXPERIENCE

5. Empirical Imagination in Perception and Experience	131
6. *A Priori* Imagination and the Conditions of Experience I: The Transcendental Deduction	177
7. *A Priori* Imagination and the Conditions of Experience II: The Schematism	212

PART III IMAGINATION IN AESTHETICS

8. Imagination and the Appreciation of Beauty	249
9. Artistic Imagination	282
10. Imagination and the Sublime	299

viii CONTENTS

PART IV IMAGINATION IN PRACTICAL AGENCY AND MORALITY

11. The Possibility of Moral Imagination	325
12. Imaginative Sight and the Faculty of Desire	334
13. Imaginative Exhibition in Morality	353
Conclusion	391
Bibliography	393
Index	425

Acknowledgments

I first started sketching this book in 2018. For all the solitary hours of writing since, there have also been countless hours of conversation and community, without which I never would have reached the end.

Imagine, if you will, all of the people who have read or heard parts of this book and given me invaluable feedback: R. Lanier Anderson, Christopher Benzenberg, Angela Breitenbach, Taylor Carman, David Cerbone, Yoon Choi, Alix Cohen, Leonard Feldblyum, Naomi Fisher, Marcela Garcia, Stefanie Grüne, Paul Guyer, Sean Kelly, Katharina Kraus, David Landy, James Messina, Irene McMullin, Alexandra Newton, Karen Ng, Karin Nisenbaum, Thomas Pendlebury, Julia Peters, Andrew Roche, Michael Rosen, Francey Russell, Joseph Schear, Janum Sethi, Nicholas Stang, Andrew Stephenson, David Suarez, Daniel Sutherland, Jessica Williams, Mark Wrathall, and the students in my Phil 229 Seminar in Spring 2019.

Imagine, too, all the people who patiently read the whole and helped me make it better: Lucy Allais, Mavis Biss, Nicholas Dunn, Thomas Land, Colin Marshall, Colin McLear, Kenneth Walden, Eric Watkins, Reed Winegar, and two anonymous referees at Oxford. This was made possible, in part, through support provided by the Philosophy Department and Provostial Funds at Harvard.

Finally picture the people who have seen me through, parts and whole, as I have written this. My Santa Cruz Lot: Vilashini Cooppan, Jennifer Derr, Renee Fox, Jody Greene, and Marc Matera. My Cambridge Lot: Eram Alam, Jeff Behrends, L.P. Hodgson, Emmanuelle Humblet, Gina Schouten, Frank and Rudy Schouten-Behrends, and Susanna Siegel. My Far-Flung Philosophical Lot: Crista Farrell, Alex King, and Nick Riggle. And my Familial Lot: Aimée Baker; Carolena, Carlos, and Gus Carmona-Ernst; Christine Catania; and Elizabeth and Roman Matherne.

How fortunate am I? Thank you, everyone.

Citation Notes

I cite Kant's texts by the volume and page number in the Academy Edition, Kant's *Gesammelte Schriften* (Berlin: de Gruyter and predecessors, 1900–) with the exception of the *Critique of Pure Reason* (Kant 1998a), which I cite in the standard A/B format to refer to the 1781/7 editions. Unless otherwise noted, italics and bold are in the original.

The quotation in the dedication is from Dinah Craik's *A Life for a Life, Volume II* (1859).

Abbreviations

AB	*Anthropology Busolt* (in Kant 2012b)
AC	*Anthropology Collins* (in Kant 2012b)
AF	*Anthropology Friedländer* (in Kant 2012b)
AMr	*Anthropology Mrongovius* (in Kant 2012b)
Anthro.	*Anthropology from a Pragmatic Point of View* (Kant 2007)
AP	*Anthropology Parow* (in Kant 2012b)
APill	*Anthropology Pillau* (in Kant 2012b)
BL	*Blomberg Logic* (in Kant 1992a)
Br.	*Correspondence* (Kant 1999)
DWL	*Dohna-Wundlacken Logic* (in Kant 1992a)
EC	*Collins's Moral Philosophy* (in Kant 1997b)
EE	"First Introduction" to the *Critique of the Power of Judgment* (in Kant 2000)
Gr.	*Groundwork of the Metaphysics of Morals* (Kant 2012a)
ID	*Concerning the Form and Principles of the Sensible and Intelligible World—* "Inaugural Dissertation" (in Kant 1992b)
JL	*Jäsche Logic* (in Kant 1992a)
KPM	*Kant and the Problem of Metaphysics* (Heidegger 1990)
KpV	*Critique of Practical Reason* (Kant 1997a)
KU	*Critique of the Power of Judgment* (Kant 2000)
Lbl	*Lose Blätter* in *Notes and Fragments*
MAM	"Conjectural Beginning of Human History" (in Kant 2007)
MD	*Metaphysik Dohna* (in Kant 1997c)
Mensch.	*Menschenkunde* (in Kant 2012b)
MN	*Metaphysical Foundations of Natural Science* (in Kant 2002)
ML1	*Metaphysics L1* (in Kant 1997c)
ML2	*Metaphysics L2* (in Kant 1997c)
MMr	*Metaphysics Mrongovius* (in Kant 1997c)
MS	*The Metaphysics of Morals* (in Kant 1996a)
MVo	*Metaphysics Volckmann* (in Kant 1997c)
OKT	"On Kästner's Treatises" (Kant 2014)
OP	*Opus Postumum* (Kant 1993)
PIK	*Phenomenological Interpretation of Kant's Critique of Pure Reason* (Heidegger 1997)
Prol.	*Prolegomena to Any Future Metaphysics That Will Be Able to Come Forward as Science* (Kant 1997d)
R	*Notes and Fragments*—"Reflections" (in Kant 2005)

Rel.	*Religion within the Boundaries of Mere Reason* (Kant 1998b)
Streit	"Conflict of the Faculties" (in Kant 1996b)
Tr.	"Dreams of a Spirit-Seer" (in Kant 2002)
VL	*Vienna Logic* (in Kant 1992a)
WF	"What Real Progress Has Metaphysics Made in Germany since the Time of Leibniz and Wolff?" (in Kant 2002)

the "productive imagination" led to
that "difference...between seeing and seeing"
...all "sensible" seeing is always already
a "seeing with the eyes of spirit."
  —Ernst Cassirer, *The Philosophy of Symbolic Forms*, Volume 3, 1929

What counts here—first and last—is not so-called knowledge
of so-called facts, but vision—seeing.
Seeing here implies <u>Schauen</u> (as in <u>Weltanschauung</u>) and is coupled
with fantasy, with imagination.
                    —Josef Albers, *Interaction of Color*, 1963

Imagination! who can sing thy force?
                    —Phillis Wheatley, "On Imagination," 1773

Introduction

> Imagination...is the most necessary of all our powers
> —AMr 25:1261

How imaginative are we? It is perhaps tempting to answer: not very. Imagining seems to involve engaging with things that are not real or absent. But we spend most of our time in the grip of what is real and present: the world around us, people in front of us, and tasks at hand. Though we no doubt find imaginative escapes from these preoccupations, the press of our dailiness would appear to leave little room for us to be imaginative most of the time.

In the philosophical tradition, there is a long-standing precedent for theorizing imagination along precisely these lines, as a capacity for "fantasy," which we exercise only when we transcend what is real and present. Consider, for example, Aristotle's theory of imagination as "phantasia": "imagination [*phantasia*] is different from both perception [*aisthêsis*] and reason [*nous*]...in [imagination], the affection is up to us, whenever we wish (for it is possible to produce something before one's eyes)" (2016, 56).[1] Here, Aristotle suggests that unlike perception and reason that are, in some sense, responsive to factual or rational matters, imagination, as fantasy, allows us to produce whatever "we wish" "before" our "eyes."

We find echoes of this conception of imagination as fantasy in the early modern period.[2] Thomas Hobbes, for instance, says,

> For after the object is removed, or the eye shut, we still see an image of the thing seen...And this is it, the Latines call *Imagination*, from the image made in seeing...But the Greeks call it *Fancy*, which signifies appearance...IMAGINATION therefore is nothing but decaying sense.   (1996, 14)[3]

---

[1] For discussions of Aristotle's theory of imagination, see Wedin (1988); Ferrarin (1995b); Frede (1995); Modrak (2016).

[2] This is not to say that all early modern philosophers define imagination just as a capacity for fantasy. In his *Treatise on Human Nature*, for example, David Hume argues that all conscious mental states ("perceptions") can be divided between "impressions" and "ideas," and that all "ideas" can be divided into "ideas of memory" and "ideas of imagination" (see Book I, Pt. I, §§1–3). He, in turn, divides ideas of imagination into "ideas of fancy" and "ideas of judgment," where the former track "mere fictions" and the latter track beliefs and judgments (see Pt. I, §3). For discussion of Hume's theory of imagination, see Garrett (2008); Cottrell (2015); Dorsch (2016); Costelloe (2018); and Magri (2023).

[3] For discussion of Hobbes's view of imagination, see Lukac de Stier (2011).

2 INTRODUCTION

Meanwhile, Alexander Baumgarten claims that, "I have...the FACULTY OF IMAGINATION [*Phantasian*]. And since my imaginations are perceptions of things that were formerly present, they are perceptions of the senses that, while I imagine, are absent" (2014, 211).[4] For Hobbes and Baumgarten, unlike perception, which involves engaging with objects in their presence, imagination, as fancy or fantasy, involves engaging with objects in their "remove" or "absence."

We find still more variations on this theme in the phenomenological tradition. Edmund Husserl, for one, glosses imagination as "Phantasie" and asserts, "In phantasy...the object itself appears...but it does not appear as present...[I]t is as though it were there, but only as though" (2005, 18).[5] And according to Jean Paul Sartre, "The act of imagination...is a magical act. It is an incantation to make the object of one's thought, the thing one desires, appear...[The] object as imaged is an irreality" (2004, 125).[6] For Husserl and Sartre, then, it is in this orientation toward what is "irreal" and only "as though" that we find what is distinctive of our imaginative activities.

What emerges at these various philosophical junctures is a view of imagination as something that is not beholden to what is real and present in the way our ordinary activities are. Theorized as fantasy, imagination is a capacity through which we, for good or ill, engage with what is not real and absent. But given that we, for good or ill, are usually in the midst of what is real and present, this philosophical view of imagination seems to lend support to the conclusion that we are not imaginative most of the time.

Though prevalent, this more limited view of imagination is precisely not what we find in the philosophy of Immanuel Kant. For Kant, we are as imaginative in our engagement with what is real and present as we are with what is not real and absent. Indeed, on Kant's view, imagination shapes the way in which we "see" (in a broad sense) and we bring this imaginatively textured "sight" to all our encounters, theoretical, aesthetic, and practical alike. It is this Kantian theory of imagination, as something that pervades our lives, that I aim to elucidate in this monograph.

This said, theorizing about imagination is notoriously difficult. There is a dizzying array of mental phenomena that are labeled "imaginative": visualization, make-believe, hallucination, fiction, creativity, dreaming, memory, supposition, empathy, to name but a handful. How are we to account for these phenomena and the relations between them, let alone whether there is anything like "the imagination" that is responsible for all of them?

---

[4] I return to Baumgarten's definition of imagination in Chapter 4.

[5] For discussion of Husserl's view of imagination, see Aldea (2013); Jansen (2016); and the articles in the special issue edited by Aldea and Jansen (2020).

[6] For discussion of Sartre's view of imagination, see Lennon (2015, chap. 3) and Hopkins (2016); and of the relationship between Sartre and Husserl's views, see Wiesing (1996).

INTRODUCTION   3

As if this was not challenging enough, theorizing about imagination in the Kantian framework introduces further difficulties. Kant not only discusses his own dizzying array of imaginative phenomena, empirical and *a priori* included, but also situates his account of imagination in a philosophical system with its own complicated idiom and infrastructure.

Beyond what Kant himself says, there is also a complex reception history surrounding his theory of imagination. According to one line of interpreters, imagination is among the most important topics in Kant's philosophical system. G.W.F. Hegel, for example, sees in Kant's theory of imagination, "what is primary and original," i.e. "reason" or the "In-itself," out of which the dichotomy between our basic sensible and intellectual capacities, "sensibility" (*Sinnlichkeit*) and "understanding" (*Verstand*), emerges (1997, 73). Martin Heidegger, likewise, finds in Kant's theory of imagination an account of the "common but unknown root" out of which sensibility and understanding stem (see KPM 97; PIK 64, 278).[7] And more recently, interpreters have emphasized the crucial mediating role between sense and intellect that imagination plays in Kant's system. In this vein, Fiona Hughes describes imagination as "the mediating faculty *par excellence*" on Kant's view (2007, 130). And Sarah Gibbons says, "imagination mediates between many of the dualisms that Kant employs throughout this work— including those between concepts and intuition, thought and sensibility, spontaneity and passivity, subject and object, and, somewhat more indirectly, nature and freedom" (1994, 2).

Though interpreters such as these underscore the centrality of imagination in Kant's philosophical project,[8] other interpreters treat it as far less significant. Sometimes the topic of imagination is simply neglected. In John McDowell's influential interpretation of Kant in *Mind and World* and *Having the World in View*, for example, imagination gets scant mention.[9] Other times, commentators suggest that though Kant emphasizes imagination, this is bound up with some philosophical missteps that we should aspire to leave behind. Notoriously in the course of defending his own preferred "austere" reading of the first *Critique* in *The*

---

[7] Heidegger here draws on Kant's claim in the introduction to the first *Critique* that, "there are two stems of human cognition, which may perhaps arise from a common but to us unknown root, namely sensibility and understanding, through the first of which objects are given to us, but through the second of which they are thought" (A15/B29). I return to Heidegger's reading in Chapter 2.

[8] Other recent book-length studies that emphasize the importance of imagination in Kant include Makkreel (1990); Freydberg (2005); Kneller (2007); the essays in Thompson (2013); Horstmann (2018); and Villinger (2018).

[9] In *Mind and World*, McDowell mentions imagination in passing in his discussion of Hume (1996, 173, 174 n10) and Nagel (1996, 121–3). And in *Having the World in View* McDowell notes the importance of imagination on Sellars's interpretation of Kant but says that he "cannot go into this here" (2009, 27 n7; though see also 114–17, 124). See also Engstrom (2006) who only mentions imagination in passing at 1726 n27 and Willaschek and Watkins (2020) who do not mention it in their overview of Kant's theory of cognition and knowledge (though they do briefly in (2017, 1726 n27).

4 INTRODUCTION

Bounds of Sense, P.F. Strawson laments Kant's account of imagination as part of his fixation on transcendental psychology:

> What is given in sense alone, in mere receptivity, is one thing; what is made out of it by understanding, the active faculty, with the help of its no less active lieutenant, imagination, the go-between of sense and understanding, is quite another...It is useless to puzzle over the status of these propositions. They belong neither to empirical...psychology nor to an analytic philosophy of mind...They belong to the imaginary subject of transcendental psychology.
>
> (1966, 97)[10]

Far from imagination having a foundational role to play in Kant's system, readers like these treat imagination as something that is, or should be, regarded as peripheral.

Given the topic of this monograph, it should come as no surprise that my sympathies lie with interpreters who recognize imagination as a vital theme in Kant's philosophical system. In this spirit, I argue that across his theoretical, aesthetic, and practical philosophy, Kant defends a systematic theory of imagination, as a capacity to see more, that permeates our lives.[11]

However, more than just defending a reading of Kant, I hope to put forward this theory of imagination as something that has promise still today. Admittedly this aspiration poses challenges of its own. For even if one regards Kant's view of imagination as a resource to draw on in theorizing about imagining now, the distinctive idiom and elaborate philosophical system in which he situates it can seem foreign from a contemporary standpoint. One strategy for dealing with this challenge would be to explore a Kantian account of imagination, rather than Kant's own account, which largely dispenses with his terminology and system.[12] This is not my strategy. I devote most of my efforts to defending an interpretation of Kant's theory of imagination that hews closely to his text and system. Nevertheless, in defending this interpretation of Kant, I aim to be defending a view of imagination that continues to merit serious attention. Though the on-going relevance of this view is something that I can only hope to motivate over

---

[10] Though, see also Strawson's (1974) emphasis on imagination in the context of a Kantian and Humean theory of perception.

[11] Of the commentators who take Kant's theory of imagination seriously, Gibbons (1994) stands out for offering a systematic account of what imagination does across Kant's theoretical, aesthetic, and practical philosophy. Other commentators tend to focus more narrowly. Banham (2005), for example, focuses on Kant's theoretical account of imagination in the first *Critique*. Makkreel (1990), Hughes (2007), and Horstmann (2018) focus on the theoretical and aesthetic account of imagination in the first and third *Critiques*. Kneller (2007) focuses on the aesthetic and moral account of imagination in the third *Critique* (she also discusses Kant's hesitation about imagination in Kneller (1993) (see also Böhme and Böhme (1996, 231)). Freydberg (2005) focuses on the moral account of imagination in the second *Critique*.

[12] See, e.g. Church's (2013) Kant-inspired account of the role imagination plays in perception, and Gaut's (2003) and Stokes's (2014) Kant-inspired theories of the role imagination plays in creativity.

the course of this monograph, in this Introduction, I set the stage with some remarks about why we should still be concerned with what Kant has to say about imagination.

To this end, I orient the following discussion around three central questions that are live in philosophical debates about imagination today, which I shall call the "unity" (§0.1), "taxonomy" (§0.2), and "use" (§0.3) questions. In each section, I map out some of the contemporary answers to these questions alongside Kant's answers. In doing so I aim not only to bring to light points of continuity and discontinuity between his view and current views, but also to gesture toward the insights I take his view to promise. However, I also use this discussion to introduce the key theses that I defend in my interpretation and to provide readers with a thematic guide to the book. After this ground laying, in §0.4, I offer a more linear overview of the book, which includes a chapter-by-chapter breakdown and some remarks on my use of Kant's texts.

0.1 The Unity Question

The unity question is this: is there any reason to think that there is something we can refer to as "the imagination"? One way to understand this question is in terms of our mental architecture: is there a single mental capacity or faculty that "the imagination" refers to? Another, by no means unrelated, way to understand this question is in terms of our mental activities: is there a single mental activity that we can refer to as "imagining"?

The unity question is particularly forceful given the wide, and seemingly heterogeneous, set of mental phenomena that are characterized as imaginative. Recall the partial list from above: visualization, make-believe, hallucination, fiction, creativity, dreaming, memory, supposition, empathy, etc. Why should we think that there is anything like a single capacity of imagination or single activity of imagining that is responsible for mental phenomena as diverse as these?[13]

Many, though not all,[14] contemporary theorists are skeptical about the prospects of a positive answer to the unity question. In this spirit in his influential

---

[13] In Amy Kind's words, "is there such a thing as the phenomenon of imagining, i.e., is there a single mental activity that can do all the explanatory work that has been assigned to imagination?" (2013, 141–2). Kind, here, draws on O'Shaughnessy's way of framing this: "What is the *imagination*? What is it to *imagine*? These perfectly natural questions already assume too much: the first question assumes there exists something that is the Imagination, presumably a distinctive faculty; the second that there is some one thing that is the phenomenon of Imagining, doubtless instantiated in diverse phenomenal forms. These assumptions may be valid, but they need not be. We ought not to prejudge these questions. Until we look more closely at 'imaginative' phenomena, we cannot really know how matters actually stand" (2000, 339–40).

[14] However, not everyone has abandoned the project of giving a unified theory of imagination. Colin McGinn, for example, defines the imagination as "a creative combinatorial faculty," the "identity" of which "consists in the same type of operation being performed by a structurally uniform faculty" (2004, 129–30). Fabian Dorsch, meanwhile, defends an agency-based account of imagination,

6 INTRODUCTION

book on imagination, *Mimesis as Make-Believe*, Kendall Walton says, "What is it to imagine? We have examined a number of dimensions along which imagining can vary; shouldn't we now spell out what they have in common? Yes, if we can. But I can't" (1990, 19).[15] In this more circumspect vein, many philosophers now just focus on elucidating different kinds of imaginative phenomena and their interrelations, rather than developing a unified theory of imagination.

The unity question is no less forceful when we cast back to Kant's theory of imagination. As in contemporary discussions, we find Kant addressing an impressively large range of imaginative phenomena in contexts such as perception, experience, memory, anticipation, visualization, dreaming, hallucination, mathematics, aesthetic appreciation, artistic creation, empathy, among others. Nevertheless, one of my main aims in this book is to argue that he defends a unified theory of imagination, according to which there is something we can refer to as "the imagination" that is responsible for this range of mental phenomena. To this end, I attribute to Kant a view of the imagination as a single capacity that is responsible for a distinctive type of representation, activity, and function in our mental lives.

More specifically, my goal is to demonstrate that Kant defends a unified theory of the imagination of human beings. He does acknowledge a (reproductive) imagination in non-human animals.[16] And though thinking through Kant's theory of imagination across the human/non-human divide is certainly an important project,[17] my project is more restricted in scope: I aim to uncover the unity of the human imagination on his view. So when I refer to imagination in my interpretation, what I have in mind is the human imagination.

My argument for the unity of imagination on Kant's view moves in two stages. In Part I, I analyze Kant's account for what kind of mental capacity our imagination is in general, and then in Parts II–IV, I explore his analysis of the various ways in which we exercise this capacity in theoretical, aesthetic, and practical contexts, respectively.

In a bit more detail, in Part I, I argue that Kant conceives of our imagination in general as a cognitive capacity. As a terminological note, to say that imagination

---

according to which, "Imaginings are essentially mental actions with the ultimate intrinsic purpose of forming one or more representations with specific and directly determined contents" (2012, 390). For another defense of the unity of imagination, with special focus on the unity of its aesthetic and cognitive use, see Breitenbach (2020).

[15] See also Ryle, "There is no special Faculty of Imagination" (1984, 257); O'Shaughnessy (2000, 339–40); and Kind (2013).

[16] See ML1 28:277; MVo 28:450; ML2 28:594. In virtue of possessing a reproductive imagination, Kant claims that animals are able to make associations and anticipate the future (see AMr 25:1272–3; AF 25:533).

[17] See Villinger (2018) for an extended interpretation of Kant's view of the relationship between the imaginations of non-human animals and human beings. For other discussions of the relationship between non-human animals and humans on Kant's view that reference imagination, see Naragon (1990); Pendlebury (1996; 2017); McLear (2011; 2020a); Fisher (2017); Callanan (2020); Golob (2020).

is a cognitive capacity, for Kant, is not to say that it is responsible for non-sensory episodes in which we suppose, entertain, hypothesize, etc., that something is the case.[18] Though "cognitive" is often used this way in contemporary discussions of imagination, when Kant describes imagination as a cognitive capacity, he has in mind a more basic idea: imagination is a capacity involved in our conscious representation of objects (see Chapter 1).

More specifically, I attribute to Kant a view of imagination as a cognitive capacity that is sensible in nature. In interpreting Kant along these lines, I take a position in a debate surrounding where to situate imagination in our cognitive architecture, as divided between two "stems": sensibility and understanding (see Chapters 2–3). At issue in this debate is not only how to locate imagination in Kant's theory of mind, but also how to make sense of what it is to imagine on his view. Does imagining, for example, involve receptivity and intuitions or spontaneity and concepts? Though these are fraught issues, I argue that Kant ultimately situates imagination in sensibility. To this end, I argue that Kant defends a bipartite account of sensibility, according to which imagination is one part of sensibility, sense being the other (see Chapter 3). I claim that each part of sensibility is responsible for a distinctive type of intuition, sensory activity, and cognitive function. More specifically, I make the case that, on Kant's view, our imagination generates a distinctive type of intuition through a spontaneous sensory activity that mediates between what is sensible and intellectual.

In order to elaborate on this basic picture of imagination, I draw on Kant's analysis of imagination as a distinctive "faculty of..." (see Chapter 4). To this end, I explore three ways in which he characterizes our imaginative faculty, each of which elucidates a different aspect of it. First, as the faculty of formation (*Bildungsvermögen*), which is responsible for sensibly organizing ("forming," "synthesizing," or "composing") what we are given through sensibility. Second, as the faculty responsible for generating intuitions "even without the presence of objects."[19] And, third, as the faculty of "exhibition" (*Darstellung, exhibitio*),[20] which is responsible for generating intuitions that "exhibit" concepts to us in a way that facilitates our concrete comprehension of them.[21]

---

[18] This sort of cognitive imagination is sometimes referred to as propositional, attitudinal, or belief-like imagining, and is contrasted with imagistic, objectual, perception-like imagining (see Yablo 1993; Gaut 2003; and Stock 2017, 23–4). I return to this issue in §0.2.

[19] See, e.g., "*Imagination* is the faculty for representing an object in intuition even **without its presence**" (B151; transl. modified).

[20] *Darstellung'* in Kant is typically translated as either "exhibition" or "presentation," and occasionally as "rendering." I shall translate it as "exhibition" because Kant gives *exhibitio* as the Latin cognate (see KU 5:192; EE 20:220; Anthro. 7:167).

[21] As I discuss in Chapter 4, the sort of concrete comprehension at issue here is different from comprehension in the sense of "*Begreifen*" that Kant attributes to reason (see JL 9:65).

8 INTRODUCTION

In attributing this account of imagination to Kant, I contend that we need to revise certain traditional assumptions about sensibility and intuition in his framework. For one thing, however heterodox it might seem, I argue that Kant is committed to imagination being a spontaneous part of sensibility. For another thing, in spite of the intuitive character of sensibility, I claim that imagination is a conceptually interfacing part of sensibility. In this vein, I weigh in on the debate about Kant's (non-)conceptualism and I maintain that he recognizes two types of intuitions: intuitions that we are given which do not require concepts, and intuitions that are imaginatively made that do require concepts.[22]

After laying out what imagination is in general for Kant, I move on to the second stage of my argument, where I explore how this capacity operates in a unified way across theoretical, aesthetic, and practical contexts, placing particular emphasis on the pervasive role of seeing more and exhibition. In Part II, I focus on the role that Kant attributes to imagination in his account of perception and experience in the first *Critique*. There, I consider the contribution he thinks our imagination makes at both the empirical (Chapter 5) and *a priori* levels (Chapters 6–7). In Part III, I turn to Kant's analysis of what our imagination does in relation to the appreciation of beauty (Chapter 8), artistic production (Chapter 9), and the appreciation of sublimity (Chapter 10). Finally, in Part IV, I argue that even though imagination is not usually recognized as an important aspect of Kant's practical philosophy, he nevertheless attributes to it a significant role in our pursuit of happiness and morality. Although over the course of this discussion I examine a wide range of imaginative phenomena, I make the case that, on Kant's view, there is a single capacity of imagination that underwrites and unifies them: the cognitive capacity that I detail in Part I.

Let's return to Walton's remark about the unity question, "What is it to imagine? We have examined a number of dimensions along which imagining can vary; shouldn't we now spell out what they have in common?" (1990, 19). What I am proposing, in effect, is that if we were to ask Kant these questions, he would not just say, "Yes, if we can," but "I can." By exploring his answer, I hope to model what a sophisticated theory of the unity of imagination looks like, which at once does justice to the core of what it is to imagine and the rich variety of ways in which we do so.

0.2 The Taxonomy Question

A second question about imagination that has received a fair amount of attention is a question about taxonomy: how should we classify imaginative phenomena? Granting that fiction, memory, visualization, dreams, and so forth are imaginative phenomena, what patterns, if any, can we discern among them? And is there any sense in which these phenomena belong to a class of mental states,

---

[22] For an overview, see McLear (2021).

"imagining," that we can contrast with other mental states, like "perceiving," "believing," or "desiring"? Call the question pertaining to how we classify different imaginative phenomena the "internal taxonomy question." Call the question about how we distinguish imaginative phenomena from non-imaginative phenomena the "external taxonomy question."

0.2.1 The Internal Taxonomy Question

Though there are a variety of ways in which recent theorists have taxonomized different kinds of imaginative phenomena, here I shall consider two distinctions that are particularly relevant to Kant's view: sensory versus non-sensory imagining and reproductive versus productive imagining.[23]

0.2.1(a) Sensory/Non-Sensory Imagining

Let's begin with the distinction between sensory and non-sensory imagining.[24] Sensory imagining is typically characterized as a kind of imagining that involves mental states that have a sensory character. Paradigmatic instances of sensory imagining include things like visualizing, dreaming, or hallucinating. These imaginings are often, though not always, characterized as "imagistic" in nature.[25]

By contrast, non-sensory imagining is taken to involve a thought process in which we consider something that departs from reality without the aid of sensory representation. Paradigmatic instances of non-sensory imagining include things like supposing, entertaining, hypothesizing, or pretending that something is the case without sensorily representing that it is the case. This mode of imagining is often characterized as "propositional" or "attitudinal" imagining insofar as it involves adopting an attitude toward a proposition, "imagining that P," which differs from other attitudes like "believing that P" or "desiring that P."[26]

Though Kant is committed to the pervasiveness of imagination, when it comes to non-sensory imagining, he defends a less encompassing view than many

---

[23] Another important distinction that I shall not thematize at length, but only touch on in passing in Part IV, is the distinction between imagining "from the inside" and "from the outside" (see Ninan 2016).

[24] This distinction has also been carved up as a distinction between imagistic, objectual, perception-like imagining, on the one hand, and propositional, attitudinal, cognitive, or belief-like imagining, on the other. For the objectual/propositional distinction, see Yablo (1993); Gaut (2003); and Stock (2017, 23–4) (though, see Kind 2016b, 10 n7, for reason to think that objectual and sensory imagining can come apart). For the perception-like/belief-like distinction, see Currie and Ravenscroft (2002). For the sensory/cognitive distinction, see McGinn (2004). For the imagistic/attitudinal distinction, see Van Leeuwen (2013; 2014); Kind (2016b); and Langland-Hassan (2020). For the imagistic or sensory/propositional distinction, see Nichols (2020).

[25] See Kind (2001); McGinn (2004); Gregory (2016); Nanay (2017); Langland-Hassan (2020); Kozak (2023).

[26] See Van Leeuwen (2014); Stock (2017, chap. 6); Langland-Hassan (2020, chap. 3); Nichols (2020).

10 INTRODUCTION

contemporary theorists do. For Kant, all imagining is sensory, or so I argue.[27] I take this to be something that follows from his commitment to imagination being a capacity that belongs to sensibility. As I discuss in Part I, in Kant's cognitive architecture, non-sensory thought processes in which we adopt an attitude toward a proposition fall on the side of understanding, rather than on the side of sensibility, and are hence outside the purview of imagination.[28] This said, I also make the case that central to Kant's analysis of imagination is an account of how our imaginative activities are responsive to our understanding and involve concepts. However, I contend that, for Kant, whatever our imagination does in relation to our understanding and concepts, it does it as a sensory capacity. If we are to find points of contact between Kant's view and contemporary ones, we thus have reason to focus on accounts of sensory, rather than non-sensory imagining.

But when we pursue a comparison between Kant's account of sensory imagination and contemporary accounts, we find another way in which his view is at odds with a certain trend in recent approaches. *Per* this trend, sensory imagining has the following two characteristics. First, sensory imagining is something that involves imagining what is not present or not real, e.g. when I see an empty vase and imagine how some irises would look in it.[29] Second, sensory imagining is something that results not from external stimuli, but rather from an internal source.[30] My iris vision, for example, is not the result of some irises impinging upon me here and now, but rather the result of an endogenous effort on my part to envision how I might fill that empty vase. Given these two characteristics, it is now typical to cast sensory imagining as restricted in scope: it is something we enact in contexts in which we are responding to objects that are not present or absent, such as memory, anticipation, visualization, hallucination, and dreams, rather than in contexts where the object is present or real, such as perception, experience, or moral action. Note, however, that this trend is not new: it has a philosophical precedent in the traditional account of imagination as fantasy that I traced above.

It might be tempting to attribute to Kant a view of sensory imagination along these lines. He certainly accords imagination a role to play in memory, anticipation, visualization, hallucination, and dreams. He, moreover, asserts, "*Imagination* is the faculty for representing an object in intuition even **without its presence**" (B151, transl. modified; see Chapter 4).[31]

---

[27] Though the label "sensory" is typically preferred in contemporary discussions, I shall use "sensory" and "sensible" interchangeably, though opting for "sensible" more often as the common translation of "*sinnlich*" in Kant.

[28] See, for example, Kant's discussion of hypotheses as involving "problematic" judgments through which reason "opines," rather than "asserts" (A769/B797), and his discussion of "having an opinion" as "an occurrence in the understanding" (A820/B848). This said, Kant allows for us to produce imaginative "inventions" in service of the intellectual activity of formulating a hypothesis or opinion (see A770/B798).

[29] See McGinn (2004, 29–30), who traces this view back to Sartre (2004).

[30] See Nanay (2010; 2015); Williamson (2016); Langland-Hassan (2020, 54, 57).

[31] For debate about how to translate this passage, see Stephenson (2015; 2017).

While this passage, and others like it, might seem to suggest that he endorses the traditional conception of imagination as fantasy, notice that Kant claims that imagination is operative "even without" the presence of an object. Though this "even without" qualifier can be easy to miss, on my reading, it is crucial: for a capacity that can operate even without the presence of objects can also operate even with their presence. Indeed, as I anticipated earlier, one of my main aims in this book is to show that, for Kant, our imagination is most fundamentally not a capacity for fantasy, but rather a capacity for seeing more, which we exercise as much in relation to objects that are real and present, as in relation to objects that are not real and absent. And acknowledging this, I submit, is central to Kant's account of the imaginative dimensions of our ordinary experience, aesthetic engagement, and practical dealings, and hence, to his sweeping vision of how imaginative we are.

0.2.1(b) Reproductive/Productive Imagining

Turning now to the distinction between reproductive and productive imagining, in recent discussions, reproductive imagining has been cast as a kind of imagining in which we "copy," "recreate," or "simulate" another mental state.[32] Paradigmatic cases of reproductive imagining include memory,[33] dreaming,[34] hallucination,[35] and perspective shifting.[36] By contrast, productive imagining is characterized as a creative form of imagining in which we imagine something novel, e.g. in the context of creating art, make-believe, problem-solving, or visualization.[37] Such productive imagining is taken to be less constrained by reality, truth, conventions, or expectations than reproductive imagining.[38]

We find more continuity between Kant's view and contemporary views regarding this distinction; indeed, his view provides a historical precedent that many theorists still draw on:[39]

> The imagination . . . is either *productive*, that is a faculty of the original exhibition of the object (*exhibitio originaria*), which thus precedes experience; or *reproductive*, a faculty of the derivative exhibition of the object (*exhibitio derivativa*),

---

[32] See Currie and Ravenscroft (2002, chap. 1); Currie (2013).

[33] For discussions of the relationship between imagination and memory, see Debus (2014; 2016); Michaelian (2016); the essays by Gregory, Hopkins, and Debus collected in part I of Dorsch and Macpherson (2018); Michaelian, Perrin, and Sant'Anna (2020); and the essays collected in Berninger and Vendrell Ferran (2023).

[34] See McGinn (2004, chaps. 6–7); Ichikawa (2009).

[35] See Casey (2003); Allen (2015); Nanay (2016).

[36] See Currie and Ravenscroft, e.g., who define perspective shifting in terms of "the capacity to put ourselves in the place of our own future, past, or counterfactual self: seeing, thinking about, and responding to the world as the other sees, thinks about, and responds to it" (2002, 8–9).

[37] See Currie and Ravenscroft (2002, chap. 18); Carruthers (2002; 2006; 2011); Gaut (2003); Stokes (2014; 2016).

[38] See, e.g., Gaut's (2003) claim that imagination, and by extension, creative imagining, is not constrained by truth or action; and Stokes's (2014) claim that creative imagining is not "truth-bound."

[39] While this precedent is often implicit, Gaut (2003) makes it explicit.

12 INTRODUCTION

which brings back to the mind an empirical intuition that it had previously...Imagination (in other words) is either *inventive* [*dichtend*] (productive) or merely *recollective* [*zurückrufend*] (reproductive).

(Anthro. 7:167; transl. modified)[40]

Here, Kant distinguishes between reproductive imagining as something that is "derivative" and "recollective," and productive imagining as something that is "original" and "inventive." His examples of reproductive imagining include memory,[41] associative habits,[42] and anticipation.[43] And he cites artistic creation,[44] dreaming,[45] and mathematical construction[46] as examples of the productive exercise of imagination.

This said, Kant offers a more expansive notion of productive imagining than is common now, indeed doubly so. For one thing, while most contemporary theorists only discuss empirical cases of productive imagining, Kant claims that there are also *a priori* acts of productive imagining. Indeed, Kant's analysis of the *a priori* activities of productive imagining plays a central role in his account of the conditions of the possibility of experience in the first *Critique* (see Chapters 6–7). For another thing, he acknowledges a wider range of empirical instances of productive imagining than is often done. Like a number of recent theorists, he thinks we engage in empirical acts of productive imagining in paradigmatically creative contexts like artistic production and aesthetic experience.[47] However, Kant accords the empirical activities of the productive imagining a central role in more ordinary activities like perception and the pursuit of happiness as well (see Chapters 5, 12). For Kant, then, it is not just that imagining pervades our lives; productive imagining pervades our lives.

0.2.2 The External Taxonomy Question

The external taxonomy question concerns how we are to classify imaginative states vis-à-vis other mental states. Are imaginative states *sui generis* or should

---

[40] For other discussions of the productive-reproductive distinction, see B152; KU 5:240; Mensch. 25:945–6; AMr 25:1257; MD 28:674. For discussion of the reproductive-productive distinction in the pre-Critical lectures, see Dyck (2019, §1).

[41] For example, when "one's school years come to mind when one goes by the school" (AF 25:513). See also Anthro. 7:182–5; AF 25:521–4; AMr 25:1272–6; Mensch. 25:974–80.

[42] For example, "to think of heavy cinnabar on the occasion of the representation of the color red" (A101).

[43] For example, anticipating dinner to follow once you hear a bell (MMr 29:884). See also Anthro. 7:186; AF 25:533; AMr 25:1289; Mensch. 1017–23; ML1 28:236; ML2 28:585.

[44] See KU §49; Anthro. §30; AF 25:526–7; AMr 25:1279–83; Mensch. 25:997–1006.

[45] See B278; Anthro. §37; AF 25:528–31; AMr 25:1283–5; Mensch. 25:995–7; MMr 29:885.

[46] See B155fn; A163/B204.

[47] See Gaut (2003); Church (2013, 4, 83, 129 n73; 2016, 171, 175). For a historical precedent, see Coleridge's claim that while everyone has a reproductive imagination ("fancy"), fewer people, like poets, possess a full productive imagination ("imagination") (2015, chap. IV).

they be analyzed in terms of other mental states? In contemporary discussions, this question has taken shape as a question about the relationship between imaginative states, on the one hand, and perceptions, beliefs, and desires, on the other.

One prevalent view is that imaginative states are not perceptions, beliefs, or desires, but are rather *sui generis* mental states[48] that are perception-like,[49] belief-like,[50] or desire-like.[51] Proponents of this view tend to offer accounts of the ways in which imagining is at once analogous to, but distinct from these other mental states. Take a belief-like imagining, for example.[52] Imagining that a bunch of irises popped up in my backyard involves adopting a cognitive attitude toward a proposition and drawing inferences, and is, to this extent, similar to belief.[53] But this imagining does not seem to aim at truth[54] and to directly motivate action in the way that belief does.[55]

However, some reject the view that imagining is merely perception-like, belief-like, or desire-like. To name but a couple of examples, Langland-Hassan (2020) argues that imagination is reducible to beliefs and desires. And Schellenberg (2013) claims that although imagination is distinct from desire, it is continuous with belief.

So, how does Kant's approach to the external taxonomy question map onto these contemporary approaches? Answering this question is complicated given the ways in which Kant's framework for the mind differs from contemporary frameworks. Though I shall have more to say about the details in Part I, here I want to try and say enough to situate his framework vis-à-vis our perception-belief-desire framework.

In Kant's map of the mind, there are three "fundamental faculties" (*Grundvermögen*): the "faculty of cognition" (*Erkenntnisvermögen*), the "faculty of desire" (*Begehrungsvermögen*), and the faculty of the "feeling of pleasure and displeasure" (*Gefühl der Lust und Unlust*).[56] Roughly, Kant conceives of the faculty of cognition as a faculty through which we consciously represent objects, the faculty of desire as a volitional faculty through which we endeavor to bring objects about, and the faculty of the feeling of pleasure and displeasure as a hedonic faculty through which we register how we are subjectively affected. Were

---

[48] The idea that imaginative states are *sui generis* is sometimes cashed out in terms of the idea that there is an imaginative "box" that is distinct from the belief "box" or desire "box" in our mind (see Nichols and Stich 2000 and Weinberg and Meskin 2006).

[49] See Kind (2001); Currie and Ravenscroft (2002); Van Leeuwen (2013).

[50] See Currie and Ravenscroft (2002); Nichols (2006); Van Leeuwen (2014); Arcangeli (2019).

[51] See Currie and Ravenscroft (2002); Goldman (2006); Doggett and Egan (2007; 2012); Currie (2010); Kind (2011).

[52] See Sinhababu (2016) for an overview.   [53] See Currie and Ravenscroft (2002).

[54] See Humberstone (1992); Shah and Velleman (2005). For criticism, see Sinhababu (2013).

[55] See Nichols and Stich (2000; 2003); O'Brien (2005); Funkhouser and Spaulding (2009); Kind (2011). For complications, see Velleman (2000); Doggett and Egan (2007).

[56] See Wuerth (2014, chap. 6) for a discussion of Kant's "map of the mind." See also Hume's description of his project in the *Enquiry* as a "mental geography" (2007, 9).

14 INTRODUCTION

we to situate perception, belief, and desire in this Kantian map,[57] insofar as perception and belief involve consciously representing objects they would fall in the purview of the faculty of cognition. And insofar as desire pertains to our volitional efforts to bring objects about, it would fall in the purview of the faculty of desire.

As for imagination, Kant locates it in the faculty of cognition (see Part I), and attending to this placement offers some clues for how to think about his classification of imaginative states vis-à-vis perception, belief, and desire. Insofar as Kant takes imagination to be part of the faculty of cognition, rather than the faculty of desire, he distinguishes imaginative states from desires. This is not to say that imaginative states and desires do not interact on Kant's view. In Part IV, I offer an extended analysis of the ways in which they do interact in our pursuit of happiness and morality. However, for Kant, whatever contribution our imagination makes to this end, it makes it as a cognitive, rather than a volitional, capacity.

But what about the relationship between imagination, perception, and belief in Kant's framework? Beginning with perception, Kant famously claims that, "Imagination is a necessary ingredient of perception" (A120n). This should alert us to the fact that Kant parts ways with contemporary theorists who draw a sharp distinction between perception and imagination.[58] He, instead, veers closer to those who accord imagination a role in perceptual phenomena, such as the "perceptual presence" of what is absent and amodal completion, e.g. when I perceive an iris as having a stem that is occluded by a white vase.[59]

However, Kant does draw a sharp distinction between imagining and sensing. Indeed, on my reading, this distinction is central to his bipartite account of sensibility, according to which the sensory activities involved in the part of sensibility he calls "sense" are distinct from those involved in the part he calls "imagination" (see Chapters 3, 5). Kant thus distinguishes imagining from another type of sensory activity; however, the contrast class is not perceiving, but sensing.

Let's turn now to the relationship between imagination and belief on Kant's view. Though there is reason to attribute to Kant a distinction between imagination and belief in the contemporary sense, appreciating this idea requires some terminological clarification. In contemporary usage, belief is tantamount to an attitude we adopt when we take something to be true. Kant, likewise, thinks belief

---

[57] I here set aside questions about where hedonic feelings and emotions fit in Kant's map of the mind, but arguably they belong to the faculty of feeling of pleasure and displeasure (see Cohen 2020).

[58] See Currie and Ravenscroft (2002, 11–12); McGinn (2004); Van Leeuwen (2013; 2014). This said, as I discuss in Chapter 5, when Kant says imagination is a necessary ingredient of perception, he has a technical notion of "perception" (Wahrnehmung) in mind, which comes apart from the way this term is often used in contemporary discussions, e.g. of perceptual content (see McLear 2016b).

[59] See Thomas (2009) and Kind (2018) for discussion of the phenomena of "perceptual presence." See Nanay (2010; 2016; 2018a) for a discussion of imagination in amodal perception. See Church (2013) for a Kant-inspired discussion of imagination in a range of perceptual phenomena, including the perception of objects in ordinary experience, persons, and aesthetic phenomena.

involves adopting an attitude toward something as true, but he situates his account of belief in an epistemic framework in which he distinguishes belief from two other states: "knowledge" (*Wissen*) and "cognition" (*Erkenntnis*).[60]

For Kant, belief and knowledge are epistemically similar insofar as they involve "an occurrence in our understanding" through which we adopt an attitude toward a judgment as true or justified (A820/B848). His word for this intellectual attitude is *Fürwahrhalten*, which is literally translated as "holding-for-true" and less literally as "assent" (A820/B848). So in both belief and knowledge, Kant thinks we engage in an intellectual act in which we hold a judgment to be true. However, he takes belief and knowledge to have different kinds of justificatory grounds. In the case of belief, he claims, we take ourselves to have "subjective" "grounds," whereas in the case of knowledge, we take ourselves to have "subjective" and "objective" "grounds" for taking a judgment to be true (A822/B850).

As for belief and cognition, as Kant understands it, cognition is not a state that requires an intellectual act in which we take a judgment to be justified as is the case with belief. Cognition, for Kant, just involves the conscious representation of an object (see Chapter 1). For example, I might consciously represent an iris in a hallucinatory episode without taking it to be the case that there is an iris in front of me; in which case, I will have a cognition of it, in Kant's sense, without adopting the "holding-for-true" attitude toward a judgment that is required for belief.

So, where does imagining fit into this epistemic framework? As I have been signaling, on my interpretation of Kant, imagination belongs to sensibility, rather than to understanding. Insofar as this is the case, the sort of intellectual acts involved in belief and knowledge in Kant's sense fall outside the purview of imagination. The sensible nature of imagination also gives us reason to be wary of attributing to him a view of imagining as belief-like: adopting attitudes toward propositions and drawing inferences without the aid of sensory representations are activities that fall to the understanding, rather than to imagination as part of sensibility, in his framework.

However, matters are quite different when we consider the relationship between imagination and cognition in Kant's sense. Working through this topic will occupy me for much of this book, but for present purposes I hope it will suffice to say that insofar as imagination is a cognitive capacity on Kant's view, he does not distinguish imagination from cognition, but rather takes imagination to be involved in our conscious representation of objects in some way. Indeed, one of my aims is to bring to light Kant's sophisticated account of imagination as a cognitive capacity that not only engages in a distinctive kind of cognitive activity and has a distinctive cognitive function, but also is cognitively flexible enough to operate across the theoretical, aesthetic, and practical domains.

---

[60] For discussion of these epistemic distinctions, see Chignell (2007); Cohen (2014); Watkins and Willaschek (2017); Tolley (2020); Willaschek and Watkins (2020).

16 INTRODUCTION

For Kant, imagining thus fits into a complicated mental taxonomy in which imagining is distinct from sensing, desiring, and believing, but is nevertheless involved in perceiving and cognizing. And though complicated, on my interpretation, attending to his conception of imagination as a cognitive capacity that belongs to sensibility helps explain what motivates him in classifying imagining vis-à-vis other mental states in this way.

0.3 The Use Question

In addition to asking broader questions about the unity and taxonomy of imagination, we can set our sights on more specific ways in which we exercise our imagination. In this vein, theorists ask questions about imaginative use: how exactly do we deploy our imagination in epistemic, aesthetic, and practical contexts?

0.3.1 The Epistemic/Theoretical Use

Let's begin with how we epistemically use our imagination in our pursuit of knowledge. First, though, a note on terminology. I frame this in terms of both the "epistemic" and "theoretical" use of imagination because the former termingology is in keeping with contemporary parlance, while the latter is in keeping with Kant's terminology for epistemic issues in the first *Critique* (see, e.g., Bx, B20, B168).[61] And I shall use these terms largely interchangeably below.

There has been a recent surge of interest in the epistemic use of imagination. In particular, philosophers have devoted their attention to the question of, one, what constraints must be in place for imagination to have this use, and, two, what different kinds of epistemic uses we can put it to.[62]

The question about constraints is motivated, in part, by a puzzle that Amy Kind and Peter Kung have called the "puzzle of imaginative use": "How can the same mental activity that allows us to fly completely free of reality also teach us something about it" (Kind and Kung 2016, 1)? Kind and Kung refer to the use of our imagination in flying free of reality, its "transcendent" use, and its use in teaching us something about reality, its "epistemic" use. And the puzzle is how we can use imagination both as a fantastic way to depart from reality and as an epistemic tool for gaining insight into it.

One recent strategy for explaining how imagination can have both a transcendent and epistemic use is to specify a set of constraints that the latter, but not the

---

[61] Kant also discusses a "practical" form of cognition, but when I speak of the epistemic use of imagination I shall focus on its use in theoretical cognition. For discussion of Kant's theory of practical cognition, see Chignell (2007a; 2010b); Kain (2010); Abaci (2022); Schafer (2023).

[62] See the essays collected in Kind and Kung (2016) and Badura and Kind (2021).

former, is subject to. Kind and Kung identify two relevant types of constraints: architectural and volitional (2016, 21).[63] Architectural constraints turn on the way in which our imagination is constrained by our mental architecture. Examples of such architectural constraints include constraint by other mental states, such as beliefs or desires, or mental processes, such as inference. Volitional constraints turn on the way in which we voluntarily impose constraints on our imagining by choosing to rein it in, say, in light of reality, a certain set of beliefs, or a given problem. And the proposal is that when certain architectural and volitional constraints obtain, we are able to exercise our imagination in epistemically productive, rather than transcendent, ways.

Assuming that we can deploy our imagination to epistemic ends, another trend has been to specify different types of epistemic uses to which we can put imagination. Though this literature is ever expanding, much attention has recently been devoted to the epistemic use of imagination in science,[64] mathematics,[65] reasoning,[66] thought experiments,[67] modal knowledge,[68] self-knowledge,[69] and understanding others.[70]

For those sympathetic to the idea that imagination is not just of transcendent use, but also of epistemic use, Kant is an ally. To be sure, Kant acknowledges that our imagination can be used in transcendent ways, e.g. in dreams, hallucination, and hypochondria. However, as I explore in Part II, in the first *Critique*, Kant argues that if our imagination is suitably constrained, then it has a crucial role to play in service of our epistemic efforts in the context of perception and experience.

This said, some caution is needed in how we approach the epistemic use of imagination in light of Kant's epistemic framework. Here, we need to return to his distinction between "knowledge" (*Wissen*) and "cognition" (*Erkenntnis*). Recall that, for Kant, knowledge involves taking a judgment to be justified on subjective and objective grounds, whereas cognition involves the conscious representation of objects. Though both epistemic states are important in his framework,

---

[63] See also Kind (2016a); Langland-Hassan (2016); Van Leeuwen (2016); Kind (2018); Badura and Kind (2021, intro.).

[64] See Toon (2012); the essays collected in Levy and Godfrey-Smith (2019) and French and Ivanova (2020); French (2020); Murphy (2022).

[65] See Mancosu (2005); Giaquinto (2007); Arana (2016).

[66] See Byrne (2005); Williamson (2007; 2016); and the essays by Myers, Berto, Badura, and Mallozzi in Badura and Kind (2021).

[67] See Ninan (2009); Gendler (2010, pt. 1); Elgin (2014); Meynell (2014); Kung (2016); Sorensen (2016); and the essays by Arcangeli, Strohminger, and Peterson in Badura and Kind (2021).

[68] See Yablo (1993); Chalmers (2002); Gendler and Hawthorne (2002); Kung (2010; 2016); Strohminger and Yli-Vakkuri (2017); and the essays by Kung, Lam, Hanrahan, and Omoge in Badura and Kind (2021).

[69] See Langland-Hassan (2015); Stokes (2019).

[70] See discussions of the role imagination plays in taking up someone else's perspective in the essays collected in Summa, Fuchs, and Vanzago (2018); Kind (2021); and Langkau (2021); and the role imaginative "simulation" and "projection" play in "mindreading" (our ability to attribute mental states to others, and to explain or predict actions on this basis) in Currie and Ravenscroft (2002) and Nichols and Stich (2003).

18   INTRODUCTION

Kant devotes far more attention to cognition than to knowledge in the first *Critique*. Indeed, he does not offer a sustained discussion of knowledge until the end of the first *Critique*.[71] But the topic of cognition is one he foregrounds from the start:[72] "All that seems necessary for an introduction...is that there are two stems of human cognition, which may perhaps arise from a common but to us unknown root, namely sensibility and understanding" (A15/B29).

More specifically, the epistemic issue that Kant devotes the most attention to in the first *Critique* is how to think about the sort of "theoretical" cognition involved in "experience" (*Erfahrung*). Under the heading of "experience," Kant discusses not only our everyday cognition of objects around us, but also the sort of cognition that we arrive at through mathematics and natural science. And he dedicates much of his epistemic efforts towards elucidating the empirical and *a priori* contours of such experience.

Given this focus, if we are to understand the epistemic use of imagination on Kant's view, then we need to focus on the contribution it makes to the sort of theoretical cognition at issue in experience. Detailing this use of imagination is my task in Part II. There I consider the sort of empirical activities that imagination engages in that conduce to the empirical cognition involved in experience, laying particular emphasis on its contribution via perception (see Chapter 5). I also address his account of the sort of *a priori* activities of imagination that make experience possible in the first place, which he addresses in the Transcendental Deduction and Schematism (see Chapters 6 and 7).

Here, however, I want to return to the question of what sort of constraints must be in place for imagination to have an epistemic use. As I see it, Kant's account in the first *Critique* is particularly salient with respect to the question of the sort of architectural constraints that need to be in place for our imagination to be epistemically productive. This is not to say that he ignores the topic of volitional constraints altogether in his theory of imagination. In the *Anthropology* and various lectures, Kant distinguishes between involuntary and voluntary exercises of imagination, which he sometimes refers to as "Imagination" and "Phantasie" ("fantasy"), respectively.[73] For Kant, this distinction turns on exercises of

---

[71] Kant's most elaborate discussion of *Wissen* is in the "Canon of Pure Reason" (see A820/B848ff).

[72] See also his opening to the preface of the A-edition: "Human reason has the peculiar fate in one species of its cognitions that it is burdened with questions which it cannot dismiss...but which it also cannot answer" (Avii); and to the B-edition: "Whether or not the treatment of the cognitions belonging to the concern of reason travels the secure course of a science is something which can soon be judged by its success" (Bvii).

[73] For this use of *Imagination*, see Mensch. 25:946; AMr 25:1258; MMr 29:885. For this use of *Phantasie*, see Anthro. 7:167, 175; Mensch. 25:946; AMr 25:1258. See Dyck (2019, 354–6) for a discussion of this distinction in the pre-Critical period. See Russell (forthcoming b) for an interpretation of Kant's theory of fantasy.

THE USE QUESTION   19

imagination that are under our conscious control and those that are not.[74] Or, as
he sometimes puts it, in voluntary cases, "*we* play with imagination," but in
involuntary cases, imagination "plays with *us*" (MMr 29:885).[75] His examples of
voluntary imagining include artistic activities,[76] planning activities (e.g. when an
architect designs a house);[77] memory (*Gedächtniß*), defined as "deliberately
visualizing [*vergegenwärtigen*] the past";[78] and foresight (*Vorsehung*), defined as
deliberately "visualizing" the future.[79] His examples of involuntary activities,
include dreaming;[80] non-veridical sensory phenomena, like hallucination;[81]
mental disorders, such as hypochondria and paranoia;[82] forming expectations of
how something or someone will appear (e.g. imagining that Hume will look

---

[74] *Per* Kant, the voluntary mode is "governed by choice" (Anthro. 7:175), and in this mode, we
"give...direction and order" to our imagination in line with "certain purposes and ends" (MMr
29:885). In the involuntary mode, Kant claims someone has "no control at all over the course of his
representations" (Anthro. 7:181), and that this imagining arises "not according to choice and intention [*Wahl und Vorsatz*]" and "not at will [*nach Belieben*]," but rather as the result of some "contingent
occasion" [*zufälligen Gelegenheit*] (Mensch. 25:946; my transl.).
[75] See also AMr 25:1258; Mensch. 25:946.   [76] See Anthro. 7:175; AMr 25:1279.
[77] See AMr 25:1279; AF 25:524. For the architect example, see ML1 28:237.
[78] Anthro. 7:182. See also AF 25:521; Mensch. 25:974; AMr 25:1273.
[79] Anthro. 7:182. See also Anthro. 7:185–6; AMr 25:1289–93; AF 25:531–5; Mensch. 25:1017–23.
Kant himself deploys imagination in this regard in "Conjectural Beginning," where he offers an imaginative "exhibition" [*Darstellung*] of the beginning of human history, which takes its cue from Genesis
(see MAM 8:108–9, 115, 123; transl. modified).
[80] See Anthro. 7:167, 175, 189; MMr 29:885–6; AF 25:528; AMron. 25:1283–5.
[81] Mensch. 25:948; my transl. See also Kant's generic description of these non-veridical phenomena: "Deception due to the *strength* of the human power of imagination often goes so far that a person
believes he sees and feels outside himself that which he has only in his mind" (Anthro. 7:178; see also
AMr 25:185). Although, on Kant's view, imagination plays a role in sensory illusion and hallucination,
he argues that judgment must also be involved (see A293–4/B349–51; Prol. 4:328; Anthro. §11). In
addition to acknowledging one-off episodes of sensory illusion and hallucination, Kant claims that
they can occur more habitually. For example, a "Schwärmer" ("fantastic," someone undergoing
"Schwämerei" ("delusion," "visionary rapture")) is under **a delusion of being able to see something
beyond all bounds of sensibility,**" e.g. being able to see a spiritual being, like an angel or a god
(KU 5:275; see also AMr 25:1262, 1287–8, Mensch. 25:1006–7, AF 25:530–1, and Kant's extensive
discussion of Swedenborg in these terms in "Dreams of a Spirit Seer."). Meanwhile, an "enthusiast" is
someone who is a "fantast of concepts," who mistakenly thinks that "ideals" can be actual (AF 25:529–30;
see also KU 5:275, Mensch. 25:1006–7, AMr 25:1287).
[82] Kant distinguishes between different kinds of "mental illnesses" that involve habitual non-
veridical episodes. In general, Kant distinguishes between "melancholia" [*Grillenkrankenheit*], where
"the patient is well aware that something is not going with the course of his thoughts," e.g. hypochondria (see also Anthro. 7:212–13; Streit 7:103–4; AMr 25:1257; MMr 29:885; ML1 28:237;
AF 25:515) and "mental derangement" [*gestörte Gemüth*] in which the patient lacks such awareness
(Anthro. 7:202; see also Mensch. 25:1008). According to Kant, mental derangement that involves sensory illusion and hallucination can either be "dementia" [*Wahnsinn*] or "amentia" [*Unsinnigkeit*]
(Anthro. 7:202, 215). With "dementia" someone's imaginings agree with the "formal laws...[of] experience," but they mistake their "self-made representations" for "perceptions," e.g. someone with paranoia who "believes they are surrounded by enemies everywhere" (Anthro. 7:215). Meanwhile with
"amentia" [*Unsinnigkeit*] someone's imaginings do not have "the coherence necessary for the possibility of experience," and their illusions and hallucinations are non-sensical and self-contradictory
(Anthro. 7:215). The former belongs to what Kant calls "unreined" [*zügellos*] and the latter to "ruleless" [*regellos*] imagination (see Anthro. 7:181; Mensch. 25:955–6).

20   INTRODUCTION

"delicate and soft" upon reading his work);[83] and being lost in a reverie while looking at something like "flickering flames" or a "brook rippling over stones."[84]

While this distinction between voluntary and involuntary imagining plays a central role in the *Anthropology*, it is not something Kant foregrounds in the first *Critique*. He, instead, focuses his attention on imaginative activities in cognition that are "the mere effect of the imagination, of a blind though indispensable function of the soul, without which we would have no cognition at all, but of which we are seldom even conscious," and that involve "a hidden art in the depths of the human soul, whose true operations we can divine from nature and lay unveiled before our eyes only with difficulty" (A78/B103, A141/B180). Insofar as these imaginative activities are "blind," "seldom even conscious," and involve a "hidden art," they do not seem to be under our conscious control in the way that paradigmatic voluntary activities like visualizing and remembering are. However, it is clear that Kant nevertheless thinks they have a pivotal role to play in the epistemically productive use of imagination in experience.

Instead of volitional constraints, then, the kind of constraints that we find operative in Kant's account of the epistemic use of imagination in the first *Critique* are architectural ones. More specifically, as I discuss at length in Parts I and II, Kant takes the epistemic use of our imagination to be subject to sensible and conceptual constraints. In the sensible vein, I explore Kant's account of how this use is formally constrained by space and time and materially constrained by the deliverances of sensibility (see Chapter 3). In the conceptual vein, I make the case that Kant regards our epistemically useful imaginative activities as constrained by concepts (see Part II).[85] And in the course of spelling out these constraints, I attribute to Kant a conceptualist position, according to which the intuitions that our imagination generates in the context of experience depend on concepts.[86] However, I also maintain that though constrained by and dependent upon concepts, he nevertheless distinguishes these imaginative activities from the intellectual activity of judgment.

---

[83] In this scenario, Kant says, "Concepts of objects often prompt a spontaneously produced image (through the productive imagination), which we attach to them involuntarily" (Anthro. 7:173; transl. modified. See also AF 25:511).

[84] Anthro. 7:173–4. See also KU 5:243–4; AMr 25:1258–9.

[85] See Wiltsher (2016) and Arcangeli (2020) for a recent discussion of the conceptual nature of imaginative content. As Arcangeli notes, in contemporary discussions of imagination, the propositional nature of imagining has received more attention than its conceptual nature, but she makes the case for distinguishing these issues and devoting more attention to the latter issue. In Kant's system, these issues also come apart as he distinguishes between propositions or judgments, on the one hand, and concepts, as the constituents of propositions or judgments, on the other.

[86] However, I do not attribute to Kant a conceptualist position about the generation of all intuitions. I argue, instead, that the intuitions generated through sense and our most basic pure intuitions of space and time do not depend on concepts on Kant's view. See Schulting (2016, intro.) and McLear (2021) for an overview of debates about Kant's conceptualism.

THE USE QUESTION   21

Setting the details aside, as the epistemic use of imagination continues to garner attention, this elaborate Kantian account of the use of, and constraints on, imagination in experiential cognition promises itself as a valuable historical resource.

0.3.2 The Aesthetic Use

While attention to the epistemic use of imagination is now on the rise, its aesthetic use is something that has long been the object of philosophical attention. And in contemporary discussions of its aesthetic use, Kant's robust account of the aesthetic exercise of imagination in the third *Critique* has served as an explicit touchstone. Here, I concentrate on two aesthetic topics that Kant's view has been especially influential with respect to: creativity and aesthetic experience.

For many contemporary theorists, imagination has a pivotal role to play in the creativity at issue in the production of art, enabling artists to reach beyond what is ordinary and familiar to what is new and surprising.[87] But beyond this artistic context, philosophers have recently made the case that imaginative creativity has a pivotal role to play in science[88] and in mundane activities, such as problem-solving and free association,[89] in which we exercise our imagination to come up with new concepts, conceptual schemes, techniques, solutions to problems, and ways of combining what is familiar.[90]

In these discussions of creativity, Kant's account of artistic genius has served as a resource (see KU §§46–9).[91] Consider, for example, Kant's claim that in genius, "The imagination (as a productive cognitive faculty) is...very powerful in creating, as it were, another nature, out of the material which the real one gives it...[nature] can be transformed by us into something entirely different, namely into that which steps beyond nature" (KU 5:314). Here, Kant identifies imagination as a powerful resource for us to draw on in our attempts to "step beyond" and "transform" nature through our creative endeavors. And in this "stepping beyond," he claims that our imagination is released from "the constraint" that it is ordinarily subject to in cognition, and "free" "in an aesthetic respect" (KU 5:316).

However, Kant insists that, for all its freedom, the creative imagination is not unbridled. Indeed, in contrast with some traditional theories of genius as involving either divine inspiration or madness,[92] Kant insists that, "To be rich and

---

[87] This formulation of creativity in terms of what is new, surprising, and valuable is in keeping with Boden's (2004, 1) definition of creativity.

[88] See Murphy (2022).   [89] See Stokes (2014).

[90] See Boden (2004); Stokes (2014; 2016); Hills and Bird (2018; 2019).

[91] See Gaut (2003); Stokes (2014; 2016); Hills and Bird (2018; 2019).

[92] See Robinson (2011, chap. 5) for a discussion of the history of the connection between genius and madness.

22 INTRODUCTION

original in ideas is not as necessary for the sake of beauty as is the suitability of the imagination in its freedom to the lawfulness of the understanding. For all the richness of the former produces, in its lawless freedom, nothing but nonsense" (KU 5:319). Though Kant here indicates that the creative activities of our imagination are "free," he also claims that if those activities are to amount to something more than "nonsense," then there needs to be some sort of "lawfulness" about them. And this picture of imaginative creativity as free, yet lawful, has served as a precedent for theorists who have offered accounts of what sort of constraints the creative use of imagination is subject to, including constraints related to reality, truth, practical ends, and value.[93]

In addition to its contribution to creativity, contemporary philosophers have accorded imagination a central role to play in aesthetic experience. In one vein, theorists have highlighted ways in which exercising our imagination enables the sort of open-ended, playful mode of engagement that the aesthetic calls for. Think, here, of how imaginatively exploring a host of associations, images, and thoughts[94] or imaginatively engaging with metaphor[95] shapes our encounters with art, nature, design, and more. In another vein, imagination has featured prominently in recent discussions of fiction, as contributing to the sort of make-believe,[96] pretense,[97] supposition,[98] perspective taking,[99] or imaginative resistance[100] that our experience of fiction involves.[101]

As was the case with creativity, Kant's treatment of imagination in the third *Critique* has served as a point of reference in contemporary discussions of aesthetic experience, particularly in the first vein.[102] Here, Kant's analysis of aesthetic appreciation as involving a kind of "free play" of imagination has been influential (KU 5:217).[103] Theorists inspired by this line of thought have developed accounts

---

[93] See Novitz (1999); Gaut (2003); Boden (2004); Stokes (2014). For criticism of the idea that imaginative creativity is constrained by value, see Hills and Bird (2018; 2019). I discuss this constraint at more length in Part III.

[94] See Elliott (1972); Savile (1993); Carroll (2014); Breitenbach (2020).

[95] See Moran (1989); Gaut (2003, §5); Camp (2009).

[96] See Walton (1990); Currie (2013).

[97] See Gendler (2003); Nichols and Stich (2003, chap. 2); Liao and Gendler (2011).

[98] See Stock (2017); Arcangeli (2019).   [99] See Camp (2009; 2017).

[100] See Gendler and Liao (2016) and Tuna (2020) for overviews. See Lambeth (2022) for a discussion of a Kantian account of imaginative resistance.

[101] Beyond fiction, for discussions of the role imagination plays vis-à-vis music, see Kania (2015) and Trivedi (2017); film, see Gaut (1998), Lopes (1998), Zinkin (2003; with a nod to Kant), and Gilmore (2019); and photography, see Benovsky (2020).

[102] I shall touch on fiction in the context of discussing Kant's theory of aesthetic ideas (Chapter 9), happiness (Chapter 12, §12.4.1), and morality (Chapter 13, §13.3). However, given Kant's commitment to imagining being sensory in nature (or so I argue), his view does not make much contact with recent discussions of the non-sensory imagining that we enact in relation to fiction.

[103] This said, Kant does not originate the notion of "free play." Lessing explicitly mentions it in *Laocoön* (1766), and it is an idea that is arguably implicit in many other British, French, and German aesthetic theories of the 18th century (see Guyer 2014, vol. 1).

of the role that playful activities, such as imaginative exploration, projection, and elaboration have in aesthetic experience.[104]

Kant's theory of so-called "aesthetic ideas" in his account of genius has also been influential in discussions of aesthetic experience (see KU §49). For Kant, aesthetic ideas are imaginatively rich representations expressed in art that open up horizons of imagining and thinking in a way that borders on the ineffable. Consider, for example, the imaginative world that Virginia Woolf gives us in *Mrs. Dalloway*: the world of Clarissa Dalloway and Peter Walsh, of Sally Seton and Miss Kilman, of Septimus Smith and Lucrezia Smith. From a Kantian perspective, this replete imaginative world amounts to an aesthetic idea, which "occasions much thinking though without it being possible for any determinate thought... to be adequate to it" (KU 5:314). In this theory of aesthetic ideas, some contemporary theorists find resources to draw on in articulating the open-ended structure of aesthetic experience and what imagining contributes therein.[105]

In keeping with this recognition of the on-going value of Kant's vision of the aesthetic use of imagination, I devote Part III to an interpretation of the contribution our imagination makes in the appreciation of beauty through free play (Chapter 8), artistic production, genius, and aesthetic ideas (Chapter 9), and the appreciation of the sublime (Chapter 10). In addition to analyzing the distinctive way in which Kant thinks we exercise our imagination in each of these contexts, I argue that he defends an overarching theory of the aesthetic use of our imagination, which turns on us exercising it in cognitive, creative, and conceptually rich ways. In defending this interpretation, I extend my conceptualist analysis of Kant's account of our imaginative activities into the aesthetic domain. And I make the case that attending to the aesthetic use of imagination is crucial for acknowledging the variety of cognitively valuable ways in which Kant thinks we can imagine, whether in the more constrained context of experience or the more creative context of the aesthetic.

0.3.3 The Practical Use

Although the practical use of imagination has not always garnered attention, there are philosophers in both the historical tradition and more recently who take this use seriously. For example, we find a defense of the practical use of

---

[104] Wiltsher and Meskin (2016) and Breitenbach (2020) discuss a Kantian approach to the role imagination plays in aesthetic engagement more generally. Carroll (2014, 63–6) discusses a Kantian approach to the exploratory role imagination plays in our aesthetic engagement with art. Brady (1998), drawing on Savile (1987), discusses the role the exploratory, projective, ampliative, and revelatory modes of imagination play in our appreciation of nature. Gaiger (2020) also discusses projective and ampliative imagination in an analysis of the role imagination plays in our aesthetic engagement with sculpture.

[105] See Nuyen (1989); Gaut (2003, §5); Pillow (2000, pt. 3); Breitenbach (2020).

24 INTRODUCTION

imagination in the moral sentimentalists of the 17th and 18th centuries, such as David Hume and Adam Smith, according to whom the sympathy required for morality involves the imaginative ability to "enter into" someone else's experience and "place" ourselves in their "situation."[106] In the American pragmatist tradition, we find thinkers like John Dewey and Ella Lyman Cabot arguing that in addition to enabling sympathy, imagination is required for moral deliberation[107] and for seeing situations in light of the practical opportunities they afford.[108] In Hannah Arendt's political theory, inspired directly by Kant, we find the claim that imagination plays a key role in the practice of judgment, impartiality, and our ability to think from the standpoint of others.[109] And in the work of the 20th century British philosopher and novelist, Iris Murdoch, we find a picture of imagination as integral to our moral perception.[110]

Building on this historical precedent, more recently, philosophers have continued to explore the role imagination plays in relation to empathy and sympathy,[111] moral deliberation and judgment,[112] and moral perception.[113] There has also been discussion of the contribution imagination makes to the possibility of moral transformation and revolution,[114] envisioning new possibilities for moral action,[115] human development,[116] and our moral engagement with fiction.[117]

For all his influence in other areas of contemporary moral philosophy, Kant has not been a major influence in these discussions of the practical use of imagination. But according to at least one way of reading Kant, this is no accident: "when [moral sentimentalist theories] were eclipsed by Kantian rationalist moral philosophy, this led to a profound neglect of moral imagination"

---

[106] See, e.g., Smith's claim that, "By the imagination we place ourselves in his situation..., we enter as it were into his body, and become in some measure the same person with him" (2002, 12). For discussion of Hume's and Smith's views, see Collier (2010); Bailey (2017); and Ilyes (2017).

[107] See, e.g., Dewey's gloss of deliberation as "imaginative rehearsal" (1922, pt. 3, §3).

[108] Making this point in the negative, in *Everyday Ethics* Lyman Cabot says, "The man of little imagination may plod along going about what is expected of him, but he can never be greatly good. Thousands of iridescent opportunities open for a moment like a rainbow before him, but he sees only the dust on the road... Everywhere he misses the sight of the delicate opportunities which pass swiftly as the shadow of a bird's wing in flight" (1906, 211–12). For discussion, see Kaag (2011); Matherne (2023b).

[109] See, e.g., sessions 11 and 12 in Arendt's *Lectures of Kant's Political Philosophy* (1982).

[110] For discussion of Murdoch's view of moral imagination, see Clarke (2006); Altorf (2008); Gomes (2022).

[111] See Sherman (1998); Stueber (2011); Langton (2019); Maibom (2020); Bailey (2021; 2022).

[112] See Fesmire (2003); Stueber (2011); Biss (2014).

[113] See Nussbaum (1990); Church (2013, chap. 5).   [114] See Babbitt (1996).

[115] See Biss (2014).

[116] Fletcher (2016), for example, identifies imagination as a basic capability required for human development.

[117] See Nussbaum (1990); Carroll (2002); Liao (2013); Gilmore (2020); Vendrell Ferran (2023).

(Johnson 2016, 356).[118] *Per* this interpretive line of thought, given his rationalist conception of morality, Kant regards imagination as something to be suppressed, rather than championed, in the moral domain.

Kant certainly does not foreground the topic of imagination in his central moral writings and sometimes cautions us against its moral subversiveness. However, in Part IV, I argue that when we think through his account of morality and practical agency in light of his theory of what imagination is in general, then we shall uncover a Kantian vision of the practical use of imagination. Given the dearth of references to imagination in his major moral writings, my efforts in this part are more reconstructive than are my efforts in Parts I–III; nevertheless, I hope to bring to light how imagination can practically serve us within the Kantian framework. To this end, I argue that, on Kant's view, our imagination aids us by providing us with concrete, sensory ways to grasp how happiness and morality can, and do, make a different to us, as human beings.

I organize this discussion, more specifically, around an account of how two of Kant's characterizations of imagination in general shed light on its practical use. First, I claim that Kant's gloss of imagination as something that enables us to see more than is immediately present has a significant role to play in our pursuit of happiness and morality (Chapter 12). Here, I explore how this imaginative seeing more contributes to activities, such as the specification of practical principles, perception of and deliberation about concrete situations, envisioning of ideals of happiness, and the assessment of maxims in light of the categorical imperative.

Second, I argue that Kant's definition of imagination as the faculty of exhibition has moral import (Chapter 13). Here I discuss a wide range of ways in which Kant thinks our imagination can exhibit moral concepts to us, including in our aesthetic engagement with beauty and sublimity, as well as in our engagement with moral examples and moral ideals. And I make the case that, on Kant's view, the imaginative exhibition of moral concepts serves us by facilitating our comprehension of what moral concepts mean for us, as human beings, and provides us with proof that, limited as we are, moral action is possible for us. In these acts of exhibition, I submit that we find a distinctively Kantian conception of moral imagination, *qua* an imagination that has been "call[ed]...into play" by "morally oriented reason" (Rel. 6:23n).

Stepping back, over the course of the past three sections, I have surveyed various points of contact between Kant's and contemporary answers to the unity, taxonomy, and use questions in the hope of motivating the idea that we still have reason to look to Kant in our efforts to make sense of what imagination is. In

---

[118] I discuss Johnson's interpretation at more length in Chapter 11. I also discuss Johnson's (1985) reconstruction of the implicit role imagination plays in Kant's theory of moral judgment vis-à-vis the universalizability test of maxims in Chapter 12.

26   INTRODUCTION

order to conclude these introductory remarks, I shall now offer a chapter-by-chapter overview of the book in which I draw together the key tenets of my interpretation.

0.4 The Plan for the Book

At the heart of my systematic interpretation of Kant's theory of imagination is the claim that he offers a unified account of what imagination is as a sensible cognitive capacity, which plays a robust role in our theoretical, aesthetic, and practical lives. I devote Part I to an analysis of what imagination is in general on Kant's view and Parts II–IV to an analysis of how our imagination operates in theoretical, aesthetic, and practical contexts, respectively.

In Part I, my main thesis is that Kant conceives of imagination as a cognitive capacity that belongs to sensibility. In defending this thesis, I proceed by way of zooming in on imagination from the perspective of Kant's broader map of the human mind. In Chapter 1, I open with a discussion of Kant's analysis of imagination as part of our faculty of cognition. In this chapter, I consider both what cognition amounts to on Kant's view and his organization of the faculty of cognition into the two "stems" of sensibility and understanding.

I then devote Chapters 2 and 3 to the argument that Kant conceives of imagination as a cognitive capacity that belongs to the stem of sensibility. In Chapter 2, I spell out the debate surrounding how to think about where imagination fits into Kant's two-stem architecture and what philosophically hangs on this. And I canvass three possible views of our imagination Kant might endorse: a view that treats imagination as a "third thing" alongside sensibility and understanding, a view that treats imagination as part of sensibility, and a view that treats imagination as a sensible exercise of understanding. In Chapter 3, I make the case that Kant's considered view is that imagination is part of sensibility. In defending this reading, I attribute to Kant a bipartite account of sensibility, according to which it has two parts: sense and imagination. And I contend that imagination is a spontaneous part of sensibility that engages in a distinctive kind of sensibility activity (formation, synthesis, or composition), generates a distinctive kind of intuition (intuition of imagination, or what I label an "intuition$_i$"), and has a distinctive cognitive function (making concepts sensible).

In Chapter 4, I go into more detail about how to understand the distinctive kind of sensible activity, intuition, and cognitive function that Kant attributes to imagination. To this end, I zoom in on three definitions Kant offers of imagination as a distinctive "faculty of...," each of which elucidates a different aspect of it: the faculty of formation (*Bildungsvermögen*), the faculty for representing objects in intuition even without their presence, and the faculty of "exhibition" (*Darstellung, exhibitio*). In my discussion of the "formation definition," I further explicate the sort of sensible activities and intuitions Kant ascribes to imagination. In my discussion of the "even-without-presence" definition, I explore Kant's account of the degree of independence our imagination has from the presence of objects and our ability to see more (i.e. to be sensorily aware of more) than is immediately present to us. While this definition echoes traditional accounts of imagination as fantasy, I argue that Kant's qualifier of "even without" signals an important way in which he innovates within this tradition and accords our imagination a significant role to play in relation to objects that are present. Finally, in my discussion of the "exhibition definition," I analyze Kant's picture of imagination as a capacity responsible for exhibiting concepts to us in intuition. Though this definition has received less attention than the other two definitions, I maintain that the exhibition definition is crucial for understanding Kant's account of the cognitive function of our imagination: the function of making concepts sensible in a way that facilitates our concrete comprehension of them.

With this interpretation of what imagination is in general in place, in Parts II–IV, I examine Kant's account of how we deploy this single cognitive capacity across the theoretical, aesthetic, and practical domains and I particularly emphasize the ubiquitous activities of seeing more and exhibition. In Part II, I focus on Kant's analysis of the theoretical (or epistemic) use of imagination in the context of perception and experience. In addition to analyzing the details of Kant's account of what our imagination theoretically contributes on both the empirical and *a priori* levels, I make the case that in order to understand this imaginative contribution, we need to attend to the theme of exhibition. Doing so, I argue, reveals Kant's commitment to the theoretical use of our imagination being constrained by concepts and his endorsement of a conceptualist position, according to which the imagination's generation of intuitions in this context depends on concepts of both the empirical and pure variety.

More specifically, in Chapter 5, I focus on the empirical level. I attribute to Kant a view of experience, according to which experience involves three stages: a sense stage, which involves sensing; an imagination stage, which involves perception; and an understanding stage, which involves empirical judgments. I contend that perception, on Kant's view, ultimately involves the imaginative activity of exhibiting empirical concepts in intuition. And I claim that Kant distinguishes the sensible, conceptually laden imaginative activity involved in perception from the sensible, pre-conceptual activities involved in the sense stage of experience, on the one hand, and the intellectual, conceptual activities of judgment involved in the understanding stage of experience, on the other.

In Chapters 6 and 7, I take up the account of the *a priori* contribution imagination makes to the possibility of experience that Kant articulates in the B-edition of the Transcendental Deduction and Schematism, respectively. One of the key questions I pursue in these chapters is how Kant understands the relationship between the *a priori* activities of imagination, the pure intuitions of space and

28 INTRODUCTION

time, and the pure concepts of the understanding ("the categories"). In Chapter 6, I argue against a reading of the Transcendental Deduction, according to which we should attribute to him a radical model of the *a priori* exercise of imagination as the source of our basic pure intuitions of space and time. I, instead, attribute to him a more moderate view, according to which the *a priori* exercise of imagination involves activities that mediate between the pure intuitions of space and time given by sensibility, on the one hand, and the categories, on the other. Turning to the Schematism, in Chapter 7, I maintain that Kant there elaborates on his position in the Transcendental Deduction in light of the pivotal claim that our imagination accomplishes this mediating work through an activity of exhibition that he calls "schematism." In attributing this mediating view of schematism to Kant, I resist another kind of radical reading, according to which the *a priori* activities of imagination are the source of the categories, *qua* concepts of objects. And in these two chapters, I continue to develop my argument to the effect that Kant regards the theoretical use of imagination as something that is constrained by concepts, the relevant concepts here being the categories.

In Part III, I address Kant's account of the aesthetic use of imagination. My overarching thesis in this discussion is that the key to understanding this use is attending to Kant's commitment to our imagination proceeding in a cognitive, creative, and conceptually rich way in the aesthetic domain. I devote Chapter 8 to Kant's account of the contribution our imagination makes to the aesthetic appreciation of beauty. I focus, in particular, on Kant's account of what our imagination contributes to the "free play" involved in appreciating beauty. I argue against so-called "precognitive" interpretations of free play, according to which it precedes independently from concepts, in favor of a so-called "multicognitive" interpretation, according to which free play involves an imaginative activity that is conceptually rich.[119] And in defending this interpretation, I expand my conceptualist reading of Kant's account of intuitions of imagination as dependent on concepts into the aesthetic domain.

I extend this interpretive line concerning imaginative creativity to Kant's account of what our imagination contributes to artistic production and genius in Chapter 9. At the core of this chapter is an interpretation of Kant's account of "aesthetic ideas," according to which they involve the creative exhibition of concepts that expands our comprehension of concepts in open-ended ways.

I then address Kant's account of what our imagination contributes in relation to the sublime in Chapter 10. Although commentators sometimes attribute to Kant a view of our imagination as having a wholly negative role to play in relation to the sublime, I argue that he not only accords our imagination a positive role to play, but also insists that in relation to the sublime we discover a higher vocation of our imagination as an instrument of reason. I analyze this positive and elevated

---

[119] The "precognitive" and "multicognitive" labels are from Guyer (2005).

role in terms of a cognitively creative activity in which our imagination treats extremely large and powerful objects in nature as an indirect exhibition of the sublimity of our rationality, which makes its greatness and might palpable to us.

In Part IV, I shift my focus to Kant's view of the practical use of imagination. In Chapter 11, I explore some reasons to be skeptical that Kant can countenance anything like a moral imagination. But I ultimately defend the thesis that he accords our imagination a valuable role to play in the practical domain. I lay particular emphasis on the role our imagination has in making practical concepts sensible to us in a way that helps us envision the difference they can, and do, make in the minds and lives of human beings.

In order to defend this thesis, I offer a reconstruction of a Kantian view of the practical value of imagination that builds upon the general picture of imagination I develop in Part I. In Chapter 12, I draw on Kant's definition of imagination as a faculty that enables us to represent objects in intuition even without their presence in order to elucidate different ways in which our imaginative ability to see more than we are immediately given contributes to our pursuit of happiness and morality. In this chapter, I focus, in particular, on what imagination contributes to general activities involved in the faculty of desire, such as principle specification, situation assessment, deliberation, the projection of happiness as a so-called "ideal of imagination," and in testing the morality of maxims in light of the categorical imperative.

In Chapter 13, I take my cue from Kant's definition of imagination as a faculty of exhibition and I make the case that he thinks that the imaginative activity of exhibiting moral concepts in intuition has moral value for us as human beings. After addressing some reasons we might worry that Kant can acknowledge the imaginative exhibition of moral ideas, I consider his account of the value that the indirect exhibition of moral concepts in beauty and sublimity and the direct exhibition of them in moral ideals and moral examples has for us. I underscore Kant's commitment to exhibition of the moral variety facilitating our comprehension of moral ideas from a human perspective and encouraging us to think that it is really possible for us, as human beings, to be moral.

In the end, by exploring Kant's systematic picture of what imagination is in general and how we deploy it in the context of ordinary experience, aesthetic engagement, and practical agency, I aim to bring to light a vision of the unity, flexibility, and ubiquity of imagination in our lives. At the same time, there are many imaginative phenomena that Kant canvasses in his philosophy, which I will not be able to offer an in-depth analysis of, including the connection between imagination and empirical concept formation,[120] memory,[121] the highest good,[122]

---

[120] See Longuenesse (1998, chap. 5); Allison (2004, chap. 1); Newton (2015); Anderson (2015, chap. 13); Ginsborg (2015, chap. 7); Sethi (2022).
[121] See Stephenson (2017).   [122] See Gibbons (1994, chap. 5); Kneller (2007).

30   INTRODUCTION

the regulative use of ideas of reason,[123] among other topics. However, I take these to be horizons of further work to be done, work that I hope might be inspired by Kant's vision of imagination as a cognitive capacity that allows us to see more in the variegated ways that we do.

The last preliminary set of remarks I want to make concern my use of Kant's texts. The anchor of my interpretation is the theory of imagination that Kant develops in the *Critique of Pure Reason* (1781/7), the *Critique of the Power of Judgment* (1790), and the *Anthropology from a Pragmatic Point of View* (1798). Given the lengthy discussion of imagination he offers in the first and third *Critiques*, my reliance on these texts should come as no surprise. However, I also lean heavily on the account of imagination that Kant offers in the *Anthropology* because in it he offers a more synoptic view of imagination than in either the first or third *Critiques*. In the first *Critique* Kant's concern is with the theoretical use of imagination in ordinary experience, especially in the *a priori* register, and in the third *Critique* with the aesthetic use of imagination vis-à-vis beauty and sublimity. But in the *Anthropology* Kant offers an account of what imagination is in general, as well as of the variety of reproductive-productive, voluntary-involuntary, and empirical-*a-priori* modes in which it is exercised. The *Anthropology* is thus an invaluable resource for thinking through Kant's approach to the unity and taxonomy of imagination; hence the central role it plays on my interpretation.

However, in my interpretation, I also draw on other published and unpublished writings, as well as student notes on Kant's lectures. These other writings provide a wealth of material that shed light on the development of Kant's views and help fill out his mature picture of imagination in crucial ways. This said, there is some question about whether we should take the student notes to be a reliable indicator of Kant's considered position.[124] I take this to be a serious concern and though I do cite the lecture notes frequently, I use passages and lines of thought that we either find recorded in other student lecture notes or that Kant affirms in his published writings. When I cite from these notes, I will use locutions like "Kant says," but in these contexts, what I mean is that "Kant is recorded as saying that."

Ultimately, insofar as my aim is to offer a systematic interpretation of how Kant understands imagination in general and its various uses across our lives, I look to the full range of texts that shed light on it in its myriad aspects. And by synthesizing these aspects together, I aspire to put forward, in its on-going promise, a Kantian picture of just how imaginative we are.

Seeing More: Kant's Theory of Imagination. Samantha Matherne, Oxford University Press.
© Samantha Matherne 2024. DOI: 10.1093/9780191999291.003.0001

---

[123] See Kraus (2020, chap. 5, §§5–6).
[124] For discussion of these concerns, see Clewis (2015, editor's intro.); Lu-Adler (2015); and Merritt (2018a, chap. 1.4).

PART I
IMAGINATION IN GENERAL

1

Imagination as a Cognitive Capacity

imagination...without which we would have no cognition at all
—A78/B103

1.1 Introduction

What is it to imagine?[1] My aim in Part I is to show that Kant has an answer to this question that turns on a theory of our imagination (*Einbildungskraft*) as a single mental capacity that we exercise in a rich range of ways. More specifically, I attribute to Kant a view of imagination as a cognitive capacity that is sensible in nature, which I often gloss as a capacity to see more.[2]

My analysis of the kind of cognitive capacity Kant takes imagination to be proceeds in two phases. In the first phase (Chapters 1–3), I zoom out and analyze Kant's account of what imagination is in light of his view of our cognitive architecture as a whole. In the second phase (Chapter 4), I fill out this basic picture by zooming in on Kant's efforts to define imagination as a specific cognitive "faculty of..."

The first phrase first, however. In order to situate imagination in Kant's cognitive architecture as a whole, I proceed by considering his treatment of imagination as a capacity that belongs to the so-called "faculty of cognition" (*Erkenntnisvermögen*). Kant famously claims that our faculty of cognition is structured by "two stems": "sensibility" (*Sinnlichkeit*) and "understanding" (*Verstand*) (A15/B29).[3] And in

---

[1] Recall Walton's posing of this question in *Mimesis as Make-Believe*: "What is it to imagine? We have examined a number of dimensions along which imagining can vary; shouldn't we now spell out what they have in common? Yes, if we can. But I can't" (1990, 19).

[2] As I noted in the Introduction, although in contemporary discussions of imagination "cognitive" is often used as a label for propositional, attitudinal, or belief-like imagining, in contrast with imagistic, objectual, perception-like imagining (see Yablo 1993; Gaut 2003; and Stock 2017, 23–4), Kant uses "cognitive" as a more generic label for mental states in which we consciously represent objects.

[3] I shall use the terms "faculty" (*Vermögen*), "capacity" (*Fähigkeit*), and "power" (*Kraft*) interchangeably in what follows. This said, in lectures Kant sometimes draws a technical distinction between these terms (see, e.g., MVo 28:434; MMr 29:823), and some interpreters emphasize this difference (see, e.g., Longuenesse's 1998, 7–8, emphasis on the difference between the faculty of judgment (*Vermögen zu urteilen*) as the "potentiality" for making judgments, and the power of judgment (*Urteilskraft*) as the "actualization" of this "potentiality"). However, in the first and third *Critiques* Kant tends to use these terms interchangeably. For example, in his discussion of sensibility and understanding in the first *Critique*, he describes them as "two faculties or capacities [*Vermögen, oder Fähigkeiten*]" (A51/B75) and as "powers" (A262/B318). And in the third *Critique*, he says, "all the

34 IMAGINATION AS A COGNITIVE CAPACITY

the next three chapters I develop an argument to the effect that Kant ultimately conceives of imagination as part of sensibility and that recognizing this is crucial for appreciating the basic kind of sensible representation, sensible activity, and cognitive function that he attributes to imagination.

In this chapter, I concentrate on the insights we can gain into Kant's basic conception of what imagination is in light of him situating it in the faculty of cognition. After I make a few preliminary remarks about the relationship between imagination and the faculty of cognition in §1.2, I devote the rest of the chapter to developing a sharper picture of what the faculty of cognition amounts to on Kant's view. To this end, in §1.3, I approach the faculty of cognition by way of considerations about exactly what Kant means by "cognition" (*Erkenntnis*) and I address the basic implications this view of cognition has for how we are to think of imagination as a cognitive capacity. In §1.4, I then turn to Kant's analysis of the architecture of the faculty of cognition, which hinges on its two stems: sensibility and understanding. And in order to clarify these two stems, I offer an account of the distinction he draws between sensibility and understanding on logical, metaphysical, and functional grounds. Though this two-stem architecture has important implications for what kind of cognitive capacity we take imagination to be for Kant, spelling out these implications is no easy matter and it will occupy me in Chapters 2 and 3.

1.2 Imagination and the Faculty of Cognition

Let's begin with some high-level considerations about how imagination fits into Kant's theory of mind. As I indicated in the Introduction, at the most basic level, Kant operates with a tripartite account of the mind, according to which it is divided into three "fundamental faculties" (*Grundvermögen*): the "faculty of cognition" (*Erkenntnisvermögen*), the "faculty of desire" (*Begehrungsvermögen*), and the faculty of the "feeling of pleasure and displeasure" (*Gefühl der Lust und Unlust*).[4] Recall that the faculty of cognition is a faculty responsible for consciously representing objects. The faculty of desire is a volitional faculty by means of which we, through our representations, bring about certain objects.[5] And the

---

faculties or capacities of the soul [*alle Seelenvermögen, oder Fähigkeiten*] can be reduced to three" (KU 5:177). Meanwhile in his discussion of imagination, though the German term for imagination, *Einbildungskraft*, includes the term "power" (*Kraft*) (see also KU 5:316), Kant also refers to imagination as a "faculty" (A94; KU 5:313) and a "capacity" (A94). My interchangeable use of capacity, faculty, and power is in keeping with this tendency in the first and third *Critiques*.

[4] See KU 5:177, 196–8; EE 20:205, 245–6. See also Kant's organization of the *Anthropology* along these tripartite lines: Book 1: "On the cognitive faculty," Book 2: "The feeling of pleasure and displeasure," Book 3: "On the faculty of desire" (see also Mensch. 25:852). For further discussion, see Frierson (2014b, chap. 2); Wuerth (2014, chap. 6).

[5] See, e.g., Kant's gloss of the faculty of desire as the "*faculty to be by means of its representations the cause of the reality of the objects of these representations*" (KpV 5:9n, quoted again at KU 5:177n; see also MS 6:211).

feeling of pleasure and displeasure is a hedonic faculty through which we register how we are subjectively affected by objects or our own subjective states.[6]

Kant locates imagination in the faculty of cognition. In this vein, he says that imagination is a "faculty" or "capacity" of cognition (see A94; KU 5:217). And this is why he situates his analysis of imagination in his discussion of the faculty of cognition, rather than in his discussion of the other faculties of the mind in the *Anthropology*, his anthropological lectures, and his metaphysics lectures.[7] Though Kant by no means denies that imagination can relate to the faculty of desire or the feeling of pleasure and displeasure, on his view, it does so as part of the faculty of cognition.[8] Hence my description of imagination, for Kant, as a cognitive capacity.

But what exactly is a cognitive capacity on Kant's view? To begin answering this question, we need to take a closer look at what Kant means by "cognition" in the first place.

1.3 Kant's Theory of Cognition

For all its importance in Kant's philosophy, pinning down what he means by "cognition" (*Erkenntnis*) is no easy matter.[9] Indeed, even the translation of "Erkenntnis" poses a challenge: some render it as "knowledge," while others insist on "cognition."[10] For reasons I noted in the Introduction, I take "cognition" to be preferable.[11] The term Kant uses for "knowledge" is "Wissen," and he characterizes *Wissen* as something that involves an intellectual act in which we take a judgment to be true.[12] But, as we shall see, *Erkenntnis* involves a more minimal state. This said, specifying exactly what sort of more minimal state cognition involves is also vexed. For, as a slew of recent interpreters have emphasized, Kant appears to use cognition in both a "broad" and a "narrow" sense.[13]

---

[6] See, e.g., Kant's description of the faculty of feeling of pleasure and displeasure in terms of how "the subject feels itself as it is affected by the representation" (KU 5:204). For discussion of the feeling of pleasure/displeasure as a "faculty," see Sorensen and Williamson (2018); Cohen (2020).

[7] See Pt. I of Anthro. §§15, 28–39; AF 25:511; AMr 25:1241; ML1 28:230; MMr 29:880–1.

[8] The relation of imagination to the faculty of desire will be important in my discussion of the practical contribution of imagination in Chapter 12, and I touch more elliptically on its relation to the feeling of pleasure and displeasure in my discussion of his account of aesthetic appreciation in Chapters 8 and 10.

[9] For recent discussions of the complications surrounding Kant's theory of cognition, see Smit (2000; 2009); Kain (2010); Gomes and Stephenson (2016); Sommerlatte (2016); Tolley (2017; 2020); Watkins and Willaschek (2017b); Willaschek and Watkins (2020); Schafer (2022a).

[10] Kemp Smith, for example, opts for "knowledge," whereas Guyer and Wood opt for "cognition" in their translation of the first *Critique*.

[11] For discussion of the knowledge-cognition distinction, see Chignell (2007a); Cohen (2014); Watkins and Willaschek (2017b); Willaschek and Watkins (2020); Tolley (2020).

[12] Kant describes this in terms of the attitude of "Fürwahrhalen," literally "holding-for-true" (see A820/B848ff).

[13] I take the "broad" and "narrow" labels from Watkins and Willaschek (2017b).

36 IMAGINATION AS A COGNITIVE CAPACITY

In the broad sense, Kant characterizes cognition as a conscious representation of an object. He offers this broad characterization of cognition in the so-called "Stufenleiter" passage in the first *Critique* (A320/B376-7).[14] There, he claims that cognition involves a particular kind of "representation [*Vorstellung*]," which he characterizes as an "objective perception [*Perception, perceptio*]" (A320/B376-7). By a "perception" in this context, Kant has in mind a "representation with consciousness"; hence a representation that is conscious, rather than unconscious (A320/B376).[15] And by an "objective" perception he has in mind a conscious representation through which we represent an object, *qua* something that stands over and against us.[16] An objective perception thus contrasts with a "subjective perception," or what Kant labels a "sensation" (*Empfindung, sensatio*), which is a conscious representation through which we represent a subjective state (A320/ B376). For example, whereas a representation of my current state of feeling cozy would count as a subjective perception, a representation of a marigold as a flower that stands over and against me would count as an objective perception, hence as a cognition in the broad sense.

In the *Stufenleiter* Kant appears to distinguish between two sub-species of cognition in the broad sense: "an objective perception [*Perception*] is a **cognition** (*cognitio*). The latter is either an **intuition** [*Anschauung*] or a **concept** [*Begriff*] (*intuitus vel conceptus*)" (A320/B376-8).[17] While I have more to say about intuitions and concepts in §1.4, roughly, intuitions amount to sensible representations of particulars, whereas concepts amount to intellectual representations of properties particulars share in common. For example, a sensible representation of a particular marigold that I see here and now in a garden would count as an intuition, whereas an intellectual representation of the properties that marigolds share in common, such as having pinnate leaves or being low maintenance, would count as a concept. Notice that the *Stufenleiter* seems to imply that either intuitions or concepts count as cognitions in the broad sense. So, whether I just have an intuition of a marigold or just think about the concept <marigold>,[18] each representation would count as a cognition in the broad sense: each involves a conscious representation through which I represent marigolds, *qua* objects that stand over and against me.

---

[14] I here focus primarily on Kant's account of cognition in the first *Critique*, but he also defends a broad characterization at JL 9:64-5.

[15] I return to issues surrounding Kant's use of "perception" in Chapter 5.

[16] There is a question as to whether this conscious representation just involves a representation with consciousness, or whether it also involves consciousness of the object (see Tolley 2020 and Schafer 2022a for the argument that cognition in the broad sense involves the latter). I am sympathetic to the latter position. However, in Chapter 5, I argue that we need to recognize a range of different kinds of objects that we can be conscious of through sense, imagination, and judgment.

[17] I say Kant "appears" to distinguish between two sub-species of cognition because there is some question as to whether we should read the *Stufenleiter* along genus-species lines, or whether he intends to describe intuitions and concepts as two "parts" of the complex that is cognition (see Tolley 2020).

[18] I shall use < > to designate concepts throughout this book.

However, elsewhere Kant offers a narrower characterization of cognition:

Intuition and concepts therefore constitute the elements of all our cognitions, so that neither concepts without intuition corresponding to them in some way nor intuition without concepts can yield a cognition...Thoughts without content are empty, intuitions without concepts are blind...Only from their unification can cognition arise. (A50–2/B74–6)[19]

In this passage, Kant construes cognition as something that involves both intuitions and concepts. In the narrow sense, then, cognition involves the conscious representation of objects by means of some sort of unification of intuitions and concepts. *Per* this narrow characterization, in order to cognize a marigold, it is not enough for me to consciously represent it through either an intuition or a concept; I need to deploy the concept <marigold> to think about a flower I intuit here and now.

While there are different ways to think through the relationship between cognition in the broad and narrow senses, what I want to focus on is the question of what Kant thinks cognition in the narrow sense achieves in our conscious representation of objects beyond what cognition in the broad sense achieves. In particular, I shall concentrate on Kant's claim that cognition in the narrow sense enables us to consciously represent objects as, one, determinate, and, two, really possible.[20] Call these the "determinacy achievement" and "modal achievement" of cognition in the narrow sense, respectively.

Starting with the determinacy achievement, according to Kant, cognition in the narrow sense enables us to consciously represent objects as determined in some way, rather than as an indeterminate something or other.[21] In this vein, he claims that, "the **cognition** of objects that we think, the determination of the object, requires intuition" (B166n). And he says, "I cannot stop with these intuitions, if they are to become cognitions, but must refer [*beziehen*] them as representations to something as their object and determine this object through them," and that, concepts are that "through which I bring about this determination" (Bxvii).[22]

---

[19] See also his description of cognition as a "complex representation (*perceptio complexa*)...since intuition and concepts are always required for it" (Anthro. 7:138; see also 7:141), and "cognition... consists of concept and intuition. Each of these two is representation, indeed, but not yet cognition [*Erkenntnis*]...By this mere intuition without concept the object is given, indeed, but not thought; by the concept without corresponding intuition it is thought but not given; thus in both cases it is not cognized [*erkannt*]" (WF 20:325; transl. modified).

[20] See Schafer (2022a) for an emphasis on both of these aspects of cognition in the narrow sense.

[21] For discussion, see Watkins and Willaschek (2017b, §3); Smit (2000, 243); Schafer (2022a).

[22] See also "With us **understanding** and **sensibility** can determine an object **only in combination**. If we separate them, then we have intuitions without concepts, or concepts without intuitions, but in either case representations that we cannot relate to any determinate object" (A258/B314), and his claim about the empirical cognition that is experience, to the effect that, "experience...is to determine the object of perception" (B423n).

38 IMAGINATION AS A COGNITIVE CAPACITY

While the details remain to be filled in, in these passages Kant indicates that cognition in the narrow sense involves us consciously representing an object as determinate in some fashion.

But what sort of determinacy does Kant think cognition in the narrow sense brings into our representation of objects? At the very least, Kant thinks cognition in the narrow sense involves us deploying concepts to represent objects as qualitatively determinate. When I, for example, think about a flower I intuit in the garden as falling under the concept <marigold>, I represent it as having certain qualitative features that marigolds share in common, e.g. having pinnate leaves, being low maintenance, or being a deer deterrent.

However, Kant also indicates that the representation of sensible, i.e. spatio-temporal, determinacy of objects is relevant to cognition in the narrow sense. Examples of representations of sensible determinacy for Kant include representations of the numerical identity, spatial shape, temporal duration, or the mereological spatio-temporal structure of something.[23] We find indirect evidence that representations of sensible determinacy are relevant to cognition in the narrow sense in the *Prolegomena*, where Kant underscores the importance of both conceptual and spatio-temporal determinations to this end:

> it would be an absurdity for us... with respect to any thing that we assume not to be an object of possible experience, to claim even the least cognition for determining it according to its nature as it is in itself; for by what means will we reach this determination, since, time, space, and all the concepts of the understanding... do not and cannot have any use other than merely to make experience possible. (Prol. 4:350)

In this passage, Kant elliptically indicates that the only way in which we can determine an object in cognition is through space, time, and concepts. For example, when I cognize the marigold in the garden, I not only qualitatively determine it as having general properties of marigolds, e.g. having pinnate leaves or being low maintenance, but also as sensibly determinate, e.g. as one thing and as a spatial whole that contains spatial parts. This line of thought suggests that, on Kant's view, the determinacy achievement of cognition in the narrow sense amounts to the way in which the use of both intuitions and concepts enables us to consciously represent objects as qualitatively and sensibly determinate.

The modal achievement of cognition in the narrow sense, i.e. our ability to consciously represent objects as really possible, will take more time to spell out. We find Kant connecting cognition and real possibility in the following passage in the first *Critique*:

---

[23] Whereas Watkins and Willaschek (2017b, 101) suggest that the relevant determination is qualitative rather than numerical, Schafer (2022a) argues it is both.

> To **cognize** an object, it is required that I be able to prove [*beweisen*] its possibility...
> I can **think** whatever I like, as long as I do not contradict myself...But in order
> to ascribe objective validity to such a concept (real possibility, for the first sort of
> possibility was merely logical) something more is required.   (Bxxvi fn)[24]

In this passage, Kant alludes to his distinction between "real" and "logical" possibility.[25] *Per* Kant, something is logically possible as long as the concept of it does not entail a contradiction. But in order for something to be really possible, he claims that it "must be able to be given in some way" (A155/B194). Insofar as this is the case, Kant claims that the concepts of really possible things are not "empty," but rather have "objective validity" (or what he also calls "objective reality"): they are concepts that are "related to an object...[that] must be able to be given in some way" (A155/B194, see also A239/B298).[26]

To illustrate, consider the contrast between the possibility of precognition (i.e. the ability to "*intuit* the future") and marigolds (A222/B270). From Kant's perspective, both are logically possible: the concepts <precognition> and <marigold> do not entail a contradiction in the way that the concept <round square> does. However, Kant denies that precognition is a real possibility: the concept of precognition is an empty concept that involves an "arbitrary combination of thoughts" that does not relate to an object that we can be given (A223/B270). By contrast marigolds count as really possible objects on Kant's view: they are objects that can be given and the concept <marigold> is, hence, not empty, but rather has objective reality.

Let's now return to Kant's claim that, "To **cognize** an object, it is required that I be able to prove [*beweisen*] its possibility" (Bxxvi fn). Here, Kant suggests that cognition in the narrow sense "requires" being able to "prove" that the object at issue is really possible. As we have just seen, this involves us being able to prove that the concept of the relevant object has objective reality, i.e. relates to objects that we can be given. So, according to Kant, what puts us in a position to prove this real possibility of objects and objective reality of concepts?

Kant typically answers this question with an appeal to intuition: "To demonstrate the reality of our concepts, intuitions are always required" (KU 5:351).[27]

---

[24] For discussion of the modal constraints Kant here places on cognition, see Chignell (2010; 2011); Grüne (2016, 245–6; 2017b, 115–6); Schafer (2022a); Watkins (forthcoming).

[25] For discussions of Kant's theory of real possibility, see Chignell (2009b; 2011); Stang (2016); Leech (2017); Marshall and Barker (forthcoming); Watkins (forthcoming).

[26] See, e.g., "The first possibility may be called logical, the second, real possibility; the proof of the latter is the proof of the objective reality of the concept" (WF 20:325). Although Kant often uses "objective validity" in a way that appears interchangeable with "objective reality" (e.g. Bxxvi n), he sometimes describes objective validity as a property of judgments, rather than concepts (e.g. B142; Prol. 4:298–9; KU 5:215). For the argument that the difference between the two terms is significant, see Heidegger KPM 61–2; Meerbote (1972); Allison (2015, 382–3).

[27] Although in this passage and others like them (e.g. OD 8:188–9) in which Kant discusses theoretical cognition, he tends to emphasize intuition, he also suggests that there can be "practical" "sources of cognition" that secure the objective reality of concepts. See Chignell (2007a; 2010); Kain

40 IMAGINATION AS A COGNITIVE CAPACITY

At more length in the first *Critique*, Kant says, "For every concept there is requisite...the possibility of giving it an object to which it is to be related. Without this latter it has no sense, and is entirely empty of content...Now the object cannot be given to a concept otherwise than in intuition" (A239/B298). As we see in this passage, Kant claims that intuition is needed to demonstrate the objective reality of our concepts because intuition is what gives us the objects that correspond to those concepts.[28] For example, having an intuition of a marigold gives me the object that the concept <marigold> relates to; hence puts me in a position to demonstrate the real possibility of marigolds and objective reality of <marigold>.

Bringing this to bear on the modal achievement, on Kant's view, the unification of concepts and intuitions in cognition in the narrow sense enables us to be conscious of objects as really possible. For when we think about the object we intuit in accordance with a certain concept, this establishes that the concept at issue is not empty, but rather has objective reality in an object that we can be given through intuition. And in this way, Kant thinks that cognition in the narrow sense enables us to represent objects not just as determinate, but as really possible.

There is, no doubt, much more to say about Kant's theory of cognition, but what interests me here are the implications that this theory has for how we are to understand what it means for imagination to be a cognitive capacity. At the most basic level, his account of cognition in the broad sense indicates that, as a cognitive capacity, our imagination contributes to our conscious representations of objects. What this suggests is that when we attend to Kant's account of imaginative activities, such "synthesis" or "composition," and imaginative representations, such as "images" or "schemata," we should be alert to how they figure in our conscious representation of objects. But what Kant's account of cognition in the narrow sense indicates is that imagination is, moreover, a capacity that has some role to play in the cognitive process through which we unite intuitions and concepts together, and, thereby, consciously represent objects as determinate and as really possible. However, in order to further specify exactly how imagination participates in this process, we need to take a closer look at Kant's analysis of the architecture of the faculty of cognition.

(2010); Abaci (2022); and Schafer (2023) for how these issues bear on Kant's account of practical cognition.

[28] There are further complications to this picture that I shall not address here, one of them being that Kant appears to allow for the demonstration of real possibility in theoretical contexts to proceed either through intuitions that give us actual objects or through intuitions that give us objects that agree with the "formal conditions" of the possibility of experience, and, hence, are "formally" possible objects (see A218/B266). For further discussion, see Chignell (2010); Gomes and Stephenson (2016, §3.4.1); McLear (2016a); Grüne (2017a).

1.4 Sensibility and Understanding

Kant's account of the architecture of our faculty of cognition pivots on its "two stems": "there are two stems of human cognition, which may perhaps arise from a common but to us unknown root, namely sensibility and understanding, through the first of which objects are given to us, but through the second of which they are thought" (A15/B29). In a similar vein, he describes sensibility and understanding as the "two fundamental sources" of cognition:

> Our cognition arises from two fundamental sources in the mind, the first of which is the reception of representations (the receptivity of impressions), the second the faculty for cognizing an object by means of these representations (spontaneity of concepts)...If we will call the **receptivity** of our mind to receive representations insofar as it is affected in some way **sensibility**, then on the contrary the faculty for bringing forth representations itself, or the **spontaneity** of cognition, is the **understanding**. (A50–1/B74–5)

In order to get a working picture of sensibility and understanding in place, in what follows I approach them, as Kant often does, by describing their "heterogeneous" natures.[29] To this end, I sketch three distinctions Kant deploys to distinguish between sensibility and understanding: a metaphysical, logical, and functional distinction.[30]

The first distinction between sensibility and understanding is what Kant calls a "metaphysical" distinction, which pertains to the sort of causality each faculty involves (JL 9:36). Sensibility, he argues, is a "receptive" faculty by means of which we are causally "affected" by objects (A19/B33; A50–1/B74–5; Anthro. 7:140).[31] By contrast, understanding is a "spontaneous" faculty because it is capable of "bringing forth representations itself" in a "self-active" way (A51/B75, AB157–8fn; see also MMr 29:880). As he sometimes draws this contrast, whereas sensibility

---

[29] Here, I have in mind Kant's claim that sensibility and understanding are "heterogeneous elements [*Stücke*]" (KU 5:401).

[30] This is not meant to be an exhaustive discussion of the distinctions Kant draws between sensibility and understanding. In addition to these discussions, Kant describes sensibility as a "sensible" faculty, and understanding as an "intellectual" faculty (see ID 2:392; ML1 28:229; AMr 25:1230). And, recently, commentators have emphasized the distinction Kant draws between them on the basis of being governed by fundamentally different laws or principles (see Watkins 2017; McLear 2020b; Schafer 2021).

[31] Kant sometimes cashes out this feature of sensibility by describing it as a "passive" power (Gr. 4:452; B153; Anthro. 7:141). However, on his view, this passivity is consistent with activity: "We can never be merely passive, but rather every passion is at the same time action" (MMr 29:823; see also "Metaphysik v. Schön" 28: 513–14). For Kant, then, sensibility is passive in the sense that its activity is determined through "an external power" (MMr 29:823). For discussion of issues surrounding Kant's characterization of sensibility as passive and as responsible for activities, see Indregard (2017, 632); Watkins (2017); and McLear (forthcoming).

42   IMAGINATION AS A COGNITIVE CAPACITY

proceeds by way of "affections," understanding proceeds by way of "functions" through which it self-actively brings forth representations (A68/B93).[32]

The second distinction between sensibility and understanding is what Kant calls a "logical" distinction between the type of representation each faculty is responsible for: sensibility gives rise to "intuitions" and understanding to "concepts" (JL 9:36; see also A50–1/B74–5). As I anticipated earlier, Kant characterizes an intuition as a "singular" (*einzeln*) representation of something particular,[33] which stands in an "immediate" (*unmittelbar*), i.e. direct or non-inferential, relation to objects.[34] And in our case, he maintains that our intuitions have a spatio-temporal form (see A26–7/B42–3; B148). By contrast, Kant attributes to the understanding concepts, defined as "general" (*allgemein*) representations of properties shared in common by several things,[35] which stand in a "mediate" (*mittelbar*) relation to objects, i.e. they represent objects by means of common "marks" (*Merkmale*).[36] So whereas the intuition of a marigold is a spatio-temporal representation of a particular flower that I stand in a direct, non-inferential relation to, the concept <marigold> relates to marigolds by way of the common properties represented by the concept, e.g. having pinnate leaves, being low maintenance, etc.

The third distinction between sensibility and understanding that Kant draws is what I shall call a "functional" distinction, which pertains to the cognitive function that he attributes to each in cognition.[37] This distinction will require a bit more time to tease out.

Kant articulates the cognitive functions of sensibility and understanding as follows in this famous passage from the first *Critique* (which I partially quoted above):

> Without sensibility no object would be given to us, and without understanding none would be thought. Thoughts without content are empty, intuitions without concepts are blind. It is thus just as necessary to make the mind's concepts

---

[32] Kant often connects this metaphysical distinction to the "sensible" status of sensibility and "intellectual" status of understanding. See, e.g., "Cognition that rests on receptivity is sensible, that which [rests] on spontaneity is intellectual" (MMr 29:880). See also his remarks in the first *Critique* that, "our (human) intuition (which is always sensible, i.e., insofar as we are affected by objects)" (A35/B51); that, "It comes along with our nature that intuition can never be other than sensible, i.e., that it contains only the way in which we are affected by objects" (A51/B75); and that, "this spontaneity is the reason I call myself an intelligence" (B158fn). And see his claim in the *Anthropology* that, "representations that comprise a sheer *activity* (thinking) belong to the *intellectual* cognitive faculty" (Anthro. 7:140; transl. modified). For discussion of what spontaneity amounts to in the context of Kant's theory of understanding, see Pippin (1987); Smit (2009); Choi (2019); Kohl (2020).

[33] See A320/B377; JL 9:91; Anthro. 7:196; WF 20:266.

[34] See A320/B377; A68/B93; WF 20:266.

[35] See A320/B377; JL 9:91; Anthro. 7:196; WF 20:266, 272.

[36] See A320/B377; A68/B93; WF 20:266.

[37] Though I here talk about "functions," I remain neutral on the question of whether Kant conceives of this function as an "end" that reason sets for our capacities and that they are teleologically oriented toward. For arguments along these lines, see Fugate (2014); Mudd (2017); Schafer (2021). See also Kern's (2017, chap. 9) analysis of this in terms of "teleological causality."

sensible [*Begriffe sinnlich zu machen*] (i.e., to add an object to them intuition) as it is to make its intuitions understandable [*Anschauungen verständlich zu machen*] (i.e., to bring them under concepts)...[T]hese two faculties or capacities cannot exchange their functions...Only from their unification can cognition arise. (A51–2/B75–6)[38]

Here Kant casts the function of sensibility in terms of giving us objects through intuition and making concepts sensible, and the function of understanding in terms of thinking about objects through concepts and making intuitions understandable.

In detailing what these functions involve, Kant sometimes casts sensibility and understanding as the "lower" and "higher" faculties of cognition, respectively:[39] "It is customary to call sensibility the *lower* [niedere] faculty, the understanding on the other hand the *higher* [obere] faculty, on the ground that sensibility gives the mere material for thought, but the understanding rules over this material and brings it under rules or concepts" (JL 9:36).[40] To elaborate this line of thought Kant employs a political analogy.[41] Understanding, he claims, acts like a "sovereign" power in relation to sensibility insofar as it provides concepts which serve as "rules" that govern the intuitions delivered by sensibility (Anthro. 7:196).[42] Kant then sometimes continues the political analogy by describing sensibility as like the "people" who are governed by the understanding (Anthro. 7:196). However, at other times, he attributes a more robust role to sensibility, claiming that it is the "executive force, through which understanding has an effect" (AF 25:486). It may come as something of a surprise that Kant uses the language of "executive force" here because we usually think of the power of choice as the "executive force" in

---

[38] See also, "sensibility gives the intuition...Hence we demand everyone to represent the matter [*Sache*] sensibly <make sensible [*versinnlichen*]>. If we did not have sensibility, our understanding would not at all have cognition of things, for then it would have no object" (AMr 25:1230).

[39] Kant relies on the distinction between sensibility as lower and understanding as higher throughout his anthropological and metaphysics lectures (see Anthro. pt. I, esp. 7:140, 196; AC 25:43, 147; AP 25:256–7; AF 25:485–7, 537; AMr 25:1228–30, 1296; AB 25:1444–5, 1476; ML1 28:228–30, 238; MMr 29:880, 888). Though he sometimes draws this distinction as he does in this passage in terms of the functional roles of sensibility and understanding, at other times he draws it on the metaphysical grounds that sensibility is receptive and understanding is spontaneous. See, e.g., his claim that, "What belongs to my faculty so far as I am passive belongs to my lower faculty. What belongs to my faculty so far as I am active belongs to my higher faculty" (ML1 28:228).

[40] See also his claim that, "*Understanding*...is also called the *higher* cognitive faculty (as distinguished from sensibility, which is the *lower*), because...[it] contains...the *rule* to which the manifold of sensuous intuitions must be subordinated in order to bring unity to the cognition of the object" (Anthro. 7:196); that understanding has "a higher rank...[b]ecause it governs and gives rules; hence everything must be subordinated to it" (AMr 25:1230), and that, "understanding has priority insofar as it must prescribe rules to sensibility" (AB 25:1445).

[41] Drawing on Alexander Pope's lines in an *Essay on Man*, "On life's vast ocean diversely we sail/ Reason the card, but passion is the gale," Kant also uses a nautical analogy, claiming that "understanding is the guide and sensibility the motive force, as Pope rightly says" (AMr 25:1232, Pope quote cited in fn 24, p. 541).

[42] See also AMr 25:1230; AF 25:486; EC 27:362–4.

44   IMAGINATION AS A COGNITIVE CAPACITY

Kant's system. But in this context what he has in mind is an executive force within the faculty of cognition. And his thought is that sensibility, in some sense, makes the understanding effective. Indeed, as he puts it in rather strident terms in the *Anthropology*, without sensibility, understanding "is not able to do anything at all" (Anthro. 7:196).[43]

This remark from the *Anthropology* requires some immediate qualification. For, technically, on Kant's view there are things we can do through our understanding without the executive force of sensibility: we can engage in acts of thought about things we cannot intuit. For example, according to Kant, God and freedom are supersensible things that we can never intuit;[44] nevertheless, he allows for us to have thoughts about them like, "freedom is the faculty of beginning a state from itself," and, "God is the *ens realissimum* (i.e., the most real being)" (A533/B561; A576/B604).[45] For Kant, then, it cannot be that the understanding needs the executive force of sensibility to engage in acts of thought. Instead, I take his position to be that the understanding needs the executive force of sensibility if it is to have thoughts that are not "empty" in the way cognition requires.

While these considerations shed more light on the cognitive functions that Kant ascribes to sensibility and understanding, it also raises the following question: does he conceive of "making concepts sensible" and "making intuitions understandable" as functions that are constitutive of all of our acts of sensibility and understanding, respectively? These are controversial issues that veer toward debates about whether he thinks that we can have intuitions without concepts and concepts without intuitions. While I shall have more to say about these debates in subsequent chapters,[46] here the preliminary point that I want to make is that Kant at least gestures toward the possibility that there are acts of sensibility and understanding that do not involve them performing their cognitive function. For example, the fact that Kant allows for us to have "empty" thoughts, like those about God and freedom I just adduced, suggests that our understanding can engage in acts of thought in which no intuitions are made understandable. So, too, does Kant seem to acknowledge cases in which we can have "blind" intuitions that do not make concepts sensible.[47] In this vein, Kant says, "The exercise of all of [the faculties of the mind], however, is always grounded in the faculty of

---

[43]   See also his claim that, "The understanding cannot carry anything out, rather sensibility must give it material" (AF 25:486), and that, "The understanding is nothing without sensibility, and only a mere faculty, just the same as the government without subjects" (AF 25:537).

[44]   See, e.g., A339/B396; KpV 5:55; KU 5:342.

[45]   See also his claim that freedom as a "causa noumenon" is a "thinkable concept" (KpV 5:55).

[46]   In Parts II and III, I make the case that the intuitions generated by imagination in the context of ordinary experience and aesthetic engagement depend on concepts; and in Part IV, I make the case for why we need to supplement practical concepts with intuitions on Kant's view.

[47]   For discussion of the possibility of "blind" intuitions on Kant's view, see McDowell (1994, 3–4); Grüne (2009); Bauer (2012); Allais (2015, 152–3); Shaddock (2018).

cognition, although not always in cognition (since a representation belonging to the faculty of cognition can also be an intuition, pure or empirical without concepts)" (EE 20:245).[48] And he illustrates a scenario in which someone has an intuition "without concepts" with the example of someone seeing a house who lacks the concept <house>:

> he admittedly has before him in his representation the very same object as someone else who is acquainted with it determinately as a dwelling established for men. But as to form, this cognition of one and the same object is different in the two. With the one it is mere *intuition*, with the other it is *intuition* and *concept* at the same time. (JL 9:33)

Given that this person lacks the concept <house>, their intuition is not something that makes this concept sensible and is hence "blind" with respect to it.[49]

Insofar as Kant, at least in these instances, appears to allow for us to have thoughts that are "empty" and intuitions that are "blind," we have reason to be cautious about attributing to him the view that sensibility, in all its acts, makes concepts sensible, and understanding, in all its acts, makes intuitions understandable.

Instead, what I would like to propose is that we conceive of the cognitive functions of sensibility and understanding as functions they perform when they are functioning cognitively well. So understood, these cognitive functions reflect a standard that sensibility and understanding are respectively oriented toward, which they meet when they are functioning well, but fail to meet when they are not functioning well.

However, caution is needed in how we interpret what it means for sensibility and understanding to function cognitively well on Kant's view. In particular, it might be tempting to attribute to Kant the view that sensibility and understanding only function well in the context of the sort of theoretical cognition Kant has in mind in the first *Critique*. His paradigms of theoretical cognition include our empirical cognition of spatio-temporal objects in experience and our synthetic *a priori* cognition about such objects captured by the Principles, e.g. "In all change of appearances, substance persists" (B224). Given that Kant orients his analysis of sensibility and understanding in the first *Critique* around clarifying what is involved in theoretical cognition of this sort, one might think he endorses the view that it is only in theoretical cognition that they function cognitively well.

---

[48] See also, "Certainly, sense representations come before those of the understanding and present themselves *en masse*. But the fruits are all the more plentiful when understanding comes in with its order and intellectual form and brings [them] into consciousness" (Anthro. 7:144).

[49] I say "with respect to this concept" because their intuition may not be "blind" with respect to other concepts, such as color concepts, shape concepts, or categorial concepts.

Yet as a number of commentators have recently emphasized, Kant speaks of other forms of cognition, including "practical" cognition, e.g. of the moral law or freedom, and "symbolic" cognition, e.g. of God.[50] What is more, one of the centerpieces of Kant's aesthetics is the claim that in the appreciation of beauty, our cognitive faculties operate in an "optimal" way that does not result in theoretical cognition (KU 5:238). The fact that Kant countenances other ways in which sensibility and understanding can function cognitively well outside the context of theoretical cognition suggests that he builds more flexibility into his account of their cognitive functions than we might initially be led to believe in the first *Critique*. And one of my goals in this book is to make the case that attending to Kant's theory of imagination confirms that he thinks there is a range of ways in which sensibility, in particular, can function cognitively well by making concepts sensible beyond the bounds of theoretical cognition.

While this argument will take time to develop, here I want to anticipate a distinction in Kant's account of the cognitive functions of sensibility and understanding that will play an important role in my interpretation: a distinction between what I shall call the "object-facing" and "subject-facing" aspects of the cognitive functions of sensibility and understanding. By the "object-facing" aspect, I have in mind the function sensibility and understanding have vis-à-vis the cognitive determination of objects we are given in an act of cognition. To borrow language from the third *Critique*, this object-facing aspect turns on the function that sensibility and understanding have with respect to "solving" the "problem" of determining an object through an act of cognition in which we think about an object we are given in intuition (KU 5:242). In this vein, Kant highlights the function sensibility has of "giving" us objects, i.e. putting us in touch with them in the first place, and the function understanding has of enabling us to "think" about the objects we are given.[51]

However, in addition to this object-facing aspect, I would like to propose that Kant acknowledges a subject-facing aspect of the cognitive function of sensibility and understanding, which turns on the way in which they function cognitively well by serving one another internally to our cognitive processes. In the third *Critique* Kant discusses this "inner relationship" under the heading of the "subjective conditions" of cognition,[52] and he claims that when sensibility and understanding function cognitively well, there is a certain "proportion" or "agreement" between them (KU 5:238, 287, 293). Although he thinks that

---

[50] For a discussion of practical cognition, see Chignell (2007a; 2010); Kain (2010); Abaci (2022); and Schafer (2023). For a discussion of symbolic cognition, see Westra (2016, chap. 7), Matherne (2021b).

[51] See, e.g., "Objects are therefore **given** to us by means of sensibility...; but they are **thought** through the understanding...all thought...must...ultimately be related to intuitions, thus in our case, to sensibility, since there is no other way in which objects can be given to us" (A19/B33).

[52] See, e.g., KU Introduction VII and §§9, 21, 35, 38.

SENSIBILITY AND UNDERSTANDING   47

sensibility and understanding achieve this proportion or agreement in acts of theoretical cognition, he introduces this line of thought in order to explain why, even though judgments of the beautiful do not amount to theoretical cognition, sensibility and understanding nevertheless achieve a certain proportion or agreement therein and, thereby, function cognitively well.[53] Reserving a discussion for why exactly he takes this to be the case in aesthetic appreciation until Chapter 8, here, what I want to draw out is Kant's commitment to there being ways in which sensibility and understanding function cognitively well in relation to one another internal to our cognitive processes—processes that may or may not result in an act of cognition in which we determine an object that we are given in intuition.

More specifically, when explicating the cognitive function of sensibility in its subject-facing guise, Kant glosses "making concepts sensible" in terms of the idea that sensibility makes concepts "comprehensible" (*faßlich*) to us (Rel. 6:65n).[54] As I discuss at more length in subsequent chapters, according to Kant, it is a "natural need of all human beings to demand for even the highest concepts... something that *can be sensibly held on to* [etwas Sinnlich-haltbares]" (Rel. 6:109; transl. modified). I take Kant's idea to be that, as beings who are at once sensible and intellectual, a purely abstract grasp of concepts does not satisfy us; to fully comprehend concepts, we need intuitions that facilitate a concrete grasp of them. And it is in these terms that Kant articulates what it means for sensibility to make concepts sensible in the subject-facing way: it generates intuitions that facilitate our concrete comprehension of concepts internal to our cognitive processes. In this vein, he describes making concepts sensible as a cognitive process that involves "distinctness in intuition, in which a concept thought abstractly is exhibited [*dargestellt*][55] or elucidated [*erläutert*] *in concreto*" (JL 9:39).[56] For Kant, then, making a concept sensible in the subject-facing sense involves having an intuition that cognitively "exhibits" to us *in concreto* the content of a concept that we intellectually grasp *in abstracto*. Suppose, for example, someone has read about the concept <marigold> without having seen one.[57] Though they have an abstract grasp of the content of this concept, e.g. <having pinnate leaves>, <being low maintenance>, or <being a deer deterrent>, unless sensibility provides them with intuitions that

---

[53] In this context, Kant treats imagination as the "greatest faculty of sensibility" (KU 5:257).

[54] To be clear, "making concepts sensible" in this sense is not a matter of forming sensible concepts in the first place, but rather a process in which we develop a concrete grasp of concepts. And the sort of "comprehension" at issue not to be confused with the sort of "comprehension" (*Begreifen*) that reason enables on Kant's view (see JL 9:65; Schafer 2022b; McLear forthcoming).

[55] I shall have much more to say about exhibition in subsequent chapters, see, e.g., Chapter 4.

[56] As I discuss in more detail later, Kant describes this as a kind of "aesthetic perfection" of cognition, where the relevant notion of "aesthetic" has to do with the "particular sensibility of man" and the "intuitive" side of cognition, rather than with phenomena like beauty or sublimity (see JL 9:36, 9:39; VL 24:806). He also describes this in terms of "intuitive clarity" (see Axvii–xviii).

[57] I take up Kant's own example of a physician who has a thorough understanding of disease concepts in the abstract, but cannot comprehend them in the concrete in Chapter 4 (see A134/B173).

48 IMAGINATION AS A COGNITIVE CAPACITY

cognitively "exhibit" this concept *in concreto, per* Kant, there will be a kind of emptiness, a "glittering poverty," in their grasp of this concept (Anthro. 7:145).

Notice, however, that in the *Religion* passage, Kant indicates that this need to have a concept made sensible to us is true "for even the highest concepts." For Kant, our "highest concepts," include concepts, such as <God> and <freedom>, that do not correspond to any object we can be given in intuition. In these cases, it is thus impossible for sensibility to fulfill its function of making concepts sensible in the object-facing sense: it cannot give us objects that correspond to these concepts. However, if sensibility can provide us with intuitions that facilitate our comprehension of these concepts, e.g. through aesthetic or symbolic means, then it can make concepts sensible in a subject-facing sense: it can exhibit or elucidate them for us. And though in theoretical cognition, sensibility fulfills both the object- and subject-facing aspects of its cognitive function, what I shall argue is that we need to recognize a range of ways in which it can successfully play its subject-facing role even when it does not fulfill its object-facing role, and so function cognitively well outside the context of theoretical cognition.

As for the subject-facing dimension of the understanding's cognitive function, I shall have much less to say about this topic.[58] But I take the basic idea to be that making intuitions understandable in a subject-facing way amounts to removing a certain "blindness" in our internal grasp of the content of an intuition. Suppose, for example, that I am daydreaming about a garden and there is an image hovering in my mind, but I am not quite sure what it is. As I reflect on it, it dawns on me that it is an image of a row of marigolds nestled between two rows of tomatoes. In this case, it seems I conceptually determine the content of my imagined intuition in a way that makes it understandable to me. However, given that the garden does not exist, I am not determining an object I am given; I am clarifying an intuition I have imaginatively wrought from myself.[59] And in this fashion, my understanding makes intuitions understandable in a way that discharges the subject-facing aspect of its cognitive function.

Though the details remain to be filled in, by my lights, recognizing the object- and subject-facing aspects of the cognitive function of sensibility and understanding is crucial for acknowledging the range of ways in which Kant thinks sensibility and understanding can function cognitively well inside and outside the bounds of theoretical cognition. And this distinction will eventually play a pivotal role in my interpretation of Kant's account of the flexibility built into our imagination, as a capacity that can function cognitively well across theoretical, aesthetic, and practical domains.

Generalizing for now, however, insofar as imagination belongs to the faculty of cognition, it thus belongs to a faculty structured by two stems, sensibility and

---

[58] These issues are bound up with Kant's account of apperception and self-consciousness, which are topics that lie beyond the scope of this monograph.

[59] There are complex issues surrounding how to think about the relationship between imagined intuitions and objects that I address in Chapters 3 and 4.

understanding, with their divergent metaphysical, logical, and functional profiles. If we are to fill out Kant's account of what kind of cognitive capacity imagination is, then we need to think through where it fits in this two-stem architecture—a complicated task I shall take up in the two following chapters.

1.5 Conclusion

In this chapter, I began exploring Kant's answer to the question "what is it to imagine" in light of his analysis of imagination as a cognitive capacity. To this end, I considered where imagination fits in Kant's mental architecture, locating it in the part of the mind he calls the "faculty of cognition." And, drawing on Kant's broad and narrow uses of cognition, I teased out some basic implications this has for understanding imagination as part of the faculty of cognition. More specifically, I gleaned the idea that as a cognitive capacity imagination contributes, at the most basic level, to our conscious representation of objects. But, *qua* something that also contributes to cognition in the narrow sense, I claimed that Kant conceives of imagination as having some role to play in the unification of intuitions and concepts, and hence in relation to our consciousness of objects as determinate and really possible.

I then sketched Kant's account of sensibility and understanding, *qua* the "two stems" that structure the faculty of cognition. To this end, I explored the metaphysical, logical, and functional distinctions he draws between the two. To recap: metaphysically, sensibility is receptive, whereas understanding is spontaneous. Logically, sensibility is a faculty of intuitions, whereas understanding is a faculty of concepts. Functionally, sensibility has the cognitive role of giving us objects and making concepts sensible, whereas understanding has the cognitive role of enabling us to think about objects and making intuitions understandable.

Given the foundational role sensibility and understanding have in Kant's account of the faculty of cognition, if we are to make headway in clarifying what it means for imagination to be a cognitive capacity, then we need to address its relationship to these two stems. Indeed, Kant's analysis of this relationship will be crucial for clarifying his conception of our imagination's metaphysical, logical, and functional profile, as well as its distinctive place in our cognitive architecture. However, Kant's position on the relationship imagination has to sensibility and understanding is one of the most fraught issues in interpreting his theory of imagination. And it is to this controversy, and my argument that Kant ultimately conceives of imagination as part of sensibility, that I shall turn in the next two chapters.

Seeing More: Kant's Theory of Imagination. Samantha Matherne, Oxford University Press.
© Samantha Matherne 2024. DOI: 10.1093/9780191999291.003.0002

2
Imagination and the Two Stems
of Cognition

> Both extremes, namely sensibility and understanding,
> must necessarily be connected by means of...imagination
>
> —A124

2.1 Introduction

In the first *Critique* Kant brings the Introduction to a close by telling us that, "there are two stems of human cognition, which may perhaps arise from a common but to us unknown root, namely sensibility and understanding" (A15/B29). As I discussed in the last chapter, if we are to make sense of what kind of cognitive capacity Kant takes imagination to be, then we need to situate it vis-à-vis this sensibility-understanding architecture. And according to some readers (notoriously Martin Heidegger) the two-stem passage, in fact, offers us a clue on this front: for Kant, *per* this reading, imagination is ultimately the "common but to us unknown root" of sensibility and understanding.[1] Others, however, have rejected this reading, insisting that Kant regards imagination as integrated into the two stems—though which stem is also a matter of debate. Whereas some interpreters maintain that Kant conceives of imagination as part of sensibility, others insist he thinks it is an exercise of the understanding.

Though there is thus little agreement about how to interpret Kant's account of the relationship that imagination has to sensibility and understanding, sorting through these issues has significant consequences. One way to appreciate what hangs in the balance is in light of what I called the "external taxonomy" question about imagination in the Introduction: how are we to classify imaginative states vis-à-vis other mental states (§0.2.2)? If we think through this question in Kant's sensibility-understanding framework, then we can come at the issue through three, by no means unrelated, angles. First, how does Kant conceive of the relationship between the representations involved in imagining and the representations involved in sensibility and understanding: intuitions and concepts? Does he regard imagining as something that involves intuitions or some other mental state

---

[1] I return to Heidegger's reading in §2.2.

distinct from intuitions? And does he take imaginative representations to be independent from, or dependent on, concepts? Second, how does Kant regard the relationship between our capacity for imagining and the capacities involved in sensibility and understanding? Does he regard imagination as a capacity that is distinct from sensibility and understanding, or does he think that these capacities have an imaginative dimension? And third, is there some distinctive function that Kant accords to imagining in cognition over and above sensibility's function of giving us objects and understanding's function of enabling us to think about objects? As this range of questions suggests, wading through the complexities surrounding how Kant classifies imaginative states in relation to other mental states given his two-stem architecture has important implications for how we think about his picture not only of imagination, but also of cognition, our cognitive architecture, and the cognitive division of labor among our various capacities.

I devote the next two chapters to these issues. After exploring the difficulties surrounding how to situate imagination in Kant's sensibility-understanding architecture in this chapter, in the next chapter, I defend the thesis that, on his view, imagination belongs to sensibility.

In this chapter, my aim is twofold. My first goal is to lay out the controversy surrounding how to read Kant's account of the relationship imagination has to sensibility and understanding. To this end, I explore the ambiguous remarks Kant makes about this relationship and three interpretations of imagination that these remarks motivate. The first interpretation is what I call the "third thing view," according to which imagination is a third faculty distinct from sensibility and understanding (§2.2). The second is what I call the "sensibility view," according to which imagination is part of the faculty of sensibility (§2.3). And the third is what I call the "understanding view," according to which imagination is an exercise of the faculty of understanding (§2.4).

My second goal is to use this discussion to start introducing some more specific claims that Kant makes about what kind of cognitive capacity imagination is. In particular, I highlight three commitments: first, to imagination being a capacity tasked with mediating between intuitions and concepts, sense and intellect (§2.2); second, to imagination being responsible for representing objects in intuition even without their presence (§2.3); and third, to the spontaneity of imagination (§2.4).

2.2 The Third Thing View of Imagination

The first possible view of imagination we might attribute to Kant is what I am calling the "third thing view," according to which imagination is a faculty that is distinct from both the faculty of sensibility and the faculty of understanding.[2]

---

[2] See, e.g., Hegel (1997, 73); Heidegger KPM, PIK; Hughes (2007, chap. 4); Ostaric (2017); Horstmann (2018); Hoerth (2020).

52 IMAGINATION AND THE TWO STEMS OF COGNITION

We find remarks that support the third thing view particularly in the A Deduction of the first *Critique*. There, Kant describes imagination as one of "three" "original" "faculties": "There are...three original sources (capacities or faculties of the soul), which contain the conditions of possibility of all experience, and cannot themselves be derived from any other faculty of the mind, namely **sense, imagination**, and **apperception**" (A94; see also A155/B194). Later in the A Deduction, Kant claims, "We...have a pure imagination, as a *fundamental* faculty of the human soul, that grounds all cognition *a priori*...Both extremes, namely sensibility and understanding, must necessarily be connected by means of this transcendental function of the imagination" (A124; my emph.). In this passage Kant treats imagination not only as a "fundamental faculty," but also as one that is tasked with mediating between the "extremes" of the other fundamental faculties, sensibility and understanding.

This latter claim about mediation is particularly significant because it helps shed light on why Kant might see the need to posit imagination as a third thing. In particular, in articulating his basic picture of cognition, Kant makes two claims that might seem to be in tension with one another. On the one hand, Kant paints a picture of sensibility and understanding in "heterogeneous" terms (KU 5:401). Sensibility is receptive, understanding is spontaneous. Intuitions are singular representations that immediately relate to objects, whereas concepts are general representations that mediately relate to objects. On the other hand, Kant claims that it is only from the "unification" of intuitions and concepts that cognition in the narrow sense can "arise" (A51/B75–6). But how can the two ever be united in cognition given the dichotomous terms in which Kant has characterized them?

In the A124 passage Kant appeals to imagination in answering this question: it is the "transcendental function of the imagination" to "connect" the "extremes" of sensibility and understanding. Indeed, if cognition is to be possible, he indicates that our imagination "must" perform this mediation. Kant thus tasks imagination with a crucial cognitive function: mediating between sensibility and intuition, on the one hand, and understanding and concepts, on the other. And from the perspective of the third thing view of imagination, Kant's recognition of this mediating function is part of what motivates him to conceive of imagination as a faculty that is distinct from sensibility and understanding.[3]

Commentators who attribute to Kant the third thing view of imagination have interpreted its status as a third thing along different lines. Some have argued that

---

[3] In her interpretation of imagination as a third faculty, Hughes glosses imagination as "the mediating faculty *par excellence*," though she also indicates that its "status as mediator *par excellence*...leads to the problem of identifying it in a definitive way" (2007, 130, 136). Gibbons likewise defends an account of imagination defined as a "mediating" capacity on Kant's view and claims that this is part of why imagination is so difficult to "pigeonhole" (1994, 2, 29). Zöller also emphasizes its mediating function, but he does so in service of a "functionalist" interpretation, according to which imagination is not "a further, third source of cognition next to—or rather, in between—sensibility and the understanding," but is rather a functional "ability to link" sensibility and understanding (2019, 78). Schaper (1964, 283) also defends a functionalist reading along these lines.

Kant treats imagination, sensibility, and understanding as three independent and equally basic cognitive faculties.[4] Others, have argued that Kant regards imagination as, in some sense, more basic than sensibility and understanding. For example, in *Faith and Knowledge* (1802), Hegel suggests a reading of Kant, according to which imagination is more basic than sensibility and understanding because it is identical with "what is primary and original," viz. "reason" or the "In-itself," out of which the dichotomy between sensibility and understanding emerges (1997, 73).[5] Meanwhile, Heidegger, in *Kant and the Problem of Metaphysics* (1929) and the parallel lecture course, *Phenomenological Interpretation of Kant's* Critique of Pure Reason (1927–8), argues that imagination is a "third fundamental faculty," that is "part of the root" out of which sensibility and understanding stem (PIK 64).[6] However, regardless of whether all three faculties are equally basic or not, these readers agree in attributing to Kant a view of imagination as a third thing alongside, and capable of mediating between, the faculties of sensibility and understanding.

Yet treating imagination as a third thing distinct from sensibility and understanding does not sit easily with Kant's account of the fundamental architecture of the faculty of cognition. As we have seen, in his discussion of this architecture, he asserts that there are "two stems" or "two elements" of human cognition, not three. And this dualism is in keeping with Kant's more general theory of mind, according to which each of the three basic faculties of the mind (the faculties of cognition, desire, and the feeling of pleasure and displeasure) are divided into two parts: a "lower" receptive part and a "higher" spontaneous part.[7] Given Kant's frequent insistence on this dualistic framework, we would thus expect him to treat imagination not as a third faculty alongside sensibility and understanding, but as somehow integrated into either sensibility or understanding. This expectation is not disappointed, as he often proceeds in this way. However, this raises a host of

---

[4] See Hughes (2007, 130–1, 136, 148–51); Ostaric (2017); Horstmann (2018); Hoerth (2020). More specifically, Horstmann (2018) argues that Kant treats imagination as autonomous in the A-edition and the third *Critique* (see also Ostaric 2017), and he claims that the texts in the B Deduction that appear to deny autonomy to imagination are symptomatic of Kant shifting his focus to the phase of experience in which imagination is under the constraint of concepts.

[5] For discussions of Hegel's reading, see Sedgwick (2001); Bates (2004, intro.); Wretzel (2018). See Pippin (1989, 77) and Nuzzo (2013, 42–5) for the argument that this is not a viable reading of Kant's position on account of his fundamental dualistic commitments regarding sensibility and understanding.

[6] The full quote reads, "But our interpretation will show that this third fundamental faculty does not grow like a third stem, as it were, next to the other two stems and also that this third faculty does not mediate between the other two as something which is placed between them. Instead our interpretation will show that this third fundamental faculty is, as it were, part of the root itself" (PIK 64; see also PIK 278, KPM 97). For criticism of Heidegger's reading as inconsistent with Kant's treatment of a common root as a regulative idea of reason that is "purely hypothetical," see Henrich (1994, 26–7, quoting A649/B67). For further discussion of Heidegger's reading, see Weatherston (2002, chap. 6); Dahlstrom (2010); Lambeth (2021; 2023); Shockey (2021, chap. 5).

[7] See, e.g., AC 25:29–30; APill 25:738; ML1 28:228; MMr 29:880–1.

54 IMAGINATION AND THE TWO STEMS OF COGNITION

new issues as Kant appears to integrate imagination sometimes into sensibility and sometimes into understanding.

2.3 The Sensibility View of Imagination

The second view of imagination we might attribute to Kant is the sensibility view, according to which imagination belongs to the faculty of sensibility.[8]

We find evidence for this view in the *Anthropology*. In his discussion of the faculty of cognition in Book One, he divides his discussion between an account of sensibility as the "lower" faculty of cognition (§§7–39) and understanding as the "higher" faculty of cognition (§§40–4) (Anthro. 7:140). And he situates his analysis of imagination in the discussion of sensibility (§§28–39), prefacing it with the claim, "*Sensibility* in the cognitive faculty (the faculty of intuitive representation) contains two parts [*Stücke*]: *sense* [*Sinn*] and the *power of imagination* [*Einbildungskraft*].—The first is the faculty of intuition in the presence of an object, the second is intuition even *without* the presence of an object" (Anthro. 7:153). Here, Kant's motivation for treating imagination as part of sensibility appears to stem from what I discussed in terms of his logical account of sensibility as a faculty of intuition in Chapter 1: imagination belongs to sensibility because it generates intuitions, viz. intuitions "even without the presence of an object" (see also Anthro. 7:167).[9]

This characterization of imagination as part of sensibility in the *Anthropology* is in keeping with a trend that persists throughout Kant's pre-Critical and Critical lectures on anthropology and metaphysics. In these texts when Kant discusses the faculty of cognition, he consistently inserts his analysis of imagination into the discussion of sensibility, *qua* the lower faculty of cognition, rather than into his discussion of understanding, *qua* the higher faculty of cognition.[10] And as in the *Anthropology* his reason for treating imagination as part of sensibility seems to turn on a commitment to imagination being a faculty responsible for a specific type of intuition: intuition even without the presence of objects.[11]

Reading Kant's view of imagination along these lines has various merits. It tracks his treatment of imagination in his anthropological and metaphysical writings, it reflects his characterization of imagination as a faculty responsible for

---

[8] See, e.g., Mörchen (1970, 15–21); Stephenson (2015, 496–8); McLear (2017, 91). Nuzzo (2008; 2013) also interprets imagination as part of sensibility, and she emphasizes the status of productive imagination as a spontaneous aspect of sensibility.

[9] I return to this issue of imagination being responsible for intuitions at length in Chapter 3.

[10] See Anthro. §§15, 28; AF 25:511; AMr 25:1258; ML1 28:230; MMr 29:881; MD 28:672–4. Dyck (2019, 353) highlights this view in Kant's pre-Critical position.

[11] See, e.g., MMr 29:881; MD 28:672.

THE SENSIBILITY VIEW OF IMAGINATION   55

intuitions even without the presence of objects, and, in contrast with the third thing view, it treats imagination as integrated into Kant's two-stem architecture.

Yet in spite of these advantages, it is not clear whether Kant can ultimately endorse the sensibility view on metaphysical grounds. Recall that Kant characterizes sensibility as a receptive, rather than spontaneous, faculty of cognition. However, if we take a closer look at how Kant characterizes imaginative activity, it does not readily fit the receptive profile of sensibility. Instead, I shall argue that he treats our imaginative activities as spontaneous.

In order to unpack this metaphysical worry, I want to begin with some preliminary remarks about how Kant characterizes imaginative activity in general, before turning to the question of its receptivity versus spontaneity. These remarks are, indeed, preliminary as I shall devote much of my attention in Chapter 3 to refining this picture of imaginative activity.

According to Kant, at the most basic level, imaginative activity involves sensibly ordering and organizing a manifold of intuition, i.e. a multiplicity of sensible representations, in spatial and/or temporal relations. For example, *per* Kant, when I look at these three dots, . ˙ ., a manifold of visual representations is generated in me, and it falls to my imagination to sensibly organize them, e.g. into a spatial representation of a triangle. Or to use a temporal example, when I hear these four notes, ♫, my imagination is responsible for sensibly ordering the multiplicity of sonic representations that arises in me into a representation of, say, a musical phrase that successively unfolds.[12]

Kant uses various terms to describe this basic activity of imagination. In the first *Critique* he uses the term "Synthesis" ("synthesis").[13] In the pre-Critical period, he uses terms related to "Bildung" ("formation") and "bilden" ("to form").[14] And in the third *Critique*, he tends to favor language of "Zusammensetzung" ("composition") and "zusammensetzen" ("to compose").[15] However, whether we refer to it as "synthesizing," "forming," or "composing," Kant's core idea is this: what our imagination does, at the most basic level, is spatially and/or temporally order and organize a manifold of representations together.

On Kant's view, this imaginative activity can manifest in a variety of different contexts. In perception he claims that our imagination sensibly orders and organizes the manifold delivered to us through our senses. For example, on a Kantian analysis, when I look at a hyacinth, a manifold of representations will be generated in me (e.g. of its green stem, its blue petals, the dirt beneath it), and it falls to my imagination to spatially synthesize the representations of the hyacinth's stem and petals as belonging together in distinction from the representation

---

[12] These notes open Beethoven's 5th Symphony (assume the key of C minor).
[13] See, e.g., A77–9/B103–4; A98–102; A118–25; B151–2; B160–4.
[14] I discuss this at length in Chapter 4 under the heading of "The Formation Definition" (§4.2).
[15] See KU 5:217, 238, 287. In the first *Critique*, Kant also uses "composition" (see B201n; B202)—a topic I discuss in Chapter 7.

56   IMAGINATION AND THE TWO STEMS OF COGNITION

of the dirt.[16] However, Kant also allows for scenarios in which our imagination connects a more disparate multiplicity of representations together. In association, for example, I might connect a current representation together with representations that are more far-flung, for example, when I associate the representation of the hyacinth that I see with a representation of, say, Sparta or spring. Or to cite a couple of "inventive" cases, in visualization Kant maintains that our imagination can synthesize together a manifold of representations that transcend what is given to us here and now, for example, when I envision what a cluster of hyacinths might look like in my currently hyacinth-less garden. Or in art, Kant indicates that an artist can imaginatively alight on more creative ways to connect representations together.[17] Think, for example, of the way T.S. Eliot weaves hyacinth-related representations together in "The Waste Land":

> "They called me the hyacinth girl."
> — Yet when we came back, late, from the Hyacinth garden,
> Your arms full and your hair wet, I could not
> Speak, and my eyes failed, I was neither
> Living nor dead, and I knew nothing,
> Looking into the heart of light, the silence.
>
> (2000, 6)

Moreover, as I discussed under the heading of the "internal taxonomy question" in the Introduction (§0.2.1), Kant acknowledges (as do many contemporary theorists following in his wake) two basic modes in which imaginative activity can proceed: reproductive or productive. In its reproductive mode, Kant claims that our imaginative activity proceeds in a "derivative" and "recollective" way, as it "bring[s] back to the mind" representations we have "had previously" (Anthro. 7:167). When sighting a hyacinth brings images from the "The Waste Land" to mind, my imagination "calls back" a representation from the past to bear on what I see here and now. Meanwhile, in its productive guise, Kant claims our imagination operates in an "inventive" or "original" way (Anthro. 7:167). Think, for example, of a landscape architect who produces an original design for a garden with hyacinths that does not just copy some garden they have seen before. For Kant, then, although our imaginative activity involves sensibly ordering and organizing a manifold, this activity can manifest in a variety of reproductive and productive ways.

With this sketch of imaginative activity in view, let's return to the issues surrounding Kant's account of the metaphysics of imaginative activity. The worry

---

[16] In Chapters 3 and 5, I discuss how this imaginative synthesis differs from what the senses afford.
[17] I discuss the creative exercise of our imagination in aesthetic contexts in Part III.

THE SENSIBILITY VIEW OF IMAGINATION   57

that I shall press against the sensibility view is that if imagination were part of sensibility, then we should expect Kant to characterize its activities as receptive. However, what I shall now argue is that Kant conceives of imaginative activity as spontaneous in the sense that it "bring[s] forth representations itself" in a "self-active" way (A51/B75; AB157–8fn).[18]

At the very least, Kant treats the productive mode of imagining as spontaneous. For example, in the B Deduction he explicitly describes the *a priori* exercise of the productive imagination as an "exercise of spontaneity" (B151).[19] Meanwhile, in the third *Critique* in describing the empirical productive exercise of imagination involved in aesthetic appreciation he uses language reminiscent of spontaneity: "the imagination must be considered in its freedom...as productive and self-active" (KU 5:241). And in terms that more elliptically suggest spontaneity, in his account of artistic creation, he claims that, "The imagination (as a productive cognitive faculty) is, namely, very powerful in creating, as it were, another nature, out of the material which the real one gives it" (KU 5:314). Insofar as the productive imagination spontaneously brings forth representations in these ways, it does not seem that it could belong to the receptive capacity that is sensibility.

Granted, this still leaves open the possibility that in Kant's taxonomy of imagining, the reproductive exercise of imagination is receptive and hence belongs to sensibility. And Kant does, indeed, seem to distinguish the productive imagination from the reproductive imagination on account of the former's spontaneity: "insofar as the imagination is spontaneity, I also occasionally call it the **productive** imagination, and thereby distinguish it from the **reproductive** imagination, whose synthesis is subject solely to empirical laws, namely those of association" (B152).[20] By empirical laws of association, Kant has in mind laws according to which,

> representations that have often followed or accompanied one another are finally associated with each other and thereby placed in a connection in accordance with which, even without the presence of the object, one of these representations brings about a transition in the mind to the other in accordance with a constant rule. (A100)[21]

---

[18] See Chapter 1, §1.4 for a discussion of the spontaneity of understanding in these terms.

[19] In this context, Kant is discussing the so-called "figurative synthesis" of the productive imagination (see Chapters 6–7 for more on this topic). See also his characterization of figurative synthesis in the *Opus Postumum*, "Space and time are products (but primitive products) of our own imagination, hence self-created intuitions, inasmuch as the subject affects itself" (OP 23:37).

[20] See also, "in the judgment of taste the imagination must be considered in its freedom, then it is in the first instance taken not as reproductive, as subjected to the laws of association, but as productive and self-active" (KU 5:240).

[21] See also B141–2, B152; KU 5:240; Anthro. 7:176; AMr 25:1273; ML1 28:236; MMr 29:883; ML2 28:585; MD 28:674.

58 IMAGINATION AND THE TWO STEMS OF COGNITION

Here, Kant appears to cast the reproductive imagination as receptive, rather than spontaneous because it is governed by empirical laws of association.[22] If this is right, then we might impute to Kant a more moderate version of the sensibility view, according to which it is not that imagination in general is part of sensibility, but rather that the reproductive imagination is part of sensibility.[23]

Nevertheless, a closer look at Kant's view of imaginative activity in general gives us reason to attribute to him a more capacious account of imaginative spontaneity, according to which all imaginative activity, whether productive or reproductive, is spontaneous. We get hints of this in various passages, for example, in the Refutation of Idealism, where he claims that we must "distinguish the mere receptivity of an outer intuition from the spontaneity that characterizes every imagining" (B277n). This is in keeping with an early remark in the ML1 lectures to the effect that imagination involves a "spontaneity of the mind" (ML1 28:230). And he hints at this later in the Dohna-Wundlacken lectures on logic from 1792: "Imagination and understanding are the only two active faculties of cognition of the human mind. But the senses are wholly passive" (DWL 24:705–6).

But beyond these textual hints, we have reason to cast imaginative activity in general as spontaneous in Kant's framework in light of his analysis of it as synthesis in the first *Critique*. In the first *Critique*, Kant describes both the productive and reproductive activities of imagination as a kind of synthesis.[24] And in the A Deduction, he insists that imaginative synthesis is a form of spontaneity. He, for example, opens the A Deduction with the claim, "If... sense... contains a manifold in its intuition, a synthesis must always correspond to this, and **receptivity** can make cognitions possible only if combined with **spontaneity**."[25] And he immediately indicates that this spontaneity is the "ground of" the imaginative synthesis of "apprehension" and "reproduction" (A97).[26] He returns to this theme later contrasting the receptivity of the senses with imagination as an "active faculty of the synthesis of this manifold in us" (A120). And he claims that imaginative synthesis involves "more than the receptivity of impressions"; it involves generating representations through a "function of the synthesis," i.e. a kind of

---

[22] See Sethi (2021).   [23] See, e.g., Nuzzo (2013).

[24] See, for example, his discussion of the imaginative syntheses of apprehension and reproduction in the A Deduction, and his account of the synthesis of the productive and reproductive imagination in §24 of the B Deduction.

[25] This echoes his opening remark in the B Deduction to the effect, "the **combination** (*conjunctio*) of a manifold... can never come to us through the senses... for it is an act of the spontaneity of the power of representation..., which we would designate with the general title **synthesis**" (B129–30).

[26] I take this claim to be applicable to imaginative synthesis insofar as Kant goes on to say that, "This is now the ground of a threefold synthesis, which is necessarily found in all cognition," which includes two forms of imaginative synthesis: the synthesis of apprehension and reproduction. See also Kant's claim in the Metaphysical Deduction, "Only the spontaneity of our thought requires that this manifold [of intuition] first be gone through, taken up, and combined [*verbunden*] in a certain way in order for a cognition to be made out of it. I call this action synthesis... Synthesis in general is... the mere effect of the imagination, of a blind though indispensable function of the soul" (A77–8/B102–3).

THE SENSIBILITY VIEW OF IMAGINATION   59

active ordering and organizing of a manifold (A120, 120n).[27] In his discussion of imaginative synthesis, Kant thus presents imaginative activity in general as spontaneous: it involves bringing forth representations in a self-active way through ordering and organizing a manifold.

But how might this picture of the spontaneity of imagination in general accommodate Kant's analysis of the reproductive exercise of imagination? There are, at least, two lines of thought to pursue in this direction. The first turns on the idea that reproductive imagining is spontaneous because it involves synthesis, and the second on the idea that the associative patterns that govern the productive imagination have their source in spontaneity.

To begin, in the first *Critique* Kant characterizes the reproductive activities of imagination as ones that involve synthesis. He only mentions this in passing in the B Deduction: attributing to reproductive imagination a "synthesis subject... solely to empirical laws" (B152). But in the A Deduction he thematizes this issue at length. He explicates "the synthesis of the reproduction in the imagination" as part of the "threefold synthesis" that is grounded in spontaneity (A100, 97). And he describes reproduction as a kind of synthesis because he thinks that we do not receive associations the way that we receive sensations. Instead, Kant claims that associations require a "combination in the imagination" in which we combine "a representation... with one representation rather than with any others"—a combination, without which, he says, our representations would be "unruly heaps" (A121). For example, when I associate a hyacinth I see with the Hyacinth girl from "The Waste Land," *per* Kant, I do not receive this association in the way I receive a sensation of the hyacinth's blue. This association is the result of my imagination actively connecting these representations together in synthesis. And to the extent that synthesis in general is a spontaneous activity through which we bring forth representations in a self-active, rather than receptive, way, then the reproductive activities of imagination count as spontaneous for Kant.

In addition to this commitment to the reproductive imagination being spontaneous insofar as it engages in synthesis, Kant, at least in his discussion of imagination in the *Anthropology*, hints that associations ultimately have a spontaneous basis (Anthro. §31). There, Kant rather surprisingly situates his analysis of association in a section titled, "On the sensible productive faculty [*sinnlichen Dichtungsvermögen*] according to its different forms [*Arten*]" (Anthro. 7:175; transl. modified).[28] As is typical, in this section he claims that reproduction follows the

---

[27] In this context, Kant picks up on language of "affections" and "functions" to distinguish sensibility and understanding from A68/B93, attributing affections to sense and functions to imagination.

[28] As he often does (see AF 25:512–3), Kant distinguishes between three different kinds of association: associations in space, associations in time, and associations of "affinity," which involves associating things together that have a "common origin," e.g. belong to the same class or have the same causal ground. But somewhat confusingly, in this section Kant only explicitly uses the term "association" for associations in time ("*associating* of intuitions in time (*imaginatio associans*)"), describing

60 IMAGINATION AND THE TWO STEMS OF COGNITION

law of association: "empirical representations that have frequently followed one another produce a habit in the mind such that when one idea is produced, the other comes into being" (Anthro. 7:176; transl. modified).[29] But what is surprising is that instead of discussing this topic under the heading of the reproductive imagination, he discusses it under the heading of the productive imagination.

Kant does not offer much by way of an explanation as to why he discusses associations under the umbrella of the productive imagination.[30] Here are two potential reasons he might do so. The first reason is more minimal: Kant's reference to the "productive faculty" of imagination in this section amounts to a reference to imagination, *qua* a faculty that engages in synthesis. So understood, association falls in the purview of the productive imagination because it involves the imaginative activity of synthesis.

The second reason is more robust, as well as more speculative, and it requires taking seriously the claim that association has its basis in the productive imagination, *qua* "original." According to this line of thought, although the law of association in general does not have its source in the productive imagination, particular associations do: a particular association is first established in an act of productive imagining in which we "originally" connect representations together.[31] Prior to establishing this association, the representations form an "unruly heap": they occur in us "dispersed and separate" (A120). And it is only if we engage in some sort of "original" productive act, in which we imaginatively connect the representations together that a particular associative pattern is established. For example, when I first listened to Mariah Carey's "Fantasy," the first notes and first verse unfolded in a "dispersed and separate" way for me. However, once I started listening to it on repeat, I came to form a temporal association, which involves an expectation of a certain verse to follow the first notes. And what I am suggesting is that the reason Kant ascribes associations of this sort to the productive imagination is because he does not think that mere exposure is enough to establish an associative pattern. We need to engage in some sort of "original" productive act in which we imaginatively hold representations together and alight on their connection. This is admittedly all rather hand-wavy, but I think it gives us another way to think about a spontaneous dimension of reproductive imagination: the associative

---

associations in space as "the *forming* [bildende] of intuitions in space (*imaginatio plastica*)" and associations of affinity just as "*affinity*" (Anthro. 7:175).

[29] He makes this claim in the sub-section devoted to associations in time, a sub-section titled, "On the Sensible Productive Faculty of Association [*Von dem sinnlichen Dichtungsvermögen der Beigesellung*]" (Anthro. 7:176).

[30] He does claim that we cannot look for a "physiological explanation" of association (Anthro. 7:176). But this remark seems to be motivated more by lacking the requisite "knowledge of the brain" that would be needed to get such an explanation off the ground (Anthro. 7:176).

[31] This reading of the source of associations thus parts ways with Ginsborg's reading, according to which the association of ideas is "simply something we are naturally disposed to do," just as animals are (2015, 162).

THE UNDERSTANDING VIEW OF IMAGINATION   61

patterns that govern the reproductive imagination are not just ones we receive; they are ones that we spontaneously generate through the productive imagination. To be clear, this does not amount to the claim that the reproductive imagination is itself spontaneous; my argument regarding synthesis was meant to motivate this idea. The claim is that the associative patterns that govern our reproductive activities are ones that are spontaneously established by the productive imagination.

Setting these complications surrounding the source of association aside, let's return to the question I have been pursuing about Kant's account of the metaphysics of imaginative activity: is it receptive or spontaneous? What I have argued is that although it might initially seem that he can only conceive of the productive imagination as spontaneous, his description of imaginative activity as synthesis points toward an important insight into Kant's account of the metaphysics of imagining in general: whether in its productive or reproductive mode, imagining is spontaneous.

However, if Kant thinks imaginative activity is spontaneous, then we have reason to be wary of attributing to him the sensibility view of imagination: the metaphysical profile of imagination as spontaneous simply does not fit with the metaphysical profile of sensibility as receptive. Indeed, its spontaneous metaphysical profile suggests that we should look away from sensibility and toward the understanding, *qua* the spontaneous stem of cognition, in order to see where imagination fits in Kant's cognitive architecture.

2.4 The Understanding View of Imagination

According to what I am calling the "understanding view" Kant conceives of imagination as a sensible exercise of the understanding.[32] In addition to the sort of metaphysical considerations about the spontaneity of imagination I just sketched, support for the understanding view comes from Kant's treatment of imagination in the B Deduction of the first *Critique*.[33] Indeed, as many readers have noted,

---

[32] See, e.g., Long (1998); Land (2011); Caimi (2012, 417). While I here present the understanding view as a view of imagination in general, there is a more restricted version of it, according to which this view only applies to the productive exercise of imagination as an "exercise of spontaneity" (B151). See, e.g., Sellars's claim that, "it turns out, most clearly in the second edition (B151–3) that this imagination, under the name 'productive imagination', is the understanding functioning in a special way" (1967, 4), and Land's claim that, "Kant draws a distinction between productive and reproductive imagination. While the reproductive imagination is indeed a merely sensible capacity, the productive imagination is not. It depends on the involvement of the understanding, for its act is a "synthesis in accordance with concepts" (A78/B104; cf. A112)" (2015a, 472). However, for reasons I adduced in §2.3, there are reasons to read Kant as committed to all imaginative activity being spontaneous, which undercuts the motivation for attributing to Kant a more restricted version of the understanding view along these lines.

[33] See also Kant's marginal note in his copy of the A-edition at A78, where he crosses out the description of imagination as a "function of the soul," and replaces it with the claim that imagination is a "function of the understanding" (see Guyer/Wood note on Kant 1998a, 211).

62   IMAGINATION AND THE TWO STEMS OF COGNITION

the B Deduction appears to mark a radical shift in Kant's conception of imagination. For in sharp contrast with his treatment of imagination as a unique "fundamental faculty" in the A Deduction, in the B Deduction he appears to deny independence to imagination, presenting it, instead, as a sensible exercise of the understanding.[34]

More specifically, when we look at the B Deduction, Kant's initial characterization of the understanding in §15, as well as his subsequent treatment of the relationship of imagination to understanding appear to lend support to the understanding view. Beginning with §15, in the opening paragraph Kant sets up his analysis of the understanding by way of a contrast with sensibility:

> The manifold of representations can be given in an intuition that is merely sensible, i.e., nothing but receptivity... Yet the **combination** [*Verbindung*] (*conjunctio*) of a manifold in general can never come through the senses...; for it is an act of the spontaneity of the power of representation, and since one must call the latter understanding, in distinction from sensibility, all combination... is an action of the understanding, which we would designate with the general title **synthesis**.
>
> (B129–30)

In this passage, Kant alludes to the metaphysical characterization of sensibility as receptive and understanding as spontaneous. And he indicates that although in its receptivity sensibility can provide a manifold of intuition, the synthesis of this manifold needed for cognition is something that requires spontaneity. Since one must "call" the spontaneity of the power of representation "understanding," Kant claims that synthesis is an action of the understanding.

If we apply these remarks in §15 to Kant's account of imagination, then we have reason to suspect that the spontaneity of imagination and its synthesis, on his view, must ultimately be regarded as actions of the understanding. And he, indeed, appears to corroborate this later in the B Deduction: "It is one and the same spontaneity that, there under the name imagination and here under the name of understanding, brings combination into the manifold of intuition" (B162fn.). For Kant, it would seem to be "one and the same spontaneity" because the "spontaneity" involved in imaginative synthesis is nothing other than the spontaneity of understanding, exercised in a particular way, precisely as the understanding view would have it.

Further support for the understanding view has been adduced from §24 of the B Deduction. In this section, Kant details the so-called "figurative synthesis" of imagination, which is an *a priori* activity of imagination that I shall discuss in more detail in Chapter 6. For my purposes here what is relevant is the fact that

---

[34] For a discussion of this apparent shift between the A and B Deductions, see Heidegger KPM §31 ("Kant shrank back" (112)); Bennett (1966, 134–8); Kitcher (1990, 158–60); Longuenesse (1998, 204–8); Allison (2001, 186–9); Horstmann (2018, pt. 1).

THE UNDERSTANDING VIEW OF IMAGINATION   63

the language he uses to characterize figurative synthesis seems to suggest that it is an exercise of understanding. As I noted above, Kant describes figurative synthesis as "an exercise of spontaneity" (B151–2). He also claims that it is "an effect [*Wirkung*] of the understanding on sensibility and its first application," and a "designation [*Bennenung*]" under which understanding acts on sensibility (B152–3). When read in light of §15, it is tempting to think that the reason Kant describes the figurative synthesis of imagination as an "exercise of spontaneity" and an "effect," "application," or "designation" of understanding is because he regards it as an exercise of the understanding carried out in intuition. Otherwise put, §24 suggests that, on Kant's view, we exercise our understanding not just in intellectual acts of synthesis in judgment, but also in sensible acts of synthesis in intuition.[35] And, according to the understanding view, the latter operation of our understanding is just what the figurative synthesis of imagination amounts to.

In addition to this seemingly more direct support for the understanding view of imagination in the B Deduction, support might be drawn more elliptically from the following infamous passage,

> The same function that gives unity to the different representations **in a judgment** also gives unity to the mere synthesis of different representations **in an intuition**…The same understanding, therefore, and indeed by means of the very same actions through which it brings the logical form of a judgment into concepts…, also brings a transcendental content into its representations by means of the synthetic unity of the manifold of intuition in general.
>
> (A79/B105)

One way of reading this passage is in terms of the claim that the "same understanding" can be exercised in two different ways: it can either be exercised intellectually when it gives unity to representations in a judgment or exercised sensibly when it gives unity to representations in an intuition.[36] And it is tempting to think that the subsequent account of imagination that Kant gives in the B Deduction is meant to clarify what exactly this sensible exercise of understanding amounts to.

Yet, in spite of this support for the understanding view, there are reasons to worry that this view reflects Kant's considered position. For one thing, it is not clear that Kant can allow for a sensible exercise of the understanding. At the outset

---

[35] See Land (2015a).

[36] See, e.g., Sellars's claim that, "since [Kant] tells us…that it is 'the same function which gives unity to the various representations *in a judgment*' which 'also gives unity to the mere synthesis of various representations *in one intuition*' (A79; B104–5), we are not surprised when, after vaguely characterizing 'synthesis' as 'the mere result of the power of imagination, a blind but indispensable function of the soul' (A78; B103), it turns out, most clearly in the second edition (B151–3) that this imagination, under the name 'productive imagination', is the understanding functioning in a special way" (1968, 4). See also McDowell's (2009, chaps. 2, 14) reading of Sellars and Kant along these lines.

64 IMAGINATION AND THE TWO STEMS OF COGNITION

of the Analytic, for example, Kant claims that, "the understanding can make no other use of these concepts than judging by means of them," and that, "we can...trace all actions of the understanding back to judgments" (A68/B93). These remarks certainly suggest that instead of allowing for understanding to have an "intellectual" and "sensible" exercise, Kant takes all exercises of the understanding to be "intellectual" and to involve judgment.[37] This would call for another reading of the "same function" passage, according to which the sort of unity the understanding gives "in an intuition" is ultimately bound up with judgment. This is a thorny issue and one that I shall address at length in Part II.[38] For now, though, I want to point out reasons to be hesitant about ascribing to Kant a view of the understanding as something that can be exercised in any way other than in an intellectual fashion in judgment.

However, a more straightforward reason to doubt the understanding view is that, with the exception of the B-edition of the first *Critique*, when we survey Kant's treatment of imagination in his pre-Critical and Critical writings on anthropology and metaphysics, as well as the three *Critiques*, the position he consistently defends is one according to which imagination is distinct from understanding. As I noted above, in his pre-Critical and Critical anthropological writings and lectures on metaphysics, Kant consistently situates his analysis of imagination in his discussion of sensibility, rather than the understanding.[39] Moreover, as I indicated, Kant either just assumes that this is the case or implies that this is the case given their logical profile: imagination is a faculty of intuition, whereas understanding is a faculty of concepts.

When we turn to the three *Critiques*, on either side of the B-edition of the first *Critique*, we likewise find Kant characterizing imagination as distinct from the faculty of the understanding. We have already seen evidence for this in the A Deduction.[40] In the second *Critique*, published just a year after the B-edition of

---

[37] Land (2015a) labels this position "judgmentalism" and raises doubts about it as the best reading of Kant.

[38] There I distinguish between acts of the understanding that involve judgment and acts of imagination, which are acts of it as a part of sensibility under the guidance of the understanding.

[39] See, e.g., "We have just run through the field of sensibility, which starts from the senses, on which all actions [*Handlungen*] of imagination [*Imagination*] rests, and thus we have run through the field of intuition" (Mensch. 25:1032); my transl.). See also Part I of Anthro., §§15, 28–39; AF 25:511; AMr 25:1241; ML1 28:230; MMr 29:880–1.

[40] It is also worth noting that in Kant's substantive discussion of imaginative activities after the Deduction, e.g. in the Schematism and Principles, he does not revise his position between the A- and B- editions. See, e.g., the unchanged claim at the outset of the Principles that, "There is only one totality in which all our representations are contained, namely inner sense and its *a priori* form time. The synthesis of representations rests on the imagination, but their synthetic unity (which is requisite for judgment), on the unity of apperception. Herein therefore is to be sought the possibility of synthetic judgments, and, since all three contain the sources of *a priori* representations, also the possibility of pure synthetic judgments" (A155/B194).

the first *Critique*, Kant suggests that the moral assessment of maxims involves "no cognitive faculty other than the understanding (not the imagination)" (KpV 5:69).[41]

So too, in Kant's lengthy treatment of imagination in the third *Critique*, we find him insisting on the distinction between imagination and understanding as two distinct faculties of cognition. For example, in rehearsing his theory of cognition in §9, Kant explicitly describes imagination and understanding as "faculties of cognition" (plural) (KU 5:217). And in his description of these two "powers of representation" (again plural), Kant aligns imagination with intuitions, and understanding with concepts: "there belongs to a representation by which an object is given, in order for there to be cognition of it in general, **imagination** for the composition [*Zusammensetzung*] of the manifold of intuition and **understanding** for the unity of the concept that unifies representations" (KU 5:217, see also KU 5:238). Kant follows a similar pattern in §35, where he treats imagination and understanding as "two powers" (two) required for cognition: "[cognition] requires the agreement of two powers of representation: namely, the imagination (for the intuition and the composition [*Zusammensetzung*] of the manifold of intuition), and the understanding (for the concept as representation of the unity of this composition)" (KU 5:287). And a few sentences later, he distinguishes between "the **faculty** of intuitions or exhibitions [*Darstellungen*] (i.e., of the imagination)" and "the **faculty** of concepts (i.e., the understanding)" (KU 5:287; transl. modified). We thus find Kant following a pattern similar to the one he follows in his writings on anthropology and metaphysics: he distinguishes imagination from understanding on the logical grounds that the former is a faculty of intuitions while the latter is a faculty of concepts.

We see similar themes operative in Kant's analysis of judgments of taste and genius. For example, in his discussion of aesthetic appreciation, Kant claims that judgments of the beautiful involve a "free play" of imagination and understanding, a play he describes in terms of the "animation of both faculties (the imagination and the understanding)" and the "play of both powers of the mind (imagination and understanding), enlivened through mutual agreement" (KU 5:219).[42] And in his description of free play, he again distinguishes between imagination and understanding along the intuition-concept lines we saw above: when the "cognitive faculties...are in play," Kant claims that, "the imagination (as the faculty

---

[41] As I discuss in more detail in Chapter 12, the assessment at issue here is the "universalizability test" in which we test whether a maxim is moral by considering whether it can serve as a universal law of nature.

[42] See also, "in the aesthetic judgment of reflection...it is that sensation which the harmonious play of the two faculties of cognition in the power of judgment, imagination and understanding, produces in the subject" (EE 20:224), and, "the ground for this pleasure [in the beautiful] is to be found in...the purposive correspondence of an object...with the relationship of the cognitive faculties among themselves (of the imagination and the understanding) that is required for every empirical cognition" (KU 5:191).

66   IMAGINATION AND THE TWO STEMS OF COGNITION

of *a priori* intuitions) is unintentionally brought into accord with the understanding, as the faculty of concepts" (KU 5:190).

Finally, in his account of genius, Kant asserts,

> The mental powers, then, whose union (in a certain relation) constitutes **genius**, are imagination and understanding. Only in the use of imagination for cognition, imagination is under the constraint of the understanding…; in an aesthetic respect, however, imagination is free to provide…unsought extensive undeveloped material for the understanding.   (KU 5:316–17)

As was the case in his account of cognition and free play, Kant indicates that artistic creation involves the operation of imagination and understanding as two distinct faculties or powers that relate to one another in a "free" way. And a bit later, he says that genius, "presupposes a determinate concept of the product, as an end, hence understanding, but also…the intuition, for the exhibition of this concept, hence a relation of the imagination to the understanding" (KU 5:317). Here, Kant suggests that genius involves the relation of imagination, *qua* a capacity responsible for intuition, and understanding, *qua* a capacity responsible for concepts.

Altogether, when we consider the trajectory of Kant's treatment of imagination from his pre-Critical through his Critical writings, the position that he most consistently endorses is one according to which imagination is distinct from the understanding. And the reason he offers for why this is the case turns on its logical profile: insofar as imagination is a faculty of intuition, it does not belong to the understanding, *qua* the faculty of concepts. However, if this is right, then it seems that the understanding view is no more satisfying as an interpretation of Kant's theory of imagination than the other two views.

2.5   Conclusion

My main aim in this chapter was to explore the complexities surrounding Kant's account of the relationship that imagination has to sensibility and understanding. In this vein, I considered reasons for and against attributing to Kant the third thing view, sensibility view, or understanding view of imagination.

In addition to laying out this debate, I used this discussion to introduce three of Kant's key claims about imagination. First, we saw that Kant tasks imagination with bridging the gap between sensibility and understanding in cognition. This line of thought points toward Kant's commitment to mediation being a crucial notion for making sense of the cognitive function of imagination. Second, we found texts in which he attributes intuitions to imagination—an attribution that is relevant to how we think about its logical profile. Third, we uncovered Kant's metaphysical commitment to imaginative activity being spontaneous. As we sort through Kant's conception of imagination as a cognitive capacity, these three intimations of its functional, logical, and metaphysical profile point us in promising directions.

At the same time, these three commitments also provide a succinct frame for seeing why it is so challenging to pin down imagination's relationship to sensibility and understanding on Kant's view. How could a spontaneous faculty of intuition tasked with mediating between sensibility and understanding fit neatly in Kant's sensibility-understanding architecture? To say that imagination is a third thing on Kant's view can capture the sense in which it is a mediating and, arguably, a spontaneous faculty of intuition, but then imagination does not clearly integrate into his two-stem architecture. To say that imagination is part of sensibility can capture its status as a faculty of intuition, its place in the two-stem architecture, and arguably, its status as a mediator, but not the sense in which it is spontaneous. To say that imagination is an exercise of the understanding can capture the sense in which it is spontaneous, integrated into this architecture, and a mediator, but not the sense in which imagination is a faculty of intuition. And at this point one may begin to wonder whether we can attribute to Kant a coherent view of imagination at all.[43]

Seeing More: Kant's Theory of Imagination. Samantha Matherne, Oxford University Press.
© Samantha Matherne 2024. DOI: 10.1093/9780191999291.003.0003

---

[43] Gibbons, for example, argues that it is ultimately "impossible" to pin down imagination's relation to sensibility and understanding on Kant's view given its status as a mediating capacity (1994, 29).

3

Imagination Is Part of Sensibility

> our imagination ... the greatest faculty of sensibility
>
> —KU 5:257

3.1 Introduction

Though no reading of Kant's view of imagination is without complications, in this chapter, I argue that his considered view is that imagination is part of sensibility. I have labeled this the "sensibility view" of imagination, and have contrasted it with the "third thing view," according to which imagination is a faculty that is distinct from the faculties of sensibility and understanding, and the "understanding view," according to which imagination is a sensible exercise of the understanding. Central to my argument is the claim that Kant defends a bipartite account of sensibility as containing two parts: sense and imagination. I, moreover, contend that appreciating the imaginative dimension of sensibility gives us reason to attribute to Kant a more cognitively sophisticated view of sensibility and intuition than he is often credited with.

However, in addition to defending the sensibility view as the best reading of Kant's theory of imagination, in this chapter, I hope to shed light on a couple of issues that I raised in the Introduction. The first concerns the fact that, unlike many contemporary theorists, Kant does not acknowledge a non-sensory mode of imagining (see §0.2.1). Recall that contemporary theorists tend to distinguish between sensory modes of imagining that involve mental states that have a sensory character, e.g. visualizing, dreaming, or hallucinating, and non-sensory modes of imagination that involve mental states that do not have a sensory character, e.g. supposing that something is the case or entertaining a proposition. I indicated that Kant, by contrast, takes all imaginative activity to be sensory and thus does not regard non-sensory activities such as these as attributable to imagination. In this chapter, I aim to clarify Kant's motivation for this restriction: insofar as he takes imagination to be a part of sensibility (*Sinnlichkeit*), he takes all of its activities to be sensory or sensible (*sinnlich*).[1] This is not to say that Kant denies that imaginative activities can relate to concepts, judgments, or propositions. To the contrary, in Parts II–IV, I make the case that the cognitive

---

[1] In translations of Kant, the German term "sinnlich" is translated as "sensible," and, for this reason, I shall typically opt for it over "sensory."

activities that Kant attributes to our imagination in the context of experience, aesthetic engagement, and our practical pursuits are conceptually rich and often have some relation to judgment. However, for Kant, in these cases, imagining is never just a matter of intellectually adopting a cognitive attitude in thought; it must involve some sort of sensible activities and sensible representations.

The second issue from the Introduction that I return to concerns Kant's distinction between sensing and imagining. I discussed this under the heading of the "external taxonomy question," i.e. the question of whether imagining is a *sui generis* mental state (§0.2.2). And in this chapter, I explore Kant's robust account of the distinction between imagining and sensing in light of his account of the different kinds of sensible representations, sensible activities, and cognitive functions they involve.

In order to spell out what it means for imagination to be part of sensibility, I proceed as follows. In §§3.2–3.5, I present my reading of Kant's bipartite account of sensibility. I begin in §3.2 with a discussion of what it means for sensibility to have two parts. I then explore his distinction between the two parts in light of the types of intuitions they generate (§3.3), the types of mental processes they involve (§3.4), and the cognitive functions they perform (§3.5). And in §3.6, I argue that once we appreciate Kant's bipartite account of sensibility, then we have reason to regard the sensibility view, rather than the third thing or understanding view, as his considered view of imagination.

Over the course of this discussion, I make the case that attending to Kant's account of imagination gives us reason to revise certain assumptions about the logical, metaphysical, and functional character of sensibility in his framework. To this end, I argue that, logically, he acknowledges two types of intuitions, intuitions of sense and intuitions of imagination, which are generated through different processes and which differ in how they relate to objects and concepts. Metaphysically, I claim that although Kant is committed to sensibility being receptive in nature, he nevertheless acknowledges a kind of spontaneous activity of sensibility that is constitutively dependent on receptivity: the activity of imagination. And, functionally, I propose that, for Kant, the two parts of sensibility have different cognitive functions: whereas sense gives us objects, imagination makes concepts sensible and facilitates our concrete comprehension of them. Although these revisions to how we understand Kant's picture of sensibility are rather radical, I submit that appreciating them reveals a more nuanced picture of what sensibility, in its bipartite manifestations, contributes to our cognitive lives.

3.2 The Bipartite Structure of Sensibility

In the following passage from the *Anthropology* Kant articulates the core of the bipartite structure of sensibility as I understand it: "*Sensibility* in the cognitive

70 IMAGINATION IS PART OF SENSIBILITY

faculty (the faculty of intuitive representation) contains two parts [*Stücke*]: *sense* [*Sinn*] and *power of imagination* [*Einbildungskraft*].—The first is the faculty of intuition in the presence of an object, the second is intuition even *without* the presence of an object" (Anthro. 7:153). Here, he treats sensibility in general as the cognitive faculty responsible for "intuitive representations," and he indicates that it has two parts: "sense" and "imagination." But, for Kant, what does it mean for sensibility to have parts?

One possible way to read this parthood language is in mereological terms. We might thus attribute to Kant a view according to which sensibility is a whole that contains sense and imagination as two mereological parts. However, the term that gets translated as "part" in this passage is "Stück," rather than "Teil," the latter being the term he typically uses in mereological contexts, and the former being a term he uses more loosely (see A25/B39). Given this terminological choice, we thus do not need to read this passage as committing Kant to the view that sensibility is a whole that contains two mereological parts.

Instead, I take Kant to be committing himself to the idea that sensibility has a set of generic features that are realized in a specific way in its two parts. I have already laid out a more encompassing account of the generic features of sensibility on Kant's view in Chapter 1. Sensibility is, logically, a faculty of intuition, which, for us, amount to spatio-temporal representations of objects. Metaphysically, sensibility is a receptive faculty. And functionally, sensibility is a faculty that functions cognitively well when it gives us objects and makes concepts sensible. Following out my line of interpretation, we should thus expect each part of sensibility to realize these features in a specific way.

Prima facie, it is plausible to think that sense fits this logical, metaphysical, and functional of sensibility. When we sense objects, we have an intuition of them, which is the result of a receptive process of causal affection, and which has the cognitive function of giving us objects by putting us in touch with them. But how could imagination fit this profile? As I stressed in the previous chapter, Kant characterizes imaginative activity as spontaneous rather than receptive; in which case, it does not seem to fit the metaphysical profile of sensibility. What is more, as we shall soon see, it is not clear that imagination fits the logical profile of sensibility either. Kant denies that imaginative representations stand in the same immediate, receptive relation to objects that intuitions of sense do in virtue of which they give us objects. Insofar as this is the case, it is not clear that Kant can attribute intuitions to imagination at all.

In spite of these concerns, in what follows I argue that if we take a closer look at the representations, metaphysical processes, and cognitive functions of sense and imagination, then we shall find that they each instantiate the general profile of sensibility in a distinctive way. However, as I noted above, appreciating this complexity in Kant's account of sensibility calls for rethinking certain assumptions about the scope and cognitive remit of sensibility, as well as the nature of intuition on his view.

3.3 The Intuitions of Sensibility

Given Kant's logical characterization of sensibility in general as a faculty of intuition, we have reason to expect both parts of sensibility to generate intuitions. This expectation appears to be met in the passage from the *Anthropology* I quoted above: "*Sensibility* in the cognitive faculty (the faculty of intuitive representation) contains two parts [*Stücke*]: *sense* [*Sinn*] and *power of imagination* [*Einbildungskraft*].—The first is the faculty of intuition in the presence of an object, the second is intuition even *without* the presence of an object" (Anthro. 7:153). In the second sentence, Kant appears to distinguish between sense and imagination on the basis of the kind of intuitions they are responsible for: sense is responsible for "intuition in the presence of an object" and imagination for "intuition even without the presence of an object." In a similar vein in his Kiesewetter notes, he says, "We have two sorts of intuition: sensible intuition, for which the object must be represented as present, and an imagining as intuition without the presence of the object" (R6314 (1790), 18:619).

This said, in the first sentence in the *Anthropology* passage, Kant characterizes the representations of sensibility in general not as "intuitions," but as "intuitive representations," and this raises some questions. Does he ultimately conceive of "intuitions" or "intuitive representations" as the generic representation type of sensibility? And does he think that both sense and imagination generate intuitions, or does he think, perhaps, that intuitions are the special purview of sense and some other representation type falls to the purview of imagination?

One reason to worry about identifying intuitions as the type of representation generated by both parts of sensibility turns on Kant's account of the relationship between intuitions and objects. Kant often characterizes intuitions as representations that depend on the presence of objects. For example, in the *Prolegomena*, he says, "An intuition is a representation of the sort which would depend immediately on the presence of an object" (Prol. 4:281). In a similar vein in the first *Critique*, he maintains that an intuition "is dependent on the existence of the object" (B72). Moreover, the idea that intuitions depend on the "presence" or "existence" of an object is a natural way of unpacking the immediacy criterion that Kant places on intuition. Recall that Kant claims that intuitions have an "immediate" relation to an object (A320/B377).[2] One might think that the reason

---

[2] As Allais puts it, "As I read Kant's immediacy claim, he thinks that intuitions are object-dependent in the sense that we have an intuition of an object only when that object is in fact present to us" (2015, 156); see also Allais (2010, 59; 2011, 395n).

72 IMAGINATION IS PART OF SENSIBILITY

he takes them to have an immediate relation to an object is because they depend on the existence and presence of objects. On the basis of these remarks, it is thus tempting to attribute to Kant a view of intuition as "strongly object-dependent,"[3] i.e. as a representation that requires the object exist and be present to the subject at the time that they have the intuition.[4]

If Kant endorses a strongly object-dependent view of intuition, then it does not seem that representations of imagination can count as intuitions. As we have seen, Kant claims that imagination produces representations "even without the presence" of objects. For example, when I hallucinate an anemone, my imagination generates a representation of a flower that is precisely not present to me at the time of the hallucination. Insofar as this is the case, the representations generated by imagination would not appear to count as intuitions, *qua* strongly object-dependent representations, but as some other representation type on Kant's view. Given that he often attributes "images" (*Bilder*) to imagination,[5] one possibility is to identify images as the alternative representation type that imagination is responsible for.[6]

Piecing this interpretive line of thought together, it seems that we should attribute to Kant a view according to which the type of representation sensibility in general is responsible for is not an intuition, but rather an intuitive representation.[7] Intuitions, *per* this interpretation, are the species of intuitive representation that sense is responsible for, while images are the species of intuitive representation that imagination is responsible for.

---

[3] Grüne (2017a, 67) frames this as "strong object-dependence"; Stephenson (2015, 488; 2017, 108) frames it as "strong-particular dependence"; and McLear (2017, 89) frames it as "strong-presence dependence."

[4] See also Hanna (2005, 259); Allais (2009, 389; 2015, 156); McLear (2016b, §5.2; 2017); Watkins and Willaschek (2017b, 89–90). Some defenders of the strongly object-dependent view connect Kant's account of intuition to a "relational" or "naïve realist" view of perception (see, e.g., Gomes 2014; 2017; Allais 2015; McLear 2016a; 2016b).

[5] See, e.g., Kant's claim that, "The mind must have a capacity to make, as it were, an image á la a mosaic from compared and combined [*zusammengefaßten*] impressions" (AC 25:45, my transl.; see also AC 25:75, AP 25:303).

[6] Although a number of commentators have attempted to distance Kant's theory of imagination from images (see, e.g., Strawson 1974, 54; Young 1988; Allison 2004, 187; Pollok 2017, 151), these pre-Critical remarks, as well as his attribution of images to imagination in the Critical period (e.g. A120; B156; A140–2/B180–1; Anthro. 7:173), reveal that he does regard images as one type of representation generated by imagination. For readings of Kant's theory of imagination along image involving lines, see Matherne (2015); Horstmann (2018, 66, 83–4, 97–100, 102); Tolley (2019); and Tracz (2020). However, my interpretation of images as intuitions differs from that of Tracz (2020), who argues that Kant distinguishes images from intuitions. On my reading, images produced by imagination are a kind of intuition. See Chapter 5 for discussion of the roles images play in perception.

[7] See, e.g., Allais (2015, 156–7 fn 23); Watkins and Willaschek (2017b, 2.6); Tracz (2020, 1097n33). In support of this reading, commentators point to the Refutation of Idealism as a text in which Kant uses "intuitive representation" as a general term to refer to representations produced through both sense and imagination (B278).

However, there are, at least, three reasons to worry about this reading of Kant's account of the representations of sensibility.[8] In the first place, Kant does not appear to observe a technical distinction between intuitive representations and intuitions. The phrase "intuitive representation" is not one that he frequently uses.[9] And when he does use it, he typically uses it interchangeably with "intuition." He does this in the *Anthropology* passage I just cited (Anthro. 7:153).[10] He also does this in §59 of the third *Critique*, where he speaks of "schemata" and "symbols" as both "intuitions" and an "**intuitive** kind of representation" (KU 5:351–2). And in "On a Discovery," Kant unpacks the notion of "intuition" in terms of "the subjective conditions of our sensibility under which alone we can receive an intuitive representation" (OD 8:210; see also 8:212).

Second, we should be hesitant in ascribing to Kant the view that images, rather than intuitions, are the distinctive representation type generated by imagination. Kant certainly describes some representations generated by imagination as images. Indeed, in Chapter 5, I argue that images play a pivotal role in Kant's analysis of what our imagination contributes to perception. However, Kant does not describe all representations generated by imagination as images. In the Schematism chapter of the first *Critique*, for example, Kant is at pains to distinguish images from another "product of imagination," which he labels a "schema" (A140–1/B179–80).[11] Meanwhile, in the third *Critique*, Kant characterizes the imaginative representations produced in the context of artistic creation not as images, but rather as "aesthetic ideas" (see KU §49).[12] Given that Kant identifies representations other than images as products of imagination, it does not seem viable to identify images, rather than intuitions, as its distinctive representation type.

The third issue is that Kant repeatedly attributes intuitions to imagination.[13] Indeed, we find Kant doing so in two veins. In one vein, he ascribes specific kinds

---

[8] Grüne (2016; 2017a; 2017b) has also recently argued that *a priori* intuitions of space and time do not appear to fit the strongly object-dependent model. According to this objection, *a priori* intuitions of space and time cannot be object-dependent because Kant denies that space and time are "objects that are intuited" (A291/B347; see also A431/B549, OP 22:12, R4673 17:638–9). There is, however, some question as to whether Kant has a thick sense of object in mind in the A291/B347 passage, *qua* spatio-temporal objects of experience, or a thinner sense of object, defined as an object of consciousness (see, e.g., "one can…call everything…insofar as one is conscious of it, an object" (A189/B234)). See Chapters 6–7 for a discussion of Kant's account of the relationship between imagination and pure intuitions of space and time.

[9] He uses the phrase twice in the first *Critique* (B160fn, B278), twice in the "On a Discovery" (8:210, 212), once in "What Real Progress" (20:267), and once in the *Anthropology* (7:154).

[10] He also refers to sensibility as the "faculty of intuition" at Anthro. 7:196.

[11] See also his claim that, "it is not images of objects but schemata that ground our pure sensible concepts," and that, "The schema of a pure concept of the understanding…is something that can never be brought to an image at all" (A142/B181).

[12] Earlier in the ML1 lectures Kant also uses "image" in a restricted way to refer to the representations our imagination generates in the "*Abbildung*" or "illustration" of an object that is present, rather than absent (ML1 28:235).

[13] Commentators in favor of attributing intuitions to imagination include Longuenesse (1998, chap. 8; 2005, 73); Wenzel (2005); Haag (2007); Grüne (2016); Land (2016, 147–8); Stephenson (2015; 2017); McLear (2017); Horstmann (2018, chap. 1); Rosefeldt (2019).

74 IMAGINATION IS PART OF SENSIBILITY

of intuitions to imagination. In the *Anthropology* Kant describes the representations of the productive imagination as "(invented) intuitions" (Anthro. 7:169). In the third *Critique* he characterizes an "aesthetic idea" and "aesthetic normal idea" as an "intuition (representation of the imagination)" and "individual intuition (of the imagination)," respectively (KU 5:314, 233). And in his discussion of mathematical construction, he ascribes *a priori* intuitions of finite spaces and times to imagination.[14]

In another vein, Kant characterizes imagination in general as a faculty of intuition. We saw this above in the *Anthropology* passage where he describes imagination as the "faculty of intuition even without the presence of an object." He repeats this claim again in §28, glossing imagination as the "faculty of intuition without the presence of the object" (Anthro. 7:167). We find echoes of this in the first *Critique*, "**Imagination** is the faculty for representing an object in intuition even **without its presence [*Einbildungskraft ist das Vermögen, einen Gegenstand auch ohne dessen Gegenwart in der Anschauung vorzustellen*]**" (B151; transl. modified).[15] Again in the third *Critique* Kant characterizes imagination in general as a "faculty of intuition" and a "faculty of *a priori* intuitions" (KU 5:287, 292, 190). And in his discussion of the beautiful, he glosses imagination as a "power of representation" that is responsible "for the intuition and the composition [*Zusammensetzung*] of the manifold of intuition" (KU 5:287).

What this third line of thought reveals is that rather than reserving the term "intuition" for the representations generated by sense "in the presence of an object," Kant is happy to use it to refer to representations generated by imagination "even without the presence of an object."[16] And in order to mark the distinction between the species of intuition generated by sense and imagination, I shall refer to the former as an "intuition of sense" or "intuition$_s$" and the latter as an "intuition of imagination" or "intuition$_i$" in what follows.

Piecing this together, on my reading, Kant endorses the following view of the logical character of sensibility. Sensibility in general is the faculty of intuition, and each of its two parts is responsible for a specific kind of intuition: sense for intuitions$_s$ and imagination for intuitions$_i$.

This ascription of intuitions to both sense and imagination certainly makes sense when we consider intuitions as spatio-temporal representations of particulars. I can, for example, spatio-temporally represent a particular anemone through either sense or imagination. However, it is much less clear how this ascription works given the immediacy criterion that Kant places on intuition. If intuitions$_i$

---

[14] See, e.g., A163/B204; A713–14/B741–2; OKT 20:411.
[15] As I noted earlier, there is some debate about how to translate this passage, see Stephenson (2015; 2017).
[16] See Roche (2011, 360–2) and Stephenson (2015; 2017) for the argument that Kant's account of imagination puts pressure on the view of intuition as strongly object-dependent.

are produced even without the presence of an object, then how can they have an immediate relation to an object?

Answering this question turns, in part, on specifying exactly what Kant means by an intuition having an immediate relation to an object. This is a contentious issue. One question especially relevant for our purposes is whether Kant thinks that the object an intuition stands in an immediate relation to needs to exist and be directly present to the subject at the time of the intuition. According to one reading, Kant endorses a relational view of immediacy, according to which it involves the subject standing in an acquaintance relation to an object that exists and is present to them at the time of the intuition.[17] But according to another reading, Kant offers a phenomenological view of immediacy, according to which what matters is not whether the object, in fact, exists and is present to the subject, but rather whether the subject experiences the object as present to them.[18] Let's consider the prospects of both of these readings of immediacy with respect to intuitions$_i$.

Prima facie, it might seem that the phenomenological reading of immediacy is a more promising route to pursue to account for how intuitions$_i$ can stand in an immediate relation to an object. For even in cases where our imagination generates intuitions$_i$ of objects that are either not present or non-existent, we often experience those objects as present. For example, if I hallucinate a bouquet of anemones, even though no such bouquet exists and is present to me, I can experience it as present.

However, some proponents of the relational reading of immediacy have argued that intuitions of imagination can meet the immediacy criterion as they interpret it.[19] In this vein, they have argued that, on Kant's view, there is an existing object that is present to the subject in imaginative episodes: an internal mental object.[20] Kant, indeed, speaks of imaginings that involve "appearances of inner sense" (Anthro. 7:161). And in his Kiesewetter notes, he writes that in imagining, "no object outside the representation is present" and that an imagining can be "an object of inner sense" (R6315 18:621). Remarks like these can be read as

---

[17] See, e.g., Allais (2015, 156ff; 2017); Gomes (2014; 2017); McLear (2016a; 2016b; 2017). See also Watkins and Willaschek's (2017b) reading, according to which Kant has in mind the relationship an intuition has to an existing object that is present and that causes the intuition as its effect.

[18] See, e.g., Heidegger's characterization of immediacy in terms of an object being "directly shown" (PIK 67) and Parson's claim that, immediacy "means that the object of an intuition is in some way directly present to the mind, as in perception" (1964, 112; see also 1992, 66). See also Carson (1997, 510); Allais (2015, 158). I take accounts according to which the relevant object is the intentional object that we are directed toward in consciousness to also fall in this category (see Prauss 1971; Aquila 1983; Pereboom 1988).

[19] Not all proponents of the relational view countenance this possibility. For example, as noted above, Allais (2015) argues that representations of imagination are "intuitive representations," rather than "intuitions" because they are not strongly object-dependent in the way that intuitions that have an immediate relation to objects are.

[20] See McLear (2017).

76 IMAGINATION IS PART OF SENSIBILITY

indicating that, on Kant's view, intuitions$_i$ have an immediate relation to an existing object after all, an "object of inner sense." According to this reading, when I
hallucinate a bouquet of anemones, there is, indeed, an object that exists and is
present to me: the bouquet that is an object of inner sense.

Yet, by my lights, if we take a closer look at the full range of intuitions$_i$ that
Kant attributes to imagination, then there are reasons to worry that these
intuitions$_i$ can count as immediate in either the phenomenological or relational
senses. According to both the phenomenological and relational readings of
immediacy, the object that our intuitions$_i$ relate to always needs to be present,
either as experienced or as an object of inner sense. However, in his analysis of
many intuitions of imagination, Kant emphasizes the idea that the object is not
present, but absent.[21] Sometimes he highlights the temporal absence of such
objects, e.g. in memory where the object represented is not present, but from the
past,[22] or in anticipation where the object represented is not present, but in the
future.[23] Other times he highlights the spatial absence of such objects, e.g. dreams
or delusions in which the object represented is an "outer thing" that does not currently "exist" outside of us (B278).[24] And in his account of certain inventive representations he underscores the idea that we represent "objects which are not there,"
which are "neither present, nor future, nor past," e.g. when I visualize my dream
house (AF 25:511).[25]

As I see it, neither the phenomenological nor relational account of immediacy
can do full justice to this range of cases in which intuitions$_i$ represent objects that
are absent, rather than present. Phenomenologically, Kant wants to allow for intu-
itions$_i$ that represent things experienced as absent, rather than experienced as
present. For example, when I remember my childhood home, I do not experience
it as present, but rather as temporally and spatially absent. Relationally, with these
cases, the point that Kant insists on is not that the intuitions$_i$ represent an object

---

[21] Stephenson (2017, §6.3) presses this line of argument against the relational approach. Stephenson
(2017, §6.4) also argues that the modified relational view saddles Kant with a bad account of memory
and is inconsistent with the original aspirations of the relational view.

[22] See, e.g., Anthro. 7:182; AF 25:511; AMr 25:1257; ML1 28:235.

[23] See, e.g., his claim that in memory, we "deliberately visualize[e] the past," which "*no longer
exists*," and in anticipation, we "visualize[e] something taking place in the future," that "*does not yet
exist*" (Anthro. 7:182; see also ML1 28:235, AF 25:511). By my lights, Kant's emphasis on the temporal
absence of these represented objects gives us particular reason to be wary of the revised version of the
relational view defended by McLear (2017). For, on McLear's reading, Kant takes imaginative intuitions to be "inner intuitions" that have a temporal, rather than a spatial form, and McLear claims that
it is the object of these inner intuitions that is present. However, this would seem to make it the case
that the objects of imaginative intuitions are always temporally present in a way that Kant appears to
deny in his account of memory and anticipation.

[24] See also his discussion of how "when a passion appears on the scene the power of imagination is
more enlivened through the absence of the object than by its presence" (Anthro. 7:180).

[25] See also, "The faculty of imagination is the faculty for producing images from oneself, independent of the actuality of objects, where the images are not borrowed from experience. E.g., an architect
pretends to build a house which he has not yet seen" (ML1 28:237), and "Our imagination is...productive
when it portrays for us an object that is not present in our senses" (AMr 25:1257).

that is present internally, but rather an object that is absent. For example, when an architect envisions a new house, Kant underscores the idea that they imaginatively proceed "independent of the actuality of objects" (ML1 28:237). Kant's account of intuitions$_i$ that represent absent objects thus cannot be counted as having an immediate relation to an object in either the phenomenological or relational senses.

So, where does this leave us with intuitions of imagination and Kant's immediacy criterion on intuition? By my lights, these considerations give us reason to rethink Kant's commitment to the immediacy criterion on intuition. To be sure, there are classic passages in which Kant indicates that intuitions have an immediate relation to an object (see, e.g., A68/B93; A320/B377; JL 9:91). However, the fact that he explicitly and repeatedly attributes intuitions to imagination, which, for reasons I just discussed, do not have an immediate relation to an object, suggests that the immediacy criterion is more restricted in scope than these passages suggest. Rather than extending the immediacy criterion to all intuition, I take Kant's considered view to be that the immediacy criterion is applicable to intuitions$_s$, rather than intuitions$_i$. And part of what I hope to clarify in the rest of this chapter is Kant's motivation for distinguishing between intuitions$_s$ and intuitions$_i$ on this count given the different metaphysical processes through which they are generated and the different functions they have in cognition.

3.4 The Processes of Sensibility

From a metaphysical perspective, we have seen that Kant characterizes the mental processes involved in sensibility as receptive: they depend on affection.[26] We should accordingly expect the two parts of sensibility to generate their respective kinds of intuition through processes that are receptive. As I anticipated above, while it is relatively easy to see how this expectation is met in the case of sense, given Kant's characterization of imagination as spontaneous (see Chapter 2), this expectation would seem to be disappointed in the case of imagination. Indeed, as I discussed, the spontaneity of imagination is one of the major stumbling blocks to attributing to Kant a view of imagination as part of sensibility.

In what follows, I argue that the key to removing this stumbling block is recognizing that although receptivity is a generic feature of sensibility, Kant allows for receptivity to be realized in a different way by sense and imagination. As I shall now claim, on Kant's view, whereas sense is receptive in all its processes (§3.4.1), imagination is at once spontaneous and constitutively dependent on receptivity

---

[26] Although interpreters sometimes contrast "receptivity" and "passivity" with "activity," Kant allows for passive activities: "We can never be merely passive, but rather every passion is at the same time action" (MMr 29:823; see also "Metaphysik v. Schön" 28: 513–14).

78 IMAGINATION IS PART OF SENSIBILITY

in a way that is consistent with it being part of sensibility (§3.4.2). On my reading, then, it is this constitutive dependence of imagination on receptivity that explains how Kant can regard imagination, for all its spontaneity, as part of sensibility, *qua* the receptive faculty of cognition.

In order to orient this discussion, I shall take my cue from what I find to be a helpful early remark that Kant makes in his ML1 lectures, in which he articulates the difference between the processes of sense and imagination (or what he then calls the "formative power"): "One can classify sensibility in the following manner: all sensible cognitions are either *given* [*gegebene*] or *made* [*gemachte*]. To the given we can reckon sense in general, or the representation of the senses themselves...To the made we reckon... [t]he representations of the formative power [*bildenden Kraft*]" (ML1 28:230). In this context, Kant uses the terms "sensible cognition" and "intuition" interchangeably,[27] so we can read this passage as him distinguishing between two processes that generate intuitions: processes of sense that "give" intuitions$_s$ and processes of imagination that "make" intuitions$_i$. Kant, moreover, indicates that being "given" an intuition$_s$ is a receptive affair that arises "entirely from the impression of the object," whereas "making" an intuition$_i$ is something that involves the "spontaneity of the mind" (ML1 28:230). In order to work through Kant's account of the metaphysical processes involved in sense and imagination, I thus want to explore what it means for sense to receptively give intuitions$_s$ and for imagination to spontaneously make intuitions$_i$, as well as what implications this has for how we are to understand the differences between these two types of intuitions.

3.4.1 The Process of Sensing

So, what does it mean for the processes involved in sense to be receptive ones that give us intuitions$_s$? Let me note straightaway that this is not the notion of givenness that is typically associated with sensibility on Kant's view. Usually, when we think of givenness in the context of his theory of sensibility, what comes to mind is his claim that sensibility is responsible for giving us objects. Though I return to this notion of givenness in §3.5, here, my interest is in Kant's account of the way in which sensing proceeds in a receptive way that gives us intuitions$_s$. And what I aim to show is that on Kant's view, being given an intuition$_s$ is a wholly receptive process in which our senses generate intuitions$_s$ as the result of causal affection.

Let's return to Kant's account of the process of sense in the ML1 lectures. As I noted above, he glosses what it means for us to be given an intuition$_s$ in terms of the idea that these intuitions "arise entirely from the impression of the object"

---

[27] For example, in addition to ascribing sensible cognition to sensibility, he claims that, "The sensible consists in intuition" (ML1 28:229).

(ML1 28:230). This picture of intuitions$_s$ "arising entirely from the impression of the object" is in keeping with his earlier characterization of sensibility as a "passive property of our faculty of cognition so far as we are affected by objects" (ML1 28:229). In these lectures, Kant thus paints a picture of being given an intuition$_s$ as a passive process in which an intuition$_s$ is generated in us as the result of being causally affected by an object through our senses.

When we look to the Critical period, we find Kant pursuing a similar line of thought regarding the process of sense, though he tends to cash out this process more in terms of "receptivity" than "passivity."[28] In the first *Critique*, for example, he describes this process as one in which, "The manifold of representations can be given in an intuition that is merely sensible, i.e. nothing but receptivity" (B129). This echoes his earlier claim that the manifold of intuition is something that is "given in the mind without spontaneity" (B68).[29] And this appears to be part of his motivation for cashing out the receptivity of sensibility in terms of our capacity "to receive representations": we "receive" these representations insofar as they are given to us through a receptive process (A51/B75). In the first *Critique*, we thus find Kant again claiming that sense involves receptive processes that give us intuitions$_s$.

Moreover, it is precisely in virtue of being the receptive result of causal affection by objects that Kant takes intuitions$_s$ to have an immediate relation to objects. In his words, "that through which [cognition] relates immediately to [objects]...is **intuition**. This, however, takes place only insofar as the object...affects the mind in a certain way" (A19/B33; see also B41).

But what exactly does Kant think the receptive process of sensing involves? He distinguishes between two types of senses: outer and inner. Outer sense involves affection by "physical things" outside the subject through sight, sound, touch, taste, and smell, whereas "inner" sense involves being affected "by the mind" in a way that results, e.g. in hedonic or affective states (Anthro. 7:153).[30] So, it is through the affection of outer and inner sense that Kant thinks sense gives us intuitions$_s$ that stand in an immediate relation to their objects.

Whether through outer or inner sense, Kant claims that sense gives us "empirical" intuitions$_s$, which he describes as follows: "The effect of an object on the capacity for representation, insofar as we are affected by it, is **sensation** [*Empfindung*]. That intuition which is related to the object through sensation is

---

[28] However, see the *Anthropology* where Kant uses language of "passivity" and sets up his discussion of sensing with the claim that, "Representations in regard to which the mind behaves passively, and by means of which the subject is therefore *affected*...belong to the *sensuous* [*sinnliche*] cognitive faculty" (Anthro. 7:140).

[29] See also Kant's claim in §21 that in the first step of the B Deduction, "I still could not abstract from one point, namely, from the fact that the manifold for intuition must already be **given** prior to the synthesis of understanding and independently from it" (B145).

[30] For discussion of the relationship between affection through outer and inner sense, see Jankowiak (2014); Schmitz (2015); Ingredgaard (2017); Kraus (2019; 2020); Liang (2020; 2021).

80 IMAGINATION IS PART OF SENSIBILITY

called **empirical**" (A19–20/B34). Here, Kant claims that being given an empirical intuition$_s$ is the result of a process in which our senses are causally affected by an object in a way that gives rise to "sensation" as an "effect" in us. According to Kant, sensation is a "merely subjective aspect of our representation," which reflects how we have been "modified" by the object (KU 5:189; A320/B376; transl. modified). Though Kant occasionally mentions the possibility of us having a single sensation,[31] he takes the paradigmatic scenario to be one in which affection results in a multiplicity of sensations. For example, when I see an anemone, I have sensations of dark blue petals, an even darker center, a green stem, etc. Kant typically refers to this multiplicity of sensations as a "manifold of intuition" and occasionally as a manifold "contained in" empirical intuition (see A99). For Kant, then, a crucial component of the senses generating empirical intuition$_s$ turns on us having sensations as the result of causal affection.

However, on Kant's view, having sensations does not amount to having an empirical intuition$_s$. According to Kant, sensations account for the "matter," but not the "form" of an empirical intuition$_s$ (A20/B34; see also A42/B60). The "form" that Kant has in mind is the spatial and/or temporal form that empirical intuitions$_s$ have insofar as they are "grounded" in the *a priori* forms of space and time.[32] And, on his view, all empirical intuitions$_s$ contain a manifold of sensations that stand in some sort of spatio-temporal relation to one another.

Kant, moreover, argues that in an empirical intuition$_s$, we "relate to the object through sensation" (A20/B34; see also A93/B126). That is to say, in an empirical intuition$_s$, we do not just represent the subjective state we are in; "through" the sensations contained in an empirical intuition$_s$ we represent an object, *qua* something that stands over and against us in space and time.[33] For example, if I have an empirical intuition$_s$ of an anemone, I do not just represent the subjective state the flower has put me in; through the sensations of dark blue petals, an even darker center, and a green stem, I consciously represent something that stands over and against me. In order to explicate how sensations figure in empirical intuitions$_s$ in this way, in the third *Critique* Kant introduces a distinction between "objective" and "merely subjective" sensations (KU 5:506).[34] An "objective" sensation, such as "the green color of the meadows," is one through which an object is represented in an empirical intuition$_s$, whereas a "merely subjective" sensation, such as a feeling of pleasure, is one "through which no object is represented" (KU 5:506). For Kant,

---

[31] See, e.g., his discussion of a sensation that "fills only an instant [*Augenblick*]" in the Anticipations of Perception (A167/B209). I return to this in Chapter 7.

[32] See, e.g., "Space is…the ground of all outer intuitions" (A24/B38), and "Time is a necessary representation that grounds all intuitions" (A31/B46).

[33] I discuss in more detail what it means for an empirical intuition$_s$ to represent an object in §3.4.2 and Chapter 5.

[34] See Jankowiak (2014) for discussion.

then, the sensations contained in an empirical intuition$_s$, through which we relate to an object, are "objective," rather than "merely subjective" sensations.

According to Kant, being given an empirical intuition$_s$ thus requires more than just having sensations as the result of objects affecting our senses; it involves representing an object through objective sensations. And it is in virtue of this receptive etiology that Kant takes intuitions$_s$ to have an immediate relation to objects.

3.4.2 The Process of Imagining

Let's turn now to Kant's account of the process involved in imagining. I begin by providing a more detailed analysis of Kant's view of what it means for imagination to make intuitions$_i$ and what distinguishes intuitions$_i$ from intuitions$_s$. I then make the case that, for Kant, although imagining is spontaneous, it is constitutively dependent on the receptivity of sensibility in such a way that warrants thinking of imagination as a part of sensibility, *qua* the receptive faculty of cognition.

3.4.2(a) Imaginative Activity and Intuitions$_i$
Recall the basic characterization of imaginative activity on Kant's view that I offered in Chapter 2. According to Kant, imaginative activity in general ("formation" (*Bildung*), "synthesis" (*Synthesis*), or "composition" (*Zusammensetzung*)) involves sensibly ordering and organizing a manifold of representations in spatio-temporal relations. We can now add the thought that through these activities our imagination makes intuitions$_i$. In order to unpack this idea, I want to again look at both Kant's early and Critical remarks on this topic.

Returning to the passage from the ML1 lectures I quoted above, Kant says the following about how imagination (or the "formative power")[35] makes intuitions$_i$: "sensible cognitions which arise from the spontaneity of the mind are called *cognitions of the formative power* [*bildende Kraft*]...sensible cognitions are either *given* or *made*...To the made we reckon...[t]he representations of the formative power [*bildenden Kraft*]" (ML1 28:230). Here, Kant indicates that our imagination makes intuitions$_i$ through a spontaneous activity he describes in terms of "formation," in which our imagination spatio-temporally "forms" a manifold delivered through the senses.[36] As he describes this activity of formation in the Friedländer lectures on anthropology,

---

[35] I return to this terminological issue in my discussion of the formation definition of imagination in Chapter 4.

[36] I take Kant's commitment to the relevant "forming" being sensible in nature to follow from his commitment to space and time being the forms of our sensible representations: "For all sensible representations we can distinguish, 1. The matter [*die Materie*], whereby the impression of the senses happen...2. The form...Space and time are the form of all sensible intuitions," a comment that immediately precedes his discussion of the formative activities of imagination (AC 25:44).

82 IMAGINATION IS PART OF SENSIBILITY

> Besides the faculty of sensation, we have in addition a faculty to illustrate objects [*Gegenstände abzubilden*], and through special power in the mind to describe [*zu schildern*] and to form [*zu bilden*] what strikes the senses. This is the faculty for forming the impressions of sense [*facultas informandi impressions sensuum*].
> (AF 25:511; transl. modified)[37]

For example, when I look at the anemone and am given a manifold of different representations, *per* Kant, my imagination makes an intuition$_i$ by sensibly "forming" this manifold into an "illustration" of the anemone: I generate an intuition$_i$ that illustrates the dark blue petals, darker blue center, and green stem as spatial parts that belong to the anemone as a spatial whole.

Notice that, for Kant, intuitions$_i$ are thus not the immediate result of us being affected by objects; they are, instead, the result of a process in which our imagination takes up and organizes the manifold delivered through the senses. So understood, intuitions$_i$ stand at a remove from that initial moment of affection. They are, as he puts it, an "imitated [*nachgeahmte*] representation of the senses," i.e. a representation of the representations delivered through the senses (ML1 28:230). And given this etiology, made intuitions$_i$ cannot stand in the same immediate relation to objects that the given intuitions$_s$ of the senses do.

Turning to the Critical period, Kant tends not to use the language of "formation" to describe imaginative activity in general; however, he preserves this basic account of how imagination makes intuitions$_i$ using language of "synthesis" or "composition" instead. For example, in the first *Critique*, Kant discusses how our imagination generates a "**determinate** intuition" through the synthesis of a manifold (B154). Kant analyzes the relevant kind of "determinate intuition" as an intuition that represents a "determinate space or time," i.e. a determinate spatial or temporal form, such as a line or circle (B202). And he describes the relevant kind of synthesis as the imaginative "action of putting different representations together," an action in which a manifold is "gone through, taken up, and combined in a certain way" (A77/B102). He, moreover, claims that this imaginative synthesis must "be in agreement with" the "forms" of space and time, which I take to mean that imaginative synthesis must order the representations in the manifold in spatial and/or temporal relations (B160). In the first *Critique*, then, Kant characterizes imagining as a process in which we make an intuition$_i$ by spatially and/or temporally synthesizing a manifold into a representation of a determinate spatio-temporal form on this basis.

Kant pursues a similar line of thought in the third *Critique* using language of "composition."[38] There, he claims that imagination is a faculty "for intuition,"

---

[37] See also BL 24:235–6; R314 15:124.
[38] As I discuss in Chapter 7, Kant also uses language of "composition" in the Analytic of Principles in the first *Critique*.

i.e. it is a faculty responsible for generating intuitions$_i$ (KU 5:287). He indicates that our imagination makes these intuitions$_i$ through "the composition [*Zusammensetzung*] of the manifold of intuition"—a process that results in the representation of determinate spatio-temporal forms, like shapes, temporal series, or mereological structures (KU 5:217, 287; see also KU 5:238). In this account of imaginative composition, we thus, once again, find echoes of the early account of the formative activity through which imagination makes intuitions$_i$ as the result of spatio-temporally "forming" a manifold and generating a representation of a determinate spatio-temporal form.

In order to further clarify the process of imagining, let's take a closer look at Kant's account of the most basic way in which imagination makes intuitions$_i$. According to Kant, at the most elementary level, our imagination is responsible for forming, synthesizing, or composing a manifold in such a way that results in an intuition$_i$ that represents a "shape" or "gestalt" (*Gestalt*) or a temporal "sequence" (*Gefolge*), "series" (*Reihe*), or "play" (*Spiel*).[39] As an example of the former, think about an intuition$_i$ that represents these dots $.\ ^{.}$. as a triangle. As an example of the latter, think about an intuition$_i$ that represents two tones you hear when a doorbell rings as a ding-dong sequence. To be clear, on Kant's view, our imagination can also engage in activities that are more elaborate: we can imaginatively represent more complex shapes, temporal sequences, or spatio-temporal forms. But, at the most basic level, Kant takes imagining to generate intuitions$_i$ that represent determinate spatio-temporal forms, like a simple shape or temporal sequence.[40]

However, one may wonder whether Kant thinks that intuitions$_i$ are unique in representing determinate spatio-temporal forms, or whether he thinks that this can happen through intuitions$_s$ as well. For example, when we simply look at this $.\ ^{.}$., do we already have an intuition$_s$ that represents a determinate triangular shape?[41] And if so, what do intuitions$_i$ contribute over and above what we can accomplish through sensing?

---

[39] See, e.g., "All form of the objects of the senses (of the outer as well as, mediately, the inner) is either **shape** [*Gestalt*] or **play**: in the latter case, either play of shapes..., or mere play of sensations (in time)" (KU 5:225). See also, "The representation of an object in accordance with the relations of space is gestalt [*Gestalt*]...The form of appearance without representation of an object consists merely in the order of sensations in accordance with temporal relation, and the appearance is called a sequence (or series or play)" (R683 15:304; transl. modified), and, "The relations of space give gestalts [*geben Gestalten*], those of time give play [*Spiel*]. Hence music, in which there is a series of tones, is called play" (AC 25:44–5; my transl.).

[40] When I speak of representations of spatio-temporal forms in Part I, I have in mind representations of spatio-temporal determinacy in general. However, in Chapter 7, I shall look at Kant's discussion of the representation of spatio-temporal forms in a more specific sense in the Axioms of Intuition, as distinct from the representation of the sensible matter that fills those forms in the Anticipations of Perception.

[41] See Allais's (2015, 169–70, 272; 2017) argument that binding is something that happens in intuition prior to imaginative synthesis, e.g. "Consider a tomato affecting our senses...We perceptually represent the tomato as round and red because it is round and red, and its roundness and redness affect our senses" (2015, 156, n.21).

84 IMAGINATION IS PART OF SENSIBILITY

To answer these questions, we need to first draw a distinction between two ways in which an intuition might be said to involve the conscious representation of a determinate spatio-temporal form. On the one hand, an intuition can be a conscious representation that is the result of a causal sequence in which we are affected by an object that has a determinate spatio-temporal form.[42] Think, for example, of an intuition that is the result of being causally affected by something with a triangular form, such as · ·. Call this the "causal sense" of consciously representing a determinate spatio-temporal form. On the other hand, an intuition can be a representation, the content of which involves consciously representing something as a determinate spatio-temporal form. Think, for example, of consciously representing the dots, · ·, as having a triangular form. Call this the "content sense" of consciously representing a determinate spatio-temporal form.[43]

Though these are vexed issues, and issues that I shall return to in Chapter 5, as I interpret Kant's position, although intuitions$_s$ can consciously represent a determinate spatio-temporal form in the causal sense, they do not do so in the content sense. That is to say, even if they result from affection by an object with a determinate spatio-temporal form, their content is not such as to involve a subject consciously representing something as a determinate spatio-temporal form.[44] I take this to be the case because, on Kant's view, in order to represent a determinate spatio-temporal form in the content sense, we need to connect a multiplicity of representations together into a representation of that form. However, in the A Deduction, Kant argues that the senses "merely afford us impressions" but do not "put them together" (A120n).[45] Indeed, he claims that in an intuition$_s$, the representations contained in the manifold "are encountered dispersed and separate in the mind" (A120n).[46] If the representations are to be put together into a representation of a determinate spatio-temporal form in the content sense, then Kant claims that

[42] That Kant thinks this is possible is something he insists on in his discussion of our aesthetic engagement with the beautiful: "in the apprehension of a given object of the senses [imagination] is of course bound to a determinate form of this object" (KU 5:240). I return to this issue in Chapter 8.

[43] By "content" here I have in mind the content of a mental state, rather than the notion of "perceptual content" as it is used in contemporary philosophy of perception to refer to the conditions under which perceptual experiences are correct (see Siegel 2010, 30). For discussion of where Kant's view parts ways with this contemporary picture of perceptual content, see McLear (2016b).

[44] I thus take the causal sense of representing a determinate spatio-temporal form to be what is at issue in the Anthropology, when Kant describes how the sense of touch can "inform us about the shape of the object" (Anthro. 7:156).

[45] Admittedly in the A Deduction, Kant hints at the idea that an empirical intuition involves the "synopsis" of the manifold of intuition through the senses (A94; A97) (for discussion, see Heidegger PIK 93; KPM 43–5, 100; Waxman (1991, 218–25). It is not entirely clear what this "synopsis" amounts to, since as we have just seen Kant insists that the senses, qua merely receptive, cannot "put representations together" or "connect" them (see A120n; B233). Instead, I think the best way to read synopsis is in terms of the idea of "containment": "If therefore I ascribe a synopsis to sense, because it contains a manifold in its intuition" (A97). So understood, synopsis amounts to the way in which the senses give an empirical intuition$_s$ that contains a manifold.

[46] As he makes this point in the Anthropology, "sense representations...present themselves en masse" (Anthro. 7:144).

THE PROCESSES OF SENSIBILITY   85

"something more than the receptivity of impressions is required"; what is needed is "an active faculty of the synthesis of this manifold in us, which we call imagination" (A120, 120n).[47]

More on imagination shortly, but first I want to consider how we are to understand the content of an empirical intuition$_s$ on my reading of Kant. In the Transcendental Aesthetic, Kant specifies the object represented by an empirical intuition$_s$ as follows: "The undetermined object of an empirical intuition is called **appearance**" (A20/B34). As I interpret this claim, Kant's point is not that the object causally responsible for the empirical intuition$_s$ is undetermined. When I am affected by the anemone, for example, *per* Kant, I am affected by "a given object of the senses" that has a "determinate form": the spatial form of an anemone (KU 5:240). I, instead, take Kant's point to be that the content of an empirical intuition$_s$ involves a conscious representation of an object as "undetermined," i.e. as a something or other that stands over and against us. More specifically, through the objective sensations contained in the empirical intuition$_s$ we are conscious of something or other "as in" space and time, the determinate form of which we do not yet grasp (A22/B37). To illustrate, consider an episode in which you have been in a darkened movie theater for a few hours and then exit into bright daylight. As your senses are affected by the parking lot, cars, and lampposts in front of you, you will have various objective sensations, e.g. of colors and sounds. Through these sensations, you are conscious not just of a subjective state in yourself; you are, instead, conscious of something like an array of colors and sounds in space and time. But overwhelmed by the daylight, you are not yet conscious of what you see as having a determinate spatio-temporal form. It is an episode of this sort that I take to involve an empirical intuition$_s$ that represents an object as "undetermined" in Kant's framework.

However, if we are to have an intuition, the content of which involves consciously representing something as a determinate spatio-temporal form, then *per* Kant, something more than sensing is required. According to Kant, we need to engage in acts of imaginative synthesis in which we "put together" a manifold into a representation of a determinate spatio-temporal form. In the anemone example, in order to consciously represent what I see as having, say, an anemone shape, then I need to imaginatively synthesize the representations of blue petals, darker blue center, and green stem into an intuition$_i$ that represents this shape. It is for this reason that I take Kant to be committed to the view that it is ultimately

---

[47] I take this line of thought to put pressure on Allais's argument that there can be "binding" ("ordering and organizing sensory input") prior to "synthesis" (2017, 29). According to Allais, synthesis is required for the higher level cognitive state, experience, that involves a relation to an object, rather than the more minimal cognitive state involved in the presentation of particulars in intuition, which involves binding. However, as I argue here and at more length in Chapter 5, this line of thought in the A Deduction suggests that, on Kant's view, the senses, *qua* merely receptive, cannot put representations together in the way that binding requires. This task, I claim, falls to imagination in perception.

86 IMAGINATION IS PART OF SENSIBILITY

through imaginative activity and intuitions$_i$, rather than through sensing and intuitions$_s$ that we consciously represent a determinate spatio-temporal form in the content sense.

3.4.2(b) The Metaphysics of Imagining

With this basic picture of imagining in place, we can now turn to considerations about its metaphysical profile and the worry that imagination cannot be part of sensibility, *qua* the receptive faculty of cognition, given Kant's characterization of imaginative activity as spontaneous. In spite of this *prima facie* concern, what I shall now argue is that if we attend to, one, the specific kind of spontaneity imagination involves, and, two, its constitutive dependence on the receptivity of sensibility, then we can make sense of how Kant can be committed to imagination being both spontaneous and a part of sensibility.

Let's start, then, with the question of what kind of spontaneity imagination involves. Often what comes to mind when we think about spontaneity in Kant's framework is his account of "transcendental" freedom defined as "a causality...through which something happens without its cause being further determined by another previous cause, i.e., an **absolute** causal **spontaneity** beginning **from itself**" (A446/B474). If we think about imaginative spontaneity along these lines, then it does, indeed, seem inconsistent for imagination to belong to sensibility, *qua* a faculty that begins states as a result of affection.

However, Kant sometimes draws a distinction between two kinds of spontaneity: "absolute" and "relative" (ML1 28:267).[48] According to Kant, absolute spontaneity is "without qualification" and involves "self-activity from an *inner principle* according to the power of free choice" (ML1 28:267). The practical species of transcendental freedom, as the faculty for "determining oneself from oneself, independently of necessitation by sensible impulses," involves absolute spontaneity in this sense (A534/B562; see also A533/B561, KpV 5:56). By contrast, relative spontaneity is "qualified in some respect," and it occurs when "something acts spontaneously *under a condition*" (ML1 28:267).[49] So understood, relative spontaneity does not require being able to begin a state from oneself, but rather beginning a state in a way that is at once self-active and conditioned.

When we consider Kant's characterization of the spontaneity of imagination in light of this absolute-relative distinction, we have reason to conceive of it as a relative kind of spontaneity. We, indeed, find Kant hinting at this in the ML1 lectures. There he claims both that imaginative activity involves "spontaneity of the mind" and that this activity can occur only "under the condition under which the mind is affected by objects" (ML1 28:230). For Kant, then, although the

---

[48] For discussion of this distinction, see Smit (2009, 241–3); Ellis (2017).

[49] This "relative" notion of spontaneity would seem to find echoes in Kant's later ascription of spontaneity to spiritual *automata* (KpV 5:97) and natural organisms (KU 5:411).

THE PROCESSES OF SENSIBILITY   87

imaginative activity of forming, synthesizing, or composing a manifold is spontaneous to the extent that it involves self-actively bringing forth intuitions$_i$, it is relatively spontaneous because it is, in some sense, "conditioned" by receptivity. But in exactly what sense does Kant think imaginative spontaneity is so conditioned, and how does this bear on the claim that imagination belongs to sensibility?

What I shall now argue is that, on Kant's view, imagining is conditioned by the receptivity of sensibility in the sense that its activities constitutively depend on receptivity. That is to say, for Kant, we cannot imaginatively act except in ways that are constitutively shaped by the receptive aspects of sensibility. More specifically, I make the case that this constitutive dependence turns on two constraints that Kant places on imaginative activity vis-à-vis the receptivity of sensibility, which I shall call the "formal constraint" and "material constraint," respectively.

By the "formal constraint," I have in mind the ways in which the formal structure of the receptivity of sensibility constitutively constrains imagining. Kant analyzes this formal structure in terms of the *a priori* forms of space and time that are built into the constitution of our sensibility (see A26/B42; A77/B102; B129). And he insists that imaginative activity (formation, synthesis, composition) "must always be in agreement with" the forms of space and time "since it can occur only in accordance with this form" (B160).[50] I have analyzed this "agreement" and "accordance" in terms of the idea that imaginative activity can only proceed by ordering and organizing a manifold in spatial and/or temporal relations. And I have argued that, on Kant's view, this activity results in intuitions$_i$, which are spatial and/or temporal in character. For Kant, then, even though imaginative activity is spontaneous, the sort of ordering and organizing it involves can only be carried out in the formal framework provided by sensibility, *qua* our capacity of receptivity. Insofar as this is the case, I take Kant to be committed to the following:

Formal Constraint on Imagination (FC$_i$):   all acts of imagination are constitutively constrained by space and time, *qua* the forms of the receptivity of our sensibility.

By my lights, FC$_i$ reflects one of the ways in which Kant thinks the spontaneity of imagining is relative to the condition of the receptivity of sensibility. However, I take FC$_i$ to also reflect one of the reasons that Kant regards imagination as something that belongs to sensibility even though its intuitions$_i$ do not have an immediate relation to objects. Kant gestures toward this in a passage from the B Deduction that I have partially quoted before, "*Imagination* is the faculty for

---

[50] Kant makes this claim specifically in the context of discussing the imagination's synthesis of apprehension; however, I take the point to extend to all forms of imaginative synthesis. See, e.g., his claim that the sort of "formative [*bildende*] synthesis" through which "we construct a figure in imagination is entirely identical with that which we exercise in the apprehension" (A224/B271).

88   IMAGINATION IS PART OF SENSIBILITY

representing an object in intuition even **without its presence**. Now since all of our intuition is sensible, the imagination, on account of the subjective condition under which it can give a[n]...intuition...belongs to **sensibility**" (B151–2; transl. modified).[51] Here, although Kant highlights the fact that our imagination generates intuitions$_i$ even without the presence of objects, he says imagination nevertheless "belongs to sensibility" because it is subject to a "subjective condition" on account of which "all of our intuition is sensible." Prior to this passage, he glosses this "subjective condition" in terms of the *a priori* form of space and time: "in us a certain form of sensible intuition *a priori* is fundamental, which rests on the receptivity of the capacity for representation (sensibility)" (B150). It is thus in virtue of being subjectively conditioned by the *a priori* forms of space and time that Kant takes all of our intuition, including the intuition$_i$ our imagination is responsible for, to be sensible.[52] For Kant, then, it is consistent to say that imagination is a faculty for generating intuitions$_i$ of objects even without their presence and to say it belongs to sensibility because imagination is subject to the subjective condition I have articulated with FC$_i$: imaginative activity through which we generate sensible intuitions$_i$ is constitutively constrained by the *a priori* forms of the receptivity of our sensibility.

However, in addition to this formal constraint, Kant is committed to a kind of material constraint on imagining:

Material Constraint on Imagination (MC$_i$):   all acts of imagination are constitutively constrained by a manifold delivered through the receptivity of our sensibility.

In order to elucidate MC$_i$, I begin with how it operates in the empirical case, before turning to the more complicated question of how it works in the case of *a priori* imagining.

In the empirical case, I understand the core of Kant's account of MC$_i$ to turn on the idea that the empirical activities of imagination are constitutively constrained by a manifold of sensation delivered through the senses: we can only imaginatively act by taking up, ordering, and organizing such a manifold.[53] To unpack

---

[51] I have elided the part of this passage where Kant says that imagination gives a corresponding intuition "to the concepts of the understanding"—a topic I take up at length in Chapter 6.

[52] See, e.g., "Space and time are the form of all sensible intuitions" (AC 25:44), and Kant's 1769–70 note, "In order for sensibility to have a determinate form in our representation it is necessary that it have an order [*Zusammenordnung*]...This order is a connection of coordination [*Verknüpfung der coordination*]...The basis of all coordination, hence the form of sensibility, is space and time" (R683, 15:304).

[53] On this issue, I disagree with Tracz, who claims that, on Kant's view, although the empirical imagination depends on sense, it does not depend on sensation because we can have "images...when we lack sensation-involving empirical intuitions that represent present objects" (2020, 1096, 1110). On my reading, by contrast, empirical imagining involves sensations because it involves ordering and organizing a manifold of sensations that we are either currently having or have had in the past.

THE PROCESSES OF SENSIBILITY   89

how this material constraint works, let's look at the reproductive and productive modes of empirical imagining, in turn.

Starting with the material constraint on reproductive imagination, recall Kant's claim that reproductive imagining involves the "derivative [abgeleiteten] exhibition of the object (exhibitio derivativa), which brings back to the mind an empirical intuition that it had previously" (Anthro. 7:167; transl. modified). We need to be careful in how we interpret this passage. Kant's claim, here, that the reproductive imagination "brings back to mind an empirical intuition that it had previously" might suggest that empirical intuitions_s we have previously had are what materially constrain the reproductive imagination. However, Kant's considered view is that, at the most basic level, "sensations" that we have had in the past are what materially constrain the reproductive imagination (Anthro. 7:168).[54] Recall that Kant discusses sensations of outer sense, e.g. of color, sound, and smell, and of inner sense, e.g. of hedonic feelings or affects.[55] Recall also that Kant distinguishes between sensations of the "subjective" variety that represent a subjective state, such as a feeling of pleasure in the taste of pistachio, and the "objective" variety that represent a quality in the object, such as the green of the meadow (see KU 5:506). For Kant, then, the most basic "material" (Stoff) that the reproductive imagination must draw on when generating its "derivative" representations are not empirical intuitions_s of whole scale objects from the past, but rather sensations, whether from inner or outer sense, or of the subjective or objective variety (Anthro. 7:168).[56] To be sure, our imagination can

---

[54] In his account of empirical imagination, I thus take Kant to be committed to what Stephenson calls "General-Affection Dependence": "If, at time t, the subject s intuits an object o utilising matter m, then at t or $t_{<t}$, m has been given to s through causal affection" (2015, 493), and McLear calls "Weak Presence Dependence": "If a subject S intuits an object O, then either O exists at T and is suitably causally related to S, or the sensory qualities characteristic of O were instantiated and suitably related to S at some time (or times) prior to T" (2017, 93), where I understand the sensory qualities to be ones that cause sensations. Stephenson (2015) and McLear (2017) contrast this more minimal view with the stronger view according to which imagination must draw on empirical intuitions of objects, which Stephenson (2015, 491) calls the "weak object-dependence" view (see also Grüne (2017a, 70), and McLear (2017, 90) calls "moderate presence-dependence."

[55] By "affect," Kant has in mind an affective state that comes upon us all of a sudden, e.g. a quick feeling of anger, and which differs from a "passion," which is an affective state that develops over time, e.g. a passion for vengeance (see KU 5:272; Anthro. 7:252–3; MS 6:408–9). There are complicated questions about Kant's account of both affects and passions, as well as their relation to the faculty of the feeling of pleasure and displeasure. For more, see Borges (2008); Deimling (2014); Frierson (2014b); Matherne (2014b, 133); Williamson (2015); Merritt (2018a, 20–1); Cohen (2020).

[56] There is a question about the relationship between the sensations of outer and inner sense. According to Schmitz (2015), "Kant did not believe in a specifically inner material of sensation" (1045). In support of this claim, Schmitz points to Kant's statements in the Transcendental Aesthetic that, "the representations of **outer sense** make up the proper material with which we occupy our mind" (B67), and in the B Introduction that, "we after all get the whole matter for our cognitions, even for our inner sense" from "the existence of things outside us" (Bxxxix fn). However, by my lights, these statements are, in part, a product of Kant's focus on theoretical cognition in the first Critique. But if we look to Kant's aesthetic philosophy and account of emotions, we find him acknowledging "merely subjective" sensations, which "absolutely cannot constitute a representation of an object," but which are the result of the subject being affected by their own mental state (KU 5:206). Kant claims that it is

90 IMAGINATION IS PART OF SENSIBILITY

reproduce empirical intuitions$_s$ from the past, e.g. when I remember an anemone that I saw yesterday. But, on Kant's view, when I do this, I am still drawing on sensations, they just happen to be the objective sensations of, say, blues and greens, contained in my empirical intuition$_s$ of the anemone. For Kant, then, sensations are what make up the most basic material that our reproductive imagination is constrained by.

Turning now to how this material constraint works in the case of our productive imagination, recall that, for Kant, paradigmatic cases of the empirical exercise of the productive imagination include things like artistic creativity, aesthetic appreciation, and dreaming. In his discussion of the empirical activities of the productive imagination in the *Anthropology*, Kant claims that the "*inventive* [*dichtend*][57] (productive)" imagination is, "not exactly creative, for it is not capable of producing a sense representation that was never given to our faculty of sense; one can always furnish evidence of the material [*Stoff*] of its representations" (Anthro. 7:167–8; transl. modified).[58] As he makes this point in the Mrongovius lectures, "our imagination cannot create anything, and it is true that it cannot produce any sensations in us that we have not already had" (AMr 25:1258). In these passages we find Kant articulating a material constraint on the creativity of the empirical productive imagination: rather than being able to create *ex nihilo*, our creative acts of productive imagining are constrained at the most basic level by sensations.[59] Indeed, even when our productive imagination draws on larger scale intuitions$_s$, it is constrained by the sensations contained in those

---

this sort of merely subjective sensation that is involved in the judgment of the beautiful (see Sethi 2019 for a discussion of the role sensation plays in these judgments). See also Cohen's (2020, §4.2) discussion of "higher" feelings that pertain to how subjects relate to themselves and to the states of their faculties.

[57] The term "dichten" and its cognates, such as "Dichtungsvermögen," are difficult to translate into English. In the translation of the *Anthropology*, Dichtungsvermögen is translated as "productive faculty" (§31), in ML1 (28:230, 237), MMr (29:881, 884–7), and MD (28:674), Dichtungsvermögen is translated as "the fictive faculty" or "fictive power," and aligned with the "*facultas fingendi*"; and in AF (25:524–5) "dichten" is translated as "to compose." The difficulty of translating *dichten*-terms is compounded by the fact that Kant deploys them to refer to uses of imagination in fiction ("erdichten") and invention ("erfinden") (see AF 25:524–5; AMr 25:1277–83). Tetens also describes one level of imaginative activity in terms of a creative capacity he calls "Dichtungsvermögen" or "Dichtkraft," which contrasts with the imagination as a faculty of perception (*Perceptionsvermögen*) and as a faculty of *Phantasie* or *Einbildung*, which is responsible for reorganizing perceptions (see *Philosophische Versuche* 24–5, 105, 110–38, 150–7). See Engell (1981, chap. 10), Dyck (2014, 643–7), Allison (2015, 153–8) for a discussion of the relationship between, and influence of, Tetens's theory of imagination on Kant, especially on Kant's theory of productive imagination.

[58] See also Anthro. 7:168, where Kant emphasizes the constraint of the "sensations produced by the given senses." In the first *Critique*, he frames this constraint as follows: "This material or real entity, however...cannot be invented by any power of imagination...Once sensation is given..., then through its manifold many an object can be invented [*gedichtet*] in imagination that has no empirical place outside imagination in space or time" (A373–4). See also Mensch. 25:944; AMr 25:1277; ML1 28:232; MMr 29:885.

[59] As I noted in the Introduction (§0.3.2), several recent discussions of the constraints on imaginative creativity have taken a Kantian starting point: see Gaut (2003) and Stokes (2014; 2016). See Part III for more discussion of imaginative creativity in Kant's aesthetics.

intuitions$_s$. For Kant, then, the real site of imaginative creativity is not producing new sensations or intuitions$_s$, but in finding new ways to put sensations or intuitions$_s$ together. As he makes this point in his lectures, productive imagination is responsible for "creat[ing] new forms" in which the material delivered through mere receptivity is "combined" in unprecedented ways (AMr 25:1257, 1241).[60] This happens, for example, when I draw on sensations of clean lines and light-filled spaces when I envision my dream house. Or to take an artistic example, this happens when Patricia Highsmith in *The Talented Mr. Ripley* draws on sensations of insecurity, ambition, and fluidity when fashioning Tom Ripley and on the sensations contained in whole scale empirical intuitions$_s$, e.g. when detailing Rome.

While this gives us a sense of how the material constraint operates in relation to the empirical activities of the productive imagination, there is a question as to whether MC$_i$ has purchase on the *a priori* activities of the productive imagination on Kant's view.[61] For Kant, *a priori* activities of the productive imagination involve the generation of "pure," rather than "empirical" intuitions$_i$, "in which nothing is to be encountered that belongs to sensation," and that "occur *a priori*, even without an actual object of the senses of sensations" (A20–1/B34–5). Rather than representing objects through sensations, Kant claims that pure intuitions$_i$ "relate to the form under which the object is intuited" (WF 20:266). A paradigmatic instance of a pure intuition$_i$, for Kant, is a "**non-empirical** intuition" generated in geometrical construction that represents a spatial form, such as a triangle or a circle (A713/B741).

As an instance of *a priori* activity, this imaginative production of pure intuitions$_i$ cannot depend on empirical affection and sensations in the way that empirical imaginative activities do. Nevertheless, Kant indicates that there is a kind of material constraint operative in the *a priori* case: constraint by the manifold contained in the *a priori* forms of space and time. In analyzing the *a priori* forms of space and time, Kant claims that they contain a manifold: the multiplicity of the parts of space and moments of time that are contained in space and time as a whole.[62] Rather than being given through causal affection via sense, Kant claims that the *a priori* manifold of space and time is "the manifold that sensibility in its original receptivity provides" (A99–100). As he makes this point about the *a priori* form of space,

> Space is nothing other than the form of all appearances of outer sense, i.e., the subjective condition of sensibility...Now since the receptivity of the subject to be affected by objects necessarily precedes all intuitions of these objects, it can

---

[60] See also his gloss of the productive imagination in terms of imagination acting as the "authoress of voluntary forms of possible intuitions" (KU 5:240).

[61] I discuss the *a priori* activities of productive imagination at more length in Chapters 6–7.

[62] See, e.g., "space and time contain a manifold of pure *a priori* intuition" (A77/B102), and, "the **form of intuition** merely gives the manifold" (B160n).

92 IMAGINATION IS PART OF SENSIBILITY

be understood how the form of all appearances can be given in the mind prior to all actual perceptions. (A26/B42)[63]

For Kant, we are thus given the forms of space and time, as well as the manifold they contain, in virtue of possessing the kind of receptive capacity of sensibility that we do.

If we now return to the question of whether Kant thinks the *a priori* productive exercise of imagination is materially constrained, although it is not constrained by a manifold of sensations, it is constrained by the *a priori* manifold of space and time that sensibility "in its original receptivity provides." That is to say, for Kant, the *a priori* productive imagination can only act by forming, synthesizing, or composing the *a priori* manifold of space and time given to us through sensibility. We find Kant making this claim, for example, in the Metaphysical Deduction, where he describes a "pure" synthesis of imagination that involves the synthesis of a "**manifold** of pure intuition" that is "given to us *a priori*" (A78/B104). Likewise in the A Deduction, he ascribes to imagination a "**pure** synthesis of apprehension" that involves "the synthesis of the manifold that sensibility in its original receptivity provides" (A99–100). And in the B Deduction, he offers an account of the "figurative synthesis" of the productive imagination, which involves the "**synthesis** of the manifold of sensible intuition" and "determining" "the form of sense *a priori*" (B151–2). Though I will have more to say about what this *a priori* productive synthesis involves in Chapters 6 and 7, for now the point I wish to make is that, on Kant's view, even the *a priori* activities of the productive imagination are materially constrained by the receptivity of sensibility: they can only proceed by way of ordering and organizing the *a priori* manifold of space and time that are given to us through the receptive structure of sensibility.

So far, I have made the case that, for Kant, all imaginative activity, whether of the empirical or pure variety is subject to a material constraint tied to the receptivity of sensibility. But does this lend any support to my argument to the effect that imagination is part of sensibility on his view? One might worry that it does not because, *prima facie*, it seems that the understanding is also subject to this material constraint.

More specifically, it seems that in virtue of characterizing our understanding as "discursive," Kant is committed to it being dependent on the material delivered through sensibility. According to Kant, unlike an "intuitive" understanding that is "completely independent from sensibility," our understanding is "discursive" and depends on sensibility to provide us with intuitions, which it subsumes under

---

[63] This sort of "givenness" is not just something that is applicable to sensibility: according to Kant, there are also *a priori* concepts, e.g. the categories, that "are given to me through the nature of my understanding" (VL 24:914; see also JL 9:93, A728/B756). There is a further question as to whether this sort of givenness involves some kind of *a priori* "self-affection," but I shall leave this controversial issue to the side here (see Heidegger KPM 103–5, 262–70; Indregard (2017); Kraus (2020, chap. 2; Jauernig (2021, 238–9).

concepts (KU 5:406). Kant, moreover, casts what sensibility provides the understanding with as a "field of matter" (A231/B283). Insofar as our discursive understanding depends on sensibility to provide it with a field of matter, isn't it materially constrained in the way that I have argued imagination is?

Though there is a kind of material constraint that Kant takes our discursive understanding to be subject to, there are reasons to distinguish it from the sort of material constraint that he takes imagination to be subject to. According to MC_i, all imaginative acts proceed by way of sensibly organizing and ordering a manifold delivered through the receptivity of sensibility. However, the sort of material constraint that Kant places on understanding is weaker. As I discussed in Chapter 2, Kant allows for certain acts of the understanding to proceed without intuitions: acts of thinking about things we cannot intuit. Recall the examples of thinking, "freedom is the faculty of beginning a state from itself" and "God is the *ens realissimum* (i.e., the most real being)." Insofar as Kant acknowledges acts of the understanding like these that do not involve forming intuitions, the material constraint on understanding cannot be as strong as it is in the case of imaginative activity. Instead of it being the case that understanding can only act by giving form to a manifold delivered through sensibility, Kant's position is that the understanding can only engage in certain acts, acts of cognition in the narrow sense, if it gives form to a manifold delivered through sensibility. We could thus formulate the material constraint he places on understanding as follows:

Material Constraint on Understanding (MC_u): some acts of the understanding, viz. those involved in cognition in the narrow sense, are constrained by a manifold delivered through the receptivity of our sensibility.

So, whereas MC_i reflects a constraint on all acts of imagination, MC_u reflects a constraint on some, but not all acts of understanding.

By my lights, MC_i is not restricted in scope the way that MC_u is precisely because MC_i reflects Kant's commitment to imagination belonging to sensibility. More specifically, I take it that the reason why Kant thinks we cannot engage in imaginative acts without drawing on a manifold of sensibility is because he regards generating intuitions$_i$ by way of forming, synthesizing, or composing a manifold to be the sensible activity that is characteristic of the imaginative part of sensibility. That is to say, on my interpretation, Kant conceives of sensibility in general as responsible for generating intuitions through sensible processes that are conditioned by receptivity. And, in his bipartite framework, whereas sense realizes this general profile in sensible processes that generate intuitions$_s$ in a wholly receptive way as a result of affection, imagination realizes this general profile in sensible processes that generate intuitions$_i$ as a result of spontaneously ordering and organizing a manifold delivered through sensibility. But because Kant regards the understanding as distinct from sensibility, he does not think that drawing on

94 IMAGINATION IS PART OF SENSIBILITY

a manifold of sensibility is constitutive of its activities; it is only constitutive of activities in which our understanding interfaces with sensibility in cognition.

Bringing these various threads together, I have argued that, on Kant's view, in virtue of belonging to sensibility, all acts of imagining are subject to two constitutive constraints. Formally, all imaginative activity proceeds under the constraint of space and time, *qua* the forms of the receptivity of our sensibility (FC_i), and, materially, it proceeds under the constraint of a manifold delivered through the receptivity of sensibility (MC_i). More specifically, I analyzed this constitutive constraint in terms of the idea that all imaginative activity involves generating spatio-temporal representations, intuitions$_i$, through the spatio-temporal forming, synthesizing, or composing of a manifold, whether empirical or *a priori*, provided through the receptivity of sensibility. And though Kant regards this imaginative forming, synthesizing, or composing as spontaneous to the extent that it brings forth representations in a self-active way, it is ultimately relatively spontaneous because it is conditioned formally and materially by the receptivity of sensibility in these ways.

Stepping back, over the course of this section, I have explored the metaphysics of Kant's bipartite account of sensibility. In particular, I have examined the specific way in which sense and imagination each realize the profile of sensibility, as our receptive faculty of cognition. As we have seen, both parts of sensibility proceed by way of activities that are constrained by the *a priori* forms of space and time that are built into the receptive structure of our sensibility. They also both generate intuitions through processes that are conditioned by receptivity. However, sense proceeds by way of processes that are wholly receptive and that depend on causal affection. And it is in virtue of its processes being wholly receptive that Kant thinks sense gives us intuitions$_s$ that stand in an immediate relation to objects. By contrast, imagining, for Kant, proceeds by way of spontaneous processes that are constitutively dependent on the receptivity of sensibility: our imagination acts by generating intuitions$_i$ as the result of sensibly forming, synthesizing, or composing a manifold delivered through the receptivity of sensibility. Though the resulting intuitions$_i$ do not stand in an immediate relation to objects the way that intuitions$_s$ do, they are still products of imagination, understood as the part of sensibility that proceeds by ways of relatively spontaneous activities that are conditioned by receptivity. And, as we shall now see, on Kant's view, this metaphysical difference goes hand in hand with a difference in the functional role that sense and imagination have in cognition.

3.5 The Cognitive Function of Sensibility

In the famous passage about blind intuitions and empty thoughts from the first *Critique*, Kant indicates that the "function" of sensibility is to "give" us objects and

THE COGNITIVE FUNCTION OF SENSIBILITY 95

"to make the mind's concepts sensible [*Begriffe sinnlich zu machen*]" (A51/B75). What I shall now argue is that we can, in fact, tease these apart as the functions that Kant ascribes to sense and imagination, respectively, when they are functioning cognitively well.

Let's start with the cognitive function of sense: giving us objects. We find Kant articulating this function in the following passage I have already cited, "Our cognition arises from two fundamental sources in the mind, the first of which is the reception of representations (the receptivity of impressions)...through [which] an object is **given** to us" (A50/B74). In a lengthier passage, Kant says,

> In whatever way and through whatever means a cognition may relate to objects, that through which it relates immediately to them...is **intuition**. This, however, takes place only insofar as the object is given to us; but this, in turn, at least for us humans, is possible only if it affects the mind a certain way. The capacity (receptivity) to acquire representations through the way in which we are affected by objects is called **sensibility**. Objects are therefore **given** to us by means of sensibility. (A19/B33)

By "giving us objects," I take Kant to have in mind the way in which sense puts us in immediate touch with objects. In this passage, he indicates that it is because its processes are receptive and involve causal affection that sense gives us objects in this immediate way.[64] And, on Kant's view, it is in virtue of giving us objects that sense puts us in a position to have thoughts that are not "empty," but rather relate to objects.

When we consider the cognitive function of imagination, there are, at least, two reasons that giving us objects cannot be its function on Kant's view. The first reason concerns the metaphysical profile of imaginative activity. As we have just seen, Kant claims that the senses give us objects through a process of causal affection. But, as we have also seen, he does not think that imaginative activities proceed in this wholly receptive way. Instead, he characterizes imaginative activities as relatively spontaneous ones that order and organize the receptive deliverances of sensibility. For Kant, imaginative activities are thus a step removed from affection and our immediate relation to objects. Insofar as this is the case, on his view, the cognitive function of imagination cannot be located in giving us objects, but must instead be bound up with the sort of spontaneous activities he ascribes to it.

The second reason for attributing to imagination a cognitive function other than giving us objects pertains to Kant's characterization of it as a mediating capacity. Recall that Kant attributes to imagination the cognitive task of mediating between the "extremes" of sensibility and understanding for the sake of

---

[64] Watkins and Willaschek (2017b, 93) emphasize this.

96 IMAGINATION IS PART OF SENSIBILITY

cognition (A124). In light of his bipartite account of sensibility, we can now formulate this mediation more precisely: Kant tasks imagination with mediating between what sensibility provides in its receptivity, on the one hand, and what understanding provides in its spontaneity, on the other.

If we piece together these two lines of thought, we can thus anticipate that, on Kant's view, rather than giving us objects, what it means for imagination to function cognitively well is bound up with spontaneous activities that not only sensibly order and organize the receptive deliverances of sensibility, but also play a mediating role in our cognitive lives. And the thesis that I shall here propose, and defend in subsequent chapters, is that the cognitive function that Kant ultimately tasks imagination with is making concepts sensible.

More specifically, I shall argue that Kant attributes to our imagination the cognitive function of making concepts sensible in, what I described in Chapter 1 as, the "subject-facing" way. There, I distinguished between the "object-facing" and "subject-facing" aspects of the cognitive functions of sensibility and understanding in Kant's framework. The object-facing aspect concerns how we use sensibility and understanding to determine objects, whereas the subject-facing aspect concerns how we use them in ways that facilitate one another internal to our cognitive processes.[65] And I argued that, from the subject-facing perspective, Kant paints a picture of what it is to make concepts sensible that involves sensibility making concepts "comprehensible" (*faßlich*) to us by facilitating our concrete grasp of them internal to our cognitive processes (Rel. 6:65n).[66] To this end, I highlighted Kant's claim that making concepts sensible in this sense involves a process of "distinctness in intuition, in which a concept thought abstractly is exhibited [*dargestellt*] or elucidated [*erläutert*] *in concreto*" by sensibility (JL 9:39). And I underscored Kant's claim that having an intuition of this sort fulfills a "natural need of all human beings" to grasp concepts not just in the abstract, but in the concrete (Rel. 6:109).[67]

Bringing this to bear on imagination, my thesis is that Kant attributes to imagination the cognitive function of making concepts sensible in this subject-facing way. That is to say, on Kant's view, our imagination functions cognitively well by facilitating our comprehension of concepts by exhibiting them *in concreto* in intuition$_i$, and thereby fulfilling one of our human cognitive needs. To be clear, on Kant's view, imaginatively making concepts sensible can, and does, have a role to play in our determination of objects (see Part II). However, I shall also argue

---

[65] Although the object- and subject-facing aspects of these cognitive functions come together in theoretical acts of cognition, I suggested that distinguishing between them is crucial for appreciating a wider range of cognitive cases in which Kant thinks our capacities function cognitively well outside the context of theoretical cognition, e.g. in judgments of taste, practical cognition, or symbolic cognition.

[66] As I claimed in Chapter 1, this sort of "comprehension" is not to be confused with the sort of "comprehension" (*Begreifen*) that reason enables on Kant's view (see JL 9:65).

[67] See also his claim that, "Aesthetic perfection consists in the agreement of cognition with the subject and is grounded on the particular sensibility of man" (JL 9:36).

that Kant countenances instances in which our imagination functions cognitively well that do not involve the determination of objects in this way in the aesthetic and practical domain (see Parts III–IV).

But for my purposes here, what I would like to stress is that, on my reading, Kant casts the cognitive function of imagination in conceptually laden terms: what it is for our imagination to function cognitively well is for our imagination to make concepts sensible. This is not to say that all imagining involves concepts for Kant. It is to say that all imaginative activities that meet his standard for what it is for imagination to function cognitively well involve concepts.

However, as I shall also argue, this does not mean that we should cast the cognitive function of sensibility in general in conceptually laden terms. To the contrary, on my interpretation, Kant does not think that the cognitive function of sense depends on concepts: we can be given objects through intuition$_s$ without concepts needing to be involved. I take this to be why Kant asserts that, "The manifold of representations can be given in an intuition that is merely sensible, i.e., nothing but receptivity," and that, "the manifold for intuition must already be **given** prior to the synthesis of understanding and independently from it" (B129; B145). By my lights, this sort of givenness of a manifold of representations through merely receptive processes that are independent from the understanding is precisely what Kant takes to be involved in sensing. For in sensing, Kant claims that we are "given" an intuition$_s$ that contains a manifold of representations through causal affection. Insofar as this sort of givenness of an intuition$_s$ occurs prior to the understanding, I take this to imply that it occurs prior to the concepts, which have their seat in the understanding. But insofar as these intuitions$_s$ nevertheless involve us standing in an immediate relation to objects, Kant can allow for sense to discharge its cognitive function of giving us objects without concepts needing to be involved. I shall develop this line of thought at more length in Part II, where I offer an extended argument to the effect that answering the question of whether Kant is a conceptualist about intuitions requires attending to the complexities introduced into his theory of intuition given his bipartite account of sensibility.

But in this chapter, my task has been to lay out the basic contours of Kant's bipartite account of sensibility. To summarize, I have analyzed Kant's account of sense and imagination as the two parts of sensibility in terms of the idea that each part realizes the general features of sensibility in a specific way. Though both parts of sensibility generate intuitions through processes that are, in some sense, conditioned by receptivity and contribute to the cognitive function of sensibility, each does so in a specific way. Sense gives intuitions$_s$ through receptive processes that have the cognitive function of giving us objects and that need not involve concepts. Meanwhile, imagination makes intuitions$_i$ that represent determinate spatio-temporal forms through relatively spontaneous processes that are constitutively constrained by the receptivity of sensibility in a formal and material way.

98 IMAGINATION IS PART OF SENSIBILITY

Moreover, as I just indicated, on Kant's view, imagination has the cognitive function of mediating between the receptivity of sensibility, on the one hand, and the understanding, on the other, by making concepts sensible in a way that facilitates our concrete comprehension of them. Insofar as this is the case, concepts will figure in imaginative activities in which we are functioning cognitively well in some robust way that they do not figure in the activities of sense. And it is on account of these specific differences in how sense and imagination realize the logical, metaphysical, and functional profile of sensibility in general that Kant ultimately taxonomizes sensing and imagining as mental states that are distinct from one another.

As I projected at the outset of this chapter, this bipartite account of sensibility turns on a more nuanced picture of sensibility than is often attributed to Kant. No doubt, Kant is partially to blame for this. Passages like the following certainly invite a view of sensibility as exhausted by its merely receptive aspect:

> Our cognition arises from two fundamental sources in the mind, the first of which is the reception of representations (the receptivity of impressions)...through [which] an object is given to us...we will call the receptivity of our mind to receive representations insofar as it is affected in some way sensibility...It comes along with our nature that intuition can never be other than sensible, i.e., that it contains only the way in which we are affected by objects. (A50–1/B74–5)

Similarly, passages in which he characterizes intuitions as having an immediate relation to an object and as strongly object-dependent do not appear to leave room for imagination, with its representations of objects even without their presence, to be part of sensibility. Nevertheless, I have argued that a closer look at Kant's view reveals that though he thinks one part of sensibility, sense, is wholly receptive and responsible for intuitions that have an immediate relation to objects and that cognitively serve us by giving us objects, this does not exhaust his view of sensibility. For in addition to sense, Kant acknowledges imagination as part of sensibility that is relatively spontaneous, that generates intuitions that do not have an immediate relation to objects, and that cognitively serves us by making concepts sensible in a subject-facing way. In this account of imagination, we thus find a spontaneous, mediating, conceptually interfacing dimension of sensibility that these more flat-footed passages might occlude, but which is nevertheless crucial for appreciating the cognitively sophisticated picture of sensibility, intuition, and imagination that Kant ultimately defends.

3.6 The Sensibility View of Imagination, *Redux*

With this bipartite picture of sensibility in place, we can now return to the question of which view of imagination Kant endorses: does he conceive of imagination as a third thing alongside sensibility and understanding, as a part of sensibility, or as a sensible exercise of the understanding? In the last chapter, we saw why this question is so vexed. For in addition to the fact that textual evidence can be mustered in support of all three views of imagination, it seems that none of these views can do justice to Kant's commitment to imagination as a mediator between sensibility and understanding, as a faculty of intuition, and as spontaneous in a way that remains in keeping with the two-stem architecture of the faculty of cognition. However, I submit, that once we appreciate Kant's account of the bipartite structure of sensibility, then we find that the sensibility view best represents his considered position.

To return briefly to the concerns about these other views, recall that although the third thing view can accommodate the sense in which imagination is mediating, a faculty of intuition, and spontaneous, it violates Kant's fundamental architectural commitment to there being two stems of cognition, not three. Meanwhile, the understanding view integrates imagination into Kant's two-stem architecture, and this view can do justice to the sense in which imagination is spontaneous and a mediator. However, the understanding view cannot easily accommodate the claim that imagination is a faculty of intuition, nor can it explain why over the course of the pre-Critical and Critical period, the position Kant most consistently articulates is one according to which imagination is distinct from understanding.

Compare, now, the prospects of the sensibility view once we take the bipartite picture of sensibility into account. Starting with the textual record, the sensibility view makes sense of why Kant not only situates his discussion of imagination in his analysis of sensibility in his pre-Critical and Critical writings on anthropology and metaphysics, but also why across the three *Critiques*, with the exception of the B Deduction, he clearly distinguishes imagination from understanding. Beyond the textual record, however, the sensibility view does justice to Kant's commitment to imagination being a faculty of intuition. And though Kant's commitment to the spontaneity of imagination was initially a stumbling block for the sensibility view, I have made the case that the bipartite account of sensibility can allow for imagination to still fit the receptive profile of sensibility. To this end, I argued that imagining involves a kind of relative spontaneity that is constitutively dependent on the receptivity of sensibility vis-à-vis the formal and material constraints receptivity places on imaginative activity. Finally, the sensibility view can accommodate Kant's commitment to the mediating nature of imagination, *qua* something that has the cognitive function of making concepts sensible in a way that bridges the gap between the receptive aspects of sensibility, on the one hand, and understanding and its concepts, on the other. The version of the sensibility view that builds on the bipartite account of sensibility can thus do justice both to the textual record and to Kant's core commitments to imagination as a mediator, a faculty of intuition, and spontaneous within his two-stem architecture in a way that neither the third thing nor the understanding view of imagination can. It is for these reasons that, I submit, we should ultimately attribute to Kant the view that imagination is part of sensibility.

3.7 Conclusion

In the past two chapters, I have explored Kant's account of what kind of cognitive capacity imagination is in light of a discussion of where imagination fits in his cognitive architecture. Though support can be found in favor of a third thing, sensibility, or understanding view of imagination, I have argued that the sensibility view best represents Kant's position. However, I have made the case that his commitment to the sensibility view only emerges once we appreciate his account of sensibility as divided into two parts: sense and imagination. Though this bipartite structure of sensibility calls for the revision of some basic assumptions about the kinds of intuitions, processes, and cognitive function of sensibility on Kant's view, I have claimed that the result is a rich account of sensibility and its cognitive remit.

In addition to clarifying Kant's bipartite theory of sensibility and his taxonomy of sensing and imagining, in this chapter, I have made headway with respect to how we are to think of imagination in general on his view. At the most basic level, I have argued that Kant conceives of imagination as part of sensibility, hence as something that is sensory, rather than non-sensory, in nature. In unpacking what this means, I have attributed to him the following basic picture of imagination. Logically, imagination is a faculty of intuitions. More specifically, it is a faculty of intuitions of imagination (intuitions$_i$), which represent determinate spatio-temporal forms, like shapes or temporal sequences, even without the presence of objects. Metaphysically, imagination is a relatively spontaneous capacity that is constitutively dependent on the receptivity of sensibility, which formally and materially constrains our imaginative activities. Finally, functionally, the cognitive function of imagination turns on it mediating between the receptive aspects of sensibility and understanding in a way that makes concepts sensible and facilitates our comprehension of them internal to our cognitive processes.

While situating imagination in Kant's theory of sensibility thus sheds more light on his answer to the question "what is it to imagine," what I now hope to show is that we can fill out further key details of his answer by attending to his formulations of imagination as a specific kind of "faculty of..."

Seeing More: Kant's Theory of Imagination. Samantha Matherne, Oxford University Press.
© Samantha Matherne 2024. DOI: 10.1093/9780191999291.003.0004

4
Three Definitions of Imagination

Imagination is the faculty for...
—B151

4.1 Introduction

Whereas in the past three chapters, I have approached Kant's theory of imagination by zooming out and considering where it fits in his broader cognitive architecture, in this chapter, I zoom in and focus on texts in which he explicitly refers to imagination as a specific "faculty of..." or "faculty for..."[1] On this basis, I tease out three Kantian definitions of imagination: imagination is the faculty of formation (*Bildungsvermögen*), the faculty of intuition even without the presence of objects (*Vermögen der Anschauung auch ohne die Gegenwart des Gegenstandes*),[2] and the faculty of exhibition (*Vermögen der Darstellung*).[3] Let me note straightaway that when I speak of "definitions," I am not using the term in Kant's technical sense to refer to a "real" definition, *qua* a definition of the essence of a thing

---

[1] In taking my cue from these "faculty of" formulations, my strategy for defining imagination differs from another strategy commentators often use, which turns on adducing a definition of imagination on the basis of the basic function he attributes to it. For example, a number of commentators define imagination for Kant as the faculty of mediation because he attributes a mediating function to it. See, e.g., Gibbons's definition of imagination as a "mediating capacity" or a "capacity to 'bridge gaps'" (1994, 2), and Hughes's definition of it as a "mediating faculty" (2007, 2). I am sympathetic to this mediating definition, and address it under the heading of the exhibition. Other commentators define imagination as the faculty of interpretation in virtue of a kind of interpretative function that they claim Kant allocates to it. Makkreel, e.g., glosses imagination as a faculty of interpretation, understood as "comprehending the coherence and significance of our experience" by "mediating" between "sense on the one hand and understanding and reason on the other" (1990, 2–3). While I am also sympathetic to Makkreel's reading in this vein, other commentators have argued that the sort of interpretation Kant attributes to imagination is pre-conceptual in nature: see, e.g., Young's gloss of imagination as the "capacity for construal or interpretation" that is perceptual and pre-conceptual in nature (1998, 142), and Allison following him (2004, 188–9). For reasons that I touched on in my discussion of the cognitive function of imagination in Chapter 3 and that I will clarify in my discussion of the exhibition definition of imagination below, insofar as I read Kant as committed to a conceptually laden view of imagination, I do not think he is committed to this pre-conceptual interpretive definition of imagination. More generally, though I by no means want to deny that attending to the functions Kant accords to imagination are crucial for understanding his view of imagination, in this chapter, I am focusing on Kant's own "faculty of..." formulations, since these appear to be his most direct and succinct effort to define what imagination is in general.

[2] This phrasing is based on Anthro. 7:153.

[3] As I noted earlier "Darstellung" in Kant is typically translated as either "exhibition" or "presentation," and occasionally as "rendering." I shall translate it as "exhibition" because Kant gives *exhibitio* as the Latin cognate (see KU 5:192; EE 20:220; Anthro. 7:167).

102 THREE DEFINITIONS OF IMAGINATION

(see A241–2n; A727–32/B755–60; JL 9:143–4). I am, instead, using "definition" in a looser sense to refer to a general characterization of something. And in what follows, I argue Kant's definitions of imagination in terms of formation, intuitions even without the presence of objects, and exhibition are complementary definitions, which shed light on different core aspects of what he takes to be distinctive about this cognitive capacity and its intuitions, activities, and cognitive function. This discussion will serve as a capstone to my analysis of what imagination is in general on Kant's view, paving the way for my discussion of the specific theoretical, aesthetic, and practical uses of it in Parts II–IV, respectively.

I begin in §4.2 with a discussion of the definition of imagination as a faculty of formation, which Kant initially offers in the pre-Critical period. This section will be somewhat brief, as I rehearse ideas that should be familiar from Chapter 3 about imaginative activity and intuitions of imagination (which I have labelled "intuitions$_i$"). In §4.3, I turn to his definition of imagination as a faculty for representing objects even without their presence. While this definition resonates with a traditional definition of imagination as fantasy, I emphasize the ways in which Kant innovates within this tradition by casting imagination as something that we exercise in both the absence and presence of objects. To this end, I argue that rather than using this definition to characterize imagination as something we exercise only in relation to objects that are not present or not real, Kant uses this definition to clarify, one, the degree of independence our imagination has in relation to objects, and, two, a kind of "seeing more" that imagination enables. Then in §4.4, I take up Kant's definition of imagination as a faculty of exhibition. Though this definition has received less attention than the other two definitions, I submit that it is crucial for understanding Kant's analysis of the cognitive function of imagination that I addressed at the end of Chapter 3: the function of making concepts sensible in a way that facilitates our concrete comprehension of them. Indeed, I contend that this definition reveals Kant's commitment to the distinctive cognitive task our imagination has as a conceptually interfacing sensory capacity that is capable of mediating between what is sensible and conceptual in our cognitive processes. What is more, I claim that once we appreciate the connection between exhibition and the cognitive function of imagination on Kant's view, we have reason to regard the imaginative activities that fall under the formation and even-without-presence definitions as oriented toward exhibition, *qua* his standard for what it is for our imagination to operate cognitively well.

4.2 The Formation Definition

The Formation Definition: Imagination is the faculty of formation (*Bildungsvermögen*).[4]

---

[4] For discussion of this definition, see Makkreel (1990, chap. 1); Goy (2012); Dyck (2019); Hoerth (2020).

THE FORMATION DEFINITION   103

This first definition should sound familiar from Chapter 3, where I discussed Kant's account of the sort of sensory activity our imagination carries out as a kind of "formation": a spatio-temporal ordering and organizing of a manifold of representations. In order to expand on this definition here, I proceed by first taking a closer look at Kant's introduction of this definition in his pre-Critical account of the imagination as the *Bildungsvermögen* ("faculty of formation," "formative faculty") or *bildende Kraft* ("formative power").[5] I then make the case that though there are significant shifts in his conception of imagination between the pre-Critical and Critical periods, the definition of imagination as the faculty of formation is one that he carries over into his Critical account of imagination as *Einbildungskraft*.

To unpack the formation definition, let's thus begin with Kant's treatment of imagination in the pre-Critical writings.[6] First, a note on terminology. Unlike in the Critical period in which Kant uses "Einbildungskraft" as his preferred term for imagination in general, in the pre-Critical period he uses "Bildungsvermögen" to refer to imagination in general and "Einbildungskraft" to refer to a power responsible for a specific kind of imaginative activity, "Einbildung," in which we represent something we have not experienced. As he makes the latter point in his ML1 lectures, the *Einbildungskraft* is "The faculty for producing images from oneself, independent of the actuality of objects, where the images are not borrowed from experience. E.g. an architect pretends to build a house which he has not yet seen" (ML1 28:237).[7] Kant contrasts the imaginative activity of *Einbildung* with other imaginative activities like *Nachbildung* ("imitation") in which we represent something from the past, and *Vorbildung* ("anticipation") in which we represent something in the future (see ML1 28:234–6; AC 25:45; AF 25:512).[8] And he treats these various imaginative activities of *Einbildung*, *Nachbildung*, and *Vorbildung* as exercises of the more general *Bildungsvermögen*, the "faculty of formation."

Terminological issues aside, in order to clarify Kant's pre-Critical account of the faculty of formation, I want to return to some ideas concerning imaginative activity and intuitions, that I introduced in Chapter 3. Recall Kant's claim from the ML1 lectures:

---

[5] See, e.g., ML1 28:230–7; AC 25:76; AF 25:511–12 (where he connects the "faculty to form [*zu bilden*] what strikes the senses" with the Latin "facultas informandi impressiones sensuum"); R332 15:131. I agree with Dyck (2019, 352n3) that, *pace* Makkreel (1990, 13), Kant treats *Bildungsvermögen* and *bildende Kraft* as interchangeable.

[5] See Makkreel (1990, chap. 1) and Dyck (2019) for a discussion of Kant's account of imagination in his pre-Critical writings.

[7] See also AC 25: 45–6; AF 25:511; APill 25:750.

[8] In addition to *Nachbildung* and *Vorbildung*, Kant also discusses *Abbildung*, which involves forming a representation of an object that is present to us in perception (I discuss this at more length in Chapter 5) (see ML1 28:231, 235; AC 25:45; AF 25:511); *Ausbildung*, which involves completing a representation as a whole, e.g. endeavoring to bring a story "to an end" (ML1 28:237; see also AF 25:512, AP 25:303–4); and *Gegenbildung*, which involves supplying a representation with a corresponding sign, e.g. attaching a word to something (see ML1 28:237).

104 THREE DEFINITIONS OF IMAGINATION

sensible cognitions that arise from the spontaneity of the mind are called: *cognitions of the formative power*...One can classify sensibility in the following manner: all sensible cognitions are either *given* or *made*. To the given we can reckon sense in general...To the made we reckon...[t]he representations of the formative power [*bildenden Kraft*]. (ML1 28:230; see also 28:235)[9]

In keeping with his bipartite account of sensibility, Kant here contrasts the formative faculty, as the spontaneous part of sensibility, with sense, as the wholly receptive part of sensibility. In this vein, he claims that whereas sensing involves a receptive process through which we are "given" intuitions of sense (intuitions$_s$) in virtue of being affected by objects, the formative faculty involves a spontaneous process through which it "makes" intuitions$_i$ on the basis of the material delivered through sense. More specifically, he claims that the formative faculty makes intuitions$_i$ by forming, i.e. spatio-temporally ordering and organizing, a manifold of representations delivered through sense.[10]

Recall that, according to Kant, the content of an intuition$_i$ is such as to involve a subject consciously representing something as a determinate spatio-temporal form. As we saw, on Kant's view, the two most basic kinds of spatio-temporal forms that intuitions$_i$ represent are a spatial shape (*Gestalt*) (e.g. the triangular shape of the three dots .˙.) and a temporal sequence (*Gefolge*), series (*Reihe*), or play (*Spiel*) (e.g. the temporal sequence of the ding-dong of a doorbell). This said, he also allows for our imagination to engage in formative activities that make more complex intuitions$_i$ that represent a complicated shape (e.g. the shape of a bouquet of flowers); a complex temporal series (e.g. the temporal sequence of the notes in Mariah Carey's "Fantasy"); or a complex spatio-temporal figure (e.g. the dynamic spatio-temporal form of a time-lapse image of a seascape). For Kant, then, as the faculty of formation, imagination is responsible for generating intuitions$_i$ that represent determinate spatial and/or temporal forms along these lines.

If we now look to the role the formation definition plays in the Critical period, there is a question of how much of the pre-Critical view of the formative faculty Kant preserves in his Critical theory of imagination. At the very least, there is a notable shift in Kant's terminology. As I noted above, in the Critical period he largely drops the term "Bildungsvermögen" as a way of referring to imagination, and uses it, instead, as a biological term.[11] And rather than using "Einbildungskraft"

---

[9] As I noted in Chapter 3, although in this passage Kant uses language of "sensible cognition," in this context he uses "sensible cognition" and "intuition" interchangeably (see ML1 28:229–30).

[10] See also Kant's 1769–70 note, "In order for sensibility to have a determinate form in our representation it is necessary that it have an order [*Zusammenordnung*]...This order is a connection of coordination [*Verknüpfung der coordination*]...The basis of all coordination, hence the form of sensibility, is space and time" (R683 15:304).

[11] See Goy (2012) for a detailed discussion of Kant's use of "Bildungsvermögen" throughout his corpus. Goy argues that after 1780 Kant no longer uses it as an epistemological term, but rather as a biological term, e.g. in the third *Critique*.

THE FORMATION DEFINITION   105

to refer to one species of imaginative activity, he begins to deploy it as his preferred term for the faculty of imagination in general.[12] It is, moreover, clear that in the Critical period, Kant's recognition of the *a priori* mode of imaginative activity marks a significant development in his theory of imagination. Indeed, in this period, much of his analysis of imagination is devoted to elucidating its *a priori* activities and the transcendental role they play in making possible the sort of cognition Kant is concerned with in the first *Critique* (see Part II).

However, in spite of his shifting terminology and his recognition of the *a priori* mode of imagining, Kant remains committed to the formation definition in his Critical theory of imagination.[13] In the first *Critique*, for example, Kant analyzes imagination as a faculty for a kind of "synthesis" (*Synthesis*), which appears to be formation by another name: imaginative synthesis is a spontaneous action in which a manifold is "gone through, taken up, and combined in a certain way," and which "can only occur in accordance with" the forms of space and time (A77/B102; B160).[14] And in the third *Critique* formative activity appears under the heading of "composition" (*Zusammensetzung*)—a spontaneous activity through which our imagination sensibly orders and organizes a manifold (see KU 5:217, 287).[15]

In the Critical period, we, moreover, find Kant characterizing the representations generated by the imagination as intuitions$_i$ that involve the representation of determinate spatio-temporal forms. In the first *Critique*, for example, Kant claims that imaginative synthesis generates a "**determinate** intuition" that represents a "determinate space or time," such as a line or a circle (B154, B202; see also A162–3/B203–4, A223–4/B271). And in the B Deduction, he closes with two examples that involve imaginative synthesis that results in the representation of a basic spatio-temporal form: the representation of the "shape" of a house and of the "temporal sequence" in freezing water (B162–3).[16] Meanwhile in the third *Critique*, Kant credits imagination with representations that involve a "whole of intuition," which "comprehend[s]" "the many in one" (KU 5:254–5). And he intimates that the holistic "forms" represented in such intuitions$_i$ are "either shape or play" (KU 5:225).

---

[12] Dyck (2019, 356) dates the shift in terms to Kant's *Anthropology Pillau* lectures from the winter semester 1777/8 (25:750–1).

[13] It is perhaps also worth noting that etymologically *einbilden* can be traced back to Eckhart's notion of *inbilden* (to form in, e.g. God forms his image in [*sich einbilden*] human beings), and is thus a cognate of *bilden* (Espagne 2014, 112).

[14] Kant alludes to the formative nature of imaginative synthesis in the Postulates, where he describes a "formative [*bildende*] synthesis by means of which we construct a triangle in imagination" (A224/B271; transl. modified).

[15] I thus disagree with Makkreel's reading, according to which Kant shifts from a synthetic conception of imaginative activity in the first *Critique* to a non-synthetic conception of imaginative activity in the third *Critique* (see 1990, 48). Kant continues to use language of "synthesis" to describe the activity of imagination in the third *Critique*, e.g. EE 20:203, 212, 230n; KU 5:177, 238. And, as I discuss in Chapter 7, in the first *Critique* Kant describes composition as a kind of synthesis (see B201n).

[16] I discuss these two examples at more length in Chapters 6–7.

106   THREE DEFINITIONS OF IMAGINATION

To be sure, unlike in the pre-Critical period where Kant only offers an analysis of the empirical manifestation of the formative activities of imagination, in the first *Critique* he develops an account of the *a priori* mode of imaginative synthesis. But as I indicated in Chapter 3, on his view, this *a priori* exercise proceeds in the same general way that the empirical exercise of imagination does: by taking up, ordering, and organizing a manifold that sensibility in its receptivity provides. The difference is that in the *a priori* case the manifold is not a manifold of empirical intuition$_s$, but rather an *a priori* manifold of space and time that sensibility "in its original receptivity" provides (see A100). For Kant, then, the *a priori* activities of imagination involve our imagination synthesizing the *a priori* manifold of space and time and generating intuitions$_i$ that represent determinate spatio-temporal forms on this basis. While spelling out what this synthesis and these intuitions$_i$ amount to is one of my major tasks in Part II, for now, what matters is the fact that even in the *a priori* case, Kant takes our imagination to proceed along formative lines.

What this cursory look at the trajectory of his view suggests is that regardless of the terminological shifts and *a priori* extension of imagination in the Critical period, Kant continues to define imagination as a faculty that makes intuitions$_i$ that represent determinate spatio-temporal forms through spontaneous activities that involve sensibly ordering and organizing a manifold delivered through the receptivity of sensibility.

4.3 The Even-Without-Presence Definition

The Even-Without-Presence Definition: Imagination is the faculty of intuition even without the presence of objects.[17]

The idea that imagination involves representing objects without their presence is certainly not new in Kant. As I discussed in the Introduction, this is a traditional philosophical view of imagination as fantasy that we find variations of, for example, in Aristotle's account of imagination as *phantasia*, Hobbes's account of imagination as fancy, and Husserl's account of imagination as *Phantasie*. This traditional view of imagination is also one put forward by Kant's Leibnizian predecessors, Christian Wolff and Alexander Baumgarten. For example, in *Psychologia empirica* (1732), Wolff says, "The faculty of producing perceptions of absent sensible things is called faculty of imagining or imagination... We call ideas produced by imagination a fantasm [*Facultas producendi perceptiones rerum sensibilium*

---

[17] For discussion of this definition, see Mörchen (1970, 14, 26, 48, 181); Arendt (1981, 75–6; 1982, 65–70, 79–80); Young (1988, 141–2); Waxman (1991, 118–19, 261–3); Longuenesse (1998, 205–6); Banham (2005, 101, 160; 2013, 76–7); Guyer (2006, 462–3); Nuzzo (2013, 27–8, 36); Stephenson (2015; 2017).

THE EVEN-WITHOUT-PRESENCE DEFINITION   107

absentium Facultas imaginandi seu Imaginatio appellatur…Ideam ab imaginatione productam Phantasma dicimus]" (§92; my transl.). And in the *Metaphysics* (1739/43), Baumgarten asserts, "I have a faculty of imagining [*facultatem imaginandi*], or the FACULTY OF IMAGINATION [*Phantasian*]. And since my imaginations are perceptions of things that were formerly present, they are perceptions of the senses that, while I imagine, are absent" (§558, 211).

It can be tempting to attribute to Kant this traditional view of imagination in general as fantasy. After all, in the first *Critique*, Kant says, "***Imagination* is the faculty for representing an object in intuition even without its presence [*Einbildungskraft ist das Vermögen, einen Gegenstand auch ohne dessen Gegenwart in der Anschauung vorzustellen*]**" (B151; transl. modified).[18] And in the *Anthropology* he claims that, "the *power of imagination…*is the faculty of intuition…even *without* the presence of an object" (Anthro. 7:153).[19]

However, one of the central tenets of my interpretation of Kant's theory of imagination is that it is a mistake to attribute to him a traditional view of imagination as fantasy. As I noted in the Introduction, this traditional view of imagination goes hand-in-hand with a more restrictive view of how imaginative we are, according to which we only exercise our imagination in relation to what is not real or not present. But one of the claims I hope to establish is that Kant endorses a more capacious view of how imaginative we are, according to which imagining pervades our engagement with what is real and present, as much as with what is not real and not present.[20] I cannot offer a complete defense of this claim until I explore Kant's commitment to imagination shaping our theoretical, aesthetic, and practical encounters with what is real and present in Parts II–IV. Here, however, I want to begin motivating this idea by underlining an important modification that Kant makes to the view of imagination as fantasy endorsed by Wolff and Baumgarten.

Notice that, as a kind of fantasy, Wolff and Baumgarten cast imagination as a faculty that only represents objects that are absent. But Kant does not claim that imagination is operative only in relation to objects that are absent; he claims that it is operative "even without" the presence of objects.[21] Though this "even without" might be easy to overlook, it is crucial for understanding Kant's

---

[18] As I noted earlier, there is some question as how to translate this passage: see Stephenson (2015; 2017) for discussion.

[19] See also Anthro 7:167; APill 25:750; Mensch. 25:944; AMr 25:1241, 25:1257; AB 25:1451, 1456; ML2 28:585; MD 28:673–4; MV 28:449; R6315 18:618.

[20] As I note in the Introduction, in attributing to imagination a more capacious role to play in our lives than traditional accounts of imagination as fantasy do, Kant's view echoes Hume's account of imagination as something that can manifest in both "ideas of fancy" and "ideas of judgment."

[21] Commentators tend to overlook this qualifier. See, e.g., Guyer's gloss of the B151 passage in terms of the idea that imagination is "the ability to form a representation of anything that is not currently given to intuition for any reason" (2006, 462); Stephenson's gloss in terms of the idea that, "it is *the object of intuition that is not present* in imaginational intuition" (2017, 114); and Rosefeldt's gloss in terms of the idea that imagination is "a faculty to have image-like representations of non actually perceived objects" (2021, 53173).

108 THREE DEFINITIONS OF IMAGINATION

view: for a faculty that can operate "even without" the presence of an object can operate "even with" its presence as well. And, indeed, as we shall see Kant accords imagination a role as much in representing absent objects, e.g. in memory, hallucination, or fiction, as in representing objects that are present, e.g. in perception, aesthetic appreciation, and practical action.[22] Hence my gloss of this second Kantian definition of imagination as the "even-without-presence definition," rather than a more traditional "without-presence definition."

This said, one of the advantages of the traditional theory of imagination as fantasy is that it promises a clear picture of what imagining involves: imagining involves representing objects that are absent. But if Kant also allows imagining to involve representing objects that are present, then what distinctive feature of imagining does the even-without-presence definition of imagination bring out? By my lights, there are two features of imagination on his view that this definition captures, the first concerns how imagination relates to objects and the second concerns a kind of "seeing more" that imagination enables.

The first feature is what I shall describe in terms of the "presence-independence" of imagination. As we have seen, according to Kant, one thing that distinguishes imagination from sense is that our imagination can generate intuitions$_i$ of objects independent of those objects being currently present to us. In his words, "sense...is the faculty of intuition in the presence of an object, [imagination] is intuition even *without* the presence of an object" (Anthro. 7:153). For Kant, the intuitions$_s$ produced through sense depend on the presence of objects because they are generated as a result of us being causally affected by objects that exist and are currently present to us. By contrast, Kant allows for imagination to generate intuitions$_i$ of objects that outstrip what is affecting us here and now. To cite some empirical examples, when I envision my ideal flower garden, hallucinate the melody of Mariah Carey's "Fantasy," or picture what Clarissa Dalloway looks like, even though none of these objects are currently present to me, my imagination is nevertheless able to generate intuitions$_i$ of them. And to cite an *a priori* example, Kant claims that in activities like geometrical construction, we are able to imaginatively generate "non-empirical" intuitions$_i$, e.g. of lines or triangles, that do not depend on an existing object being present to us and causally affecting us (see A713/B741).

However, we must be careful in just how independent from the presence of objects we take imagination to be on Kant's view. For, as I discussed in Chapter 3, in virtue of its constitutive dependence on receptivity, our imagination is materially constrained by the receptivity of sensibility: we can only imaginatively act by sensibly ordering and organizing a manifold delivered through sensibility in its receptivity. What this means for the presence-independence of imagination,

---

[22] This said, as I discuss in Chapter 5, even when imagination operates in relation to present objects, e.g. in perception, it is not constrained to representing what is immediately present.

at least in the empirical case, is that although Kant allows for our imagination to generate intuitions$_i$ of objects that do not currently exist and are not currently present to us, it is nevertheless bound by material that has been delivered to us through the presence of objects, or properties of objects, at some point. As I specified in Chapter 3, at the most basic level, Kant claims that our empirical imagining must draw on sensations that we have had in the presence of objects in the past. For example, when I envision my ideal flower garden, I draw on sensations that I have had in the presence of, say, peonies, dahlias, and ranunculi in the past. To draw on some recent literature to make this point, on Kant's view, although our empirical imagining is not "strongly" dependent on the presence of objects, it is "weakly" dependent on the presence of objects in the ways I have just specified.[23] The even-without-presence definition thus sheds light, in part, on the way that our empirical imagining relates to objects: it is weakly, not strongly, dependent on their presence.

Matters are more complicated when it comes to the *a priori* case. As I also discussed in Chapter 3, on Kant's view, although the *a priori* exercise of imagination is not constrained by a manifold of sensations, it is constrained by the manifold of space and time that sensibility "in its original receptivity" provides (A100). While I shall have more to say about this in Chapter 6, for now, I want to indicate that cashing out the presence-independence of the *a priori* exercise of imagination will require taking this kind of constraint into account.

The second feature of imagination that I want to glean from the even-without-presence definition is what I shall describe in terms of "seeing more." By "seeing more" I have in mind the way in which imagination enables us to "see" more than we are immediately given, where "seeing" is to be understood as a loose way to refer to our sensory awareness of something. So the basic idea behind the seeing more feature is that imagination enables a kind of sensory awareness of more than is currently given to us.

To illustrate, let's start with a case in which we imagine an object that is absent. Here, consider these lines about Dido from the *Aeneid*,

> In the empty hall, lying alone on Aeneas's couch,
> Seeing and hearing him although he is gone.
>
> (2005, 97–8)

Though Aeneas is absent, Dido finds herself "seeing and hearing him" nonetheless. On a Kantian analysis, this involves her imaginatively making Aeneas present by generating an intuition$_i$ of him. And as a result of this imaginative activity, she is able to see more than the empty hall around her.

---

[23] This notion of weak dependence is a variation on what Stephenson calls "General-Affection Dependence" (2015, 493), and McLear refers to as 'Weak Presence Dependence' (2017, 93).

110   THREE DEFINITIONS OF IMAGINATION

However, as I have emphasized, on Kant's view, our imagination is not just operative in relation to objects that are absent; it is also operative in relation to objects that are present. So, what does it mean to see more even when the object is present to us? According to Kant, when an object is present to us, what is immediately given to us through the senses will be limited by our bodily point of view, and will shift with each successive now and change in our spatial perspective or spatial environs. And, on his view, our imaginative activities extend our sensory awareness of what is present to us beyond what is immediately given to us at a particular moment or place, e.g. to spatio-temporal features of objects that have passed out of, or lie beyond, our current point of view. To use some more contemporary language to make this point, on Kant's view, in our encounter with objects that are present, our imagination is able to make more "perceptually present" to us than we are immediately given.[24] Let's consider two examples.

The first is an example of amodal perception, i.e. perception in which we represent parts of an object that are not immediately present to us. Suppose I am looking at a burgundy ranunculus in a vase. Even though I am only immediately given the part of the ranunculus stem and petals that are not occluded by the vase, I nevertheless amodally perceive it as having a stem hidden from my view. On Kant's analysis, this amodal perception is made possible by my imagination making the hidden stem perceptually present to me.[25]

The second example is an example of a temporally extended perception. Suppose I visit the Gropius House in Lincoln, Massachusetts.[26] As I walk up to the Gropius House, what I am given shifts with each step, as I take in the whites and blacks of the façade; the angularity of the covered walkway and adjacent walls; the admixture of wood, brick, glass block, and steel; the surprise of the external spiral staircase; etc. Over the course of my approach, some of the things I initially see pass out of view, e.g. as I spy the spiral staircase, I lose sight of the covered walkway. Nevertheless, when I look at the staircase, I am still sensorily aware of the covered walkway.[27] And what I am proposing is that on a Kantian analysis, the walkway and other features of the house no longer in view continue

---

[24] The language of "perceptual presence" is drawn from Noë (2004). For further discussion of how Kant's view bears on explicating perceptual presence, see Sellars (1978); Thomas (2010); Matherne (2015); Kind (2018).

[25] For discussion of Kant's account of the role imagination plays in amodal perception, see Sellars (1978); Matherne (2015). For contemporary discussions of the contribution imagination makes to amodal perception, see Nanay (2010; 2018a).

[26] This example recalls Kant's example of the perception of a house at B162, which I shall discuss in Chapters 6–7.

[27] For an example from Kant, consider his discussion of the *Abbildung* or "illustration" of a city that is "present": "when I see a city, the mind then forms an image of the object which it has before it while it runs through the manifold...The mind must undertake many observations in order to illustrate an object so that it illustrates the object differently from each side. E.g., a city appears differently from the east than the west. There are thus many appearances of a matter according to the various sides and points of view. The mind must make an illustration [*Abbildung*] from all these appearances by taking them all together" (ML1 28:235–6).

to be perceptually present to me because my imagination makes them present and, thereby, enables me to see more.

Though I shall have more to say about what it means to imaginatively see more in later chapters, my point for now is that one of the features of imagination suggested by the even-without-presence definition is that it enables us to be sensorily aware of more than we are immediately given through the senses at any particular moment in time or location in space. To be sure, this is related to the presence-independence feature of imagination: we are able to see more through our imagination because it does not depend on objects being currently present to us. However, whereas the presence-independence feature pertains to how imagination relates to objects, the seeing more feature pertains to the kind of sensory awareness of more than we are currently given enabled by our imagination.

As I understand the even-without-presence definition of imagination, then, although it has traditional antecedents in theories of imagination as fantasy, Kant innovates within this tradition. For Kant's even-without-presence definition does not convey the thought that our imagination operates only in relation to objects that are absent. Instead, this definition reflects the fact that our imagination operates in a way that involves a degree of independence from the presence of objects and enables us to see more than we are currently given, even of objects that are present to us.

If we now consider the relationship between the formation and even-without-presence definitions, the latter supplements the former in helpful ways. From the formation definition, I adduced the idea that, on Kant's view, the characteristic sensory activity of imagination is one in which it makes intuitions$_i$ that represent determinate spatio-temporal forms through a spontaneous process in which it sensibly orders and organizes a manifold. What the even-without-presence definition adds is the thought that this formative activity occurs with a degree of independence from the presence of objects, and that through intuitions$_i$ thereby produced we are able to imaginatively see more than is immediately given to us.

4.4 The Exhibition Definition

Exhibition Definition: Imagination is the faculty of exhibition (*Vermögen der Darstellung*).[28]

The third, and final, Kantian definition of imagination that I shall consider is a definition that he articulates most explicitly in the third *Critique*: "the faculty of

---

[28] As I noted earlier, I translate "Darstellung" as "exhibition" in keeping with Kant's Latin gloss of it in terms of *exhibitio*' (see KU 5:192; EE 20:220; Anthro. 7:167).

112   THREE DEFINITIONS OF IMAGINATION

exhibition [*Darstellung*] is the imagination" (KU 5:232; transl. modified).[29] Though this definition has received less attention,[30] one of my aims in this book is to show that we should take this definition seriously as a guide to understanding Kant's theory of imagination. Indeed, I hope to show that attending to the exhibition definition sheds light on his conception of it as a mediating faculty tasked with the cognitive function of making concepts sensible, which we exercise across the theoretical, aesthetic, and practical domains.

But, here, I want to preface my discussion of the exhibition definition with a couple of preliminaries. The first is a rather brief preliminary that concerns Kant's terminology. Kant uses "Darstellung" in a somewhat unusual way. Typically, "Darstellung" is used to refer to something that depicts or presents something else, e.g. Vanessa Bell's 1912 portrait of Virginia Woolf (her sister) is a "Darstellung" of Woolf. Kant, however, uses "Darstellung" in a broader way to refer to an intuition that exhibits a concept. In this vein, he glosses *Darstellung* in terms of the act of "placing a corresponding intuition beside the concept" and "the act of appending [*Hinzufügung*] the intuition to the concept" (KU 5:192; WF 20:325). He also characterizes a *Darstellung* as an intuition that involves the *Versinnlichung*, the making sensible, of a concept (KU 5:351). For Kant, then, an intuition of a ranunculus counts as a *Darstellung* if it, in some yet to be specified sense, exhibits the concept <ranunculus>. And it is *Darstellung* in this broader sense that is at issue when Kant asserts that, "the faculty of exhibition is the imagination."

The second is a more involved preliminary that pertains to a set of interpretive issues surrounding defining imagination in terms of exhibition on Kant's view. Though there are texts in which Kant explicitly asserts that imagination is the faculty of exhibition, there are also various reasons why this gloss on imagination has received less attention. For one thing, as I noted, Kant does not explicitly characterize imagination as the faculty of exhibition until the third *Critique*. What is more, in the third *Critique* Kant is not always consistent in which faculty he attributes exhibition to. For in addition to describing imagination as the faculty of exhibition, he appears to claim that the power of judgment is responsible for exhibition: "If the concept of an object is given, then the business of the power of judgment in using it for cognition consists in **exhibition** (*exhibitio*), i.e., in placing a

---

[29] See also Kant's claim that in judgments of taste, "the faculty of exhibition or imagination is considered, in the case of a given intuition, to be in accord with the **faculty of concepts**" (KU 5:244; transl. modified); that in judgments of the beautiful, "the imagination, as the faculty for exhibiting [concepts], feels [itself] strengthened" (KU 5:366); and that, "the **faculty** ... of the exhibition of [concepts] (which is one and the same as that of apprehension)" is imagination (KU 5:279; transl. modified).

[30] For example, in the following comprehensive treatments of imagination, *Darstellung* is mentioned only in passing: Makkreel (1990, 4–5, 55–6, 128–9); Gibbons (1994, 139, 150, 151n36); Banham (2005, 141); Kneller (2007, 4–5, 14, 106). However, more attention is paid to the relationship between imagination and *Darstellung* in Henrich (1992, 47–50); Helfer (1996, chap. 1); Rush (2001, 45–6, 56–8); Gasché (2003); Ferrarin (2008, §2); Haag (2013, §5.1); Rosefeldt (2019).

THE EXHIBITION DEFINITION   113

corresponding intuition beside the concept" (KU 5:192; transl. modified).[31] Kant defines the power of judgment, in general, as "the faculty for thinking the particular as contained under the universal" (KU 5:179). And it is certainly tempting to think that an act of judgment in which we think a particular contained under a universal amounts to an act in which we exhibit a concept in an intuition. But if this is the case, then exhibition would not seem to be something that uniquely defines imagination for Kant.

In addition to these concerns, there might be reason to doubt that exhibition can be definitive of imagination in general. For, on the face of it, exhibiting concepts through intuitions seems more like a particular kind of imagining, rather than characteristic of imagining as such.[32] For example, it seems that even if certain activities, like mathematically constructing the concept <triangle>,[33] writing a poem that expresses the concept <fame>,[34] or doing an anatomical dissection to demonstrate the concept <human eye>[35] involve intuitions$_i$ that exhibit concepts, why should we think that other paradigmatic imaginative activities, like association or hallucination, involve exhibition? Indeed, what about imaginative activities that Kant claims conflict with the understanding, such as the *"ruleless* [regellos]...inventions" that "have no place in any world at all, because they are self-contradictory" or the "nonsense" an artist's imagination produces in "lawless freedom" (Anthro. 7:181; KU 5:319)? How could these "ruleless," "self-contradictory," "nonsensical," "lawless," imaginative activities exhibit concepts?[36]

I take these to be serious concerns, and one of my main tasks in this chapter and ensuing ones is to make the case that the exhibition definition is, indeed, a core definition of imagination on Kant's view. To this end, in Parts II–IV, I endeavor to show that the theme of exhibition provides us with a through line for making sense of a mediating feature of our imaginative activities that remains constant across its use in theoretical, aesthetic, and practical domains: these activities make concepts sensible for us in a way that facilitates our concrete comprehension of them. In the rest of this chapter, however, my aim is to defend the basic idea that Kant conceives of imagination as the faculty responsible for

---

[31] See also Kant's description of "the **exhibition** (*exhibitio*) of the object corresponding to this concept in intuition" as an "action" that "requires" the "power of judgment" (EE 20:220), and, "Nature is necessarily harmonious with...the **power of judgment** and its capacity for exhibiting [empirical] laws [of nature] in an empirical apprehension of its forms through the imagination" (EE 20:233).

[32] Gibbons, e.g., defines imagination in general as a "mediating capacity" (1994, 2) and treats exhibition as one imaginative function among others, viz. a "productive" and "constructive" function that plays a role in schematism, mathematical construction, aesthetic ideas, and the sublime (1994, 139, 150, 151n26). Makkreel also distinguishes imagination as a faculty of representations (*Vorstellungen*), which has "primarily a perceptual function," from imagination as a faculty of exhibition, which has the function of "relat[ing] sensibility to the intellect" (1990, 129, 55).

[33] See A713–14/B741–2.   [34] See KU 5:314.   [35] See KU 5:343.

[36] For Kant's emphasis on concepts as "rules," see, "All cognition requires a concept...that serves as a rule" (A105), and for his emphasis on laws as "rules," see the understanding is "the **faculty of rules**...Rules, so far as they are objective...are called laws" (A126).

114 THREE DEFINITIONS OF IMAGINATION

exhibition. I, first, take a closer look at what Kant means by exhibition (§4.4.1). I then address why we should read him as committed to imagination being the faculty of exhibition (§4.4.2).

4.4.1 Exhibition in General

Prescinding for the moment from the question concerning the connection between imagination and exhibition, let's take a bigger picture look at Kant's account of exhibition in general and why he thinks it cognitively matters.

As I alluded to above, in his analysis of exhibition in general Kant makes two sorts of broad claims. In the first place, he characterizes exhibition as a process through which an intuition is added to a concept. In this vein in the third *Critique* he describes exhibition as the activity of "placing a corresponding intuition beside the concept" (KU 5:192). And in the "What Real Progress" essay, he says exhibition is "the act of appending [*Hinzufügung*] the intuition to the concept" (WF 20:325).

The second set of claims Kant makes about exhibition turns on the idea that exhibition is a process through which a concept is made "sensible" (*sinnlich*) or "intuitable" (*anschaulich*) (A240/B299; KU 5:343, 351). Drawing on language from rhetoric to elucidate what this "Versinnlichung" (making sensible) of concepts amounts to, he describes exhibition as something that involves the "hypotyposis" or "subjecto sub adspectum" of a concept, i.e. throwing the concept before the eyes (KU 5:351).[37] So understood, exhibition involves displaying a concept to ourselves in a concrete, sensible form.

Piecing these two claims together, on Kant's view, exhibition involves adding an intuition to a concept in such a way that makes the concept sensible to us. To illustrate this basic picture of exhibition, let's consider Kant's description of the exhibition involved in an anatomical dissection: "the anatomist [exhibits] the human eye when he makes intuitable [*anschaulich macht*] the concept, that he has previously expounded discursively, by means of the dissection of this organ" (KU 5:343; transl. modified). Prior to the dissection, perhaps as a result of reading textbooks or attending lectures, Kant suggests that the anatomist has a "discursive" grasp of the concept <human eye>: he has some sort of intellectual understanding of the common properties ("marks") of human eyes, such as having a cornea, an iris, and a lens. According to Kant, when the anatomist then dissects the human eye, he makes the concept <human eye> "sensible" to himself by exploring how its marks concretely show up, and show up as a whole, in intuition. For example, if prior to the dissection the anatomist understood *in abstracto* that

---

[37] See Gasché (2003) and Stroud (2014, chap. 2) for a discussion of the influence of the rhetorical notion of hypotyposis on Kant's account of *Darstellung*.

THE EXHIBITION DEFINITION 115

the human eye has a cornea, iris, and lens, the dissection provides him with the opportunity to learn how those marks manifest, and manifest in relation to one another, in actual eyes.

However, on Kant's view, the exhibition involved in the dissection is not just a matter of there being some object on the dissection table that displays the concept <human eye>. As we have seen, Kant conceives of exhibition as a cognitive activity in which we "add" or "append" an intuition to a concept in a way that makes that concept sensible to us. This being the case, in the dissection, the exhibition that is ultimately of interest to Kant is a cognitive activity in which the anatomist makes the concept <human eye> sensible to himself by somehow adding an intuition of the human eye to the concept of it.[38] When I discuss exhibition in what follows it is this cognitive activity that I have in mind.

So why does Kant think that exhibition matters for us cognitively? Here, I explore two ways in which it matters: the first turns on its connection to sensibility's cognitive function of making concepts sensible (see Chapter 3), and the second on its contribution to the modal achievement of cognition in the narrow sense (see Chapter 1).

To address the first cognitive benefit of exhibition, let's return to Kant's picture of sensibility's cognitive function of making concepts sensible. Recall that according to Kant, as human beings, we have a "natural need" to grasp our concepts not just intellectually and abstractly, but sensibly and concretely (Rel. 6:109). And in order for our concepts to be "comprehensible" (*faßlich*) to us in the latter way, Kant claims that we need intuitions in which "a concept thought abstractly is exhibited... *in concreto*" (Rel. 6:65n; JL 9:39). I described this as a "subject-facing" way to think about what it means for a concept to be made sensible: exhibiting concepts in intuition facilitates agreement between sensibility and understanding internal to our cognitive processes. But what exactly does Kant think exhibition contributes to this end?

From Kant's perspective, in facilitating our concrete comprehension of concepts, exhibition accomplishes something that we cannot accomplish through the intellect alone. According to Kant, although through the understanding we can intellectually grasp concepts *in abstracto*, this does not guarantee that we grasp how they show up *in concreto*. That is to say, although we might intellectually understand the logical content of a concept or its relations to other concepts, this does not mean that we have a sense of how this content or these relations actually manifest in space and time. Indeed, as Kant says suggestively in the *Anthropology*, "abstract concepts of understanding are often only glittering poverty" (Anthro. 7:145).

---

[38] I return to exactly what this adding involves in §4.4.2.

116 THREE DEFINITIONS OF IMAGINATION

To put the point another way, on Kant's view, possessing a concept does not guarantee that we grasp how it manifests in concrete, sensible terms.[39] He illustrates this scenario with another medical example,

> a physician...can have many fine pathological...rules in his head, of which he can even be a thorough teacher, and yet can easily stumble in their application...he...to be sure understands the universal *in abstracto* but cannot distinguish whether a case *in concreto* belongs under it. (A134/B173)

Suppose this physician has a good understanding of the concept <cholera> *in abstracto*: he is able to rattle off the key symptoms and underlying causes of cholera in his lectures and to explain how cholera relates to other diseases. Yet, *per* Kant, this physician may nevertheless be unable to identify a case of cholera when it presents in a patient. As we might put this point, for all his "knowledge" about the concept <cholera>, the physician lacks the "know-how" required to identify cases of it "in actual business" (A134/B173).[40]

Though there are different lessons to be drawn from the physician example, by my lights, when we read it in tandem with the anatomist example, we learn something about why Kant thinks exhibition serves us cognitively.[41] On Kant's view, exhibition involves intuitions that "demonstrate" or "illustrate" to us how the marks contained in our concepts and relations between concepts actually show up, and, thereby, facilitates a concrete comprehension of concepts that we lack through the understanding alone (KU 5:342–3). Indeed, this is part of why Kant draws on language from rhetoric, "hypotyposis" and "subjecto sub adspectum," to describe exhibition. For just as a speaker intentionally deploys devices to throw a concept before their audience's eyes in order to make it concrete and vivid, so too do we engage in the cognitive activity of exhibition to throw a concept before our mind's eye in order to make it concrete and vivid.

---

[39] I thus read Kant as rejecting Warnock's (1949) assumption that possessing a concept involves the ability to use that concept in concrete cases.

[40] I am drawing the distinction between know-how and knowing from Kant's analysis of the difference between "art" and "science" in the third *Critique* in terms of the difference between "**to be able** [*können*]" and "**to know** [*wissen*]," where the former involves a kind of "skill" that the latter does not (KU 5:304). I return to these topics in Chapters 5 and 7. For discussion of know-how in the context of Kant's theory of imagination and judgment in the first and third *Critiques*, see Bell (1987) and Matherne (2014a).

[41] In addition to the lesson that I am adducing about exhibition, Kant uses this example to motivate his picture of the power of judgment as a "special talent that cannot be taught but only practiced," which can explain how subsumption of particular cases under rules is possible without running into a rules-regress problem (A133/B172; see Bell 1987 for discussion). However, the fact that Kant's next step in explicating how subsumption is possible turns on his account of a special product of the imagination that he calls a "schema" reveals that imagination has a crucial role to play in his analysis of how such subsumption is possible. See Gibbons (1994, chap. 2); Hughes (2007); and Ferrarin (2008) for extended accounts of the role imagination has to play in making subsumption possible.

THE EXHIBITION DEFINITION   117

Although the anatomy example might make it seem as if Kant thinks exhibition is only something we rely on when we are first learning how a concept concretely manifests, he, in fact, treats it as something that has an on-going role to play as we deepen our comprehension of concepts over time. This commitment emerges in Kant's account of comprehensibility-via-exhibition as a kind of "perfection" (*Vollkommenheit*) of cognition in his logic lectures. There, he connects the comprehensibility of concepts facilitated by exhibition with a kind of "aesthetic perfection" of cognition, which he calls "aesthetic distinctness" (*Deutlichkeit*) (see JL 9:39; BL 24:45, 56–7; VL 24:806–10; DWL 24:709).[42] In this context, Kant is not using "aesthetic" in a narrow way to refer to what concerns beauty or sublimity; he is using it more generally as a term to refer to what is "grounded on the particular sensibility of man" (JL 9:36).[43] And his claim is that we can aesthetically perfect cognition by deepening and refining our grasp of how concepts manifest *in concreto* through on-going engagement with intuitions that exhibit those concepts in new and expansive ways.

Suppose, for example, that as I am reading Jeff Chang's *Can't Stop, Won't Stop: A History of the Hip-Hop Generation*, I come across the following passage about the musical genre dub:

> One studio session could now produce multiple "versions." A single band session with a harmony trio could be recycled as a DJ version for a rapper to rock *patwa* rhymes over, and a dub version in which the mixing engineer himself became the central performer—experimenting with levels, equalization and effects to alter the feel of the riddim, and break free of the constraints of the standard song.   (2005, 30)

This passage might give me an intellectual grasp of some of the marks of the concept <dub>, such as <being a version of a song>, <being the product of a sound engineer experimenting with levels, equalizations, and effects>, <emphasizing rhythm>, etc. However, in order to concretely comprehend this concept, I need some intuitions that exhibit how these marks actually show up, and show up together, in music. To this end, I might listen to some of the classic dub music that grew out of the reggae scene in Jamaica in the 1960s and 1970s by artists, such as King Tubby and Lee "Scratch" Perry, that Chang cites.[44] By listening, I can develop a more aesthetically distinct grasp of the concept <dub> through intuitions that

---

[42] See Cohen (2018) and McQuillan (2018) for a discussion of the influence of Meier's and Baumgarten's notion of aesthetic perfection on Kant's account of cognition and aesthetics.

[43] Hence his gloss of aesthetic perfection as perfection with respect to the "laws of sensibility" (see JL 9:38; VL 24:806–7). Insofar as aesthetic perfection hinges on agreement with the subject and our sensibility, he sometimes describes this as "subjective" perfection (see BL 24:45; VL 24:809–10). This is also why he sometimes describes aesthetic distinctness as "subjective clarity...through *intuition*" (JL 9:62; see also VL 24:810).

[44] See Chang (2005, chap. 2); Veal (2007).

118 THREE DEFINITIONS OF IMAGINATION

exhibit to me how being a version of a song, the product of a sound engineer's experimentations, or emphasizing rhythm musically manifest. However, it is not as if I will have thereby developed an exhaustive comprehension of the concept <dub>. For example, I might begin listening to Bauhaus's "Bela Lugosi's Dead" and discover new ways in which <dub> can musically manifest in a dark glam context.[45] From a Kantian perspective, the intuitions that I have when I listen to this song can make the concept <dub> more aesthetically dis- tinct to me, as I come to learn how a band, rather than an engineer might engage in the requisite experimentation, or as I discern ways that rhythm can be emphasized through, say, other uses of drum and bass. What this example reveals is that, on Kant's view, while exhibition is something that plays an important role in helping us first learn how concepts manifest concretely, this learning process is on-going, as intuitions that exhibit concepts can provide us with an ever richer sense of how concepts, including their content and relations, show up.

The last point I wish to stress here on this topic is that, for Kant, the cognitive value exhibition has in virtue of making concepts sensible is something it has in relation to all types of concepts, whether they be concepts of experience or con- cepts of what transcends experience. With respect to concepts of experience, Kant indicates that exhibition and the comprehensibility of concepts that it provides is part of the "know-how" with these concepts that allows us to identify instances of them in experience. In the physician case, unless <cholera> is made comprehen- sible to the physician through exhibition in intuition, then he will not have the know-how needed to identify when his patients have it. Indeed, this seems to be why Kant suggests that one of the faults of this physician is that he has not engaged with enough "examples" in intuition (A134/B173).[46]

However, even when it comes to concepts that are the most remote from experience, "supersensible" concepts, like the idea of God or the morally good, Kant claims that we need to make them comprehensible to ourselves through exhibition.[47] As we have seen, Kant claims that, it is a "natural need of all human beings to demand for even the highest concepts ... something that *can be sensibly held on to* [*etwas Sinnlich-haltbares*]" (Rel. 6:109; transl. modified). In a similar vein, he says, "It is plainly a limitation of human reason, one which is ever inseparable from it, that ... we always need a certain analogy with natural being in order to make supersensible characteristics comprehensible to us" (Rel. 6:64–5n).[48]

---

[45] See Carpenter (2012).

[46] Kant glosses examples as a kind of exhibition at KU 5:351 and WF 20:235–6. I take up this issue in Chapters 5 and 13.

[47] I return to the topic of the exhibition of supersensible ideas at more length in Chapters 9, 10, and 13.

[48] Although in this passage Kant frames this point in terms of "analogies," on his view analogies are a form of exhibition (see KU §59).

THE EXHIBITION DEFINITION   119

For Kant, then, even with concepts that transcend experience, given our "limitations" and "needs" as human beings, if we are to fully comprehend them, then we need to sensibly exhibit them to ourselves in intuition. Granted, exhibition in this context will not enable us to identify instances of these concepts in experience; nevertheless, internal to our cognitive processes, it can facilitate our comprehension of the content of, and relations between, these concepts.

In addition to making concepts sensible, Kant thinks exhibition cognitively matters on account of a certain modal role it plays in cognition in the narrow sense. Recall from Chapter 1 that while Kant characterizes cognition in the broad sense in terms of the conscious representation of objects, he characterizes cognition in the narrow sense as something that involves the conscious representation of objects through some sort of unification of intuitions and concepts. And, according to Kant, one thing we achieve through this unification is the conscious representation of objects as "really possible." As a reminder, for Kant, a really possible object is one that we can be given, and the concept of a really possible object has objective reality in virtue of relating to an object that we can be given. As we also saw, on his view, intuition, insofar as it gives us objects, plays a key role in putting us in a position to prove the real possibility of objects and, hence, the objective reality of our concepts. While this much should be familiar, what I would now like to add is the idea that Kant accords exhibition, *qua* the activity of "adding" or "appending" intuitions to concepts, a vital role to play vis-à-vis the modal achievement of cognition in the narrow sense.[49]

We find Kant pursuing the connection between exhibition and proof of real possibility in two texts composed around the same time: the third *Critique* and the "What Real Progress" essay.[50] In the third *Critique*, Kant develops this line of thought in §59, which includes one of his most sustained discussions of exhibition. Indeed, it is in §59 that Kant introduces the idea that exhibition involves the "making sensible" (*Versinnlichung*) of concepts through "hypotyposis" or "subjecto sub adspectum" in intuition (KU 5:351). However, he frames this section by claiming that, "To demonstrate the reality of our concepts, intuitions are always required" (KU 5:351). For Kant, then, in order to understand how intuitions demonstrate the objective reality of concepts, we need to situate them in the context of exhibition.

He returns to these issues later in the third *Critique* in his discussion of the anatomist example that I cited above (KU 5:342–3). In this stretch of text,

---

[49] See Rosefeldt (2021) for a discussion of the epistemic contribution our imagination makes to modal knowledge in light of the idea of "exhibition." Watkins (forthcoming) also alludes to the role imagination plays vis-à-vis the proof of real possibility under the heading of the "subjective sources condition" on cognition.

[50] The third *Critique* was first published in 1790 and the "What Real Progress" essay appears to have been composed a couple of years later for submission in an essay contest that the Académie Royal des Sciences et des Belles-Lettres in Berlin announced in 1790 (with a deadline in 1792), though it was only published posthumously in 1804.

120 THREE DEFINITIONS OF IMAGINATION

Kant considers what it means for a concept to be "demonstrable" (KU 5:242). And he distinguishes between two senses of demonstration: demonstration in a "logical" sense that proceeds by way of "propositions" in a proof and demonstration in a more literal sense, where "to demonstrate (*ostendere, exhibere*) means the same as...to exhibit its concept at the same time in intuition" (KU 5:343; transl. modified).[51] Kant introduces the anatomist example to clarify what demonstration in the latter sense involves. And he argues that in order to be in a position to prove that a concept "is not empty, i.e., without any object," this kind of literal demonstration, in which we actively take an intuition to exhibit a concept, is needed (KU 5:243).

In the "Progress" essay Kant pursues a parallel line of thought. Indeed, in the following long passage, he sketches his picture of the relationship between cognition in the narrow sense, the modal achievement, and exhibition:

> As to man..., cognition in him consists of concept and intuition. Each of these two is representation, indeed, but not yet cognition...; for a cognition we in fact require both combined together...[T]he act of appending the intuition to the concept is called...exhibition (*exhibitio*) of the object, without which...there can be no cognition whatever. The possibility of a thought or concept rests on the principle of contradiction...But the thing of which the concept is possible is not on that account a possible thing. The first possibility may be called logical, the second, real possibility; the proof of the latter is the proof of the objective reality of the concept...But it cannot be furnished otherwise than by exhibition of the object corresponding to the concept; for otherwise it always remains a mere thought, of which, until it is displayed in an example, is always uncertain whether any object corresponds to it, or whether it be empty.
>
> (WF 20:325–6; transl. modified)[52]

Kant sets up this passage by indicating that cognition in the narrow sense requires both intuitions and concepts. He then claims that exhibition is required for cognition in the narrow sense. He argues that this is the case because exhibition "displays" to us in intuition that there is an object that corresponds to the concept, and, thereby, enables proof of the real possibility of the object and objective reality of the concept required for cognition in the narrow sense. For example, if I am to have cognition in the narrow sense of dub, then, *per* Kant, I need

---

[51] He sometimes distinguishes logical from literal demonstration in terms of the distinction between "mediate" proof "by means of inferences" and as "immediate" proof by means of "description" (OKT 20:411).

[52] While I have been emphasizing the idea that exhibition involves the exhibition of a concept in intuition, in this passage Kant emphasizes the exhibition of an object that corresponds to the concept. However, I take it that these two ideas come together in cognition in the narrow sense: we exhibit an object that corresponds to a concept by exhibiting a concept in an intuition through which we are conscious of a given object.

THE EXHIBITION DEFINITION   121

to be able to engage in an act of exhibition that displays <dub> to me in an intuition of a really possible object, e.g. a song like "King Tubby Meets Rockers Uptown."

Kant articulates a similar thought earlier in the "Progress" essay in a section titled, "How to Confer Objective Reality on the Pure Concepts of Understanding and Reason" (WF 20:279–80). There, he claims that, "To represent a pure concept of the understanding as thinkable in an object of possible experience is to confer objective reality upon it, and in general to exhibit it. Where we are unable to achieve this, the concept is empty, i.e., suffices for no cognition" (WF 20:279; transl. modified). As in the other "Progress" passage, Kant here indicates that if we are to "confer" objective reality on concepts, here the pure concepts of the understanding, then we need to do so through exhibition of concepts in intuition.[53]

While the details remain to be filled in, what these passages indicate is that, on Kant's view, the modal achievement of cognition in the narrow sense is something that ultimately depends on exhibition. For, according to Kant, in order to demonstrate that a concept has objective reality, hence is a concept of a really possible object, we need to add an intuition to that concept through exhibition.

For Kant, then, exhibition cognitively matters for us not just because it makes our concepts sensible, but also because it provides evidence that our concepts are not empty. Notice that in both cases, exhibition serves us in virtue of cognitive activities that mediate between what is sensible and what is intellectual in some way. And as we now return to the question of the relationship between exhibition and imagination, I hope to show that it is precisely this sort of mediation that Kant thinks imagination, as the distinctive cognitive mediator it is, is uniquely positioned to accomplish.

4.4.2 Exhibition Is an Imaginative Activity

As I noted above, motivation for ascribing to Kant the exhibition definition of imagination stems, in part, from his repeated description of imagination as the "faculty of exhibition" in the third *Critique*. This finds echoes in a *Reflexion* from 1788–90 in which Kant describes exhibition as, "The action of the imagination in giving an intuition for a concept" (R5661 18:320). However, as I also noted, there are at least two reasons to be wary of attributing the exhibition definition of imagination: his comments about the relationship between exhibition and judgment, and concerns about exhibition characterizing some, but not all imaginative acts. I shall now address each of these concerns, in turn, and make the case that we

---

[53] Kant goes on to suggest that it is also possible to confer objective reality on pure concepts of reason in a more attenuated way through a kind of "indirect" exhibition, which I discuss in Chapters 9 and 13.

122 THREE DEFINITIONS OF IMAGINATION

nevertheless have good reason to conceive of imagination, on Kant's view, as the faculty of exhibition.

Beginning with the concerns related to the connection Kant draws between exhibition and the power of judgment, recall his claim that, "If the concept of an object is given, then the business of the power of judgment in using it for cognition consists in **exhibition** (*exhibitio*), i.e., in placing a corresponding intuition beside the concept" (KU 5:192; transl. modified). To repeat the worry: if Kant thinks that the power of judgment can also engage in exhibition, then it does not seem that imagination can be *the* faculty of exhibition on his view.

However, just because exhibition is part of the business of the power of judgment, this does not mean that exhibition is carried out by the power of judgment. This is also consistent with exhibition being something imagination carries out in service of the power of judgment. And what I shall propose is that once we situate Kant's account of exhibition in the context of his overarching view of the cognitive relationship between sensibility and understanding, then we have reason to conceive of exhibition as something the power of judgment demands and imagination executes.

Recall from Chapter 1 that Kant describes a certain functional dynamic between sensibility and understanding in cognition: understanding acts as a "sovereign" power that "rules" sensibility, and sensibility acts as an "executive force" through which the understanding becomes "effective." Bringing this dynamic to bear on the third *Critique*, we can read the power of judgment, *qua* a faculty that belongs to the understanding in "general," as a "sovereign," and imagination, *qua* a faculty that belongs to sensibility, as an "executive."[54] And when we consider exhibition in light of this sovereign-executive relationship, then we have reason to conceive of it as something the power of judgment demands as part of its business and as something that imagination executes in service of that business.

More specifically, on Kant's view, insofar as the power of judgment's business is to think of a particular as contained under a universal, this business requires an act of exhibition to "place a corresponding intuition beside the concept." However, though the power of judgment requires exhibition, Kant continues by suggesting that "placing a corresponding intuition beside the concept" is "done through our own imagination" (KU 5:192–3).[55] What this indicates is that even though Kant

---

[54] Kant uses "understanding" in two senses: first, in the "general" sense to refer to the faculty of thinking in general, and, second, in a "specific" sense to refer to a specific faculty of thinking in general: the "faculty of concepts" (A130–1/B169, see also Anthro. 7:197). Kant distinguishes understanding in the "specific" sense from two other species of the faculty of thinking in general: the power of judgment, *qua* the faculty of judgments, and reason, *qua* the faculty of inference.

[55] More expansively, in this passage Kant says that exhibition is "done through our own imagination, as in art…, or through nature, in its technique (as in the case of organized bodies)" (KU 5:193). However, I take it to be the case that even in the latter context, there is some mental faculty required for exhibiting the concept of purposiveness in an organism, and which, I am claiming, is imagination.

maintains that the power of judgment requires exhibition, he takes imagination to be what executes exhibition, which is precisely what we would expect of it as the executor to the power of judgment's sovereign.

What is more, the sort of relationship between intuitions and concepts involved in exhibition fits better with Kant's account of how our imagination relates to intuitions and concepts than how judgment relates to them. In the context of judgment, Kant tends to characterize the relationship between intuitions and concepts in terms of "subsumption": a judgment is a predicative act in which an intuition is subsumed under concepts (see A132/B171; KU 5:179).[56] For example, when I see a ranunculus and make the judgment, "The ranunculus is burgundy," I engage in a predicative act of thought in which I subsume my intuition under the concepts <ranunculus> and <burgundy>. But the language that Kant uses to describe exhibition does not have the same sort of subsumptive overtones: exhibition, instead, involves "placing" an intuition "beside" a concept and "appending" or "adding" an intuition to a concept. An exhibition of <ranunculus>, for example, involves an intuition that shows or displays this concept in spatio-temporal form. Exhibition thus involves a more complementary relationship between intuitions and concepts in which the two are, in some sense, fitted to one another, rather than a hierarchical relationship in which one is subsumed under the other. And I take it that the imaginative activity of generating an intuition$_i$, which sensibly shows or illustrates a concept *in concreto* is more in keeping with this complementary picture than is the subsumptive profile of judgment.

At this point, though, one might wonder why imagination alone is needed for exhibition; couldn't Kant allow for the other part of sensibility, sense, to execute exhibition? On my interpretation, Kant's account of the sort of activities involved in sense precludes this. At the end of Chapter 3, I argued that, on Kant's view, sensing gives us intuitions$_s$ through processes that are "merely sensible, i.e. nothing but receptivity," and that proceed "independently from" the understanding and concepts (B129; B145). But exhibition does not proceed in a merely receptive, concept-free way for Kant. He, instead, regards exhibition as an activity in which a concept is made sensible in intuition in a way that facilitates our concrete comprehension of that concept internal to our cognitive processes. And given his characterization of imagination as uniquely capable of mediating between intuitions and concepts, he has reason to conceive of exhibition as an "action of the imagination," rather than an action of sense (R5661 18:320).

To piece all this together, and help bring out what is distinctive about what our imagination accomplishes through exhibition that neither the power of judgment

---

[56] Kant speaks of the subsumption of both intuitions under concepts and objects under concepts in judgments (A137–8/B176–7; KU §35; EE 20:212). Though I take these issues to be related, here I am focusing on the former. For discussion of subsumption involving objects, see Longuenesse (1998, 92–7); Stang (2023).

124 THREE DEFINITIONS OF IMAGINATION

nor sense can accomplish, let's return to my quest to learn more about dub. Suppose I am at a party and "King Tubby Meets Rockers Uptown" comes on. I hear the music, but I am like the physician: though I have dutifully learned key marks of <dub> by reading *Can't Stop, Won't Stop*, I fail to hear this song as an instance of <dub>. Though, from a Kantian perspective, this failure manifests, in part, in my inability to make a judgment in which I think of what I hear as falling under the concept <dub>,[57] there is also a failure at the sensible level: I am not hearing it as dub. However, this is not a failure of sense: I sonically sense the song. My sensible failure is different: I am not hearing this song as a sensible rendering of the concept <dub>. And what I am proposing is that, on Kant's view, this sort of sensible failure, which is neither a failure of sense nor a failure of judgment, is a failure of my imagination: my imagination has not made the concept <dub> sensible through the concept-involving process of exhibition.[58]

However, what about the concern that exhibition only characterizes some, but not all, cases of imagining? As I put it above, even if we concede that Kant casts certain imaginative activities like mathematical construction or poetic illustration as involving exhibiting concepts in intuition, why think other imaginative activities like association, hallucination, let alone "ruleless," "self-contradictory," "nonsensical," "lawless" ones, involve exhibition? In order to address this worry, I need to provide a sharper picture of exactly what sort of imaginative activity is involved in exhibition for Kant. And in so doing, I hope to show that although on his view not all imaginative activity involves exhibition, all imaginative activity is oriented toward exhibition, *qua* Kant's standard for what it means for our imagination to function cognitively well.

To clarify Kant's picture of imaginative exhibition let's return to the passages that I cited earlier in which he characterizes it as "placing a corresponding intuition beside the concept," "appending" the intuition to the concept', and "giving an intuition for a concept" (KU 5:192; WF 20:325; R5661 18:320). On the face of it, the language of "placing," "appending," or "giving" an intuition to a concept might invite a view of exhibition as something that involves our imagination tacking an intuition delivered from elsewhere onto a concept. However, as I argued in Chapter 3, on Kant's view, imaginative activity proceeds by way of making intuitions$_i$. Insofar as this is the case, we should expect the intuitions that our imagination places, appends, or gives to a concept in exhibition to be intuitions$_i$ that it makes by taking up representations delivered through receptivity and sensibly ordering and organizing them. And insofar as exhibition involves making concepts sensible, we should expect this imaginative activity to involve ordering

---

[57] As I noted earlier, in his discussion of the physician example Kant diagnoses the problem as a problem with the physician's power of judgment, *qua* a "special talent that cannot be taught but only practiced," and his not having "received adequate training for this judgment through examples" (A133–4/B172–3).

[58] I have more to say about the relationship between sensing, perceiving, and judging in Chapter 5.

and organizing representations into an intuition$_i$ that represents a concept manifesting *in concreto*. For example, the intuition of "King Tubby Meets Rockers Uptown" that exhibits the concept <dub> to me and facilitates my comprehension of this concept is not just the intuition$_s$ I am given when I hear it. It is an intuition$_i$ that my imagination makes by organizing the manifold contained in that intuition$_s$ into a representation of how, say, experimenting with levels, equalizations, and effects sensibly manifest in this track. Hence, at the party when I hear this song, but fail to hear it as dub, this is a sensible failure not of sensing, but rather of me imaginatively failing to make an intuition$_i$ that makes this concept sensible.

With this picture of the imaginative activity of exhibition in place, let's return to the worry that exhibition characterizes some, but not all, imagining. The first point to make is that it is not difficult to think of cases of association and hallucination that involve exhibition: when I associate dub with reggae or hallucinate a ranunculus, the intuitions$_i$ involved exhibit concepts, like <dub>, <reggae>, and <ranunculus>.

But the more substantive proposal that I would like to make is this: the commitment to exhibition being relevant for all imagining is something that follows from Kant's account of the cognitive function of imagination. At the end of Chapter 3, I claimed that, on Kant's view, the cognitive function of our imagination is to make concepts sensible in a way that facilitates our concrete comprehension of them. So understood, making concepts sensible is Kant's standard for what it is for our imagination to function cognitively well. And I suggested that this cognitive function is in keeping with his conception of our imagination as a cognitive capacity that is tasked with mediating between the receptive deliverances of sensibility, on the one hand, and concepts and the understanding, on the other. What I have been arguing in this section is that, for Kant, exhibition just is the activity through which our imagination makes concepts sensible. Insofar as this is the case, in Kant's framework, we can cast the cognitive function of imagination in general in terms of exhibition. So understood, exhibition is not just one activity among others that our imagination can engage in; exhibition is what our imagination does when it is functioning cognitively well. Indeed, as I shall discuss at length in subsequent chapters, it is in exhibition that Kant thinks we engage in imaginative activities that cognitively matter with respect to our basic human need to have concepts rendered in sensible terms, and with respect to our need in the context of cognition in the narrow sense to prove the real possibility of objects and objective reality of concepts.[59] For Kant, then, exhibition serves as the cognitive standard for all imaginative activity, and in this sense, I take it that all imaginative activity is oriented toward exhibition. To be clear, this does not mean that

---

[59] I discuss the ways in which exhibition cognitively matters vis-à-vis this first need throughout the rest of the book and the ways in which it matters vis-à-vis the second need in a theoretical context in Chapter 5 and in a practical context in Chapter 13.

all imaginative acts are acts of exhibition for Kant. He can allow for imaginative acts that do not, in fact, make concepts sensible. However, in these cases, it is not that exhibition is irrelevant; exhibition remains the standard that these imaginative acts fall short of.

Appreciating Kant's commitment to exhibition serving as the standard of cognitively well-functioning imagining has important implications for how we think about the formation and even-without-presence definitions of imagination. For insofar as Kant regards exhibition as the activity that our imagination engages in when it is functioning cognitively well, then we have reason to regard the imaginative activities implicated in the formation and even-without-presence definitions as oriented toward the standard of exhibition. Indeed, attending to this dimension of exhibition is crucial for understanding how the sort of activities at stake in the formation and even-without-presence definitions play a role in our imagination fulfilling its cognitive function in Kant's framework. For what neither of these definitions capture on their own is the sense in which our imagination is cognitively tasked with bridging the gaps between what is sensible and what is conceptual. The formation definition tells us that our imagination engages in the spatio-temporal forming of the receptive deliverances of sensibility, and the even-without-presence definition tells us that our imagination has a degree of independence from the presence of objects and enables us to see more than we are immediately given. However, on Kant's view, though our imagination contributes to cognition through sensory activities such as these, he locates its distinctive cognition function in the way in which its sensory activities mediate between what is sensible and conceptual and, thereby, make concepts sensible. And it is the exhibition definition that captures this distinctive cognitive function of imagination in Kant's framework. So, if we are to understand how the activities at issue in the formation and even-without-presence definitions perform the cognitive function of imagination on Kant's view, then we need to situate them in the context of the exhibition definition.

This is not to say that we should collapse the formation and even-without-presence definitions to the exhibition definition of imagination. The first two definitions highlight features of imaginative activity on Kant's view that are not fully reflected by the exhibition definition. However, I take it that there is a kind of primacy that the exhibition definition has insofar as it articulates Kant's standard for what it means for our imagination to function cognitively well—a standard that the imaginative activities that fall under the formation and even-without-presence definitions are subject to.

This said, attributing to Kant the view that our imagination in general is oriented toward making concepts sensible through exhibition raises the question of how exactly he conceives of the relationship between imagination and concepts. This is a complicated issue. For one thing, Kant discusses a wide range of concepts that can be imaginatively exhibited: empirical concepts, mathematical concepts, pure concepts of the understanding ("the categories"), and pure concepts of reason ("ideas"). For another thing, he describes a range of different kinds of imaginative exhibition of concepts, including "direct" exhibition through "demonstration" and "indirect" exhibition through "symbols" and "analogies" (see KU 5:343, 351–2). Finally, Kant explores various ways in which concepts can figure in imaginative exhibition. Sometimes, he claims, concepts "constrain" how our imagination proceeds, but other times he claims that our imagination proceeds in a "free" and "creative" way that is in "harmony" with concepts (see KU 5:315, 317). What this all suggests is that Kant builds a fair amount of leeway into what the imaginative exhibition of concepts involves. And one of my tasks in Parts II–IV will be to analyze how exhibition operates in different ways across the theoretical, aesthetic, and practical domains. However, as I work through these nuances, one Kantian idea that will remain constant throughout is his commitment to understanding imagination as the faculty of exhibition, which cognitively serves us by facilitating our concrete comprehension of concepts.

4.5 Conclusion

In this chapter, my goal was to bring into sharper focus Kant's account of what imagination is in general in light of his three definitions of imagination as a "faculty of..." To summarize, I claimed that the formation definition clarifies Kant's view of the basic sensible activity and type of intuition$_i$ imagination is responsible for. More specifically, this definition reveals that, according to Kant, imagination spontaneously makes intuitions$_i$ that represent determinate spatio-temporal forms as the result of sensibly ordering and organizing (forming, synthesizing, or composing) a manifold delivered through sensibility. I then argued that the even-without-presence definition reveals Kant's commitment to, one, the presence-independence of imagination: in order to imaginatively represent an object, the object does not need to currently exist and be present to us. And, two, it points toward how our imagination enables us to see more, i.e. to be sensibly aware of more, than we are immediately given through the senses. Finally, I made the case that although it has received less attention, we should acknowledge the exhibition definition as a third Kantian definition of imagination. I argued that this definition sheds light on Kant's conception of imaginative activity as something that makes concepts sensible in a way that facilitates our comprehension of them and why this cognitively matters for us. And though I insisted that all three definitions of imagination are complementary, I maintained that the exhibition definition serves as a kind of anchor in Kant's theory of imagination insofar as it reflects his standard for what it means for our imagination to function cognitively well.

This analysis of the three definitions of imagination brings to a close my interpretation of Kant's theory of what imagination is in general. However, before moving on to a discussion of the various uses to which he thinks we put this capacity, I want to pause and consider the Kantian answer to the question "what is it to imagine" that I have sketched over the course of Part I. As I discussed under the heading of the "unity question" in the Introduction (§0.1), while many contemporary theorists are skeptical that we can give an answer to this question, I intimated there, and have now argued, that Kant offers an answer to this question that turns on a sophisticated analysis of the imagination as a distinctive kind of cognitive capacity and imagining as a distinctive kind of cognitive activity. To summarize, for Kant, to imagine is to exercise a cognitive capacity, which like any cognitive capacity, contributes to our conscious representation of objects. More specifically, I have argued that to imagine is to exercise a cognitive capacity that belongs to sensibility; hence it is to engage in cognitive activities that are sensory, rather than non-sensory, in nature. I have analyzed the sensory nature of what it is to imagine in terms of the way in which imagination realizes the logical, metaphysical, and functional profile of sensibility in a way that is distinct from sense. To this end, I have claimed that to imagine, whether in the presence or absence of objects, involves having intuitions$_i$ even without the presence of objects, which represent determinate spatio-temporal forms, and through which we are able to see more than we are immediately given. I have maintained that these intuitions$_i$ are generated through spontaneous imaginative processes that involve sensibly ordering and organizing a manifold—processes that, though spontaneous, are also constitutively dependent on, and constrained by, the receptivity of sensibility. And I have made the case that when we are functioning cognitively well, to imagine is to engage in mediating activities that result in intuitions$_i$ that exhibit concepts to us in a way that facilitates our concrete comprehension of them.

With this general account of what it is to imagine in place, we are now in a position to explore Kant's analysis of how we use this single capacity, the imagination, in the rich and varied ways we do, across the theoretical, aesthetic, and practical domains.

Seeing More: Kant's Theory of Imagination. Samantha Matherne, Oxford University Press.
© Samantha Matherne 2024. DOI: 10.1093/9780191999291.003.0005

PART II

IMAGINATION IN PERCEPTION AND EXPERIENCE

5

Empirical Imagination in Perception and Experience

> Imagination is a necessary ingredient of perception
> —A120n

5.1 Introduction

Having laid out Kant's theory of what imagination is in general in Part I, my aim in Part II is to explore his analysis of our theoretical (or epistemic)[1] use of it in perception and experience. Appreciating the role that Kant attributes to imagination in this context is especially important for understanding one of the core commitments of his theory of imagination: the pervasiveness of imagination in our lives. As I noted in the Introduction, in contrast with more restrictive views of imagining as a kind of fantasy that we only enact in relation to objects that are not real or not present, Kant takes imagining to be something we do in relation to objects that are very much real and present. And his account of imagination as a "necessary ingredient" of perception and experience is foundational to this more encompassing picture of how imaginative we are.

However, attending to the contribution of imagination in this context is also pivotal for making sense of Kant's theory of experience in the first *Critique*. Sometimes when interpreters explicate this theory, they do so without any explicit reference to imagination, and utilize, instead, the more general framework of "sensibility and understanding" and "intuitions and concepts."[2] Though we certainly cannot navigate Kant's theory of experience without this general

---

[1] As I noted in the Introduction (§0.3.1), I draw the language of the "theoretical" use of imagination from Kant's framing of his interest in "theoretical" cognition in the first *Critique* (see, e.g., Bx, B20, B168), and the language of the "epistemic" use of imagination from contemporary discussions of the role imagining plays in knowledge (see, e.g., Kind and Kung 2016 and Badura and Kind 2021). As I also noted, there are interpretive issues surrounding how to think about the relationship between "cognition" (*Erkenntnis*) and "knowledge" (*Wissen*) on Kant's view that we need to be mindful of when we think about the "epistemic" use of imagining (for discussion, see Chignell 2007a; Cohen 2014; Watkins and Willaschek 2017b; Willaschek and Watkins 2020).

[2] See McDowell (1994); Engstrom (2006); Hanna (2008); Gomes (2014); Watkins (2017); Shaddock (2018).

framework in mind, part of what is distinctive about his theory is his appeal to imagination at pivotal junctures. He, for example, asserts that, "The imagination is a necessary ingredient of perception," and that, "Both extremes, namely sensibility and understanding, must necessarily be connected by...the imagination... since otherwise...there would be no experience" (A120n, A124). If we are to do justice to the content and originality of Kant's view of perception and experience, then we need to address the distinctive contribution that imagination makes in it.

In emphasizing the role of imagination in experience Kant's project finds echoes in contemporary analyses of what imagining contributes to phenomena, such as amodal perception,[3] recognition,[4] and experiencing more as "perceptually present" than we are immediately given.[5] We, moreover, find Kant concerned with issues that are familiar in debates today about how imagining relates to, and differs from, activities like sensing and judging, and about what sort of constraints imagining must be subject to in order to have an epistemic use.[6]

However, Kant's analysis of what imagination does vis-à-vis experience operates on two levels: an empirical and *a priori* level. And once his analysis moves to the *a priori* level, his attention shifts toward issues that are less prominent today, such as how imagination relates to the pure intuitions of space and time and to the pure concepts of the understanding ("the categories"). Needless to say, at the *a priori* level, Kant's analysis unfolds in an abstract way, and it can be difficult to keep track of what purchase this *a priori* edifice has on familiar phenomena like perceiving a flower or experiencing a song. Nevertheless, central to Kant's argument in the first *Critique* is the claim that if we are to make sense of these familiar phenomena, then we need to acknowledge the *a priori* exercise of imagination that enables them.[7]

Understanding Kant's account of the theoretical use of imagination in experience thus calls for attending to both the empirical and *a priori* levels of his analysis and how they relate to one another. In this spirit, I devote the rest of this chapter to laying out Kant's picture of the empirical exercise of imagination in perception and experience, and Chapters 6 and 7 to exploring his *a priori* picture of imaginative activity in the B-edition of the Transcendental Deduction and Schematism chapter of the first *Critique*, respectively. Though this discussion will move in increasingly abstract registers in these latter two chapters, I shall orient it around the question of how Kant thinks the *a priori* exercise of imagination enables the sort of familiar empirical activities that I detail in this chapter.

---

[3] See, e.g., Nanay (2010; 2018a).   [4] See Strawson (1974).
[5] See Noë 2004; Kind 2018.
[6] See, e.g., the essays collected in Kind and Kung (2016); Badura and Kind (2021); and my discussion of this issue in §0.3.1 of the Introduction.
[7] Indeed, Kant takes this to be something that his empiricist predecessors, like Hume, neglect in their account of perception and experience. See Landy (2015, chap. 3) for discussion.

INTRODUCTION 133

In order to clarify Kant's account of what imagination contributes to experience, I anchor my interpretation in the general theory of imagination that I developed in Part I. I thus draw on Kant's account of imagination as a spontaneous part of sensibility that makes intuitions of imagination (intuitions$_i$), and that, in keeping with its mediating character, has the cognitive function of making concepts sensible (see Chapter 3). I also make use of his definitions of imagination as the faculty of formation, faculty for representing objects in intuition even without their presence, and the faculty of exhibition (see Chapter 4).

This said, though attending to these various general features of imagination illuminates Kant's analysis of what imagination does in relation to experience, I mount an argument to the effect that conceiving of imagination as the faculty of exhibition is especially crucial to this end. Recall that, as the faculty of exhibition, Kant construes imagination as a faculty that generates intuitions$_i$ that make concepts sensible and that, thereby, facilitates our concrete comprehension of concepts. Though scant attention has been paid to the role that imaginative exhibition plays in Kant's account of perception, experience, and cognition in the first *Critique*, I submit that it is key to understanding the theoretical use of imagination in this context.[8]

What is more, in stressing the importance of exhibition, I attribute to Kant a conceptually laden picture of what our imagination contributes to experience: our imagination generates intuitions$_i$, at both the empirical and *a priori* level, that make concepts sensible. In developing this line of thought, I defend a so-called "conceptualist" interpretation of the imaginative dimension of experience on Kant's view. This said, the debate about Kant's (non-)conceptualism is vast and I cannot pretend to address its many complexities here.[9] But one central question is whether, in the first *Critique*,[10] Kant commits himself to the view that the generation of intuitions depends on concepts.[11] Over the next three chapters, I mount

---

[8] For example, in their analyses of what imagination does in this context, exhibition is not mentioned: Strawson (1974); Sellars (1978); Young (1988); Pendlebury (1996); Allison (2004, chap. 7); Ginsborg (2008); Land (2014); Merritt and Valaris (2017); and Tolley (2019). However, exhibition is discussed in this context by Ferrarin (1995a), who analyzes it in light of the implications that Kant's theory of mathematical construction has for experience; by Longuenesse (1998, 116–18, pt. III) who addresses it in the context of her interpretation of schematism; and by Rosefeldt (2021) who discusses it in his analysis of Kant's account of the epistemic use of imagination for modal knowledge.

[9] See McLear (2021) for an overview.

[10] I take up questions concerning the relationship between intuitions and concepts in the third *Critique* in Part III.

[11] In the literature, there are various ways in which the conceptualist debate about Kant has been framed, but McLear (2021) has helpfully distinguished between two main frames. In one vein, the vein I shall focus primarily on, the debate can be framed as one about whether the generation of intuitions depends on the intellect. According to the "intellectualist" reading of Kant, "the generation of intuition is at least partly dependent on the intellect," but according to the "sensibilist" reading, "at least some intuitions are generated independently of the intellect itself" (McLear 2021). McLear casts the former as "intellectualism," rather than "conceptualism" in order to accommodate interpretations of Kant, according to which the generation of intuitions does not depend on concepts, but rather on an exercise of the understanding or apperception that does not involve concepts (see, e.g.,

134 EMPIRICAL IMAGINATION IN PERCEPTION AND EXPERIENCE

an argument to the effect that Kant is committed to the generation of intuitions$_i$ in the context of experience, at both the empirical and *a priori* levels, depending on concepts. In this chapter, I make this case with regard to empirical concepts and in the next two chapters with regard to the pure concepts of the understanding ("the categories"). However, I also insist that this does not amount to a commitment to all the intuitions involved in experience depending on concepts for Kant. Instead, in keeping with the bipartite account of sensibility that I defended in Chapter 3, I argue that Kant regards certain intuitions that we are given through sensibility, including empirical intuitions of sense (intuitions$_s$) and the pure intuitions of space and time, as intuitions, the generation of which, does not depend on concepts. By bringing out these non-conceptual and conceptual aspects of Kant's account of intuition, I aim to not only weigh in on the debate about his conceptualism, but also to bolster my case for why we should attribute to him a more sophisticated account of sensibility than he is often credited with.

In this vein in this chapter, my focus is on Kant's account of empirical intuitions and empirical concepts, and whether the generation of the former depends on the latter in the context of perception and experience. Given my bipartite reading of Kant's theory of sensibility, I think we need to distinguish between the question of whether empirical intuitions$_s$ depend on empirical concepts and whether empirical intuitions$_i$ depend on empirical concepts. And I shall argue that while empirical intuitions$_s$ do not depend on empirical concepts, empirical intuitions$_i$ do. In order to make my case, I devote sustained attention to Kant's distinction between sensing and perceiving, where the latter requires imagination as a "necessary ingredient" in the way that the former does not. And I argue that in perception, Kant thinks our imagination generates empirical intuitions$_i$ through a process that involves making concepts sensible through the activity of exhibition. However, I also claim that, for Kant, the role empirical concepts play in the empirical intuitions$_i$ at issue in perception differs from the role that they play in the empirical judgments carried out by the understanding in experience. By

---

Waxman 1991, pt. 1; Longuenesse 1998, chap. 8; Ginsborg 2008; Messina 2014; Friedman 2015; Williams 2018; Indregard 2021; I discuss this in Chapter 6). While I address these latter sorts of intellectualist positions below, I present my own position on this issue as a conceptualist one to the extent that I argue that the imaginative generation of intuitions$_i$ depends on concepts. In a second vein, the debate can be framed as a debate about the conceptual content of intuition, where the "conceptualist" position holds that, "The 'content' (*Inhalt*) of an intuition is conceptual, and constitutes its cognitive relation to a (putatively) mind-independent object," and the "non-conceptualist" position holds that, "The 'content' of an intuition is at least partly nonconceptual, and is sufficient to constitute a cognitive relation to a (putatively) mind-independent object" (McLear 2021). Though I will have things to say about the relationship between concepts and the contents of intuition below, I will not presuppose the contemporary notion of perceptual or representational content as tied to correctness conditions that McLear (2016a; 2016b; 2020a) and Gomes (2017a) worry that this framing anachronistically imports into Kant. I will instead be concerned with content in the sense of what is "in the mind," i.e. with what sort of representations are contained in an intuition (see Siegel 2021 for this as a contrast with contemporary uses of "content"). For an alternative way to frame the debate, see Grüne (2022) who draws on the contemporary debate about "state" versus "content" non-conceptualism.

INTRODUCTION 135

drawing these distinctions, I endeavor to bring to light the subtlety in Kant's position concerning the relationship between empirical intuitions and concepts in the context of experience, which only comes to the fore when we attend to the contribution imagination makes therein.

In order to develop this argument, I begin in §5.2 with a sketch of Kant's technical account of "experience" (*Erfahrung*). There, I argue that Kant defends a three-stage view of experience, according to which the cognitive capacities of sense, imagination, and understanding are each responsible for a distinctive stage of experience. I refer to these as the "sense stage," "imagination stage," and "understanding stage" of experience, respectively. On the interpretation I develop, these three stages should be understood not as aspects of a single conscious episode, but rather as three different conscious states that we can be in, which involve sensing, perceiving, and judging, respectively. And, as I read Kant, the conscious states of sensing and perceiving that occur in the sense and imagination stages are states we can be in prior to, and independently of, the sort of conscious state of judging that occurs in the understanding stage, which is required for full-blown experience in Kant's technical sense.

In developing this interpretation of the three stages of experience, I return to questions that I raised under the heading of the "external taxonomy" question in the Introduction, which concern whether imagining is a *sui generis* mental state (§0.2.2).[12] There, I indicated that, unlike many contemporary theorists, Kant does not distinguish imagining from perceiving, and one of my main aims in this chapter is to lay out his imagination-dependent theory of perception. However, I also continue to explicate why Kant distinguishes imagining from sensing, which I began addressing in Chapter 3, as well as why he distinguishes imagining from judging, which I began addressing in Chapter 4.

Since my primary concern is with the imagination, I orient the rest of the chapter around an analysis of what the imagination stage contributes in the course of experience, and how this differs from what the sense and understanding stages contribute on Kant's view. This will be a lengthy discussion, which I divide between an analysis of what our imagination contributes to perception in §5.3 and to the relationship between the imagination stage and the sense and understanding stages in §§5.4–5.5, respectively.[13]

In §5.3, I argue that the crux of Kant's account of the imagination stage turns on the claim that imagination is a "necessary ingredient of perception" (A120n). I contend that to fully understand the imagination-dependent view of perception

---

[12] As I indicated there, in contemporary discussions, the external taxonomy question is usually framed in terms of the question of how imagining relates to perception, desire, and belief, and I offered an account of how we can map this perception-desire-belief framework onto Kant's theory of mind.

[13] This is, indeed, the longest chapter in the book, and should readers be looking for a place to pause, the transition between §5.3 to §5.4 is a natural place to do so.

he defends in the first *Critique*, we must look not only to the Transcendental Deduction, but also to the Schematism chapter. I claim that when we take the latter into account, we find that Kant is committed to perception involving the imaginative activity of exhibiting concepts in intuition$_i$. I submit that it is through these acts of exhibition that our imagination mediates between sense and concepts, and performs its cognitive function of making concepts sensible in perception. And on the basis of these considerations I attribute to Kant a conceptually laden view of what our imagination contributes to perception, and a conceptualist view of the imaginative generation of intuitions$_i$ in perception as dependent on empirical concepts.

With this analysis of perception in place, I turn to the question of how Kant conceives of the relationship between the imagination stage and the two other stages of experience. In §5.4, I focus on the relationship between the imagination stage and the sense stage. I argue that whereas the imagination stage involves concepts, the sense stage does not. I thus carve out a place for non-conceptual representations in Kant's theory of experience: the empirical intuitions$_s$ produced in the sense stage.[14] And I contrast these intuitions$_s$ with the conceptually dependent intuitions$_i$ involved in the imagination stage. In this section I also analyze what accomplishment vis-à-vis empirical cognition in the narrow sense Kant takes perception to achieve over and above sensing.

Then in §5.5, I address the relation between the imagination stage and understanding stage of experience. I contend that Kant conceives of the understanding stage of experience as something that involves a form of recognition that requires judgment. And I argue that, on his view, although perception, *qua* a form of exhibition involves empirical concepts, it does not involve judgments. I thus conclude that Kant regards the imagination stage of experience as something that occurs independently from the understanding stage of experience, hence judgment, but not independently from empirical concepts.

By the end of this chapter, I aim to have shown how nuanced Kant's theory of experience and perception is, and how attending to imagination as a "necessary ingredient of perception" helps bring out this nuance. Moreover by underscoring the contribution our imagination makes to our experiential encounters with objects that are very much real and present, I hope this discussion sheds light on Kant's commitment to imagining being something that plays a more pervasive role in our lives than traditional accounts of imagination as fantasy acknowledge. However, in order to get a complete picture of what imagination does vis-à-vis experience, we need to shift our focus to the *a priori* level of Kant's analysis, which I shall undertake in Chapters 6 and 7.

---

[14] I reserve questions for how empirical intuitions$_s$, *qua* conscious representations of objects, can be independent from the categories for Chapter 6.

5.2 The Three Stages of Experience

While we often use "experience" to refer to any "lived" or phenomenally conscious episode,[15] Kant has a technical way of characterizing experience: "experience is an empirical cognition [*Erfahrung ist ein empirisches Erkenntnis*]" (B218).[16] More specifically, Kant conceives of experience as involving cognition in the narrow sense, which requires both intuitions and concepts: "all experience contains in addition to the intuition of sense, through which something is given, a **concept** of an object that is given in intuition" (A93/B126).[17] For Kant, then, when I have an experience of a mum, I do not just intuit a flower, nor do I just think about the concept <mum>; I use this concept to think about a flower I intuit.[18]

Recall that, on Kant's view, there are two things that the unification of intuitions and concepts in cognition in the narrow sense enables us to achieve in our conscious representation of objects. The first achievement is what I called the "determinacy achievement": cognition in the narrow sense involves us consciously representing objects as sensibly determinate (e.g. as numerically distinct, as having a determinate spatio-temporal form or mereological structure), and as qualitatively determinate (e.g. as having properties shared by objects of a certain kind). The second achievement is what I called the "modal achievement": cognition in the narrow sense involves us consciously representing objects as really possible; hence as objects that can be given and the concepts of which, are not empty, but rather have objective reality. So, when Kant glosses experience as cognition in the narrow sense, he commits himself to the view that experience involves the unification of intuitions and concepts in a way that enables us to consciously represent objects as determinate and really possible.

However, Kant does not just gloss experience as "cognition," but as "empirical" cognition, and he does so because he takes it to involve the unification of empirical intuitions and empirical concepts. More specifically, as we saw above, Kant claims that experience "contains...intuitions of the senses"; hence it must involve empirical intuitions$_S$. Meanwhile, the need for empirical concepts of objects, i.e. concepts "drawn from" experience,[19] is not something that Kant makes fully

---

[15] Often in the phenomenological tradition, the term "Erlebnis," rather than "Erfahrung" is used to refer to "lived experience."

[16] See also B147, B165–6, B234, B277; Anthro. 7:144; EE 20:203. See Chapter 1 for discussion of cognition in the "narrow" and "broad" sense on Kant's view.

[17] See also his claim that, "we cannot **cognize** any object that is thought except through intuitions that correspond to those concepts. Now all our intuitions are sensible, and this cognition, so far as its object is given is, empirical. Empirical cognition, however, is experience" (B165–6).

[18] I thus attribute to Kant a view of experience as something that happens in our everyday lives, rather than a view of experience as tantamount to the experience involved in mathematical-natural science as the Marburg-Neo-Kantians, like Hermann Cohen, Paul Natorp, and Ernst Cassirer do (for discussion, see Richardson 2003).

[19] See A23/B38; A30/B46.

138 EMPIRICAL IMAGINATION IN PERCEPTION AND EXPERIENCE

explicit until the third *Critique*.[20] There, Kant makes clear that in experience we do not represent objects as "things of nature in general"; we represent objects "specifically, as such and such particular beings in nature" (KU 5:183).[21] On his view, in order to represent objects "specifically," we cannot just rely on *a priori* concepts of objects, like <substance> and <cause>; we need empirical concepts of objects, like <flower> or <photosynthesis>. For Kant, then, experience is empirical cognition that involves using empirical concepts to think about the objects we empirically intuit through the senses.

But what exactly does the unification of empirical intuitions and empirical concepts in experience involve on Kant's view? Does Kant conceive of this as a process in which we, in some sense, hold an isolable intuition and concept together? Kant's language of "subsuming" intuitions under concepts might seem to suggest this model (see A137/B176; KU 5:287). Or does Kant think that experience involves a process through which intuitions are somehow transformed to align with concepts?

As an initial piece of evidence in favor of the transformative model, consider the following remark Kant makes in a letter to Jacob Sigismund Beck in 1792:

> Two sorts of representations are needed for cognition: 1) intuition, by means of which an object is given, 2) concept, by means of which it is thought. To make a single cognition out of these two *pieces of cognition* [*Erkenntnisstücke*] a further activity is required: the composition [*zusammenzusetzen*] of the *manifold given in intuition*. (Br. 11:315–16)

Here, Kant suggests that cognition does not just involve holding together an intuition and a concept; it involves "making" a "single cognition" out of these two representations through some cognitive process in which the manifold given in intuition is "composed" in a certain way.

In what follows, I argue that Kant offers an elaborate story of the sort of transformation required for experience, which I articulate in terms of the three stages of experience: the "sense stage," "imagination stage," and "understanding stage."[22]

---

[20] Kant seems to make an oblique reference to the need for empirical concepts at the end of both Deductions, where he indicates that the categories can only give us laws for "nature in general," and that "particular laws" that "**cannot** be **completely derived** from the categories" are also needed for experience of particular objects in nature (B165; see also A127–8).

[21] For discussion, see Allison (2001, 20).

[22] My three-stage reading of experience differs from the two-phase reading offered by Horstmann, according to which experience involves a first phase in which intuitions are generated from sensations through an imaginative activity that is not constrained by the understanding or concepts, and a second phase in which cognitions are generated from intuitions on the basis of imaginative activity that is constrained by the understanding (2018, 27, 31–5, 42–3). By contrast, I not only read Kant as acknowledging three stages of experience, rather than two, but also I argue that in the sense stage Kant allows for the senses to generate empirical intuitions$_s$ prior to the involvement of the imagination, and

THE THREE STAGES OF EXPERIENCE   139

I shall argue that each stage involves a different kind of conscious cognitive state that we can have in relation to objects: sensing, perceiving, and judging. I shall also claim that, for Kant, we only arrive at experience of objects in the full-blown sense through judgment at the understanding stage, although we can be in the cognitive states of sensing and perceiving prior to this. And it is in terms of a progression through these three stages that I shall analyze the transformative picture of experience that Kant offers us in the first *Critique*—a picture in which the mediating activities of imagination have a central role to play.

While a full defense of this picture will require the rest of this chapter, let me begin by motivating why we should think of these three stages as separable conscious states by returning to the example of listening to "King Tubby Meets Rockers Uptown" that I offered in Chapter 3. In order to have an experience of this song in Kant's technical sense, I need to be able to think about what I hear as an instance of some empirical concept like <dub>. But remember that in this example, when this track comes on at a party, though I listen to the music, I fail to identify it as an instance of <dub>. Recall, however, that I suggested that there are two ways in which I fail to identify the song as an instance of <dub>. On the one hand, I intellectually fail: I am unable to judge that the track is dub. On the other hand, I perceptually fail: I am unable to hear the track as dub. In Kant's framework, then, we can distinguish between three different ways I might relate to this song in the course of experience: I might sense it without the concept <dub> being involved; I might perceive it as an instance of <dub>; or I might judge it as an instance of <dub>. And in the party scenario, though I relate to the song in the first way, I fail to relate to it in the latter two ways. What I now hope to show is that Kant's account of the three stages of experience reflects this range of experiential possibilities. Indeed, by exploring these three stages, I aim to shed light not only on Kant's taxonomy of sensing, imagining, and judging, but also on his recognition that we have multiple ways of being conscious of objects in the experiential context.

Since my primary concern is with imagination, what is of particular interest to me is how Kant conceives of the imagination stage of experience. So, in what follows, I shall focus on the following three questions that pivot around this stage. What does Kant mean by perception and why is imagination a "necessary ingredient of it" (§5.3)? How does imagination interact with the sense stage and what does perception add to experience over and above the empirical intuitions of sense (§5.4)? And how does the imagination stage relate to the understanding stage: does perception involve the sort of judgments at stake in the understanding stage (§5.5)?

---

that in the imagination stage he thinks the generation of intuitions; through imaginative synthesis in perception depends on empirical concepts.

5.3 Imagination Is a Necessary Ingredient of Perception

5.3.1 Perception

In order to begin exploring Kant's account of the imagination stage of experience, let's take a closer look at what he means by "perception."[23] At the outset, it should be noted that Kant does not appear to have an entirely consistent account of perception.[24] There are two terms in the first *Critique* that are translated as "perception": "Perception" and "Wahrnehmung." "Perception" does not appear frequently, and Kant uses it to refer to "a representation with consciousness" (A320/B376). He identifies "sensations," "intuitions," and "concepts" as instances of *Perception* in this sense (A320/B376).[25]

The term "Wahrnehmung" appears more frequently, e.g. in the Transcendental Deduction, the Anticipations of Perception, and the Analogies. But here too Kant does not use "Wahrnehmung" in an entirely consistent way. Sometimes Kant aligns *Wahrnehmung* with sense. In the A Deduction, for example, he says that, "**Sense** represents the appearances empirically in **perception** [*Wahrnehmung*]" (A115). And he indicates that perceptions are part of a manifold of empirical intuition$_s$: "every appearance contains a manifold, thus different perceptions [*Wahrnehmungen*] by themselves are encountered dispersed and separate in the mind" (A120; see also B422–3n).

However, at other times, Kant insists that *Wahrnehmung* involves empirical consciousness *of* an intuition$_s$. In this vein in the B Deduction, Kant asserts, "by the **synthesis of apprehension** I understand the composition [*Zusammensetzung*] of the manifold in an empirical intuition through which perception [*Wahrnehmung*], i.e., empirical consciousness of it…, becomes possible" (B160).[26] In this passage, Kant indicates that perception is not a matter of being given a manifold of intuition through the senses, but rather of consciously "apprehending" that manifold through "synthesis." Though both apprehension and consciousness play an important role in Kant's account of this kind of perception, I shall focus on the former because this is what he credits to imagination.[27] Indeed, it is in service of explicating the role apprehension plays in perception that Kant

---

[23] See McLear (2016b) for discussion of how Kant's account of perception differs from contemporary theories of perception, particularly on the issue of perceptual content.

[24] For discussion of the ambiguity in Kant's use of "perception," see Longuenesse (1998, 219–20 fn 14); McLear (2014); Tolley (2017; 2020); Horstmann (2018, 50–1).

[25] See also his gloss of perception as "sensation of which one is conscious" (A225/B272).

[26] See also his claim that perception requires that we, in some sense, "make the empirical intuition…into perception through apprehension of its manifold" (B162). I take these passages to count against Horstmann's reading of Kant's view, according to which we only arrive at an intuition as the result of our imagination taking up "perceptions" (2018, 19–20, 31, 38).

[27] Kant's account of the consciousness of empirical intuition is ultimately bound up with his account of apperception and self-consciousness, which is, of course, a central topic in the Deduction, but which I shall not address here. For discussion, see Kitcher (2011); Kraus (2019; 2020, pt. I); Sethi (2021).

IMAGINATION IS A NECESSARY INGREDIENT OF PERCEPTION 141

claims, "No psychologist has yet thought that the imagination is a necessary ingredient of perception [*Wahrnehmung*] itself...for which without doubt something more than the receptivity of impressions is required, namely a function of the synthesis of them" (A120fn).[28] And it is *Wahrnehmung* in this imagination-dependent sense that I refer to as "perception" in what follows.

In order to work through the details of the role Kant attributes to imagination in perception, let's continue with the "necessary ingredient" passage:

> No psychologist has yet thought that the imagination is a necessary ingredient of perception itself. This is so partly because...it has been believed that the senses do not merely afford us impressions but also put them together, and produce *images* of objects, for which without doubt something more than the receptivity of impressions is required, namely a function of the *synthesis* of them.
> (A120fn; my emph.)

Here, Kant highlights two features of perception in the imagination-dependent sense. First, as I have just emphasized, he denies that perception is a passive affair of sense. Instead, Kant insists that perception involves our imagination actively taking up a manifold of intuition$_s$ through synthesis. Second, as the full quote reveals, he regards perception as something that involves a certain kind of representation, which he calls an "image" (*Bild*). Hence Kant's claim that in perception, "the imagination is to bring the manifold of intuition into an **image**" (A120). Recall that, on my reading of Kant, since imagination is part of sensibility, we have reason to conceive of all its representations as intuitions$_i$. I thus understand images, for Kant, to be a particular type of intuition$_i$. Taking these two claims together, on Kant's view, perception in the imagination-dependent sense is a site of transformation in the experiential process in which our imagination generates an intuition$_i$, an image, as the result of synthesizing an intuition$_s$.[29]

While this imagination-dependent picture of perception is the one that we find in the Transcendental Deduction, in what follows, I argue that Kant augments his account of it in significant ways in the Schematism chapter in the first *Critique*. More specifically, I contend that to fully understand Kant's view of perception, we need to take into account his theory of schemata and his claim that "the schema...[is that] through which and in accordance with which the images

---

[28] See also Kant's remark in the Analogies that, when "I perceive that appearances succeed one another...I really connect two perceptions in time," and "connection is not the work of mere sense and intuition, but is rather the product of a synthetic faculty of the imagination" (B233), and his remark in the B Deduction that, "that which connects the manifold of sensible intuition is imagination" (B164).

[29] Insofar as I take this passage to point toward images having a central role to play in Kant's theory of perception, I disagree with Young (1988) and Allison (2004, 188–90) who deny to images such a role. For other discussion of Kant's theory of perception that emphasize the role of images, see Sellars (1978); Kitcher (1990, chap. 6); Matherne (2015); Tolley (2019).

142 EMPIRICAL IMAGINATION IN PERCEPTION AND EXPERIENCE

[*die Bilder*] first become possible" (A142/B181). I accordingly explore Kant's account of perception and the imagination stage of experience in light of his account of the role that images (5.3.2), imaginative synthesis (5.3.3), and schemata play in it (5.3.4).[30] And it is in this last sub-section that I make the case that Kant ultimately conceives of the imagination's contribution to perception in the conceptually laden terms of exhibition.

5.3.2 Perceptual Images

Although Kant sometimes uses "image" to refer to representations of imagination in general, in the context of perception he is concerned with a particular type of image: an image our imagination generates of an object that is present to us and currently affecting our senses (see Chapter 3).[31] Call this a "perceptual image." Though the language of an "image" might suggest that these representations are visual in character, Kant uses "image" in a wide enough way to include representations from other sense modalities. For Kant, a sensible representation of a song I hear can thus count as a perceptual image just as much as a sensible representation of a flower I see can.

We find one of Kant's most helpful accounts of perceptual images in the early Metaphysics L1 Lectures. Recall that during this period, Kant's general term for imagination is the "faculty of formation" (*Bildungsvermögen*), and that he describes formation as a spontaneous activity through which imagination makes intuitions$_i$ by spatio-temporally organizing the receptive deliverances of sensibility (see Chapter 4). When this formative activity is directed toward objects that are present to us, Kant describes it as "illustration" (*Abbildung*) (ML1 28:235).[32] And the result of this illustrative activity, he claims, is an "image of the manifold"; hence what I have labeled a "perceptual image" (ML1 28:235).

Kant describes the perceptual process of forming images through illustration as follows,

> My mind is always busy with forming the image of the manifold while it goes through [it]. E.g., when I see a city, the mind then forms an image of the object which it has before it while it runs through the manifold...This illustrative [*abbildende*] faculty is the formative faculty of intuition. The mind must undertake many observations in order to illustrate [*abzubilden*] an object so that it

---

[30] Here, I further develop the account of perception I advance in Matherne (2015).

[31] In the ML1 lectures, for example, Kant explicitly claims that the images produced in perception are of objects that are currently "present" to us, and contrasts them with images of objects from the "past" and "future" (ML1 28:235–6; see also AF 25:511).

[32] When it is exercised in relation to objects that are past, he calls it the faculty of "imitation" (*Nachbildung*), and when related to the future, he calls it the faculty of "anticipation" (*Vorbildung*) (ML1 28:235).

IMAGINATION IS A NECESSARY INGREDIENT OF PERCEPTION 143

illustrates the object differently from each side. E.g., a city appears differently from the east than from the west. There are thus many appearances of a matter according to the various sides and points of view. The mind must make an illustration [*Abbildung*] from all these appearances by taking them all together.

(ML1 28:235–6)

As this passage suggests, on Kant's view, when our senses are causally affected by an object, this gives rise to a manifold of intuition$_s$ in us, which includes a multiplicity of representations of an object from "various sides and points of view." He then characterizes illustration as an activity in which our imagination "runs through" these multiple representations and "takes them all together" in a way that results in a perceptual image that illustrates the object as a whole from multiple sides and points of view.[33] For example, suppose someone walks across the room and hands me a yellow mum. As this happens, my senses generate a manifold of empirical intuition$_s$ in me, which includes representations of the yellow petals, a thin green stem, alternating green leaves, etc., from across the room and in hand. But according to Kant, in order to perceive the mum, my imagination needs to actively "run through" and "take together" these representations in order to generate a perceptual image that illustrates the mum as a whole from these different sides and points of view.

As we now turn to Kant's account of perceptual images in the first *Critique*, though his view of imagination has certainly undergone important shifts,[34] I aim to show that he retains this basic picture of perception as something that involves our imagination generating a perceptual image that represents an object from multiple sides and points of view, as a result of "running through" and "taking together" a manifold of intuition$_s$ delivered through the senses.

5.3.3 Synthesis and Perceptual Images

Let's return to Kant's account of imagination as a necessary ingredient of perception in the Transcendental Deduction. Though he also addresses this topic in the B Deduction (e.g. §26), since he offers a more detailed analysis of it in his discussion of the so-called "threefold synthesis" in the A Deduction, the latter shall be my focus here (A97).[35] As we shall see, though he remains committed to

---

[33] In Matherne (2015) I describe this as a "phenomenological" view of images as complex, holistic representations of an object from multiple spatio-temporal perspectives, and I contrast it with a "snapshot" view of images, as a representation that captures only a single spatio-temporal instance.

[34] For discussion of these shifts, see Chapter 4.

[35] There is some question as to whether Kant changes his views about imagination between the A and B Deductions, especially with regard to whether he in the B Deduction denies to imagination an independence from the understanding that he granted it in the A Deduction (see Heidegger KPM §31; Bennett 1966, 134–8; Kitcher 1990, 158–60; Longuenesse 1998, 204–8; Allison 2001, 186–9;

144 EMPIRICAL IMAGINATION IN PERCEPTION AND EXPERIENCE

perception involving perceptual images, he refines his pre-Critical analysis of the sort of spontaneous imaginative activities required for image formation with an account of two empirical forms of imaginative synthesis: the synthesis of apprehension and reproduction.

Kant describes the synthesis of apprehension in language reminiscent of the Metaphysics lectures: in apprehension imagination is "to run through [*Durchlaufen*] and then to take together [*Zusammennehmung*]" a manifold of intuition$_s$ (A99).[36] Kant tends to emphasize this point with respect to the "succession" of a manifold, his idea being that we need to take up a manifold of intuition$_s$ as it unfolds over time (see A99).[37] As he puts it in the third *Critique*, apprehension is something that "proceeds merely progressively," by taking up the manifold as it temporally develops (KU 5:254). For example, *per* Kant, as I track the mum as someone carries it across the room, my imagination "takes up" the representations of it from far and near. Or to take a non-visual example, as I listen to Mariah Carey's "Fantasy," my imagination "takes up" the representations of the notes as they unfold over its 4' 03".

By contrast, Kant claims that the synthesis of reproduction is something that operates retrospectively: it "call[s] back" representations that have passed (A121). For example, by the time I hold the mum in hand, the synthesis of reproduction calls back representations of it from across the room, just as when I get to the final chorus of "Fantasy," the synthesis of reproduction calls back representations of the opening verse. *Per* Kant, reproduction is governed by the law of association, according to which we associate representations together "that have often followed or accompanied one another" (A100).[38]

In perception, Kant claims that apprehension and reproduction work together in order to produce a perceptual image:

Horstmann 2018, pt. 1). For reasons I offered in Chapter 3 and will continue to discuss in Chapter 6, I do not think Kant changes his mind regarding the status of imagination in the B Deduction: it remains something that "belongs to **sensibility**" (B151). For my purposes in this chapter, however, I proceed under the assumption that Kant's account of the empirical activities of imagination in perception are consistent across the A and B Deductions.

[36] Although Kant often attributes apprehension to imagination (see B164, B233, B257; KU 5:251–4), in his summary of the threefold synthesis, he says, "**Sense** represents the appearances empirically in **perception**, the **imagination** in association (and reproduction)" (A115), which some take to mean that he thinks apprehension falls to sense (see, e.g., Hughes 2007, 122–6). However, this reading saddles Kant with an empiricist view of imagination as "limited to reproduction" that he rejects (A120n). It also conflicts with Kant's insistence beginning in the Metaphysical Deduction and continuing throughout the Analytic that the senses, *qua* something receptive, provide a manifold, and imagination, *qua* something spontaneous, synthesizes that manifold (A78–9/B103–4; A94, A120n; B151; A155/B194).

[37] See Chapter 7 for an argument to the effect that Kant also allows for apprehension to involve the imaginative synthesis of a single "moment" or "instant" (*Augenblick*).

[38] See Chapter 3 for a discussion of reproductive imagination and the law of association.

IMAGINATION IS A NECESSARY INGREDIENT OF PERCEPTION 145

> There is thus an active faculty of the synthesis of this manifold in us, which we call imagination...For the imagination to bring the manifold into an image; it must therefore...apprehend [impressions]. It is, however, clear that even this apprehension of the manifold alone would bring forth no image...were there not...a reproductive faculty of the imagination. (A120–1)[39]

According to Kant, apprehension and reproduction are "inseparably combined" in the perceptual process because in order to form a perceptual image of an object that represents it from multiple sides and points of view, we need to both take up representations of the object as they unfold and hold on to the prior representations of the object as we move forward in our apprehension (A102). Emphasizing the importance of reproduction to this end, Kant says, "if I were always to lose the preceding representations...from my thoughts and not reproduce them when I proceed to the following ones, then no whole representation...could ever arise" (A102).[40] For example, suppose I am looking attentively at a mum. If by the time I am looking at the base of the stem of the mum, I no longer retain any representations of the yellow petals at the top, then I am not able to form a "whole representation," i.e. a perceptual image the represents the mum as a whole. So too in the case of "Fantasy," if by the end of the 4' 03". I do not retain representations of the preceding parts of the song, then I will not be able to form a perceptual image of the song as a whole. For Kant, then, to form a perceptual image, a representation of "the many in one intuition," then our imagination needs to engage in the synthesis of both apprehension and reproduction (KU 5:254).

We can flesh out the details of the process of perceptual image formation through synthesis by bringing to bear Kant's definitions of imagination in general (see Chapter 4). Beginning with the formation definition, recall that as the faculty of formation imagination makes intuitions$_i$ that represent determinate spatio-temporal forms, like shapes or temporal series, as a result of spatio-temporally ordering and organizing the manifold of intuition$_s$. Applying this to his account of perception, on Kant's view, through the syntheses of apprehension and reproduction we imaginatively order and organize a manifold of empirical intuition$_s$ that contains representations of different aspects of an object, the result being an empirical intuition$_i$ (a perceptual image), that represents those aspects organized into a determinate spatio-temporal form. When I look at the mum, for example, I will have a manifold of representations of different parts of it, including its yellow petals, green stem, alternating leaves, etc. Through the syntheses of

---

[39] I thus disagree with Waxman's (1991, pt. II) treatment of apprehension, rather than reproduction, as the synthesis required for perception.

[40] I take this "whole representation" to coincide with what Kant refers to as "**one representation**" in his discussion of apprehension (A99). Although in the first *Critique*, Kant does not have a label for the imaginative act through which we produce a holistic representation, in the third *Critique* he labels it "aesthetic comprehension [*Zusammenfassung*] [*comprehensio aesthetica*]" (KU 5:252).

apprehension and reproduction, my imagination organizes this manifold in a way that results in an empirical intuition$_i$ (a perceptual image) that represents the mum as a determinate spatial whole that includes the petals, stem, and leaves as its parts. Likewise, with "Fantasy," my imagination generates a perceptual image of this song as a whole by synthesizing together, through apprehension and reproduction, the manifold of representations that arises in me as I listen to the notes, beginning to end.

It is also helpful to think about perception through the lens of the even-without-presence definition of imagination. Recall that, *per* this definition, imagination generates intuitions$_i$ with a degree of independence from objects and enables us to see more than is immediately affecting our senses at any given moment. In perception, the presence-independence of imagination manifests not in our imagination representing an object that is wholly absent, as it does in, say, memory or anticipation, but rather in our imagination perceptually representing parts of the object we perceive that are not immediately affecting our senses. And as a result we are able to see more, i.e. be sensorily aware of more, of an object as "perceptually present" than is immediately given to us.[41] For example, after I put the mum in a vase, even though its stem is no longer in view, I still amodally perceive it as having a stem.[42] And, on Kant's view, this involves my imagination generating a perceptual image through which I am sensorily aware of the mum as a whole with present parts, such as the stem, now occluded from my view. For Kant, then, in the perceptual context, we need imagination to represent objects "even without their presence," not because the objects are absent, but rather because we need imagination to fill out our representation of the objects that are present in a way that extends our sight beyond what is immediately affecting our senses.

But what of the exhibition definition of imagination? Nothing that I have said so far commits Kant to the view that image formation and synthesis in perception ultimately involve our imagination exhibiting concepts in intuition$_i$. However, what I shall now argue is that Kant does not complete his account of what our imagination contributes to perception until the Schematism chapter of the first *Critique*, and that once we look to that text, we find him glossing this contribution ultimately in terms of the imaginative exhibition of concepts.[43]

---

[41] As I note in Chapter 4, the description of this phenomenon in terms of "perceptual presence" is one I draw from Noë (2004). For further discussion of how Kant's view bears on explicating perceptual presence, see Sellars (1978); Thomas (2010); Matherne (2015); and Kind (2018).

[42] For recent discussions of the role imagination plays in amodal perception, see Nanay (2010; 2018a).

[43] For analyses of Kant's theory of perception that do not take the Schematism into account, see, e.g., Rohs (2001); Wenzel (2005); Ginsborg (2008); Hanna (2008); Griffith (2012); and Allais (2015). Exceptions include Paton (1936), Sellars (1978), and Longuenesse (1998; 2005, chap. 1) (I return to how my reading of the Schematism and its role in perception differs from hers below).

5.3.4 Perception and Schematism

In the Schematism chapter, Kant introduces a distinctive "product of imagination" that he labels a "schema" (*Schema*) (A140/B179). Though schemata serve different functions on his view,[44] what is relevant for our purposes here is the role they play in perception. As I noted above, in the Schematism, Kant claims that, "the **schema**...[is that] through which and in accordance with which the images [*die Bilder*] first become possible" (A142/B181). What this suggests is that if we are to understand the sort of image formation involved in perception, then we need to take schemata into account. When we do so, I submit, we shall discover that Kant understands perception to be a conceptually laden process. More specifically, I argue that we discover perception to be a process in which imaginative synthesis is guided by empirical concepts and that results in empirical intuitions$_i$, viz. perceptual images, that exhibit empirical concepts. However, before we can consider the role they play in perception, we need to spend some time exploring Kant's theory of schemata.

5.3.4(a) Schemata

Kant introduces his theory of schemata in the first *Critique* as part of the "Transcendental Doctrine of the Power of Judgment (or Analytic of Principles)" (A137/B17–A147/B187). Kant organizes the Schematism chapter around the question of how it is possible to "subsume" an intuition under a concept in judgment (A137/B176).[45] When we subsume an intuition under a concept in a judgment, Kant claims that we think of the object we intuit as "contained under a concept," e.g. when I judge that the flower I intuit falls under the concept <mum> (A137/B176). According to Kant, in order to subsume intuitions under concepts in judgment there must be something "homogeneous" between the two representations (A137/B176). That is to say, the content of the intuition must, in some sense, correspond to the content of the concept. For example, if I am to subsume my empirical intuition of a mum under the concept <mum>, then there needs to be something in that intuition that maps onto marks, like <having alternate leaves>, <oval-shaped>, <fuzzy-stemmed>, etc.

However, given Kant's dichotomous treatment of intuitions and concepts, it is not entirely clear how the two could ever be "homogeneous." As he makes this point about pure concepts of the understanding ("the categories") and empirical

---

[44] Kant, for example, accords schemata an important role in his theory of mathematics and mathematical construction (see Young 1982; 1984; Friedman 1990; 2015; Longuenesse 1998, chap. 9; Ferrarin 1995a; Domski 2010; Dunlop 2012; Sutherland 2022, chap. 3).

[45] This is why in the Schematism, Kant talks about both subsuming intuitions under concepts and subsuming objects under concepts. See Stang (2023) for a helpful discussion of the different notions of subsumption at issue in the Schematism. Given my interest here, however, my focus shall be on the issue of subsuming intuitions under concepts.

148 EMPIRICAL IMAGINATION IN PERCEPTION AND EXPERIENCE

intuitions: "pure concepts of the understanding...in comparison with empirical...
intuitions, are entirely unhomogeneous...Now how is the **subsumption** of the
latter under the former...possible" (A137/B176)? Though the categories, *qua*
pure, are unhomogeneous with empirical intuitions, *qua* empirical, the worry
about homogeneity is more general than this pure-empirical mismatch.[46] Given
Kant's characterization of intuitions as sensible, singular representations that
immediately relate to objects and concepts being intellectual, general representations that mediately relate to objects, there is a question of how we can ever subsume the former under the latter, even if the intuitions and concepts at stake are
empirical in kind.[47]

It is as part of his effort to explain how such subsumption is nevertheless possible that Kant introduces his theory of schemata. Kant's basic idea is that in order
for subsumption to be possible, we need a "third thing [*ein Drittes*]," a "mediating
representation," that is at once "sensible" and "intellectual" that can bridge the gap
between intuitions and concepts (A138/B177). This "third thing" is the "product
of imagination" that Kant labels a "schema" (A140/B179). And in order to clarify
his account of a schema, I shall briefly look at its sensible and intellectual features,
in turn, before addressing his characterization of them as a kind of imaginative
exhibition of concepts.

Beginning with the sensible features of a schema, as I just noted, Kant describes
a schema as a "product of imagination." I have argued that insofar as imagination
is part of sensibility, we have reason to identify all of its representations as intu-
itions$_i$. I take this to be why he refers to schemata as intuitions in the second and
third *Critiques*.[48]

This said, in the Schematism, Kant also distinguishes the sort of intuition$_i$
involved in a schema from the sort involved in an image. According to Kant,
whereas an image represents a particular, insofar as a schema needs to be homogeneous with concepts, then it must involve some sort of "generality": "No image
of a triangle would ever be adequate to the concept of it. For it would not attain
the generality of the concept, which makes this valid for all triangles, right or
acute, etc., but would always be limited to one part of this sphere" (A141/B180).
The fact that Kant describes a schema both as an intuition$_i$ and as involving

---

[46] I thus disagree with Walsh (1957/8), Chipman (1972), and Pippin (1976) who take this worry to
only apply in the pure case.
[47] See, e.g., his claim that "concepts and sensible intuition" are "two heterogeneous elements"
(KU 5:401).
[48] See, e.g., his description of schemata for the categories as "intuitions to which pure concepts of
the understanding could be applied, and...can be given a priori" (KpV 5:68); "To demonstrate the
reality of our concepts, intuitions are always required...If they are pure concepts of the understanding, then the latter are called **schemata**" (KU 5:351), and "All intuitions that are ascribed to concepts
a priori are thus either **schemata** or **symbols**" (KU 5:352). More elliptically in the "Progress" essay,
he says, "If objective reality is accorded to the concept directly (*directe*) through the intuition that
corresponds to it...this act is called schematism" (WF 20:279).

generality is surprising. As we have seen, Kant frequently insists that generality is a feature of concepts, rather than intuitions. However, what his theory of schemata reveals is that in the case of a schema, we have an intuition$_i$ that "attains the generality of a concept." But one wonders, what could this generality of a schematic intuition$_i$ amount to?

In the Schematism, Kant's analysis of the generality of a schema turns on an account of it being a kind of rule. More specifically, he claims that a schema involves "a rule of the synthesis of imagination," and "a rule for the determination of our intuition in accordance with a certain general concept" (A141/B180). Kant thus conceives of a schema as a rule that guides our imagination in synthesizing a manifold of intuition in accordance with a concept. What I take this to mean is that a schema provides us with a rule that guides us in synthesizing representations in a manifold that belong together insofar as they accord with a certain concept in distinction from other representations. For example, when I look at the mum in the vase, my manifold of intuition$_s$ will include representations not just of various parts of the mum, but also of the vase, the table it sits upon, and the background of my living room. For Kant, my mum-schema serves as a rule that guides my imagination in synthesizing the mum representations in this manifold together in distinction from the non-mum representations. And when I imaginatively synthesize my representations in this way, per Kant, I "determine" my intuition "in accordance with a certain general concept," the concept <mum>.

But how can the intuition$_i$ involved in a schema serve as such a rule? In order to answer this question, we need to take a closer look at the content of a schema. And what I now hope to show is that Kant understands the content of a schema in terms of an intuition$_i$ that sensibly exhibits a concept.

In the third *Critique* Kant explicitly describes the intuitions$_i$ involved in schemata as exhibitions (KU §59). In his words, schematic intuitions involve the "**hypotyposis** (exhibition, *subjecto sub adspecctum*)" and "making-sensible [*Versinnlichung*]" of a concept (KU 5:351; transl. modified). More specifically, Kant claims that the intuition$_i$ involved in a schema is one that "directly" exhibits a concept in sensible form (KU 5:352). That is to say, the sensible content of a schema "corresponds" to the logical content of a concept, i.e. the "marks" it contains (KU 5:351).[49] For example, the schema of a mum contains sensible representations that directly exhibit the marks contained in the concept <mum>, like <having alternate leaves>, <oval-shaped>, <fuzzy-stemmed>, etc.[50]

---

[49] As Stang (2023) points out, in the case of organisms, like a flower or animal, Kant's account of their schemata will be complicated by the claim he introduces in the third *Critique* to the effect that we represent organisms as having an internally purposive structure. Though important I shall set this complication aside here.

[50] One way to understand these sensible representations is as "intuitive marks" (R 2286 16:299–300). For discussion, see Smit (2000) and Stang (2023, §2.1).

150 EMPIRICAL IMAGINATION IN PERCEPTION AND EXPERIENCE

Kant, furthermore, indicates that the intuition_i involved in a schema directly exhibits how the marks contained in a concept show up together as a whole. Hence his description of a schema as an "outline" (*Umriß*), "sketch" (*Zeichnung*), or "silhouette" (*Schattenbild*) (A833/B862; A570/B598).[51] As we might think of this point, a schema is a kind of *Gestalt* (albeit one "in our heads"[52]) that represents how the marks contained in a concept show up in a sensible, holistic way. The schema of a mum, for example, is an intuition_i that sketches a mum *Gestalt*: how having alternate leaves, being oval-shaped, and being fuzzy-stemmed sensibly show up together in a mum as a whole.

This said, Kant is not exactly forthcoming about how our imagination generates a schematic intuition_i. Indeed, in the Schematism, Kant says that schematism is "a hidden art [*Kunst*] in the depths of the human soul" (A141/B180). However, his characterization of schematism as involving direct exhibition in the third *Critique* is helpful. For what this suggests is that the imaginative process of generating a schema is constrained by concepts in the following sense.[53] Insofar as schematism is an activity that involves our imagination rendering the logical content of a concept in sensible form, this logical content constrains our imagination as it generates a schematic *Gestalt*. For example, in the schematism of the concept <mum>, my imaginative activities are constrained by the marks contained in this concept, as I imaginatively project how marks, such as <having alternate leaves>, <oval-shaped>, <fuzzy-stemmed>, etc., sensibly manifest as a whole.

While the notion of direct exhibition gives us a way to start unpacking what schematism involves, Kant's gloss of it as a "hidden art" is, in fact, also helpful. Indeed, though some commentators read this as Kant's metaphorical way of telling us schematism is something too obscure to explain,[54] I think it provides an important literal clue for how he understands schematism: it is a kind of art.[55]

In particular, I take the kind of art at issue to be what Kant describes in the third *Critique* as follows: "**Art** as a skill [*Geschicklichkeit*] of human beings is...distinguished from science [*Wissenschaft*] (**to be able** from **to know** [*Können vom Wissen*]), as a practical faculty from a theoretical one, as technique [*Technik*]

---

[51] I take this description of a schema as an "outline," "sketch," or "silhouette" to be what he has in mind in the Schematism chapter when he describes a schema as a "monogram" (*Monogramm*) (A142/B181). See A833/B861 for Kant's alignment of an outline with a monogram.

[52] See, e.g., Kant's claim that, "The schema of the triangle can never exist anywhere except in thought" (A141/B180).

[53] On this issue, my reading of schematism parts ways with readings of schematism as a preconceptual process that leads to concept formation (see Pendlebury 1995, 784, 787–8; Longuenesse 1998, 115–18; Allison 2001, 25–8; and Filieri 2021). I take this pre-conceptual analysis of schematism to be ruled out by Kant's characterization of it as a mode of direct exhibition of concepts, a commitment that he is explicit about in the third *Critique* and that I take him to be implicitly committed to in the first *Critique*.

[54] See, e.g., Bennett (1966, 142); Strawson (1974, 47); Pippin (1976, 170); Guyer (1987, 158; 2006, 96).

[55] See Matherne (2014a), where I also discuss the relationship between schematism and the art involved in genius.

IMAGINATION IS A NECESSARY INGREDIENT OF PERCEPTION   151

from theory" (KU 5: 303). Here, Kant distinguishes art as something that requires skill, technique, and know-how from science, which requires theory and knowledge.[56] And by my lights, it is this conception of art as involving a kind of know-how that Kant has in mind in the Schematism.

More specifically, when Kant says that schematism is an art, I understand him to mean that schematism is a process that involves an imaginative kind of know-how with how the logical content of a concept manifests sensibly and as a whole. As I read this imaginative art, it involves skills for projecting and anticipating how the various marks of a concept show up and show up together in space and time, as well as for adjusting and readjusting our sense of this showing up on the basis of further sensible encounters. And as is the case with any art, central to Kant's conception of this imaginative art is the idea that it involves something more than knowledge of the logical content of concept. Kant, indeed, prefaces the Schematism chapter with the discussion of the doctor who, as you will recall, has advanced knowledge of disease concepts *in abstracto*, but who lacks the ability to apply these concepts to actual patients *in concreto*. Though Kant uses this example to make various points,[57] it is not incidental that he dedicates the subsequent chapter to the topic of schematism (A133/B172).[58] For, on his view, part of what the physician lacks is an imaginative art or know-how with these concepts, which would provide him with a sense of how the disease concepts he understands in the abstract actually show up in the concrete.

As I understand the process of schematism, then, on Kant's view, in generating a schema, our imaginative activities are constrained by the logical content of a concept, as that which we are to directly exhibit in sensible form. However, in producing a schema, we cannot just rely on our intellectual knowledge of that content; we must rely on our imaginative skills or know-how with how that content sensibly and holistically manifests. And it is through this conceptually constrained art that our imagination produces a schematic intuition$_i$ that represents how the marks contained in a concept show up as a whole in general.

With this picture of the content and process underlying schemata in place, let's return to Kant's conception of a schema as a kind of rule. As I understand Kant's view, although a schema involves an intuition$_i$, it is an intuition$_i$ that represents how marks of a concept show up as a whole in general, and in virtue of this generality it can serve as a rule. More specifically, I take it that a schematic intuition$_i$ provides us with a sensible pattern that guides how we imaginatively synthesize a

---

[56] Kant illustrates this art-science distinction with the example of Pieter Camper, who wrote the *Treatise on the Best Form of Shoes* and could "describe quite precisely how the best shoe must be made, but he certainly was not able to make one" (KU 5:304).

[57] As I noted in Chapter 4, Kant also uses this example to make points about the "special talent" that is the power of judgment.

[58] For discussion of the relationship between the "art" of schematism and judgment, see Schaper (1964); Bell (1987); and Dahlstrom (2018).

152   EMPIRICAL IMAGINATION IN PERCEPTION AND EXPERIENCE

manifold in accordance with the relevant concept. As we might think of it, a schema serves as a kind of stencil that guides imaginative synthesis, where this stencil reflects the *Gestalt* of a concept, i.e. how its marks show up as a sensible whole.[59] This stencil, in turn, guides us across various situations in which we imaginatively synthesize certain representations in a manifold together in distinction from others in accordance with the relevant concept. My mum schema, for example, is a schematic intuition$_i$ for the concept <mum> that provides me with a stencil for imaginatively synthesizing representations in a manifold together, which can guide me whenever I encounter a mum, whether in my vase, at a flower shop, or in your garden.

Piecing this together, on Kant's view, a schema is a distinctive kind of intuition$_i$, a "mediating representation," that our imagination generates through the artful activity of schematic exhibition. In this activity, our imagination, on the one hand, is constrained by concepts, but, on the other hand, evinces a kind of know-how or skill with how concepts sensibly manifest as a whole, which outstrips our abstract knowledge of them. The schemata that result from this activity of exhibition are sensible, *qua* intuitions$_i$ that directly exhibit how the logical content of a concept manifests in a sensible, holistic way. But they are intellectual insofar as they provide us with a general rule, a kind of stencil or pattern, that guides us in imaginatively synthesizing manifolds of intuition in accordance with the relevant concept. According to Kant, schemata thus provide an important bridge between intuitions and concepts, enabling us to synthesize the former in accordance with the latter. And it is in virtue of this schematic meditation that Kant thinks we can ultimately be in a position to subsume intuitions under concepts in acts of judgment.

5.3.4(b) Schemata in Perception

With this picture in place of what schemata are, we can now turn to the role they play in Kant's theory of perception. As I indicated earlier, I take his key claim to be that a schema is that "through which and in accordance with which the images first become possible" (A142/B181). As I read this claim, Kant commits himself to the idea that in order to produce a perceptual image, our imaginative synthesis needs to be guided by a schema.

Let's take a closer look at this process. The relevant passage reads in full: "[a schema is that] through which and in accordance with which the images first become possible, but which must be connected with the concept, to which they are in themselves never fully congruent, always only by means of the schema that

---

[59] Though "Gestalt" has spatial connotations, I here intend for the term to be understood in a wider sense to capture the way in which a concept shows up as a spatial and/or temporal whole. So understood, a doorbell can have a temporal *Gestalt* (ding-dong) or a pop song can have a temporal *Gestalt* (intro-verse-chorus-verse-chorus-bridge-chorus-outro).

IMAGINATION IS A NECESSARY INGREDIENT OF PERCEPTION   153

they designate [*bezeichnen*]" (A142/B181). There are two lessons about Kant's view of perception that I want to draw out of this passage that he does not make explicit in the Transcendental Deduction, both of which pertain to it being conceptually laden: the first concerns the conceptual content of perceptual images and the second the role empirical concepts play in guiding perception.[60]

Regarding the content of perceptual images, note that in the above passage Kant claims that images "must" be connected with a concept. As he clarifies this point in "On a Discovery," "images...always presuppose a concept of which they are the *exhibition*" (OD 8:222; transl. modified). For Kant, then, the content of a perceptual image is to be understood in terms of the exhibition of a concept: a perceptual image is an intuition$_i$ that represents a particular as exhibiting a concept *in concreto*. For example, the perceptual image of a mum I have when I look at the one in my vase is an intuition$_i$ that represents that particular flower as exhibiting the concept <mum> *in concreto*.

One way to make this point about the content of a perceptual image in Kant's framework is in terms of exhibition via an "example" (*Beispiel*).[61] Kant is not unequivocal in his use of "example," but the use I am interested in here pertains to his characterization of an example as an "exhibition of a concept" that involves "a particular (*concretum*), represented in accordance with concepts as contained under a universal (*abstractum*)" (MS 6:480n; transl. modified).[62] He further specifies that an example is something that involves exhibition through an empirical intuition: "If, to a concept, the corresponding intuition...is merely empirical intuition, it is called simply an example [*Beispiel*] of the concept" (WF 20:325, transl. modified; see also KU 5:351). Note that here Kant describes not a particular object, but rather the empirical intuition that represents a particular "in accordance with concepts" as an example. But I take these two thoughts to be connected: in order to regard a particular object as an example of a concept, *per* Kant, we need to have an empirical intuition that represents the particular as exemplifying the concept. Bringing this to bear on the content of a perceptual image, for Kant, insofar as a perceptual image involves an empirical intuition$_i$ of a particular represented in accordance with an empirical concept, it involves exhibition via an example. My perceptual image of the mum, for instance, is an

---

[60] In this chapter, my focus is on the role empirical concepts play in perception, but in the following two chapters, I address the question of the role the pure concepts of the understanding ("the categories") play in perception.

[61] For discussions of Kant's theory of examples more generally, see Arendt (1982, 43–4, 76–7, 80, 84) and Summa (2022). And for a Kant-inspired theory of examples, see Ferrara (2008). I take up Kant's account of moral examples in Chapter 13.

[62] "*Beispiel*" is translated as "instance" in this passage because, here, Kant distinguishes between a *Beispiel* and an *Exempel*: "An example [*Exempel*] is a particular case of a *practical* rule..., whereas an instance [*Beispiel*] is only a particular (*concretum*), represented in accordance with concepts as contained under a universal (*abstractum*), and is an exhibition of a concept merely for theory" (MS 6:480n; transl. modified). See also his claim in the *Metaphysical Foundations* that examples involve us representing "instances" of concepts "*in concreto*" (MN 4:478).

154 EMPIRICAL IMAGINATION IN PERCEPTION AND EXPERIENCE

empirical intuition$_i$ that represents the flower I perceive as exemplifying the concept <mum>.

The second lesson about perception that I want to adduce turns on Kant's commitment to empirical concepts guiding the imaginative synthesis that generates perceptual images.[63] This commitment emerges specifically when we attend to what is implied by the claim that a schema is that "through which and in accordance with which" an image becomes possible. For Kant, a schema makes perceptual images possible because it provides the rule that guides the imaginative synthesis of apprehension and reproduction through which we generate perceptual images. However, on Kant's view, schemata, in turn, depend on concepts: our imagination generates a schema under the constraint of a concept, which is itself a kind of rule. We see him make this point in the following passage, "The concept of a dog signifies [bedeutet] a rule in accordance with which my imagination can delineate [verzeichnen] the shape [Gestalt] of a four-footed animal in general, without being restricted to any single particular shape [Gestalt] that experience offers me" (A141/B180; transl. modified). Here, Kant indicates that the concept <dog> involves a rule "in accordance with which" my imagination "delineates" a schema. I take the content of the relevant conceptual rule to be the marks contained in the concept, such as <four-footed>, <animal>, etc. And I take the schema that delineates that rule to be an intuition$_i$ that represents how the marks of that concept show up as a whole in dogs in space and time.[64]

This said, there is a question as to why we should think that there is any distinction between an empirical concept and an empirical schema at all.[65] In the dog case, for example, why think that the empirical concept <dog> is distinct from the schema of this concept? Aren't they both rules that guide our imagination in synthesizing a manifold of intuition in accordance with a concept?[66]

---

[63] Insofar as I take the imaginative synthesis involved in perception to be guided by concepts on Kant's view, my reading differs from three readings. First, it differs from readings of this imaginative synthesis as pre-conceptual (see, e.g., Young 1988; Gibbons 1994, chap. 1; Pendlebury 1996; Longuenesse 1998, 116–20; Rohs 2001; Allison 2004, 187–9; Horstmann 2018, 23–6, 40 (who makes this point regarding the production of "intuition" on the basis of "perceptions" through imaginative synthesis)). Second, it differs from readings according to which this imaginative synthesis only depends on a priori concepts, not empirical concepts (see Griffith 2012, 2, 6–7; Williams 2012). Third, it differs from readings of this imaginative synthesis as something that depends on the understanding, but not on concepts (see Ginsborg 2008). I return to some of these interpretations in my discussion of conceptualism later in this section.

[64] See Williams (2020) for emphasis on the importance of spatial form in this context and Stang (2023) for emphasis on temporal form.

[65] See Bennett (1966, 151), Chipman (1972, 42), and Guyer (2006, 97) for the argument that Kant collapses the distinction between empirical concepts and schemata.

[66] See, e.g., Kant's description of a concept as a "rule of intuition" that "represents the necessary reproduction of the manifold of given intuitions" (A106).

IMAGINATION IS A NECESSARY INGREDIENT OF PERCEPTION 155

However, we have at least two reasons to preserve the distinction between empirical concepts and schemata on Kant's view.[67] In the first place, Kant conceives of empirical concepts and empirical schemata as fundamentally different types of representations produced by fundamentally different cognitive capacities.[68] An empirical concept is a product of the understanding that involves an intellectual representation of the marks contained in the concept. Meanwhile, an empirical schema is a product of imagination, a part of sensibility, that involves an intuition$_i$ that represents how the marks contained in the concept show up as a whole in space and time.

Second, on Kant's view, it is possible to possess an empirical concept without possessing the correlative schema. To see this, recall once again the example of the learned physician who understands certain disease concepts in the abstract, but cannot apply them to concrete cases (A24/B173). The physician's problem is not that he lacks the requisite concepts: Kant tells us he is even capable of lecturing about them. Instead (at least part of) the physician's problem is that he lacks schemata for these concepts that are bound up with the imaginative know-how required to identify actual cases. The fact that possessing an empirical concept can come apart from possessing an empirical schema for that concept gives us another reason to maintain the distinction between the two in Kant's framework.

Let's return now to the lesson about the role empirical concepts play in perception that I have been drawing from the Schematism. On my reading, since the imaginative synthesis of apprehension and reproduction responsible for generating perceptual images is guided by schemata, and schemata, in turn, depend on empirical concepts, then we have reason to conceive of perception as ultimately guided by empirical concepts. If we piece this lesson together with the first lesson about perceptual images exhibiting concepts through examples, then the Schematism chapter reveals that, in the end, Kant conceives of perception as a conceptually laden process that involves the imaginative exhibition of empirical concepts in empirical intuitions$_i$. Indeed, perception involves imaginative exhibition of empirical concepts doubly so. For, on the one hand, the perceptual images our imagination generates in perception are empirical intuitions$_i$ that represent particulars as examples that exhibit empirical concepts. On the other hand, the imaginative synthesis through which these perceptual images are generated is

---

[67] Another strategy for distinguishing between empirical concepts and schemata turns on interpreting the latter as pre-conceptual and as playing a role in empirical concept formation (see Pendlebury 1995, 784, 787–8; Longuenesse 1998, 115–18; and Allison 2001, 25–8). However, since I take Kant to be committed to schemata as direct exhibitions of concepts, I do not think they should be read along these pre-conceptual lines.

[68] Though proponents of what I call the "understanding view" of imagination, according to which imagination is just a sensible exercise of understanding, would not concede this point, I argued against this view in favor of a "sensibility view," according to which imagination is part of sensibility, rather than understanding in Chapters 2 and 3.

156 EMPIRICAL IMAGINATION IN PERCEPTION AND EXPERIENCE

guided by schemata, which are themselves intuitions[i] that exhibit empirical concepts.

Notice that attending to the role that imaginative exhibition and concepts play on Kant's view of perception casts a particular light on his claim that imagination is a necessary ingredient of perception. For Kant, imagination is a necessary ingredient of perception not just in virtue of its formative and even-without-presence activities (see Chapter 4). Though our imagination certainly acts in these formative and even-without-presence ways in perception, on Kant's view, these activities are ultimately underwritten by, and contribute to, our imagination exhibiting empirical concepts vis-à-vis perceptual images. And in this regard, we find that attending to Kant's definition of imagination as the faculty of exhibition is crucial for making sense of its distinctive contribution, as a capacity that mediates between sense and concepts, in perception.

These two lessons about perception, in turn, have implications for how we approach the debate surrounding Kant's conceptualism with regard to the generation of intuitions. For what his account of perception reveals, at least on my interpretation, is a commitment to the generation of at least one kind of intuition depending on empirical concepts: the intuitions[i] of perception, i.e. perceptual images. As we have just seen, according to Kant perceptual images are intuitions[i] generated through imaginative syntheses that are guided by empirical concepts by way of schemata, and their content is such as to represent particulars as exemplifying empirical concepts.[69] I shall have more to say about this issue below, but for now, what I want to stress is that these conceptualist commitments are ones we are liable to miss if we do not attend to the role that schematism and schematic exhibition play in Kant's theory of perception.

Over the course of this section, I have been analyzing the imagination stage of experience by taking a closer look at Kant's theory of perception and why imagination is a "necessary ingredient" of it. However, various questions remain concerning how the imagination stage relates to the sense and understanding stages of experience. For example, what does the sort of perception involved in the imagination stage cognitively accomplish in the course of experience that is different from what we accomplish through either the sense or understanding

---

[69] To situate this reading in relation to other (non-)conceptualist readings of Kant's theory of perception, I take Kant's account of the role imagination plays in perception to cut against non-conceptualist readings of his theory of perception (see Young 1988; Rohs 2001; Allison 2004, 187–9; Hanna 2005: 249, 267; Allais 2009; 2015). However, my reading also parts ways with other conceptualist readings of his theory of perception, including what I in Matherne (2015) call "weak conceptualism," according to which perception is guided by the understanding, but not by concepts (see Ginsborg 2008); "strong conceptualism," according to which perception is guided by concepts and the synthesis of recognition (see Grüne 2009, chaps. 3.3, 4; Landy 2015, 138–9; more on the synthesis of recognition in §5.5); and a kind of "moderate conceptualism," according to which perception is guided by the categories, but not by empirical concepts (see Griffith 2012; Williams 2012). I, instead, endorse a different kind of moderate conceptualism, according to which perception is guided by empirical and pure concepts (see also Kitcher 1990, chap. 6).

stages? How does perception transform what we are given through the sense stage? And how are we to think about the role concepts play vis-à-vis these various stages?

5.4 The Sense and Imagination Stages of Experience

In order to navigate the relationship between the sense and imagination stages of experience, I shall here presuppose the interpretation of Kant's account of sensing and imagining that I developed in my discussion of his bipartite theory of sensibility in Chapter 3. Applying that reading of sensing to the sense stage, this stage involves the generation of intuitions$_s$ through processes that are "nothing but receptivity," and, hence, do not depend on empirical concepts (B129).[70] And these intuitions$_s$ have the cognitive function of giving us objects, i.e. putting us in touch with them. By contrast, the imagining at issue in the imagination stage involves spontaneous processes in which we make intuitions$_i$, viz. perceptual images, by sensibly ordering and organizing a manifold of intuition$_s$ under the guidance of a schema, and, by extension, an empirical concept. As I understand Kant's position, then, perception involves the imaginative transformation of intuitions$_s$ that are not conceptually laden into intuitions$_i$ that are conceptually laden through imaginative synthesis that is guided by schemata for empirical concepts. And, as a case in which our imagination functions cognitively well as a mediator, the intuitions$_i$ our imagination generates in this context, i.e. the perceptual images that exhibit empirical concepts, have the cognitive function of making empirical concepts sensible.

Note that given this dynamic, there is a kind of asymmetrical dependence relation between these two stages of experience on my interpretation. The sense stage does not depend on the imagination stage: being given an empirical intuition$_s$ does not require imaginative synthesis of the sort that perception requires.[71] Instead, Kant claims that the senses give us a "manifold of intuition...that is...nothing but receptivity," and that they "merely afford us impressions" but do not "put them together" (B129; A120n). But the imagination stage does depend on the sense stage: insofar as it involves the synthesis *of* a manifold of empirical

---

[70] Recall Kant's example of someone who sees a house, but lacks the concept <house>: "he admittedly has before him in his representation the very same object as someone else who is acquainted with it determinately as a dwelling established for men. But as to form, this cognition of one and the same object is different in the two. With the one it is mere *intuition*, with the other it is *intuition* and *concept* at the same time" (JL 9:33). I also take this to be one kind of scenario that Kant has in mind when he says that "sense representations" "certainly" "come before...the understanding and present themselves *en masse*" (Anthro. 7:144).

[71] I thus disagree with readings according to which the empirical intuitions of the senses can only be generated through imaginative synthesis (see Ginsborg 2008; Gomes 2014; Horstmann 2018, 4, 45, 64–6, 100–2; Grüne 2009; 2022 (who speaks of "sensible synthesis")).

158 EMPIRICAL IMAGINATION IN PERCEPTION AND EXPERIENCE

intuition$_s$ into a perceptual image, our imaginative activities in perception depend on the deliverances of sense. Hence his remark that, "There is thus an active faculty of synthesis *of* this manifold in us, which we call imagination...For the imagination is to bring the manifold of intuition into an **image**" (A120; my italics).[72]

To further clarify the relationship between these two stages, let's consider the question: what does the imagination stage cognitively accomplish beyond the sense stage? Part of the answer to this question turns on Kant's account of the different cognitive functions of sense and imagination. Whereas the sense stage delivers us empirical intuitions$_s$ that have the function of giving us objects, the imagination stage provides empirical intuitions$_i$ (perceptual images) that have the function of making concepts sensible. In discharging this function, our imagination plays an important mediating role internal to our cognitive processes, bridging the gap between the deliverances of sensibility and concepts, in a way that sense, in its merely receptive character, cannot.

The imagination stage, moreover, contributes to how we consciously represent objects in a way that the sense stage cannot. Although both stages, according to my reading, involve consciously representing an object, *qua* something that stands over and against the subject, I take it that they involve different kinds of conscious representations of objects. And in order to bring out this point, I want to consider what the imagination stage accomplishes beyond the sense stage with respect to what I described in Chapter 1 as the two achievements involved in cognition in the narrow sense: the "determinacy achievement" and the "modal achievement."

Beginning with the determinacy achievement, as a reminder, on Kant's view, cognition in the narrow sense involves us consciously representing objects as both sensibly and qualitatively determinate. Recall that representing an object as sensibly determinate includes representing it as numerically identical or as having a determinate spatio-temporal form or mereological structure, whereas representing it as qualitatively determinate involves representing it as having properties shared by objects of a certain kind. On my reading of Kant's view, the imagination stage contributes to our conscious representation of objects as both sensibly and qualitatively determinate in a way that the sense stage does not. This said, as will emerge in comparison with the understanding stage, there are also limits to this imaginative contribution, which I discuss in §5.5.

Let's start with the issue of sensible determinacy. According to my interpretation, Kant is committed to the imagination stage involving a perceptual representation of spatio-temporal determinacy that outstrips what is possible at the sense stage. As I argued in Chapter 3, on Kant's view, in sensing although our empirical

---

[72] See also the passages in which Kant describes imaginative synthesis as the synthesis of the manifold at A79/B104; A99; B164.

THE SENSE AND IMAGINATION STAGES OF EXPERIENCE   159

intuitions$_s$ can be caused by objects with a determinate spatio-temporal form, the content of intuitions$_s$ is not such as to involve a conscious representation of an object as having a determinate spatio-temporal form.[73] According to Kant, in order to consciously represent a determinate spatio-temporal form in the latter sense, we need to connect representations in a manifold together. However, on his view, given the receptive nature of the senses, they cannot connect representations in a manifold together. Instead, he claims that the empirical intuitions$_s$ that the senses give us contain a manifold of representations that have not yet been "put...together" and are "encountered as dispersed and separate in the mind" (A120, 120n).[74] When I look at the mum, for example, per Kant, my senses give me a multiplicity of representations, e.g. of yellow petals, green leaves, and a green stem, but they do not put these representations together into a representation of the mum as a spatial whole. Instead of representing objects as spatio-temporally determinate, in Chapter 3 I claimed that Kant thinks that through the objective sensations contained in an empirical intuition$_s$, we consciously represent an appearance as an "undetermined object," a something or other that stands over and against us in space and time (A20/B34). Recall the example of exiting a movie theater into bright daylight. In this episode, through sensations of colors and sounds contained in my empirical intuition$_s$, I am conscious of something or other in space and time, but not yet of anything with a determinate form, such as a car shape or lamppost shape.

By contrast, as I also argued, on Kant's view, the content of empirical intuitions$_i$ is such as to involve the conscious representation of something as a determinate spatio-temporal form. Recall his claim that our imagination is responsible for making a "**determinate** intuition" that represents a "determinate space or time" (B154; B202). Recall also that, on Kant's view, the most basic determinate spatial form is a "shape" (Gestalt) and the most basic determinate temporal form is a "sequence" (Gefolge), "series" (Reihe), or "play" (Spiel). Applying this to Kant's account of the imagination stage of experience, in perception our imagination generates a perceptual image, the content of which involves a conscious representation of a particular with a determinate spatio-temporal form, such as a spatial shape or

---

[73] In the Anthropology, Kant does claim that we can only "form a concept of the shape of a body" through the sense of touch; however, I take his position to be that if we are to successfully form a concept of shape, then we cannot just be given shapes through touch; we must become conscious of shapes by forming images of them in imagination (Anthro. 7:154). I take a similar line of thought to be applicable to Kant's analysis of the connection between touch and the perception of impenetrability, hence the repulsive force of bodies (see MN 4:510; for discussion, see Marshall 2017).

[74] See also, "connection is not the work of mere sense and intuition, but is rather the product of a synthetic faculty of the imagination" (B233). As I discussed in Chapter 3, I take these claims to give us reason to resist readings according to which the senses are capable of "binding" (see Allais 2017), or any other synthesis in perception (see Hanna 2005, 249, 267; Allais 2009, 394–5). Instead of connecting representations together, I take an intuition$_s$ to contain a manifold.

temporal duration.[75] For example, in the perception of the mum, my imagination generates a perceptual image, the content of which involves a conscious representation of a particular as having a mum shape that contains petals, leaves, and a stem as its spatial parts. Indeed, I take the latter kind of mereological representation to be what Kant has in mind when he suggests that in perception our imagination synthesizes the representations contained in a manifold together into a "whole representation" (A102).[76]

On my interpretation of Kant, then, the imagination stage of experience accomplishes something with respect to the sensible determinacy of our representations of objects that the sense stage does not. Whereas sensing gives rise to intuitions$_s$ that represent appearances as undetermined objects, perceiving involves perceptual images that represent them as having a determinate spatio-temporal form.

However, for Kant, the imagination stage does not just contribute to our representation of objects as sensibly determinate; it also contributes to our representation of objects as qualitatively determinate in a way that the sense stage does not. On his view, representing an object as qualitatively determinate involves representing it as determined with respect to an empirical concept it instantiates. However, on my interpretation, since empirical intuitions$_s$ are the result of merely receptive processes that do not involve empirical concepts, the sense stage cannot give rise to our consciousness of objects as qualitatively determinate. But since the imagination stage does involve empirical concepts, it is in a position to contribute to our conscious representation of objects as qualitatively determinate. As I have argued, in perception, our imagination is guided by a schema, defined as "a rule for the determination of our intuition in accordance with a certain general concept" (A141/B180). The perceptual images that our imagination produces in perception are empirical intuitions$_i$ that represent particulars as examples that exhibit empirical concepts. When I perceive the mum, for example, *per* Kant, my mum schema guides my imagination in synthesizing a manifold of intuition$_s$ in accordance with the concept <mum>, and the perceptual image that is thereby generated is an intuition$_i$ through which I consciously represent this flower as qualitatively determinate: as exhibiting the concept <mum>.

Stepping back, when we compare the sense and imagination stages of experience through the lens of the determinacy achievement of cognition in the narrow sense, we find that Kant attributes to the imagination stage a representation of objects as sensibly and qualitatively determinate, which we do not yet arrive at through the sense stage. There are, of course, further questions about how to

---

[75] Below, I argue that in perception we do not represent a particular as an existing object that has this form, but rather as something that subjectively "appears" to us as having this form.

[76] See also his description of this in the third *Critique* as a representation of "the many in one intuition" (KU 5:254). See Rosefeldt (2019, 51–2) for a discussion of Kant's account of how apprehension takes up a manifold of intuition "as such" along these mereological lines (A99).

think about this contribution to representing determinacy in comparison to understanding stage which I shall address shortly. Before doing so, however, I want to address the second kind of cognitive achievement that Kant thinks the imagination stage contributes to experience in a way the sense stage does not: the modal achievement of cognition in the narrow sense.

Recall Kant's commitment to cognition in the narrow sense involving us being conscious of an object as really possible. As I discussed in Chapter 1, Kant tends to emphasize the idea that this involves us being able to have an intuition that demonstrates that the concept of the relevant object is not empty, but rather has objective reality, hence relates to objects that we can be given in intuition. As I intimated in Chapter 4, Kant maintains that proof of real possibility depends on exhibition: when we exhibit a concept in intuition, this literally demonstrates to us that the concept has objective reality, and hence is a concept of a really possible object. For Kant, given that exhibition is moreover an imaginative activity, imagination thus plays a pivotal role in enabling us to be conscious of an object as really possible in cognition in the narrow sense.[77]

When we reflect on the sense and imagination stages of experience in light of the modal achievement, we have reason to identify the latter as contributing to our consciousness of objects as really possible in a way the former does not. To be sure, the sense stage involves empirical intuitions$_s$ that give us objects in the first place, and this is crucial for being in a position to prove the real possibility of objects. However, empirical intuitions$_s$ do not suffice for the proof of real possibility. For, as we have seen, on Kant's view, proof of real possibility involves proving that the relevant concept has objective reality. And in order for this to happen, we need to be conscious that the relevant concept is not empty, but has objective reality. But since concepts are not involved in the sense stage of experience, this stage does not involve this sort of concept-interfacing consciousness. Perhaps another way to put the point is this: insofar as empirical intuitions$_s$ occur without concepts, they do not "throw" concepts "before our eyes" (see KU §59).

Matters are different with the imagination stage. As we have seen, according to Kant, in perception, our imagination generates a perceptual image that represents a particular as exhibiting a concept in an intuition$_i$. In this way, perception has something important to contribute to our awareness that a concept relates to an object we can be given, and, hence, has objective reality. And, indeed, in the third *Critique*, Kant suggests that, "To demonstrate the reality of our concepts, intuitions are always required. If they are empirical concepts, then the latter are called **examples**" (KU 5:351). As I suggested above, we can think of perceptual images as providing us with examples of concepts on Kant's view; in which case, an implication of this passage is that the perceptual images involved in perception

---

[77] See Rosefeldt (2021) and Watkins (forthcoming) for discussion of the relevance of imagination in this context.

provide evidence of the reality of our empirical concepts and put us in a position to prove their objective reality, *qua* concepts that relate to really possible objects. In this way, perception contributes not only to our consciousness of objects as determinate, but also as really possible in the way cognition in the narrow sense requires—topics which I shall return to in §5.5.

Taking stock, my aim in this section has been to clarify the relationship between the imagination and sense stages of experience, and the distinctive cognitive contribution that Kant thinks the former makes over and above the latter. As we have seen, the involvement of concepts in the imagination stage plays a decisive role in the distinct kind of consciousness of objects that we arrive at in perception. However, the involvement of concepts also raises questions concerning the relationship that the imagination stage has to the understanding stage and whether Kant distinguishes between the cognitive state involved in the imagination stage from the one involved in the understanding stage at all.

5.5 The Imagination and Understanding Stages of Experience

Before turning to the relationship between the imagination and understanding stages, we need to take a closer look at the latter, hence at the stage in which Kant thinks we arrive at full-blown experience, at least on my interpretation. I shall argue that he ultimately conceives of this stage as involving judgment, and that appreciating this is crucial for seeing why he distinguishes the conscious state involved in this stage from the one involved in perception and the imagination stage of experience.[78]

Kant offers one of his most extended discussions of the empirical activities involved in the understanding stage of experience in his analysis of the threefold synthesis required for experience in the A Deduction. There, he claims that in addition to the imaginative syntheses of apprehension and reproduction, experience requires a synthesis of understanding that he calls the "synthesis of recognition [*Rekognition*] in the concept" (A103). *Prima facie*, the label for this synthesis might make it seem as if what is at stake here is perceptually recognizing an instance of a concept, e.g. perceptually recognizing a particular flower as an instance of the concept <mum>.[79] If this is what is involved in the synthesis of recognition, then it would seem that rather than being posterior to the imagination stage of experience, the understanding stage coincides with it.[80] According to

---

[78] For other readings according to which the synthesis of recognition involves judgment, see Pippin (1982, 130); Tolley (2019). These readings contrast with readings according to which the synthesis of recognition generates intuitions or perceptions, rather than judgments (see Longuenesse 1998, chap. 2; Grüne 2009, chaps. 3.3, 4; 2022; Landy 2015, 138–9; Schulting 2017).

[79] See, e.g., Kitcher's (1990, 153) gloss of this in terms of perceptual recognition.

[80] See, e.g., Longuenesse (1998, 44–7); Schulting (2017, 278–9); Grüne (2022, 99–100).

THE IMAGINATION AND UNDERSTANDING STAGES OF EXPERIENCE 163

this reading, then, although Kant presents the threefold synthesis in sequence, he does not regard the imaginative syntheses of apprehension and reproduction as temporally separable from the synthesis of recognition; they are rather three inseparable aspects of perceptual recognition.[81]

Support for this reading can be adduced from the way Kant introduces the synthesis of recognition:

> Without consciousness that that which we think is the very same as what we thought a moment before, all reproduction in the series of representations would be in vain. For it would be a new representation in our current state, which would not belong at all to the act through which it had been gradually generated, and its manifold would never constitute a whole, since it would lack the unity that only consciousness can obtain for it.   (A103)

Just as the synthesis of reproduction cannot proceed without the synthesis of apprehension in perception, in this passage Kant seems to claim that the synthesis of reproduction (and presumably the apprehension with which it is "inseparably combined") cannot proceed without the synthesis of recognition (A102). More specifically, Kant's thought appears to be that in order for reproduction and apprehension to not be "in vain," they need to result in a "whole" representation: a conscious representation of an object that remains "the same" through a series of representations. However, in this passage, Kant suggests that this requires "consciousness that that which we think is the very same as what we thought a moment before." And he goes on to argue that this consciousness depends on us synthesizing the relevant representations in accordance with a concept. As he puts it, a concept "is the **one** consciousness that unifies the manifold that has been successively intuited, and then also reproduced, into one representation" (A103). Insofar as this is the case, it seems that the synthesis of recognition is not a synthesis that occurs over and above the imaginative synthesis that issues in perception; it is a synthesis that occurs inseparably from these imaginative syntheses in acts of perceptual recognition.

Though appealing, what I shall argue is that Kant is ultimately committed to the understanding stage of experience and the synthesis of recognition involving an act of judgment, which is distinct and separable from the act of perception at issue in the imagination stage of experience. To begin laying the groundwork for this, it is important to note that elsewhere Kant is clear that the understanding stage of experience involves judgment. For example, in the *Prolegomena*, he claims, "Experience consists of intuitions, which belong to sensibility, and of judgments, which are solely the understanding's business" (Prol. 4:304). In the

---

[81] See Paton (1936, 271–2); Kemp Smith (1962, 245–6); Longuenesse (1998, 35–6); Allison (2015, chap. 5); Anderson (2015, 354–5); Ginsborg (2015, 37); Schulting (2017); Grüne (2022, 99–100).

164 EMPIRICAL IMAGINATION IN PERCEPTION AND EXPERIENCE

unpublished Introduction to the third *Critique*, he says, "The possibility of an experience in general is the possibility of empirical cognitions as synthetic judgments" (EE 20:203n). And in the *Anthropology*, he asserts, "Experience is empirical cognition, but cognition (since it rests on judgments) requires reflection (*reflexio*), and consequently consciousness of activity in combining the manifold of representations according to a rule of the unity of the manifold; that is, it requires concepts and thought in general (as distinct from intuition)" (Anthro. 7:141; transl. modified).[82] This characterization of what our understanding contributes to experience in terms of judgment is, moreover, in keeping with his claim that, "the understanding can make no other use of these concepts than that of judging by means of them" (A68/B93). And what I now hope to show is that if we return to Kant's account of the synthesis of recognition in the first *Critique*, then we have reason to read him as implicitly committed to the understanding stage of experience involving judgment, and as, therefore, distinct from the imagination stage of experience.[83]

In order to bring out this implicit commitment to judgment in the A Deduction, it is important to note that Kant does not just present the synthesis of recognition as a matter of recognizing an instance of a concept; he presents it as a matter of recognizing that there is an "an object corresponding to, and therefore also distinct from" our representations, which "makes" our representations "necessary" (A104–5). I take this object to be the one that Kant says we think of as "the same" through a series of representations (A103). But what does this recognition of "the same" object "corresponding to," "distinct from," and "necessitating" our representations amount to?

Here, in order to cash out recognition, one might appeal to Kant's characterization of cognition in the *Stufenleiter*: recognition involves the conscious representation of an object (A320/B377). If this is right, then Kant would appear to be committed to the view that whenever we consciously represent an object, this requires deploying concepts in the synthesis of recognition. This would, in turn, lend support to a conceptualist reading of intuition, according to which the

---

[82] In the first *Critique*, see "The synthesis of representations rests on the imagination, but their synthetic unity (which is requisite for judgment), on the unity of apperception" (A155/B194). See also A7–8/B11–12 for a gloss of experience in terms of synthetic judgments. There are thorny issues that bear on the distinction Kant draws between "judgments of experience" and "judgments of perception" in the *Prolegomena* that I shall have to set aside here (see Prol. §18). For discussion, see Longuenesse (1998, chap. 7), Sethi (2020).

[83] I take the implicit role of judgment in the A Deduction to be part of Kant's downplaying of the theme of judgment in the A Deduction, which he corrects for in the B Deduction, and in the *Metaphysical Foundations* (see, e.g. his claim that his argument in the Deduction can "almost be accomplished through a single inference from the precisely determined definition of a *judgment* in general (an action through which given representations first become cognitions of an object)" (MN 4:475–6)). For discussion, see Guyer (2010).

THE IMAGINATION AND UNDERSTANDING STAGES OF EXPERIENCE   165

generation of intuitions, *qua* conscious representation of objects, depends on the understanding deploying concepts in the synthesis of recognition.[84]

However, on my reading, Kant is not committed to there being just one way of consciously representing an object: he acknowledges different modes of consciously representing an object. I already began developing this interpretive line in §5.4, where I contrasted the sort of sensory consciousness of objects we are given through the sense and imagination stages. Recall that, according to my interpretation, in the sense stage, we have an empirical intuition$_s$ that we are given through the receptive process of sensing, through which we consciously represent an undetermined appearance, a something or other that stands over and against us in space and time. Meanwhile, in the imagination stage, we have an empirical intuition$_i$ that we make through an active imaginative process, through which we consciously represent a particular as having a determinate spatio-temporal form and as exhibiting a concept. But in his discussion of the understanding stage, Kant highlights a different mode of conscious representation and different sense of object: the synthesis of recognition involves "thought" in which we are conscious of an object that remains the same across, corresponds to, and necessitates our representations (A104). Notice that this emphasis on thought is in keeping with how Kant describes the cognitive function of the understanding: its task is to think about objects we are given in intuition (see Chapter 1). And, what I aim to show is that through the synthesis of recognition, we realize this cognitive function in acts of empirical judgment in which we think about existing objects that remain the same and that our representations correspond to and are necessitated by.[85]

Let's begin with the idea that the synthesis of recognition involves being conscious of existing objects that our representations correspond to. In the Principles, Kant makes clear that what we are concerned with in "empirical thinking in an experience" is the correspondence of our representations to the "existence [*Dasein*] of appearances" (A160/B199). A bit more expansively, in the Analogies he claims that what is at issue is the correspondence of our representations to the "existence" of appearances and "their **relation** to one another with regard to this their existence" (A178/B220). Kant identifies the relevant existing appearance as an "**object** of the senses" (B218). So, I take his basic idea to be that in the synthesis of recognition, what we are conscious of in thought is an object we sense that is distinct from us, that exists in space and time, that stands in relation to other objects that exist in space and time, and that our representations correspond to.

According to Kant, when we are conscious of our representations as corresponding to an existing object in thought, we are conscious of those

---

[84] For conceptualist readings of intuition that appeal to the synthesis of recognition, see Griffith (2012); Schulting (2017); Grüne (2022, 99–100).

[85] I am thus sympathetic to Tolley's reading of the synthesis of recognition as involving something that "takes us...beyond consciousness of sensible representations and on to a consciousness of the object to which these representations are related" (2020, 3326).

166 EMPIRICAL IMAGINATION IN PERCEPTION AND EXPERIENCE

representations as having a certain kind of unity: the "unity that the object makes necessary" (A105).[86] As he describes this unity, "our thought of the relation of all cognition to an object carries something of necessity with it, since namely the latter is regarded as that which is opposed to our cognitions being determined at pleasure or arbitrarily" (A104).[87] For Kant, our representations have "the unity that the object makes necessary" when they have the character of "being determined" by an existing object rather than being "arbitrarily" produced by a subject.

As he draws this necessary-arbitrary contrast in the B Deduction, in the former case our representations have "objective" unity, whereas in the latter case only "subjective" unity (§§18–19). He cites as a paradigmatic example of subjective unity the sort of unity our imaginative representations have on the basis of association (B141). Suppose, for example, I associate mums with my mother. From Kant's perspective, when upon seeing a mum my imagination reproduces a representation of my mother, this synthesis has a "subjective" rather than "objective" basis: it is not a synthesis that is based in the mum, but rather based in an arbitrary associative pattern I happen to have. By contrast, when upon seeing a mum, I synthesize together the representations of its petals, leaves, and stem, this synthesis has an objective basis: this pattern of connection is one that is "determined" by the flower in front of me. For Kant, then, the synthesis of recognition involves being conscious in thought of an objective unity among our representations, an order among our representations that has been necessitated by an existing object.

What we now need to add to this picture is Kant's claim that the sort of thought at issue in the synthesis of recognition involves judgment. According to Kant, the synthesis of recognition involves the "thought" of the "relation" that our representations have to the object corresponding to them.[88] As I have now specified, this amounts to the thought that there is an existing object (or relation among existing objects) that necessitates a certain objective unity among our representations. According to Kant, the way that we, in thought, become conscious of this objective unity among our representations is by synthesizing them in accordance with a "concept of an object" (A105). Recall that Kant describes a concept of an object as "the **one** consciousness that unifies the manifold that has been successively intuited, and then also reproduced, into one representation" (A103). So, in the synthesis of recognition, Kant takes it that we engage in an act of thought in which we synthesize the manifold of representations we apprehend and reproduce in accordance with a concept of an object and think of those representations as having objective unity. As I discussed in Chapter 4, Kant tends to characterize

---

[86] For discussion of how this sort of unity differs from the sort of unity our representations have through sensibility, see McLear (2015).

[87] See also his description of this necessitation in terms of a **"relation to an object,"** which "mak[es] the combination of representations necessary in a certain way" (A197/B242).

[88] See Allais (2015, chap. 11) for discussion of this in terms of "referential thought."

this kind of intellectual act in terms of subsumption: we subsume intuitions under concepts in thought. Insofar as this is the case, synthesizing a manifold of representations in accordance with a concept, here, will involve subsuming it under concepts. And through this subsumption, Kant claims that we become conscious of those representations as having objective unity, i.e. as belonging together insofar as they are necessitated by an existing object.

To illustrate, consider Kant's example of perceiving a body. Suppose as I am perceiving a body, I apprehend and reproduce a manifold of representations, which includes representations of the body's extension, impenetrability, and shape (see A106). In order to be conscious of this manifold of representations as having objective unity, *per* Kant, I need to engage in a synthetic act of thought in which I subsume them under the concept <body> because it is "through" this concept that "the unity of the manifold...is thought" (A106). From Kant's perspective, then, it is through this act of subsumption in thought that I become conscious of those representations of extension, impenetrability, and shape as necessarily belonging together: they are necessitated by an existing body that is extended, impenetrable, and has a shape.

But what reason is there to interpret the thought and deployment of concepts involved in the synthesis of recognition in terms of judgment? Couldn't this thought be involved in perception, prior to any act of judgment?

It is true that in the discussion of the synthesis of recognition in the A Deduction, Kant does not explicitly reference judgment. He, instead, references "thought": recognition involves "consciousness that that which we think is the very same as what we thought a moment before," and the "thought of the relation" of representations to an object. He also illustrates the synthesis of recognition with the example of using the concept <triangle> to "think of a triangle as an object" (A105). However, there are several reasons to interpret the thinking at stake in the synthesis of recognition as involving judgment.

First of all, this is in keeping with Kant's general remarks to the effect that, "thinking is the same as judging," and that, "the understanding can make no other use of these concepts than that of judging by means of them" (Prol. 4:304, A68/B93; see also A69/B94). For another thing, when we look at his account of the understanding stage in the first step of the B Deduction, Kant does emphasize judgment. In §19 of the B Deduction, for example, Kant claims,

> If...I...distinguish the relation, as something belonging to the understanding, from the relation in accordance with the laws of the reproductive imagination..., then I find that a judgment is nothing other than the way to bring given cognitions to the **objective** unity of apperception. That is the aim of the copula **is** in them: to distinguish the objective unity of given representations from the subjective. (B141–2)

168 EMPIRICAL IMAGINATION IN PERCEPTION AND EXPERIENCE

Here, Kant addresses the distinction between the objective and subjective unity of representations I mentioned earlier. And in this passage, he indicates that it is through the act of judgment that we "distinguish the objective unity of given representations from the subjective." As I understand Kant's idea, when we subsume representations under concepts in predicative acts of judgment, we take our representations to have objective unity, i.e. the unity necessitated by the existing object they correspond to. For example, when I look at a mum and make the empirical judgment, "The flower is a mum," I subsume my representations of, say, the petals, stem, and leaves under the empirical concepts <flower> and <mum>, and through this conceptual subsumption, I am aware that those representations have an objective unity, the unity corresponding to and necessitated by this flower, which is a mum.

Piecing this trajectory together, on my reading of Kant, the sort of conscious representation of objects that the synthesis of recognition enables involves acts of empirical judgment in which we subsume a manifold of representations under empirical concepts and, thereby, become conscious, in thought, of an existing object that remains the same across our representations, and that our representations correspond to and are necessitated by. It is this consciousness of an object in judgment that I take to be involved in the "thought" of the "relation" of our representations to an existing object and that I understand to be at stake in Kant's account of the synthesis of recognition.

With this picture of the synthesis of recognition in place, we can now return to the question of how Kant conceives of the relationship between the understanding stage and imagination stage of experience. Does Kant think that these stages are inseparable, or does he think that we can arrive at the sort of perception at stake in the imagination stage independently from the understanding stage? By my lights, once we acknowledge that the understanding stage involves judgment, then we have reason to attribute to Kant the latter position.[89] For on Kant's view, although both stages involve concepts, the sort of activities involved in the imagination stage are distinct in kind, and independent from, those involved in judgment.[90]

More specifically, Kant regards the perceptual activities at stake in the imagination stage as sensible in nature: they involve us sensibly ordering and organizing a manifold of intuitions into a perceptual image under the guidance of a schema for

---

[89] For a contrasting "intellectualist" reading of Kant, according to which perception involves judgment, see Merleau-Ponty's *Phenomenology of Perception* (see intro, chap. 3; pt. II, chap. 3) (see also Dreyfus 2006). However, for discussion of certain Kantian commitments that Merleau-Ponty nevertheless takes on board in his theory of perception given Kant's theory of imagination, see Matherne (2014a; 2016).

[90] I am thus sympathetic to commentators who read Kant as attributing concepts a role in perception and sensible synthesis that is prior to the role they play in judgment (see, e.g., Sellars 1978; Longuenesse 2005, chap. 1; Haag 2007; Ginsborg 2008; Grüne 2009; 2022; McDowell 2009; Land 2015a).

THE IMAGINATION AND UNDERSTANDING STAGES OF EXPERIENCE   169

an empirical concept.[91] And through these perceptual images, we consciously represent what appears to us as exhibiting that concept. In recognitional judgment, by contrast, we engage in intellectual activities in which we subsume intuitions under concepts in predicative acts of judgment.[92] And through these judgments, we deploy concepts in order to consciously represent existing objects that remain the same and that our representations correspond to and are necessitated by.

But what of Kant's prefacing his account of the synthesis of recognition with the claim that,

> Without consciousness that that which we think is the very same as what we thought a moment before, all reproduction in the series of representations would be in vain. For it would be a new representation in our current state, which would not belong at all to the act through which it had been gradually generated, and its manifold would never constitute a whole, since it would lack the unity that only consciousness can obtain for it.   (A103)

Doesn't this commit Kant to the sort of sensible activities involved in perception depending on the understanding's synthesis of recognition?

Ultimately, I do not think that the A103 passage forces a reading of perception, hence the imagination stage of experience, along these lines. In this passage, Kant does not commit himself to the idea that reproduction and apprehension happen "in vain" *tout court* without the synthesis of recognition. He commits himself to the idea that without the synthesis of recognition, reproduction and apprehension happen "in vain" vis-à-vis an act of thinking: "Without consciousness that that which we *think* is the very same as what we *thought* a moment before, all reproduction in the series of representations would be in vain" (A103; my emph.). I have argued that, for Kant, this thought amounts to an act of judgment in which we think that our representations relate to an existing object that remains the same throughout our representations and that our representations correspond to

---

[91] Grüne (2009; 2022) and Land (2015a) also place emphasis on the idea that intuitions or perceptions are the product of sensible synthesis, rather than the intellectual synthesis involved in judgment. However, Grüne and Land argue that sensible synthesis is an activity of the understanding; in which case, they take the understanding to be involved in the imagination stage. However, given my analysis of imagination as part of sensibility (see Chapters 2–3), on my reading, though concepts supplied by the understanding guide and constrain the imagination stage, the activities at stake are not a sensible exercise of the understanding, but rather a sensible exercise of imagination, *qua* part of sensibility, carried out in service of the understanding. As I see it, then, Kant is, indeed, committed to the view that, "the understanding can make no other use of these concepts than that of judging by means of them" because the only concept-using activities that the understanding can itself carry out involve acts of judging (A68/B93). Nevertheless, I take this to be consistent with the possibility that the understanding, as the "sovereign" of cognition, supplies concepts that guide and constrain the imagination, as the "executor" of cognition, in its sensible activities (see Chapter 2).

[92] See Land (2015a) for emphasis on the distinction between the predicative structure of a judgment and the spatio-temporal structure of an intuition.

and are necessitated by. I accordingly understand the "wholeness" in our representations that is at issue in this passage to be the wholeness of representations that have objective unity, *qua* representations we have judged to correspond to and be necessitated by an object. As I interpret the stakes of this passage, then, Kant's claim is that without the synthesis of recognition, our imaginative apprehension and reproduction is in vain in the sense that it does not culminate in an act of judgment in which we are conscious of an existing object that remains the same throughout this apprehension and reproduction. Otherwise put, without the synthesis of recognition, our imaginve efforts are in vain given the cognitive function of the understanding: we do not think about objects that we are given through intuition.

However, this does not mean that this imaginative synthesis is cognitively in vain altogether. Even if we do not make a judgment, we can engage in imaginative activities in perception that generate intuitions$_i$ through which we consciously represent particulars as spatio-temporally determinate and as exhibiting concepts. In this, we cognitively progress beyond the consciousness of objects as undetermined that we have through the senses stage. And in these activities, our imagination fulfills the cognitive function that Kant ascribes to it: making concepts sensible. For example, even if I do not judge that the flower in my hand is a mum, my imagination can generate a perceptual image of it that exhibits the concept <mum>. And in this activity, my imagination mediates between the deliverances of sense, on the one hand, and concepts, on the other, in a way that befits its cognitive function.

Still, one might worry that in the A103 passage Kant forecloses the possibility of perception without the synthesis of recognition because the latter is what enables us to be conscious of an object as "the same" in the way perception requires. However, I think that this worry can be dispelled if we take a closer look at the difference in the consciousness of objects involved in perception versus in judgment on Kant's view.

I have argued that, according to Kant, at the understanding stage, we judge that there is an existing object (or relation among existing objects) that remains the same across our representations, which our representations relate to and are necessitated by. And he claims that in virtue of being necessitated by an existing object we take our representations to have "objective unity." This, I take it, is what is involved when we consciously represent an object in thought as "the same."

But at the imagination stage, Kant does not think we represent existing objects that necessitate our representations, nor does he think that we take our representations to have objective unity. Instead of representing existing objects, Kant claims that imaginative synthesis is "always sensible, for it combines the manifold only as it **appears** in intuition, e.g. the shape of a triangle" (A124). As I understand his position, then, the sort of particulars that we consciously represent to ourselves in perception are not existing objects, but rather how things sensibly "appear" to us in their spatial

THE IMAGINATION AND UNDERSTANDING STAGES OF EXPERIENCE 171

and/or temporal form in intuition. Kant connects this consciousness of how things sensibly appear to the idea that in perception our representations only have "subjective unity":

> no necessity of the connection [of perceptions] can become evident in the perceptions themselves, since apprehension is only a juxtaposition of the manifold of empirical intuition, but no representation of the necessity of the combined existence of the appearances that it juxtaposes in space and time is to be encountered in it. (B219)

Here, Kant indicates that in perception our imagination does not represent necessary connection among representations, but only their "juxtaposition in space and time." As Kant makes this point a bit later, "I am...only conscious that my imagination places one state before and the other after, not that the one state precedes the other in the object; or, in other words, through the mere perception the **objective relation** of the appearances that are succeeding one another remains undetermined" (B233–4). For example, when I form a perceptual image of the melody of Mariah Carey's "Fantasy," my imagination places a certain string of notes in a temporal sequence. However, as a failed attempt to sing along might reveal, the way I have imaginatively sequenced these notes may come apart from the objective sequence of notes. For Kant, then, at the imagination stage of experience, we do not yet represent how things objectively are, but rather how things seem to us juxtaposed in space and time. And I take this to be why Kant says that in imaginative synthesis we "combine the manifold only as it appears in intuition": in representing juxtaposition in space and time, our imagination is thus representing how things subjectively appear to us in intuition, but not how objects, in fact, are. Insofar as this is the case, on Kant's view, in the imagination stage, we do not yet consciously represent how objects, in fact, are; we only consciously represent how things spatio-temporally seem to us.

Returning to the A103 passage, as I read it, the consciousness of an object as "the same" that is at issue in this passage is consciousness of an object in judgment, i.e. consciousness of an existing object that we think our representations correspond to and are necessitated by. And without the synthesis of recognition, our imaginative synthesis of representations is, indeed, in vain vis-à-vis this kind of consciousness of objects. However, I have been urging that perception, on Kant's view, involves a different kind of consciousness of objects: it involves consciousness of objects as they subjectively appear to us in perception. And as I interpret Kant's position, without the synthesis of recognition, our imaginative synthesis need not be in vain in relation to this way of consciously representing objects. To the contrary, through reproduction and apprehension, we can generate a perceptual image through which we are conscious of how things seem to us. And this sort of consciousness of how things seem or appear is what I take the cognitive state of perception, independently from the synthesis of recognition and judgment, to deliver on Kant's view.

According to my interpretation of Kant, then, the imagination stage does not depend on the understanding stage of experience: it is possible for us to engage in the sensible activities that result in perception without engaging in the intellectual activities required for judgment. For example, I take it to be possible on Kant's view to have a perceptual image of a particular as something that sensibly appears with a determinate spatial form and that exhibits the concept <mum>, perhaps when I reach for it while making a bouquet, without making a judgment, such as "The flower is a mum."

However, as was the case with the sense and imagination stages, I take it that the understanding stage does depend on the imagination stage for Kant. Recall Kant's claim that, "Experience is empirical cognition, but cognition (since it rests on judgments) requires reflection (*reflexio*)" (Anthro. 7:141). In the third *Critique* Kant describes this reflection in terms of "reflected perception [*reflektierte Wahrnehmung*]" (KU 5:191). And as I read this claim, Kant takes empirical judgment to involve reflecting on perception; hence on the representations that have been apprehended and reproduced in the imagination stage of experience. In this reflection, we subsume what we have apprehended and reproduced under concepts of objects, which, recall, "unif[y] the manifold that has been successively intuited, and then also reproduced, into one representation" (A103). For Kant, then, just as the imagination stage proceeds by transforming what we sense through imaginative acts of sensible synthesis, the understanding stage proceeds by transforming what we perceive through reflective acts of intellectual synthesis in judgment.

The final point I wish to make to clarify the distinction between what sort of consciousness of objects we arrive at through the imagination and understanding stages of experience turns on what each stage enables us to achieve vis-à-vis experience, *qua* cognition in the narrow sense. What I shall argue is that, on Kant's view, though both the imagination and understanding stages contribute to our conscious representation of objects as determinate and really possible, the judgment involved in the understanding stage contributes to these cognitive achievements in a way that the perception involved in the imagination stage cannot.

Beginning with the determinacy achievement, although Kant thinks that both the imagination and understanding stages involve us being conscious of objects as sensibly and qualitatively determinate, in the former case we are conscious of what subjectively appears to us as determinate, whereas in the latter case we are conscious of an existing object that necessitates our representations as determinate. For example, when I perceive the mum, through my imaginative activities, I am conscious of what subjectively appears to me as having a determinate spatial form and as exhibiting the concept <mum>. But when I judge the mum, I am conscious of the mum as an existing object with properties, e.g. as having

THE IMAGINATION AND UNDERSTANDING STAGES OF EXPERIENCE   173

alternating leaves, as a perennial, as boilable for tea, etc., which my representations correspond to and are necessitated by.

To help motivate the difference let's consider a non-veridical case of me hallucinating a mum.[93] In this hallucination, my imagination engages in imaginative synthesis that results in an empirical intuition$_i$ of a mum.[94] Since, on Kant's view, image formation depends on schemata, this intuition$_i$ will be the result of imaginative synthesis that is guided by a schema for the concept <mum> and that exhibits the concept <mum> in sensible form. However, just in virtue of generating an empirical intuition$_i$ that exhibits the concept <mum>, Kant does not think that I have yet committed the error of taking there to, in fact, be an existing mum in front of me: "truth and illusion are not in the object, insofar as it is intuited, but in the judgment about it insofar as it is thought" (A293/B350).[95] So, according to Kant, as long as I do not issue a judgment about the mum, I do not make the mistake of taking there to be an existing mum that necessitates my representations. Nevertheless, my hallucination of the mum involves concepts: my imaginative synthesis has been implicitly guided by a the schema for <mum> and the intuition$_i$ my imagination generates exhibits this concept.

By my lights, the hallucination case is instructive because it points toward the different role concepts play in the imagination and understanding stages of experience and why the determination of objects in each stage differs. In the sort of perception involved in the imagination stage of experience, concepts play a role via schemata, which provide us with sensible patterns in accordance with which we imaginatively synthesize a manifold in accordance with concepts and thereby generate perceptual images that represent particulars as exemplifying concepts. And though through these perceptual images we are conscious of objects as determinate, this amounts to being conscious of a particular, *qua* what subjectively appears to us, as determinate. Meanwhile, in the understanding stage of experience, we deploy concepts in predicative acts of judgment in which we subsume what we intuit under concepts. And in these judgments, concepts serve as predicates by means of which we think about existing objects that have certain properties that necessitate our representations.

But what of the modal achievement of cognition and our consciousness of objects as really possible: how do the contributions of the imagination and understanding stages differ on this count?[96] My remarks about this will be more succinct. Above I suggested that, on Kant's view, the imagination stage contributes to

---

[93] For other discussions of the role imagination plays in Kant's theory of hallucination, see Stephenson (2011; 2015; 2017); McLear (2017).

[94] See Anthro. 7:167; AF 25:511–12; ML1 28:237.

[95] See also Anthro. 7:146; BL 28:83ff; DWL 24:720ff; VL 24:825.

[96] See Watkins (forthcoming) for a discussion of the contributions our various capacities make to the modal achievement of cognition under the heading of the "subjective sources condition" on cognition.

174 EMPIRICAL IMAGINATION IN PERCEPTION AND EXPERIENCE

the modal achievement in the context of experience insofar as the intuitions$_i$ it furnishes demonstrate the objective reality of empirical concepts in the literal sense: they show or present a concept in intuition, throwing it before our eyes.[97] However, there is a question here of whether having the perceptual image suffices for the proof of the objective reality of a concept, or whether it is what puts us in a position to prove this. It seems to me that, on Kant's view, although perception can demonstrate the objective reality of an empirical concept in the literal sense, proof of the objective reality of an empirical concept requires reflection on this demonstration (KU 5:343). More specifically, we need to reflect on the literal demonstration furnished to us through an intuition$_i$ and issue a judgment to the effect that our representations are necessitated by an existing object, to which our concepts relate. As I read Kant, then, it is only when this reflection happens in the understanding stage that we become conscious of an existing object as really possible in the way requisite for "proof"; hence it is only through the understanding stage that we accomplish the modal achievement of cognition in the narrow sense.

To sum up, on my interpretation, although, on Kant's view, the imagination and understanding stages of experience differ from the sense stage insofar as they involve concepts, he ultimately distinguishes between the two with respect to the sort of cognitive state they involve. Though both stages involve a kind of conceptually laden consciousness of objects, on my interpretation of Kant, there is a distinction between the sort of consciousness of how things seem to us that we arrive at through the sensible activities of imagination in perception and the intellectual consciousness of how existing objects, in fact, are, that we arrive at through the intellectual activities of the understanding in judgment. And, for Kant, it is only through the latter activities that we arrive at the empirical cognition required for experience in his technical sense.

5.6 Conclusion

In this chapter, my main aim has been to clarify the empirical contribution that Kant attributes to imagination in perception and experience in light of his three-stage account of experience. To recap, I argued that, on Kant's view, the sense stage involves the generation of empirical intuitions$_s$ through receptive processes of sensing, which do not depend on empirical concepts. And I claimed that, for Kant, these intuitions$_s$ involve the conscious representation of objects as undetermined appearances and have the cognitive function of giving us objects. The imagination stage, meanwhile, involves spontaneous sensible activities of imaginative synthesis that are guided by empirical concepts by way of schemata. These

---

[97] Recall, "to demonstrate (*ostendere, exhibere*) means the same as...to exhibit its concept at the same time in intuition" (KU 5:343; transl. modified).

concept-guided imaginative activities generate intuitions$_i$ (perceptual images) through which we see more in perception, are conscious of how appearances seem to us, and represent those appearances as spatio-temporally determinate and as exhibiting empirical concepts. And this stage has the cognitive function of making empirical concepts sensible. Finally, the understanding stage involves spontaneous processes of intellectual synthesis in which we subsume representations under empirical concepts in acts of recognitional judgment through which we consciously represent existing objects that remain the same and that our representations correspond to and are necessitate by. And these acts of judgment have the cognitive function of enabling us to think about the objects that we intuit in the way that is required for cognition in Kant's technical sense, *qua* empirical cognition.

In addition to defending an interpretation of the three stages of experience and laying out Kant's taxonomy of sensing, perceiving, and judging in an experiential context, over the course of this discussion I hope to have clarified Kant's commitment to imagination being a "necessary ingredient" of perception. For it is through its distinctive acts of synthesis that Kant thinks our imagination forms the sort of perceptual images posterior to sensing, but prior to judging, that animate our perceptual lives and enable us to see more therein.

I also hope to have begun clarifying in what sense Kant endorses a conceptualist picture of what our imagination contributes vis-à-vis experience. In particular in this chapter, I have focused on his commitment to the imagination's generation of empirical intuitions$_i$ in perception depending on empirical concepts. I have argued that the key to understanding this dependence on Kant's view is attending to the ways in which perception involves the imaginative exhibition of empirical concepts. Indeed, I claimed that, for Kant, the generation of intuitions$_i$ in perception involves the imaginative exhibition of empirical concepts on a couple levels. In the first place, the schemata that guide perception are a kind of intuition$_i$ generated through imaginative acts that are constrained by the logical content of empirical concepts and evince our imaginative know-how with how that logical content shows up in a sensible, holistic way. In the second place, perceptual images are another kind of intuition$_i$, which are produced through imaginative synthesis that is guided by empirical concepts vis-à-vis schemata, and which represent a particular as exhibiting an empirical concept *in concreto*. Unlike sensing, then, which I claimed can generate empirical intuitions$_s$ without the involvement of empirical concepts, perceiving, for Kant, must involve empirical concepts. However, I also maintained that the role empirical concepts play in generating empirical intuitions$_i$ in perception is distinct from the role they play in judgment. Whereas in perception, concepts guide imaginative synthesis of how things appear and figure in the content of perceptual images, in judgment concepts serve as predicates through which we think about the existing objects that our representations correspond to and are necessitated by.

Finally in this chapter, I hope to have brought out the importance of attending to Kant's definition of imagination as a faculty of exhibition in order to understand its theoretical use in the context of experience. To be sure, as I also claimed, in this context, our imagination acts as a faculty of formation and a faculty that represents objects in intuition even without their presence. However, if we are to ultimately understand how those formative and even-without-presence activities unfold in cognitively well-functioning ways in perception, then we need to situate them in Kant's account of the imaginative exhibition of concepts in perception. For it is in the course of directly exhibiting a concept that our imagination sensibly orders and organizes a manifold and represents objects even without their presence in perception. To put the point another way, for Kant, imagination is a "necessary ingredient" of perception in virtue of sensible activities of exhibition that ultimately mediate between the deliverances of sense, on the one hand, and empirical concepts, on the other.

However, as I noted at the outset, Kant analyzes what our imagination contributes in the context of experience at both an empirical and an *a priori* level. And it is to the latter level, in all its complexity, that I shall now turn.

Seeing More: Kant's Theory of Imagination. Samantha Matherne, Oxford University Press.
© Samantha Matherne 2024. DOI: 10.1093/9780191999291.003.0006

6

A Priori Imagination and the
Conditions of Experience I

The Transcendental Deduction

Is it therefore certainly strange,
yet from what has been said... obvious
that it is only by means of this transcendental function of
the imagination that... experience itself, become[s] possible

—A123

6.1 Introduction

Although in the first *Critique* Kant addresses the empirical contribution imagination makes in experience, given the transcendental orientation of this text,[1] his main concern is with the *a priori* contribution it makes to the possibility of experience in the first place. As I noted in the last chapter, in the *a priori* vein, Kant's theory of imagination veers in increasingly abstract directions, as he explores how imagining can bridge the gap between pure intuitions of space and time and pure concepts of the understanding, like <substance> and <cause>. He explicates this *a priori* imaginative activity in two notoriously difficult stretches of the first *Critique*, the Transcendental Deduction and Schematism, in which he introduces some notoriously difficult topics, such as figurative synthesis, formal intuitions of space and time, and transcendental schemata. Yet for all its abstraction and difficulty, Kant's analysis of the *a priori* exercise of imagination is central to his account of the theoretical use our imagination has vis-à-vis experience, for without this exercise, he thinks experience would not be possible at all.

My aim in the two following chapters is to elucidate Kant's picture of this *a priori* exercise of imagination and to clarify how it helps makes possible the sort of empirical activities involved in experience that I discussed in Chapter 5. In this

---

[1] See, e.g., Kant's description of a "**critique** of pure reason" as something that is concerned with "transcendental" "cognition" "that is occupied... with our mode of cognition of objects insofar as this is to be possible *a priori*" (A11/B25).

178 A PRIORI IMAGINATION AND THE CONDITIONS OF EXPERIENCE I

chapter, I focus on Kant's account in the Transcendental Deduction (specifically the B-edition),[2] and in the next chapter on the Schematism. Indeed, I make the case that though Kant begins developing his picture of the *a priori* exercise of imagination in the Deduction, it is not until the Schematism that he settles many of the key issues on this topic.

Over the course of these chapters, I address three main questions about the theoretical use of *a priori* imagining. First, I consider the question of Kant's account of the relationship between imagination and the two *a priori* conditions on the possibility of experience he introduces in the Aesthetic and Analytic of the first *Critique*, respectively: the pure intuitions of space and time and the pure concepts of the understanding ("the categories"). What is of particular interest to me is the question of whether he defends a radical view, according to which the *a priori* imagination is, in some sense, the source of either space and time or the categories. The notorious footnote in §26 of the B Deduction in which he intimates that space and time are "first **given** as intuitions" through the figurative synthesis of imagination, and his claim that space and time are "*ens imaginarium*" might suggest the former (B161n; A291/B347).[3] Whereas his remark in the Schematism chapter that "without schemata" produced by imagination, "the categories are only functions of the understanding for concepts, but do not represent any object" might suggest the latter (A147/B187; A140/B179).[4]

Though one can find evidence pointing in these radical directions, in what follows I argue that we should attribute to Kant a mediating, rather than a radical, model of the *a priori* imagination, according to which it mediates between the pure intuitions of space and time given through sensibility, on the one hand, and the categories given through the understanding, on the other. Like other interpreters who defend a mediating model, I proceed on the basis of a detailed

---

[2] As I have noted, some commentators argue that Kant changes his view about imagination between the A and B Deductions, denying to imagination an independence from the understanding that he accords it in the A Deduction (see Heidegger KPM §31; Bennett 1966, 134–8; Kitcher 1990, 158–60; Longuenesse 1998, 204–8; Allison 2001, 186–9; Horstmann 2018, pt. 1). On my reading, however, he does not change his mind about the status of imagination in the B Deduction: it remains a faculty that "belongs to **sensibility**," rather than to the understanding (B151). So, in focusing on the B Deduction, I do not take it to represent a substantively different account of the *a priori* exercise of imagination than the one we get in the A Deduction. We, indeed, find a considerable amount of continuity in his discussion of the *a priori* exercise of imagination across both texts. In both the A and B Deductions Kant speaks of a "transcendental synthesis" of the "productive" imagination (see, e.g., A118–19; B151–3, B157). And as in §24 of the B Deduction, Kant argues in the A Deduction that this transcendental synthesis plays a pivotal role in securing the objective validity of the categories: "the **categories**...[are] related to all objects of the senses, though only by means of intuition, and to their synthesis by means of imagination" (A119). However, I focus on the B Deduction because I think he offers a more streamlined account of the *a priori* exercise of imagination, specifically in §§24 and 26.

[3] See, e.g., Heidegger PIK chap. 2, §7; KPM §28; Waxman (1991, pt. 1; 2014); Longuenesse (1998, chap. 8; 2005, chap. 5); Banham (2013); Nuzzo (2013, 41–2).

[4] See, e.g., Heidegger PIK 291–2; KPM 77–8; Longuenesse (1998, 252–3); de Boer (2016, §6; 2020, chap. 6, §4).

INTRODUCTION 179

interpretation of the first *Critique*.[5] However, I supplement this interpretive line of thought with an argument to the effect that the mediating model is supported by Kant's theory of imagination in general.[6] More specifically, I argue that the mediating model is underwritten by Kant's analysis of the distinctive kind of intuition (intuition$_i$), activity, and cognitive function that he ascribes to imagination in general (see Chapters 3–4).

The second main question that I address concerns how exactly Kant thinks the *a priori* exercise of imagination conditions experience. I shall cast this question as a question about how imagination contributes to the possibility of the three stages of experience that I detailed in Chapter 5: the sense stage, the imagination stage, and the understanding stage. According to one version of the radical interpretation, Kant intends for his account of *a priori* imagination to explain how the most basic stage of experience is possible: the sense stage in which we have empirical intuitions of sense (intuitions$_s$).[7] Against this, I make the case that Kant conceives of the *a priori* exercise of imagination as a condition not of sensing, but rather of the perception involved in the imagination stage and the judgments involved in the understanding stage. More specifically, I contend that, on his view, what the *a priori* exercise of imagination conditions, at the most basic level, is our ability to represent appearances as spatially and/or temporally determinate in the way that is required for perception and experience.

The third question I take up pertains to Kant's conceptualism and whether he commits himself to the view that the generation of intuitions in the context of experience depends on concepts. I began addressing this question in Chapter 5, where I focused on empirical intuitions and empirical concepts, and I argued that he offers a nuanced view with conceptualist and non-conceptualist dimensions. To this end, I claimed that Kant is not committed to the generation of empirical intuitions$_s$ depending on empirical concepts, but he is committed to the generation of empirical intuitions$_i$ in perception depending on empirical concepts. In the next two chapters, I pursue the question of whether the intuitions generated in the context of experience depend on the pure concepts of the understanding, i.e. the categories. This question is especially pressing, as some conceptualist interpreters have argued that one of the upshots of Kant's argument in the Transcendental Deduction is that the generation of intuitions depends on the categories.[8] However, in keeping with the trajectory of my interpretation from Chapter 5, I argue that Kant does not commit himself to the view that the

[5] See, e.g., Allison (2004, chap. 7); Hughes (2007, chap. 4); Onof and Schulting (2015); Schulting (2017, chap. 7): Tolley (2019).
[6] For example, Onof and Schulting (2015) defend a mediating model on the basis of a non-conceptualist interpretation of the pure intuitions of space and time as articulated in the Transcendental Aesthetic. For other non-conceptualist readings of the pure intuitions of space and time that are consistent with the mediating model, see Allais (2009); McLear (2015); and Tolley (2016).
[7] See Longuenesse (1998, chap. 8; 2005, chap. 5).
[8] See, e.g., Bowman (2011); Griffith (2012); Land (2015b); Schulting (2017); Shaddock (2018).

generation of all intuitions depends on the categories in the Deduction. I, instead, defend a more restricted conceptualist reading, according to which he is only committed to the generation of intuitions$_i$, at both the empirical and *a priori* levels, depending on the categories. And I claim that he acknowledges other intuitions, at both the empirical and *a priori* levels, that do not depend on the categories.

In this chapter, I approach these questions in the context of the B-edition of the Transcendental Deduction, focusing in particular on issues surrounding Kant's account of the relationship that the *a priori* exercise of imagination has to space and time.[9] In §6.2, I lay out the debate surrounding whether Kant, in the footnote in §26, commits himself to the radical view that the *a priori* exercise of imagination is the source of our most fundamental pure intuitions of space and time, which condition empirical intuitions$_s$. My aim in the rest of the chapter is to argue that he endorses a more moderate mediating model that is in keeping with his theory of imagination more generally.

This argument shall move in two stages. In the first stage (§§6.3–6.4), I work through the implications that Kant's account of imaginative activity in general has for how we frame its *a priori* exercise. To this end, I claim that as is in keeping with his account of imaginative activity in general, the *a priori* activities of imagination involve making intuitions$_j$, here, pure intuitions$_i$ of space and time, as the result of spontaneously ordering and organizing a manifold given through the receptivity of sensibility, here the manifold of the pure intuition of space and time. In §6.3, I pursue this line of thought in light of the distinction between "given" versus "made" pure intuitions of space and time that Kant explicitly articulates in his 1790 remarks, "On Kästner's Treatises." And in §6.4, I argue that the given-made distinction serves as an important backdrop to his analysis of the relationship that our imagination has to the "forms of intuition," *qua* given, and "formal intuitions," *qua* made, in §26 of the B Deduction.

In the second stage of my argument (§§6.5–6.6), I offer a close reading of §26 in which I draw on Kant's analysis of what it means for our imagination to function cognitively well in general in order to elucidate the complicated and seemingly contradictory details of his position. I have argued that, for Kant, our imagination functions cognitively well by generating intuitions$_i$ that make concepts sensible, and I claim that this is no less true in the *a priori* case, the relevant intuitions, here, being formal intuitions of space and time, and the relevant concepts being the categories. After detailing the process of so-called "figurative synthesis" through which our imagination generates these formal intuitions in §6.5, in §6.6, I take up the question of how this *a priori* exercise of imagination contributes to the possibility of experience. To this end, I argue that rather than explicating how

---

[9] See Henrich's (1969) now classic division of the B Deduction into two steps, the first of which culminates in §20 and the second of which culminates in §26.

it is possible for us to have intuitions$_s$, his account of the *a priori* imagination is meant to elucidate how we actively take up intuitions$_s$ through the activity of perception and experience. In this section, I explore issues surrounding what role Kant's account of the imagination plays vis-à-vis his aim and strategy in the second step of the B Deduction, as well as how these issues bear on his conceptualism.

At the end of this chapter, though I hope to have made headway with respect to the three main questions I listed above, I flag several key junctures where the details of Kant's answers remain underdeveloped in the Deduction. And in Chapter 7, I hope to show that we do not, in fact, get clarity about many of these issues until we look to Kant's elaboration of his position in the Schematism chapter, where we discover that conceiving of imagination as the faculty of exhibition is crucial in this context.

6.2 The Radical Interpretation of Imagination as the Source of Space and Time

In the so-called "Table of Nothing" with which Kant concludes the Transcendental Analytic, he provocatively describes space and time as *"ens imaginarium"* (A291/ B347).[10] According to some readers, this remark points toward one of Kant's most radical commitments: he conceives of space and time as products of imagination. Defending this radical interpretation, Heidegger claims, "space and time...are rooted in the transcendental power of imagination. Hence space as well as time were designated as *ens imaginarium*" (PIK 84; see also KPM 101). Pursuing this interpretation more recently, Wayne Waxman attributes to Kant the *"entia imaginaria* thesis," according to which "space and time, together with the manifold they contain, were for Kant *wholly* products of imagination" (1991, 33). Béatrice Longuenesse, meanwhile, argues that, "we should conclude that the space and time described in the Transcendental Aesthetic are products of the figurative synthesis of imagination" (1998, 216).[11]

When one begins reading the first *Critique*, the idea that Kant conceives of space and time as products of imagination is not readily apparently. He introduces his theory of space and time in the Transcendental Aesthetic, a stretch of text he describes as an "investigation" that "**isolate[s]** sensibility by separating off everything that the understanding thinks through its concepts" (A22/B36). In this investigation, Kant presents space and time as the "two pure forms of sensible

---

[10] See also, "Space and time are products (but primitive products) of our own imagination, hence self-created intuitions, inasmuch as the subject affects itself" (OP 23:37).

[11] She develops this reading in (1998, chap. 8) and (2005, chaps. 1, 3 (referencing "ens imaginarium" explicitly at 73–6)).

182   A PRIORI IMAGINATION AND THE CONDITIONS OF EXPERIENCE I

intuitions," which make up the *a priori* "constitution" of our sensibility (A22–3/B36–38; see also B41). And he dedicates the "expositions" to explicating his theory of space and time. He dedicates the so-called "Metaphysical Exposition" to the question: "what are space and time" (A23/B37). And he answers this question by arguing that space and time are pure "intuitions" rather than "concepts";[12] "singular";[13] wholes that "precede" their parts,[14] "infinite given magnitudes,"[15] and the "ground" of empirical intuitions.[16] Then in "Transcendental Exposition" he explores how space and time, so understood, make "synthetic *a priori* cognition" in fields, such as geometry, arithmetic, and mechanics possible. Nowhere in this discussion does Kant suggest that space and time have their source in imagination. Indeed, he mentions imagination only once in the Aesthetic, as part of a critique of the Leibnizian view of space and time as "only creatures of the imagination" (A40/B57).

As the first *Critique* continues, Kant appears to confirm the picture of space and time he presents in the Aesthetic. In the Metaphysical Deduction, he says that, "space and time contain a pure *a priori* intuition, but belong nevertheless among the conditions of the receptivity of our mind" (A76/B102). And at the outset of the B Deduction, Kant asserts, "The manifold of representations can be given in an intuition that is merely sensible, i.e. nothing but receptivity, and the form of this intuition can lie *a priori* in our faculty of representation without being anything other than the way in which the subject is affected" (B129).[17] Up until this point in the first *Critique*, Kant thus gives us little reason to suspect that he regards space and time as products of imagination.

However, as the radical interpreters emphasize, once we get to the end of the B-edition of the Transcendental Deduction, Kant appears to complicate this origin story, offering an account of how space and time are "first **given** as intuitions" (B161). To this end, in the footnote to §26, he introduces a distinction between space and time as "forms of intuition" and "formal intuitions" (B160n). He says that the latter involve the "determination of the **unity**" of the manifold contained in the forms of intuition (B160). He, rather surprisingly, claims that although in the Aesthetic he credited these formal intuitions "to sensibility," they actually "presuppose a synthesis" (B160–1n). And his citation of §24 at the end of this footnote suggests that the synthesis through which we are first given space and time as formal intuitions is an imaginative synthesis, he calls "figurative synthesis" or "*synthesis speciosa*" (B151). The Transcendental Deduction thus appears to give us reason to "reread the Aesthetic," as we come to learn that the pure intuitions of space and time under discussion in the Aesthetic are not just given to us

---

[12] See A23/B38–A25/B39; A30/B46–A32/B47.   [13] See A25/B39; A31–2/B47.
[14] See A25/B39; A438/B466.   [15] See A25/B39; A31/B47–A32/B48.
[16] See A24/B38; A31/B46.
[17] See also his claim at the outset of the A Deduction to the effect that there is a "manifold [of space and time] that sensibility in its original receptivity provides" (A100).

THE RADICAL INTERPRETATION OF IMAGINATION   183

through sensibility, but depend on some sort of *a priori* imaginative activity (Longuenesse 1998, 213). And it is in this spirit that commentators have attributed to Kant the radical view of space and time as "ens imaginarium."[18]

While the basic idea animating the radical interpretation is relatively clear (space and time are products of imagination), the details are anything but. As these interpreters stress, Kant speaks of space and time in different ways, describing them variously as "forms of intuition," "pure intuitions," and "formal intuitions." The content of each of these terms is debatable, as are the relations between them.[19] But attending to these distinctions is important for thinking through in exactly what sense space and time might, or might not, be products of imagination for Kant. Indeed, in contrast with Heidegger who reads Kant as committed to the view that space and time are nothing but products of imagination,[20] Waxman and Longuenesse argue that Kant acknowledges one sense in which space and time are not products of imagination: space and time understood as "forms of intuition" that are built into our sensibility.[21] Waxman glosses a form of intuition in this sense as the "*innate nonrepresentational faculty ground* of space and time" (1991, 95–7). And Longuenesse describes it as the "*merely potential form*" that is "contained in receptivity," and that is a "mere form of manifoldness" (1998, 221; 2005, 69). So, according to their interpretations, Kant never intends to establish that space and time as forms built into the constitution of sensibility are products of imagination. Instead, they argue that his aim is to show that the representations of space and time as "pure intuitions" and "formal intuitions" are products of imagination. They emphasize that these pure or formal intuitions involve a "determination of the **unity**" of the manifold of space and time. And they argue that this unified intuition of space and time maps onto the account of the pure intuition of space and time as singular, wholes that precede their parts, and infinite magnitudes that Kant gives in the Metaphysical Exposition.[22] On this

[18] Commentators have also argued that the footnote gives us reason to reread the pure intuitions of space and time as products of the understanding. See, e.g., the reading defending by Marburg Neo-Kantians, such as Hermann Cohen, Paul Natorp, and Ernst Cassirer (for discussion, see Matherne 2021a, chap. 2). And, more recently, see Henrich 1969; McDowell 1996, 73–6; 2009, 73–4; Keller 1998, 107–12; Dufour 2003; Gomes 2010; Bauer 2012; Griffith 2012; Messina 2014; Conant 2016; 2017; Williams 2018. I will address the role the understanding plays in this argument in §6.5.

[19] See, e.g., Heidegger PIK chap. 2, §7; KPM §28; Waxman (1991, pt. I); Longuenesse (1998, chap. 8; 2005, chap. 3).

[20] See also Banham who argues that forms of intuition involve "the manifold as unified by *a priori* intuitions," where this unification depends on the transcendental synthesis of imagination (2013, 92). And see Nuzzo (2013, 41–2) who argues that the transcendental synthesis of imagination is what makes receptivity possible in the first place because the manifold as a form of intuition can only be given if it is "*gathered together* in a 'formal intuition'" (2013, 41).

[21] This is how Waxman and Longuenesse understand forms of intuition, *qua* the "first formal ground" of sensibility (OD 8:222); see Waxman (1991, 45–6) and Longuenesse (1998, 222; 2005, 34–5, 70–2).

[22] See Waxman (1991, 80–2); Longuenesse (1998, 214–15; 2005, 35–6, 69). Onof and Schulting (2015) describe these features of space and time under the heading "unicity," and they, like Allais (2009), McLear (2015), and Tolley (2016), resist this radical reading and defend an alternative non-conceptualist reading of the pure intuition of space and time at issue in the Metaphysical Exposition.

version of the radical interpretation, then, the aspect of Kant's account of space and time from the Aesthetic that we need to "reread" in light of the Deduction is not the account of space and time as forms of intuition built into the constitution of our sensibility, but rather the account of space and time as pure intuitions that Kant offers in the Metaphysical Exposition.

This said, in her defense of the radical interpretation, Longuenesse nevertheless attributes to Kant a view according to which there is another sense in which space and time are forms of intuition that have their source in imagination. To this end, she argues that although by "form of intuition" Kant sometimes has in mind the "merely potential form" of our sensibility, at other times he identifies "form of intuition" with our most basic "pure intuitions" and "formal intuitions" of space and time (see 1998, 219; 2005, 67–73).[23] And she makes the case that conceiving of forms of intuition in this latter sense as products of imagination is crucial for understanding why he appeals to imagination as part of his argumentative strategy in the Transcendental Deduction. For, according to Longuenesse, in order to prove that "everything that may ever come before our senses must stand under" the understanding in the Deduction, Kant's strategy is to prove that "*the manner in which things are given to us*, that is, the forms of intuition expounded in the Transcendental Aesthetic" must stand under the understanding (B159) (1998, 212; 2005, 32—referencing B144).[24] This argument, she claims, goes by way of Kant showing that the forms of space and time, in the relevant sense, are first generated through the figurative synthesis of imagination—a synthesis through which understanding affects sensibility (see 1998, chap. 8; 2005, 32–6). If Longuenesse is right, then in order to make sense of Kant's project in the Deduction, we need to acknowledge his radical commitment to imagination being the source of the forms of space and time, *qua* pure intuitions of space and time as singular, wholes that precede their parts, infinite given magnitudes, and the ground of empirical intuitions.

By my lights, the radical interpretation rightly brings to the fore the importance of attending to Kant's account of the *a priori* exercise of imagination if we are to make sense of his theory of space and time, in all its nuance, and his strategy in the Transcendental Deduction. However, in what follows, I argue that approaching these issues through the lens of Kant's theory of imagination more generally points toward a more moderate mediating, rather than a radical, model

---

[23] See, e.g., her claim that, "We must then conclude, in light of sections 24 and 26 of the Transcendental Deduction, that the figurative synthesis...generates the *pure intuition* of space and time and thereby the *form of appearances*, or form of intuition, or form of sensibility, all of which were expounded in the Transcendental Aesthetic" (1998, 219). In support of this line of interpretation, she also draws on Kant's remark in the Dialectic to the effect, "Space is merely the form of outer intuition (formal intuition)" (A429/B457).

[24] More specifically, she argues that, in the second step, "he argues that space and time themselves, the forms of our sensibility, stand under the very same unity of apperception," which she takes to be that "in which the categories originate as 'concepts of an object'" (2005, 32).

of the imagination's relation to space and time. To be clear, there is a kind of mediation that radical interpreters like Waxman and Longuenesse can acknowledge: the way in which the *a priori* imagination mediates between the forms of space and time that are given through the constitution of sensibility, on the one hand, and the understanding, on the other. But because they distinguish these forms of intuition from our most basic intuitions of space and time as singular, wholes that precede their parts, infinite given magnitudes, and the ground of empirical intuitions described in the Metaphysical Exposition, they do not cast this imaginative mediation as mediation between pure intuitions and the understanding. It is thus mediation in this latter sense that I take to be at issue between our interpretations. And I make the case that attending to Kant's commitments concerning imagination in general, including to the nature of imaginative activity and its cognitive function, lends support to a mediating, rather than a radical, reading, according to which Kant does not conceive of imagination as the source of our most basic pure intuitions of space and time, but rather as the source of pure intuitions$_i$ of space and time that our imagination makes on this basis.

6.3 Pure Intuitions: Given and Made

In order to begin developing my argument that Kant's theory of imagination in general lends support to a mediating, rather than a radical, model of its relationship to space and time, let's pick up the thread of his basic picture of imaginative activity. As I discussed in Chapter 3, according to Kant, imaginative activity in general involves spontaneous processes in which our imagination makes intuitions$_i$ by sensibly ordering and organizing a manifold that is given through sensibility. In the empirical case, I identified the relevant manifold as the one we are given through the receptivity of sense, and in the *a priori* case as the *a priori* manifold of space and time that sensibility "in its original receptivity provides" (A100).[25] While this much is relatively uncontroversial, what I argue in the next two sections is that Kant does not regard this *a priori* manifold of space and time just as a "potential form" built into sensibility, but rather as a manifold inseparable from the pure intuition of space and time that we are given through the formal constitution of sensibility. On my reading, then, the distinction between pure intuitions of space and time that are given versus those that are made is a key piece of Kant's story concerning the relationship imagination has to space and time.

First, however, a few words are in order about Kant's conception of what a pure intuition of space and time is. He describes a pure intuition in general as one "in which nothing is to be encountered that belongs to sensation," and that "occurs *a*

---

[25] I discussed this under the heading of the "material constraint" on imagining in Chapter 3.

priori, even without an actual object of the senses or sensations" (A20–1/B34–5). Unlike empirical intuitions, then, which "relate to the object through sensation," pure intuitions are devoid of sensational matter (A20/B34). Instead of relating to actual objects through sensations, Kant claims that pure intuitions "relate to the form under which the object is intuited" (WF 20:266). By this, I take Kant to mean that pure intuitions represent the spatial and/or temporal form of objects we intuit, e.g. their shape or duration.

So, what is Kant's distinction between pure intuitions of space and time that are given versus those that are made? While I shall turn to how this bears on the B Deduction in §6.4, I want to introduce this distinction by way of Kant's explicit discussion of it in "On Kästner's Treatises" (1790), which is a set of unpublished remarks he wrote to Johann Schultz about Abraham Kästner's mathematical views (OKT 20:419; transl. modified).[26] In these remarks, Kant draws the distinction between pure intuitions of space that are "given" (*gegeben*) and those that are "made" (*gemacht*) as part of an analysis of two perspectives that we can take on space: a metaphysical and geometrical perspective (OKT 20:419; transl. modified). From the metaphysical perspective, Kant claims that our interest is in how our most basic representation of space is given to us, whereas from the geometrical perspective our concern is with how representations of space can be made through acts of geometrical construction (OKT 20:420).

In more detail, in his discussion of the metaphysical perspective, Kant claims we are concerned with our "original" or "foundational" representation of space (OKT 20:219–20). This space, he maintains, is "subjectively given" "on the side of the thinker" (OKT 20:420–1).[27] More specifically, he asserts that this space is given as "the pure form of the sensible mode of representation of the subject, as *a priori* intuition" (OKT 20:420). By glossing space as a "subjectively given" "pure form" of this sort, he alerts us to the idea that space is originally given to us in virtue of the formal constitution of our sensibility. However, notice that he identifies this given form with an *a priori* intuition. What this suggests is that Kant does not here distinguish between space as the form of sensibility from our original pure intuition of space, but rather identifies them.

Kant goes on to characterize this pure intuition of space in terms familiar from the Metaphysical Exposition in the Transcendental Aesthetic. He claims that it is an intuition of space as "singular" (*einigen*): "all spaces are only possible…as parts of one single space" (OKT 20:419–20; transl. modified). He also maintains that it is an intuition of space as "infinite": "a magnitude, in comparison with which

---

[26] For discussions of the context of this treatise, see Allison (1973, 12–13); Onof and Schulting (2014). For discussion of how this treatise bears on Kant's account of space and time in the first *Critique*, see Carson (1997, 497–8); Friedman (2000, 188–93); Onof and Schulting (2014; 2015); Tolley (2016); Chaplin (2022); Winegar (2022).

[27] See Chaplin (2022) for a reading of what it means for space and time to be "given" in a metaphysical, rather than in a phenomenological sense.

each assignable [unit] of the same type is only equal to a part of it" (OKT 20:419). And he argues that it is the "ground" on the basis of which all other intuitions of space are "derived" (OKT 20:420).

Switching to the geometrical perspective on space, Kant suggests that in geometry we are concerned with pure intuitions of space that are "made," e.g. intuitions of circles, lines, or triangles (OKT 20:419; transl. modified).[28] These pure intuitions, he claims, are "derivative": they are formed on the basis of the original pure intuition of space (OKT 20:419). And he analyzes the process through which such pure intuitions of space are made in terms reminiscent of mathematical "construction" (*Konstruktion*) from the first *Critique*.[29]

By way of a bit of background, in the first *Critique* Kant defines mathematical construction as an imaginative process in which we "**construct** a concept" by "exhibit[ing] *a priori* the intuition corresponding to it," whether "on paper" or "through mere imagination" (A713/B741). For example, we construct the concept <circle> by imaginatively "describing" a curve all points of which are equidistant from a given point (see B154; Br. 11:43). Though Kant does not mention construction by name in the Transcendental Exposition, it is in the background of his account of how we come to have synthetic *a priori* cognition in geometry: through the pure intuitions$_i$ of space provided by construction, we come to cognize certain "properties of space synthetically and yet *a priori*" (B40). For example, through constructing a pure intuition$_i$ of space by "**placing** three lines perpendicular to each other at the same point," we arrive at the synthetic *a priori* cognition that, "space has only three dimensions" (B154, B41).

Alluding to this theory of mathematical construction in the "Kästner" piece, Kant characterizes the process through which pure intuitions$_i$ of space are made in geometry as one that involves "exhibition" and "the determination of [space] in conformity with a certain concept of an object" (OKT 20:419; transl. modified). So understood, our imagination makes pure intuitions$_i$ by "determining" the space we are given in accordance with a "concept of an object," such as <circle>, and the result is a pure intuition$_i$ that represents a determinate spatial form that exhibits the relevant concept to us. Kant, moreover, claims that when we determine space in accordance with a concept of an object in this way, we become conscious of space as "objectively given" (OKT 20:420). By this, I understand Kant to mean that when we geometrically construct a concept, we become conscious of a spatial form as an object, and through this we can come to cognize

---

[28] Kant explicitly calls these "pure intuitions" at OKT 20:422.

[29] For more discussion of Kant's account of mathematical construction and the role imagination plays in it, see Young (1982; 1984; 1988); Friedman (1990; 2015); Longuenesse (1998, chap. 9); Ferrarin (1995a); Shabel (1998); Domski (2010); Dunlop (2012); Land (2014); Breitenbach (2015); Sutherland (2022, chaps. 2, 4); Kravanja (2023).

188   A PRIORI IMAGINATION AND THE CONDITIONS OF EXPERIENCE I

certain properties of that spatial form synthetically and *a priori*.[30] To take another example, through the intuitions$_i$ I imaginatively generate when I describe a circle and draw lines, I become conscious of a circle as a determinate spatial object, and through this constructive activity I can arrive at synthetic *a priori* cognition of "many splendid properties," e.g. "If a point be taken within a circle, from which two equal straight lines can be drawn to the circumference, that point must be the center of the circle" (KU 5:362; Euclid Book III, Proposition 9).

Although in the "Kästner" piece, Kant focuses on space, I take it that he has a similar story about the pure intuitions of time. The given pure intuition of time is our original intuition of time that we are subjectively given in virtue of the formal constitution of our sensibility. This intuition is an intuition of time as singular and infinite and it is the ground of all other intuitions of time. Meanwhile pure intuitions$_i$ of time are derivative intuitions of determinate temporal forms, e.g. durations or sequences, that we generate through an imaginative process in which we determine the given pure intuition of time in accordance with certain concepts. Through these pure intuitions$_i$ time is "objectively given" to us in a way that puts us in a position to have synthetic *a priori* cognition of time, e.g. in mechanics or arithmetic.

Though there are various productive angles from which we might think through Kant's distinction between given and made pure intuitions, what I would like to stress is that this framework is in keeping with Kant's picture of imaginative activity in general. Our imagination proceeds in this *a priori* register as it always does: by taking up the deliverances given through sensibility (here, our given pure intuitions of space and time), and making its own intuitions$_i$ (here, derivative pure intuitions$_i$ of space and time) on this basis. And what I shall now argue is that this framework should inform how we read what our imagination accomplishes, and does not accomplish, in relation to space and time, as Kant articulates it in the B Deduction.

6.4 Given and Made Pure Intuitions in the B Deduction

As I noted above, in §26 of the B Deduction, Kant complicates his earlier account of space and time from the Aesthetic by drawing a distinction between space and time as "forms of intuition" and "formal intuitions." However, I shall argue that this distinction maps onto the distinction between given and made pure intuitions that I just pursued,[31] and provides a helpful frame for the *a priori* imaginative

---

[30] Here, we must be careful, as Kant suggests that mathematical objects are not self-standing objects, but are rather to be understood in terms of the "form" of "**Things in space and time**" (B147).
[31] Onof and Schulting (2015) resist mapping the distinction between subjectively given versus geometrically constructed space in the "Kästner" treatise onto the form of intuition versus formal intuition distinction because they argue subjectively given space can be identified both as a form of

GIVEN AND MADE PURE INTUITIONS IN THE B DEDUCTION   189

activity he articulates in the B Deduction: our imagination proceeds by taking up an intuition, viz. the given one involved in space and time as forms of intuition, and making an intuition$_i$ of its own, viz. a formal intuition, on this basis.

Beginning with forms of intuition, in the B Deduction, Kant characterizes them in a way that indicates that they are subjectively given. He says, for example, that the forms of space and time are "a certain form of sensible intuition *a priori*" that is "fundamental" "in us," and which "rests on the receptivity of the capacity for representation (sensibility)" (B150). While this much is relatively straightforward, recall Longuenesse's suggestion that Kant acknowledges two senses in which space and time are forms of intuition: in the first sense, they are "potential" forms, "mere forms of manifoldness," that are built into the constitution of sensibility, and, in the second sense, they are "forms of the unity of the manifold," where this unity is understood in terms articulated in the Metaphysical Exposition: the unity of space and time as singular, wholes that precede their parts, and infinite given magnitudes (1998, 221; 2005, 69).[32] And according to Longuenesse's radical interpretation, whereas a form of intuition in the former sense is one we are given, Kant uses the B Deduction to establish that a form of intuition in the latter sense, which amounts to our most basic pure intuition of space and time, requires imagination.

To be sure, in §26, Kant claims that, "the **form of intuition** merely gives the manifold" of space and time (B160n; see also B68, A76–7/B102, B129). However, there are several reasons to be wary of attributing to Kant the view that being given a manifold of space and time through a form of intuition can come apart from being given a manifold of space and time through a pure intuition.

In the first place, the distinction between a form of intuition and a pure intuition is one that Kant tends to elide. We saw this in the "Kästner" piece. However, we also see this in the first *Critique*, where he claims, "This pure form of sensibility itself is called **pure intuition** ... [T]he pure intuition ... occurs *a priori* even without an actual object of the senses ..., as a mere form of sensibility in the mind" (A20–1/B34–5).[33] Similarly in the *Prolegomena* he asserts, "the pure intuition is nothing but the mere form of sensibility," and that, "by the very fact that [space and time] are pure intuitions *a priori*, they prove that they are mere forms of sensibility" (Prol. 4:283–4). This gives us some initial reason to doubt that forms of intuition can come apart from pure intuitions.

---

intuition and as the formal intuition in which space is "represented as *object* (as is really required in geometry)" (2014, 293). However, when Kant speaks of space "represented as object," he is not talking about space, *qua* the subjectively given space we represent in geometry; rather, his reference to §24, where he discusses examples of geometrical construction, suggests that he has the made intuition$_i$ of space in mind.

[32] As I noted earlier, Onof and Schulting (2015) describe these features of space and time under the heading "unicity."

[33] See also, "it can be understood how the form of all appearances can be given in the mind ... *a priori*, and how as a pure intuition ... it can contain principles of their relations prior to all experience" (A26/B42).

The way that Kant treats the relationship between manifolds and intuitions in general in the B Deduction also suggests that he thinks they are inseparable in the pure case. He, for example, opens the Deduction with the claim that a manifold of intuition is given through intuition: "The manifold of representations can be given in an intuition that is merely sensible, i.e. nothing but receptivity" (B129). He repeats this characterization of the manifold as "given in an intuition" over the course of the Deduction (see B132-3, B139, B144-5). And he moves seamlessly from the claim that his proof in the B Deduction presupposes that "the manifold for intuition must already be given prior to the synthesis of understanding and independently from it" to the claim that thinking involves "the synthesis of the manifold that is given to it in intuition from elsewhere" (B154). Applying this line of thought to space and time, as is the case with any manifold-intuition relationship, the manifold of space and time is given in an intuition prior to and independently from synthesis—the relevant intuition, here, being the pure intuition of space and time.

Finally, the Metaphysical Exposition gives us reasons related to the mereological structure of space and time to doubt that we can be given the manifold of space and time apart from being given the pure intuition of space and time on Kant's view. More specifically, in the Metaphysical Exposition, Kant offers a mereological account of the manifold of space and time, i.e. the multiplicity of parts of space and time, as dependent on the whole of space and time. To this end, he claims that the whole of space and time are prior to the parts of space and time, and the parts are dependent on that whole. Regarding space, for example, Kant claims that the parts of space "cannot as it were precede the single all-encompassing space as its components... [space] is essentially single; the manifold in it...rests merely on limitations" (A25/B39). And about time, he says, "Different times are only parts of one and the same time" (A31-2/B47-8). Insofar as the manifolds of space and time are mereologically dependent on the wholes of space and time, it is not possible for us to be given the manifolds without being given the wholes. However, the givenness of the whole is precisely what Longuenesse denies: on her view, it is only by "actualizing" the "potential" form that contains the manifold of space and time that we have a pure intuition of the whole of space and time (Longuenesse 1998, 221). But what I am suggesting is that Kant's mereological commitments preclude this: the only way to be given the manifold of space and time is by being given the whole of space and time, and this, Kant claims, happens through a pure intuition. So, when Kant claims in §26 that the form of intuition gives us the manifold of space and time, I take this to be shorthand for the idea that the form of intuition gives us a pure intuition of the whole of space and time that contains the manifold of space and time. On my reading, then, it is this pure intuition that is given through the formal constitution of sensibility on Kant's view.

Turning now to Kant's treatment of formal intuitions in the B Deduction, there are various reasons to interpret them as pure intuitions$_i$ of the made variety.

For one thing, in explicating what formal intuitions amount to, Kant alludes to geometry in a way that resonates with his discussion of the made pure intuitions$_i$ of space we are interested in from a geometrical perspective in the "Kästner" piece.[34] He, for example, opens the §26 footnote by suggesting that formal intuitions involve representations of space "as **object**" "as is really required in geometry" (B160n).[35] This echoes his claim in the "Kästner" treatise that space is "objectively given" through made intuitions$_i$. And his citation of §24 at the end of the §26 footnote directs us to a section in which he discusses examples of geometrical construction: "drawing" "a line," "describing" "a circle," "placing three lines perpendicular to each other" to represent the "three dimensions of space," and "drawing a straight line" to "represent time" (B154).

However, more than just alluding to geometry, Kant's characterization of the activity involved in generating formal intuitions suggests that he has made pure intuitions$_i$ in mind. Though I shall have more to say about this topic in §6.5, for now, hopefully it will suffice to note that his citation of §24 indicates that he thinks formal intuitions are generated through an imaginative activity that he designates "figurative synthesis." More specifically, he claims that figurative synthesis is an act of the *a priori* productive imagination, which involves "determining...the form of sense *a priori*," and which results in "determinate intuition[s]," that represent the manifold of space and time as "determined" and "unified" in some way (B151–2, B154). And, as Kant suggests earlier in the Deduction, through such intuitions$_i$, space is "first cognized" by us "as object": "the mere form of outer sensible intuition, space, is not yet cognition at all...[I]n order to cognize something in space, e.g. a line, I must **draw** it...and thereby is an object (a determinate space) first cognized" (B138).[36] This framing of formal intuitions thus echoes Kant's analysis of made pure intuitions$_i$, understood as intuitions$_i$ that we imaginatively make by determining and unifying the given pure intuition of space and time in a certain way, and through which space and time are "objectively given" in a way that enables us to have synthetic *a priori* cognition of them, e.g. in geometry.

This said, though Kant's examples in §24 suggest that he thinks formal intuitions represent determinate spatial and temporal forms, such as shapes or

---

[34] This distinction between forms of intuition and formal intuitions also finds echoes in the *Prolegomena*, where Kant distinguishes between space as a "form of sensory intuition" and the "space of the geometer" (Prol. 4:287). As in the "Kästner" piece, he claims that the former serves as the "foundation" and "base" for geometry (Prol. 4:282–3). Later in §38, Kant describes space, as a "form of intuition," that is the "substratum" of the geometrical representations of "determinate" spaces, e.g. a circle, conic section, and sphere (Prol. 4:322).

[35] For emphasis on the connection between formal intuitions and geometry, see Finchant (2004); Friedman (2012); Tolley (2016).

[36] See Onof and Schulting for the argument that what is ultimately at stake in the formal intuitions under discussion in §26 is "*the grasp of the unicity of space by the faculty of the understanding*" (2015, 27).

192   A PRIORI IMAGINATION AND THE CONDITIONS OF EXPERIENCE I

sequences, there is a further question as to whether he also allows for them to represent space and time as a whole. On the one hand, in order to represent space and time as a whole, it seems we would need to represent them as infinite wholes. However, Kant insists that our imagination, finite as it is, cannot generate an intuition; that represents something infinite.[37] On the other hand, Kant does talk about representations of space and time as a whole. In the Schematism, he refers to the "pure image" of space and time as a whole (A142/B182). And, about time, he claims,

> we...represent the temporal sequence through a line progressing to infinity, in which the manifold constitutes a series that is of only one dimension, and infer from the properties of this line to all the properties of time..., it is also apparent that the representation of time itself is an intuition.   (A33/B50)[38]

While no line represented by imagination is itself infinite, Kant suggests that we can represent a finite line as progressing toward infinity, e.g. through →.[39] With this finite line, it seems we represent time as an infinite whole by representing the parts of time as successively unfolding without limit. In a similar vein, it would seem that we can represent space as infinite with a finite representation of three such lines perpendicular to one another at the same point (see §24). I shall return to these issues again briefly in Chapter 7, but, for now, what I want to emphasize is the idea that Kant appears to leave open the possibility that formal intuitions; represent space "as object" not only by way of representations of finite spaces and times, but also by way of a representation of infinite space and time as such.

Stepping back, I have been arguing that we have reason to read Kant's distinction between "forms of intuition" and "formal intuitions" as mapping onto the distinction between given and made pure intuitions. So interpreted, the forms of intuition in §26 amount to our most fundamental pure intuitions of space and time as singular, wholes that precede their parts, and infinite given magnitudes, which we are subjectively given in virtue of possessing the sensibility that we do.

---

[37] See, e.g., his argument in his discussion of the mathematical sublime to the effect that reason demands our imagination generate "**one** intuition" that represents "the infinite (space and past time)," a demand with respect to which "our imagination, even in its greatest effort...demonstrates its limits and inadequacy" (KU 5:254, 257). For discussion, see Winegar (2022). See also McLear (2015) for the argument that the mereological structure of space and time as wholes that precede parts cannot be represented through imaginative synthesis because imaginative synthesis is a successive synthesis that can only generate representations by preceding from part to whole.

[38] See also, "time...cannot be made representable to us except under the image of a line, insofar as we draw it, without which sort of exhibition we could not know the unity of its measure at all" (B156; transl. modified), and, "we must be able to grasp time, as the form of inner sense, figuratively through a line" (B292).

[39] See Friedman (2000, 192–3) for discussion of such representations of time (and space) in "kinematic" terms. See also Blomme (2017) and Chaplin (2022, 891). And for discussion of such representations as the result of a "decomposing" synthesis, see Rosefeldt (2022).

THE FOOTNOTE AND FIGURATIVE SYNTHESIS   193

Meanwhile formal intuitions amount to derivative pure intuitions$_i$, which are made as a result of our imagination synthesizing the given pure intuitions of space and time. These pure intuitions$_i$, represent space and time as "determined" or "unified" in a certain way. And through them, we first cognize space and time "as object," as is required, e.g. in geometry. Insofar as I interpret formal intuitions as products of imaginative activity, I shall add the "$_i$" subscript to them in what follows.

Bringing this to bear on the debate about how to interpret Kant's account of the relationship that imagination has to space and time, I thus do not take the form of intuition/formal intuition distinction that he draws in §26 to support the radical view, according to which our most basic pure intuitions of space and time are products of imagination. I have argued that Kant, instead, aligns these most basic intuitions with the forms of intuition that we are given in virtue of having the kind of sensibility that we do. Rather than being responsible for these given pure intuitions of space and time, I have made the case that Kant attributes to our imagination made pure intuitions$_i$ of space and time, viz. formal intuitions$_i$, which it produces as the result of synthesizing the manifold contained in a given pure intuition of space and time in a determinate and unified way. And in this process, I have insisted that our imagination proceeds as Kant claims our imagination always does: it makes intuitions$_i$ by taking up what is given through the receptivity of sensibility.

While this sheds some light on Kant's account of the *a priori* exercise of imagination, as I now work through the full details of §26, I argue that attending to his conception of the cognitive function of imagination is also elucidatory with respect to his position. Indeed, I make the case that part of what is, indeed, radical in the B Deduction is Kant's recognition of the ways in which our imagination functions cognitively well in the *a priori* register by engaging in mediating activities that generate intuitions$_i$ (formal intuitions$_i$) that make the categories sensible (§6.5) and that make experience possible in the first place (§6.6).

6.5 The Footnote and Figurative Synthesis

In this section, my goal is to work through Kant's account of the *a priori* process through which our imagination makes formal intuitions$_i$ of space and time in light of this stretch of the footnote in §26:

> In the Aesthetic I ascribed this unity [of formal intuitions] merely to sensibility, only in order to note that it precedes all concepts, though to be sure it presupposes a synthesis, which does not belong to the senses but through which all concepts of space and time first become possible. For since through it (as the understanding determines sensibility) space or time are first **given** as intuitions,

the unity of this *a priori* intuition belongs to space and time, and not to the concept of the understanding (§24). (B160–1fn)

It is not obvious how the various claims Kant makes in this passage are compatible.[40] On the one hand, he claims that the imaginative synthesis through which formal intuitions$_i$ are generated involves understanding determining sensibility. On the other hand, he indicates that this synthesis "precedes all concepts," and generates a unity that "belongs to space and time, and not to the concept of the understanding." However, given that the understanding is the "faculty of concepts," how could it determine an imaginative synthesis that "precedes all concepts," and how could the unity of a formal intuition$_i$ not belong "to the concept of the understanding" (A126)?

In order to navigate this set of claims, I shall follow the clue of Kant's reference at the end of the footnote and look to §24. As we shall see, in §24, Kant's description of the figurative synthesis of imagination fits the requisite profile: it is a synthesis through which understanding determines sensibility, that precedes concepts (of space and time), and that generates intuitions$_i$ that belong to space and time. And I aim to show that this imaginative synthesis is best understood in accordance with the mediating model that I sketched above, according to which our imagination functions cognitively well in this context by making pure intuitions$_i$ of space and time that make the categories sensible.

6.5.1 "The Understanding Determines Sensibility"

Let's begin with the idea that figurative synthesis is an imaginative process through which "the understanding determines sensibility." According to Kant, at the *a priori* level our understanding's "first application" is determining sensibility "in accordance with the unity of apperception" and "**in accordance with the categories**" (B152). And he identifies the figurative synthesis of imagination as the means through which this determination takes place.

More specifically, as I gestured toward earlier, on Kant's view, figurative synthesis is an *a priori* "synthesis of the manifold of intuition" carried out by the productive imagination (B151). Indeed, it is this imaginative synthesis that he identifies as the activity that, "determine[s] the form of sense *a priori* in accordance with the unity of apperception...and..., **in accordance with the categories**" (B151–2).[41] He, moreover, asserts that this synthesis results in a "**determinate**

---

[40] For an in-depth discussion of these seemingly incompatible claims, see Onof and Schulting (2015).

[41] I return to how the involvement of the categories bears on his claim in §26 that this synthesis "precedes all concepts" in §6.5.3.

intuition" that represents the manifold of space and time determined and unified "as object" in some fashion (B154). And he illustrates "determinate intuitions" with examples of our imaginatively "drawing" "a line," "describing" "a circle," and "representing[ing] the three dimensions of space" by "**placing** three lines perpendicular to each other at the same point" (B154).

Although Kant indicates that figurative synthesis is the means through which the understanding determines sensibility, he also distinguishes it from "intellectual synthesis" (B152). Recall that, on Kant's view, intellectual synthesis involves the predicative combination of concepts together in a judgment (see Chapter 5). Insofar as figurative synthesis involves the sensible synthesis of representations together in intuition, he thus contrasts it with the intellectual synthesis of concepts involved in judgment.[42]

As I discussed in Chapter 2, Kant's characterization of figurative synthesis can be seen as evidence in favor of attributing to him what I labeled the "understanding view" of imagination, according to which imagination just is a sensible exercise of the understanding.[43] After all, Kant describes figurative synthesis as a process through which the understanding determines sensibility, as an "exercise of spontaneity," as "an effect of the understanding on sensibility and its first application … to objects of the intuition that is possible for us," and as the "designation" (*Benennung*) under which understanding "affects" sensibility (B152–4). This language certainly invites a reading of imagination, as Kant presents it in the B Deduction, as an exercise of understanding in a sensible guise.

However, in Chapter 3, I argued that Kant's considered view of imagination is the "sensibility view," according to which imagination is part of sensibility. And in §24, Kant, in fact, reminds us that imagination "belongs to sensibility": "*Imagination* is the faculty for representing an object in intuition even **without its presence**. Now since all of our intuition is sensible, the imagination, on account of the subjective condition under which alone it can give a corresponding intuition to the concepts of understanding, *belongs to sensibility*" (B151; transl. modified; last italics mine). Here, Kant rehearses the even-without-presence definition of imagination that he often offers when he is distinguishing imagination from sense, as the two parts of sensibility (see Anthro. 7:153). To be sure, he immediately goes on to suggest that the synthesis of imagination is "an exercise of spontaneity"; however, according to the interpretation of imagination I have developed, this is in keeping with his general analysis of imagination as the spontaneous part of sensibility, which he distinguishes from the merely receptive part

---

[42] For a discussion of the difference between intellectual synthesis and figurative synthesis, *qua* sensible, see Land (2015a); Grüne (2022).

[43] See, e.g., Sellars's claim that, "it turns out, most clearly in the second edition (B151–3) that this imagination, under the name 'productive imagination', is the understanding functioning in a special way" (1967, 4). Land (2011; 2015) also reads the productive imagination along these lines. Long (1998) and Caimi (2012) read imagination in general along these lines.

that is sense. As I understand this passage, then, Kant is telling us that figurative synthesis, *qua* a spontaneous synthesis of imagination that generates intuitions$_i$, belongs to sensibility.

But how can this interpretive line be consistent with Kant's treatment of figurative synthesis as an "effect" or "designation" of the understanding? What I would now like to suggest is that we should read these remarks in light of Kant's conception of the cognitive function of imagination. The basic thought is that in figurative synthesis our imagination, as part of sensibility, functions cognitively well as it always does: it serves the understanding by generating intuitions$_i$ that make concepts sensible.

In more detail, recall from Chapter 1 that, on Kant's view, the cognitive function of understanding in general turns on it being a "sovereign" that provides concepts that "rule" the deliverances of sensibility, and that the cognitive function of sensibility turns on it being an "executive force, through which understanding has an effect" (Anthro. 7:196; AF 25:486). I have argued that imagination contributes to the executive force of sensibility by generating intuitions$_i$ that make the understanding's concepts sensible and facilitate our comprehension of those concepts *in concreto* (see Chapters 3–4). And I take it that when our imagination functions in this way, there is, indeed, a sense in which it is an "effect" or "designation" of the understanding: it is an imaginative activity that serves the understanding.

Applying this line of thought to figurative synthesis, for Kant, this synthesis is an *a priori* way in which our imagination functions cognitively well by generating formal intuitions$_i$ that make the categories sensible, and, thereby, serves the understanding. This, at least, is how I read Kant's claim that figurative synthesis involves determining the *a priori* manifold of space and time "**in accordance with the categories**," and generating "determinate" intuitions$_i$ of space and time (i.e. formal intuitions$_i$) that, in some sense, represent the categories as manifest in spatio-temporal form (B152). I say "in some sense" because in the Deduction, Kant does not offer much in the way of details about what it might mean for our imagination to make the categories sensible in this way. He gives us a gloss of the categories as, "concepts of an object in general, by means of which its intuition is regarded as determined with regard to one of the logical functions for judgments" (B128). So, we know that formal intuitions$_i$ in some sense represent space and time "as object," by representing the manifold of space of time as determined with regard to the logical functions contained in the categories. But, by my lights, it is not until the Schematism that he offers us a complete story of how this works, a story I shall have to postpone until Chapter 7. Nevertheless, in the Deduction, I take it that insofar as figurative synthesis is a case in which our imagination functions cognitively well on Kant's view, we should conceive of it and the formal intuitions$_i$ it generates as part of a process in which our imagination makes the categories sensible, and, thereby, serves as an "effect" or "designation" of the understanding. And as I suggested earlier, attending to this line of thought is important for appreciating one of the innovative moves in Kant's theory of imagination: he acknowledges an *a priori* way in which our imagination functions cognitively well that not only makes it possible for us to "first cognize" space and time "as objects," but also makes experience possible in the first place.

With this picture of figurative synthesis in §24 in place, let's return to the footnote in §26 and Kant's claim that formal intuitions$_i$ are generated through an imaginative process in which "understanding determines the sensibility." As I interpret Kant's view, formal intuitions$_i$ are generated through the process of figurative synthesis, understood as a synthesis carried out by the imaginative part of sensibility in service of the understanding. Through this synthesis, the imagination mediates between the pure intuition of space and time that we are given, on the one hand, and the categories, on the other. And when our imagination enacts its cognitive function in this context it generates formal intuitions$_i$ that, in some way, make the categories sensible.

6.5.2 "Belongs to Space and Time"

Although in both §§24 and 26, Kant treats figurative synthesis as the imaginative means through which understanding determines sensibility, in the §26 footnote he also claims that the unity of a formal intuition$_i$ "belongs to space and time, and not to the concept of the understanding." How can this be the case if formal intuitions$_i$ are the result of an imaginative process through which understanding determines sensibility in accordance with the categories?

As I see it, the "belongs to space and time" remark is a rather infelicitous way for Kant to remind us of a point he has made in §24: formal intuitions$_i$ are produced not through intellectual synthesis but through the figurative synthesis of imagination. Kant, indeed, repeats the distinction between intellectual and figurative synthesis three times in §24 (see B151–2). And, as I just indicated, unlike intellectual synthesis which is an activity of the understanding in judgment, figurative synthesis is an activity of imagination, as something that "belongs to sensibility," which it carries out in service of the understanding. My suggestion, then, is that when in the footnote Kant says that the unity of a formal intuition$_i$ "belongs to space and time, and not to the pure concept of the understanding," he is reminding us that formal intuitions$_i$ are generated through figurative, rather than intellectual, synthesis; hence through the imagination, *qua* part of sensibility, rather than through the understanding. This is not a maximally felicitous way for Kant to make this point because, on my reading at least, there is, indeed, a sense in which the unity of a formal intuition$_i$ "belongs to the pure concepts of the understanding": our imagination produces formal intuitions$_i$ through synthesis that is, in some sense, "in accordance with the categories." But I take it that the

198 A PRIORI IMAGINATION AND THE CONDITIONS OF EXPERIENCE I

categorial dependence of formal intuitions$_i$ is not what he is worried about in the footnote. Instead, what he wants to warn against is the idea that formal intuitions$_i$ depend on intellectual synthesis in judgment, given that they are, in fact, the result of a figurative synthesis of imagination, which "belongs to sensibility," and, as such, "belongs to space and time."

6.5.3 "Precedes All Concepts"

The last claim in the §26 footnote that I shall address is Kant's claim that the imaginative synthesis that generates formal intuitions$_i$ "precedes all concepts." According to some interpreters, this means that figurative synthesis is something that precedes all concepts, the categories included, and that it proceeds, instead, in accordance with the understanding and apperception in their "prediscursive" or "preconceptual" guise.[44] However, as I have been emphasizing, in §24, Kant is clear that figurative synthesis occurs "in accordance with the categories." He reiterates this point in the main text of §26, claiming that the unity of a formal intuition$_i$, "can be none other than that of the combination of the manifold of a **given intuition in general** in an original consciousness, in agreement with the categories, only applied to our **sensible intuition**. Consequently all synthesis... stands under the categories" (B161). And I take it that Kant has good reason for insisting that the categories are involved in figurative synthesis. For one thing, in the Deduction, Kant insists that the categories are "concepts of an object in general, by means of which its intuition is regarded as determined" (B128). To the extent that figurative synthesis involves representing space and time "as objects," then the categories need to be guiding this synthesis in some fashion (more on this in Chapter 7). Moreover, I have just argued that in order to understand why Kant thinks figurative synthesis is an instance of our imagination functioning cognitively well, we need to frame it as an activity in which our imagination generates intuitions$_i$ (here: formal intuitions$_i$) that make concepts (here: the categories) sensible. For these reasons, I read Kant's claim that the generation of formal intuitions$_i$ through figurative synthesis "precedes all concepts" as an overstatement: it cannot precede the categories.

Rather than endorsing the view that figurative synthesis precedes all concepts, I interpret Kant as being committed to a view that is narrower in scope: figurative synthesis precedes a particular set of concepts that he refers to later in this

---

[44] See, e.g., Waxman (1991, pt. 1; 2014, 116–18, 138–40, 395–8); Longuenesse (1998, 222, 72; 2005, 69); Friedman (2012, 248); Williams (2018); Indregard (2021). There are further complications surrounding whether the categories play a role in figurative synthesis prior to their "reflected" or "schematized" state as concepts of objects (see Longuenesse 1998, 123, 222–3; 2005, 24–6; Friedman 2000, 197–9; 2012, 246–9; and Kraus 2020, 70–1), which I shall take up in Chapter 7.

THE FOOTNOTE AND FIGURATIVE SYNTHESIS 199

sentence as the "concepts of space and time."[45] I understand "concepts of space and time" to include the concepts <space> and <time> in general,[46] as well as more specific concepts, such as <triangle>, <circle>, <simultaneity>, and <succession>.[47] And what I shall now propose is that, for Kant, figurative synthesis "precedes" these concepts insofar as it contributes to our formation of them.

Support for reading the concepts at issue along these lines can be found in the portion of the "Progress" essay that parallels the Deduction, where Kant claims,

> Space and time, subjectively regarded, are mere forms of sensibility, but in order to make [*machen*] a concept of them, as objects of pure intuition (without which we could say nothing at all about them), we require...the composition [*Zusammensetzung*] (synthesis) of the manifold, and thus...combining [*Verbindung*] this manifold; which...requires...different functions to combine them; these are called categories. (WF 20:276; transl. modified)

This passage suggests that, on Kant's view, part of what is involved in forming concepts of space and time is generating an intuition$_i$ of them as "object." As I discussed in §6.3, on Kant's view, when we have intuitions$_i$ through which we are conscious of space and time as "object," we grasp "many splendid properties" of space and time, which synthetically inform our concepts of them (KU 5:362). In other words, through these intuitions$_i$ we discover marks of concepts of space and time, which we synthetically add to them. To be clear, in Kant's analysis of mathematical construction, he allows for the process through which we generate intuitions$_i$ to, at least sometimes, be guided by concepts of space and time, the content of which we analytically grasp.[48] For example, my construction of a circle can be guided by the concept of a curve all points of which are equidistant from a given point, which I analytically grasp through mere definition. However, on Kant's view, when we construct concepts of space and time in intuition$_i$, we are able to go synthetically beyond these mere definitions and discover properties, hence marks, of these concepts, which are not analytically contained in these mere definitions. To return to an example from above, through construction, I can learn that, "If a point be taken within a circle, and more than two equal straight lines

---

[45] I am thus sympathetic to Allison's (2004, 192–3) reading.

[46] I take these concepts to be the concepts he "expounds" in the Metaphysical Exposition (B38). See Onof and Schulting (2015) for emphasis on this kind of concept of space and time in the context of the §26 footnote.

[47] I take these specific concepts to be the ones he references in the Transcendental Exposition, which belong to geometry, as the science of space; and arithmetic and mechanics, as the sciences of time.

[48] See Kravanja (2023) for a discussion of *prima facie* tensions in Kant's account of mathematical construction, insofar as he sometimes suggests that construction produces intuitions that are "equivalent" to mathematical concepts, and sometimes that it produces intuitions that "overstep" the mere definition of mathematical concepts.

fall from the point on the circle, the point taken is the center of the circle," and thereby synthetically augment my concept <circle> on the basis of the intuition$_i$ involved.

Notice that in the "Progress" passage, although Kant is offering an account of what is needed "in order to make" concepts of space and time, he also insists that the requisite intuitions$_i$ are generated as the result of combining the manifold of space and time in accordance with the categories. And as I just suggested, Kant takes this to be the case because the categories, *qua* our most basic concepts of objects, must guide our imagination in determining and unifying the manifold in this objective way. In this passage, Kant thus offers us a picture of the categorially guided synthesis that we need "in order to make" concepts of space and time; hence of a synthesis that precedes concepts of space and time, but which is nevertheless dependent on the categories. And my proposal is that this is a repetition of the account that Kant offers in the B Deduction.

Kant, in fact, makes his interest in the conditions of forming concepts of space and time explicit in §24. As I alluded to earlier, Kant illustrates his account of figurative synthesis and the determinate intuitions$_i$ it generates with the following remark about construction: "We cannot think of a line without **drawing** it in thought, we cannot think of a circle without **describing** it, we cannot represent the three dimensions of space at all without **placing** three lines perpendicular to each other at the same point" (B154–5).[49] He also says that figurative synthesis is what "first produces the concept of succession at all," and that, "**drawing** a straight line (which is to be the external figurative representation of time)" is how we make time "representable" to ourselves in the way that is required to "know [*erkennen*] the unity of its measure at all" (B154–5).[50] As I read these passages, in describing that without which we "cannot think" or "know" lines, circles, the three dimensions of space, succession, or the measurability of time, Kant is articulating the conditions for "making" concepts of them. And he emphasizes figurative synthesis and its determinate intuitions$_i$ as conditions for making these concepts because this is how we synthetically discover properties of space and time that we cannot cognize through an analysis of mere definitions alone.[51]

---

[49] These first two examples are examples of constructions that belong to "elementary" rule and compass geometry, by means of which we construct basic spatial concepts. Kant contrasts "elementary" geometry, through which we construct simpler figures, such as circles and lines, with "higher" geometry by means of "more complex machines" of construction, through which we construct more complicated figures like conic sections (EE 20:198; see also OD 8:191n).

[50] For discussion, see Dunlop (2009).

[51] Onof and Schulting (2015, 13) object to readings of the §26 footnote according to which the concepts that figurative synthesis cannot "precede" are mathematical concepts, because Kant thinks that mathematical construction is guided by mathematical concepts. However, although Kant sometimes suggests that construction is guided by antecedent concepts, he also allows for cases in which construction can "**make** the concept itself"; hence, he opens the door to the possibility of acquiring new concepts through construction (A730/B758) (see Shabel 2007, 106–7; Dunlop 2012; Callanan 2014; Kravanja 2023). But even in cases where construction is guided by a mathematical concept that we analytically grasp the content of, there are certain synthetic marks of mathematical concepts that we only discover through construction, and I take the sort of formation of concepts through this

As I read the §26 footnote, then, when Kant claims that formal intuitions$_i$ are generated through a synthesis that "precedes all concepts," he has in mind concepts of space and time, not the categories. Indeed, I understand this claim to be part of his conception of what role our imagination has to play in our formation of concepts of space and time vis-à-vis a figurative synthesis, which is guided by the categories, and which enables us to generate formal intuitions$_i$ that represent space and time "as objects" in the way that allows us to synthetically discover properties of them.

At this point, I have laid out the various pieces of my interpretation of §26 and I now want to take stock. As I read the footnote, Kant characterizes formal intuitions as follows. Formal intuitions are pure intuitions$_i$ that are made by the figurative synthesis of imagination and that represent space and time as determined in a unified way, which is required in order to first cognize space and time "as objects," e.g. in geometry. Formal intuitions$_i$ are "derivative," rather than "original" or "foundational" pure intuitions of space and time because they are made through a mediating process in which our imagination synthesizes the given pure intuitions of space and time in accordance with the categories. In this process, our imagination, as part of sensibility, functions cognitively well as an "executor" to the understanding by generating intuitions$_i$ that make the categories sensible, i.e. that represent the categories as manifesting in spatial and/or temporal form, and thereby mediates between our given pure intuitions of space and time, on the one hand, and the categories, on the other. And though this imaginative synthesis does not precede all concepts, it does precede concepts of space and time because it provides pure intuitions$_i$ of space and time that synthetically contribute to our formation of these concepts.

With this picture of formal intuitions$_i$ in view, we can now return to the question of how radical a view Kant endorses concerning the relationship that imagination has to our most basic pure intuitions of space and time as singular, wholes prior to their parts, and infinite given magnitudes. I have argued that, as is in keeping with Kant's understanding of imaginative activity in general, rather than casting our most basic pure intuitions as products of imagination, he, instead, regards them as providing the manifold that our imagination takes up and synthesizes in the course of making the derivative set of pure intuitions$_i$ of space and time that he labels "formal intuitions." I have also claimed that, as is in keeping with Kant's conception of the cognitive function of imagination in general, our imagination functions cognitively well in this *a priori* context by mediating between the given pure intuitions of space and time, on the one hand, and the categories, on the other, the result being pure intuitions$_i$ of space and time that make the categories sensible. I thus take it that we have reason to attribute to Kant not the radical view,

---

synthesis to be what is at stake in the footnote. See Anderson (2015, pt. III) for the argument that, on Kant's view, "analytic concept containment (as he understood it) does in fact lack the expressive power to capture even the simplest mathematical truths" (2015, 211).

according to which our most basic pure intuitions of space and time are products of imagination, but rather a mediating view, according to which it generates derivative pure intuitions$_i$ (formal intuitions$_i$) by figuratively synthesizing the given pure intuitions of space and time in accordance with the categories. But I have also stressed the cognitive significance that Kant accords these intuitions$_i$, as the imaginative vehicle through which the categories are made sensible, and as playing a crucial role in our cognition of space and time "as objects" and in enabling experience in the first place.

However, what of Longuenesse's contention that Kant's endorsement of the radical view is central to his argumentative strategy in the B Deduction? In attributing to Kant a mediating, rather than a radical, view of what our imagination does in §26, is my reading in tension with his aims in the Deduction? Though I cannot here hope to wade through the enormous literature surrounding Kant's aims and strategy in the second step of the B Deduction, in the next section my goal is to say enough to elucidate why he appeals to the *a priori* exercise of imagination in this context and why exactly he thinks this exercise is needed if experience is to be possible at all.

6.6 Imagination and the Possibility of Experience

To set the stage, I want to make a few brief remarks about how Kant initially frames his aim and strategy for the B Deduction in §13. In this section, Kant articulates his aim in terms of showing how the categories as "**subjective conditions of thinking** should have **objective** validity, i.e. yield conditions of the possibility of all cognition of objects" (A89–90/B122). To this end, he needs to show that rather than being "entirely empty" as Hume would have it, the categories are applicable to objects we experience (A90/B123). Kant compares this task with the task of proving that the pure forms of space and time have objective validity, which he undertook in the Aesthetic. However, he suggests a particular "difficulty" arises in the case of the categories that does not arise in the case of space and time (A89/B122). When it comes to the pure forms of space and time, Kant claims it is relatively easy to prove that they are applicable to objects we experience because "an object can appear to us only by means of them" (A89/B122). By contrast, he asserts that "appearances can certainly be given in intuition without functions of the understanding," and that, "The categories of the understanding...do not represent to us the conditions under which objects are given in intuition at all, hence objects can indeed appear to us without necessarily having to be related to functions of the understanding" (A89–90/B122).[52] Insofar as this is the case,

---

[52] Below, I return to the debate about whether this passage reflects Kant's considered position at the end of the Deduction, which I think it does.

proving that the categories have objective validity poses a particular challenge: if appearances can be given in intuition without the categories, then what reason do we have to think the categories are applicable to them?

Kant then sketches the following strategy for meeting this challenge: in order to show that the categories are valid with respect to objects of experience, he will show that the categories are *a priori* conditions of the possibility of experience (see A93/B126). He is convinced that this strategy will work because he thinks there is a kind of dependence relation between objects of experience and conditions of the possibility of experience. More specifically, he claims that an "object of experience" is an object that has a certain kind of "form," and that the conditions of the possibility of experience are "determinant" of that form (A93/B126). Whereas in the Aesthetic he takes himself to have established that the form of an object of experience is "grounded" in the pure intuitions of space and time, the task of the Deduction is to show that "nothing is possible as **an object of experience**" without the "form of thinking" provided by the categories (A93/B125–6).

From this, we can glean a basic scheme for Kant's aim and strategy in the Deduction. He aims to show that the categories are objectively valid with respect to objects of experience by showing that the categories are conditions of the possibility of experience, which determine the form of objects of experience.

Fast-forwarding now to the second step the B Deduction, Kant fills out this scheme in a particular way. In §21 he describes his aim as showing the categories' "*a priori* validity in regard to all objects of our senses" (B144). Or as he puts it in §26, his goal is showing "why everything that may ever come before our senses must stand under the laws that arise *a priori* from the understanding alone" (B160). And he glosses his strategy as follows: "it will be shown from the way in which the empirical intuition is given in sensibility that its unity can be none other than the one the categories prescribe to the manifold of a given intuition in general" (B144–5). Notice that instead of talking about "objects of experience" and "conditions of experience" in general, in these passages Kant articulates his intention in the second step of the Deduction in terms of showing that the categories are valid with respect to objects of the senses by showing that the categories are, in some sense, conditions of empirical intuition. As he puts it in the Schematism, he sets his sights on showing that the categories are bound up with "*a priori* formal conditions of sensibility" that condition empirical intuition (A140/B179). For Kant, then, the purpose of the second step of the B Deduction is to establish the categories as some kind of "formal condition of sensibility," which condition empirical intuition, and, by extension, the form of objects of the senses. We could thus specify the argumentative scheme for the second step as follows: he aims to show that the categories are objectively valid with respect to objects of the senses by showing that the categories provide formal conditions of sensibility, which condition empirical intuition and, by extension, the form of objects of empirical intuition.

Turning now to Longuenesse's reading of the second step, she identifies the relevant objects as the ones we are given through empirical intuition, and the relevant formal conditions of sensibility as the forms of space and time from the Transcendental Aesthetic, *qua* the pure intuitions of space and time as singular, wholes that precede their parts, and infinite given magnitudes, through which we are given objects in empirical intuition (see 1998, 213; 2005, 33). And, on her reading, Kant reaches his conclusion that, "the forms of our sensibility, stand under the very same unity of apperception...in which the categories thus originate" in §26 by arguing that the forms of space and time so understood are products of the figurative synthesis of imagination in which the understanding determines sensibility (2005, 32).

Yet if my mediating reading is correct, then this is not what happens in the second step of the B Deduction. As I interpret Kant, he assumes that the forms of space and time, which coincide with our most basic pure intuitions of space and time, are given to us through sensibility. Indeed, I take this to be why Kant frames his strategy as he does in §26, claiming that his goal is "explaining," "the possibility of cognizing *a priori* **through categories** whatever objects **may come before our senses,** not as far as the form of their intuition but rather as far as the laws of their combination are concerned" (B159). Here, Kant explicitly says that his aim is not to establish a connection between the categories and our form of intuition, but rather between the categories and the "combination" of the objects that come before our senses. I have argued that this is in keeping with his presupposition in the Deduction of space and time, as forms of intuition, being given, and with his argumentative focus being, instead, on how we actively take up those given intuitions through categorially dependent imaginative synthesis. But, to return to the worry: doesn't this deprive Kant of the strategy he needs to establish the objective validity of the categories with respect to objects of the senses?

Here, we need to be mindful of a distinction that I claimed is integral to Kant's bipartite theory of sensibility: there are two different kinds of empirical intuitions generated by sensibility, empirical intuitions$_s$ generated by sense and empirical intuitions$_i$ generated by imagination (see Chapter 3). As I discussed in Chapter 5, both kinds of empirical intuition play a role in Kant's theory of experience: the former are involved in the sensing at issue in the senses stage of experience and the latter in the perception at issue in the imagination stage of experience. Given this distinction, we need to ask which kind of empirical intuition Kant wants to show the categories are a condition of in §26.

Kant's references to objects of sense in §§21 and 26 certainly makes it tempting to identify the relevant intuition as the empirical intuition$_s$ involved in sensing. This is the interpretive line that Longuenesse pursues in her analysis of how Kant uses §26 to establish that the way we are given objects in empirical intuitions$_s$ depends on the generation of the pure intuitions of space and time through figurative synthesis.

IMAGINATION AND THE POSSIBILITY OF EXPERIENCE   205

However, this is also a line pursued by proponents of a conceptualist reading of the Transcendental Deduction that I alluded to in the introduction to this chapter.[53] According to this interpretation, in the Deduction, Kant commits himself to the generation of empirical intuitions$_s$, *qua* conscious representations of objects, depending on the categories. To this end, interpreters argue that in the Deduction, Kant seeks to establish the categories as *a priori* conditions of us being able to have conscious representations that relate to objects at all. In the first step of the Deduction, for example, Kant claims,

> An **object**... is that in the concept of which the manifold of a given intuition is **united**. Now, however, all unification of representations requires unity of consciousness in the synthesis of them. Consequently the unity of consciousness is that which alone constitutes the relation of representations to an object.
>
> (B137; see also A253/B309)

Per the conceptualist reading, Kant here casts the categories as our most basic concepts of objects, in accordance with which we must unify a manifold if we are to be able to consciously relate to objects through our representations. Pursuing this interpretive line with regard to the second step of the Deduction, conceptualist interpreters argue that it is through this lens that we should read Kant's claim, "In the sequel (§26) it will be shown from the way in which the empirical intuition is given in sensibility that its unity can be none other than the one the categories prescribes" (B144–5). According to this reading, Kant here indicates that in §26 his aim is to establish the dependence of empirical intuitions$_s$ on the categories by establishing that the categories condition the figurative synthesis of space and time, which is, in turn, a condition of us being able to have empirical intuitions$_s$, *qua* conscious representations that relate to objects of the senses that appear in space and time.

However, when we look at how Kant actually proceeds in §26 the empirical intuitions that he targets as categorially dependent are not the empirical intuitions$_s$ involved in sensing, but rather the empirical intuitions$_i$ involved in perception, i.e. the empirical intuitions$_i$ our imagination generates by actively taking up the empirical intuitions$_s$ delivered by sense.[54] This is evident in the arc of the

---

[53] See Bauer (2012); Land (2014; 2015b); Conant (2016); Shaddock (2018). As I indicated above, instead of defending a "conceptualist" reading according to which the categories are involved, some interpreters defend an "intellectualist" reading according to which Kant's argument proceeds not by way of an appeal to the categories, but by way of an appeal to the understanding and the synthetic unity of apperception in a prediscursive or preconceptual guise (see Waxman 1991, pt. 1; Longuenesse 1998, chap. 8; 2005, chaps. 1, 3; Ginsborg 2008; Messina 2014; Friedman 2015; Williams 2018; Indregard 2021).

[54] For other readings that emphasize the idea that Kant's concern in §26 is not with how we are given an intuition through sense, but rather with how we take up those intuitions through synthesis, see Hanna (2005); Haag (2007); Allais (2009; 2015; 2017); McLear (2015); Tolley (2013; 2019; 2020);

argument Kant offers in §26. He frames the argument with reference to perception: "First of all I remark that by the **synthesis of apprehension** I understand the composition [*Zusammensetzung*] of the manifold in an empirical intuition, through which perception, i.e., empirical consciousness of it (as appearance), becomes possible" (B160).[55] And he concludes: "all synthesis, through which even perception itself becomes possible stands under the categories, and since experience is cognition through connected perceptions, the categories are conditions of the possibility of experience" (B161).

In between, he argues that the synthesis of apprehension that perception requires "must be in agreement with" not just the forms of space and time, but also formal intuitions$_i$ of space and time (B160). His argument for why this is the case turns on a feature of perception that I highlighted in Chapter 5: the empirical intuitions$_i$ (i.e. perceptual images) generated in perception represent appearances "as determined in space and time" (B161). And what he here indicates is that in order for the imaginative synthesis of apprehension to generate perceptual images that represent appearances as spatio-temporally determinate, that synthesis needs to "agree" and be "in accordance with" the basic spatio-temporal forms of determinacy and patterns of unity represented by formal intuitions$_i$ (B160–1). His next move is to claim that the "unity" of formal intuitions$_i$ depends on the categories: this unity "can be none other than that of the combination of the manifold of a given **intuition in general** ... in agreement with the categories, only applied to our **sensible intuition**" (B161). He takes this to be the case because formal intuitions$_i$, through which we represent space and time as unified, are generated through the figurative synthesis of imagination that occurs in accordance with the categories. Insofar as this is the case, he concludes that the categories are conditions of the possibility of experience because they are conditions of the synthesis upon which perception depends, and experience is "cognition through connected perceptions." The complicated details notwithstanding, the empirical intuitions at the center of this argument are thus not empirical intuitions$_s$, but rather the empirical intuitions$_i$ involved in perception, which we connect in experience.

The two examples that Kant offers in §26 also points in this direction. The first is an example of perception in which "I make the empirical intuition of a house into perception through apprehension of its manifold," and the second is an

---

Sá Pereira (2017); Golob (2016a; 2016b); Schulting (2017, chap. 7). This is in keeping with the fact that in the A Deduction, Kant presupposes that sense delivers a manifold of intuition, which is taken up through the "threefold synthesis" (see A94–5, A97–8). That his focus in the Deduction is on the imaginative synthesis of apprehension, rather than on sense is something he hints at in a note, likely for the A Deduction, in the 1780s, "All appearances concern me not insomuch as they are in the senses but as they can at least be encountered in apperception. In this, however, they can only be encountered by means of the synthesis of apprehension, i.e., of imagination" (Lbl B12 23:19).

[55] He also emphasizes perception in his summary remarks about §26 to the effect: "all possible perception depends on the synthesis of apprehension" and "this empirical synthesis depends, on the transcendental one" (B164).

example of experience in which when "I perceive the freezing of water, I apprehend two states (of fluidity and solidity) as ones standing in a relation of time to each other" (B162–3). Notice that neither of these examples are just examples of us having empirical intuitions$_s$ at the sense stage of experience. The house example is an example of how we "make" something of an empirical intuition$_s$ in the perception involved in the imagination stage, and the freezing water example is an example of how we determine an objective sequence in perception through the sort of full-blown experience involved in the understanding stage (which I have argued requires judgment). As is in keeping with my interpretation of the latter two stages of experience, Kant underscores the fact that they involve a representation of something as spatially or temporally determinate: we "draw" the shape of the house and fix the two states of water as "standing in" a sequential "relation of time" (B162). And the upshot of the examples is that our ability to represent this spatial and temporal determinacy depends on the category-dependent "unity" of space and time that he has just offered in his account of formal intuitions$_i$ (B162–3). Though I shall have more to say about these examples in Chapter 7, for now, my point is that as was the case with the argument in §26, in neither of these examples is Kant concerned with proving the categories as conditions of the empirical intuitions$_s$ involved in the sense stage of experience. His concern is with proving that the sort of spatially and/or temporally determinate representations that we generate in the perception involved in the imagination stage and, ultimately, in the full-blown experience involved in the understanding stage of experience depends on the categories.

When we thus consider, at the most basic level, what kind of empirical intuition Kant seeks to establish the categories are a condition of in §26, his argument and examples suggest it is an empirical intuition$_i$ rather than an empirical intuition$_s$ that is at issue. But what of the conceptualist argument to the effect that the latter must be at issue, *qua* a conscious representation of an object? Notice that in §26, the sort of conscious representation of objects in space and time that Kant focuses on is the conscious representation of objects "as determined in space and time." But in Chapter 5, I mounted an argument to the effect that this is not how we consciously represent objects in sensing on Kant's view. I argued that, for Kant, empirical intuitions$_s$ involve conscious representation of objects as undetermined appearances, i.e. as something or other that stands over and against us in space and time. And in his framework, I claimed that conscious representations of objects as spatially and/or temporally determinate only arise when we actively take up what we sense in perception in the imagination stage.[56] As I read §26, then, Kant's aim is not to show that, at the most basic level, the categories condition conscious representation of objects in empirical intuition$_s$, but rather conscious

---

[56] In Chapter 5, I discussed this in light of what I have labelled the "determinacy achievement" of cognition in the narrow sense.

representation of objects as spatially and/or temporally determinate in the empirical intuition$_i$ involved in perception.[57] To repeat, Kant takes this to be the case because the categories condition the figurative synthesis of imagination that generates the formal intuitions$_i$ that supply the most basic patterns of spatio-temporal determinacy that the imaginative synthesis of apprehension in perception "must always be in agreement with, since it can only occur in accordance with this form" (B160).

On my reading, then, Kant's argument in §26 is consistent with a non-conceptualist position, according to which empirical intuitions$_s$ that involve conscious representations of objects as undetermined appearances can be generated without the categories. At the end of the Deduction I thus take Kant to remain committed to his claims from §13 to the effect that, "appearances can certainly be given in intuition without functions of the understanding," and that, "The categories... do not represent the conditions under which objects are given in intuition" (A89–90/B122).[58] But when it comes to empirical intuitions$_i$ of the sort involved in perception, I read Kant as committed to a conceptualist position, according to which their generation depends on the categories vis-à-vis the figurative synthesis of imagination that generates formal intuitions$_i$.

To summarize, let's return to the argumentative scheme in the second step that I sketched above: Kant aims to show that the categories are objectively valid with respect to objects of the senses by showing that the categories provide formal conditions of sensibility, which condition empirical intuition and, by extension, the form of objects of empirical intuition. According to my interpretation, we should fill out this scheme as follows. The relevant formal conditions of sensibility are not formal conditions of sensing, i.e. the forms of intuition/given pure intuitions of space and time, but rather formal conditions of perception, i.e. the formal intuitions$_i$ generated through figurative synthesis. The relevant empirical intuitions are not empirical intuitions$_s$, but rather empirical intuitions$_i$ through which we represent appearances as spatially and/or temporally determinate in perception. And the relevant objects of the senses are not the undetermined appearances that we are conscious of through empirical intuitions$_s$, but rather the spatio-temporally determinate appearances that we are conscious of through perception.

---

[57] I am thus sympathetic to Golob's reading of the second step, according to which Kant seeks to establish that the "representation of a certain privileged class of spatial or temporal relations," including the distinction between subjective and objective succession and mereological relations, depends on the categories (2016b, 38). Like Golob, I take this representation of spatio-temporal determinacy to be more basic than the sort of dependence of referential thought on the categories, which Allais (2015, chap. 11) argues is at stake in the Deduction.

[58] I thus disagree with readings of these passages to the effect that they articulate a position that Kant aims to overturn by the end of the Deduction (see, e.g., Paton 1936, v1 324–6; Ginsborg 2008, 70–1; Grüne 2011, 475–6; Griffith 2012, 199–200; Allison 2015, 188–91; Indregard 2021). My reading is thus in the spirit of Hanna (2001, 199; 2005, 259–60) and Allais (2015, 162–3) who take these passages to reflect Kant's considered view.

On my reading, then, in the second step of the B Deduction, Kant shows that, at the most basic level, the categories are objectively valid with respect to the spatio-temporally determinate objects of perception because the categories provide the formal conditions of sensibility, which condition the empirical intuitions$_i$ and, by extension, the form of objects, at stake in perception. And I take it that Kant appeals to the *a priori* exercise of imagination in this argument because he regards figurative synthesis and formal intuitions$_i$ as the mediating work of imagination, carried out in service of the understanding, through which objects of perception are conditioned by the categories.

This said, in §26, Kant does not fully spell out the details of how the categorial conditioning of perception and experience by way of formal intuitions$_i$ and figurative synthesis works. Indeed, his examples of perceiving a house and experiencing freezing water in some ways raise more questions than they answer. To be sure, the examples are illustrative of the idea that our ability to represent objects as spatially and/or temporally determinate in perception and experience depends on formal intuitions$_i$ generated by imaginative synthesis that is in accordance with the categories. But these examples also raise a whole host of new questions concerning the *a priori* exercise of imagination.

One set of questions pertains to how we are to understand the *a priori* activities of imagination and formal intuitions$_i$ Kant has in mind here. How exactly does Kant conceive of the formal intuitions$_i$ involved in these examples? In the house case, he implies that the relevant formal intuition$_i$ is connected to "the **necessary unity** of space and of outer sensible intuition in general," and in the water case to the "necessary synthetic **unity** of the manifold" of time (B162–3). But how are we to understand the "necessary unity" of space and time at issue? And how does our imagination generate a formal intuition$_i$ that represents the "necessary unity" of space and time?

Another set of questions concerns how we are to understand the role of the categories in relation to this imaginative synthesis. How exactly do our imaginative activities proceed in accordance with the categories? And is it significant that the formal intuition$_i$ involved in the perception example is that of a mathematical category of quantity and in the experience that of the dynamical category of causality?

A third set of questions turns on how exactly Kant thinks the *a priori* exercise of imagination grounds perception and experience. Does a formal intuition$_i$ somehow guide the empirical activities involved in perception and experience? Or is there some relation other than guidance at play here?

In the end, although in §26 Kant takes himself to have shown that the *a priori* exercise of imagination conditions perception and, by extension, experience, many of the important details of his position remain unclear. However, Kant himself indicates that the question of "how" exactly this is all possible is not something he is attempting to fill out in the Deduction (B167). All he wants to establish is the objective validity of the categories in general, and he reserves an answer to the "how" question for the Analytic of Principles. Thus, in order to fully understand Kant's picture of how the *a priori* activities of imagination contribute to the possibility of experience, we need to look at how he elaborates his view in the Principles, particularly in the Schematism, to which I turn next.

6.7 Conclusion

In this chapter, I began exploring Kant's account of the *a priori* dimensions of the theoretical use of imagination, which pivots on his analysis of the *a priori* contribution imagination makes to the possibility of experience. As I noted earlier, my analysis of this contribution is motivated by three questions: how does Kant understand the relationship between the *a priori* exercise of imagination and the *a priori* conditions of the possibility of experience (the pure intuitions of space and time and the pure concepts of the understanding); exactly what stages of experience does he take the *a priori* exercise of imagination to enable; and what implications, if any, does this account have for how we understand Kant's (non-) conceptualism about intuitions. In this chapter, I explored the answer to these questions we find in the B-edition of the Transcendental Deduction.

With regard to the first question, I indicated that though the second step of the B Deduction might make it tempting to attribute to Kant the radical view of our most basic pure intuitions of space and time as "ens imaginarium," reading his argument in light of his account of the activity and cognitive function of imagination in general points toward a mediating model instead. According to this mediating model, rather than generating our most basic pure intuitions of space and time, our imagination makes derivative pure intuitions$_i$ of space and time by synthesizing the pure intuitions of space and time we are given through the "original receptivity" of sensibility in accordance with the categories. Though imagination is thus not responsible for our most basic pure intuitions of space and time on my reading, I have insisted that, on Kant's view, this derivative set of pure intuitions$_i$ that our imagination generates, i.e. formal intuitions$_i$, have the cognitive function of making the categories sensible, and that they pave the way for us being able not only to "first cognize" space and time "as objects," but also to have experience at all.

With regard to the second question, I emphasized that in the second step of the B Deduction, instead of arguing that these formal intuitions$_i$ of imagination make the sense stage of experience possible, Kant maintains that they make the representation of objects as spatio-temporally determinate at issue in perception in the imagination stage and full-blown experience involved in the understanding stage possible. And I claimed that when we thus ask what aspect of experience Kant thinks the *a priori* exercise of imagination conditions, at the most basic level, the answer is our representation of objects as spatially and/or temporally determinate in perception.

As for the third question, over the course of this chapter, I further elaborated on the interpretation that I began developing in Chapter 5, according to which Kant, in the context of experience, is not a conceptualist about the generation of intuitions across the board; he is only committed to the generation of intuitions$_i$ depending on concepts. Whereas in the last chapter, I defended this interpretation with respect to empirical concepts, in this chapter, I defended it with respect to the categories. In particular, I argued that Kant does not endorse a conceptualist position regarding the generation of either our most fundamental pure intuitions of space and time or empirical intuitions$_s$ as dependent on the categories. He regards these intuitions as given to us through the receptivity of sensibility, without the need of categorial involvement. However, *per* my reading, he does mount an argument to the effect that the generation of derivative pure intuitions$_i$ of space and time (the formal intuitions of §26) and the empirical intuitions$_i$ in perception depends on the categories.

Though in this chapter, I hope to have shown that Kant commits himself to a view of the *a priori* exercise of imagination along mediating, rather than radical, lines, as I also suggested the details of how this all works remain rather vague at the end of the Deduction and that we need to look to the Schematism in order to gain more clarity. And what I now aim to show is that, in the Schematism, we learn that we cannot fully make sense of what the imagination contributes to the possibility of experience on Kant's view unless we take into account his definition of imagination as the faculty of exhibition.

Seeing More: Kant's Theory of Imagination. Samantha Matherne, Oxford University Press.
© Samantha Matherne 2024. DOI: 10.1093/9780191999291.003.0007

7

A Priori Imagination and the Conditions of Experience II

The Schematism

schematism ... is a hidden art in the depths of the human soul,
whose true operations we can divine from nature
and lay unveiled before our eyes only with difficulty

—A141/B180–1

7.1 Introduction

Reading Kant as committed to imagination being the source of our most basic pure intuitions of space and time is not the only radical way of reading his account of the theoretical use of its *a priori* activities. According to another radical reading, in the Schematism chapter of the first *Critique* Kant commits himself to imagination being the source of our most basic pure concepts of objects: the categories.[1] As Heidegger puts it, "In the Transcendental Schematism the categories are formed first of all as categories" (KPM 77–8).[2] Or as Longuenesse has argued more recently, for Kant, the categories are "originally acquired" as "concepts of an object," through the schematizing activities of imagination (1998, 252–3; quoting B128).[3] In this way, just as Kant's account of the *a priori* exercise of imagination in the Transcendental Deduction can be interpreted as giving us reason to reread

---

[1] There are complicated issues surrounding how Kant conceives of the categories as "concepts of an object in general," and their relationship to the logical functions of judgment, which I shall address below (B128).

[2] See, e.g., Heidegger's claim that, "If these are the true 'primal concepts', however, then the Transcendental Schematism is the original and authentic concept-formation as such" (KPM 77–8; see also PIK 291–2). For discussion, see Lambeth (2021; 2023).

[3] In developing her interpretation of the "original acquisition" of the categories, Longuenesse draws on Kant's remarks to Eberhard: "universal transcendental concepts of the understanding, which are likewise acquired and not innate, though their *acquisitio*, like that of space, is no less *originaria* and presupposes nothing innate save the subjective conditions of the spontaneity of thought" (OD 8:22–3). See also de Boer's claim that, the categories are to be understood in terms of pure concepts of the understanding that have been "deschamatized" (2016, §6; 2022, chap. 6, §4). Guyer also argues that the Duisburg Nachlass (R5637 18:271–2) points toward the view that "the categories should be derived from the transcendental schemata of time-determination" (1987, 176).

Kant's account of space and time from the Aesthetic, so too can his account of it in the Schematism be interpreted as giving us reason to reread the earlier parts of the Transcendental Analytic in which he claims that the understanding is the "birthplace" of the categories (A66/B90). For what we realize in the Schematism, *per* this radical reading, is that the categories have their birthplace in imagination, instead.

However, against this reading, I shall argue that in the Schematism chapter Kant continues to endorse the more moderate mediating model of *a priori* imaginative activity that I claimed he puts forward in the Transcendental Deduction: at the *a priori* level, our imagination mediates between the pure intuitions of space and time given through sensibility and the categories given through the understanding. But in this chapter, I supplement this interpretive line with an argument to the effect that by casting this mediating activity in terms of "schematism," Kant expands his account in elucidatory ways, giving us reason to interpret this activity in light of his definition of imagination as the faculty of exhibition (see Chapter 4). In this vein, I maintain that Kant ultimately conceives of the *a priori* exercise of imagination as a categorially constrained activity in which our imagination generates so-called "transcendental schemata," which are pure intuitions of imagination (intuitions$_i$) that exhibit the categories in sensible form and that facilitate our concrete comprehension of these pure concepts.

In the course of defending this reading of the Schematism, I continue to be guided by the three questions about the *a priori* exercise of imagination that I introduced in Chapter 6: how does Kant understand its relationship to the pure intuitions of space and time and the pure concepts of the understanding, exactly what stages of experience does he think the *a priori* exercise of imagination enables, and how does this all bear on Kant's (non-)conceptualism concerning intuitions.[4] Though I hope to have made some headway with respect to Kant's answers to these questions with my interpretation of the B Deduction, in this chapter, I endeavor to show that in the Schematism Kant elaborates on his position in a way that clarifies many of the key issues that remain unsettled at the end of the Deduction.

With regard to the first question, as I already anticipated, I argue that the Schematism reveals Kant's commitment to the *a priori* exercise of imagination being a mode of exhibition ("schematism") in which our imagination makes pure

---

[4] Though I read the Schematism through the lens of Kant's theory of imagination in general and his account of the *a priori* dimensions of its theoretical use, there are other valuable lenses through which the Schematism can be read. See, e.g., Longuenesse's (1998, pt. III) reading with an eye to schematism as a process in which "the power of judgment (*Urteilskraft*) schematizes for its reflective use" (1998, 251); de Boer's (2016; 2020, chap. 6) reading with an eye to the role the Schematism plays in Kant's critique of Wolffian metaphysics; and Stang's (2023) reading of Schematism with an eye to the question of whether sensible objects are subsumable under the categories.

intuitions$_i$ ("transcendental schemata") that exhibit the categories in sensible form. And I contend that we should ultimately read Kant's account of figurative synthesis and formal intuitions$_i$ from the B Deduction in light of this account of imaginative schematism and transcendental schemata.

With regard to the second question, I continue developing the interpretation of Kant that I put forward in the last chapter, according to which the *a priori* exercise of imagination does not condition our having empirical intuitions of sense (intuitions$_s$), but rather the way we take up what we sense and represent appearances as spatially and temporally determinate in perception and experience. Recall, here, Kant's examples of representing the shape of a house in perception or representing the temporal sequence in freezing water in experience (B162–3). In this chapter, I make the case that in the Schematism Kant develops an argument to the effect that the most basic way in which we represent appearances in perception and experience is as temporally determinate, e.g. as having a duration, as persisting, as standing in successive relations, as occurring simultaneously, and that this kind of representation depends on the *a priori* schematizing activities of imagination. By my lights, what the Schematism thus reveals is that, for Kant, enabling the representation of temporal determinacy is the most basic way in which the *a priori* exercise of imagination contributes to the possibility of experience.

Finally, with regard to Kant's (non-)conceptualism, I have been attributing to him a restricted conceptualism according to which the generation of intuitions$_i$ depends on concepts, empirical and categorial, but the generation of given intuitions, whether of sense or the pure intuitions of space and time, does not. In this chapter, I explore how Kant elaborates on his picture of the dependence of intuitions$_i$ on the categories in his account of both the pure intuitions$_i$ involved in transcendental schemata and the empirical intuitions$_i$ generated in perception that depend on those schemata. And I make the case that attending to the role that transcendental schemata play in Kant's conceptualism can stem the worry that this commitment saddles him with an overly intellectualized view of perception.

In order to develop my interpretation of the Schematism, I begin in §7.2 with a discussion of the relationship between the Transcendental Deduction and the Schematism in which I map Kant's account of figurative synthesis and formal intuitions$_i$ in the former onto his account of transcendental schematism and transcendental schemata in the latter. However, I argue that Kant uses the Schematism to elaborate on his view in the Deduction in vital ways, most centrally, by clarifying that the *a priori* exercise of imagination involves the exhibition of the categories. I submit that reading his account of the *a priori* activity of imagination in light of his theory of exhibition illuminates what transcendental schematism involves, why it matters for us cognitively, and how it conditions our ability to represent appearances as temporally determinate in perception and full-blown experience.

ELABORATION OF THE TRANSCENDENTAL DEDUCTION   215

In what remains of the chapter, I offer an interpretation of Kant's view of the transcendental schemata for the so-called "mathematical" categories of quantity and quality (§7.3) and the "dynamical" categories of relation (§7.4). I analyze his account of how the relevant schemata are generated by imagination, as well as of the representation of temporal determinacy that they enable in perception and experience in the technical sense, respectively. I here set aside the schemata for the categories of modality (<possibility>, <actuality>, <necessity>) because they are outliers with respect to Kant's analysis of how the *a priori* exercise of imagination enables experience. Instead of treating these schemata as conditions that enable experience, he treats them as conditions of our "metaphysical" understanding of the connection between objects and the possibility of experience (see p. 285n of the Guyer/Wood 1998a translation, citation to *Nachlaß* 23:28). So understood, the schemata for the modal categories do not appear to directly condition the empirical activities involved in experience in the way that the categories for quantity, quality, and relation do, which is why I shall set them aside.[5]

In addition to clarifying Kant's account of transcendental schematism, over the course of this discussion, I hope to show that just as attending to the notion of exhibition is crucial for making sense of his empirical account of the theoretical use of imagination internal to perception and experience, so too is it crucial for understanding his *a priori* account of its use vis-à-vis the possibility of perception and experience in the first place. Indeed, I argue that attending to imagination as the faculty of exhibition in this context sheds light on the distinctive cognitive function that Kant accords our imagination vis-à-vis perception and experience. For, although on Kant's view, sensibility in its receptive guise can give us intuitions, and understanding can provide us with concepts, imagination alone can engage in the cognitive activity of exhibition that mediates between the two in the way that perception and experience require. And while I bring my interpretation of Kant's account of the theoretical use of imagination to a close in this chapter, the thread of exhibition is one that I shall continue to pursue as I move ahead in my analysis of its aesthetic and practical uses, as providing a unifying framework for our diverse imaginative activities across these domains.

7.2 The Schematism as an Elaboration of the Transcendental Deduction

The Schematism chapter is notorious not just for its obscurity, but also for its potential redundancy. Given what Kant has accomplished in the Transcendental

---

[5] According to Kant, these schemata enable us to have modal thoughts in which we determine the relationship between objects and "time itself" (A145/B184). The schema for <possibility> enables the "determination of the representation of a thing to some time"; the schema for <actuality> enables the determination of an object's "existence at a determinate time"; and the schema for <necessity> is the representation of "the existence of an object at all times" (A144–5/B184).

216   A PRIORI IMAGINATION AND THE CONDITIONS OF EXPERIENCE II

Deduction, some commentators have called into question whether he needs the Schematism at all.[6] To see why, consider how Kant opens the Schematism chapter: "how is the **subsumption** of [empirical intuition] under the [categories], thus the **application** of the category to appearances possible, since no one would say that the category, e.g. causality, could also be intuited through the senses and is contained in the appearance" (A137–8/B176–7). This question can seem rather puzzling: what was the point of the Deduction if not to show that the subsumption of empirical intuition, hence appearances, under the categories is possible?

To be sure, in the Schematism Kant covers some of the same territory that he covers in the Deduction. However, this is not something that he is oblivious to. In the Schematism, he explicitly addresses the overlap between the texts and makes clear what he intends to add in a passage that I shall quote at length,

> After what has been shown in the deduction of the categories, hopefully no one
> will be in doubt about...whether, as conditions of a possible experience, they
> relate *a priori* solely to appearances...For we have seen that concepts...cannot
> have any significance [*Bedeutung*], where an object is not given...; that, further,
> the modification of our sensibility is the only way in which objects are given to
> us; and finally, that pure concepts *a priori* in addition to the function of the
> understanding in the category, must also contain *a priori* formal conditions of
> sensibility (namely of the inner sense) that contain the general condition under
> which alone the category can be applied to any object. We will call this formal
> and pure condition of the sensibility, to which the use of the concept of the
> understanding is restricted, the **schema** of this concept.   (A139–40/B178–9)

Though there are many things going on in this passage, Kant's basic claim is that in the Deduction he has shown that the categories only have "significance," i.e. applicability, with respect to objects that we empirically intuit through a "modification of our sensibility." He then reminds us of his argument to the effect that the categories are connected to empirical intuition via an "*a priori* formal condition of sensibility," which I argued in Chapter 6 amounts to formal intuitions$_i$ generated through the figurative synthesis of imagination.

While this much is familiar from the Deduction, in the last sentence of the passage Kant makes a new claim: the formal condition of sensibility generated through imagination should be understood as a "schema" of a category. Kant here signals his intention for the Schematism to serve as an elaboration of his account of the *a priori* exercise of imagination from the Deduction.[7] And far from being

---

[6] For the charge of superfluity, see, e.g., Prichard (1909, 246–7); Warnock (1949); Bennett (1966, 150–1).

[7] In defending a reading of the Schematism as an elaboration of the argument in the Deduction, I am sympathetic to the readings offered by Gibbons (1994, chap. 2); Longuenesse (1998, pt. III); Allison (2004, chap. 8); Banham (2005, chap. 5); Hughes (2007, chap. 6); Birrer (2017, pt. III); de Boer (2016; 2020, chap. 6).

superfluous, I shall argue that this elaboration reveals the importance of conceiving of imagination as a faculty of exhibition in this context, for what we shall find is that, on Kant's view, the *a priori* exercise of imagination amounts to the generation of pure intuitions$_i$ that exhibit the categories in sensible form. Appreciating the frame of exhibition, I submit, not only clarifies the sort of imaginative activity and cognitive function involved in this *a priori* exercise, but also why we should attribute to him a mediating, rather than a radical, model of the imagination's relation to the categories. To this end in this section, I consider the ways in which Kant's account of schematism as a kind of exhibition maps onto and extends his account of the *a priori* activities of imagination (§7.2.1) and how it conditions experience (§7.2.2) from the Transcendental Deduction, before addressing how this works in the case of the categories of quantity, quality, and relation in subsequent sections.

7.2.1 From Figurative Synthesis and Formal Intuitions to Transcendental Schematism and Transcendental Schemata

In the Schematism chapter, Kant does not use the language of "figurative synthesis" or "formal intuitions" to characterize the *a priori* exercise of imagination familiar from the Deduction; however, if we look at his characterization of the activity of schematism and schemata themselves, then we have reason to read the latter as continuous with the former.[8]

To see this, let me briefly rehearse my interpretation of figurative synthesis and formal intuitions$_i$ in the B Deduction. On my reading, Kant conceives of figurative synthesis as a transcendental synthesis of our productive imagination through which it "determine[s] the form of sense *a priori*... in accordance with the categories" (B152).[9] I identified this "form of sense" with the pure intuitions of space and time and the manifold they contain that we are given through sensibility. And I argued that, *per* Kant, figurative synthesis results in formal intuitions$_i$, which are "made" pure intuitions$_i$ that represent space and time "as object," i.e. as "determined" or "unified" in some way (B160). I, in turn, claimed that,

---

[8] Some commentators have objected to the identification of transcendental schemata with formal intuitions. Waxman (1991, 104–6), for example, contrasts formal intuitions, which precede all concepts, with transcendental schemata, which presuppose concepts. And Guyer argues that the schemata of the categories are neither intuitions nor forms of pure imaginative synthesis, but should rather be understood just as "rules *in accordance with* which particular syntheses of empirical intuitions... can and must be conducted" (2006, 473). However, I shall argue that though Kant conceives of transcendental schemata as rules for empirical synthesis, his theory of schemata in general and his account of the schemata of the categories in particular commit him to regarding them as intuitions$_i$ that exhibit the categories. For other interpreters who take the account of schematism to be continuous with the account of figurative synthesis and formal intuitions in the B Deduction, see Longuenesse (1998, pt. 3); Allison (2004, 215–16); Birrer (2017, 294–5).

[9] See also Kant's discussion of the "transcendental synthesis of imagination" that is "contained" in the categories (A119).

218 *A PRIORI* IMAGINATION AND THE CONDITIONS OF EXPERIENCE II

according to Kant, our imagination engages in figurative synthesis and produces formal intuitions$_i$ in service of the understanding and the understanding's effort to "determine sensibility" at the *a priori* level (B161n). When our imagination proceeds in this way, I suggested that it meets Kant's standard for functioning cognitively well: it performs its cognitive function of generating intuitions$_i$ that make concepts (here, the categories) sensible. And I made the case that when our imagination functions cognitively well in the *a priori* register, Kant accords it a role in making possible not only our "first" cognition of space and time, but also our experience (B138).

In the Schematism chapter, we find Kant characterizing the activity and result of schematism along similar lines. Beginning with the activity, as was the case with figurative synthesis, Kant describes schematism as a "transcendental synthesis of imagination" in its "productive" guise, and, more specifically, as a transcendental synthesis of the "*a priori* manifold in pure intuition" "in accord with... the category" (A141–2/B181; A138/B177).[10] Granted, he also glosses schematism as a "procedure of the understanding" (A140/B179; A142/B181). However, I take this to amount to the claim that schematism is an activity our imagination executes in service of the understanding (A142/B181).

As for the representation that results from schematism, though Kant introduces new terminology for it, "transcendental schema," it maps onto his account of a formal intuition$_i$ from the Deduction. According to Kant, a transcendental schema is a "transcendental product of imagination" that involves a representation of a "transcendental time-determination [*Zeitbestimmung*]" (A140/B179; A138/B177). As I shall discuss in more detail below, a "transcendental time-determination," for Kant, is a representation of the *a priori* form of time (i.e. the pure intuition of time that contains a manifold) as determined in accordance with a particular category. And though in the Schematism, he does not explicitly label a transcendental schema an intuition, he does in the second and third *Critiques*, as well as in the "Progress" essay.[11] For Kant, transcendental schemata are thus a

---

[10] The more extended quote reads, "The schema of a pure concept of the understanding... is rather only the pure synthesis, in accord with a rule of unity according to concepts in general, which the category expresses" (A142/B181).

[11] In the second *Critique*, he glosses schemata as "intuitions... given *a priori*" (KpV 5:68). And in the third *Critique*, he says, "To demonstrate the reality of our concepts, intuitions are always required... If they are pure concepts of the understanding, then the latter are called **schemata**," and he glosses schematism as a process, "where to a concept grasped by the understanding the corresponding intuition is given *a priori*" (KU 5:351). He makes a similar claim about the categories in the "Progress" essay, where he claims, "If objective reality is accorded to the concept directly (*directe*) through the intuition that corresponds to it, i.e., if the concept is immediately exhibited, this act is called schematism" (WF 20:279; transl. modified). This is also in keeping with Kant's commitment to all representations of imagination, *qua* products of a part of sensibility, being intuitions (see Chapter 3).

ELABORATION OF THE TRANSCENDENTAL DEDUCTION   219

kind of pure intuition$_i$ that represent the *a priori* form of time as determined in accordance with the categories, and hence map onto formal intuitions$_i$.[12]

This said, as this talk of time suggests, one notable difference between the B Deduction and the Schematism is that Kant presents transcendental schematism in exclusively temporal terms, which is not something he did in his account of figurative synthesis and formal intuitions$_i$ of space and time in the Deduction.[13] As I just noted, Kant characterizes a transcendental schema as a "transcendental time-determination" and transcendental schematism as "the determination of the inner sense in general, in accordance with conditions of its form (time) in regard to all representations" (A142/B181). The reason Kant offers for focusing exclusively on time is that time, unlike space, is a "formal condition... of *all* representations" (A138/B177). Kant takes this to be the case because all representations, whether of something "inner" or "outer," are "inner states," and all inner states, according to Kant, "belong under the formal condition of... time" (A34/B50; see also A99–100). By contrast, Kant claims that space is a more "limited" form of intuition because it is only a condition of "outer intuitions," i.e. of intuitions that represent what is "outside" of us (A34/B50). By concentrating exclusively on time in the Schematism chapter, Kant thus narrows his focus to the *a priori* formal conditions of sensibility upon which all perception and experience depends. However, in spite of this exclusively temporal focus, for reasons I adduced above, the account of the *a priori* imaginative synthesis and intuitions$_i$ offered in the Schematism is continuous with the one he offers in the B Deduction. As we might think of it, for Kant, transcendental schematism and transcendental schemata are figurative synthesis and formal intuitions$_i$ in a temporal key.

What I would now like to propose is that appreciating figurative synthesis and formal intuitions$_i$ in light of the notion of schematism clarifies not only the *a priori* exercise of imagination, but also its cognitive function. In Chapter 6, I suggested that one of Kant's original moves in the Deduction is to acknowledge an *a priori* way in which our imagination functions cognitively well in service of the understanding by generating intuitions$_i$ that make the categories sensible and that play a role in enabling both our cognition of space and time and experience. However, as I also indicated in Chapter 6, in the Deduction, Kant does not fully explicate how our imagination proceeds "in accordance with the categories" in this way. But in the Schematism, Kant adds the idea that this process involves the

---

[12] Further evidence of this mapping can be drawn from a combination of passages from the Schematism and the *Prolegomena*. The relevant text in the Schematism is Kant's description of the transcendental schema for the category of quantity as a "pure image" (A142/B182). And in the *Prolegomena* he appears to identify an "image" of <quantity>, viz. of the sort a geometer has, with a "formal intuition" (and, indeed, he indicates that "formal intuition" is a "better" label for this than "image") (Prol. 4:287).

[13] In the §§24 and 26 of the B Deduction, for example, Kant discusses figurative synthesis and formal intuitions$_i$ of both space and time.

schematization of the categories. And in later texts, such as the third *Critique* and the "Progress" essay, Kant is even more precise: this process is one in which a "concept grasped by the understanding" is "directly" "exhibited" through the "corresponding intuition" that is a schema (KU 5:351–2; transl. modified).[14] And what I shall now argue is that if we attend to Kant's account of schematism as a kind of direct exhibition of concepts, then we gain insight into the *a priori* exercise of imagination as a kind of categorially constrained process, which has the function of making the categories sensible in a way that facilitates our concrete comprehension of them.

In more detail, as I discussed in Chapter 5, Kant characterizes schematism in general as an activity in which our imagination "directly" exhibits a concept in an intuition$_i$ by representing how the logical content of a concept manifests in a concrete, holistic way in space and time (see KU §59; WF 20:279). For example, the schema of a snapdragon involves an intuition$_i$ that represents a kind of *Gestalt* for how the marks contained in the concept <snapdragon>, such as <having bilaterally-symmetrical flowers>, <having lance-shaped leaves>, <blooming from the bottom of the stalk>, etc., show up, and show up as a whole, in space and time. I suggested that, on Kant's view, insofar as schematism involves directly exhibiting a concept through an intuition$_i$ that corresponds to the marks contained in a concept, we should conceive of schematism as something that is constrained by the relevant concept. However, I also suggested that, according to Kant, in generating a schema our imagination has to rely on some "art," i.e. skill or know-how, with how concepts sensibly and holistically show up, which outstrips our purely abstract knowledge of them. Finally, as a form of imaginative exhibition, I claimed that Kant conceives of schematism as something that has the cognitive function of making concepts sensible to us and facilitating our concrete comprehension of how they manifest in space and time.[15]

Applying this general picture of schematism to transcendental schematism, on Kant's view, this is an *a priori* activity in which our imagination directly exhibits the categories in pure intuitions$_i$ (transcendental schemata) that represent how the logical content of the categories manifests in a concrete, holistic way in time. More specifically, Kant thinks a transcendental schema exhibits a category through a "time-determination," i.e. through a representation of a particular temporal form or pattern that reflects how the logical content of the category manifest in a concrete, holistic way in time. As is the case with all schematism, *per* Kant, transcendental schematism relies on some sort of imaginative art, i.e. skill or

---

[14] See also, "To represent a pure concept of the understanding as thinkable in an object of possible experience is to ... exhibit it. If objective reality is accorded to the concept directly (*directe*) through the intuition that corresponds to it, i.e., if the concept is immediately exhibited, this act is called schematism" (WF 20:279; transl. modified).

[15] As I have noted before, this sort of "comprehension" is not to be confused with the sort of "comprehension" (*Begreifen*) that reason enables on Kant's view (see JL 9:65).

ELABORATION OF THE TRANSCENDENTAL DEDUCTION   221

know-how, with how a category manifests in temporal terms (A141/B181).[16] And through this art, Kant thinks our imagination makes a category "grasped by the understanding" concretely comprehensible to us (KU 5:351). It seems that we are especially in need of this when it comes to the categories. For as challenging as it might be to have a concrete grasp of how empirical concepts, such as <snapdragon>, <dub>, or <cholera>, sensibly manifest, how much more challenging is it to have a concrete grasp of how the highly abstract concepts of <quantity>, <substance>, and <cause> sensibly manifest? Nevertheless, on Kant's view, in order to cognitively deploy a concept in relation to intuition, the concept must be made sensible to us. So, if we are to be able to deploy the categories in relation to what we intuit, then, *per* Kant, it falls to our imagination and its art of transcendental schematism to first make the categories sensible and concretely comprehensible to us through transcendental schemata. Were we to be without this imaginative art, this skill or know-how with how the categories sensibly manifest, then we would be like the physician: in possession of the categories but unable to use them in cognition to think about objects we are given. For all its abstruseness, then, I take the Schematism chapter to be pivotal in appreciating this cognitive function of the *a priori* exercise of imagination—a significance that, I submit, only comes to light once we attend to the theme of exhibition.

This said, one might wonder how exactly transcendental schematism as a mode of exhibition can work given the distinctive nature of the categories. Consider the contrast of the schematism of the categories with the schematism of an empirical concept like <snapdragon>. On Kant's view, <snapdragon> contains various marks, such as <having bilaterally-symmetrical flowers>, <having lance-shaped leaves>, <blooming from the bottom of the stalk>, etc., which are derived from experience. When our imagination schematizes this concept, *per* Kant, it is constrained by these marks as that which it endeavors to make sensible to us. The marks of <snapdragon> thus constrain our imagination, as it sketches a schematic intuition; that represents how those marks show up as a whole in a spatio-temporal form.

But as *a priori* concepts, the categories do not contain marks derived from experience in this way. So, how exactly does our imagination go about schematizing them? Indeed, at this point, one might object that direct exhibition is a misguided way to be thinking about the schematism of the categories at all. For according to a radical model of the *a priori* exercise of imagination of the sort I suggested above, transcendental schematism is not a process through which our imagination exhibits concepts already possessed by the understanding;

---

[16] See Bell (1987) and Matherne (2014a) for discussion of the relevance of the notion of "art" to schematism.

transcendental schematism is the process through which the categories, *qua* concepts of objects, are "formed" or "acquired" in the first place.[17]

Here, however, we must be cautious. As was the case with Kant's account of space and time, specifying in exactly what sense imagination might, or might not, be the source of the categories requires attending to the different ways in which Kant speaks of the categories. Sometimes Kant aligns the categories with logical functions of judgment, which amount to the basic logical patterns in accordance with which concepts can be combined in judgment.[18] But other times, he specifies the categories as concepts of objects, e.g. "**the categories**... are concepts of an object in general, by means of which its intuition is regarded as **determined** with regard to one of the **logical functions** for judgments" (B128). In this latter vein, the categories are not just logical functions that concern the combination of concepts in judgments, but rather concepts of objects that concern the combination of representations together in intuition.[19] What is at issue in the debate I am concerned with here is not whether the categories as logical functions have their source in imagination; all parties concede that the logical functions have their source in the understanding on Kant's view. The question is whether Kant thinks the categories, as concepts of objects, have their source in imagination.

Defending the radical interpretation, Heidegger claims that Kant's considered position, distilled in the Schematism, is that,

> the pure concept of understanding is not given at all through a pure formal-logical function of judgment. Rather, this concept springs from the imaginative synthesis which is related to intuition and that means to time. The birthplace of pure concepts of understanding is not the faculty of understanding, which is pure, isolated, and functions logically. (PIK 193)[20]

---

[17] Heidegger uses language of "formation" (see KPM 78), whereas Longuenesse uses language of "acquisition" (1998, 252).

[18] See, for example, "The categories of the understanding...do not represent to us the conditions under which objects are given in intuition at all, hence objects can indeed appear to us without necessarily having to be related to functions of the understanding...Thus a difficulty is revealed here..., namely how **subjective conditions of thinking** should have **objective validity**...; for appearances can certainly be given in intuition without functions of the understanding" (A89–90/B122).

[19] Following Paton (1936, 41–60, 458) interpreters sometimes refer to the logical functions as "unschematized" categories, and the categories as concepts of objects as "schematized" categories (see Detel 1978; Langton 1998, 48–52; Symington 2011). Recently, de Boer (2016, §6; 2020; chap. 6, §4) has argued that the Schematism gives us reason to distinguish between a pure concept of the understanding that "contains" both a schema and a logical function of judgment (A139–40/B179), and a category as a "deschematized" pure concept of the understanding, which only contains the logical function. I, however, do not find Kant observing a strict distinction between categories and pure concepts of the understanding (see, e.g., his title of the Metaphysical Deduction: "On the pure concepts of the understanding or the categories" (A76/B102); "**the categories**, i.e., pure concepts of the understanding" (A119); "the categories, as concepts of the understanding" (A85/B118)).

[20] See also, "Thus we agree that the logical function of judgment, of understanding, is not the primary and exclusive source of the origin of concept of understanding. Rather this source lies in the pure synthesis of the time related power of imagination" (PIK 197).

ELABORATION OF THE TRANSCENDENTAL DEDUCTION 223

Longuenesse, meanwhile, argues that, for Kant, although the categories are, in one sense, "engrained in the mind as logical functions," they are only "acquired" as concepts of objects through the *a priori* imagination (1998, 244, 253).[21] Notice that insofar as Heidegger and Longuenesse interpret the logical functions of judgment as playing some role in this process, they can acknowledge a kind of mediation that happens in schematism: our imagination mediates between the *a priori* form of time and the logical functions of judgment.[22] But what the radical reading rules out is the possibility that schematism involves our imagination mediating between the *a priori* form of time and the categories, *qua* concepts of objects, because the latter are precisely what are said to be acquired through this process.

However, there are several reasons to worry that this radical interpretation of schematism as preceding the categories, *qua* concepts of objects, can reflect Kant's considered view. In the first place, this reading is not in keeping with how Kant characterizes the schematism of the categories in the third *Critique*. Kant does not describe schematism as the process through which the categories are generated. He, instead, describes it as a process of exhibition, "where to a concept grasped by the understanding the corresponding intuition is given *a priori*" (KU 5:351). Here, Kant intimates that a category is a concept that is "grasped by the understanding," and that schematism is a process in which that intellectually grasped content is exhibited, or "made sensible," through a "corresponding intuition" (KU 5:351).

Granted this claim occurs in the third *Critique*, but if we look at the Schematism chapter itself, then I submit that we find Kant implicitly articulating the same view. In particular, I have in mind Kant's claim in the passage that I quoted above, "pure concepts *a priori* in addition to the function of the understanding in the category, must also contain *a priori* formal conditions of sensibility" (A139–40/B178–9). What I would like to propose is that we understand this "function of the understanding" as bound up with the logical content that the categories, as concepts of objects, have independent of any *a priori* imaginative activity.

In more detail, I take the logical content of the categories to be what Kant refers to at the end of the Schematism as the "logical significance" they have apart from

---

[21] While this is part of the acquisition process, Longuenesse argues that although the categories are originally acquired through the generation of schemata, they are only acquired as "'clear concepts', that is 'universal representations' of pure synthesis according to rules," through a process in which we reflect on schemata (1998, 253). Given my focus on imagination, I shall leave the latter aspect of Longuenesse's reading aside.

[22] See, e.g., her claim that, "the schemata enumerated in the Schematism...are nothing other than the specific results of the *synthesis speciosa*, that is the results of the "determination of inner sense by the understanding" that aims at reflecting the sensible given under concepts combined according to the logical forms of judgment" (1998, 245; quoting A142/B181).

224 A PRIORI IMAGINATION AND THE CONDITIONS OF EXPERIENCE II

schemata: a "pure significance, without any condition of sensibility" (A147/B186).[23] To illustrate, he offers the example of substance, claiming that apart from its transcendental schema, the category of substance logically signifies "a something that can be thought as a subject (without being a predicate of something else)" (A147/B186). So understood, the logical content of the category of substance amounts to the concept of an object that can only be thought of as a subject, rather than as a predicate of something else. And the source of this logical content, *per* Kant, is not schematism, but rather the understanding.

But notice that, on Kant's view, the categories are also distinct from the mere logical functions of judgment, which he outlines in the Metaphysical Deduction. For, unlike the mere logical functions of judgment, Kant defines the categories as concepts of objects: "**the categories**...are concepts of an object in general, by means of which its intuition is regarded as **determined** with regard to one of the **logical functions** for judgments" (B128). For Kant, then, a category "contains" a logical function of judgment insofar as a category is a concept of an object that represents the intuition of an object as determined with respect to a logical function of judgment. To return to the category of substance, on Kant's view, it is a concept of an object that represents the intuition of an object as determined as something that can be thought as a subject without being the predicate of something else.

To be sure, the logical content of the categories is very thin according to Kant: "it shows me nothing at all about what determinations the thing that is to count as such...is to have" (A147/B186-7). That is to say, all we can say about a category in light of its logical content is that, from an intellectual perspective, it is a concept of an object that represents an intuition of an object as determined with respect to a logical function of judgment. This logical content thus gives us no insight, from a sensible perspective, into the sort of spatio-temporal determinations the relevant object will have. Nevertheless, this logical content is enough for us to be able to distinguish between different categories as concepts of objects that have their "birthplace" in the understanding (A66/B90).[24]

According to my reading, then, Kant does not appeal to the schematizing activities of imagination to explain the generation of the categories, *qua* our most

---

[23] It should be noted that at the end of the Schematism, Kant suggests that apart from schemata, "a logical significance...is left to the pure concepts of the understanding, but no object and thus no significance is given to them that could yield a concept of the object" (A147/B186). However, as Guyer and Wood note, in Kant's copy to the first edition, he changes "concept of the object" to "cognition of the object," and I take this change to be reflective of his considered view. For apart from a schemata, I take it that categories do count as concepts of objects for Kant, e.g. the category of substance is the concept of an object of intuition that can be thought as a subject without being a predicate of something else. But apart from the schemata, he claims that the categories cannot be used in the cognition of an object because they are lacking conditions of application.

[24] I take a full story of what it means for the categories to have their "birthplace" in the understanding to turn on vexed issues surrounding how we are to understand the "derivation" of the categories in the Metaphysical Deduction—an issue I shall here have to set aside.

basic concepts of objects, as the radical interpretation would have it. These concepts have their source in the understanding. Schematizing activities have a different role to play: they generate the pure schematic intuitions$_i$ that directly exhibit the logical content of the categories in temporal form. And with this picture of the logical content of the categories in place, I can now fill out the details of how I understand this process to work on Kant's view.

For Kant, transcendental schematism is a process in which our imagination synthesizes the *a priori* form of time under the constraint of the logical content of a category, and the result of this process is a transcendental schema, i.e. a pure intuition$_i$ that directly exhibits that logical content in a determinate temporal pattern. For example, in the case of the category of substance, the logical content of this category (the representation of an object of intuition that can be thought as a subject without being a predicate of something else) constrains our imagination in synthesizing the *a priori* form of time. And the result of this schematizing process is a schema that directly exhibits this logical content in a determinate temporal pattern: "the persistence of the real in time...which endures while everything else changes" (A144/B183). And by exhibiting the categories in this temporal way, the schematizing activities of imagination give us a concrete grasp of how the categories sensibly manifest, which our intellectual grasp of the categories through the understanding alone does not provide.

Thus, on my interpretation, rather than generating the categories, Kant casts transcendental schematism as a mediating activity in which our imagination mediates between the *a priori* form of time, *qua* our most basic pure intuition of time given through sensibility, on the one hand, and the categories, *qua* our most basic concepts of objects given through the understanding, on the other. I take this mediating model of the *a priori* exercise of imagination to be in keeping with the one I argued Kant endorses in the B Deduction. However, by my lights, appreciating Kant's commitment to this mediating activity being a form of direct exhibition elucidates certain aspects of figurative synthesis and formal intuitions$_i$ that were not entirely clear in the B Deduction. We learn, for example, that figurative synthesis is an artful activity in which our imagination, under the constraint of the logical content of the categories, synthesizes the *a priori* form of time in such a way that directly exhibits this logical content in a temporal pattern. About formal intuitions$_i$ we discover that, as transcendental schemata, they amount to pure intuitions$_i$ that represent temporal patterns ("time-determinations") that directly exhibit the logical content of the categories. What is more, as I intimated above, conceiving of figurative synthesis and formal intuitions$_i$ along the lines of exhibition provides us insight into their cognition function on Kant's view: they are part of the imaginative process in which the categories are made sensible to us in a way that facilitates our concrete comprehension of them and enables us to deploy them in relation to what we intuit. However, in order to fully understand this

226 A PRIORI IMAGINATION AND THE CONDITIONS OF EXPERIENCE II

latter point, we need to take a closer look at Kant's account of how the *a priori* activity of imagination enables the empirical activities involved in perception and experience in the Schematism.

7.2.2 Imagination and the Possibility of Experience from the Deduction to the Schematism

In Chapter 6, I defended a reading of the Transcendental Deduction, according to which Kant argues that what the *a priori* exercise of imagination enables at the most basic level is the representation of appearances as spatially and/or temporally determinate in perception and experience. Making this point in terms of the three-stage theory of experience I have attributed to Kant (see Chapter 5), I claimed that he seeks to show that the *a priori* imagination conditions not the having of empirical intuitions$_s$ at the sense stage of experience, but rather the ways in which we take up what we sense and represent appearances as spatio-temporally determinate at the imagination and understanding stages of experience. Recall, here, Kant's choice to illustrate the upshot of his argument in §26 of the B Deduction with the examples of perceiving a house and experiencing freezing water. However, as I noted at the end of Chapter 6, though Kant indicates that this enabling turns on our imagination generating formal intuitions$_i$, which serve as the "ground" of the empirical synthesis required for perception and experience, he does not go into detail about how exactly this enabling works. As I read it, filling in this lacuna is another function of the Schematism for Kant. For, what we learn in this chapter is that, on Kant's view, what transcendental schemata "make representable" at the most basic level in perception and experience is temporal determinacy (A145/B184). Representations of temporal determinacy include things like representations of duration, persistence, succession, and simultaneity. And what I shall argue is that, on Kant's view, transcendental schemata are rules that provide us with the most basic temporal patterns that guide us in representing temporal determinacy along these lines in perception and experience.

Though my full analysis of how this works will require looking at what Kant says about the transcendental schemata for each category below, here I shall sketch the general picture. To repeat, on my interpretation of Kant, perception involves us imaginatively generating empirical intuitions$_i$ (perceptual images) that represent appearances as having a determinate temporal form, e.g. as having a three-second duration. And, *per* my reading, experience involves us making an empirical judgment through our understanding in which we recognize objects, which our representations correspond to and are necessitated by, as existing in time and standing in temporal relations. Turning now to the Schematism, as I see it, what Kant wants to argue in this chapter is that the transcendental schemata of the categories enable the temporal determination involved perception and experience because they provide us with the rules that guide the synthetic acts required to represent temporal determinacy.

More specifically, Kant describes transcendental schemata as "rules" for "the determining of our intuition in accordance with a certain general concept," where the relevant concept is a category (A141/B180). For Kant, then, in order to represent temporal determinacy in perception and experience, we need to be guided by transcendental schemata, *qua* rules for determining our intuition in accordance with a category. However, as I discussed in Chapter 5, on Kant's view, schemata are rules of a particular sort: they involve intuitions$_i$ that represents how the logical content of concepts shows up in a sensible, holistic way and that serve as patterns that guide us in synthesizing a manifold in accordance with those concepts. I accordingly understand the rules involved in transcendental schemata to be a kind of pure intuition$_i$ that reflects how the logical content of the categories shows up in a sensible, holistic way and that serves as a pattern that guides us in synthetic acts in perception and experience through which we represent temporal determinacy.

On Kant's view, the categories *sans* transcendental schemata cannot suffice for this guidance because they do not, on their own, provide us with temporal patterns of determinacy; they provide us with logical patterns for thinking about objects. The logical content of the category of substance, for example, gives us a pattern for thinking of an object as a subject rather than a predicate, but not a temporal pattern that reflects how such a subject would show up temporally. So, if the categories are to play a role in guiding the activity of temporal determination involved in perception and experience, then Kant claims this needs to be mediated by the art of transcendental schematism that first gives us a concrete grasp of how the logical patterns involved in the categories manifest temporally. It is thus the transcendental schemata that result from this process that, according to Kant, provide us with the basic patterns of temporal determinacy that serve as the rules that guide the empirical activities of temporal determination involved in perception and experience. This, at least, is how I understand the basic trajectory of Kant's account of how the *a priori* exercise of imagination enables perception and experience in the Schematism and how he uses it to elaborate on the role figurative synthesis and formal intuitions$_i$ play to this end in the Deduction.

However, in the Principles, Kant introduces a distinction between two types of synthesis, which I take to be important for understanding the details of how this enabling works: the distinction between "composition" (*Zusammensetzung*) and "connection" (*Verknüpfung*) (B201n).[25] Though Kant deploys the

---

[25] Though Kant explicitly emphasizes the distinction between composition and connection in the Principles, they are also implicit in the Transcendental Deduction. Regarding composition, in the A Deduction he refers to the representation of a triangle involving "being conscious of the composition

composition-connection distinction to various ends, what is of interest to me is its relevance to his account of the empirical activities involved in the perception at issue in the imagination stage of experience and the judgments of recognition at issue in the understanding stage of experience, respectively.

Kant glosses composition in general as the synthesis of a "homogeneous" manifold of intuition, i.e. a multiplicity made up of homogeneous representations, such as spatial or temporal representations (B201n). He, in turn, distinguishes between two kinds of composition: composition that pertains to the "form" and to the "matter" of homogeneous representations (B202; A167/B209).[26] As we shall see, in the context of experience, Kant takes these two kinds of composition to be involved in the imagination's generation of perceptual images in perception, *qua* empirical intuitions$_i$ that represent appearances as having a determinate spatio-temporal form and matter.[27]

By way of a bit more background, however, the first kind of composition, composition related to form, is a topic that Kant discusses in the Axioms of Intuition. According to Kant, this composition is a "successive synthesis" of the productive imagination in which we successively synthesize representations of homogeneous spatio-temporal parts into a representation of a spatio-temporal whole, e.g. a shape or duration (A163/B204). And he describes the intuition$_i$ that results from this imaginative synthesis as a representation of "a determinate space or time" (B202). He illustrates this with the example of our productive imagination representing a line: "I cannot represent to myself any line...without drawing it in thought, i.e. successively generating all its parts from one point, and thereby first sketching this intuition" (A162–3/B203). In order to represent a line as a determinate spatial form, Kant thus claims we need to imaginatively "compose" a line, by imaginatively "sketching" it as a whole through this sort of successive synthesis of its parts.

Kant discusses the second kind of composition, composition of matter, in the Anticipations of Perception. He glosses the relevant matter in terms of sensations, which are the result of the subject being affected by some "real" qualities that "fill"

---

of three straight lines in accordance with a rule" (A105; see also A118), and in the B Deduction he characterizes the synthesis of apprehension in perception as "composition of the manifold in an empirical intuition" (B160). Regarding connection, in his discussion of the synthesis of recognition in the A Deduction, he describes how apperception "subjects all synthesis of apprehension...to a transcendental unity, and first makes possible their connection in accordance with rules" (A103; see also A107, A110–11, A125).

[26] Kant also distinguishes between these two kinds of composition in terms of the idea that the first generates representations of "extensive magnitude" and the latter "intensive magnitude"; however, I shall set this complication aside here. See Zinkin (2006), Golob (2014), Land (2014), Sutherland (2022) for discussion of Kant's theory of magnitude (*Größ*) and its relevance to his account of experience (and in Zinkin's case, to his account of taste).

[27] Recall that, in Part I, I spoke of the imaginative representation of spatio-temporal form as shorthand for the representation of spatio-temporal determinacy in general (see, e.g., Chapter 3); however, I indicated that in this chapter, I would speak of the representation of spatio-temporal form in a more specific sense, as contrasting with the representation of matter.

ELABORATION OF THE TRANSCENDENTAL DEDUCTION   229

space or time (B207; A167/B210). Think, here, of the sensation of the vibrant orange of a snapdragon, the gentle warmth of sunlight, or the soft tone of Mariah Carey's first note in "Fantasy." On Kant's view, composition of matter in this sense involves apprehending sensation, and, by extension, the quality that gives rise to the sensation, in such a way that results in a representation of space or time materially "filled" with some "degree" (B207; A167/B210).[28] The composition of the gentle warmth of sunlight, for example, involves apprehending a sensation of warmth in such a way that involves representing the sensation, and, by extension, the quality of the sunlight, as filling space or time with some degree (see Prol. 4:306; A169/B211).

According to Kant, whereas the composition involved in representing a determinate spatio-temporal form proceeds diachronically, the composition involved in representing a determinate matter can occur in a single "instant" (*Augenblick*) (A167/B209).[29] He nevertheless maintains that this synchronic composition involves a kind of synthesis because it involves "apprehending" a sensation, and, in turn, a sensible quality, as filling space or time with some degree (A167–8/B209–10). Though Kant does not explicitly mention imagination in the Anticipations, as we have seen, he conceives of the synthesis of apprehension as an activity of imagination.[30] He is thus committed to this composition of matter of a manifold involving the activity of imaginative apprehension.[31]

Bringing this to bear on Kant's account of the empirical stages of experience, when we look at his discussion of composition in the Axioms and Anticipations, the empirical activities he highlights are imaginative activities that bear on perception. Kant, for example, opens the B-edition of the Axioms with the claim that, "appearances...cannot be apprehended..., i.e., taken up into empirical consciousness, except through the synthesis of the manifold through which the

---

[28] Though in this context Kant describes intensive magnitudes as the magnitude of something real that fills space and time, he also describes sensations of what is real as having an intensive magnitude (see A169/B210–11). See Jankowiak (2014) and Landy (2020) for discussion of Kant's argument for the former on the basis of the latter.

[29] Although Schulting (2017) denies that apprehension of a single instant depends on the categories, I take this argument in the Anticipations to commit Kant to the view that the categories must be involved. For discussion of the apprehension of an instant, see also Tolley (2019, 40–1; 2020, 235–6).

[30] See, e.g., "There is thus an active faculty of the synthesis of this manifold in us, which we call imagination, and whose action exercised immediately upon perceptions I call apprehension" (A120).

[31] This said, it is not entirely clear what the manifold is that Kant thinks is apprehended in the case of a single sensation. One possibility is that composition involves apprehending the multiplicity of a sensation and the time it fills. Another possibility is that composition involves apprehending the degree of the sensation (and corresponding reality) as belonging to a manifold of other degrees (see Sutherland 2022, 90). For example, if I apprehend a sensation of sunlight (or sunlight itself) as having a certain degree of intensity, then it would seem that there needs to be some sort of scale of degrees of intensity that I am operating with in the background. Apprehending the manifold in this latter sense would thus seem to be something more indirect and sophisticated than in the first case: I apprehend the manifold of degrees on the scale indirectly when I take my current sensation (and, by extension, the reality that grounds my sensation) to have a certain degree. I will not try and settle this issue here. Instead, I will focus on the basic claim that composition involves the apprehension of a sensation (and, by extension, a reality) as filling space or time with some degree.

representation of a determinate space or time are generated, i.e., through the composition of that which is homogeneous" (B202). The beginning of this passage echoes Kant's characterization of imagination-dependent perception in the B Deduction: "by the **synthesis of apprehension** I understand the composition of the manifold in an empirical intuition, through which perception, i.e., empirical consciousness of it (as appearance), becomes possible" (B160). In the Axioms, Kant thus signals that perception involves our imagination engaging in the sort of composition that generates an intuition$_i$ (a perceptual image) that involves a representation of a "determinate space or time," i.e. of an appearance having a determinate spatio-temporal form. When we read Kant's account of the imagination's activities in perception in the Deduction in this light, we should accordingly conceive of the coordination between the synthesis of apprehension and reproduction involved in the formation of perceptual images as a process of composition in which our imagination successively apprehends and retains[32] representations of parts contained in a homogeneous manifold and generates a perceptual image that represents an appearance as a spatio-temporal whole. To return to Kant's example of perceiving a house, when we "make the empirical intuition of a house into perception through apprehension of its manifold" and "as it were draw its shape," this involves us imaginatively composing the representations of the spatial parts of the house contained in the homogeneous manifold (e.g. its roof, windows, and door) into a perceptual image that represents the house as a spatial whole that contains those spatial parts. In the Axioms, Kant thus gives us another helpful lens, the lens of composition of form, as one through which we can understand the acts of imaginative synthesis in perception that generate a perceptual image of an appearance as having a determinate spatio-temporal form.

Turning from form to matter in the Anticipations of Perception, Kant there extends his account of composition in a way that sheds light on another aspect of perception: the determination of the "matter" of an appearance. The latter topic is not one that Kant highlights in the discussion of perception in §26 of the Deduction; however, in the Anticipations he emphasizes the fact that perception involves the "empirical consciousness," through "sensation," of something "real" that fills space or time, viz. some sensory quality like a vibrant orange, a gentle

---

[32] Although Kant does not make the role of reproduction explicit in the Axioms, if we are to represent a whole on the basis of successive synthesis of its parts, we need to retain those parts in representation. See, e.g., Kant's claim that, "if I draw a line in thought...I must necessarily first grasp one of these manifold representations after another in my thoughts. But if I were to lose the preceding representation (the first parts of the line...) from my thoughts and not reproduce them when I proceed to the following ones, then no whole representation...could even arise" (A102). This commitment to reproduction being required for drawing a line would seem to be implicated in his rehearsal of this example in the Axioms ("I cannot represent to myself any line...without drawing it in thought, i.e., successively generating all its parts from one point" (A162/B203)).

ELABORATION OF THE TRANSCENDENTAL DEDUCTION   231

warmth, or a soft tone (B207; see also A169/B211). So one way to think about Kant's point about perception in the Anticipations is that in perception, we do not just represent a determinate spatio-temporal form; we represent a determinate spatio-temporal form filled by sensory qualities. To return to the house example from the B Deduction, when I perceive the house, I do not just "draw" a spatial shape devoid of all sensory qualities; I represent a spatial form filled by, say, the red of the façade, the white of the door, etc. (B162). And what Kant tells us in the Anticipations is that the latter involves us imaginatively apprehending and composing a sensation, and, by extension, a sensible quality, as filling a moment of space or time with some degree.

Stepping back, with his account of composition in the Principles, Kant elaborates on his account of the sort of imaginative synthesis of apprehension and reproduction involved in perception in helpful ways.[33] We gain insight into how this imaginative synthesis composes a manifold of intuition into a representation of a determinate spatio-temporal form and matter. And this, in turn, sheds light on how we are to think about the content of a perceptual image: it is an intuitionᵢ that represents a determinate spatio-temporal form that is filled by sensory qualities.

Let's turn now to the kind of synthesis that Kant contrasts with composition in the Principles: "connection." My discussion of this kind of synthesis will be much briefer. Kant describes connection, in general, as the "synthesis of that which is manifold insofar as they **necessarily** belong **to one another**" (B201n). According to Kant, representations in the manifold "necessarily belong to one another" in the relevant sense when they are grounded in the "existence" of objects (A160/B199). For Kant, connection thus involves synthesizing certain representations as necessarily belonging to one another, *qua* representations corresponding to existing objects. As examples of connection, he cites the way in which we synthesize representations of an accident and substance together or a cause and effect as necessarily belonging together (B201n).

Kant further clarifies what connection involves in his discussion of the role that it plays in experience in his technical sense. To this end in the Analogies, he claims that, "**Experience is possible only through the representation of a necessary connection of perceptions**" (B218). In explicating what this necessary connection amounts to, he contrasts it with the way we synthesize representations in perception:

apprehension is only a juxtaposition of the manifold of empirical intuition, but no representation of the necessity of combined existence of the appearance that

---

[33] As I discuss in Chapter 8, in the third *Critique* Kant also stresses the notion of composition in his analysis of the sort of cognitive activity we imaginatively enact in the aesthetic appreciation of beauty.

it juxtaposes in space and time is to be encountered in it. But since experience is a cognition of objects through perception, consequently the relation in the existence of the manifold is to be represented in it not as it is juxtaposed in time but as it is objectively in time.   (B219)

In this passage, Kant indicates that unlike in perception where we imaginatively apprehend how things subjectively seem to us as "juxtaposed" in space and time, in experience we connect representations together in a necessary way that corresponds to how things "objectively" are. As I made this point in Chapter 5, in the latter case, our representations have "objective unity": the unity that is necessitated by existing objects and their relations to one another. For example, when I experience freezing water, on Kant's view, I do not just apprehend the representation of liquid water and solid water as they subjectively seem to me as juxtaposed in time; I connect the representation of the liquid water and solid water together as necessarily sequential in virtue of corresponding to the existing water that is in the causal process of freezing. It is thus this sort of representation of necessary connection and objectivity in experience that Kant takes the synthesis of connection to be responsible for.

Kant, in turn, attributes the synthesis of connection to the understanding. In the Second Analogy, for example, he argues that the representation of necessary connection involved in causality requires that, "the relation between the two states must be *thought* in such a way that it is thereby necessarily determined which of them must be placed before and which after rather than vice versa" (B234, my emphasis). Kant goes on to gloss the relevant thought as the "empirical judgment in which one thinks that the sequence is determined" (A201/B246).[34] In my interpretive framework, this signals Kant's commitment to connection being the mode of synthesis that is operative at the understanding stage of experience: the synthesis of recognition. As I argued in Chapter 5, the synthesis of recognition involves us making an empirical judgment in which we subsume an intuition under concepts in a way that involves recognizing an existing object as that which necessitates our representations and which our representations correspond to. And it is only when we make this sort of judgment that we arrive at experience in Kant's technical sense.[35] To return to the water example, to experience the water freezing, we need to make a subsumptive empirical judgment in which we recognize that there is a causal sequence in the water we intuit that necessitates a successive order in our representations. And what the discussion of connection in the Analogies reveals is that Kant conceives of this recognitional process as one that involves us objectively connecting the successive

---

[34] See also his gloss of what the category of causality makes possible: "the relation of cause to effect, is the condition of the objective validity of our empirical judgments with regard to the series of perceptions, thus of their empirical truth, and therefore of experience" (A202/B247).
[35] Indeed, I take this to be why Kant glosses experience in §26 of the B Deduction in terms of "cognition through connected perceptions" (B161).

representation of the liquid water and freezing water as necessarily belonging together in virtue of corresponding to the existing causal sequence in the states of the water.

So just as Kant's discussion of composition sheds light on the sort of imaginative activities operative in perception, hence on the imagination stage of experience, his analysis of connection sheds light on the sort of intellectual activities of recognition and judgment involved in the full-blown experience we arrive at through the understanding stage. However, what is ultimately relevant for my purposes in this chapter is how the notions of composition and connection bear on how the Schematism elucidates Kant's account of how the *a priori* exercise of imagination enables perception and experience from the Deduction. As I see it, the idea that perception and experience require the empirical activities of composition and connection, respectively, provides us with a better target to focus on in trying to make sense of how figurative synthesis and formal intuitions$_i$, hence transcendental schemata, enable perception and experience. For granting that the Schematism invites us to think about these issues through a temporal lens, what the account of composition tells us to focus on is how transcendental schemata guide the imaginative synthesis of a manifold of empirical intuition$_s$ into the perceptual image of an appearance as having a determinate temporal form and matter. What the account of connection tells us to think through is how transcendental schemata bear on the intellectual synthesis required for the representation of existing objects and their relations in time, which our representations correspond to and are necessitated by. And, as I suggested above, I understand Kant's basic claim to be that transcendental schemata provide a pattern-like rule that figures in the empirical activities of composition and connection through which we represent temporal determinacy.

However, in order to make good on this suggestion, I shall now turn to Kant's account of the transcendental schemata for the categories of quantity, quality, and relation (as I noted above, I here set aside the categories of modality).[36] I divide this discussion between an analysis of the transcendental schemata for the mathematical categories of quantity and quality and the dynamical categories of relation. And I argue that, for Kant, the schemata for the mathematical categories provide rules that guide the sort of composition in perception required for the imagination stage of experience, and the schemata for the dynamical categories of relation provide rules that pertain to the sort of connection required for the recognition involved in the understanding stage of experience.[37]

---

[36] For other discussions of the schemata of specific categories, see Guyer (1987, 172–5); Longuenesse (1998, pt. III); Stang (2023).

[37] I am thus sympathetic to Allison's (2004, 199) claim that the mathematical categories condition perception and the dynamical categories condition experience.

234 A PRIORI IMAGINATION AND THE CONDITIONS OF EXPERIENCE II

7.3 The Schemata of the Mathematical Categories as Conditions of Perception

In order to work through Kant's account of the transcendental schemata for the mathematical categories I open with his origin story, as it were, about the *a priori* synthesis through which our imagination makes these schemata and then address the role they play in enabling the representation of temporal determinacy in perception.

7.3.1 The Schemata of the Categories of Quantity

Although Kant distinguishes three categories of quantity, <unity>, <plurality>, and <totality>, in the Schematism, he groups them all under the heading of <magnitude> (*Größe, quantitas*).[38] As I understand the implications of this for the schematism of the categories of quantity, though Kant allows for there to be patterns of time-determination that reflect <unity>, <plurality>, and <totality>, respectively, they each need to be understood in light of the basic pattern of time-determination involved in <magnitude>.[39]

Like any other transcendental schema, according to Kant the generation of the transcendental schema for <magnitude> involves our imagination figuratively synthesizing the *a priori* form of time in accordance with the logical content of this category. Kant defines the logical content of <magnitude> as "the unity of the synthesis of the manifold of a homogeneous intuition in general" (A143/B182).[40] So, in the schematism of <magnitude>, our imagination generates a pure intuition$_i$ that exhibits the concept of the unity of the synthesis of a manifold that contains homogeneous units or parts in temporal terms.

Though Kant ultimately identifies "number" (*Zahl*) as the transcendental schema of <magnitude>, before doing so he makes an opaque remark to the effect that, "The pure image of all magnitudes (*quantorum*)...for all objects of the senses in general...is time" (A142/B182).[41] Kant does not explain what this means; however, one possible reading of this remark is in line with an idea I alluded

---

[38] Here, Kant aligns <magnitude> with the notion of "quantitas," a notion that he, in turn, defines as follows: "Quantum is one thing, in which there is a quantity [*Quantum: est unum, in quo est quantitas*]" (*Metaphysik Herder* 28:21; for discussion, see Longuenesse (1998, 264–71) and Sutherland (2004, 427–35; 2022, chap. 3). Kant thus aligns the category of magnitude with *quantitas*, hence with the quantity of a quantum.

[39] See Longuenesse (1998, 253–5) and Stang (2023, §2.6) for discussion of how to think about the relationship between the schema of <magnitude> and the three categories of quantity.

[40] See also his gloss of this logical content as, "the synthesis of the homogeneous in an intuition in general" (B162) and the "consciousness of the homogeneous manifold in intuition in general" (B203).

[41] Since I am here focused on time, I am skipping over his remark that, "The pure image of all magnitudes (*quantorum*) for outer sense is space," but I take what I say here about time to apply likewise to space (A142/B182).

THE SCHEMATA OF THE MATHEMATICAL CATEGORIES   235

to in Chapter 6, according to which he appears to allow for the possibility that our imagination, finite as it is, can generate formal intuitions$_i$ that represent the whole of time, infinite as it is. Drawing on Kant's claims to the effect that we represent time as a whole "through a line progressing to infinity," I suggested that even though no line represented by imagination can be infinite, a representation of a finite line, such as →, can capture the sense in which the parts of time successively unfold without limit (A33/B50; see also B156, B292). And I take his remark about the "pure image" of time in the Schematism to suggest that it is also possible to imaginatively represent time as a whole through a transcendental schema for <magnitude> that exhibits the concept of the unity of the synthesis of the manifold of time as a whole, which contains all of the homogeneous units of time. Such a schema would amount to something like a pure intuition$_i$ that represents the unity of time as such in accordance with the category of magnitude. And it seems that this sort of representation maps onto Kant's account of the formal intuition$_i$ that represents the "necessary synthetic **unity** of the manifold" of time, which he mentions in the freezing water example in §26 of the B Deduction (B162). This said, Kant does not develop this line of thought in the Schematism, so I shall leave it here as a promissory note and turn to his account of number.

In his discussion of number as the schema for <magnitude>, Kant glosses number not in terms of a representation of any specific number like three, but rather in general terms as "a representation that summarizes the successive addition of one (homogeneous) unit to another [*die sukzessive Addition von Einem zu Einem (gleichartigen) zusammenbefaßt*]" (A142/B182).[42] Number in this sense is a representation of a unity that contains homogeneous units that have been successively added together. For example, when I count four beats in a measure of music, I represent a unity (four beats) that contains homogeneous units (beats) that I have successively added together. On Kant's view, number counts as a temporal pattern that reflects the category of magnitude because it reflects how we successively synthesize a homogeneous manifold in order to represent a temporal unity. And, for Kant, the categories of unity, plurality, and totality are implicated in this enumeration process: each unit we pick out is a unity, each sub-set of units we add along the way is a plurality, and the unity we represent as containing all the successively added units is a totality. For Kant, then, understanding the transcendental schema for the categories of quantity in terms of number captures the various aspects involved in successively synthesizing a manifold in the representation of magnitude, *qua* the unity of the synthesis of the manifold of a homogeneous intuition in general.

Turning now to the question of the role the transcendental schema for <magnitude> plays vis-à-vis the possibility of experience, I read Kant as conceiving

---

[42] For discussion of this sense of number, see Young (1982); Longuenesse (1998, 255–63); Sutherland (2017).

236 A PRIORI IMAGINATION AND THE CONDITIONS OF EXPERIENCE II

of this schema as a stencil-like rule that guides our imagination in the composition of perceptual images that represent appearances as having a temporally determinate form. In Kant's words, in perception the schema of magnitude makes possible "the generation (synthesis) of time itself, in the successive apprehension of an object" (A145/B184). By the "generation (synthesis)" of time, I take Kant to have in mind the composition of a manifold of temporal representations that have successively unfolded into a perceptual image of a single temporal whole that contains temporal moments. For example, when I listen to Mariah Carey's "Fantasy," my imagination composes the manifold of representations of the different parts of the song that unfold successively over time into a perceptual image that represents the song as a determinate temporal whole that contains various temporal moments. And on Kant's view, number, *qua* the schema of <magnitude>, is what makes possible this sort of composition in perception: it provides our imagination with a basic temporal pattern or stencil to follow as it composes the temporal parts contained in a manifold of empirical intuition$_s$ that it successively apprehends and reproduces into a perceptual image that represents an appearance as a determinate temporal whole that contains temporal moments.[43]

Now, Kant's appeal to number here might give us some pause. Is he really committed to the idea that each time I perceive an object, my imaginative synthesis in perception is guided by a number? Wouldn't that over-mathematize perception in some sense?[44] Here, we must be cautious: when Kant claims that number serves as a rule that enables perception, he is not committing himself to the idea that a specific number must guide our imaginative activity in perception. Though this can happen,[45] once again, the notion of number he is focused on is the transcendental schema for <magnitude>, defined very generally as a basic temporal pattern that represents the "successive addition of one (homogeneous) unit to another" in an intuition$_i$ that represents a whole that contains those homogeneous units. So, when Kant indicates that number guides perception, I take him to mean that number, *qua* this kind of general temporal representation, guides perception as we imaginatively compose representations that have successively unfolded together into an intuition$_i$ that represents them as moments of a temporal whole. In my perception of "Fantasy," for example, though I might count the beats throughout the entire song, even without counting, when my imagination synthesizes the representations of the temporal moments of the song that unfold over

---

[43] Insofar as I take the representation of a temporal whole in perception to be made possible by the schema of <quantity>, I disagree with Longuenesse's reading, according to which we are "immediately 'given'" a 'whole' in intuition and perception involves "subjecting the immediate sensible given…to the act of attention by which it can also eventually be measured" (1998, 271). On my reading, by contrast, what we are immediately given is a manifold, which we only represent as a whole as the result of imaginative acts of synthesis. I thus understand imaginative synthesis guided by the schema of <quantity> to be operating at a more basic level in our sensory representation than Longuenesse does.

[44] See Guyer (2006, 472).

[45] See, e.g., Kant's discussion of the "logical estimation" of magnitude in KU §26.

time into a perceptual image of a temporal whole, this activity is guided by number, understood as the transcendental schema of <magnitude>. For Kant, then, number, *qua* the transcendental schema of <magnitude>, conditions perception insofar as number provides us with the most basic temporal pattern that our imagination follows in perception when composing a manifold that successively unfolds over time into a perceptual image that represents a temporal form, viz. a temporal whole that contains temporal moments. And it is ultimately this temporal form that Kant claims the schema of <magnitude> "makes representable" in perception (A145/B184).

7.3.2 The Schemata of the Categories of Quality

Turning now to the transcendental schema for <quality>, although elsewhere Kant discusses three categories under this heading, <reality>, <negation>, and <limitation>, in the Schematism he only explicitly discusses the first two. But as was the case with <quantity>, it seems that there are patterns of temporal determination that he thinks can be associated with all three categories, but which need to be understood ultimately in light of <reality> and <negation>. Let's again look at Kant's account of how the relevant schemata are generated before considering how they enable perception.

Kant glosses the logical content of <reality> as the representation of "a being [*ein Sein*]" and <negation> as the representation of "a non-being [*ein Nichtsein*]" (A143/B182). So, in the schematism of <reality>, the imagination's synthesis of time is constrained by the notion of "a being" and in the schematism of <negation> by the notion of a "non-being." In the Schematism chapter, Kant claims that the transcendental schema our imagination develops to exhibit <reality> in temporal terms is the representation of "the quantity of something insofar as it fills time" (A143/B182). Kant's thought is that "the quantity of something insofar as it fills time" amounts to a temporal way to make the notion of "a being" sensible. And although in the Schematism he does not mention what the schema for <negation> might be, in the "Phenomena-Noumena" chapter he suggests that it is a representation of "time... that is... empty," i.e. a moment of time that is not filled by anything (A242/B300). This echoes his reference to a representation of "empty time" in the Schematism (A143/B182). Here, again, I take the idea to be that the notion of a "non-being" can be temporally exhibited through the representation of a time that is empty. For Kant, then, the transcendental schema of <quality> temporally exhibits the logical content of the category of reality through "the quantity of something insofar as it fills time" and negation through an "empty time." We might, by extension, attribute to Kant the view that the transcendental schema of <limitation> is a temporal representation of a "reality combined with negation"; hence as something that fills time with a degree that is somewhere

238 A PRIORI IMAGINATION AND THE CONDITIONS OF EXPERIENCE II

between full plenitude and emptiness (B111). So understood, the schema for <reality> and <negation> would provide us with a kind of scale that diminishes to "0" in light of which we determine the degree to which a time is filled or empty (A143/B182).[46]

Bringing this schema to bear on perception, the relevant kind of composition bears not on the representation of the spatio-temporal form of what we perceive, but its matter. And Kant claims that in this composition, we imaginatively apprehend a sensation, and, by extension, the sensible quality that gives rise to this sensation, as filling time with a degree. In the Schematism, Kant refers to this as "the synthesis of sensation (perception) with the representation of time, or the filling of time" (A145/B184). And he argues that this imaginative composition of sensation in perception depends on the transcendental schema for the categories of quality. In the Schematism, Kant focuses, in particular, on how this works with the schema for <reality>. He argues that this schema involves a basic temporal pattern, the representation of a being in time, that serves as a rule that our imagination follows in perception as it empirically composes sensations in a material way. The result of this composition will thus be a perceptual image that represents an appearance as having a temporally determinate matter. For example, when I hear the first soft note of "Fantasy," the transcendental schema for <reality> provides me with a basic temporal pattern of a being that fills time that guides my imagination as I synthesize the sensation of this tone with the time it fills, and thereby generate a perceptual image that represents the matter of this perception (here, the tone) as a reality that fills time with some degree. And this sort of representation of matter in perception is what Kant claims the schema of <reality> "makes representable" (A145/B184).

However, as I also suggested, one way to understand the transcendental schemata for <reality> and <negation> is as providing a kind of scale we can use to determine the degree to which time is filled or empty on a given occasion. So, when we determine the degree to which a sensation, and, by extension, the sensible quality that gives rise to this sensation, fills time in perception, it seems that we are also guided by this scale in the background, as a kind of framework in which we can determine the degree of reality possessed by the quality of which we have a sensation.

Stepping back, for Kant the schemata for the categories of quantity and quality provide the imagination in perception with the stencil-like rules that guide its composition of the temporal representations contained in a manifold of empirical intuition$_s$ into a perceptual image that represents what we perceive as having a temporally determinate form and matter. The transcendental schemata for <quantity> and <quality> do this insofar as they provide us with basic temporal

---

[46] In the Anticipations, Kant refers to this scale as a kind of "continuous nexus" (A168/B210).

patterns of determinacy that guide our imagination in this empirical composition of a manifold into a representation of what we perceive as a determinate temporal whole that contains parts and that qualitatively fills time with a degree.

The final point that I wish to make about the transcendental schemata for the mathematical categories concerns the implication that this account has for how we are to understand Kant's conceptualism. In Chapter 5, I argued that, on Kant's view, the generation of empirical intuitions$_i$ (perceptual images) in perception depend on empirical concepts by way of schemata, and that their content is such as to exhibit empirical concepts. In Chapter 6, I extended this conceptualist reading of perception to include Kant's commitment to the generation of perceptual images depending on the categories by way of the figurative synthesis of imagination and formal intuitions$_i$ that condition perception. Kant's theory of transcendental schematism adds a further layer to this conceptualist story, as we learn that the most basic perceptual act of generating empirical intuitions$_i$ that represent an appearance as having a determinate temporal form and matter is guided by the transcendental schemata of the mathematical categories of quantity and quality.[47] This, indeed, is something that Kant explicitly argues for in the Axioms and Anticipations, where he asserts that the composition of form and matter in a perceptual image depends on the categories of quantity and quality, respectively.[48] And though one might perhaps worry that conceiving of perception in these categorially dependent terms might "over-intellectualize" perception in some way and somehow implicate judgment in it,[49] what the Schematism reveals is that Kant thinks the mathematical categories play this role not through judgment, but through the imaginative mediation of transcendental schemata for <quantity> and <quality>. For, according to Kant, it is the transcendental schemata of the mathematical categories which provide the stencil-like rules or basic temporal

---

[47] I am thus broadly sympathetic to Land's (2014) argument that Kant's account of the mathematical categories and their relation to imagination have import for how we understand empirical aspects of Kant's view. However, whereas Land argues that they are conditions of us having intuitions of outer sense, I have argued that they condition how we take up intuitions of sense and generate intuitions$_i$ in perception.

[48] See, e.g., the claim in the Axioms that, "appearances...cannot be apprehended..., i.e., taken up into empirical consciousness, except through the synthesis of the manifold through which the representation of a determinate space or time are generated, i.e., through the composition of that which is homogeneous and the consciousness of the synthetic unity of this manifold (of the homogeneous)...Now the consciousness of the homogeneous manifold in intuition in general...first becomes possible [through] the concept of a magnitude (*Quanti*). Thus even the perception of an object, as appearance, is possible only through...the concept of a **magnitude**" (B202–3), and the more elliptical claim in the Anticipations that, "the real, which corresponds to sensations in general...only represents something whose concept in itself contains a being...In inner sense, namely, the empirical consciousness can be raised from 0 up to any greater degree...All sensations are thus, as such, given only *a posteriori*, but their property of having a degree can be cognized *a priori*" (A175–6/B217–8).

[49] As I noted in Chapter 5, Merleau-Ponty criticizes Kant for an overly intellectualist theory of perception in the *Phenomenology of Perception* (see, e.g., intro, chap. 3; pt. II, chap. 3). However, Merleau-Ponty regards Kant's theory of imagination and schematism as cutting against this intellectualism (see Matherne 2016).

240 A PRIORI IMAGINATION AND THE CONDITIONS OF EXPERIENCE II

patterns that guide our imagination in composing an empirical intuition$_i$ in perception. So, although this discussion gives us reason to conceive of the empirical intuitions$_i$ involved in perception as dependent on the mathematical categories on Kant's view, it also gives us reason to recognize that this categorial guidance is routed through the imagination's schematizing these categories. And when we recognize that the categorial dependence of perception proceeds by way of schemata, this can stem the worry about over-intellectualizing perception to some extent, as it encourages us to recognize that the categories, at least on my reading, do not guide perception through some act of judgment, but rather through the art of schematism.

7.4 The Schemata of the Dynamical Categories of Relation as Conditions of Experience

Let's now turn to Kant's account of the transcendental schemata for the categories of relation, <substance>, <causality>, and <community>. As above, I initially look at Kant's account of the generation of these schemata and then at their enabling role, here, vis-à-vis the understanding stage of experience.

Beginning with the schema for <substance>, as we have seen, Kant describes the logical content of this category in terms of the concept of "something that can be thought as a subject (without being a predicate of something else)" (A147/B186).[50] In the schematism process, this logical content constrains our imagination in how it synthesizes the *a priori* form of time into a schema that exhibits this content in temporal form. According to Kant, the temporal representation of "the persistence of the real in time... which endures while everything else changes" is the transcendental schema that our imagination comes up with that exhibits this content in temporal form (A144/B183). For Kant, then, the temporal pattern of the persistence of the real is the time-determination that our imagination generates that renders the concept of an object that can be thought as a subject without being the predicate of something else in temporal terms.

Regarding the schema for <causality>, Kant articulates the logical content of this category in terms of the representation "in which given something A something entirely different B is posited according to a rule" (A90/B122).[51] Under the constraint of this logical content, our imagination represents the something

---

[50] See also, "the logical representation of the subject, which I try to realize by representing to myself something that can occur solely as subject (without being predicate of anything)" (A242/B300); "something can exist only as **subject**, not a mere determination of other things" (B288); "the notion of a something whose existence must be thought only as that of a subject, and not as a mere predicate of something else" (OD 8:225).

[51] See also, "the concept of a relation of something to something else in existence, whereby if I posit the first, the other is also determined and necessarily posited" (OD 8:225), and "something that allows an inference to the existence of something else" (A243/B301).

THE SCHEMATA OF THE DYNAMICAL CATEGORIES   241

A and B as real things that exist in time. And, according to Kant, in order to capture the necessary relation between the two, our imagination generates a schema that involves the representation of "the real upon which, whenever it is posited, something else always follows. It therefore consists in the succession of the manifold insofar as it is subject to a rule" (A144/B183). In this schema, Kant thus takes the necessary relation between A and B thought in the category of causality to be exhibited through the temporal pattern of necessary succession: succession that is subject to a rule.

Finally, concerning the schema for <community>, Kant glosses the logical content of this category in terms of, "if several things exist, from the existence of one of them something about the others follows and vice versa" (B288). Constrained by this logical content, Kant claims that our imagination develops a schema for <community> that represents things that exist in time as standing in a relation of "the simultaneity of the determination of one with those of the other, in accordance with a general rule" (A144/B183–4). Here, then, our imagination temporally exhibits the logical content of the category of community in a schema that represents a temporal pattern of simultaneity among the determinations of things subject to a rule that exist in community.

Turning now to the question of what role these transcendental schemata play vis-à-vis the *a priori* conditions of experience, in the Schematism, Kant claims that what these schemata "make representable" in experience is "the relation of the perceptions among themselves to all time (i.e., in accordance with a rule of time-determination)" (A145/B184). In the Analogies, Kant specifies this sort of representation of the relation among perceptions in accordance with rules of time determination as "experience":

> Experience is empirical cognition, i.e., a cognition that determines an object through perceptions. It is therefore a synthesis of perceptions, which is not itself contained in perception...[S]ince experience is a cognition of objects through perception, consequently the relation in the existence of the manifold is to be represented...as it is objectively in time...[E]xperience is possible only through a representation of the necessary connection of the perceptions...The three *modi* of time are **persistence, succession,** and **simultaneity**. Hence three rules of all temporal relations of appearances, in accordance with the existence of each can be determined with regard to the unity of all time.   (B218–19)[52]

In this passage, Kant claims that experience involves representing "objective" and "necessary" temporal relations among perceptions, i.e. the objective unity and necessary connection that perceptions have insofar as they correspond to the

---

[52] The last two sentences are also in the A-edition (A177).

242 A PRIORI IMAGINATION AND THE CONDITIONS OF EXPERIENCE II

persistence, succession, or simultaneity among existing objects. Notice also that in this passage, Kant uses the language of "connection" to describe this representation. As I argued above, I read the sort of connection at issue here to be the objective and necessary connection of our representations via the synthesis of recognitional judgment in the understanding stage of experience. So, in the Schematism, when Kant tells us that the schemata for the categories of relation "make representable" "the relation of the perceptions among themselves to all time (i.e., in accordance with a rule of time-determination)," I take him to mean that these schemata contribute to our connection of perceptions in relations of persistence, succession, and simultaneity in recognitional judgments. For example, when we experience a snapdragon, the schema for <substance> guides us in intellectually connecting our perceptions of it together, as we judge it to be a (relatively) persisting object.[53] Or to return to the example of freezing water one last time, for Kant, when we experience the freezing water, the schema for <causality> guides us in intellectually connecting the perceptions of the liquid water and solid water together into a representation of an objective order of succession that we judge to obtain. Likewise, when we judge that, say, the moon and earth exist simultaneously, our schema for <community> guides us in intellectually synthesizing our perceptions of them together in this simultaneous order (B257). In these ways, Kant treats the transcendental schemata for the categories of relation as having a crucial role to play vis-à-vis our recognitional judgments concerning existing objects as temporally determinate, i.e. as persisting, successive, and simultaneous, in the understanding stage of experience.

Stepping back, I have argued that, on Kant's view, just as the schemata for the mathematical categories help make the imagination stage of experience possible by providing rules that guide the imaginative synthesis and composition of perceptual images in perception, the dynamical categories of relation help make the understanding stage of experience possible by providing rules that guide the intellectual synthesis involved in connecting perceptions together in recognitional judgments in which we represent existing objects in their temporal determinacy.

---

[53] In the first Analogy, Kant argues that, strictly speaking, only something that persists absolutely is a substance that exists "at all time" (A185/B228); in which case, it would seem that the schema for <substance> is only apt in our representation of what persists absolutely. However, it seems that the schema of <substance>, *qua* the representation of the persistence of the real in time, could also guide us in representing a "relative" substance, i.e. a relatively persistent accident of matter, like a house, dog, or flower. And this latter idea is perhaps what Kant has in mind when he describes the upshot of the first Analogy in terms of the idea that the empirical time determination at issue is the determination of a "magnitude of existence, i.e., duration" (A215/B262).

7.5 Conclusion

In this chapter, I continued to pursue Kant's account of the *a priori* dimensions of the theoretical use of our imagination in experience in light of the Schematism chapter of the first *Critique*. I considered the question of whether the Schematism gives us reason to attribute to Kant a radical model of the *a priori* exercise of imagination, according to which it serves as the source of the categories, *qua* concepts of objects. But just as I argued against attributing to Kant a radical model of imagination as the source of our most basic pure intuitions of space and time in the previous chapter, in this chapter, I argued against attributing to him a view of imagination as the source of the categories, as our most basic pure concepts of objects. As in the previous chapter, I, instead, advocated for ascribing to Kant a mediating model of the *a priori* exercise of imagination, according to which our imagination mediates between the pure intuitions given through sensibility and the categories given through the understanding. However, in this chapter I made the case that what the Schematism reveals is the need to ultimately situate Kant's account of this mediating activity in his account of imagination as the faculty of exhibition.

In this spirit, I endeavored to show that with his account of the schematic exhibition of the categories, Kant fills out his picture of what the *a priori* exercise of imagination involves, what its cognitive function is, and how it conditions experience. To this end, I claimed that conceiving of the figurative synthesis and formal intuitions$_i$ from the B Deduction as transcendental schematism and transcendental schemata, respectively, elucidates Kant's commitment to the *a priori* exercise of imagination as a mode of exhibition, in which our imagination, through its art, makes the categories sensible to us and facilitates our concrete grasp of them that extends beyond the purely logical grasp of them we have through the understanding alone.

I, moreover, argued that Kant clarifies how the *a priori* exercise of imagination conditions perception and experience with his analysis of how transcendental schemata provide the basic patterns of temporal determinacy that serve as stencil-like rules that guide us in representing temporal determinacy in the imagination and understanding stages of experience. And over the course of this discussion, I highlighted the ways in which the Schematism chapter supports my conceptualist reading of Kant, according to which the generation of intuitions$_i$ in the context of experience, whether they be the pure intuitions$_i$ involved in transcendental schemata or the empirical intuitions$_i$ involved in perception depend on the categories.

Though the Schematism is thus crucial for making sense of the *a priori* exercise of imagination on Kant's view, as I gestured toward above, it still does not exhaust his story about how this exercise enables perception and experience. A full story would require thinking through the role the *a priori* activities of imagination play in enabling the representation of spatial determinacy in experience, not just temporal determinacy.[54] And though I hope the interpretation of the *a priori* exercise of imagination that I have offered in the last two chapters provides the resources for telling this full story, it is not something I shall pursue here. Instead, this discussion of schematism serves as the capstone to my analysis of the *a priori* exercise of imagination and, indeed, to my analysis of Kant's account of the theoretical use of imagination in the context of experience.

Before moving forward, however, I want to underscore a certain through line that I have pursued in this discussion: in order to make sense of the cognitive contribution Kant attributes to imagination vis-à-vis experience at both the empirical and *a priori* levels, we need to attend to his conception of imagination as the faculty of exhibition. For whether we think about its empirical syntheses, perceptual images, and empirical schemata, or its *a priori* synthesis, formal intuitions$_i$, and transcendental schemata, I have made the case that he ultimately casts what our imagination does in terms of it making concepts sensible in intuition$_i$ through the activity of exhibition. Indeed, I have argued that we need to attend to this theme of exhibition in order to appreciate why Kant thinks our imagination functions cognitively well in the theoretical context and plays its cognitive role of bridging the gaps between sense and intellect in the way cognition requires in both the empirical and *a priori* register.

To be sure, we also have reason to interpret the sort of activities Kant attributes to imagination in perception and experience in light of his general definition of it as faculty of formation and faculty for representing objects in intuition even without their presence (see Chapter 4). For example, on both the empirical and *a priori* levels, I have emphasized Kant's claim that our imagination engages in the formative activity of synthesizing a manifold of intuition delivered from elsewhere in such a way that results in an intuition$_i$ that represent spatio-temporal determinacy. And with respect to Kant's even-without-presence definition of imagination (which he cites at B151–2), at the empirical level, I have highlighted his commitment to perception involving our imagination operating with a degree of independence from what we are immediately given and enabling us to see more. So too at the *a priori* level, I have emphasized Kant's commitment to our imagination being able to productively generate pure intuitions$_i$ with a degree of independence from what is immediately present to us, by way of an *a priori* synthesis of the pure intuition of space and time we are given through sensibility.

However, though I take Kant's formation and even-without-presence definitions of imagination in general to bear on his account of its empirical and *a priori* role in experience, I hope to have motivated the idea that these formative and presence-independent activities need to be situated in the context of the

---

[54] For discussion of the spatial schematism of the categories, see Franzwa (1978); Guyer (1987, 167–8; 2005, 98–9); Hughes (2007, chap. 6).

exhibition definition of imagination, for it is in an effort to exhibit concepts in intuition, that our imagination engages in these activities in the context of experience. It is thus imagination, as the faculty of exhibition, that I take to serve as the key to Kant's account of the cognitive function of imagination vis-à-vis perception and experience.

In order to bring to a close this discussion of the theoretical use of imagination on Kant's view, I want to return to two of the bigger questions about imagination that are live in contemporary debates that I sketched in the Introduction.[55] One question I raised is what makes it the case that our imagination does not just "fly completely free of reality," but can "also teach us something about it" (Kind and Kung (2016, 1) (see §0.3.1). Recall that in order to explain the latter epistemic use, theorists have recently appealed to the idea that the relevant imaginative activities need to be suitably constrained, whether through voluntary or through architectural constraints. And I suggested that, in the first *Critique*, Kant provides a robust account of the architectural constraints of both the sensible and conceptual variety. I am now in a position to make good on this suggestion.

In the sensible vein, I have argued that, as part of sensibility, Kant takes our imaginative activity to be constrained formally by space and time and materially by the manifolds that are delivered to us through the receptivity of sensibility (see Chapter 3). However, insofar as these sensible constraints are constitutive of imaginative activity as such, they are not sufficient to explain its epistemic use. To explain the latter in Kant's theory of experience, we need to look to the conceptual constraints I have emphasized throughout Part II. As we have seen, whether we consider the empirical or *a priori* contribution our imagination makes vis-à-vis experience, on Kant's analysis, our imagination functions cognitively well in this context because it acts under the constraint of concepts. This, indeed, is one of the lessons that I take to emerge when we attend to the central role that exhibition plays: for, on Kant's view, it is precisely by engaging in the activity of exhibition under the constraint of concepts, whether empirical or pure, that our imagination has a cognitively robust role to play both internal to experience and in enabling experience. At the same time, however, we have seen that Kant thinks that in its exhibiting activity our imagination also displays a kind of art or know-how with concepts, which outstrips our abstract grasp of them, and, thereby, facilitates our concrete comprehension of those concepts in a way that the understanding alone cannot accomplish, but that we epistemically need. Though an account of conceptual constraint is thus central to Kant's analysis of how we epistemically use our imagination, also central is his account of how our imaginative art with concepts serves us in this needed way.

---

[55] See, e.g., Kind and Kung (2016) and Badura and Kind (2021).

The other bigger picture question about imagination from the Introduction that I want to return to is the unity question and whether it makes sense to think there is anything like "the imagination" that is responsible for the diverse array of phenomena that get called "imaginative" (§0.1). In response to the unity question in Part I, I argued that Kant offers a theory of the imagination as a single cognitive capacity, which is responsible for a distinctive kind of intuition, sensible activity, and cognitive function, and which we can exercise in a wide variety of ways. Although in Part II, I hope to have shed light on the array of ways in which Kant thinks we exercise this capacity in the theoretical context of experience, I here want to emphasize the fact that the lens of exhibition sheds considerable light on the unity of what our imagination does across the empirical and *a priori* levels in this context. To see this, let's step back and survey the wide range of imaginative phenomena I have discussed in Part II: the empirical synthesis of apprehension and reproduction that leads to the formation of images in perception and non-veridical perceptual episodes like hallucination; empirical schematism; figurative synthesis and formal intuitions$_i$ of space and time; mathematical construction; and transcendental schematism and transcendental schemata. In spite of this wide range of imaginative phenomena, I have argued that Kant situates them in the framework of exhibition, as activities and representations that are oriented toward our imagination's cognitive function of making concepts sensible in intuition$_i$. And in this way, attending to the theme of exhibition provides us with important insight into the unity of the theoretical use of imagination on Kant's view that underwrites this diversity.

As I now turn my attention toward Kant's account of how we use our imagination to see more in aesthetic contexts, this will bring new imaginative phenomena to the fore: the appreciation of beauty and sublimity and the production of art. However, I shall continue to pursue this argumentative line: to understand the unity of imagination on Kant's view, while we need to bear in mind his theory of imagination in general, we need to be especially attentive to his definition of it as the faculty of exhibition and the cognitive function it has of making concepts sensible. This said, although in the aesthetic domain Kant continues to describe what our imagination does in terms of the cognitive activity of exhibition, he also accords it more freedom than in perception and experience. However, in Part III, I shall argue that, on Kant's view, this imaginative freedom is not a freedom that operates beyond concepts; it is a freedom that operates in relation to concepts, as we function well imaginatively by finding creative ways to expand our conceptual horizons.

Seeing More: Kant's Theory of Imagination. Samantha Matherne, Oxford University Press.
© Samantha Matherne 2024. DOI: 10.1093/9780191999291.003.0008

PART III
IMAGINATION IN AESTHETICS

8

Imagination and the Appreciation of Beauty

imagination...at play in...observation
—KU 5:230

8.1 Introduction

As necessary an ingredient as imagination is in Kant's theory of experience in the first *Critique*, it is no less necessary for his theory of aesthetic engagement in the third *Critique*. Whether in the appreciation of beauty and sublimity or the production of art, Kant insists that our imagination animates our aesthetic lives. However, as necessary as an account of constraint was for his explication of the theoretical use of imagination in the first *Critique*, in the third *Critique* he argues that freedom is what is necessary for its aesthetic use: "in the use of the imagination for cognition, the imagination is under the constraint of the understanding and is subject to the limitation of being adequate to its concept; in an aesthetic respect, however, the imagination is free" (KU 5:316). For Kant, as for many contemporary theorists, then, our aesthetic lives are marked by a particularly free and, I shall argue, creative use of our imagination.[1]

However, for Kant, this free and creative exercise of imagination does not proceed in a void. As we have seen, Kant conceives of imagination in general as a cognitive capacity, and this has important implications for his analysis of its aesthetic use. Indeed, rather than conceiving of our imaginative freedom and creativity as something that swings free from the cognitive domain altogether, Kant conceives of it as a freedom and creativity realized within a cognitive framework. And I aim to show that recognizing this is critical not only for understanding Kant's account of the aesthetic use of imagination, but also for appreciating a certain leeway built into his view, which allows for us to imaginatively see more and function cognitively well not only in constrained ways in the theoretical domain, but also in creative ways in the aesthetic domain.

---

[1] See, e.g., Gaut (2003) and Stokes (2014; 2016) who draw on Kant's ideas in developing their theories of imaginative creativity.

In order to explore Kant's account of the cognitive creativity that marks the aesthetic use of our imagination, I begin with a discussion of the appreciation of beauty in this chapter, before turning to an account of artistic creation and so-called "genius" in Chapter 9 and the appreciation of sublimity in Chapter 10. Though the details of exactly what our imagination does in these three aesthetic contexts varies, I shall argue that, as was the case in his account of the theoretical use of our imagination, attending to Kant's conception of our imagination as a faculty of exhibition is pivotal for making sense of his account of its aesthetic use. Indeed, as I noted in Chapter 4, it is in the third *Critique* that he starts to explicitly refer to imagination as the "faculty of exhibition," and I hope to show that following the thread of exhibition is crucial for understanding Kant's account of the cognitive creativity we imaginatively display in the aesthetic domain.

However, following this thread also leads to some surprising results. One of Kant's central tenets in the third *Critique* is that beauty and sublimity "please...without a concept" (KU 5:219; see also KU 5:244). This can make it tempting to attribute to him a view of the aesthetic freedom and creativity of our imagination as something that proceeds without concepts. But what I shall argue is that, on Kant's view, this freedom and creativity, in fact, manifests in relation to concepts, as we find original and open-ended ways to expand our conceptual horizons through our encounters with the beautiful and sublime. And in attributing this position to Kant, I endeavor to not only shed light on what is distinctive about the cognitive way in which we aesthetically exercise our imagination on his view, but also to continue to develop my argument from Part II to the effect that he endorses a conceptualist view of intuitions of imagination (intuitions$_i$) being dependent on concepts, here extending this argument from the experiential to the aesthetic context.[2]

In this chapter, my focus is on the contribution that Kant thinks our imagination makes to the appreciation of beauty. To orient this discussion, I begin in §8.2 with an overview of Kant's account of judgments of the beautiful and the free play that they involve, which will take some time, as his account of free play is notoriously vexed.[3] While no interpretation of free play is without its difficulties, I argue that it should be understood as a dynamic state of mind in which we engage with the beautiful in imaginative and intellectual ways that are cognitive, creative, and conceptually rich. In defending this interpretation, I argue against so-called "precognitive" interpretations of free play, according to which it proceeds without

---

[2] As Heidemann (2016, 116) notes, debates over Kant's (non-)conceptualism tend to focus on his views in the first *Critique* and overlook the relevance of the third *Critique*. However, while Heidemann (2016) argues that Kant's theory of judgments of the beautiful points in a non-conceptualist direction, in this chapter, I argue that Kant's account of what our imagination contributes therein points in a conceptualist direction.

[3] For overviews of the debate about free play, see Guyer (2005; 2009); Küplen (2015, chap. 3); Ostaric (2017); Geiger (2022, chap. 5); Williams (2022).

concepts, in favor of a "multicognitive" interpretation, according to which free play involves a conceptually rich interplay between imagination and understanding.[4]

I then devote the rest of the chapter to an analysis of what our imagination does in this free play. In §8.3, I focus on the cognitive dimensions of how we imaginatively engage with beauty; and in §8.4, on the creativity and freedom that this involves. Though this analysis will be multifaceted, I lay particular emphasis on the idea that, for Kant, free play involves a creative deployment of imagination as the faculty of exhibition and new, surprising, and cognitively valuable ways in which we make concepts sensible to ourselves via the beautiful.

As I work through Kant's vision of what role our imagination has in free play, my analysis will veer in admittedly technical directions. However, in this analysis I am motivated by the desire to explore how his vision of imaginative activities that are cognitive, creative, and conceptually rich can shed light on the sort of appreciative activities we actually undertake in our engagement with beauty. In order to not lose sight of this, I orient the following discussion around two examples of appreciation: appreciating the natural beauty of a pink peony and appreciating the artistic beauty of William Blake's poem, "Ah! Sun-Flower," which opens with this stanza:

> Ah Sun-flower! weary of time,
> Who countest the steps of the Sun
> Seeking after that sweet golden clime
> Where the traveller's journey is done.

(2005, 122)

[4] The "precognitive" and "multicognitive" labels are from Guyer (2005; see also Kern 2000, 50–3 who refers to these as the "material" and "hermeneutical" interpretations, respectively). Proponents of the precognitive interpretation include Henrich (1992, 44–54); Guyer (1997, 80); Zuckert (2007, 304–5); Hughes (2007, 263–5, 281–4, 296); Gorodeisky (2011); Ginsborg (2015, chaps. 3, 7); Heidemann (2016); Horstmann (2018, §II); Makkai (2021, chap. 2); Geiger (2022, chap. 5). Proponents of the multicognitive interpretation include Seel (1988, 344–9); Rush (2001; 2008); Allison (2001, 171); Breitenbach (2021; 2020 to the extent that she claims free play involves imaginative reflection on "ideas": see 2020, 74); and Sweet (2023, 77–9). Evidence for this interpretation is sometimes adduced from Kant's theory of fine art, specifically his theory of aesthetic ideas (KU §49) (see Allison 2004, 256; Rueger and Evren 2005; Chignell 2007b; Rueger 2008; Rogerson 2008; Ostaric 2017). However, I focus here on the case that can be made for this interpretation internal to Kant's account of aesthetic appreciation in the Analytic of the Beautiful and reserve a discussion of aesthetic ideas for Chapter 9. Guyer himself defends a so-called "metacognitive" interpretation, according to which free play involves a state of mind in which we both recognize an object as falling under a determinate concept, as we do in ordinary cognition, and feel that we are encountering "even more unity and coherence" that *"goes beyond* anything required for or dictated by satisfaction of the determinate concept or concepts on which mere identification of the object depends" (2005, 99). Though I am sympathetic to the idea that we find something in the beautiful that "goes beyond" what is required for ordinary cognition, rather than analyzing this in terms of a surplus of unity, I shall analyze it, in part, in terms of an open-ended conceptualization that Guyer denies is involved in free play ("nor must the experience of beauty consist in a play among alternative…conceptualizations of the object" (Guyer 2005, 99)).

252   IMAGINATION AND THE APPRECIATION OF BEAUTY

By recurring to these examples throughout, I aim to show that for all its complexity, Kant's theory of what we imaginatively do in free play is a valuable tool for understanding how we appreciatively see more to natural and artistic beauty.

8.2 Judgments of the Beautiful and Free Play

In the third *Critique*, Kant situates his account of what is involved in appreciating beauty in an account of what is involved in judging something to be beautiful. So in order to set the stage for my discussion of what imagination contributes to appreciating beauty, I want to take a closer look at what he takes to be distinctive about judgments of the beautiful.

According to Kant, judgments of the beautiful are "reflecting," rather than "determining" judgments (see KU 5:179; EE 20:211). In a determining judgment, Kant claims, we "subsume" a particular under a "given" universal, for example, when I judge that a flower I see is an instance of the concept <peony>.[5] But in a reflecting judgment, he says, "the particular is given, for which the universal is to be found" (KU 5:179). As a reflecting, rather than determining judgment, Kant thus regards judgments of the beautiful as ones in which we, in some sense, "linger" over the particular without subsuming it under a concept in a determining way (KU 5:222).

In the Analytic of the Beautiful, Kant further clarifies what is distinctive about judgments of the beautiful by insisting that they are "aesthetic," rather than "cognitive" judgments:

> In order to decide whether or not something is beautiful, we do not relate the representation by means of the understanding to the object for cognition, but rather relate it...to the subject and its feeling of pleasure and displeasure. The judgment of taste is therefore not a cognitive judgment..., but is rather aesthetic, by which is understood one whose determining ground **cannot** be **other than subjective.**   (KU 5:203)

Here, Kant contrasts cognitive judgments, which we relate to the object and which have as their "determining ground" an object with various properties, with aesthetic judgments, which we relate to the subject and which have as their "determining ground" a subject's hedonic response to an object. For example, when I make the cognitive judgment, "The peony is pink," I take there to be an object, a peony that has the property of being pink, that warrants this judgment. But when I make the aesthetic judgment, "The peony is beautiful," *per* Kant, I do so on the basis of a feeling of pleasure I have in response to it.

---

[5] Although I did not use language of determining judgment in Chapter 5, the judgments of recognition that I discussed there are an instance of determining judgment in Kant's theory of experience.

Kant moreover maintains that judgments of the beautiful are a specific kind of aesthetic judgment. As we just saw, he glosses an aesthetic judgment as one whose determining ground is something subjective: a subject's feeling of pleasure or displeasure. He, in turn, distinguishes between three species of aesthetic judgments on the basis of the kind of pleasure involved: judgments of the agreeable, judgments of the good, and judgments of taste (which include judgments of the beautiful and the sublime).

In more detail, according to Kant, aesthetic judgments of the agreeable and the good are based on an "interested" feeling of pleasure (see KU 5:204, 209). On his view, an interest amounts to a desire that we have for the existence of an object; interested pleasure is thus pleasure we take in an object that satisfies this desire. In a judgment of the agreeable, Kant aligns the relevant interest with what "**pleases the senses in sensation**" (KU 5: 205). For example, I might take pleasure in a peony because it satisfies my penchant for pink things; in which case I should judge it to be agreeable. As for judgments of the good, though Kant maintains that they are also based on interested pleasure, he takes the source of this pleasure to be more intellectual in nature. To this end, he claims that the interested pleasure we feel in the good is tied to an interest we have in things measuring up to our "concept" of "what sort of thing the object is supposed to be" (KU 5:207). For example, suppose I have a concept of what Romantic poetry should be like. I might then take pleasure in "Ah! Sun-Flower" as something that measures up to that concept and issue the aesthetic judgment that it is good on this basis.

By contrast with judgments of the agreeable and good, Kant claims that judgments of taste have their basis in a "disinterested" form of pleasure (see KU §§2, 5). Disinterested pleasure, according to Kant, is pleasure that has its source not in any desire for the existence of the object, but rather in a "merely **contemplative**" relation to the object that is not "biased in favor of" its existence and is, in that sense, "indifferent" to it (KU 5:209). In this vein, he says, "if the question is whether something is beautiful, one does not want to know whether there is anything that is or that could be at stake, for us or for someone else, in the existence of the thing, but rather how we judge it in mere contemplation" (KU 5:204–5). Here, Kant indicates that our pleasure in the beautiful does not have its basis in what is "at stake" for us given our interests and desires, but rather in a less self-involved mode of reflective engagement that he, like many in the tradition, calls "contemplation."

In choosing to emphasize the notions of reflection and contemplation, Kant rejects a picture of aesthetic appreciation as something that is a matter of being wholly receptive to, or struck by, beauty.[6] For Kant, aesthetic appreciation does not just happen to us; it is something active, something that we do.

---

[6] Think, for example, of Sontag's description of beauty as "gladness to the senses" (2002, 21), and her claim that, "What is important now is to recover our senses. We must learn to *see* more, to *hear* more, to *feel* more...In place of a hermeneutics we need an erotics of art" (1961, 14).

254 IMAGINATION AND THE APPRECIATION OF BEAUTY

More specifically, Kant conceives of aesthetic appreciation as something that we do cognitively. To this end, he claims that it involves us reflectively engaging with the beautiful through an exercise of our spontaneous cognitive capacities: imagination and understanding.[7] More specifically still, he maintains that aesthetic appreciation involves a distinctive cognitive "state of mind [*Gemützustand*]" in which our imagination and understanding are in "free play [*freie Spiel*]" (KU 5:217). And according to Kant, it is this cognitive free play, rather than any interest or desire that gives rise to the pleasure we feel in the beautiful.

Though I shall have more to say about exactly what free play involves shortly, it is worth briefly noting that Kant also uses his discussion of free play to clarify the normativity involved in judgments of the beautiful. On his view, judgments of the beautiful involve a robust form of intersubjective normativity, according to which judging something to be beautiful involves "demanding" or "laying claim" to universal agreement, i.e. the agreement of everyone (KU 5:212–13). For example, if I judge the peony to be beautiful, then *per* Kant, I think that everyone else "should" agree with this judgment (KU 5:237). To be clear, for Kant, this is a normative demand: I am committed to thinking that everyone should agree that the peony is beautiful, whether or not they, in fact, do.[8]

According to Kant, appreciating the role that free play has in judgments of the beautiful is crucial for understanding how they can involve a demand for universal agreement.[9] To this end, he argues that judgments of the beautiful can only lay normative claim to universal agreement if the pleasure that we feel in the beautiful is universally "shareable" (*Mitteilbar*), i.e. is something that anyone else could feel in response to the beautiful object (KU 5:217). Were our pleasure in the beautiful like our pleasure in the agreeable, *qua* a pleasure that has its basis in our "private" penchants and preferences, then Kant thinks judgments of the beautiful would have "private," rather than "universal" "validity" (KU 5:217). However, Kant makes the case that the pleasure we feel in the beautiful is, indeed, universally shareable because it is grounded in the free play of imagination and understanding, *qua* capacities for "cognition in general" that we universally share (KU 5:217). To be clear, in order to share this state of mind, we need not exercise our imagination and understanding in the exact same way in relation to a beautiful object. For example, in free play with the Blake poem, I might explore imaginative and intellectual perspectives on weariness, while you concentrate on time and hope. But even though the content of our free play differs, the fact that we are both in a state of cognitive play is something we share. And it is this latter shareability, the shareability of this playful state of mind, that Kant takes to be the

---

[7] See Chapter 2 for the argument that Kant conceives of imagination as spontaneous.

[8] I thus understand the "should" not in predictive terms (see Guyer 1997, 123–33, 144), but rather in normative terms (see Rind 2002; Hamawaki 2006, 123–4; and Ginsborg 2015, chap. 2).

[9] Kant, indeed, argues for this position at several key junctures in the text, including KU §§9 and 21 and in the official Deduction in §38. Here, however, I shall focus on the argument in §9.

source of our universally shareable pleasure in the beautiful. For Kant, then, the normative force of judgments of the beautiful depends on the fact that they are based on a pleasure induced by the state of free play in response to a beautiful object—a state which anyone with our cognitive capacities can share in.

Let's turn now to Kant's description of exactly what sort of cognitive state of mind free play involves. Here, I shall focus on two sets of claims Kant makes about free play: the first concerns the play involved, and the second the freedom.

On Kant's view, free play is not just a state in which we cognitively play with a beautiful object; it is also a state in which our cognitive capacities play with one another. Indeed, he argues that there is a particularly animated way in which we deploy our cognitive capacities in relation to one another when we contemplate beauty. In this vein, he describes free play as a state in which our imagination and understanding are "enlivened through mutual agreement" and engaged in a "reciprocally expeditious [beförderlich]" way (KU 5:219; EE 20:224).[10] They are animated, he says, "the one through the other" (KU 5:238–9). For Kant, then, free play is not a matter of us engaging with the beautiful object through some imaginative activities that occur alongside some intellectual activities.[11] Free play involves a mutually enlivening, reciprocally expeditious, animating exchange between these activities.

As I understand it, this play involves an open-ended, dynamic process in which how we imaginatively engage with a beautiful object shapes how we intellectually engage with it, and vice versa. For example, consider how we might freely play with the opening lines of "Ah! Sun-Flower": "Ah Sun-flower! weary of time, / Who countest the steps of the Sun." Here, imagining how a sunflower tracks the sun might lead to thoughts about time, while thinking about time might lead us to imagine the sunflower's face as a clockface. So too thoughts about weariness might prompt us to imagine the droop of a sunflower's head, or imagining counting steps might prompt us to think of the weary march of time. For Kant, it is this sort of animating exchange, which we carry out in an open-ended way in relation to the beautiful that marks the play of free play.

The second set of claims about free play that I shall consider here concerns the sense in which it is free. This is a much more thorny issue, and it will take more time to work through. Kant often frames the freedom of free play by way of a contrast with the more constrained way we exercise our imagination and understanding in ordinary theoretical cognition. In ordinary cognition, Kant claims that our

---

[10] I take this picture of mutual reinforcement to be why Kant sometimes says that in free play, "understanding is in service of the imagination" and sometimes imagination is "subsumed" under our understanding (KU 5:242, 287).

[11] I take this to put pressure on Ostaric's claim that in free play our imagination is "entirely independent of the understanding" but happens to "contingently" agree with the understanding (2017, 1377, 1398), and Horstmann's claim that in free play our imagination operates "independently from the understanding" though in a way that is "suitable for conceptualization" (2018, 66, 97).

cognitive capacities are "restricted" by a "determinate concept": the way we imaginatively take up an object and intellectually think about it is guided by a particular concept that we determine the object in accordance with (KU 5:217). For example, when I ordinarily cognize a peony, *per* Kant, I am constrained by the concept <peony>: imaginatively, I organize and order what I sense in accordance with this concept, and intellectually, I make a determining judgment in which I subsume what I intuit under this concept (see Chapter 5). In the reflective context of free play, by contrast, Kant maintains that we have a freedom that we do not have in ordinary cognition: "The powers of cognition…are hereby in a free play, since no determinate concept restricts them to a particular rule of cognition" (KU 5:217). For Kant, then, part of the freedom of free play turns on some sort of "restriction" or "limitation" connected to a "determinate concept" operative in ordinary cognition being lifted.

In light of these remarks, it can be tempting to attribute to Kant a view of free play as free insofar as it proceeds without concepts.[12] This has been dubbed the "precognitive" interpretation of free play.[13] According to the precognitive reading, free from concepts, we are free to imaginatively explore a beautiful object in ways that we do not in ordinary cognition. For example, released from the restriction of representing a flower I perceive as an instance of <peony>, I am free to imaginatively engage with it, perhaps by attentively exploring it[14] or synthesizing the manifold in a variety of creative ways.[15] And though our understanding must also make some contribution to free play, *per* the precognitive reading, it is not through concepts, but rather through some extra-conceptual contribution, such as providing a kind of "lawfulness"[16] or "unity" to our playful activities.[17]

One can see the appeal of analyzing the freedom of free play in terms of independence from concepts: it is not only consistent with Kant's remarks about free play, but also it is in keeping with his general insistence that, in contrast with judgments of the good, judgments of the beautiful are "neither **grounded** on concepts nor **aimed** at them," and that, "That is **beautiful** which pleases universally without a concept" (KU 5:209, 219). However, the precognitive reading does not sit easily with certain aspects of how Kant characterizes the contribution of the understanding to free play. While in his analysis of free play Kant describes this contribution in terms of "lawfulness" and "unity," he also consistently glosses it as a contribution made by the understanding, *qua* the faculty of

---

[12] See, e.g., Henrich (1992, 44–54); Guyer (1997, 80); Zuckert (2007, 304–5); Hughes (2007, 263–5, 281–4, 296); Gorodeisky (2011); Ginsborg (2015, chaps. 3, 7); Heidemann (2016); Horstmann (2018, §II); Makkai (2021, chap. 2); Geiger (2022, chap. 5).
[13] See Guyer (2005).   [14] See Zuckert (2007, 285); Williams (2021; 2022).
[15] See Rush (2001, 56).
[16] See, e.g., Makkreel (1990, 47), who glosses this in terms of conformity to the categories, and Ginsborg (2015, chap. 3, 7), who glosses this lawfulness in terms of a primitive normativity.
[17] See, e.g., Crawford (1982), Gorodeisky (2011), Heidemann (2016), Horstmann (2018, §II), who argue that free play involves sensitivity to patterns of unity that are not conceptual patterns.

concepts. For example, he says, free play involves "the imagination [being]... unintentionally brought into accord with the understanding, as the faculty of concepts," and the "subsumption" "of the **faculty** of intuitions or exhibitions (i.e., of the imagination) under the **faculty** of concepts (i.e., the understanding)" (KU 5:190, 287; transl. modified; see also KU 5:244, 292; EE 20:220).[18] Though this reference to the "faculty of concepts" might be read just as Kant's epithet for the understanding, he also indicates that the basic cognitive activity that the understanding is responsible for in free play is connected to concepts. In this vein, he says that, in free play, the understanding supplies "the concept that unifies" our representations and "the concept as representation of the unity of" our representations (KU 5:217, 287; transl. modified).[19] To be sure, in the vicinity of these remarks Kant also denies that any "determinate concept... restricts" free play and that any "concept of the object is the ground of" the judgment of the beautiful (KU 5:287). However, just because a concept does not restrict or ground a judgment of the beautiful (as it does in ordinary cognition or judgments of the good), this does not mean that concepts cannot play any role at all. This is consistent with concepts playing a role other than a restricting or grounding one. And the fact that in analyzing what the understanding contributes to free play, Kant chooses to emphasize its status as the faculty of concepts and the conceptual nature of its activities suggests that he accords concepts some substantive, albeit non-restricting, non-grounding role in free play.

Kant, in fact, gestures toward an alternative way in which concepts might contribute in free play, viz. via the "**exhibition** of a concept of the understanding (though which concept be undetermined)" and the "exhibition of an indeterminate concept of the understanding" (EE 20:220; KU 5:224; transl. modified).[20] Granted it is not yet at all clear what exhibition of an "undetermined" or "indeterminate" concept might mean, but in these passages Kant at least opens the door to a so-called "multicognitive" interpretation of free play, according to which, rather than being devoid of concepts altogether, free play involves us deploying concepts in some sort of "undetermined" or "indeterminate" fashion.[21]

This said, one might worry that unless free play is free from concepts, then Kant cannot account for what distinguishes the cognitive state of mind involved

---

[18] I address Kant's claim in the KU 5:287 context that free play involves schematizing "without a concept" in §8.3.

[19] See also Kant's emphasis on concepts in the following remark: "The freedom of imagination agreeing with the concept of the understanding. Without the former, which gives it intuition, the latter would accomplish nothing—the object would disappear for it. The understanding comes to the aid of imagination and brings unity into its products" (DWL 24:707).

[20] See also Kant's claim that judgments of the beautiful "lead to some sort of concept (it is indeterminate which)" (KU 5:207), and that, "the imagination in its free play with the **understanding**... agree[s] with its **concepts** in general (without determination of them)" (KU 5:256).

[21] See, e.g., Seel (1988, 349); Allison (2001, 170–1); Rush (2001, 58).

258 IMAGINATION AND THE APPRECIATION OF BEAUTY

in free play from the one involved in ordinary cognition.[22] However, in the General Remark, Kant indicates that there is something in ordinary cognition other than concepts that free play is free from: an "end [*Zweck*] with regard to cognition" (KU 5:242). More specifically, he says that free play is free from the end of "grasping the object in a single representation and determining the manifold in its form" (KU 5:242). I take this "grasping" and "determining" the object in a single representation to be what is involved in making a determining judgment in which we subsume an object under a concept.[23] For Kant, then, ordinary cognition is guided by the end of making determining judgments in which we recognize the object we are given as falling under a concept. And when we are guided by this end, Kant suggests that we orient toward objects and our cognitive activities in a particular way: we encounter the object as a "problem" that our cognitive activities, culminating in a determining judgment, should provide a "solution" to (KU 5:242). In the General Remark, it is thus this end of cognition, with its concomitant orientation, that Kant tells us free play is free from.

In order to fill out the details of Kant's account of what this kind of freedom amounts to, I find it helpful to approach the end he thinks we are free from in free play through the lens of what I described as the object-facing function of our cognitive capacities in Chapter 1. There, I argued that, on Kant's view, we can distinguish between two aspects of the cognitive function of sensibility and understanding: an object- and subject-facing aspect. The object-facing aspect concerns the function these capacities have vis-à-vis objects and the cognitive determination of them. In this vein, Kant emphasizes the role sensibility has in giving us objects and understanding has in thinking the objects we are given. And, as we have, on Kant's view, when sensibility and understanding both perform their object-facing function, the result is a determining judgment in which we conceptually determine the object we are given in intuition.

Meanwhile, according to my interpretation, the subject-facing aspect concerns the function that our cognitive capacities have in facilitating one another internal to our cognitive processes. In this vein, Kant stresses sensibility's function of making concepts sensible, and understanding's function of making intuitions understandable. And what I would like to suggest is that we can cast the end that Kant thinks free play is free from in terms of the object-facing function of cognition: in free play, we are no longer guided by the end of cognitively determining the object, and hence, we are no longer oriented toward the object as a problem to solve, nor toward our cognitive activities as meant to provide the solution.

---

[22] As commentators often press, if Kant cannot distinguish between these states of mind, then he is open to the "everything is beautiful" objection: every time we exercise our imagination and understanding in cognition, we should find the object to be beautiful—a conclusion Kant seems to resist (see Meerbote 1982; Guyer 1997, 264; Rind 2002).

[23] Think, here, of the sort of empirical judgments of recognition that Kant thinks are involved in ordinary experience (see Chapter 5).

JUDGMENTS OF THE BEAUTIFUL AND FREE PLAY 259

Though free play is free from this object-facing end of cognition, as I interpret Kant, we are nevertheless still oriented by the end related to the subject-facing function of our cognitive capacities. That is to say, our sensibility, here in the guise of the imagination, is still oriented toward making concepts sensible,[24] and the understanding toward making intuitions understandable. However, unlike in ordinary cognition, where fulfilling this subject-facing function goes hand-in-hand with fulfilling the object-facing function, in free play we are oriented by the subject-facing function alone. And when we are so-oriented, Kant claims that we find our way to a distinctive "proportion" between our cognitive capacities that is "optimal for the animation of both powers (the one through the other)": the proportion of free play (KU 5:238). As I understand this optimal proportion, unlike in ordinary cognition where our cognitive activities are brought to a conclusion once we have solved the problem of determining the object through a recognitional act of judgment, in free play we are free to keep imaginatively and intellectually lingering over the beautiful object in an open-ended, mutually reinforcing way.

Here, however, we must be cautious. Given Kant's commitment to judgments of the beautiful involving disinterested pleasure he insists that no end, including "no subjective end [Zweck]," can govern free play (KU 5:221). While this might seem to rule out the possibility that the subject-facing end of cognition can orient free play, this is not the sort of subjective end Kant is worried about. When Kant speaks of subjective ends in this context, he has in mind ends related to the agreeable, hence to what we are subjectively interested in given our penchants and preferences.[25] Though subjective ends in this sense do not orient free play, he insists that some orientation toward "subjective purposiveness [Zweckmaßigkeit]" does: we are oriented toward how our "way of representing" an object promotes "the activity of the subject with regard to the animation of its cognitive powers" (KU 5:221-2). And insofar as this orientation toward subjective purposiveness amounts to an orientation toward how our cognitive capacities "animate" one another, I take it to amount to what I have described as an orientation toward the subject-facing end of cognition.

At this point, I would like to bring together the various interpretive threads that I have been developing and propose that the freedom of free play on Kant's view amounts to a kind of creativity that is cognitive and conceptually rich. To orient this discussion, I shall take my cue from Margaret Boden's influential definition of creativity as "the ability to come up with ideas...that are *new, surprising* and *valuable*" (2004, 1).[26] Instead of focusing on "ideas," however, I shall focus on the newness, surprise, and value involved in the cognitive state of mind that is free play.

---

[24] See Chapters 3 and 4 for discussion.
[25] In KU §11, Kant mentions subjective ends in the first paragraph and glosses them in terms of agreeableness in the second paragraph.
[26] In developing their Kant-friendly accounts of creativity, Stokes (2014) and Gaut (2014) also draw on Boden's definition of creativity.

260 IMAGINATION AND THE APPRECIATION OF BEAUTY

Let's begin with the new and surprising dimensions of free play. On Kant's view, once we are released from the object-facing end of cognition, we can exercise our cognitive capacities in ways that lead us down fresh cognitive paths that we do not pursue in ordinary cognition. As we have seen, in ordinary cognition Kant thinks that the way we imaginatively and intellectually engage with an object is "restricted" by the "determinate concept" that we subsume the object under, and that once we have arrived at a recognitional judgment, we have "solved" the "problem" the object poses and can move on. But in free play, Kant insists that we neither proceed in this conceptually restricted way, nor bring our cognitive activities to this kind of recognitional conclusion.[27] As we reflectively linger over the object, we, as it were, "try on," different imaginative and intellectual perspectives on the object, which lead us in new and surprising cognitive directions. For example, in an ordinary encounter with a peony, under the constraint of the concept <peony>, the way I imaginatively organize and conceptually think about the peony is oriented toward, and culminates in, a recognition of the flower I intuit as an instance of the concept <peony>. In free play, by contrast, I dwell on the peony and find new imaginative perspectives on, say, its graded pinks and pom-pom form, and new conceptual perspectives on, say, how showy a flower it is or how apt a "glut" for "sorrow."[28] And these imaginative and conceptual perspectives spur one another on.

Bearing this picture of creative interplay in mind, I would like to now return to Kant's remarks that free play involves the exhibition of "undetermined" or "indeterminate" concepts. To be sure, this language is vague and open to different interpretations.[29] However, I think this line of thought can be productively read in light of the idea that part of what free play involves is a kind of open-ended conceptualization in which how we imaginatively organize the beautiful object stimulates how we conceptually think about it, and vice versa. More specifically, I would like to suggest that there are two, by no means exclusive, senses in which

---

[27] I am, however, sympathetic to Guyer's (2005, 94–8) argument to the effect that free play can involve the deployment of empirical concepts in recognizing the object we freely play with (see also Küplen 2015, chap. 4). However, this only commits Kant to the view that the recognitional deployment of determinate concepts plays a preliminary role in a judgment of the beautiful. But once this conceptual recognition has taken place, the determinate concept need not constrain how we freely play with the beautiful, nor will it be the source of our pleasure in the beautiful (otherwise the judgment would be a judgment of the good).

[28] "But when the melancholy fit shall fall /... Then glut thy sorrow.../...on the wealth of globèd peonies" (Keats 2001, 250).

[29] The reading I offer here is in the spirit of the reading that Allison (2001, 71) and Breitenbach (2021, 1011–14) offer. And it contrasts with another reading according to which the relevant indeterminate concepts are the indeterminate concepts of reason that Kant discusses in §57 of the Antinomy (see Ostaric 2017; Winegar 2021). As I see it, it is important to recognize that the indeterminate concept under discussion in the Antinomy is the "transcendental concept of reason of the supersensible," which Kant explicitly contrasts with concepts of the understanding, which are "determinable by means of predicates of the sensible intuition that can correspond to it" (KU 5:339). Insofar as Kant describes the "undetermined" or "indeterminate" concept at issue in his discussion of free play as a concept of the understanding, I take it to be distinct from an indeterminate concept of reason.

the exhibition of "undetermined" or "indeterminate" concepts in free play involves open-ended conceptualization.

In the first place, this exhibition involves the exhibition of a range of concepts. Free from the constraint of the object-facing end of cognition, hence the constraint of exhibiting a particular determinate concept, we are free to imaginatively and intellectually explore the beautiful object through the lens of different concepts. Think, once again, about what is involved in contemplating the first stanza of "Ah! Sun-Flower": we can adopt a variety of conceptual perspectives on it, related to, say, the concepts of <time>, <time weariness>, <travel>, <travel weariness>, <sunflower>, and <sun>, which shape and are shaped by how we imagine, say, the sunflower, the traveler, or the course of the sun.

Furthermore, I would like to propose that free play involves the exhibition of concepts of the understanding that, Kant claims, are always open to further determination. He alludes to this idea in the Antinomy of Taste, where he asserts that concepts of the understanding are "determinable by means of predicates of the sensible intuition" (KU 5:339).[30] This echoes Kant's claims elsewhere to the effect that concepts of the understanding are "determinable" insofar as synthetically adding marks to them is something that "can never be completed" (JL 9:59). About the concept <gold>, for example, he says, "Gold is heavy, extensible, refractory, does not rust, etc., etc., There is still no completeness here. For one could discover 1000 more such marks" (VL 24:834). On Kant's view, then, concepts of the understanding can be said to be "indeterminate" or "undetermined" insofar as they are "determinable": through intuition we can always discover new marks to synthetically add to them. And I take it that this kind of determinability is also relevant to free play. For in addition to exploring a range of concepts, free play can involve exploring just one concept through a range of new perspectives. For example, when we read the Blake poem, even if we focus on the concept <weariness>, we can imaginatively and intellectually explore this concept in fresh ways, e.g. through images of a sunflower's droop or thoughts of a traveler's journey.

Notice that in this open-ended conceptualization, whether via a range of concepts or via a single concept, we are not constrained by a determinate concept the way we are in ordinary cognition: we do not simply judge that the beautiful object instances a concept and move on. We, instead, play around with how we conceptualize the object, drawing on resources from our imagination and understanding to this end. And far from concepts somehow depriving us of freedom here, the open-ended deployment of them is vital for us entering into a kind of cognitive *Spielraum*, or space of play, in which we reflectively linger over the beautiful and find ourselves going down new and surprising cognitive paths.[31]

---

[30] As I just noted contra Ostaric (2017) and Winegar (2021), I identify the "undetermined" or "indeterminate" concepts involved in free play as these "determinable" concepts of the understanding, rather than the "indeterminable" concepts of reason Kant discusses in the Antinomy.

[31] I take this to be "psychological," rather than "historical" creativity in Boden's sense (2004: 2).

262   IMAGINATION AND THE APPRECIATION OF BEAUTY

This said, while it might be relatively easy to motivate the idea that appreciation of poetry involves this kind of creative state of mind, why think that it is involved in appreciation of beauty across the board? Don't some aesthetic encounters with natural beauty and art have a more immediate character, as we are simply rapt by the beauty at hand? Kant certainly concedes that there are some aesthetic encounters that proceed in an immediate way without open-ended conceptualization being involved. However, as I read him, aesthetic encounters with nature or art that proceed without concepts fall in the domain of the agreeable and what pleases, or "charms," us immediately "**in sensation**" (KU 5:223, 205). So, if upon encountering a pink peony, I feel sensorily struck, as I interpret Kant, the sort of aesthetic judgment that I should make is one of the agreeable, rather than the beautiful. But according to Kant, a response to beauty proper, requires contemplation and reflectively lingering over the object through a dynamic exchange between our imagination and understanding. And this dynamic exchange, I have claimed, involves a mode of cognitive creativity in which concepts play a robust role.

But what purchase, if any, can this picture of free play have on how we aesthetically appreciate the beauty of something like a pink peony? Here, I propose we think through Kant's claim that aesthetic appreciation involves lingering over beauty. As I understand this claim, rather than our response to beauty being an immediate one, Kant conceives of free play as a kind of temporally extended process in which we take our cognitive time with the object. And it is because we allow ourselves to cognitively explore the object over time, free from the object-facing end of cognition, that I think we are able to find our way to fresh imaginative and conceptual perspectives on even seemingly straightforward beautiful objects. In the peony case, for example, it may well be that when I first see it, I am imaginatively focused on its sensory character, taking up the lushness of its colors and the opulence of its form. But as I linger over it, I can find my way to fresh conceptual perspectives on it. For example, I might find myself thinking about how delicate its petals are, how like a sea anemone it is, or how fitting it is as a symbol of good luck. This, in turn, might feed into how I imaginatively engage with it, and so I linger. As I see it, then, on Kant's view, part of what is involved in reflectively dwelling on a beautiful object is cognitively exploring even seemingly straightforward objects, whether in nature or art, in ways that lead us to discover new and surprising cognitive points of view on them.

Here, it might be also helpful to think about the ways in which engaging with art can teach us how to apprehend natural beauty in cognitively creative ways. Think of how prose and poetry can give us new conceptual lenses to bring to what we perceive: a sunflower, for me, cannot but evoke <time weariness> now.[32]

---

[32] I take the following remark Kant makes about appreciating the ocean as sublime to be in this spirit: "one must consider the ocean as the poets do, in accordance with what its appearance shows, for instance, when it is considered in periods of calm, as a clear watery mirror bounded only by the heavens, but also when it is turbulent, an abyss threatening to devour everything" (KU 5:270).

Painting, too, can offer us such lenses. For example, engaging with Van Gogh's *Sunflowers* (1889) might make us imaginatively attentive to yellow as a "symphony" of "light on light" or conceptually attentive to sunflowers as expressions of "gratitude"[33]—an attentiveness we might then draw on in our encounters with actual sunflowers. So too with other artistic media, architecture, sculpture, music, and the like can guide us down cognitive paths that open up natural beauty, not to mention other artistic beauty, in ways that are cognitively new and surprising. To be clear, I do not think that aesthetically engaging with nature through this artistic lens is the only route to the sort of cognitive creativity that free play involves on Kant's view. But I think that it is one way in which we learn to see even seemingly simple beauty through a rich cognitive lens.

However, in order for free play to count as creative in Boden's sense, it cannot just lead us down new and surprising cognitive paths; it needs to be valuable. It seems that part of Kant's picture of the value of free play turns on the idea that free play generates pleasure;[34] however, as we have seen, he thinks that our aesthetic encounters with the agreeable and the good have hedonic value as well.[35] For Kant, though, there is something distinctive about the pleasure involved in free play insofar as it has its source in the playful exercise of our cognitive capacities. And what I would like to explore here is the cognitive value that free play has.[36] More specifically, I would like to suggest that the pursuit of new and surprising cognitive directions in free play is something that has a particular kind of cognitive value for us vis-à-vis a need that Kant thinks we have as human beings: the need to have our concepts made sensible. As I stressed in my discussion of the subject-facing function of cognition in Chapters 2 and 3 and exhibition in Chapter 4, according to Kant, as creatures who are at once sensuous and intellectual, we need to have our concepts rendered to us in a sensible way that facilitates our concrete comprehension of them. And my proposal is that, on Kant's view, part of the cognitive value of free play is that it puts us in an "optimal" cognitive state that brings our concepts to life in a particularly animated and enlivened way.

In order to motivate this line of thought, I shall take my cue from Kant's discussion of the "aesthetic perfection" of cognition in his logic lectures. Recall from Chapter 4 that, on Kant's view, we aesthetically perfect our cognition by

---

[33] Bakker and Riopelle (2019, 39).
[34] See, e.g., Kant's claim that, "The attainment of every aim is combined with the feeling of pleasure" (KU 5:187).
[35] See Lopes (2021) for discussion of the role that hedonic normativity as well as normativity related to autonomy play in Kant's aesthetics.
[36] More specifically, the cognitive value I am interested in pertains to the cognitive value that free play itself has, rather than the downstream cognitive value free play can have for science (see Breitenbach 2018), empirical knowledge (see Geiger 2022), and empirical concept formation (see Ginsborg 2015, essay 8; Sethi 2022). My reading is thus in the spirit of Cohen's analysis of the cognitive value of free play in light of how it "stimulates our cognitive powers and thereby enhances our cognitive activity," and I intend for my account to shed further light on what this stimulation and enhancement involves (2018, 140).

264 IMAGINATION AND THE APPRECIATION OF BEAUTY

deepening and refining our grasp of how "a concept thought abstractly is exhibited...*in concreto*" (JL 9:39; transl. modified). He sometimes describes this in
terms of the "liveliness" of cognition (BL 24:126; VL 24:809; DWL 24:709; JL
9:62). And in order to illustrate aesthetic perfection, Kant appeals to the example
of a poet who exhibits the concept <spring> in a particularly "lively" way by
"showing" how the concept sensibly manifests in "the budding flowers, the new
green of the forests, the cavorting herds, the renewed rays of the sun, the lovely,
charming air[,] the revival of the whole of nature" (BL 24:126).[37] According to
Kant, the poet here represents <spring> through "a multitude of marks coordinate with one another," which makes this concept lively "with the help of much
combination" (BL 24:126; see also VL 24:835).[38] And when we, as appreciators,
engage with this poetic rendering, our cognition can be aesthetically perfected as
our concept <spring> is synthetically "augmented" or "supplemented" through
the discovery of marks that we did not "already think" in the concept and that we
"add...synthetically as predicate[s]" to it (A721/B740; JL 9:59; A8/B12).[39] From
Kant's perspective, the poem thus has cognitive value insofar as it makes the concept <spring> sensible in new and surprising ways that brings it to life and broadens our conceptual horizons.

By my lights, we should understand the cognitive value of free play along similar lines: once we are free from the object-facing end of cognition, we are free to
pursue new and surprising cognitive perspectives on objects, including perspectives that make our concepts sensible in particularly lively and animating ways.
For example, when we read the Blake poem and linger over the weary sunflowers,
golden climes, and traveler's journey, we can discover new marks of the concept
<time> and how <time> relates to other concepts such as <weariness> or
<travel>.[40] So too in the case of the peony, instead of simply subsuming the flower
under the concept <peony> in a judgment of recognition, in free play we cognitively explore the flower in a way that can lead us to augment our concept
<peony> through the discovery of marks related to, say, lushness, showiness, or
pom-poms. And in creatively expanding our conceptual horizons in these new
and surprising directions, free play has cognitive value for us: it makes our concepts

---

[37] In Chapter 9, I take up Kant's related claim that artists add "aesthetic attributes" to concepts,
which are "supplementary representations of the imagination" that "aesthetically enlarge" concepts
(KU 5:315).

[38] For Kant, a coordinate mark is "an *immediate* mark of the thing," i.e. a mark through which we
directly grasp some aspect of it, and he contrasts them with subordinate marks, which represent the
thing by way of another mark (see JL 9:59; VL 24:834). The latter, he claims, are the sort of marks that
are the concern of the "dry" and "thorough" business that occupies philosophers (VL 24:835; see also
BL 24:126-7).

[39] In the first passage I have cited here from the first *Critique*, Kant suggests that we can augment or
supplement our concept <gold> through "the intuition in which it is given" and by "initiat[ing] perceptions of it" (A721-2/B749-50).

[40] I develop this line of thought in more detail in my discussion of aesthetic ideas and aesthetic
attributes in Chapter 9.

sensible in a particularly dynamic, lively, and expansive way that fulfills one of our needs as cognizers.

Piecing this together, on my interpretation of Kant's view, the freedom of free play turns on a kind of cognitive creativity in which how we imaginatively and intellectually explore a beautiful object leads in new, surprising, and cognitively valuable directions. We are able to enter into this kind of creative *Spielraum* because free play is free not from concepts, but rather from the object-facing end of our cognitive capacities. And once we are set free from this end, we are free to strike on fresh perspectives on a beautiful object that expand us cognitively. And it is this picture of the cognitive, creative, and conceptually rich exercise of our cognitive capacities, whether in the face of natural or artistic beauty, that is the core of my version of the multicognitive interpretation of free play.

However, given my overarching concern with Kant's theory of imagination, in the following sections, I want to develop a sharper picture of what the imaginative contribution to free play amounts to. To this end, I examine the cognitive and creative dimensions of what our imagination does in free play in turn.

8.3 The Cognitive Dimensions of Imagination in Free Play

Central to Kant's analysis of what our imagination contributes to free play is the idea that it contributes as a "faculty" or "power" of cognition (see KU §§9, 35); in which case, we should expect it to engage in basic cognitive activities, such as the ones I discussed under the heading of the formation, even-without-presence, and exhibition definitions of imagination in Chapter 4 (see, e.g., KU §§9, 35). Kant, moreover, suggests that free play involves "reflected perception [*reflektierte Wahrnehmung*]"; in which case, we should expect our imagination to engage in cognitive activities familiar from the perceptual context, which I detailed in Chapter 5 (KU 5:191). And, indeed, as I shall now show, in the third *Critique*, Kant characterizes what our imagination does in terms of cognitive activities familiar from his account of how we see more in perception in the first *Critique*: it engages in apprehension, composition, and exhibition. As a reminder, Kant conceives of apprehension as an activity in which our imagination takes up a manifold of representations delivered through the senses, e.g. when I imaginatively take up the manifold of pink and green representations given to me while I gaze at a peony. Composition is an activity in which our imagination synthesizes a manifold into a perceptual image that represents something spatially and/or temporally determinate, e.g. when I imaginatively compose those pink and green representations into a perceptual image that represents a peony shape filled by a lush pink and vibrant green.[41] And

---

[41] See Chapter 7 for a discussion of composition in particular.

266 IMAGINATION AND THE APPRECIATION OF BEAUTY

exhibition is an activity in which our imagination generates a perceptual image that exhibits a concept in sensible form, e.g. a perceptual image that represents the concept <peony> as manifesting sensibly. What I shall now argue is that it is the combination of all three of these perceptual activities that provides the basic cognitive framework in which Kant situates our imaginative contribution to free play, and that attending to this framework brings to light complex dimensions of this contribution that we might otherwise overlook.[42]

Beginning with apprehension, according to Kant, in free play, our imagination is responsible for taking up the beautiful object that we are given through the senses. In the Introduction, for example, Kant claims that in free play, our imagination is responsible for the "apprehension [*Auffassung*] (*apprehensio*) of the form of an object of intuition," and that our "apprehension of a given object of the senses is of course bound to a determinate form of this object" (KU 5:189, 240; see also KU 5:292, EE 20:220–4).[43] For example, when I encounter the beautiful peony, my imagination needs to apprehend its spatial form. Or when I read the Blake poem, my imagination needs to apprehend the words and punctuation on the page, as well as the poetic images conveyed by those words. However, as we have seen, in Kant's theory of perception, our imagination does not directly apprehend the object; rather our imagination apprehends objects by apprehending a manifold of intuition of the senses (intuition$_s$) generated by an object affecting us. So, I take Kant's position to be that in free play our imagination apprehends the object by apprehending a manifold of intuition$_s$ given to us through the senses.

In addition to apprehension, Kant claims that in free play our imagination engages in the cognitive activity of composition. In §9, for example, Kant claims, that in free play our imagination is responsible for "the composition [*Zusammensetzung*] of the manifold of intuition" (KU 5:217). He reiterates this in §35, attributing "the composition [*Zusammensetzung*] of the manifold of

---

[42] Henrich (1992, 47–50), for example, focuses on exhibition, but not apprehension or composition. Makkreel (1990, chap. 3), Guyer (1997, chap. 3), Rush (2001), Rueger and Evren (2005), Zuckert (2007, chap. 7), Rueger (2008), Ostaric (2017), and Filieri (2021) focus on apprehension and exhibition (sometimes under the heading of "schematism" or "symbolism"), but not composition. Vogelmann (2018) and Williams (2022) focus on apprehension and composition, but not on exhibition. In her Kant-inspired view, Breitenbach (2020, 74–5) describes a set of activities that we can engage in under the heading of "imaginative reflection," including imaginative exploration, fictive imagining, imaginative elaboration, and imaginative construction. I am sympathetic to these imaginative activities being able to play a role in free play, but I take it that they ultimately need to be anchored in the framework of apprehension, composition, and exhibition.

[43] In his more formalist sounding moments in the third *Critique*, Kant sharply distinguishes the "form" of an object, *qua* its spatio-temporal form, from the "matter" of an object, *qua* its sensory qualities, such as colors and tones, and suggests that only the former is the proper target of judgments of the beautiful (see KU §14). However, in Matherne (forthcoming) I argue that we can imaginatively represent a "perceptual form" that incorporates the latter into the former in perception, and that engaging with colors and tones as part of a perceptual form can be involved in judgments of the beautiful.

intuition" to imagination (KU 5:287).[44] For readers of the first *Critique*, Kant's use of "composition" in these passages might seem surprising: wouldn't "synthesis" have been the more obvious choice?[45] However, as I discussed in Chapter 7, in the first *Critique*, Kant defines "composition" as a particular mode of imaginative synthesis that involves ordering and organizing a manifold of intuition in such a way that results in an intuition$_i$ that represents a determinate spatio-temporal form (e.g. a shape or temporal sequence) and matter (e.g. a sensation or sensory quality that fills space and time to some degree). And in the context of perception, I suggested that the intuition$_i$ generated through composition is a perceptual image through which we see more. Recall the example of perceiving a house. *Per* Kant, when I perceive, say, a red house, my imagination composes the manifold of intuition$_s$ that I have when I look at it into a perceptual image that represents a determinate spatial form and matter: a house shape filled by a bright red. When Kant describes what our imagination does in free play as composition, he thus has in mind the activity of synthesizing the manifold into perceptual images that represent a determinate spatio-temporal form and matter. From Kant's perspective, then, when I imaginatively engage with a beautiful peony in free play, I do not just apprehend what I am given through the senses; I see more by imaginatively composing the manifold I am given into some sort of perceptual image (or perhaps perceptual images) that represents a determinate spatio-temporal form (e.g. a typical flower or bomb shape), and a determinate matter (e.g. a lush pink with a high degree of intensity).[46]

However, though it is not often acknowledged, over and above these mentions of apprehension and composition, Kant indicates that free play involves the cognitive activity of imaginative exhibition.[47] For example, Kant claims that in our encounter with the beautiful, "the faculty of exhibition or the imagination is

---

[44] See also Kant's gloss of the "subjective condition of cognizing" in §21: "when, by means of the senses, a given object brings the imagination into activity for the composition [*Zusammensetzung*] of the manifold, while the imagination brings the understanding into activity for the unity of this composition in concepts" (KU 5:238; transl. modified).

[45] Makkreel (1990, chap. 3) argues that Kant consciously drops the language of "synthesis" in the third *Critique* because he distinguishes what our imagination does in free play from what it does in cognition in the first *Critique*. However, Kant sometimes uses language of synthesis in the third *Critique* (see EE 20:203, 212, 230n; KU 5:177, 238), and given that he identifies composition as a kind of synthesis in the first *Critique*, his references to composition in the third *Critique* also imply that synthesis is involved.

[46] This sort of composition appears to map onto what Kant describes as "comprehension [*Zusammenfassung*] (*comprehensio aesthetica*)" in the Analytic of the Sublime (KU 5:251).

[47] For example, "Darstellung" ("exhibition" or "presentation") does not feature in the account of free play defended by Guyer (2005); Zuckert (2007, chap. 7); Williams (2022). Exceptions include Allison (2001, 51, 171) who explores the notion that free play involves the exhibition of an "undetermined" concept (EE 20:221); Rush (2001, 45–6, 56–8) who aligns exhibition with schematism; and Rueger and Evren (2005) and Rueger (2008) who explore the role of symbolic exhibition in free play. Hughes (2007, chap. 8) discusses the notion of "exemplary exhibition," but her focus is on how aesthetic judgment exhibits the possibility of cognition, rather than on imagination as a faculty of exhibition.

considered, in the case of a given intuition, to be in accord with the **faculty of concepts** of the understanding...as promoting the latter" (KU 5:244; transl. modified). And in §35 he says that free play involves "the **faculty** of intuitions or exhibitions (i.e., of the imagination)" acting "**in its freedom**...in harmony with" "the **faculty** of concepts (i.e., the understanding)" (KU 5:287; transl. modified). Given that Kant defines imagination as the faculty of exhibition, these passages should come as no surprise. They should, instead, alert us to a familiar theme: part of the cognitive remit of imagination is to mediate between the senses and understanding by generating intuitions$_i$ that exhibit concepts in a spatio-temporal fashion. And, indeed, I have argued that, on Kant's view, in these acts of exhibition our imagination performs its cognitive function of making concepts sensible in a way that facilitates our concrete comprehension of them. Insofar as imagination operates as a cognitive capacity in free play, then we should expect it to act as Kant says it does: through exhibition.

What is more, I submit that Kant needs exhibition to be operative in free play if he is to have an explanation for why our imaginative engagement with the beautiful gives rise to pleasure. For, as some commentators have worried, there is some doubt that our imaginative engagement with beauty can give rise to pleasure because cognitively it seems to amount to a kind of failure.[48] According to this line of thought, the successful case of the cognitive exercise of our imagination happens in experience (in Kant's technical sense), i.e. in empirical cognition (in the narrow sense) in which we conceptually determine the object we are given through empirical intuition$_s$ (see Chapter 5). But Kant is clear that free play does not result in the sort of cognition at issue in experience. Yet, if we fail to cognitively succeed in this way, how can we feel anything other than displeasure in our imaginative activities in free play?

On my reading, the key to answering this question turns on Kant's account of how our imaginative activities in free play fulfill the subject-facing end of cognition through exhibition. For Kant, in order for our imagination to succeed vis-à-vis the subject-facing end of cognition, it needs to execute its cognitive function: making concepts sensible. However, what we learn in the third *Critique* is that in order to execute this function, Kant does not think our imagination has to contribute to cognition in the narrow sense, hence to the conceptual determination of objects we are given in intuition$_s$ in a determining judgment. All the execution of this cognitive function requires is that our imagination make concepts sensible through exhibition. Kant can thus acknowledge a rich variety of ways in which we imagine well, in and beyond, acts of ordinary cognition. And by according exhibition a role in free play, he thus has the resources to explain how our imagination

---

[48] See, e.g., Longuenesse (1998, 164; 2003). For a critique of this line of thought in the context of Kant's theory of judgment, see Dunn (2021).

THE COGNITIVE DIMENSIONS OF IMAGINATION IN FREE PLAY   269

functions cognitively well in this context and can, thereby, contribute to the pleasure we feel in the beautiful.

This said, attributing to Kant the view that free play involves our imagination exhibiting concepts returns us to the thorny issues surrounding whether he thinks concepts are involved in free play. In addition to the claims I discussed in §8.2 that seem to support the precognitive reading, in his analysis of what our imagination does in free play Kant says, "the freedom of the imagination consists precisely in the fact that it schematizes without a concept" (KU 5:287).[49] *Prima facie*, this remark would seem to call for a precognitive interpretation of what our imagination does in free play, according to which it proceeds without concepts.[50]

There are, nevertheless, reasons to worry that Kant thinks our imaginative activities in free play involve schematizing or exhibiting "without a concept" full stop. For one thing, in his more systematic remarks about schematism in §59 of the third *Critique*, he insists that schematism involves the "direct" exhibition of concepts (KU 5:352). This echoes his treatment of schematism as involving concepts in the first *Critique* and in the "Progress" essay (see A140/B179–A141/B181; WF 20:279). For another thing, as we have seen, Kant defines exhibition as an activity in which our imagination makes concepts sensible and thereby facilitates our comprehension of them (see Chapter 4). We should thus be wary of attributing to Kant the view that our imagination can schematically exhibit "without a concept" altogether in free play.

Indeed, at this point, we should once more return to Kant's remarks to the effect that free play involves the "**exhibition** of a concept of the understanding (though which concept be undetermined)" and the "exhibition of an indeterminate concept of the understanding" (EE 20:220; KU 5:224). In these passages, rather than asserting that imaginative exhibition proceeds without concepts altogether, Kant claims that imaginative exhibition is connected to concepts of the understanding that are in some sense "undetermined" or "indeterminate." In §8.2, I suggested that we should read this claim in terms of free play involving a kind of open-ended conceptualization in which we exhibit both a range of concepts and a single "determinable" concept in a more wide-ranging way than we do in ordinary cognition. And it is in this light that I think we need to read the "schematizes without a concept" claim: in free play, we are not imaginatively beholden to schematizing just one concept in just one way as we do in ordinary cognition, but are rather free to exhibit a range of concepts or even just one concept in a more expansive way as part of our creative exploration of the beautiful object.

---

[49] See also his claim earlier in the third *Critique* that, in free play, "the mere apprehension (*apprehensio*) of the form of an object of intuition" occurs "without a relation of this to a concept for a determinate cognition" (KU 5:189).

[50] See Gorodeisky (2013); Ostaric (2017); and Filieri (2021).

270 IMAGINATION AND THE APPRECIATION OF BEAUTY

While I shall have more to say about this kind of exhibition below, for now, what I want to stress is Kant's commitment to free play involving not only apprehension of what we sense and composition of perceptual images, but also the exhibition of concepts in this open-ended way. At the same time, though these cognitive activities of apprehension, composition, and exhibition are familiar from Kant's theory of perception, insofar as free play involves not just "perception," but "reflected perception," they need to unfold in free and playful ways as we linger over the beautiful, which is distinct from how they unfold in ordinary cognition. Indeed, as we have seen, according to Kant, "in the judgment of taste the imagination must be considered in its freedom" and "in an aesthetic respect...the imagination is free" (KU 5:240, 316).[51] Though there is much debate about what this imaginative freedom amounts to, in what follows I take up the thread that I began developing earlier by arguing that it should be understood in terms of a kind of cognitive creativity.[52]

8.4 The Creative Dimensions of Imagination in Free Play

In order to explore Kant's account of the sort of imaginative freedom we have in free play, I shall tease apart two related questions. The first question is: what is our imagination "free from" in free play? Call this the "negative freedom question." The second is: what is our imagination "free to do" in free play? Call this the "positive freedom question."

8.4.1 The Negative Freedom of Imagination

Beginning with the negative freedom question, for reasons I rehearsed in §8.2, it can be tempting to attribute to Kant a precognitive view of what our imagination does in free play as free from concepts altogether. However, I argued that although Kant denies that we deploy concepts in free play in the same way that we deploy them in cognition, insofar as he accords to our understanding, *qua* the faculty of concepts, and its conceptual activities a role in free play, then free play cannot be free from concepts altogether. Here, I want to offer further support for thinking that free play cannot proceed without concepts on the basis of Kant's commitment to free play involving the imaginative activities of exhibition and composition.

---

[51] Although Kant makes this latter claim in the course of discussing genius, it nicely encapsulates the sort of freedom that he takes our imagination to have in the context of aesthetic appreciation as well. I discuss the imagination's contribution to genius in Chapter 9.

[52] See Williams (2022) for an overview of debates concerning how to interpret Kant's account of our imaginative freedom in free play.

THE CREATIVE DIMENSIONS OF IMAGINATION IN FREE PLAY   271

Starting with the point about exhibition, as we have seen, Kant characterizes exhibition in general as the imaginative activity of exhibiting concept in intuitions$_i$, which has the cognitive function of making concepts sensible in a way that facilitates our comprehension of them. As we have also seen, Kant claims that free play involves the exhibition of an "undetermined" or "indeterminate" concept of the understanding in free play—a claim I have glossed in terms of the exhibition involved in an open-ended process of conceptualization. In ascribing exhibition a role in free play, I thus take Kant to be committed to the imaginative exhibition of a range of concepts or a single concept in a wide-ranging way to be a key component of what our imagination does in free play.[53]

Kant's claim that our imagination engages in the cognitive activity of composition also puts pressure on a concept-free reading of free play. In my discussion of Kant's theory of perception in Chapter 5, I argued that he conceives of the composition of perceptual images as something that is guided by empirical concepts vis-à-vis empirical schemata. And in Chapter 7, I showed that Kant is committed to imaginative composition being something that is guided by the pure concepts of the understanding ("the categories") as mediated through their transcendental schemata.[54] More specifically, in the first *Critique*, Kant argues that the imaginative composition of a perceptual image that represents a determinate spatio-temporal form and matter depends on the mathematical categories of quantity and quality. To the extent that imaginative composition is involved in free play on Kant's view, it thus cannot proceed without concepts altogether; it must, at least, proceed under the guidance of empirical concepts and the mathematical categories.[55]

But what about the dynamical categories, like <substance>, <cause>, and <community>: does Kant think they also figure in our imaginative activities in free play? Here are some reasons to think the answer is "no." Recall that on my reading of Kant's view, instead of making perception possible, the dynamical categories and their schemata make experience in the full-blown sense possible. That is to say, they make it possible for us to make empirical judgments in which we recognize that there is an existing object that our representations correspond to

---

[53] As will emerge below, I understand this range of concepts to include empirical and pure concepts (including categories and ideas of reason). I thus disagree with readings that restrict the concepts relevant to free play to ideas of reason (see Rueger and Evren 2005; Rueger 2008; and Ostaric 2017). Though I think free play can involve ideas of reason, in passages in the Analytic where Kant discusses the basics of free play (e.g. §§9, 35), he does not indicate that only some concepts, but not others, are relevant. He makes the generic claim that our understanding, as the faculty of concepts, needs to be involved.

[54] Gregor (1985), Makkreel (1990, chap. 3), and Filieri (2021, 516) also argue that the categories must be involved in free play.

[55] Zinkin (2006) also lays emphasis on the relevance of Kant's account of the mathematical categories for understanding judgments of taste, though she focuses on the relevance of Kant's account of extensive and intensive magnitudes.

272 IMAGINATION AND THE APPRECIATION OF BEAUTY

and are necessitated by.[56] Kant, however, insists that judgments of the beautiful do not concern themselves with the existence of an object: "the judgment of taste is merely **contemplative**, i.e., a judgment that is indifferent with regard to the existence of an object" (KU 5:209). Instead of being concerned with the existence of the object, Kant suggests that we are concerned with the "representation" of an object and what we can "make of" that representation in free play (KU 5:205). Given that judgments of the beautiful are thus indifferent to the existence of objects, we might have reason to attribute to Kant the view that the dynamical categories of substance, cause, and community are likewise indifferent to free play.

On the other hand, once we conceive of free play as involving the sort of open-ended, animated exchange between imaginative and intellectual perspectives that I suggested in §8.2, then it seems there is room for the dynamical categories to be involved. For example, when we engage with the Blake poem, even if we are not focused on an existing object that corresponds to what the poem represents, exploring the poem would seem to involve deploying dynamical categories in order to grasp its content. To imagine a sunflower tracking the sun or the sun in its golden clime, for instance, we need to grasp an objective order of succession, which, *per* Kant, requires deploying the category of causality. Likewise, when we imagine a traveler finishing their journey, we represent them as a substance in which accidents inhere. In these cases, I take it that our imaginative composition vis-à-vis the content of the poem is guided by the dynamical categories. On balance, then, it seems we have reason to accord both the mathematical and dynamical categories, as well as empirical concepts, a role to play in relation to our imaginative activities of composition in free play.

Stepping back, the fact that Kant thinks free play involves imaginative exhibition and composition indicates that rather than being free from concepts altogether, our imaginative contribution to free play interfaces with concepts in some fashion. This said, it also cannot be the case that the sort of imaginative exhibition and composition at stake in free play involves concepts in the way the exhibition and composition at stake in ordinary cognition does. If it did, then every time our imagination engaged in conceptually laden exhibition and composition, it would be in a state of free play, and we should accordingly find every object we cognize to be beautiful—a commitment that Kant does not appear to take on board.[57] So even though Kant thinks free play involves conceptually laden composition and exhibition, he also owes us an account of what is nonetheless distinctive about how this unfolds in our encounter with the beautiful.

Addressing this issue, in part, requires that we look at Kant's analysis of the positive freedom of imagination—a topic I shall take up in §8.4.2. However, in

---

[56] In Kant's words, whereas the mathematical categories pertain "merely to the **intuition**," the dynamical categories pertain to the "**existence** of an appearance" (A160/B199).

[57] This is a version of the "everything is beautiful" objection that I noted earlier.

THE CREATIVE DIMENSIONS OF IMAGINATION IN FREE PLAY 273

§8.2, I advanced an alternative way to understand the negative freedom of free play that is also pertinent to this discussion. There, I argued that, on Kant's view, free play is free from the object-facing end of cognition: the end of "solving" the "problem" of the object by making a determining judgment in which we subsume the object we intuit under a concept. Let's consider the implications this has for Kant's conception of the negative freedom of imagination in free play.

According to Kant, in ordinary cognition, our imagination proceeds under the constraint of a "determinate concept" that "restricts" it (KU 5:217). For example, in the context of ordinary cognition, when I come across a peony in a garden, the way that I imaginatively apprehend the manifold is guided by the concept <peony> (vis-à-vis a schema), and the result of my imaginative composition is a perceptual image that represents what I perceive as exemplifying this concept. What is more, on Kant's view, I engage in these imaginative activities in the service of the object-facing end of cognition: deploying my cognitive capacities in a way that culminates in my subsuming the object I intuit under a concept in a determining judgment.

Though conducive to us fulfilling the object-facing function of cognition, Kant claims that these sorts of constrained activities are ones that can leave us "bored" imaginatively (KU 5:243).[58] According to Kant, a sign of being imaginatively bored is "grow[ing] tired" of something rather quickly (KU 5:243). And he illustrates imaginative boredom with the example of encountering objects, such as "geometrically regular shapes—a circle, a square, a cube," that strike us as so "stiff" or "regular" that "they cannot be represented except by being regarded as mere exhibitions of a determinate concept, which prescribes the rule for that shape" (KU 5:241–2; transl. modified). His thought seems to be that in encounters in which we feel compelled to represent an object only in accordance with the concept the understanding "prescribes," we imaginatively "grow tired" of the object (KU 5:243). Indeed, it seems that once we have done our imaginative part to "solve" the "problem" that is the object, there is nothing left for us to imaginatively do.[59]

---

[58] See also KU 5:270, 314, 330.

[59] To be clear, Kant does not think geometrical figures are entirely boring. Later in the third *Critique*, he claims that discovering their "serviceability for the solution of many problems in accordance with a single principle, and indeed of each of them in infinitely many different ways," can be a source of "true joy" (KU 5:262–3). However, Kant insists that this joy is responsive to the "objective and intellectual" "purposiveness" of geometrical figures as conducive to mathematical cognition (KU 5:363). From the perspective of the imagination, however, as long as what we do with these figures is "prescribed" by concepts, they impose on us a burdensome, boring constraint. See, however, Breitenbach's (2015) argument that Kant can also acknowledge judgments of the beautiful in regard to mathematics, which turn on a "response felt in light of our own creative activities involved in the process of mathematical reasoning" (2015, 956). Though I shall not pursue this issue here, I am sympathetic to her account, and I take my analysis of free play to be consistent with cases of mathematical creativity in which we are not imaginatively compelled by prescribed concepts.

274 IMAGINATION AND THE APPRECIATION OF BEAUTY

But once we are set free from the object-facing end of cognition, Kant claims that we are no longer "compelled" to imaginatively represent objects under the constraint of the determinate concept prescribed by the understanding (KU 5:292). And free from this constraint, we find our way to being imaginatively "entertained" by a beautiful object, which "we are never tired of looking at it" and strikes us as "always new" (KU 5:243).[60] While this "never" and "always" may be something of an overstatement, I take Kant's idea to be that when we are imaginatively entertained by beauty we find something in this encounter to reflectively linger over. But far from this imaginative entertainment being something that proceeds free from concepts, Kant conceives of it as something that proceeds in tandem with them. Indeed, as I intimated in §8.2, for Kant, this imaginative entertainment is bound up with the subject-facing end of cognition and our need to have concepts made sensible to us, and this gives this entertainment a cognitive weight. And what I shall now argue is that, on Kant's view, the positive freedom of our imagination in free play turns precisely on the creative, conceptually rich ways in which we, in a dynamic exchange with our understanding, imaginatively engage with beautiful objects.

8.4.2 The Positive Freedom of Imagination

In order to explore Kant's account of the positive freedom of imagination in free play, I want to take a look at what it means to imaginatively engage in the cognitive activities of apprehension, composition, and exhibition in a creative and conceptually rich way.[61]

Kant addresses the question of what a free version of apprehension looks like in the General Remark in a passage that I partially quoted above,

> if...the imagination is to be considered in its freedom, then it is in the first instance taken not as reproductive, as subjected to the laws of association, but as productive and self-active (as the authoress of voluntary forms of possible intuitions), and although in the apprehension of a given object of the senses it is of course bound to a determinate form of this object and to this extent has no free

---

[60] Here, I am reminded of Elisa Gabbert's remark about W.H. Auden's "Musée des Beaux Arts," "No matter how familiar a poem is, rereading it always gives me a sense of first encounter, as though I've gone back to sleep and re-entered the dream through a different door" (https://www.nytimes.com/interactive/2022/03/06/books/auden-musee-des-beaux-arts.html).

[61] In her account of the sort of imaginative reflection involved in free play, Breitenbach (2015; 2018; 2020; 2021) also emphasizes the importance of the cognitive creativity of imagination on Kant's view. While I tend to place more explicit emphasis on the role concepts play in this process, I am broadly sympathetic to Breitenbach's account, and I take it that my analysis of the sort of apprehension, composition, and exhibition involved in cognition and free play is another way of articulating the sort of "imaginative reflection" that Breitenbach argues is operative across both contexts.

play (as in invention [*Dichten*]), nevertheless it is still quite conceivable that the object can provide it with a form that contains precisely such a composition of the manifold as the imagination would design in harmony with the **lawfulness of the understanding** in general if it were left free by itself. (KU 5:241)

At the outset of this passage, Kant describes the positive freedom of imagination in terms of the freedom to act in a productive and self-active way. But he distinguishes the sort of productivity involved in free play from the productivity involved in "invention" (e.g. in "fantasies" when we "look at the changing shapes of a fire...or...a rippling brook") because the former is "bound to" the determinate form of an object in the way the latter is not (KU 5:243–4). So, on Kant's view, somehow in apprehension that is bound to the form of the object, our imagination has to find ways to be productive and self-active. Or, to borrow another one of his phrases, in our appreciation of beauty, it must somehow be possible for us to be imaginatively "at play in the observation" of the beautiful object (KU 5:230).

Kant goes on to gloss what is involved in this free mode of apprehension by claiming that the form we apprehend is a form our imagination "would" compose if it were free to design something in harmony with the understanding.[62] But what might this free, yet bound mode of apprehension amount to? In order to answer this question, we might appeal to the notion of attention.[63] According to this reading, on Kant's view, free play involves a free mode of attention in which we attend to the form of the object, but not in a way that is guided by any interest in conceptual recognition. For example, in ordinary experience, when I attend to a peony, my imagination is directed toward whatever generic features enable me to recognize it as a peony. But in free play I am free to imaginatively attend to the peony's rich detail and complexity in a way that outstrips what is needed for recognition.[64]

While this model of attention nicely captures one dimension of what our imagination is free to do in free play, it does not fully capture the creativity at stake. In

---

[62] On one reading of this claim, Kant here defends a counterfactual claim, according to which our imagination engages with the form it apprehends as one it would have produced were it free (I draw the "counterfactual" language from Williams 2022). Vogelmann (2018), for example, argues that our imagination does not proceed in a free way at all; its activities merely mirror what it would do if it were free. However, this counterfactual reading cannot do justice to the sense in which our imagination is not just "as if" free, productive, and self-active in free play, but is, in fact, all of these things in free play.

[63] While intimations of this line of thought can be found in Zuckert (2007, 285), Williams (2021; 2022) offers the most fully developed version of this view. See also Makkai's (2021, 164–5) account of the role our imagination plays in being "responsive" and "receptive" to the beautiful object.

[64] See, e.g., Williams's claim that free play is guided by the imagination's interest in the "manifoldness" of an object's form, i.e. in its "intricacy of detail, irregularity, and variety" (2022, 52). See also the idea that in free play, our imagination takes in more than is needed for cognition in Guyer's (2005) "metacognitive" reading of free play and Küplen's (2015, 67–70) reading of free play.

free play, our imaginative attention cannot just be free to take in different details of an object; there must be something playful and entertaining about how our imagination does this. Consider the following example. Suppose you and I are on a walk, and we come across a very large house. I spend time perceptually scanning the details of the house, while you engage in free play. What exactly distinguishes our acts of attention? We are both interested in and attuned to the rich detail and complexity of this house. We both notice, say, the bright red of the paint, the mixture of brick and wood, the trim around the windows, and so forth. But there is something fresh and entertaining about how you imaginatively engage that is different from the rather staid and boring way in which I imaginatively engage. In short, what you do that I do not is "play in the observation."

In Kant's framework, part of what accounts for the difference between how we observe objects in ordinary cognition and in free play is the fact that in the latter case, our imaginative apprehension is neither "restricted" by a "determinate concept," nor "subjected to the laws of association"; it is, instead, "productive" and "self-active" (KU 5:217, 240). For example, the way I imaginatively apprehend the house in the above example is guided by the concept <house> vis-à-vis a schema for a building with four walls and a roof, and habitual associative patterns, such as associating the frontside of a house with a backside. But in your apprehension, you do not default into these familiar imaginative routines. You, perhaps, apprehend the frontside of the house as an extension of the landscape or as a façade about to teeter over.

To be clear, though Kant indicates that the creative apprehension we enact in free play is not governed by a determinate concept or the laws of association in the way it is in ordinary cognition, this does not mean that it is devoid of activity that is conceptually laden or associative. I have already stressed the relevance of concepts to our imaginative activities in light of the open-ended conceptualization that free play involves, and we should expect that the way we creatively apprehend an object is shaped by, and feeds into, this process. But I have not yet stressed this point about association.[65] However, I take it that, on Kant's view, we can distinguish between Humean-style associations that arise in us as a matter of course and playful associations that arise in us as part of a reflective effort to imaginatively explore a beautiful object in a creative way. In some cases, these playful associations will be new to us, e.g. associating sunflowers and time weariness for the first time after reading Blake. In other cases, though, these playful associations will be familiar patterns made anew. For example, when I observe the peony, I might imaginatively tread a familiar pattern of association, for example, associating it with a pavilion or the start of something. But insofar as this familiar

---

[65] See Breitenbach (2018) for discussion of the role imaginative association plays in judgments of beauty in science. For a more recent discussion of the role imaginative association plays in our engagement with fiction, see Moran (1994).

association is one that I enter into as part of a reflective engagement with this beautiful object, it is not one that I default into in a Humean style. It is an association that I productively deploy in apprehension, in the creative spirit of "play in observation."

Though creative apprehension is thus one component of Kant's picture of the positive freedom of imagination in free play, he is also committed to it involving creative modes of composition and exhibition. Beginning with composition, on Kant's view, if our imagination is to creatively engage, then its activities cannot just issue in one way of composing a manifold of intuition$_s$. The latter is what happens in the context of ordinary cognition in which we proceed under the restriction of a determinate concept and are imaginatively bored. In creative composition, by contrast, free from the object-facing end of cognition, we are free to compose a manifold in different ways, seeing more as we strike on different perceptual images that organize what we apprehend in different imaginative lights. Indeed, it seems that this is part of why Kant claims that in free play, our imagination acts in a "productive" way, as the "authoress" of "voluntary forms" of intuition: though our imagination cannot "invent" the form of the object *ex nihilo*, the way it creatively composes and recomposes the form of that object can involve a touch of invention. For example, when I look at the peony, though the way I compose the manifold must be based on observing the flower's form, I am nevertheless free to imaginatively compose this manifold in a whole host of perceptual images. I might initially compose it into a perceptual image of a traditional peony structure, but as I continue to play in my observation of the peony's shape I compose different perceptual images, e.g. seeing it as a bomb atop a spindly stem or a cascade of pink. And one of the reasons I keep imaginatively finding something more to see is because I am able to creatively compose and recompose the form of the peony that I apprehend in fresh ways.

However, in addition to apprehension and composition, on Kant's view, free play needs to involve some form of creative exhibition. This said, Kant typically describes exhibition as something that involves our imagination exhibiting a determinate concept in an intuition$_i$, e.g. when our imagination exhibits the concept <circle> in the intuition$_i$ of a circle. But, as we have seen, in free play, Kant claims that our imagination engages in the "**exhibition** of a concept of the understanding (though which concept be undetermined)" and the "exhibition of an indeterminate concept of the understanding" (EE 20:220; KU 5:224). According to the interpretation I developed above, Kant has in mind imaginative exhibition that occurs as part of an open-ended process of conceptualization in which we exhibit either a range of concepts or a single concept in a wide-ranging way. In the former vein, for example, we might imaginatively treat the image of a drooping sunflower as an exhibition of the concepts <sunflower>, <time>, and <time weariness>. In the latter vein, we might imaginatively treat the peony as exhibiting the concept <peony> through fresh marks, such as <showy>, <lush>, or

278 IMAGINATION AND THE APPRECIATION OF BEAUTY

<pom-pom-shaped>. And through these activities, imaginative exhibition plays a crucial role in broadening our conceptual horizons in ways I discussed in §8.2.[66] Recall that, there, I argued that, for Kant, part of the cognitive value of free play turns on the ways in which it brings concepts to life for us through a "multitude" of marks and "much combination." By exhibiting a range of concepts or a single concept in fresh ways, our imagination contributes to this cognitively valuable process, animating our concepts in our engagement with the beautiful.

Once again, we must be cautious here. It cannot be the case that free play is simply a matter of exhibiting a range of concepts or exhibiting a single concept through a multitude of marks. Were this all that free play involved, then every time we exhibited multiple concepts or a concept through multiple marks, then we should find the object beautiful. But there is no reason to think that in Kant's framework just because I imaginatively represent a house, say, as exhibiting the concepts <red> and <A-frame>, I should judge it to be beautiful.

According to my interpretation, however, what distinguishes the sort of exhibition involved in free play from ordinary cognition turns on the creativity involved, which is made possible by the suspension of the object-facing end of cognition and the concomitant demand to "solve" the "problem" of the object in a determining judgment. The sort of exhibition of multiple concepts or multiple marks of a concept that happens in accordance with this end in ordinary cognition is the sort that Kant designates as imaginatively boring. To take a geometrical example, suppose I imaginatively represent a triangle circumscribed by a circle. Though I here exhibit the concepts <triangle> and <circle>, according to Kant, however exciting this might be from an intellectual point of view, it is boring from an imaginative perspective because this exhibition is prescribed by the understanding and is dictated by our effort to "solve" the "problem" that is the object in an act of determining judgment (see KU 5:241–3, 362–3). But I have urged that on Kant's view, when we are in a state of free play, our imagination is not oriented toward this object-facing end of cognition; it is oriented toward the subject-facing end of making concepts sensible in a way that internally promotes our cognitive processes. So oriented, our imagination is able to creatively engage with our understanding and its concepts in a reciprocal, dynamic, and open-ended way. The activity of making concepts sensible in this creative context thus does not have the function of determining how the object is in an act of cognition; it has the function of facilitating our grasp of concepts by leading us in new and surprising directions that expand our conceptual horizons. For example, exhibiting the concept <sunflower> through marks related to tracking the sun or time is not something that ordinary experience typically suggests to us, but the Blake poem invites us to expand this rather mundane concept in these fresh directions.

---

[66] I take this to be in line with Breitenbach's claim that free play can lead to "a more unified and comprehensive grasp of an idea, and a more unified conception of its relation to other concepts" (2020, 82).

THE CREATIVE DIMENSIONS OF IMAGINATION IN FREE PLAY   279

This line of thought, in turn, bears on an issue that I raised earlier: as with exhibition, on Kant's view, it cannot be the case that each time we engage in imaginative composition in relation to an object, we are in a state of free play and thus in a position to judge the object to be beautiful. The composition at stake in free play needs to involve a touch of creativity. And here I want to propose at least one sense in which this creativity of composition is bound up with creative exhibition: it is bound up with the creative exhibition of the mathematical categories. Recall that, on Kant's view, composition is ultimately guided by the mathematical categories vis-à-vis their transcendental schemata and to this extent involves the exhibition of the mathematical categories. But unlike in ordinary cognition, in free play, we play around with our imaginative composition and exhibition of the mathematical categories: we arrange the manifold we are given in different spatio-temporal forms, we organize it into different spatio-temporal wholes with different spatio-temporal parts, we dwell in different degrees of intensity, etc. And I take this to point toward a distinctively creative way in which the mathematical categories figure in free play: in free play, we find ourselves in a *Spielraum* in relation to the mathematical categories, where engagement with a single given object can open us up to playing around with just how new and surprising <quantity> and <quality> can be. And though mathematics can also involve engaging with just how interesting <quantity> and <quality> can be, on Kant's view, insofar as this mathematical engagement is governed by the object-facing end of cognition, it ultimately lacks the freedom of free play.[67] But released from this end in free play, Kant thinks we are free to pursue <quantity> and <quality> in directions that are at once imaginatively entertaining and cognitively illuminating.

As I see it, this point about creative composition and exhibition in relation to the mathematical categories can be extended to other concepts as well. Whether it be pure or empirical concepts at issue, for Kant, what distinguishes the activities of composition and exhibition involved in free play from those involved in ordinary cognition is the creative way in which we imaginatively carry them out. Free from the object-facing end of cognition, Kant thinks we are free to imaginatively expand our conceptual horizons and alight upon new and surprising conceptual connections that have cognitive value for us.

Drawing these threads together, on my interpretation, Kant's analysis of the positive freedom of free play turns not just on the idea that it involves a creative mode of apprehension, but also on the idea that it involves creative modes of composition and exhibition in which we, released from the constraint of the

---

[67] As I noted above, Breitenbach (2015) argues that there is nevertheless a sense in which mathematics can involve judgments of the beautiful on Kant's view. She also argues that science can involve judgments of the beautiful (see 2018; 2020; see also Cohen 2018). I am sympathetic to the idea that Kant can accommodate judgments of the beautiful in both mathematics and science on certain occasions, and I take it that this requires engaging with mathematics and science in a way that involves suspending the object-facing end of cognition in order to freely play (albeit in a way that might have a downstream effect in mathematical or scientific inquiry) (see Breitenbach 2020, 86).

280 IMAGINATION AND THE APPRECIATION OF BEAUTY

object-facing end of cognition, find ways of imaginatively engaging with a beautiful object that are at once entertaining and conceptually enriching. And in this heightened creative state, our imagination functions cognitively well by expanding our conceptual horizons in unprecedented directions.

8.5 Conclusion

In this chapter my aim has been to elucidate Kant's account of the contribution our imagination makes in our aesthetic appreciation of the beautiful and the free play he takes to be characteristic of such appreciation. I began by advancing a multicognitive interpretation of the free play of our imagination and understanding as an activity that is cognitive, creative, and conceptually rich. In contrast with precognitive readings of free play as something that proceeds without concepts, I argued that free play, for Kant, is an open-ended activity in which the imaginative perspectives we adopt on a beautiful object spur our conceptual perspectives on it, and vice versa, leading us in new, surprising, and cognitively valuable directions. And I hope to have shown that for all its complications, Kant's theory of free play can illuminate ways in which we actually engage with beauty, whether it be the artistic beauty of something like "Ah! Sun-Flower" or the natural beauty of a pink peony.

Focusing on the imaginative component of free play, I then analyzed the cognitive aspects of what Kant takes our imagination to contribute to free play in terms of us engaging in the activities of apprehension, composition, and exhibition familiar from a perceptual context. But I argued that in the context of free play, free from the object-facing end of cognition, these cognitive activities manifest in a distinctively creative fashion that ultimately involves us making concepts sensible in a way that brings them to life in a rich and fresh manner.

In attributing this view to Kant, I have continued to develop my conceptualist reading of his account of the generation of intuitions$_i$ depending on concepts. Having made my case for this conceptualism as it pertains to the intuitions$_i$ involved in experience in Part II, I here argued that it is also applicable to his analysis of intuitions$_i$ involved in our appreciation of beauty. For the rest of the book, I shall continue to explore Kant's account of how the generation of intuitions$_i$ in the aesthetic and practical context depends on concepts: however, this marks the last occasion on which I shall directly address how this pertains to the debate over his conceptualism.

In addition to clarifying Kant's account of the aesthetic use of our imagination in the appreciation of beauty, I hope this discussion has shed more light on the unity of Kant's theory of imagination. For though our imaginative activities in free play take on a creative character, I argued that these activities are still cognitive in character. What is more, I made the case that in free play, we find our imagination enabling us to see more and performing the cognitive function it performs in ordinary experience: making concepts sensible. But this account of free play points toward a certain flexibility that Kant takes to be built into our imagination, such that it can operate as a cognitive capacity, help us see more, and fulfill its cognitive function not just when it is constrained by the understanding and the object-facing end of cognition in the theoretical context, but also when it, in accordance with the subject-facing end of cognition, operates in harmony with the understanding as part of our creative and free engagement with the beautiful. And it is this latter theme, of the flexibility built into the cognitive capacity that is our imagination, that I shall continue to pursue in my discussion of artistic production and the sublime in the next two chapters.

Seeing More: Kant's Theory of Imagination. Samantha Matherne, Oxford University Press.
© Samantha Matherne 2024. DOI: 10.1093/9780191999291.003.0009

9

Artistic Imagination

> if we add to a concept a representation of the imagination...,
> which aesthetically enlarges the concept itself,
> then in this case the imagination is creative
>
> —KU 5:315

9.1 Introduction

As Kant's account of our aesthetic use of imagination in the third *Critique* unfolds, he eventually shifts his focus away from the role it plays in the appreciation of beauty to the role it plays in the creation of beauty. The latter discussion turns on an analysis of "genius" (*Genie*) and the production of "beautiful" or "fine" art (*schöne Kunst*) (KU §§43–54). Foundational to Kant's analysis of the artistic process is a claim about imaginative creativity: "The imagination (as a productive cognitive faculty) is, namely, very powerful in creating, as it were, another nature, out of the material which the real one gives it" (KU 5:314).[1] And in this creativity, as I have cited before, Kant insists that the artist displays a kind of imaginative freedom that we do not have in ordinary cognition: "in the use of the imagination for cognition, the imagination is under the constraint of the understanding and is subject to the limitation of being adequate to its concept; in an aesthetic respect, however, the imagination is free" (KU 5:316).

However, as was the case with aesthetic appreciation, in analyzing artistic production Kant argues that for all their creativity, artists do not imaginatively proceed in a wholly unfettered way. Instead of "lawless freedom," he maintains that the creation of artistic beauty involves "the suitability of the imagination in its freedom to the lawfulness of the understanding" (KU 5:319). Kant thus situates his account of the imaginative contribution to artistic production in a

---

[1] For other interpretations of Kant's theory of genius that explicitly emphasize creativity, see Crawford (1982; who explores the analogies between the creativity involved in genius and the creativity involved in mathematical construction in contrast with philosophy); Sassen (2003); Kneller (2007, chap. 7; who explores the creativity involved in genius "creating another nature" and how this bears on Kant's theory of bringing about moral change in the world and his connection to the Romantics); Chaouli (2017, pt. II; who explores the creativity involved in "making a new kind of sense" (116)); Walden (in progress; who explores the implications of the creativity involved in genius for a theory of practical agency). For recent discussions of creativity that take their cue from Kant's theory of genius, see Stokes (2014) and Gaut (2014).

INTRODUCTION 283

broader account of the "union" or "relation" between the artist's "cognitive powers" of "imagination and understanding" involved in this creative process (KU 5:316–17). In stressing the cognitive dimension of artistic production, Kant's theory of genius thus parts ways with accounts of genius as a kind of "madness" or "divine inspiration."[2] He, instead, defends a view according to which the creativity of genius occurs in a cognitive framework.[3]

As was also the case in his account of aesthetic appreciation, at least on my reading, Kant defends a view of artistic production as conceptually rich. In this vein he claims not only that artists are guided by some sort of concept of the "end" of their work of art, but also that they deploy their imagination in a "creative" way that "aesthetically enlarges the concept itself" (KU 5:317, 315). For Kant, then, part of the cognitive creativity of an artist turns on their ability to expand our conceptual horizons in some way.

My aim in this chapter is to elucidate Kant's picture of the cognitive, creative, conceptually rich use of imagination involved in the production of art. I argue that he identifies a distinctive form of imaginative exhibition at the heart of artistic creativity: exhibition through so-called "aesthetic ideas." For Kant, an aesthetic idea involves an "intuition of imagination" that an artist generates by means of which they exhibit concepts in rich and original ways in works of art (KU 5:343). And I hope to show that attending to the theme of exhibition in Kant's account of artistic production sheds light not only on this process, but also on his commitment to the aesthetic exercise of our imagination having a distinctive kind of cognitive value for us: the value of bringing our concepts to life in new and surprising ways.

To clarify Kant's account of artistic imagination, I begin in §9.2 with a brief overview of the model of artistic production that Kant offers in his theory of genius. In §9.3, I then explore his account of the cognitive dimensions of artistic production. I argue that Kant identifies the exhibition of concepts through aesthetic ideas as the type of cognitive activity imagination is responsible for in artistic production. In §9.4, I address his account of how these cognitive activities are carried out in a free and creative way in the artistic process. As in my discussion of aesthetic appreciation, I divide this discussion between an account of the negative

---

[2] See, e.g., Socrates's claim in *Ion* that, "a poet is a delicate thing, winged and sacred, and unable to create until he becomes inspired and frenzied, his mind no longer in him" (Plato 2008, 534b). Or from Shakespeare, see Theseus's lines in *A Midsummer Night's Dream*, "The lunatic, the lover, and the poet / Are of imagination all compact.../ The poet's eye, in a fine frenzy rolling, / Doth glance from heaven to earth, from earth to heaven; / And as imagination bodies forth / The forms of things unknown, the poet's pen / Turns them to shapes, and gives to airy nothing / A local habitation and a name" (2013, 124). See Robinson (2011, chap. 5) for a discussion of the history of the connection between genius and madness.

[3] Although I shall not discuss it here, in addition to the constraints of this cognitive framework, Kant argues that in order to produce beautiful art, genius must be constrained by taste (see KU 5:312–13).

284 ARTISTIC IMAGINATION

freedom of imagination, i.e. what it is "free from" (§9.4.1), and the positive freedom of imagination, i.e. what imagination is free to do in artistic production (§9.4.2). I endeavor to show that, for Kant, this freedom consists not in artists imaginatively swinging free from concepts, but rather in their finding creative ways to exhibit concepts And I claim that this artistic freedom invites a creative seeing more in the audience as we engage with works of art in ways that advance our comprehension of concepts in open-ended directions.

9.2 Kant on Artistic Production

Section 43 of the third *Critique* marks a transition in the text away from questions about aesthetic appreciation and toward questions about genius and the production of beautiful art. Kant opens this discussion with an account of what beautiful art amounts to (§§43–5), before turning to the question of how artists produce it (§§46–50), and how we should think of, and rank, the various arts, such as poetry, music, painting, and gardens (§§51–3).

In his account of what beautiful art amounts to, Kant begins with a discussion of what art is in contrast with nature, on the one hand, and science, on the other. In contrast with nature, he argues that art involves "production through freedom, i.e., through a capacity for choice that grounds its actions in reason" (KU 5:303).[4] Kant cashes out the relevant "choice" in terms of an artist "conceiving of an end" that they endeavor to bring about through their activities (more on this choice in §9.3) (KU 5:303). And he claims that although we sometimes refer to a natural product, such as a honeycomb, as a "a work of art," insofar as it is a "product...of instinct" rather than of rational choice, it cannot count as "art" *per* Kant's definition (KU 5:303).

Meanwhile, in contrast with science Kant asserts the following: "*Art* as a skill [*Geschicklichkeit*] of human beings is also distinguished from science [*Wissenschaft*] (to be able from to know [*Können vom Wissen*]), as a practical faculty from a theoretical one, as technique [*Technik*] from theory" (KU 5:303). Whereas science requires theoretical knowledge (*Wissen*), Kant claims that art requires practical abilities which I have glossed as "know-how" (see Chapters 4 and 5). To illustrate, Kant uses the example of Pieter Camper, author of the *Treatise on the Best Form of Shoes*, who could "describe quite precisely how the best shoe must be made, but he certainly was not able to make one" (KU 5:304). On Kant's analysis, although Camper possesses theoretical knowledge about shoes, he lacks the know-how, hence the art, required to produce them. So, *qua* art, Kant conceives of beautiful

---

[4] Though Kant says that art in this sense involves "production through freedom," I do not take this to mean that it must involve autonomous action in the moral sense. As long as the artist is engaging in the activity as the result of "rational consideration," then they are producing through freedom in the sense relevant here (KU 5:303).

art as something that not only is guided by the rational adoption of an end, but also evinces know-how.[5]

However, Kant also argues that, *qua* beautiful, beautiful art is distinct from other forms of art, particularly from "handicraft" (*Handwerke*) (KU 5:304). In handicraft, Kant claims the artist regards their activity as "labour" and is motivated by the remuneration they will receive, whereas with beautiful art, the artist regards their activity as "free" and is motivated by the "play" it involves:

> [Free *art*] is regarded as if it could turn out purposively (be successful) only as play, i.e., an occupation that is agreeable in itself; [handicraft] is regarded as labour [*Arbeit*], i.e., an occupation that is disagreeable (burdensome) in itself and is attractive only because of its effect (e.g., the remuneration). (KU 5:304)

Beyond this sort of motivational discrepancy, Kant highlights several other features of the genius involved in the production of beautiful art that is not required for the production of handicraft. In the first place, he describes genius as an "inborn predisposition of the mind" (KU 5:307). It is thus a "natural endowment" or "natural gift" that the artist finds themselves in the possession of, rather than something they are taught (KU 5:307, 318).

Kant furthermore claims that genius involves a kind of originality: "Genius...is a talent for producing that for which no determinate rule can be given..., consequently...originality must be its primary characteristic" (KU 5:307). On this issue, he contrasts genius with science: whereas science proceeds on the basis of "rules that...come first and determine the procedure in it," artistic production proceeds on the basis of the artist's talent, which takes them in unprecedented directions (KU 5:317).

Yet for all its originality, Kant also claims that genius must involve an ability to produce something that "can be communicated to others" (KU 5:317). On this issue, he distinguishes the art of genius from "original nonsense [*Unsinn*]," and insists that a work of art that is original, but incomprehensible to others, falls in the latter camp (KU 5:305).[6] He, in turn, highlights different dimensions of the communicability of genius. In one vein, he stresses the importance of an artist being able to "express" themselves in a way that the audience can understand (KU 5:317). In another vein, he underscores the way in which an artist should be "exemplary" for other artists, by providing them with an example to "emulate" (see KU 5:308, 318).[7] According to Kant, this emulation is not to be confused with "imitation": whereas imitation involves aping what another artist has done,

---

[5] For discussion of the role this notion of art plays in Kant's account of genius and schematism, see Matherne (2014a).

[6] See Walden (n.d.) for a discussion of the challenge of balancing creativity and intelligibility in genius, which manifests not just in art, but also in practical agency.

[7] See Gammon (1997) for discussion of what this "exemplary originality" involves.

286 ARTISTIC IMAGINATION

emulation involves an artist being "awakened to the feeling of his own originality" by another artist (KU 5:318).

Finally, stressing the cognitive dimensions of genius, Kant says that, "The mental powers..., whose union (in a certain relation) constitute **genius**, are imagination and understanding" (KU 5:316). For Kant, then, genius is underwritten by a certain cognitive talent of the artist. More specifically, he claims that genius involves the artist's talent for a "free use" of these "cognitive faculties" (KU 5:318). This emphasis on the cognitive creativity of genius echoes his earlier account of the cognitive creativity of free play involved in aesthetic appreciation. And as was the case in my analysis of free play in Chapter 8, in order to explicate what imagination contributes to genius on Kant's view, I focus on his account of how an artist exercises their imagination in ways that are both cognitive and creative.

9.3 The Cognitive Dimension of Artistic Imagination

Let's return to his claim that in genius, "The imagination (as a productive cognitive faculty) is, namely, very powerful in creating, as it were, another nature, out of the material which the real one gives it" (KU 5:240, 314). As we have just seen, Kant insists that this imaginative "creating" "another nature" happens in a dynamic interplay with an artist's understanding. And what I shall now argue is that Kant ultimately identifies exhibition as the cognitive activity through which the artist imaginatively proceeds that is at once productive and in harmony with their understanding.

First, however, we need to take a closer look at exactly what role Kant attributes to the artist's understanding in the production process. As I noted above, according to Kant, in order for something to count as art, it must be produced on the basis of some rational choice: "only production through freedom, i.e., through a capacity for choice that grounds its actions in reason, should be called art" (KU 5:303). Kant, more specifically, glosses this choice in terms of the artist, through their understanding, setting "a determinate intention" to "express" a "determinate concept" in their work of art (KU 5:306, 317).[8] I take this "determinate concept" to amount to a theme or subject matter in a work of art. And although some commentators attribute to Kant the view that beautiful art can only express moral or rational ideas,[9] his examples also include works of art that express ordinary

---

[8] I thus disagree with Chaouli's reading of the relevant intention simply in terms of "bringing forth *this* artwork" (2017, 147). According to Chaouli, if specific concepts are involved in the artist's intention, then this would undermine the creativity of their process on Kant's view (see Chaouli 2017, 147, 151, 167). However, as I argue below, for Kant, there is a creative way in which the artist operates vis-à-vis specific concepts: creatively exhibiting them through imagination.

[9] See, e.g., Guyer (1977, 63; 1993, 39); Crawford (1982, 177); Allison (2001, 258, 282–3); Rueger and Evren (2005); Chignell (2007b, 420n); Rogerson (2008, 28); Friedlander (2015, 84); Reiter and Geiger (2018); Geiger (2021); Reiter (2021).

THE COGNITIVE DIMENSION OF ARTISTIC IMAGINATION   287

empirical concepts, such as "death, envy..., all sorts of vices, as well as love, fame, etc." (KU 5:314). Kant thus endorses a more inclusive view of what sort of concepts an artist can express, which range from the mundane to the moral, the routine to the rational.[10] And, *per* Kant, in the production process, the task of the artist's understanding is to orient them toward a "determinate concept" to express. This said, we should be careful in how demanding we take this choice to be. The language of determinacy may make it seem as if Kant expects artists to have a fully worked-out idea of what they want to present through their art, which remains unwavering over the course of production. But, as I read Kant, all this requirement amounts to is that the artist, through their understanding, needs to select some theme or subject matter, whether inchoate or fully developed, to orient their creation process, and which they may revise or even discard in favor of another concept along the way.[11]

So, when Kant claims that the artist's imagination, as a "productive cognitive capacity," operates in union with their understanding, this means that it must operate in union with the determinate concept the artist wants to express in their work of art. And as we would expect from imagination as the faculty of exhibition, Kant claims that in this dynamic "the imagination...is...purposive for the exhibition of the given concept" (KU 5:317; transl. modified). A bit more expansively, he says, "**genius**...presupposes a determinate concept of the product, as an end, hence understanding, but also...the intuition, for the exhibition of this concept, hence a relation of the imagination to the understanding" (KU 5:317; transl. modified). According to Kant, then, having oriented toward a concept to express in a work of art, the artist's imaginative task is to generate an intuition of imagination (intuition$_i$) that exhibits that concept in a way that "makes" that concept "sensible" (KU 5:314).

To illustrate, let's consider Ralph Ellison's *Invisible Man*. As the title and opening lines, "I am an invisible man," suggest, one of the concepts Ellison explores in this novel is <invisibility> (1995, 3). More specifically, in his introductory remarks, Ellison contrasts the concept of invisibility that is of interest to him with the "pseudoscientific sociological concept which held that most Afro-American difficulties sprang from our 'high visibility'" (1995, xv). "Despite the bland assertions of sociologists," Ellison says, "high visibility" actually rendered one

---

[10] I defend this "inclusive" interpretation of aesthetic ideas in Matherne (2013).

[11] Think, for example, of Ralph Ellison's description of how *Invisible Man* emerged from what he originally planned as a novel about a Black pilot in a Nazi prisoner-of-war camp: "while I had conceived of [the story] in terms of a black-white, majority-minority conflict, with white officers refusing to recognize the humanity of a Negro who saw mastering the highly technical skills of a pilot as a dignified way of serving his country while improving his economic status, I came to realize that my pilot was also experiencing difficulty in seeing *himself*...A man of two worlds, my pilot felt himself misperceived in both and thus was at ease in neither. In brief, the story depicted his conscious struggle for self-definition and for an invulnerable support for his individual dignity. I by no means was aware of his relationship to the invisible man, but clearly he possessed some of the symptoms" (1995, xiii–xiv).

un-visible" (1995, xv). And it is this concept of invisibility that he identifies as the one that oriented him in writing *Invisible Man*.

In these introductory remarks, Ellison also describes the process through which the concept of invisibility took shape in the narrator of the novel. At first, Ellison says, he came to "a taunting, disembodied voice," "the voice of invisibility" for the narrator (1995, xiv). But eventually, "how crazy-logical that I should finally locate its owner living—and oh, so garrulously—in an abandoned cellar" (1995, xviii). From a Kantian point of view, the process Ellison here describes is an imaginative one in which he alighted on the narrator, with this voice and this location, as a way of exhibiting the concept of invisibility, rendering it, as it were, visible in *Invisible Man*.

In analyzing the cognitive dimensions of artistic imagination, Kant thus highlights the aspects of the production process that involve an artist figuring out how to imaginatively exhibit the concept they have oriented toward through their understanding. Insofar as this involves the generation of an intuition$_i$ that exhibits a concept *in concreto*, this imaginative activity is of a piece with imaginative activity in other contexts, such as perception, in which we engage in exhibition. However, central to Kant's picture of artistic production is the claim that there is something free and creative in how an artist imaginatively exhibits a concept in a work of art: "if we add to a concept a representation of the imagination that belongs to its exhibition..., which aesthetically enlarges the concept itself in an unbounded way, then in this case the imagination is creative" (KU 5:315; transl. modified). In a similar vein, he says (in a passage I have partially quoted before):

> in the use of the imagination for cognition, the imagination is under the constraint of the understanding and is subject to the limitation of being adequate to its concept; in an aesthetic respect, however, the imagination is free to provide, beyond that concord [*Einstimmung*] with the concept, unsought extensive undeveloped material for the understanding, of which the latter took no regard in its concept. (KU 5:316–17)

Here, Kant contrasts the sort of conceptual constraint our imagination is subject to in ordinary cognition with the sort of freedom it has in artistic production to exhibit the concept in "aesthetically enlarging" ways. And as I shall now argue, in order to capture what is free in this process, Kant introduces the notion of an "aesthetic idea" as the unique kind of intuition$_i$ that an artist imaginatively generates to exhibit concepts in this expansive way.

9.4 The Creative Dimension of Artistic Imagination

As was the case in my discussion of free play in Chapter 8, I shall frame Kant's account of the sort of imaginative creativity involved in artistic production in terms of cognitive activities that are new, surprising, and cognitively valuable.[12] Here, however, I take the newness, surprise, and cognitive value to turn on the creative ways in which an artist imaginatively exhibits a concept through aesthetic ideas in a work of art. And as was the case in Chapter 8, in order to explore what this creativity amounts to, I shall proceed by considering the negative and positive freedom of imagination it requires, in turn.

9.4.1 The Negative Freedom of Artistic Imagination

In explicating what sort of constraints an artist is imaginatively free from in generating aesthetic ideas, Kant highlights two kinds of constraints: intellectual and imaginative constraints.

Beginning with freedom from intellectual constraints, as we saw above, Kant insists that in generating an aesthetic idea to exhibit the relevant concept, the artist's imagination is not "under the constraint of the understanding and...subject to the limitation of being adequate to its concept" (KU 5:316–17). More specifically, he claims that the artist is not under the constraint of having to provide a "logical exhibition" of a concept, where this amounts to an exhibition of the "**logical attributes**" that are analytically contained in the concept (KU 5:315; transl. modified). In Part II, I described these logical attributes in terms of the logical content of a concept, and, as we saw, Kant thinks that the sort of schematizing activities that our imagination carries out in ordinary cognition are constrained by this logical content, as what we "directly" exhibit in a schematic intuition$_i$ (see KU §59; WF 20:279). But in artistic production, Kant claims that the artist's imaginative exhibition of a concept is not dictated by its logical content in this way. To return to the *Invisible Man* example, the way Ellison imaginatively exhibits the concept <invisibility> is not confined to directly exhibiting the logical attributes contained in this concept, such as <being imperceptible to vision>.

Nevertheless, as we have seen, Kant insists that what the artist imaginatively does needs to be "purposive for the exhibition of the given concept" (KU 5:317; transl. modified). Hence Kant's claim that the artist's exhibition must, in some sense, remain "within the limits of a given concept" (KU 5:326). For Kant, then, the imagination's freedom from intellectual constraints in artistic production amounts not to freedom from concepts, but freedom from a certain kind of conceptual constraint: how the artist imaginatively exhibits a concept is not dictated by the logical content of that concept.

---

[12] See Boden's (2004, 1) definition of creativity along these lines. In their recent accounts of creativity that draw on Kant's theory of genius, Stokes (2014) and Gaut (2014) also draw on Boden's definition. However, Hills and Bird (2018; 2019) have recently argued that Kant's view of genius is consistent with their own view of creativity as something that requires originality and imagination, but that does not require value.

290 ARTISTIC IMAGINATION

In addition to this freedom from intellectual constraint, Kant argues that in creating beautiful art, the artist's imagination is free from a certain kind of imaginative constraint: "freedom from the law of association" (KU 5:314). As we have seen, on Kant's view, the "law of association" amounts to the law of associating representations together that "have often followed or accompanied one another" through the reproductive imagination (A100). And Kant insists that, "as a productive cognitive faculty," the artist's imagination does not simply default into habitual patterns of association familiar from "mundane" experience (KU 5:314). What this means for exhibition is that in alighting on how to imaginatively exhibit a concept, the artist is not governed by habits of association that shape the exhibition of that concept in ordinary experience. For example, consider the opening lines of *Invisible Man*,

> I am an invisible man. No, I am not a spook like those who haunted Edgar Allan Poe; nor am I one of your Hollywood-movie ectoplasms. I am a man of substance, of flesh and bone, fiber and liquids—and I might even be said to possess a mind. I am invisible, understand, simply because people refuse to see me.
>
> (1995, 3)

By presenting the invisible narrator as a "man of substance," Ellison resists the familiar association of invisibility with the sort of unsubstantial figures like ghosts and specters, which cannot be seen, in order to investigate the invisibility that results from a "refusal" to see, from "a peculiar disposition of the eyes" that refuses recognition (1995, 3). And, from a Kantian perspective, this evinces the fact that in imaginatively exhibiting the concept of invisibility, Ellison relies not on his reproductive imagination and staid patterns of association, but rather on his productive imagination and its power to create something fresh. To be clear, this is not to deny that artists can deploy familiar associations in exhibiting concepts.[13] However, from Kant's perspective, in order for the incorporation of such associations to be a part of the artistic process, they need to be ones the artist actively comes to through a productive imaginative effort, rather than through a reproductive routine.

For Kant, then, part of what enables an artist to exhibit a concept in a work of art in a creative way is the fact that this exhibition is not governed by the sort of conceptual and associative constraints that are operative in ordinary cognition. Though in coming up with how to imaginatively exhibit a concept, the artist is free to draw on conceptual and associative patterns, *per* Kant, this cannot be carried out under the logical dictates of the understanding or the associative dictates of the reproductive imagination; it must proceed in a way that is productive and free.

---

[13] See Chapter 8 for an analogue discussion about association in aesthetic appreciation.

THE CREATIVE DIMENSION OF ARTISTIC IMAGINATION   291

9.4.2 The Positive Freedom of Artistic Imagination

At the center of Kant's account of what the artist is imaginatively free to do in producing a work of art is the claim that they generate aesthetic ideas through which they exhibit concepts in intuitions$_i$ in creative ways. As I intimated above, I take this creativity to amount to the artist exhibiting concepts in ways that are new, surprising, and cognitively valuable. And, as we shall see, Kant thinks that aesthetic ideas, in fact, involve a double kind of creativity: creativity in how the artist generates them and creativity in how the audience receives them.

Turning first to the artist, recall Kant's gloss of artistic creativity in terms of the artist "add[ing] to a concept a representation of imagination that belongs to its exhibition..., which aesthetically enlarges the concepts itself in an unbounded way" (KU 5:315; transl. modified). The relevant "representation" or "intuition of imagination" is what Kant identifies as an aesthetic idea (KU 5:343). So, what do these aesthetic ideas involve and what makes the generation of them creative on Kant's view?

As we just saw, for Kant, in producing a work of art, the artist's imaginative activities are not dictated by the sort of rote conceptual or associative patterns that govern us in exhibiting concepts in mundane experience. Free from these constraints, Kant claims that the artist is free to find new and surprising modes of exhibition. More specifically, he says that instead of exhibiting a concept through its "logical" attributes, an artist is free to exhibit a concept through "aesthetic" attributes (KU 5:315). According to Kant, aesthetic attributes are "supplementary representations of the imagination" that "express only the implications connected with [a concept] and its affinity with other [concepts]" (KU 5:315). Though these aesthetic attributes must be purposive for exhibiting a concept, hence they must, in some sense, remain "within the limits of a given concept," in coming up with them, Kant thinks the artist can explore new and surprising implications of, or connections between, concepts (KU 5:326). To cite another example from *Invisible Man*, a cellar, while not a logical attribute of the concept <invisibility>, nevertheless vividly captures an implication of this concept, a version of invisibility in which someone is "neither dead nor in a state of suspended animation," but "in a state of hibernation" (Ellison 1995, 6). Or to cite one of Kant's examples that I mentioned in Chapter 8, a poet exhibits the implications of the concept <spring> through a "multitude" and "combination" of marks related to "the budding flowers, the new green of the forests, the cavorting herds, the renewed rays of the sun, the lovely, charming air[,] the revival of the whole of nature" (BL 24:126).

This said, there is some question as to exactly what sort of imaginative representations Kant thinks an artist creatively includes in an aesthetic idea. The sort of representations Kant most explicitly emphasizes are ones that involve some sort

292 ARTISTIC IMAGINATION

of "indirect" exhibition through symbolism and metaphor (KU 5:352).[14] A peacock, he claims, is an aesthetic attribute of the concept "the splendid queen of heaven," i.e. Juno, because the peacock indirectly represents Juno's royalty, power, watchful eye, vanity, etc. (KU 5:315). Or consider these lines from Frederick the Great's poem: "everything agreeable in a beautiful summer day, drawn to a close, which a bright evening calls to mind" (KU 5:315–16).[15] According to Kant, this image of a summer day drawing to a close is an aesthetic attribute that indirectly captures the concept of a "cosmopolitan disposition even at the end of life" (KU 5:316).

However, it is not clear that Kant is committed to the position that the artist's creativity is restricted to exhibiting concepts through indirect means in aesthetic ideas. Kant's poet of spring, after all, uses representations that have a more straightforward relation to <spring>: budding flowers and cavorting herds. But even in this case, Kant intimates that there is something that is creative in how the poet deploys these more familiar representations of spring: the poet gathers together a "multitude" or "combination" of marks that illustrate <spring> in a particularly "lively" way (BL 24:126). And this claim, I think, points to another dimension of Kant's account of the creativity involved in generating an aesthetic idea: artists exhibit concepts with a certain kind of completeness that outstrips how we ordinarily exhibit them.

In this vein, Kant says that in producing an aesthetic idea an artist makes a concept sensible "beyond the limits of experience, with a completeness that goes beyond anything of which there is an example in nature" (KU 5:314). As I read this claim, Kant is not saying that an aesthetic idea, in fact, exhibits a concept with maximal completeness: no finite work of art could exhaustively exhibit a concept, nor could any concept be exhaustively exhibited.[16] I also do not read him as

---

[14] There is debate over whether Kant conceives of this indirect mode of representation as a symbolic or metaphorical process. Nuyen (1989) and Rueger and Evren (2005), for example, argue that aesthetic ideas involve symbolization. However, Kant has a rather strict definition of what is involved in symbolism: it involves exhibiting a concept indirectly "by means of an analogy" (KU 5:352). Kant, more specifically, defines analogies as something that have a four-part comparative structure, a : b :: c : d (see Matherne 2021b). Given this stricture on symbolic exhibition, other commentators like Pillow (2000, 80–6; 2001), have argued that the sort of indirect exhibition involved in aesthetic ideas is better understood in terms of more open-ended metaphors than symbols. But it seems to me that Kant's examples of aesthetic ideas in §49 can be read either way. For example, Frederick the Great's image of a setting sun as an aesthetic idea for the concept of a "cosmopolitan disposition even at the end of life" could be read as an open-ended metaphor or as a symbol, the structure of which would be something like a cosmopolitan disposition : the end of life :: the sun : the end of a day (KU 5:316). I thus take it to be a live possibility that aesthetic attributes can exhibit concepts in both symbolic and metaphorical ways on Kant's view. I return to these issues in Chapter 10.

[15] The lines Kant quotes are, "Let us depart from life without grumbling and without regretting anything, leaving the world behind us replete with good deeds. Thus does the sun, after it has completed its daily course, still spread a gentle light across the heavens; and the last rays that it sends forth into the sky are its last sighs for the well-being of the world" (KU 5:315–16). Frederick the Great was a prolific poet; for a sample, see Epistles XVIII and XX in *Frederick the Great's Philosophical Writings* (2020). For discussion of the Epicurean flavor of his poetry, see Rosen (2022, 276–8).

[16] Recall, for example, Kant's claim that synthetically adding marks to a concept is something that "can never be completed" (JL 9:59).

THE CREATIVE DIMENSION OF ARTISTIC IMAGINATION   293

saying that works of art only exhibit ideas of reason: as I indicated earlier, Kant endorses a more inclusive view, according to which works of art can exhibit empirical concepts (e.g. "love," "fame," "death"), as well as ideas (e.g. "hell," "a cosmopolitan disposition") (KU 5:314, 316).[17] Instead, as I understand his claim, aesthetic ideas involve "completeness" because they involve an artist imaginatively exhibiting a concept in a more holistic way than the more partial way we exhibit concepts in ordinary experience.[18] In ordinary experience, our imaginative exhibition proceeds in a more schematic way: whether we are generating a schema for a concept or generating a perceptual image, we selectively focus on some common spatio-temporal features that characterize objects of a certain kind (see Chapter 5). By contrast, with an aesthetic idea, the artist holistically weaves together "supplementary representations of imagination" that capture the implications of that concept and its relation to other concepts in a more complete way.

Notice that in generating this holistic imaginative representation, artists do not just have to avail themselves of indirect means: though symbolic and metaphorical representations can be used to exhibit a concept in this more complete way, an apt curation of representations that have a more direct relation to the concept can also be used to this end. And, as I read Kant, this fashioning of an imaginative whole, which captures a concept in a more replete way, is also part of artistic creativity.

To elaborate, I want to return to Kant's claim that, "The imagination (as a productive cognitive faculty) is, namely, very powerful in creating, as it were, another nature, out of the material the real one gives it. We entertain ourselves with it when experience seems too mundane to us; we transform the latter" (KU 5:314). In this spirit, we might think of an aesthetic idea as a kind of imaginative world that the artist creates by drawing on the material the real world provides, in order to exhibit concepts in a more holistic way than we do in mundane experience. Consider, for example, the imaginative world that Ellison says he needed to develop to explore the concept of invisibility:

> I would have to provide [the narrator] with something of a worldview, give him a consciousness in which serious philosophical questions could be raised, provide him with a range of diction that could play upon the richness of our shared vernacular speech and construct a plot that would bring him in contact with a variety of American types as they operated on various levels of society. Most of all, I would have to approach racial stereotypes as a given fact of the social

---

[17] Some commentators interpret this claim in terms of a commitment to aesthetic ideas being representations of rational ideas (see, e.g., Friedlander 2015, 84; Geiger 2021). For more on my inclusive interpretation of aesthetic ideas, see Matherne 2013.

[18] In his lectures, Kant describes an imaginative activity he describes in terms of "Ausbildung" ("cultivation"), which involves completing a representation as a whole, e.g. endeavoring to bring a story "to an end" (ML1 28:237; see also AF 25:512, AP 25:303–4).

process and proceed, while gambling with the reader's capacity for fictional truth, to reveal the human complexity which stereotypes are intended to conceal.

(1995, xxii)

In the novel, we thus find a complete imaginative world, populated by a narrator with this worldview, consciousness, and diction, and a plot that takes the narrator through various levels of American society (e.g. an all-Black college, a paint factory, a political organization called "the Brotherhood," etc.) and attendant patterns of racism. And though in building this world, Ellison sometimes draws on symbols or metaphors (e.g. "Like the bodiless heads you see sometimes in circus shows, it is as though I have been surrounded by mirrors of hard, distorting glass"), he also draws on more direct ways of exhibiting <invisibility> (e.g. "people refuse to see me") (1995, 3). But from a Kantian point of view, part of Ellison's creativity is manifest in his ability to draw together this full suite of imaginative representations into a whole that brings to light the implications of <invisibility>, and its relation to other concepts, in ways that we do not ordinarily attend to.

This said, not all aesthetic ideas provide us with an imaginative world on the scale that a novel does; a four-line poem is nowhere near as imaginatively complex. And, indeed, even in more elaborate works of art, we can distinguish between different scales of aesthetic ideas. For example, in *Invisible Man*, Ellison exhibits <invisibility> both through the narrator's adventures over the course of the novel and through lines such as,

Invisibility, let me explain, gives one a slightly different sense of time, you're never quite on the beat. Sometimes you're ahead and sometimes behind. Instead of the swift and imperceptible flowing of time, you are aware of its nodes, those points where time stands still or from which it leaps ahead. And you slip into the breaks and look around. (1995, 8)

Insofar as this is the case, it seems that we should acknowledge a fair bit of leeway in Kant's account of what is involved in an artist exhibiting a concept in a holistic way. Though this creativity will sometimes manifest in aesthetic ideas that present a large-scale imaginative world, other times it will manifest in something smaller in scale, such as a perspective on a moment, emotion, or person. But even on this smaller scale, it seems there is a kind of world opened to us, as the moment, emotion, or person is portrayed with a kind of completeness and wholeness that brings to light conceptual implications and relations that we ordinarily overlook. So, regardless of the scale of the aesthetic idea, it seems that Kant is committed to them involving the artist creatively producing a new imaginative world that exhibits a concept in a holistic way that opens up a horizon on it.

However, in addition to emphasizing the artistic creativity involved in generating an aesthetic idea, Kant intimates that aesthetic ideas invite a creative style of seeing more in the audience, which expands our comprehension of concepts in new, surprising, and cognitively valuable directions. In this vein, he says that engaging with works of art in light of their aesthetic ideas "occasion[s] much thinking," "animate[s] the mind by opening up for it the prospect of an immeasurable field of related representations," and gives our "imagination an impetus to think more" (KU 5:314–15).[19] Kant does not specify exactly what this "immeasurable field of related representations" is, but we could perhaps fill out the details by drawing on his remarks in the *Anthropology* to the effect that there are three patterns of connection that belong to the "productive faculty [*Dichtungsvermögen*]" of imagination: connections in space, in time, and based on "affinity," which amount to conceptual connections (Anthro. 7:175, 177; see also AF 25:512–13). Applying this to the "immeasurable field" related to an aesthetic idea, we could think of it as a field of representations that are connected to the target concept by way of spatial, temporal, or affinitive connections. For Kant, then, aesthetic ideas invite a kind of creativity in the audience in which we see more by deploying our productive imaginations in relation to a work of art to explore the concept exhibited in it in light of, say, spatial images, temporal patterns, or conceptual implications opened up by its aesthetic ideas.

In this exploration, Kant, moreover, claims that the audience "aesthetically enlarges" their concepts: free from the rote conceptual and associative patterns that they default into in "mundane" experience, the audience is free to consider concepts from fresh perspectives (KU 5:315).[20] As was the case in generating an aesthetic idea, I take it that, on Kant's view, sometimes this aesthetic enlargement proceeds in a more indirect way, as the audience comes to connect concepts with certain symbols or metaphors, e.g. connecting bodiless heads in circus shows with <invisibility>. But sometimes this aesthetic enlargement proceeds in a more direct fashion: as the audience engages with the holistic way in which an artist exhibits a concept, they can discover more straightforward implications of, and relations between, concepts that they were insensitive to before, but in light of which they now synthetically augment their concepts, e.g. connecting a refusal to see with <invisibility>. However, regardless of how indirect or direct this enlargement is, on Kant's view, by seeing more to works of art by engaging with their aesthetic ideas, the audience comes to expand their conceptual horizons, as they grasp concepts in new and surprising ways.

Indeed, Kant suggests that the audience grasps a concept through an aesthetic idea in so creative a way that it borders on the ineffable: "by an aesthetic idea, however, I mean that representation of the imagination that occasions much thinking though without it being possible for any determinate thought, i.e.,

---

[19] See also his claim that the aesthetic ideas involved in poetry, "expand the mind by setting the imagination free and exhibiting, within the limits of a given concept and among the unbounded manifold of forms possibly agreeing with it, the one that connects its exhibition with a fullness of thought to which no linguistic expression is fully adequate, and thus elevates itself aesthetically to the level of ideas" (KU 5:326; transl. modified).

[20] See Sweet (2023, chaps. 146–7) for emphasis on this aspect of Kant's theory of aesthetic ideas.

296 ARTISTIC IMAGINATION

concept, to be adequate to it, which, consequently, no language fully attains or can make intelligible" (KU 5:314). Continuing in this vein, he says,

> the aesthetic idea is a representation of the imagination, associated [*beigesellte*] with a given concept, which is combined with such a manifold of partial representations in the free use of the imagination that no expression designating a determinate concept can be found for it, which therefore allows the addition to a concept of much that is unnamable.   (KU 5:316)

Of course, an appreciator can say that an aesthetic idea exhibits a particular concept, e.g. *Invisible Man* exhibits the concept <invisibility>. And, indeed, on Kant's view, the cognitive value of aesthetic ideas turns, in part, on the ways in which they aesthetically enlarge the audience's concepts; in which case, concepts need to figure in our engagement with a work of art in some fashion. However, from Kant's perspective, identifying the concept, or concepts, at issue in a work of art can never do justice to the "field" on a concept that an aesthetic idea opens up to us. And should we try and put words to it, it seems the most we can hope for is a non-exhaustive interpretation that gestures toward some aspect of how the aesthetic idea gives us "impetus to think more" (KU 5:315).

To illustrate this picture of how the audience creatively sees more, let's consider reading the following passage from *Invisible Man* in which Ellison describes the cellar in which his narrator lives,

> My hole is warm and full of light. Yes, *full* of light...Perhaps you'll think it strange that an invisible man should need light, desire light, love light. But maybe it is exactly because I *am* invisible. Light confirms my reality, gives birth to my form...Without light I am not only invisible, but formless as well; and to be unaware of one's form is to live a death...This is why I fight my battle with Monopolated Light & Power...In my hole in the basement there are exactly 1,369 lights. I've wired the entire ceiling, every inch of it.   (1995, 6–7)

From a Kantian perspective, in these lines, Ellison offers us an aesthetic idea that invites us to creatively explore the concept of invisibility in a more open-ended way than we do in ordinary experience. There is, for example, nothing in the logical content of the concept <invisibility> that dictates an imaginative representation of a cellar lit up by 1,369 lights. But reading this passage with an eye to this imaginative representation occasions in us much productive imagining about <invisibility>, as we, for example, envision the atmosphere of this cellar and wonder why the narrator's invisibility demands light, what kind of light is demanded (monopolated light? The "eye" as "the light of the body"[21]?), and why 1,369 lights are called for.

---

[21] Matthew 6:22, King James Version of the Bible.

CONCLUSION 297

Through this open-ended engagement, the concept <invisibility> is made sensible to us in new, surprising, cognitively valuable ways, which our words can never quite do justice to. And it is in seeing more to works of art through the lens of their aesthetic ideas in this way that Kant locates the cognitive creativity of the audience that acts as a counterpart to the cognitive creativity of the artist.

9.5 Conclusion

In his account of how our imagination contributes to the process of artistic production, Kant weaves together two claims. On the one hand, Kant insists, as many contemporary theorists do, that this aesthetic use of imagination is marked by creativity and freedom.[22] On the other hand, parting ways with theories of genius as involving madness or divine inspiration, Kant insists that these creative activities are exercises of imagination, *qua* a cognitive capacity that has the cognitive function of making concepts sensible. More specifically, I have argued that Kant anchors his account of artistic creativity in an account of the creative way in which the artist imaginatively exhibits a concept through an aesthetic idea in a work of art. And I have claimed that by seeing more to works of art by seeing them in light of their aesthetic ideas, the audience creatively opens up their conceptual horizons. For Kant, then, the sort of imaginative creativity and freedom involved in art is not in any sense non-cognitive; it is rather a creative and free way of engaging with the cognitive activity paradigmatic of the imagination, *qua* the faculty of exhibition.

This picture of the creative, cognitive, and conceptually rich profile of artistic imagination, of course, echoes the picture of the creative, cognitive, and conceptually rich profile of free play that I argued is at the heart of Kant's account of the aesthetic use of our imagination in appreciating beauty. To return to a theme that I stressed in my interpretation of free play, in his discussion of genius, Kant offers a picture not only of the creative nature of the aesthetic use of imagination, but also of the flexibility of our imagination as a capacity that can function cognitively well in both theoretical and aesthetic contexts. As he makes this point in his discussion of aesthetic ideas (in a passage I have partially quoted before): "in an aesthetic respect...the imagination is free to provide, beyond that concord with the concept, unsought extensive undeveloped material for the understanding... which it applies not so much objectively, for cognition, as subjectively, for the animation of the cognitive powers" (KU 5:317). Here, Kant claims that unlike in ordinary cognition in which our imagination serves us "objectively," in its aesthetic use it serves us "subjectively." As I drew this contrast in Chapter 8, in the former case, we deploy our imagination in service of the object-facing end of

---

[22] See, e.g., Gaut (2003); Stokes (2014; 2016).

cognition: the end of conceptually determining the object we are given in an act of determining judgment. But in the latter case, we are free from this object-facing end and free to, instead, deploy our imagination solely in service of the subject-facing end of cognition: the end of exercising our cognitive capacities in a way that promotes their interaction internal to our cognitive processes. Though Kant, of course, thinks there is much cognitive value to be had by our imagination serving the object-facing end of cognition, in his aesthetics he is at pains to emphasize the cognitive value our imagination can have vis-à-vis the subject-facing end in suspension from the object-facing end. Indeed, he claims that this subjective orientation of our imagination animates and even "strengthens" our cognitive capacities, as we find opportunities to exercise them in expansive and creative ways (KU 5:313). However, as we have also seen, in this subjective orientation, our imagination aesthetically enlarges our concepts, broadening our horizons on them by bringing them to life in creative ways. And in this fashion, Kant thinks our imaginative engagement with beauty, whether through appreciation or production, has a cognitive function: making concepts sensible and facilitating our comprehension of them in creative ways.

Although so far I have focused on Kant's analysis of the robust role our imagination plays in relation to beauty, he also offers an account of its role in relation to the sublime to which I shall now turn.

Seeing More: Kant's Theory of Imagination. Samantha Matherne, Oxford University Press.
© Samantha Matherne 2024. DOI: 10.1093/9780191999291.003.0010

10
Imagination and the Sublime

> nature... raises the imagination
> to the point of exhibiting those cases in which
> the mind can make palpable to itself
> the sublimity of its own vocation
>
> —KU 5:262 (transl. modified)

10.1 Introduction

Given the laudatory story Kant tells about the positive contribution our imagination makes in our aesthetic engagement with beauty, one might expect him to tell a similar story about its contribution to our engagement with the sublime. However, in the opening section of the Analytic of the Sublime, Kant says,

> The most important and intrinsic difference between the sublime and the beautiful... is this: natural beauty... seems as it were to be predetermined for our power of judgment..., whereas that which... excites in us the feeling of the sublime, may to be sure appear... unsuitable for our faculty of exhibition, and as it were doing violence to our imagination. (KU 5:245; transl. modified)

Kant then details the ways in which extremely large and extremely powerful objects, such as vast canyons and raging thunderstorms, are "unsuitable for" and "do violence to" our imagination. Indeed, he argues that being imaginatively thwarted is part of the complex hedonic structure of "negative pleasure" that marks our aesthetic encounter with the sublime (KU 5:245). It is thus not surprising that some readers have attributed to him a wholly negative reading of what our imagination contributes to the sublime, according to which our imaginative activities are thwarted, rather than promoted by extremely large or powerful objects.[1]

Though this story of imaginative frustration is certainly part of Kant's analysis, we also find him making strikingly positive remarks about our imaginative

---

[1] See, e.g., Matthews (1996, 169–71, 175, 177); Allison (2001, 315, 326); Bielefeldt (2003, 60–2); Kirwan (2005, 62–3, 77); Abaci (2008, 240); Merritt (2012, 39); Doran (2015, 239); Moore (2018); and Wang (2020).

300 IMAGINATION AND THE SUBLIME

engagement with sublimity. He, for example, claims that the sublime involves "the necessary enlargement of the imagination to the point of adequacy to that which is unlimited in our faculty of reason" (KU 5:259). He, indeed, describes this "enlargement" in terms of a "vocation" our imagination has in relation to reason, a vocation in which our imagination is "subordinated to freedom" and serves as "an instrument of reason and its ideas" (KU 5:257, 269). And he maintains that this vocation involves a "purposive use that the imagination makes of [nature's] representation": "a use of its intuition to make palpable [fühlbar] in ourselves a purposiveness that is entirely independent of nature" (KU 5:246). In these passages, Kant does not just ascribe a positive role to imagination in the sublime; he indicates that in relation to the sublime, we discover that our imagination has a higher vocation, a vocation tied to the ways in which it serves reason and makes reason and our rational purposiveness palpable to us. What this suggests is that far from just illustrating the limitations of our imagination, Kant uses his account of the sublime to articulate a distinctive kind of imaginative elevation, or so I shall argue in this chapter.[2]

Central to my interpretation is the claim that, as was the case with the beautiful, in relation to the sublime, Kant maintains that our imagination engages in activities that are marked by cognitive creativity. More specifically, I make the case that there is a creative kind of exhibition that Kant takes our imaginations to enact in relation to the sublime: we imaginatively treat extremely large and powerful objects as indirect exhibitions of the idea of the sublimity of our rational capacities.[3] As I interpret Kant, this idea bears on both the greatness of theoretical reason and the might of practical reason and, hence, our freedom. And I claim that, on Kant's view, this imaginative exhibition serves us subjectively by "making" this idea "palpable" to us (KU 5:268, 246). In the end, in spite of initial appearances to the contrary, I thus submit that Kant's analysis of what our imagination contributes to the sublime follows the same pattern that his analysis of the beautiful does: in its aesthetic use, our imagination operates in ways that are cognitively creative and that serve us subjectively by facilitating our concrete comprehension of concepts—the relevant concepts, here, pertaining to the idea of the sublimity of our rationality.

---

[2] Other commentators who highlight the positive contribution imagination makes to the sublime include, Makkreel (1984; 1990, chap. 4); Guyer (1993, chap. 6; 2005, chap. 9); Gibbons (1994, chap. 4); Lyotard (1994); Pillow (2000, chaps. 3–4); Clewis (2009, 79–83); Brady (2012; 2013a, chap. 3; 2013b; 2019). See also Matherne (2023c) in which I emphasize symbols, freedom, and moral vocation in this context.

[3] The majority of commentators who have noted the relevance of the notion of exhibition to the sublime do so in their analysis of the connection between sublimity and Kant's doctrine of aesthetic ideas, e.g. Crowther (1991, 155–61); Gibbons (1994, 139–43); Pillow (2000, chap. 3); and Doran (2015, 280–5). Exceptions to this include Guyer (2005, 229, 230) and Brady (2013a, 77), who allude to exhibition in the sublime in its own right. While there are fruitful connections to be made here, I think that in order to fully appreciate the relationship between aesthetic ideas and sublimity, we need to situate it within the broader framework of exhibition.

JUDGMENTS OF THE SUBLIME   301

In order to develop this interpretation, I begin in §10.2 with a brief overview of Kant's account of judgments of the sublime, contrasting them with judgments of the beautiful. In §10.3, I turn to his analysis of the ways in which we are imaginatively frustrated in relation to the sublime. Then in §10.4, I take up his positive account of what our imagination does in relation to the sublime. There I mount an argument to the effect that in relation to the sublime, Kant thinks that we discover a higher vocation for our imagination, which turns on it making the idea of our rationality palpable to us through a creative mode of exhibition in which we see extremely large and powerful objects in nature outside of us as more: as indirect exhibitions of the greatness and might of our rationality within.

10.2 Judgments of the Sublime

In the Analytic of the Sublime, Kant orients his discussion around two kinds of judgments of the sublime: judgments of the "mathematical" sublime, which concern extremely large objects in nature, such as a huge canyon or a towering mountain (§§25–7), and judgments of the "dynamical" sublime, which concern extremely powerful objects in nature, such as a thunderstorm or volcano (§§28–9).[4]

As was the case in his analysis of judgments of the beautiful,[5] Kant argues that judgments of the sublime are "judgment[s] of reflection," rather than "determining judgment[s]": in them we do not subsume a particular object under a universal the way we do in ordinary cognition, but rather reflect on the particular we are given (KU 5:244). He, likewise, describes judgments of the sublime as aesthetic, rather than cognitive judgments: their "determining ground" is not the object with its various properties, but rather the subject's hedonic response (KU 5:203). He, moreover, claims that judgments of the sublime and judgments of the beautiful belong to the same species of aesthetic judgment: judgments of taste. Recall that in contrast with aesthetic judgments of the agreeable and the good, which are based on interested pleasure, judgments of taste are based on a disinterested form of pleasure that arises through reflective contemplation and some sort of playful interaction between "the faculty of exhibition or the imagination" and "the faculty of concepts" (KU 5:244; transl. modified).[6]

---

[4] Here, I shall focus on Kant's account of judgments of sublimity in nature and shall set aside the complicated issues surrounding the possibility of sublimity in art (see, e.g., Abaci 2008; 2010; Clewis 2010) and the possibility of moral sublimity (see, e.g., Clewis 2009, chap. 2, §3; and Merritt 2012; 2018b, §4).

[5] See Chapter 8.

[6] As will emerge below, in the case of judgments of the beautiful Kant identifies the relevant faculty of concepts as the understanding and in the case of the sublime as reason.

302 IMAGINATION AND THE SUBLIME

However, in the opening stretch of the Analytic of the Sublime, Kant also underscores several ways in which judgments of the sublime differ from judgments of the beautiful. As I gestured toward in the introduction to this chapter, one major difference that he adduces concerns their hedonic structure. According to Kant, whereas judgments of the beautiful are entirely pleasurable, judgments of the sublime involve "negative pleasure" (KU 5:245). The pleasure is "negative" because the objects at issue in judgments of the sublime are either so large or so powerful that when we initially encounter them, they overwhelm us as sensible creatures and make us feel displeasure (KU 5:245). The pleasure we feel in the sublime emerges subsequently as we recognize that, *qua* rational creatures, we are "independent of... and superior over nature," regardless of how large or powerful its objects might be (KU 5:261).

A second way in which Kant distinguishes judgments of the sublime from judgments of the beautiful concerns the predication involved. To be clear, on Kant's view, neither of these judgments involve predicating beauty or sublimity as properties of objects; were this the case, they would be cognitive, rather than aesthetic judgments.[7] Nevertheless, Kant claims that we can "correctly" "call" objects in nature "beautiful" because they have a "form" that is "purposive" with respect to the free play of our imagination and understanding (KU 5:245). For example, when I judge a foxglove to be beautiful, I do so because there is something about it, with its lavender-colored tubular flowers, speckled with maroon on the inside, cascading down a tall spike, that is "purposive" with respect to my free play. But when it comes to judgments of the sublime, Kant asserts that, "we express ourselves on the whole incorrectly if we call some **object of nature** sublime" (KU 5:245). Unlike the purposive way that beauty strikes us, Kant maintains that the form of these extremely large or powerful objects strikes us as "contrapurposive" (KU 5:245). For example, instead of inviting us to play, the vastness of a canyon or force of a thunderstorm overwhelm us. Moreover, as we shall see below, according to Kant, instead of nature being the site of sublimity, the only thing that is "properly sublime" is our rationality (KU 5:245).

A third way in which Kant distinguishes judgments of the sublime from the beautiful turns on the mental capacities involved. According to Kant, whereas the reflection at issue in judgments of the sublime involves the free play of our imagination and understanding, judgments of the sublime involve the "play" of "imagination and reason" (KU 5:258, see also 244). More specifically, he claims that judgments of the mathematical sublime involve the play of imagination and theoretical reason, and judgments of the dynamical sublime involve the play of imagination and practical reason.[8] Moreover, for reasons that will emerge below, he

---

[7] In his discussion of judgments of the beautiful, he claims that we can speak of beauty "as if" it "were a property of the object" (KU 5:211).

[8] For Kant, theoretical reason is, here, reason internal to the "faculty of cognition" and practical reason, the reason internal to the "faculty of desire" (KU 5:247).

argues that the play between imagination and reason with the sublime is more complicated than the play between imagination and understanding with the beautiful. Whereas in the case of the beautiful, Kant maintains that our imagination and understanding cooperate in a straightforwardly harmonious way, in the case of the sublime our reason and imagination initially "conflict" with one another and "play" "in their contrast" (KU 5:258).

For all their similarities, then, given that judgments of the sublime involve a more complicated hedonic structure, predicative status, and mental activity than judgments of the beautiful do, it should not surprise us that Kant's account of what our imagination contributes to judgments of the sublime is likewise more complicated. In order to explore these complications, I first consider Kant's account of how the sublime thwarts certain cognitive activities of imagination (§10.3), before turning to his argument that there are nevertheless ways in which our imagination is cognitively enlarged in relation to the sublime as an instrument of reason (§10.4).

10.3 The Failure of Imagination in the Sublime

Let's return to Kant's claims that in our engagement with the sublime, objects appear "unsuitable for," indeed, "do violence to," the imagination (KU 5:245). What exactly does this unsuitability, let alone violence, amount to? In order to answer this question, let's consider the mathematical and dynamical case, in turn.

10.3.1 Imaginative Failure in the Mathematical Sublime

In our encounter with the extremely large objects involved in the mathematical sublime, Kant claims that our imagination is thwarted in its perceptual activities. Kant situates this account of frustration in a discussion of what is involved in the "aesthetic estimation" of the magnitude, or size, of an object (KU 5:251). According to Kant, we can estimate the magnitude of an object in two ways. The first way is "mathematical," and it involves using "numerical concepts" to determine magnitude, e.g. when I measure a foxglove to be three feet tall with a measuring tape (KU 5:251). The second way is "aesthetic," and it involves measuring magnitude "by eye" "in mere intuition," e.g. when I estimate a foxglove to be a medium-sized one just by looking at it (KU 5:251).[9] This latter kind of estimation, Kant claims, is an imaginative act: it involves "tak[ing] up a quantum in the imagination intuitively" (KU 5:251). More specifically, he maintains that aesthetic estimation

---

[9] The "aesthetic" here does not have anything to do with beauty or sublimity, but rather with measuring something in intuition, rather than through numerical concepts.

304 IMAGINATION AND THE SUBLIME

involves the sort of cognitive activities that our imagination enacts in perception (see Chapter 5). And, as we shall see, it is these perceptual activities that he takes to be unsuccessful in the case of the mathematically sublime.

In more detail, Kant argues that aesthetic estimation depends on two perceptual activities of imagination: "apprehension" (*Auffassung*) and "comprehension" (*Zusammenfassung*) (KU 5:251–2).[10] As I have discussed, on Kant's view, in apprehension our imagination takes up a successively unfolding manifold of representations delivered through the senses. For example, as I scan the foxglove from bottom to top, I imaginatively apprehend the manifold delivered to me through my senses by successively taking up the representations of its slender green stem, its oblong-shaped leaves, and its lavender flowers with their maroon speckled throats.

Meanwhile, in what Kant here calls "comprehension," our imagination is responsible for synthesizing the multiplicity of representations we have apprehended together into a perceptual image, which is an intuition of imagination (intuition$_i$) that represents a single "whole" (KU 5:252). As he succinctly puts it, comprehension involves "the **comprehension** of the many in one intuition" (KU 5:254). For example, in the comprehension of the foxglove, I imaginatively synthesize the representations of the stem, leaves, and flowers together into a perceptual image that represents the foxglove as a spatial whole containing various parts. Though Kant primarily uses language of "comprehension" for this activity in this discussion of the sublime, he occasionally refers to it as "composition" (*Zusammensetzung*) (see KU 5:253–4).[11] This is in keeping with his characterization of composition in the first *Critique* as an activity in which our imagination synthesizes a manifold together into an intuition$_i$ that represents a determinate spatio-temporal form and matter (see Chapter 7).[12] I thus take the imaginative activity of comprehension that Kant discusses in the context of the sublime to be tantamount to the sort of imaginative activity of composition that he discusses in

---

[10] In contrast with Makkreel (1990, chaps. 3–4) who argues that the activities of apprehension and comprehension that Kant describes here differ from the synthesizing activities of imagination in the first *Critique*, I take apprehension in the third *Critique* to map onto what Kant calls the synthesis of apprehension in the A Deduction (A98–100), and comprehension to map onto what Kant in the A Deduction describes as the coordination of the synthesis of apprehension and reproduction involved in generating an image (A120–1) and as "composition" (*Zusammensetzung*) in the Principles (see Chapter 7 and B201n).

[11] This is somewhat obscured by the fact that in this passage Guyer and Matthews occasionally translate "Zusammenfassung" as "composition" at KU 5:253–4. For example, *Zusammensetzung* is translated as "composition" in the lines, "in the composition that is requisite for the representation of magnitude" and "the further generation of magnitude in composition." *Zusammenfassung* is also translated as "composition" in the lines, "the composition of the units up to the number 10" and "apprehension, but not composition is possible in an intuition of the imagination," though as "comprehension" in the lines, "the **comprehension** of the many in one intuition."

[12] As I discussed in Chapter 8, Kant also uses language of "composition" for the imaginative activity involved in our free play with the beautiful (see KU §§9, 21, 35).

THE FAILURE OF IMAGINATION IN THE SUBLIME   305

the first *Critique*. And since I have referenced the latter activity in previous chapters, I shall follow suit here.

Bringing this to bear on the mathematical sublime, according to Kant, in order to aesthetically estimate the magnitude of an object "by eye," we must not only imaginatively apprehend the representation of the various parts of an object we sense, but also imaginatively compose the representations of parts together into a perceptual image that represents a whole, the size of which we are to estimate. With objects of ordinary size, Kant claims that apprehension and composition can proceed fluidly. When I look at the foxglove, its size poses no challenge to me as I apprehend its parts and compose those parts into a perceptual image that represents a whole that I estimate to be medium in size for a foxglove.

But when we encounter extremely large objects of the sort involved in the mathematical sublime, such as a canyon or mountain, Kant claims that our imagination hits a barrier in these perceptual activities: though we can imaginatively apprehend the object part by part, we cannot compose those representations of parts into a perceptual image that represents a whole. As he puts it,

> when apprehension has gone so far that the partial representations... that were apprehended first already begin to fade in the imagination... then it loses on one side as much as it gains on the other, and there is in the comprehension a greatest point beyond which it cannot go.   (KU 5:252)

To illustrate what this failure of imaginative composition amounts to, Kant uses the example of walking into St. Peter's for the first time. Although we can successively apprehend representations of the various parts we see, e.g. the sculptures, mosaics, columns, altars, etc., St. Peter's is so large that we fail in our attempts to compose those parts into a perceptual image that represents the whole.[13] Describing this failure, Kant says, "there is a feeling of the inadequacy of [one's] imagination for exhibiting the ideas of a whole, in which the imagination reaches its maximum and, in the effort to extend it, sinks back into itself" (KU 5:252; transl. modified). Thus, in our encounter with the extremely large objects of the mathematical sublime, Kant claims that we imaginatively fail in our cognitive effort to compose an intuition$_i$, a perceptual image, that represents a whole.

However, Kant maintains that there is a second kind of cognitive failure of imagination involved in the mathematical sublime, which arises in virtue of our imagination's relation to theoretical reason. *In nuce*, Kant argues that in relation to the mathematical sublime, theoretical reason places a demand on our imagination: it demands that our imagination compose an intuition$_i$ that exhibits one of

---

[13] I am here using the St. Peter's example only to illustrate what happens when we fail at composition. But, as I noted earlier, I leave aside whether this example has implications about the possibility of the sublime in art for Kant.

306 IMAGINATION AND THE SUBLIME

its pure concepts: the idea of the infinite (see KU 5:254).[14] But this demand, Kant claims, is one that our imagination cannot meet.

More specifically, according to Kant, when we encounter extremely large objects, we feel that they are so large that the only standard or "basic measure" by which they could be measured is by nature as an "absolute whole" or "absolute totality" that is actually infinite (KU 5:257, 255). And at this point Kant claims that theoretical reason becomes relevant to aesthetic estimation, demanding that the imagination compose an intuition$_i$ of a nature as whole that exhibits the idea of the infinite:

> the voice of reason...requires totality for all given magnitudes...hence comprehension in **one** intuition, and it demands an **exhibition** for all members of a progressively increasing numerical series, and does not exempt from this requirement even the infinite (space and past time), but rather makes it unavoidable for us to think of it...as **given entirely** (in its totality).
>
> (KU 5:254; transl. modified)

As he makes this point in §27, "the idea of the comprehension of every appearance that may be given to us into the intuition of a whole is one enjoined on us by a law of reason" (KU 5:257). So, on Kant's view, theoretical reason places a demand on our imagination to compose an intuition$_i$ of nature as an absolute infinite whole. However, he claims that in this the imagination is doomed to failure: *qua* a supersensible idea of reason, the infinite "admit[s] of no intuition" (KU 5:255). And in failing to meet this demand, Kant claims that our imagination cognitively fails in a second way in relation to the sublime: it cannot engage in composition that fulfills this demand of theoretical reason.

Given the double cognitive failure of our imagination in relation to the sublime, Kant asserts that the extremely large objects involved in the mathematical sublime appear unsuitable and violent from an imaginative perspective.

10.3.2 Imaginative Failure in the Dynamical Sublime

While Kant is explicit about the inadequacy of the imagination in the case of the mathematical sublime, there is some question as to whether the imagination plays any role in Kant's account of our encounter with the extremely powerful objects at issue in the dynamical sublime.[15] In sharp contrast with the sustained attention

---

[14] See Winegar (2022) for discussion of how the idea of the infinite at issue in the sublime (and at MN 4:559), which he interprets as the representation of infinite objective space, relates to Kant's account of space and time as infinite in the Aesthetic and the First Antinomy in the first *Critique*.

[15] See Crowther (1991, 119–20); Myskja (2001, 139–41).

THE FAILURE OF IMAGINATION IN THE SUBLIME   307

he devotes to imagination in relation to the mathematical sublime, he mentions imagination only a few times in his discussion of the dynamical sublime.[16] What is more, imagination might seem like the wrong kind of mental capacity to be at work in the dynamical sublime. For according to Kant, what is at issue in the dynamical sublime is the relation that extremely powerful objects have not to the "**faculty of cognition**," but rather to the "**faculty of desire**," i.e. to the volitional faculty through which we bring about objects or states of affairs (KU 5:247).[17] Insofar as imagination belongs to the faculty of cognition, rather than the faculty of desire, it might seem there is no role for imagination to play in Kant's account of the dynamical sublime.

However, as we have seen, at the beginning of the Analytic of the Sublime, Kant claims that the sublime in general involves "the satisfaction....connected to...the faculty of exhibition or the imagination [being] considered, in the case of a given intuition, to be in accord with...reason, as promoting the latter" (KU 5:244). The unrestricted scope of this passage indicates that Kant is committed to the sublime in all of its manifestations involving some interplay between imagination, as the faculty of exhibition, and reason, such that the former somehow "promotes" the latter. Moreover, in sketching the contrast between the mathematical and dynamical sublime, Kant says,

> the feeling of the sublime brings with it as its characteristic mark a **movement** of the mind..., this movement is related through the imagination either to the **faculty of cognition** or to the **faculty of desire**...: for then the first is attributed to the object as a **mathematical**, the second as a **dynamical** disposition of the imagination.   (KU 5:247)

What this passage suggests is that in both the mathematical and dynamical sublime our imagination has some role to play: in the former case it relates to the faculty of cognition and in the latter case to the faculty of desire. So even though in his discussion of the dynamical sublime Kant does not make this explicit, there is some "dynamical disposition of the imagination" that we need to reconstruct.

Given the practical orientation of our imagination in the context of the dynamical sublime, in order to reconstruct its contribution, we need to shift our focus away from the sort of cognitive activities Kant attributes to our imagination in ordinary experience and toward the sort of cognitive activities he attributes to it in the practical domain. This said, the topic of the practical use of our imagination on Kant's view is the topic that shall occupy me in Part IV, so, what I say about the practical exercise of imagination here is not meant to be exhaustive. I, instead, intend to say enough to make sense of the role he attributes to imagination in the

---

[16] He mentions imagination at KU 5:262–3, 265.
[17] I discuss the faculty of desire at more length in Chapter 12.

308 IMAGINATION AND THE SUBLIME

dynamical sublime and to offer a kind of prelude to the more in-depth account of its practical use to come.

In his account of the dynamical sublime, the most explicit comment Kant makes about the role of our imagination is this: when it comes to "our feeling of well-being [*Wohlbefindens*]…the imagination, in accordance with the law of association, makes our state of contentment physically dependent" (KU 5:269).[18] Here, Kant highlights the relation our imagination has to our "well-being" or happiness. And he suggests that our imagination represents our well-being or happiness as something that is "physically dependent," i.e. dependent on goods we can acquire through experience, such as riches or health. This line of thought echoes Kant's claims about happiness in the *Groundwork* to the effect that happiness (defined as "a maximum of well-being, in my present and every future condition") is "not an ideal of reason, but of the imagination, which rests merely on empirical grounds," such as wealth, intelligence, or health (Gr. 4:418; see also KU 5:430, MS 6:452, KpV 5:61). In his analysis of what our imagination contributes to the sublime, I thus take Kant to have in mind some "dynamic disposition" our imagination has in relation to the ideal of happiness. But what exactly is this connection between happiness and imagination, and why does he think it is at stake in our encounter with extremely powerful objects?

Let's begin with the claim that happiness is an "ideal of imagination."[19] In the third *Critique* Kant defines an ideal in general as "the representation of an individual being as adequate to an idea" (KU 5:232).[20] For Kant, an "idea" is a concept of reason that represents some sort of "perfection" or "maximum," e.g. the idea of friendship represents perfect friendship, and the idea of wisdom represents perfect knowledge (A316–17/B372–3). An ideal, on his view, thus involves a representation of an individual as an "archetype" (*Urbild*), who realizes some idea of perfection (see A569–70/B598–7; KU 5:232; BL 24:47; ML2 25:577). An ideal of imagination, in turn, is a representation generated by our imagination, hence an intuition$_i$, that represents an individual being as embodying some idea.[21] Think, for example, of an intuition$_i$ that represents someone who is the perfect friend. Insofar as the intuitions$_i$ involved in ideals of imagination represent an archetypal individual as embodying an idea, the process through which they are generated can be understood as one of exhibition: our imagination finds a way to exhibit a concept, here, an idea, in sensible form, and, thereby, facilitates our concrete comprehension of it.

---

[18] The reconstruction that I provide here owes much to Clewis's (2009, 79–80) discussion of the connection between the imagination and happiness as it bears on the dynamical sublime.

[19] I return to this issue in Chapter 12.

[20] See also his gloss of the ideal as "the idea not merely *in concreto* but *in individuo*, i.e., as an individual thing which is determinable, or even determined, through the idea alone" (A568/B596).

[21] I discuss the relationship between ideals generated by imagination versus ideals generated by reason in Chapter 13.

THE FAILURE OF IMAGINATION IN THE SUBLIME   309

Applying this to Kant's account of happiness as an ideal of imagination, I take his point to be that this ideal is one that our imagination generates as part of an effort to exhibit the idea of happiness in sensible form.[22] More specifically, I understand his view to be that when we try and grasp what happiness is, we imaginatively "project" an intuition$_i$ of an individual who has achieved maximal well-being through some empirical means (KU 5:430; transl. modified). If we think happiness consists in prioritizing wealth, for example, we might project an intuition$_i$ of a Gatsby-style figure (who does not meet a tragic end).[23] Or if we think it consists in prioritizing intelligence, we might project an intuition$_i$ of a George-Eliot-style figure.[24] While I shall fill in more of the details in Chapter 12, for now the point I want to stress is that in this account we find Kant attributing to imagination a kind of cognitive activity of exhibition in the practical domain: the exhibition of the idea of happiness.

Let's return now to Kant's remark in the dynamical sublime that, "the imagination, in accordance with the law of association, makes our state of contentment physically dependent" (KU 5:269). In the background, I take Kant to have in mind the ways in which our imagination projects an ideal of happiness in the form of an archetypal individual achieving maximal well-being through empirical means. And when he says that our imagination "makes our state of contentment physically dependent," I take him to be saying that each of us projects our own happiness as a matter of us being able to realize an ideal vision of happiness in our own lives.

So, in what sense does Kant think this imaginative projection of happiness is thwarted in the dynamical sublime? According to Kant, when we engage with the extremely powerful objects at issue in the dynamical sublime, we must do so from a place of safety, otherwise fear, rather than aesthetic reflection, would orient us (see KU 5:260–1). But from a place of safety, Kant claims that, "we merely **think** of the case in which we might wish to resist [the object] and think that in that case all resistance would be completely futile" (KU 5:260). For example, when I think of a case in which I might want to resist a "volcano with [its] all-destroying violence," on Kant's view, I realize that my "capacity to resist" is "an insignificant trifle in comparison with [its] power" (KU 5:261). Scenarios like this, Kant maintains, "make us, considered as natural beings, recognize our physical powerlessness" (KU 5:261). And recognizing this has implications for projecting the possibility of our own happiness. For as physically powerless, we do not have the

---

[22] As I discuss in Chapter 12, Kant also describes happiness as an "unstable" and "indeterminate" concept, which complicates what this exhibition involves (KU 5:430; Gr. 4:418).

[23] See F. Scott Fitzgerald's *The Great Gatsby*. This said, in the case of the fictional Gatsby, it is arguably love that is his ultimate priority. However, as I discuss in Chapter 12, on Kant's view, part of the "indeterminacy" of happiness turns on us having a difficult time knowing how to compare and weight different sources of pleasure and desire satisfaction.

[24] As he makes this point in the *Groundwork*, happiness is an "end" that is "actual" in all human beings, *qua* sensible beings (Gr. 4:415).

310 IMAGINATION AND THE SUBLIME

ability to realize the sort of "physically dependent" vision of happiness that is embodied in the ideal of happiness we have embraced. As a result, we are no longer able to project the possibility that we, ourselves, could be happy by realizing this ideal, and our imaginative ideal of happiness comes to be a source of displeasure for us, a vision of what we cannot have. For example, if my ideal of happiness is being someone who prioritizes wealth, Gatsby-style, but in the face of a volcano I realize that I am physically powerless, then this ideal comes to be a source of frustration, as I realize I, myself, have no chance of achieving the happiness I have imaginatively projected. And it is in this way that the "dynamical disposition" of our imagination is thwarted in the face of the dynamical sublime.

All told, in his account of both the mathematical and dynamical sublime, Kant highlights the respective theoretical and practical ways in which the objects at issue appear "unsuitable" and "violent" from the perspective of our imagination. And it is in light of these failures of our imagination that Kant claims that, "The feeling of the sublime is thus a feeling of displeasure from the inadequacy of the imagination" (KU 5:257).[25]

Though Kant's remarks in this vein might make it tempting to attribute to him a wholly negative account of what our imagination contributes to the sublime, as we have seen, this is at odds with his more optimistic claims about the kind of enlargement, elevation, and freedom our imagination ultimately achieves in relation to the sublime. And it is to his account of this positive contribution that I shall now turn.

10.4 The Elevation of Imagination in the Sublime

As was the case with the appreciation and production of beauty, on my interpretation, the key to understanding the positive contribution that Kant takes our imagination to make in relation to the sublime is attending to its cognitive creativity. In particular, I shall argue that on Kant's view, there is a kind of creative exhibition that our imagination enacts in relation to the sublime that has the function of making the idea of the sublimity of our rationality, theoretical and practical included, sensible to us in a distinctive way vis-à-vis our encounter with extremely large and powerful objects in nature.

Beginning with the cognitive dimensions of what our imagination positively contributes to the sublime, Kant pursues a familiar theme: our imagination engages in the activity of exhibition. Recall his claim that,

the satisfaction [in the sublime] is connected to the mere exhibition or to the faculty for that, through which the faculty of exhibition or the imagination is

---

[25] Kant makes this claim in the context of the mathematical sublime, but for reasons I discussed earlier I think it can be extended to the dynamical sublime as well.

THE ELEVATION OF IMAGINATION IN THE SUBLIME 311

considered, in the case of a given intuition, to be in accord with the **faculty of concepts**...of reason, as promoting the latter. (KU 5:244; transl. modified)

For Kant, then, whatever our imagination cognitively does in relation to the sublime will involve the activity of making concepts sensible through exhibition and thereby facilitating our comprehension of them (see Chapter 4). And insofar as this exhibition is something our imagination carries out in relation to reason, he identifies the relevant concepts as "concepts of reason" or "ideas."

More specifically, Kant glosses the relevant concepts of reason in terms of ideas of what is "properly sublime":

we express ourselves wholly incorrectly if we call some **object of nature** sublime...We can say no more than that the object serves for the exhibition of a sublimity that can be found in the mind; for what is properly sublime cannot be contained in any sensible form, but concerns only ideas of reason.

(KU 5:245; transl. modified)

In this passage, Kant claims that although it is inappropriate to think of an object in nature as itself sublime, we can nevertheless treat it as an "exhibition of" what is "properly sublime": the idea of our rationality within.[26] This exhibition, Kant claims, involves a "purposive use of the imagination": the "**use** of...intuitions [of nature] to make palpable [*fühlbar*] in ourselves a purposiveness that is entirely independent of nature" (KU 5:246). Or, as he puts it later, "nature is here called sublime merely because it raises the imagination to the point of exhibiting those cases in which the mind can make palpable to itself the sublimity of its own vocation even over nature" (KU 5:262; transl. modified). According to Kant, then, in our encounter with extremely large or powerful objects in nature, our imagination can engage in a kind of exhibition that "makes palpable" to us the idea of the "sublimity" of our own rationality, with its "purposiveness" and "vocation" that is independent from nature. And over the course of the Analytic of the Sublime, Kant explores how our engagement with the mathematical sublime involves the imaginative exhibition of ideas related to theoretical reason and our engagement with the dynamical sublime involves the imaginative exhibition of ideas related to practical reason and our freedom.

---

[26] Over the course of the sublime, Kant identifies a wide range of rational things as properly sublime, including ideas of reason (KU 5:244, 245, 254, 255, 257, 264), reason (KU 5:250, 254, 255, 258, 261, 262, 269), our rational vocation (KU 5:257, 262, 268, 269), the mind (KU 5:245, 256, 264), and dispositions of the mind (KU 5:250, 256, 264, 265, 268, 269, 273). He perhaps intimates that freedom belongs on this list at KU 5:271, but his focus in the Analytic is on reason- and mind-related notions. For my purposes here, I shall prescind from these complexities and refer to what is properly sublime more generally in terms of our rationality. See Guyer (1993, chap. 6) and Matherne (2023c) for more of a focus on freedom, and the question of how the sublime helps bridge the "chasm" between nature and freedom on Kant's view (KU 5:195).

312 IMAGINATION AND THE SUBLIME

Yet one wonders what kind of exhibition this could be. As we just saw, Kant claims that what is properly sublime "cannot be contained in any sensible form." But given that exhibition proceeds by way of our imagination generating intuitions$_i$ that exhibit concepts in sensible form, shouldn't Kant rule out the possibility of the exhibition of what is properly sublime? And, indeed, it might seem that this is precisely what he does in the following passage: "One can describe the sublime thus: it is an object (of nature) **the representation of which determines the mind to think of the unattainability of nature as an exhibition of ideas.** Taken literally, and considered logically, ideas cannot be exhibited" (KU 5:268; transl. modified). At this point, however, we need to attend to the creativity in how our imagination carries out exhibition in relation to the sublime. For, as we shall now see, Kant casts the exhibition at issue as a kind of indirect exhibition, which I shall suggest creatively makes the idea of the sublimity of our rationality palpable to us in a new, surprising, and cognitively valuable way.[27]

In more detail, in §59 of the third *Critique*, Kant draws a distinction between two different kinds of imaginative exhibition: direct and indirect.[28] Although both forms of exhibition involve our imagination generating intuitions$_i$ that make concepts sensible, he claims that the intuition$_i$ relates to the concept in a different way in each case.

As I discussed in Chapter 5, in the direct exhibition of a concept, Kant claims that the intuition$_i$ "corresponds" to or "demonstrates" a concept in a straightforward way (KU 5:351–2). As I understand this correspondence or demonstration, the sensible content of the intuition$_i$ maps onto the logical content of a concept in a straightforward way. For example, a direct exhibition of the concept <foxglove> will involve an intuition$_i$ that contains sensible representations that correspond to the marks contained in this concept, like <having tubular flowers>, <having oblong leaves>, <having a spikey stem>, etc.

By contrast, Kant maintains that indirect exhibition involves intuitions$_i$ that exhibit concepts by a more circuitous route. In §59, he describes this more circuitous route in a couple of different ways. In one vein, Kant claims that an intuition$_i$ indirectly exhibits a concept because the way we reflect on the former is conducive to reflecting on the latter. As he puts it, "it is...merely the form of the reflection, not the content [of the intuition], which corresponds to the concept" (KU 5:351). Or, as he says a bit later, indirect exhibition involves "transportation of the reflection on one object of intuition to another, quite different concept" (KU 5:352–3). For Kant, this "transportation" turns on us parlaying reflection on something more concrete and sensible into reflection on something more abstract and

---

[27] As was the case in Chapters 8 and 9, in glossing creativity in terms of what is new, surprising, and cognitively valuable, I am taking my cue from Boden's (2004, 1) definition of creativity.

[28] Although Kant does not explicitly describe exhibition as imaginative in §59, I take him to be implicitly committed to this view given his characterization of imagination as the "faculty of exhibition" in the third *Critique*.

THE ELEVATION OF IMAGINATION IN THE SUBLIME   313

conceptual. For example, an intuition$_i$ of a foxglove can serve as an indirect exhibition of the concept <pride> because the concrete way we reflect on how a foxglove holds itself high is conducive to the more abstract reflection that <pride> calls for.[29] For Kant, then, through indirect exhibition we leverage reflection on something more concrete and sensible into reflection on something more abstract and conceptual. And it is through this indirect process, mediated by reflection, that Kant thinks indirect exhibition facilitates our comprehension of concepts.

In addition to emphasizing this point about reflection, in §59 Kant analyzes the circuitous route through which indirect exhibition proceeds in terms of "symbols" that exhibit concepts "by means of an analogy" (KU 5:352; see also WF 20:279–80, Anthro. 7:191).[30] Elsewhere Kant analyzes analogies as having a four-part comparative structure, a : b :: c : d (see A179–80/B222; ML1 28:292).[31] And he claims that what gets an analogy off the ground is not "an imperfect similarity between things, but rather a perfect similarity between two relations in wholly dissimilar things" (Prol. 4:357–8). That is to say, an analogy does not require any similarity between the a and b terms, on the one hand, and the c and d terms, on the other. It only requires a similarity in the relation, the :, between the a and b terms and c and d terms. So, in §59 of the third *Critique*, when Kant says that indirect exhibition involves symbols that exhibit concepts "by means of an analogy," this suggests that, on his view, indirect exhibition involves intuitions$_i$ that symbolize concepts vis-à-vis some sort of analogy. For example, we might spell out the sense in which a foxgloves serves as a symbol of <pride> in terms of the analogy, a stem of a foxglove : a foxglove :: pride : one's sense of self. And although the *relata* in this analogy do not have anything in common, the way in which a stem holds a foxglove high is similar to how someone's pride holds their sense of self high.

Note that this claim that indirect exhibition involves symbols and analogies is more robust than the claim that it involves a certain pattern of reflection: the former claim specifies that the intuitions$_i$ involved need to symbolize a concept vis-à-vis an analogy. This said, there is a question as to whether Kant thinks that all indirect exhibition proceeds by way of analogies. Given Kant's technical view

---

[29] Or to cite one of Kant's examples, the intuition$_i$ of a "handmill" (think: peppermill) indirectly exhibits the concept of a "despot" because the way we reflect on the "machine"-like "causality" of a handmill is conducive to reflecting on the concept of a despot (KU 5:352).

[30] There is some question of whether Kant is committed to all symbols involving analogies as this discussion would suggest (see also Prol. §§57–9), or whether he acknowledges symbols that do not have an analogical structure. In this discussion, I focus on the more restricted description of symbols as involving analogies. For a discussion of the relation between analogies and symbols in Kant, see Cohen (1982); Allison (2001, 254–3); Chignell (2009a; 2010). In the *Religion*, Kant refers to symbolic exhibition as "*schematism of analogy*" in which we "*schematize* (render a concept comprehensible through analogy with something of the senses)"; however, following KU and WF, I shall reserve the term "schema" for direct exhibition (Rel. 6:65n).

[31] For discussions of Kant's theory of analogies in general, see Munzel (1995, §1); Pillow (2000, 81–3); Maly (2012); Nassar (2015, §1); Westra (2016, chap. 7); Matherne (2021b).

of analogies, this would amount to a rather restrictive view of what indirect exhibition involves: it would have to involve intuitions$_i$ that stand in an analogical relation to concepts and that facilitate our comprehension of concepts through analogical means.[32] But though the way Kant proceeds in §59 might appear to commit him to this more restrictive view of indirect exhibition, if we look to the account of indirect exhibition that he offers in his account of aesthetic ideas, then we have reason to attribute to him a less restrictive view.

As I discussed in Chapter 9, on Kant's view, an aesthetic idea is an intuition$_i$ an artist generates by means of which they exhibit a concept through "aesthetic" attributes: "supplementary representations of the imagination" that "express only the implications connected with [a concept] and its affinity with other [concepts]" (KU 5:315). As I also discussed, in this context, Kant describes cases in which the "supplementary representations" exhibit a concept by more indirect means: the peacock indirectly exhibits the concept of Juno, "the splendid queen of heaven," and the sun setting on a summer day indirectly exhibits the concept of a "cosmopolitan disposition" (KU 5:315–16). But it is not clear that either of these examples turn on an analogy in Kant's technical sense. The peacock seems to be a kind of metaphor that invites us to think about Juno in an open-ended way, e.g. as proud, beautiful, watchful, powerful, vain, royal, etc.[33] And though if pressed, we might be able to formulate an analogy in the sunset case (the end of a summer day : sun :: the end of one's life : a cosmopolitan disposition), it too seems more like the image of the setting sun on a summer's day is a kind of metaphor that invites us to think about a cosmopolitan disposition in an open-ended way, e.g. as peaceful, content, gentle, beautiful, etc. Indeed, this sort of open-ended engagement is precisely what Kant thinks aesthetic ideas call for: they "animate the mind by opening up for it the prospect of an immeasurable field of related representations" (KU 5:315). So even though aesthetic ideas can involve an indirect exhibition of concepts, they seem to have a more open-ended structure and call for more open-ended engagement than do analogies in Kant's technical sense.

For these various reasons, rather than attributing to Kant the restrictive view that indirect exhibition requires symbols that exhibit concepts by way of analogies, we should attribute to him the less restrictive view that indirect exhibition requires intuitions$_i$ that do not directly map onto concepts, but nevertheless exhibit concepts because they are conducive to reflecting on them. And within this more general framework, Kant can allow for different forms of indirect exhibition, whether through analogies, metaphors, or other circuitous means.

---

[32] Pillow (2000, chap. 3; 2001) emphasizes this restriction in his discussion of the relation between symbols, analogies, and metaphors.

[33] For discussion of the relationship between imagination and metaphor in Kant, see Nuyen (1989); Pillow (2000, pt. 3); Gaut (2003, §5); Sassen (2003, 176). For discussion of why imagination plays an important role in our engagement with metaphors via imagery and force, see Moran (1989).

THE ELEVATION OF IMAGINATION IN THE SUBLIME   315

With these caveats about indirect exhibition in place, let's return to the question of exhibition and the sublime. Significantly for my purposes, in §59 of the third *Critique* Kant argues that ideas of the supersensible can be exhibited indirectly. In his words, in indirect exhibition, "to a concept which only reason can think, and to which no sensible intuition can be adequate, an intuition is attributed" (KU 5:351). Pursuing a similar line of thought in the "Progress" essay, Kant claims that indirect exhibition is "expedient for concepts of the supersensible" (WF 20:279). For Kant, then, whatever the limits of the direct exhibition of ideas of the supersensible might be, they can be indirectly exhibited through intuitions$_i$ that invite patterns of reflection that are similar to the patterns of reflection the relevant ideas call for.

If we now return to the question of what the exhibition of the idea of our rationality as what is properly sublime might amount to for Kant, the distinction between direct and indirect exhibition is elucidatory. Kant does not think that we imaginatively use intuitions$_i$ of extremely large or powerful objects to directly exhibit the idea of the sublimity of our rationality. Indeed, the possibility of such direct exhibition in this context is what I take Kant to foreclose at the end of the Analytic of the Sublime, when he says, "taken literally, and considered logically, ideas cannot be exhibited" (KU 5:268; transl. modified). However, Kant immediately goes on to say that we can nevertheless treat "nature in its totality, as the exhibition of something supersensible, subjectively" (KU 5:268; transl. modified).[34] This comment suggests that even though Kant has foreclosed the possibility of us treating intuitions$_i$ of extremely large or powerful objects in nature as "literal" or "direct" exhibitions of the idea of the sublimity of our rationality, he still allows for us to treat them as indirect exhibitions of this idea. And though the latter proceeds through a more circuitous route, he claims that it is something that can serve us "subjectively." By this subjective service, I take Kant to have in mind what he described earlier in terms of this exhibition "making" this idea "palpable" to us. And it is in Kant's account of this indirect mode of exhibition that, I submit, we find the kind of cognitive creativity of our imagination that marks its elevation in the sublime, as we use intuitions$_i$ of extremely large and powerful objects in nature in new and surprising ways to make the idea of the sublimity of our rationality palpable to ourselves.

To fill out the details, I want to note that we, in fact, find a kind of precedent for conceiving of intuitions$_i$ from the aesthetic domain as indirect exhibitions of supersensible ideas in Kant's analysis of the beautiful as "the symbol of the morally good [*Sittlichguten*]" in §59 (KU 5:353).[35] Kant's basic idea is that although the intuition$_i$ of a beautiful object does not straightforwardly map onto the idea of

---

[34] See also "in judging a thing to be sublime the [imagination] is related to **reason**, in order to correspond subjectively with its **ideas**" (KU 5:256).
[35] I return to this claim in Chapter 13.

316   IMAGINATION AND THE SUBLIME

the morally good, the former can serve as a symbol of the latter because the way we reflect on this intuition$_i$ is conducive to how we reflect on the idea of the morally good.[36] If a similar pattern is at work in Kant's account of the sublime, then we would expect him to endorse the view that we can imaginatively generate intuitions$_i$ of very large or powerful objects in nature that indirectly exhibit the idea of what is properly sublime.[37]

If this is Kant's view, then it would need to be the case that he thinks the way we reflect on the intuitions$_i$ of very large or powerful objects, conduces to the way we reflect on the idea of what is "properly sublime." And in the Analytic of the Sublime, we, indeed, find Kant arguing that the sort of "disposition" involved in reflecting on an intuition$_i$ of an extremely large or powerful object is similar and conducive to the sort of disposition involved in reflecting on the idea of the sublimity of our rationality (KU 5:256). In his words, the former involves "a disposition of the mind which is in conformity with [ideas] and compatible with that which the influence of determinate (practical) ideas on feeling would produce" (KU 5:256).

More specifically, Kant glosses this parallel disposition in terms of the notion of "respect," which he here defines as, "The feeling of the inadequacy of our capacity for the attainment of an idea **that is a law for** us," "but at the same time" a feeling of "its vocation for adequately realizing that ideas as a law" (KU 5:257). I understand this inadequacy to be tied to our limitations as sensible creatures and this vocation to our calling as creatures who are also rational. And I take Kant's thought to be that the way we reflect on the intuitions$_i$ at issue in the sublime involves a sense of both our sensible limits and higher vocation in the face of the greatness and might of nature that is similar to our sense of our sensible limits and higher vocation in the face of the greatness and might of our rationality. This said, Kant insists that the sort of disposition of respect that we feel in response to the object in nature is not exactly the same as what we feel toward reason.[38] In

---

[36] More specifically, Kant adduces two common features of how we reflect on the beautiful and morally good: first, he claims that in both cases we are "aware of a certain ennoblement and elevation above the mere receptivity for a pleasure from sensible impressions," and, second, that we "esteem the value of others in accordance with a similar maxim of their power of judgment" (KU 5:353). He, moreover, claims that our reflection on beauty as a symbol of the morally good is something that encourages us to develop reflective patterns that are conducive to morality; hence his claim at the end of §59 that, "Taste as it were makes possible the transition from sensible charm to the habitual moral interest without too violent a leap" (KU 5:355).

[37] Guyer (2005, 227–30) and Clewis (2015) also explore the parallels between Kant's account of beauty as a symbol of morality and the sublime. I develop this line of interpretation specifically with an eye to what our imagination positively contributes in relation to the sublime in Matherne (2023c).

[38] I take this to put pressure on readings, according to which the respect at issue in the sublime is moral respect (see Crawford 1974, 145–59; Crowther 1991, 99, 134–5, 165–6; and Schaper (1992, 382–4). I am, instead, sympathetic to readings, according to which the feeling of respect we have in the sublime is similar to, but not identical with, the feeling of respect we have in morality (see Matthews 1996, 176; Allison 2001, 326–7; Clewis 2009, chap. 3; Merritt 2012, 43–8; 2018b; Brady 2013a, chap. 3; and Doran 2015, 249–52).

this vein, he claims that there is a "subreption (substitution of a respect for the object instead of for the idea of humanity in our own subject), which as it were makes intuitable the superiority of the rational vocation of our cognitive faculty over the greatest faculty of sensibility" (KU 5:257). Here, Kant suggests that the parallel ways in which we reflect on the intuition$_i$ and idea of what is properly sublime involves a kind of "substitution" of respect for an object in nature for respect for our rationality. But this substitution, he claims, is one in which our reflection on the object facilitates our reflection on our rationality. Insofar as this is the case, it stands to reason that, on Kant's view, the way we reflect on the intuitions$_i$ of extremely large or powerful objects maps onto, and invites, the way we reflect on the idea of our rationality as what is properly sublime. Insofar as this is the case, we can attribute to him a position according to which our intuitions$_i$ of extremely large or powerful objects serve to indirectly exhibit the idea of our rationality as sublime.

Returning now to the positive role that our imagination plays in the sublime, my proposal is that, on Kant's view, in spite of the imaginative frustration we feel when we encounter extremely large and powerful objects, we are nevertheless able to engage in a successful imaginative activity: the indirect exhibition of the idea of the sublimity of our rationality. And I have proposed that we think of this exhibition as involving a kind of cognitively creative exercise of imagination. It is cognitive, and cognitively valuable, to the extent that it involves the imaginative activity of exhibition and the execution of the imagination's cognitive function of making concepts sensible. However, it is creative to the extent that our imagination executes its function in new and surprising ways in this context.

To appreciate this creative dimension, let's return to Kant's claim that imaginative activity is free in an "aesthetic respect" insofar as it is free from the "constraint of the understanding and...the limitation of being adequate to its concept" (KU 5:316). Were our imagination restricted by this constraint in relation to the sublime, it would not engage in any exhibition of the properly sublime at all, for, as we have seen, in his discussion of the sublime he rules out intuitions$_i$ of nature as "adequate" for a direct exhibition of the idea of what is properly sublime. But in indirectly exhibiting this idea to us, our imagination displays freedom in an aesthetic respect in relation to the sublime. Indeed, free from this constraint, our imagination is able to "make" this idea "palpable" to us in new and surprising ways vis-à-vis intuitions$_i$ of extremely large or powerful objects in nature (KU 5:246).

What is more, according to Kant, in this cognitive creativity, far from being thwarted, our imagination is "enlarged" in the sublime: it becomes an "instrument of reason and its ideas" and "subordinated to freedom" (KU 5:259, 269). Indeed, as an instrument of reason, Kant claims that we discover a "purposive" or "supersensible" "use" of our imagination: "the possible **use** of its intuitions to make palpable in ourselves a purposiveness that is entirely independent of nature" (KU 5:246, 267). For Kant, then, our engagement with the sublime reveals a kind

318 IMAGINATION AND THE SUBLIME

of higher calling of our imagination, as a cognitive capacity that can serve reason through its creative exercise vis-à-vis the sublime.

In order to complete this picture of the cognitively creative ways our imagination engages in indirect exhibition in the sublime in service of reason, let's consider the mathematical and dynamical case, in turn. In his discussion of the mathematical sublime, we find Kant making the following remarks: the sublime involves "the necessary enlargement of the imagination to the point of adequacy to that which is unlimited in our faculty of reason, namely, the idea of the absolute whole," and that, "our imagination...demonstrates its limits and inadequacies, but at the same time its vocation for adequately realizing the idea [of reason] as a law" (KU 5:259). Here, Kant suggests that in relation to extremely large objects of the mathematical sublime, our imagination is "enlarged" because it "demonstrates" a "higher vocation" that is responsive to the demands of reason.

This said, Kant's account of this higher imaginative vocation that we discover in the mathematical sublime is complex. On the one hand, as we have seen, he argues that this vocation involves a demand of reason that our imagination can never meet: the demand to exhibit the idea of nature as an absolute infinite whole. In his words, although reason "enjoins" our imagination to generate such an exhibition, "our imagination, even in its greatest effort with regard to the comprehension of a given object in a whole of intuition (hence for the exhibition of the idea of reason) that is demanded of it, demonstrates its limits and inadequacy" (KU 5:257; transl. modified). According to Kant, there is a sense in which this kind of cognitive frustration is part of the imagination's vocation. For, on Kant's view, part of the vocation of imagination turns on it serving reason by "mak[ing] intuitable the superiority of the rational vocation of our cognitive faculty over the greatest faculty of sensibility" (KU 5:257). And when our imagination, as the greatest faculty of sensibility, fails to meet reason's demand to exhibit the idea of the infinite, this manifests the imagination's vocation, as a sensible faculty that is inferior to theoretical reason.

On the other hand, I have suggested that Kant also acknowledges a way in which our imagination meets the demands of reason in relation to extremely large objects: our imagination generates intuitions$_i$ of those objects that indirectly exhibit the sublimity of our theoretical reason in a way that makes the latter palpable to us. This successful activity also plays a role in Kant's account of the higher vocation of our imagination that we discover in the mathematical sublime. For part of how Kant cashes out what it means for our imagination to "demonstrate its vocation" in the mathematical sublime is in terms of the "subreption" in which we "substitute" "respect for the object" in nature for respect for the sublimity within us (KU 5:257). Above, I indicated that this subreption proceeds by way of us imaginatively treating the intuition$_i$ of an extremely large object in nature as an indirect exhibition of what is properly sublime insofar as the way we reflect on the former conduces to the way we reflect on the latter. And I take it that engaging in

THE ELEVATION OF IMAGINATION IN THE SUBLIME   319

this sort of indirect exhibition is also part of the higher vocation our imagination discovers in relation to the mathematical sublime. For in this aesthetic activity, our imagination serves reason through this "purposive" use of its intuitions; of extremely large objects to make the sublimity of our theoretical reason "intuitiable" (KU 5:257).

Turning now to the higher imaginative vocation we uncover in the dynamical sublime, let's return to this passage (which I partially quoted above):

> For the imagination, in accordance with the law of association, makes our state of contentment physically dependent; but the very same imagination...(...to the extent that it is subordinated to freedom), is an instrument of reason and its ideas, but as such a power to assert our independence in the face of the influence of nature, to diminish the value of what is great according to these, and so to place what is absolutely great only in its (the subject's) own vocation.
>
> (KU 5:269)[39]

As I argued above, in this passage, Kant alludes to what is involved in our imaginative projection of happiness, and the ways in which our imaginative vision of achieving the ideal of happiness in our own lives is imperiled in the face of the extremely powerful objects involved in the dynamical sublime. However, Kant goes on to suggest that in the dynamical sublime "the very same imagination" also comes to be "subordinated to freedom" and becomes an "instrument of reason." I take being subordinated to freedom and becoming an instrument of reason to be the higher vocation of imagination that we discover in the face of the dynamical sublime.

Once again, we find Kant highlighting two aspects of this imaginative vocation. On the one hand, Kant claims that part of this vocation turns on recognizing that the empirical goods that we imaginatively project our happiness as contingent upon, such as "goods, health and life," are "trivial" in comparison with the "authority" of reason (KU 5:262). And I take it that, as in the theoretical case, part of the higher imaginative vocation we discover vis-à-vis the dynamical sublime turns on recognizing that our greatest imaginative aspirations are inferior to the demands of practical reason. On the other hand, Kant maintains that in the dynamical sublime, "nature is here called sublime merely because it raises the imagination to the point of exhibiting those cases in which the mind can make palpable to itself the sublimity of its own vocation even over nature" (KU 5:262; transl. modified). Here, Kant suggests that our imagination is "raised" in the face

---

[39] In emphasizing the imagination's freedom from acting in accordance with the law of association, Kant is distancing his view from other accounts of the sublime, e.g. Addison's, Gerard's, and Alison's, according to which the imagination engages in association. See Brady (2013b, chap. 1) for a discussion of the role association plays in these alternative accounts.

320 IMAGINATION AND THE SUBLIME

of the dynamical sublime because it engages in an activity of exhibition that "makes" the sublimity of our practical reason and freedom "palpable" to us through intuitions$_i$ of extremely powerful objects in nature that indirectly exhibit to us its power.[40]

As I read Kant's view of the dynamical sublime, then, what it means for our imagination to have a higher vocation as an instrument of reason is not just for our imagination to be humbled in relation to practical reason in virtue of its inadequacies. This vocation also involves us discovering that we can engage in a successful activity in relation to the sublime that makes our practical reason and freedom palpable to us through indirect exhibition. And it is only if we bring both this limitation and this expansion into view that we can fully appreciate what Kant envisions for our imagination when it is "subordinated to freedom" in the dynamical sublime.

For Kant, then, although part of our encounter with the sublime involves imaginative failure, it also involves imaginative success: the success of the cognitively creative ways in which we imaginatively exhibit the idea of the sublimity of our reason to ourselves through intuitions$_i$ of extremely large and powerful objects in nature. And though this does not amount to a direct exhibition of what is properly sublime, which exhibits it "objectively," it counts as an indirect "exhibition of something supersensible," that serves us "subjectively" by making the greatness and might of our rationality sensible to us in a new, surprising, cognitively valuable way (KU 5:268).

10.5 Conclusion

I devoted this chapter to Kant's account of the aesthetic use of our imagination in our engagement with the sublime. I argued that, on Kant's view, as is the case in the appreciation and production of beauty, in our aesthetic engagement with the sublime our imagination operates in a cognitively creative way. I analyzed this cognitive creativity in terms of the indirect imaginative exhibition of the idea of our rationality as what is properly sublime through intuitions$_i$ of extremely large or powerful objects in nature. And I claimed that, according to Kant, in enacting this sort of indirect exhibition, our imagination finds its way to a higher vocation as an instrument of reason—a vocation it realizes by making the sublimity of our reason palpable to us.

To be sure, we saw that Kant also emphasizes the ways in which we are imaginatively frustrated in the face of the sublime, as extremely large objects thwart our imaginative activities of composition and extremely powerful ones frustrate our

---

[40] For discussions of the sublime that emphasize the way in which it discloses our freedom to us, see Guyer (1993, chap. 6); Brady (2013a); Merritt (2018b); and Matherne (2023c).

projections of happiness. But though Kant thinks these theoretical and practical efforts of imagination are hindered in the face of the sublime, I made the case that he also thinks that beyond these confines, the sublime provides us with a new way to orient our imaginations toward reason. In this orientation, Kant suggests that we find a new "supersensible" use of our imagination as an "instrument of reason," "subordinated to freedom."

This discussion of the sublime concludes my analysis of Kant's account of the aesthetic use of imagination. At the most general level, what I hope to have shown is that, on Kant's view, the aesthetic exercise of our imagination in relation to beauty and sublimity is no less cognitive and conceptually laden than is its theoretical exercise in experience—the difference is that the aesthetic exercise involves cognitive activities that are free and creative in a way that the more constrained activities involved in experience are not.

But this difference notwithstanding, I have also made the case that whether we consider its aesthetic or theoretical use, we find Kant attributing to our imagination a common cognitive profile. For Kant, in both contexts, we imaginatively engage in cognitive activities that enable us to see more in objects present to us. Moreover, he maintains that, in both contexts, our imagination has the cognitive function of making concepts sensible through exhibition. This is, indeed, what we would expect given his definition of imagination as the faculty of exhibition. And what this analysis of the aesthetic use of imagination has brought to light is Kant's commitment to a variety of ways in which imaginative exhibition can facilitate our concrete comprehension of concepts. For in addition to the sort of direct exhibition of concepts through intuition$_i$ involved in perception and experience, we have discovered a variety of creative ways Kant thinks we can imaginatively exhibit concepts in an aesthetic context. In the appreciation and production of beauty, our imaginations exhibit concepts in new and surprising ways that broaden our conceptual horizons. And in our engagement with the sublime, Kant indicates that in our imaginative encounter with extremely large and powerful objects, we indirectly exhibit the idea of the sublimity of our rationality in a way that makes this idea palpable to us.

Though these creative modes of exhibition do not contribute to the sort of theoretical cognition involved in experience that Kant focuses on in the first *Critique*, he nevertheless treats them as something that cognitively serve us. For one thing, Kant claims that creative exhibition serves us "subjectively" by animating our cognitive capacities in playful and expansive directions (KU 5:317). In this vein, I have suggested that the aesthetic use of imagination enables us to fulfill the subject-facing end of cognition, which turns on deploying our cognitive capacities in ways that promote one another internal to our cognitive processes, in a heightened way.

Kant, moreover, maintains that the indirect exhibition involved in the aesthetic context serves us by giving us, sensible creatures that we are, sensible ways to comprehend even our supersensible concepts. In this vein, Kant says that indirect exhibition fulfills a "natural need of all human beings to demand for even the highest concepts... something that *can be sensibly held on to* [etwas Sinnlich-haltbares]" (Rel. 6:109; transl. modified). So even though, for Kant, the aesthetic use of our imagination does not result in theoretical cognition, it involves robust cognitive activities that make concepts sensible to us and, thereby, fulfills some of our basic needs as human beings who are at once sensible and rational.

Having explored Kant's account of how we exercise our imagination in theoretical and aesthetic contexts, in the final part of this book, I turn to the question of its practical use. *Prima facie*, one might think that, on Kant's view, imaginative activity is either irrelevant or a detractor in our moral lives. However, the account of the sublime I developed in this chapter should already put pressure on this reading. For in relation to the sublime, we have seen Kant argue that our imagination finds a rational orientation as an instrument of reason. And in what remains of this book, I hope to show that this aesthetic exercise is but one way Kant thinks our imagination makes a significant contribution in the practical domain.

Seeing More: Kant's Theory of Imagination. Samantha Matherne, Oxford University Press.
© Samantha Matherne 2024. DOI: 10.1093/9780191999291.003.0011

PART IV
IMAGINATION IN PRACTICAL AGENCY AND MORALITY

11

The Possibility of Moral Imagination

> then the morally oriented reason
> (through imagination) calls sensibility into play
>
> —Rel. 6:23n

11.1 Introduction

Looking over the first and third *Critiques*, it is clear that Kant accords imagination an important role in our theoretical and aesthetic lives. As we have seen, Kant argues that imagination is a necessary ingredient not only of perception and experience, but also of our aesthetic engagement with beauty and sublimity. In ascribing imagination a role to play across this wide range of contexts, we find Kant defending a pervasive, rather than restrictive, view of imagining, as something we do as much in relation to what is real and present, as in relation to what is not real and absent. However, when we look at Kant's account of our practical lives in writings like the *Groundwork to the Metaphysics of Morals* and the *Critique of Practical Reason*, imagination does not figure prominently.[1] Indeed, Kant mentions imagination by name only three times in the *Groundwork*[2] and eight times in the second *Critique*.[3] Of these few references, none appear to pertain to a

---

[1] Kant also only mentions imagination by name five times in the *Metaphysics of Morals*. Most of these refer to a role imagination plays in what Kant considers to be immoral activities related to lust (MS 6:424–5), drunkenness (MS 6:427), and malice (MS 6:460). However, he also lists it as a "power of the soul [*Seelenkräfte*]" that we have a duty to cultivate (MS 6:445). And he alludes to a positive role imagination can play in sympathy (MS 6:457) (see Vilhauer 2021; 2022).

[2] See "one cannot better serve the wishes of those who ridicule all morality as the mere phantasm of a human imagination overreaching itself through self-conceit, than by conceding to them that the concepts of duty had to be drawn solely from experience" (Gr. 4:407); "happiness is not an ideal of reason, but of the imagination" (Gr. 4:418); and "wit, lively imagination and humour have a fancy price" (Gr. 4:435).

[3] One reference is to the role that expectation in accordance with a "rule of imagination" plays in induction (KpV 5:51). Three references occur in Typic chapter in the context of Kant claiming that in morality imagination cannot play the role that it does in the Schematism, which I shall return to in Chapter 13 (KpV 5:68–9). Two references occur in the Dialectic, as part of Kant painting the position of his opponent. The first involves the worry that the highest good is an "empty imaginary end" (KpV 5:114), and the second involves the worry that practical reason "infringes upon the interest of speculative reason to the extent that it removes the bounds which the latter has set itself and hands it over to every nonsense or delusion of imagination" (KpV 5:120). Finally, Kant references what imagination does in the "contemplation" of the beautiful, as an activity in which "we feel our entire cognitive faculty (understanding and imagination) strengthened" (KpV 5:160).

specifically moral use of imagination. He, instead, discusses a hedonically oriented use of imagination, when he describes happiness as "not an ideal of reason, but of the imagination" (Gr. 4:418). He also mentions a delusional use of imagination, which he describes as a kind of "mysticism" in which we take ourselves to have sensible intuitions of moral concepts, e.g. "of an invisible kingdom of God" (KpV 5:7–71).[4] But nowhere in these references do we find him explicitly ascribing to imagination a significant use in the sorts of activities he takes to be paradigmatic of our moral lives, such as acting on the basis of the moral law or respecting persons. This raises the question of whether, for all its pervasiveness in other domains, imagination reaches its limits in the moral domain on Kant's view.

A theory of moral imagination is certainly not something that is typically heralded as a major part of the legacy of Kant's moral theory.[5] And, indeed, among readers who have addressed the topic of imagination in this context, some have argued that Kant cannot, in fact, acknowledge a moral use of imagination. As Mark Johnson has recently put it, "moral imagination" seems to be an "oxymoron" for Kant on account of his rationalist commitment to morality being a "system of rational moral principles," on the one hand, and his dualist commitment to "imagination and reason [being] fundamentally different and nonoverlapping cognitive faculties," on the other (2016, 357).[6] In this vein, Johnson quotes Kant's

---

[4] Kant, elsewhere, refers to this "mysticism" as "delusion" of imagination or "visionary rapture" (*Schwämerei*), which he glosses as a **a delusion of being able to see something beyond all bounds of sensibility** (KU 5:275, see also AMr 25:1262, 1287–8, Mensch. 25:1006–7, AF 25:530–1, Tr. 2:339–48). And though he thinks "mysticism" and "delusion" of this sort are morally problematic, in the second *Critique* he immediately goes on to say that mysticism is not particularly prevalent because "it is not natural and not in keeping with the common way of thinking to strain one's imagination to supersensible intuitions" (KpV 5: 71). We might tease out a similar negative role in Kant's remarks about "enthusiasm" (KpV 5:84–6; Gr. 462), which he classifies elsewhere as a misuse of our imagination (see KU 5:275; AF 25:529–30; Mensch. 25:1006–7; AMr 25:1287).

[5] This is not to say that imagination is wholly neglected in discussions of Kant's moral philosophy. See Freydberg (2005) who offers a reconstruction of the role imagination plays throughout the second *Critique* in light of the idea that imagination is the source of synthesis and images; Johnson (1985), Ferrarin (2008), Freydberg (2013), and Kneller (2013, §5) who emphasize the role imagination plays in Kant's account of moral judgment; Gibbons (1994, chap. 5) and Kneller (2007) who discuss the connection between imagination and the highest good on Kant's view; Mattos (2013) who explores a role for imagination to play in Kant's account of the Postulates of Practical Reason; Varden (2020, 43–5, 117–21, 124–4, 134) who discusses the role aesthetic and teleological exercises of imagination play with regard to sex, love, and gender in Kant's practical framework; Vilhauer (2021; 2022) who explores the role imagination plays in Kant's account of sympathy and the duties of sympathy and beneficence; and Reath (2006, 46) and Timmermann (2022, chap. 2) who consider the role imagination plays vis-à-vis happiness. See also Biss (2014) for a broadly Kant-inspired discussion of the role imagination plays in creatively generating possibilities for moral action. There are also a set of commentators who focus on the moral significance of Kant's account of the aesthetic use of imagination in the third *Critique*, including Guyer (1993, chap. 6) who focuses on moral symbolism in the context of beauty and sublimity; Kneller (2007) who focuses on the relevance of aesthetic activities to the highest good; Clewis (2009) and Brady (2012; 2013a; 2013b; 2019) who focus on the sublime; McMahon (2014, chap. 7) and Walden (in progress) who focus on genius; Kemal (1992) and Geiger (2021) who focus on aesthetic ideas; and Eldridge (1989) who focuses on the role that literature plays in a historicized Kantian ethics.

[6] This said, Johnson (1985) also offers a reconstruction of the role imagination should play in Kant's theory of moral judgment, which I discuss in Chapter 12.

INTRODUCTION   327

remark in the second Critique that, "the moral law has no other cognitive faculty to mediate its application to objects of nature than the understanding (not the imagination)" (Johnson 2016, 357, quoting KpV 5:69). And Johnson underscores Kant's wariness of imagination in his Lectures on Ethics: "If he surrenders authority over himself, his imagination has free play; he cannot discipline himself, but his imagination carries him away . . . ; he yields willingly to his senses, and, unable to curb them, he becomes their toy" (Johnson (2016, 357, quoting EC 27:362). On Johnson's reading, what we find in the latter passage is not just the rationalist thought that reason and imagination do not overlap, but the thought that imagination, as part of sensibility, threatens to carry us away from reason's authority in the moral domain.

In a way, the charge that Kant's rationalist orientation in his moral philosophy prevents him from acknowledging a moral use of imagination is a more specific version of a charge that has long been leveled against his moral philosophy: it unduly neglects the moral prospects of our sensibility. We find an early critic of Kantian moral philosophy along these lines in Friedrich Schiller.[7] In "On Grace and Dignity" (1793), for example, Schiller says,

> In Kant's moral philosophy, the idea of duty is presented with a severity that repels all graces and might tempt a weak intellect to seek moral perfection by taking the path of a somber and monkish asceticism. However much this great philosopher tried to defend himself against this misinterpretation, which, to his serene and free spirit has to be the most outrageous one, he himself, it seems to me, has provided strong grounds for it (although, for his purpose, this was unavoidable), in his strict and harsh opposition of the two principles that have an effect on the human will.   (2005, 150)

Though sensitive to the subtlety in Kant's position, Schiller worries that the "severity" with which Kant presents moral duty can invite an overly "ascetic" view of our moral lives, according to which our sensibility is in need of repression insofar as it is governed by a practical principle fundamentally different from, and opposed to, the moral principle of reason. And to the extent that imagination is part of sensibility, it would seem we likewise need to repress it.

To get a sense of this asceticism worry, think about the following example of a philanthropist that Kant offers in the *Groundwork*:

> Suppose, then, that the mind of this philanthropist were overclouded by his own grief, which extinguished all sympathy with the fate of others, and that while he

---

[7] For discussion of Schiller's critique of Kant's moral philosophy, see Beiser (2005, chap. 2, 5–7); Deligiorgi (2006; 2020); Baxley (2008; 2010); Winegar (2013); and the essays in the Special Issue, "Introduction: Schiller's Challenge to Moral Philosophy—Schillers Herausforderung für die Moralphilosophie," ed. Falduto (2020).

328 THE POSSIBILITY OF MORAL IMAGINATION

still had the means to benefit others in distress their troubles did not move him because he had enough to do with his own; and suppose that now, when no longer incited to it by any inclination, he nevertheless tears himself out of this deadly insensibility and does the action without any inclination, simply from duty; not until then does it have its genuine moral worth. (Gr. 4:398)

Kant then intensifies the example,

if nature had put little sympathy in the heart of this or that man; if... he is by temperament cold and indifferent to the sufferings of others...; if nature had not properly fashioned such a man... for a philanthropist, would he still not find within himself a source from which to give himself a far higher worth than what a mere good-natured temperament might have? By all means! It is just that the worth of character comes out, which is moral and incomparably the highest, namely that he is beneficent not from inclination but from duty. (Gr. 4:398)

Kant's decision to hold out a philanthropist, who is either by circumstance or temperament cold and indifferent, as an exemplar of "incomparably the highest" kind of moral action and character certainly invites the worry that he condones a "gloomy and monkish ascetism" in our moral lives. To be sure, in a Schillerian spirit, we can regard this as ultimately a "misinterpretation," and, instead, attribute to Kant the intention of picking an extreme example to illustrate his conception of moral worth. However, there is undeniably a strand in Kant's moral philosophy which promotes a hierarchical view of the relationship between reason and sensibility in morality, according to which reason should "rule" and sensibility should be "subject" to this rule (see KpV 5:159; Gr. 5:343–5). And Schiller's criticism is that this hierarchical model does not represent the best thing we can aspire to in our moral lives. For better than a sensibility repressed by reason, Schiller claims, is a sensibility integrated with reason, which animates our moral efforts with "grace." And if we are looking for an account of moral imagination in this latter vein, then it might seem we need to look elsewhere than Kant's moral theory.

Then again, in the *Religion within the Boundaries of Mere Reason*, we find Kant making a rather surprising remark in response to Schiller's criticism,

Professor Schiller... disapproves of this way of representing obligation... Since we are however at one upon the most important principles, I cannot admit disagreement..., if only we can make ourselves clear to one another... And if we consider the gracious consequences that virtue would spread throughout the world, should it gain entry everywhere, then the morally oriented reason (through the imagination) calls sensibility into play. (Rel. 6:23n)

INTRODUCTION 329

In this passage, Kant insists that he and Schiller are "at one upon the most important principles."[8] And when it comes to virtue, Kant indicates that this unanimity is reflected in his commitment to there being a way in which a "morally oriented reason" should "call sensibility into play." In other words, Kant here stresses his sympathy with Schiller's more integrative model of how reason and sensibility should operate in our moral lives. And Kant claims that it is "through the imagination," in particular, that this integration can occur. Given Kant's sparse treatment of imagination in his moral writings, it comes as something of a surprise that he would task imagination with this important integrative role. From another perspective, however, this is not surprising at all. For as we have seen, on Kant's view, imagination is the cognitive capacity tasked with mediating between our sensible and intellectual sides. Why wouldn't we expect it to continue to play this role in Kant's account of our moral lives?

Making good on this suggestion by reconstructing the robust moral use imagination has on Kant's view is one of my main aims in the final part of this book. To this end, in Chapter 12, I explore the role it plays vis-à-vis our pursuit of moral principles through our faculty of desire; and in Chapter 13, I consider its role in relation to our moral development, moral judgment, morally relevant aesthetic activities, and moral perception.

However, in addition to bringing out the moral use of imagination in Kant's framework, I aim to bring to light its non-moral, but practically relevant use. In particular, in Chapter 12, I examine the contribution that Kant takes our imagination to make to our non-moral (though not necessarily immoral) pursuit of happiness and well-being vis-à-vis the imaginative projection of an "ideal of happiness."

Given the paucity of Kant's references to imagination in his practical writings, this analysis will proceed by way of a fair bit of reconstruction on my part. I shall anchor this reconstruction in Kant's theory of what kind of cognitive capacity imagination is in general that I developed in Part I. Reserving the details for subsequent chapters, as a kind of preliminary here, I would like to note some important implications that this framing has for the work we should, and should not, expect imagination to do in Kant's practical framework.

In the first place, recall that in Kant's map of the mind, there are three fundamental mental faculties: the "faculty of cognition" (*Erkenntnisvermögen*), the "faculty of desire" (*Begehrungsvermögen*), and the faculty of the "feeling of pleasure and displeasure" (*Gefühl der Lust und Unlust*). In his practical writings, Kant's primary concern is with the "faculty of desire," which he defines as "the faculty to

---

[8] More specifically, in this context, Kant claims that although Schiller's account of grace does not have purchase on the moral concept of duty (which is a matter of "The majesty of the law"), it does have purchase on the concept of virtue ("the firmly grounded disposition to fulfill one's duty") (Rel. 6:23n).

330   THE POSSIBILITY OF MORAL IMAGINATION

be, by means of one's representations, the cause of the objects of these representations" (MS 6:211; see also KpV 5:9, EE 20:206, MV 29:1012–22). So understood, the faculty of desire involves a causal capacity by means of which we act to bring about particular objects or states of affairs that we represent. However, as we have seen, on Kant's view, imagination is a capacity that belongs not to the faculty of desire, but rather to the faculty of cognition, and this has important consequences for how we are to think about the practical exercise of imagination in Kant's framework. For Kant, the practical use of imagination will turn on cognitive activities of imagination that contribute, in some way, to the practical activities at issue in the faculty of desire.

Moreover, as I argued in Chapter 3, on Kant's view, imagination is a cognitive capacity that belongs to sensibility, the faculty of intuition; in which case, the practical use of imagination will turn on cognitive activities of imagination that involve intuitions of imagination (intuitions$_i$). As I have stressed, given this commitment, Kant, in contrast to many contemporary theorists, does not countenance as imaginative non-sensory activities, such as supposing or entertaining that some proposition is the case without the aid of sensory representations. For Kant, all episodes of imagining are sensory in character. Insofar as this is the case, his account of the practical use of imagination will not include activities that some contemporary theorists describe as "imaginative," such as coming up with a creative solution to a moral problem in thought,[9] thinking that is not governed by rules,[10] metaphorical thinking,[11] or non-pictorial thought experiments in ethics.[12] For Kant, it is only practical activities that have a sensible, intuition$_i$-involving component that can fall under the umbrella of the practical use of imagination.

However, within the domain of sensory imagining, Kant is committed to our imagination playing a distinctive role in our practical lives: it has the cognitive function of making practical concepts sensible in intuitions$_i$. I have emphasized the subject-facing ways in which the imaginative activity of making concepts sensible serves us, by facilitating our concrete comprehension of concepts (see Chapters 3, 4, and 8). Indeed, as I intimated at the end of the last chapter, according to Kant, it is a "natural need of all human beings to demand for even the highest concepts...something that *can be sensibly held on to* [etwas Sinnlich-haltbares]" (Rel. 6:109; transl. modified).[13] On his view, this need is operative in the practical domain as much as any other domain. And, for Kant, it is precisely as a sensory, rather than a non-sensory, capacity, tasked with the subject-facing

---

[9] See Biss (2014, §2.4).   [10] See Larmore (2001).
[11] See Johnson (1985). I return to this metaphorical reading of the role imagination plays vis-à-vis the categorical imperative and the universalizability test of maxims in Chapter 12.
[12] See Kung (2016b).
[13] See also my discussion of Kant's account of this in the context of the "aesthetic perfection" of cognition, which is "grounded on the particular sensibility of man" (JL 9:36) in Chapters 4 and 8.

cognitive function of making concepts sensible through intuitions$_i$, that our imagination can help satisfy this need of ours.

However, in the context of Kant's practical philosophy, there is an even more specific idea about the sensory orientation of imagination that I would like to stress, which pertains to the specific way in which our imagination exhibits practical concepts. Here, I shall take my cue from another one of Kant's claims in the *Religion*: "It is plainly a limitation of human reason, one which is ever inseparable from it, that we cannot think of any significant moral worth in the actions of a person without at the same time portraying this person or his expression in human guise" (Rel. 6:64–5n).[14] In this passage, we find Kant articulating another need that we have as human beings: when we try and make moral actions concretely "comprehensible" to ourselves, we cannot help but represent them "in human guise" (Rel. 6:65n). Indeed, Kant claims that, "to become subjectively practical" our moral concepts "must be considered in relation to human beings and to individual human beings" (KpV 5:157). Although he does not explain exactly why this anthropomorphizing is required, I take his thought to be that one of our limitations as humans is that the only real touchstone we have for what moral action concretely looks like is a human one.[15] Insofar as this is the case, even when we attempt to envision moral action of non-human creatures, like aliens or divine beings, *per* Kant, we will need to anthropomorphize it to some extent.

While this line of thought speaks to certain anthropomorphic assumptions Kant held, I think it also clues us into a kind of substantive contribution that our imagination can make in our practical lives: our imagination facilitates our comprehension of practical concepts by intuitively exhibiting them in human guise. That is to say, the way our imagination enables us to "hold on to" practical concepts, such as <moral worth> or <happiness>, is by illustrating how they manifest in human lives. Indeed, though Kant does not explicitly explore this thought, I take it that in the practical context, imagining gives us a grip on how these concepts manifest not only externally in our conduct and interaction with others, but also internally in our thoughts, feelings, desires, and characters.[16] As I discussed in Chapter 3, on Kant's view, our imaginative activities proceed by ordering and organizing material delivered to us through sensibility. There, I flagged the possibility of our imagination drawing on material from both our outer senses, such as sight, sound, touch, taste, and smell, through which we are affected by

---

[14] He continues, "for we always need a certain analogy with natural being in order to make supersensible characteristics comprehensible to us" (Rel. 6:64–5n).

[15] See, e.g., "It is noteworthy that we can think of no other suitable form for a *rational* being than that of a human being... Therefore we populate all other planets in our imagination with nothing but human forms, although it is probable that they may be formed very differently" (Anthro. 7:172).

[16] To borrow some contemporary language to make this point, imagining "from the inside," not just "from the outside" has an important role to play in the practical use of imagination that I sketch (see Ninan 2016).

332 THE POSSIBILITY OF MORAL IMAGINATION

"physical things," and our inner sense, through which we are affected "by the mind" (Anthro. 7:153). I take it that in the practical domain, our imagination will draw, in part, on representations from inner sense and generate intuitions$_i$ that represent how choice, deliberation, and action consciously manifest in our inner lives. Here, our ability to imagine what it is first-personally like for us, as the individuals that we are, to choose, deliberate, and act will matter, as will the sympathetic ability to imagine what it is like for others, as the individuals that they are, to do the same.[17] And, on my interpretation at least, it is by facilitating our comprehension of how practical and moral concepts manifest in human guise, as much externally as internally, that our imagining broadens our horizons with respect to these concepts in an especially illuminating way. As I shall read Kant, then, one of the distinctive functions of sensory imagining in the practical domain is that it gives us a way to refract practical concepts through a human lens, and in so doing fulfills a need we have, as the kind of sensible-rational creatures we are.

The final point that I wish to make by way of set up concerns the practical use of imagination and the three definitions of imagination that I introduced in Chapter 4. Recall that, on Kant's view, our imagination in general is responsible for engaging in formative activities that generate intuitions$_i$ that represent objects even without their presence and that exhibit concepts to us. We should thus expect the practical exercise of imagination to proceed by way of these sorts of formative, even-without-presence, and exhibiting activities. However, I shall just take for granted that in the practical domain, our imagination engages in formative activities that involve spatio-temporally organizing a manifold delivered through sensibility. What I shall, instead, concentrate my efforts on is teasing out the role that the latter two sorts of imaginative activities play in the practical domain. Drawing on the even-without-presence definition in the next chapter, I make the case that our imaginative ability to "see more" than is immediately present to us serves us in exercising the faculty of desire in the pursuit of both happiness and morality. And drawing on the exhibition definition of imagination in Chapter 13, I argue that even though Kant is committed to morality having a rational basis, he is also committed to us, as human beings, needing to engage in imaginative activities that make moral concepts sensible, as concretely manifesting in our lives. This said, though I discuss separately the practical relevance of the imaginative activities of seeing more and exhibition in these chapters, since I take seeing more and exhibition to both be definitive of imagination on Kant's view, the imaginative activities I discuss will involve elements of each. So even though I am presenting them separately, I do not mean to deny that exhibition plays a role in the cases that I discuss under the heading of seeing more or vice versa.

---

[17] See Vilhauer (2021; 2022) for discussion of the role imagination plays in Kant's theory of sympathy.

INTRODUCTION 333

I instead mean to highlight an aspect, whether seeing more or exhibition, of the more complex imaginative endeavors that serve us practically well.

In the end, by anchoring my discussion of the practical use of imagination in Kant's theory of imagination more generally I hope to bring to light the way in which imagination pervades even our practical lives on his view. And, ultimately, with this practical use in view, I aim to bolster my overarching argument to the effect that Kant offers a unified theory of imagination, as a single cognitive capacity that operates in a rich variety of ways across the theoretical, aesthetic, and practical domains.

Seeing More: Kant's Theory of Imagination. Samantha Matherne, Oxford University Press.
© Samantha Matherne 2024. DOI: 10.1093/9780191999291.003.0012

12

Imaginative Sight and the Faculty
of Desire

> Without imagination we cannot see truly,
> for to be lukewarm in a glowing world is to miss the truth
> —Ella Lyman Cabot, *Everyday Ethics*

12.1 Introduction

In order to begin exploring Kant's account of the role imagination plays in our practical lives, I orient this chapter around the question of how imagination, as a cognitive capacity that enables us to see more than is immediately present to us, contributes to our pursuit of happiness and morality through what Kant calls "the faculty of desire." I introduced the imaginative ability to see more in Chapter 4 in my discussion of Kant's definition of imagination as "the faculty for representing an object in intuition even **without its presence**" (B151; transl. modified). While this might sound like a traditional definition of imagination as fantasy, I argued that Kant innovates within this tradition by defending a view, according to which our imagination operates not wholly in the absence of objects, but rather with a degree of independence from the presence of objects. And in elucidating this even-without-presence definition, I suggested that Kant commits himself to our imagination enabling us to see more, whether of an object that is absent or one that is present to us, where "seeing" is here used loosely as a term for sensory awareness. In this chapter, I offer an account of what role seeing more has vis-à-vis the faculty of desire on Kant's view. And what I aim to bring to light are various ways in which this imaginative mode of sight attunes us to practical realities and possibilities in a way that serves us as we find, refine, and perhaps even radically transform our practical pursuits as human agents.

I open in §12.2 with a discussion of Kant's conception of the faculty of desire and its relationship to our pursuit of happiness and morality. In §12.3, I then offer a reconstruction of how the imaginative activity of seeing more bears on three basic ways in which we exercise this faculty: the specification of practical principles, the assessment of concrete situations in light of particular practical principles, and deliberation about which course of action to pursue in concrete situations. In §12.4, I then take up Kant's account of the connection between imagination

THE FACULTY OF DESIRE   335

and our pursuit of happiness. I analyze his characterization of happiness as an "ideal of imagination,"[1] and I argue that he ascribes to this ideal not only a practical use internal to the lower faculty of desire, but also a moral use in relation to the higher faculty of desire. In §12.5, I turn to another role that imaginatively seeing more can play in relation to the higher faculty of desire: its contribution to testing the moral value of particular practical principles ("maxims") in light of the categorical imperative.

12.2 The Faculty of Desire

As I have discussed, Kant defines the faculty of desire as a causal capacity by means of which we act to bring about particular objects or states of affairs that we represent.[2] For example, when I think that some dahlias would look quite pretty on my table and then go purchase some at a flower shop, *per* Kant, I have exercised my faculty of desire in a way that causally brings about a state of affairs I represented.

When discussing the faculty of desire of the human being, Kant often references the "will" (*Wille*).[3] His account of the will is complex and controversial, but for my purposes here, hopefully it will suffice to say that, for Kant, the will pertains to a particular way of exercising the faculty of desire, viz. according to principles and reasons.[4] For example, if I have a principle of buying myself flowers on Thursdays, when I go to the flower shop this Thursday and buy myself flowers, I will be acting on the basis of that principle; hence exercising my will. Though the notion of will is certainty central to Kant's analysis of our practical agency, I focus on the faculty of desire in order to keep in view his tripartite map of the mind, as divided between the three basic faculties of cognition, desire, and the feeling of pleasure and displeasure, that has oriented me throughout.

As is the case in his account of the faculty of cognition, Kant distinguishes between a "lower" and "higher" faculty of desire.[5] He characterizes the lower faculty of desire as a practical form of sensibility, which proceeds in a sensible and receptive way, and the higher faculty of desire as a practical form of reason, which proceeds in an intellectual and spontaneous way. And he argues that there is a different fundamental principle, or "determining ground," that governs each: the

---

[1] I began addressing this in my discussion of the dynamical sublime in Chapter 10.
[2] For overviews of Kant's account of the faculty of desire, see Frierson (2014b, chap. 2); Wuerth (2014, chap. 6); Wood (2018). Here, I focus on the faculty of desire that human beings possess, setting aside questions about what kind of faculty of desire non-human animals possess.
[3] For discussion of the relationship between the faculty of desire and will, see Herman (2007, chap. 10); Engstrom (2010).
[4] See Gr. 4:412, 427; KpV 5:32; MS 6:213.
[5] See KpV 5:22–4; ML1 28:228–9, 258; MV 29:1013–16; MMr 29:897–901; AP. 25:438; AMr 25:1334.

336 IMAGINATIVE SIGHT AND THE FACULTY OF DESIRE

lower faculty is governed by the principle of happiness (or self-love) and the higher by the moral law (KpV 5:21). Let's take a closer look at each faculty, in turn.

Beginning with the lower faculty of desire, Kant claims that, "To be happy is necessarily the demand of every rational but finite being and therefore an unavoidable determining ground of its faculty of desire" (KpV 5:25, see also 22). As we see here, Kant takes our lower faculty of desire to be bound up with our nature as finite, sensible beings who want to be happy.[6] In detailing what the demand to be happy amounts to, Kant defines happiness as a "maximum of well-being [*Wohlbefindens*] in my present condition and in every future condition" (Gr. 4:418). And he characterizes this "maximum of well-being" in hedonic terms, as "based on the feeling of pleasure or displeasure," and in terms of desire satisfaction, as "the entire satisfaction" of our "needs and inclinations" (KpV 5:26, Gr. 4:405; see also A806/B834; Gr. 4:395, 399; KU 5:208, 422, 208).[7] For Kant, then, the principle of happiness directs us toward pursuing objects and states of affairs that will be conducive to our pleasure and desire satisfaction in some maximal way.

Though the principle of happiness involves the demand to be happy, Kant also asserts that, "Happiness is so indeterminate a concept that, even though every human being wishes to achieve it, yet he can never say determinately and in agreement with himself what he actually wishes and wants" (Gr. 4:417–18; see also KU 5:340). In explicating the indeterminacy of the concept of happiness, Kant emphasizes the fact that what we take pleasure in and desire not only varies from person to person, but also varies over the course of each of our lives: "where each has to put his happiness comes down to the particular feeling of pleasure and displeasure in each, and even within one and the same subject, to needs that differ as this feeling changes" (KpV 5:25). What is more, even if we are able to identify some of our hedonic preferences and desires, he claims that we cannot be in a position to know that they will, in fact, lead to happiness:

> If he wants riches, how much worry, envy and intrigue might he not by this bring down upon his shoulders! If he wants much cognition and insight, that might perhaps only sharpen his eyes all the more, to show him as all the more terrible the ills that are still concealed from him now...If he wants long life, who will guarantee him that it would not be a long misery?...In short, he is not able to determine with complete certainty...what will make him truly happy. (Gr. 4:418)

---

[6] See also, "there is *one* end that can be presupposed as actual in all rational beings (...as dependent beings)" (Gr. 4:415), and "we find our nature as sensible beings so constituted that the matter of the faculty of desire (objects of inclination, whether of hope or fear) first forces itself upon us" (where "matter" is a reference to happiness as the "material practical rule" that governs the faculty of desire) (KpV 5:74, 21).

[7] While some commentators insist that happiness, for Kant, only involves desire satisfaction (see Allison 1990, 102–103), most acknowledge his emphasis on its hedonic dimensions (see Johnson 2005; Hills 2006; Kohl 2017; Timmermann 2022, chap. 2).

To compound matters further, *per* Kant, happiness involves fitting our hedonic preferences and desires into the "absolute whole" that is our well-being over time; however, formulating a determinate concept of happiness along these lines would require being able to compare, weigh, and temporally anticipate our preferences and desires in a totalizing way that seems to outstrip what we are capable of (Gr. 4:418).

Nevertheless, since the pursuit of happiness is something that the principle of happiness demands of us, Kant insists that each of us must at least try and navigate the "problem" of determining our hedonic preferences and desires and how they might fit into the whole of our well-being (KpV 5:26). And though Kant thinks there are no *a priori* resources we can draw on to this end, he thinks that we can at least "empirically" try and sort through, and update, our sense of what happiness consists in for us, as the individuals that we are (KpV 5:25; see also Gr. 4:418; more on this in §12.4).

Whereas our lower faculty of desire is organized around the pursuit of happiness, Kant claims that our higher faculty of desire is oriented around the pursuit of morality. This faculty is one that Kant takes us to have insofar as we are rational creatures; hence his alignment of it with practical reason. And instead of being governed by the principle of happiness, Kant maintains that the principle that governs the higher faculty of desire is the moral law (see KpV 5:21). For finite rational creatures like us, Kant argues that the moral law takes shape as the categorical imperative: "So act that the maxim of your will could always hold at the same time as a principle in a giving of universal law" (KpV 5:30; see also Gr. 4:402, 421). For Kant, a maxim is a "subjective" principle on the basis of which someone acts, e.g. "I will express gratitude in order to honor those who help me" or "I will cut in line when I am short on time" (Gr. 4:421). His basic thought is that the moral law requires that we only act on maxims that could "hold" as a "universal law," i.e. that could be a principle on the basis of which everyone could act. For, on Kant's view, it is only if a maxim has a universalizable form, as something that could be binding on everyone, that it can be said to have moral worth (see Gr. 4:402, 421; KpV 5:27–8).

In order to figure out whether one's maxim could hold as a universal law, Kant proposes a test: could your maxim hold as a universal law of nature, or would some sort of contradiction arise in such a world (see Gr. 4:421–4; KpV 5:69–70)?[8] Consider my maxim: I will cut in line whenever I am short on time. Were this maxim a universal law of nature, a contradiction would arise. On the one hand, this maxim requires that there be a practice of forming lines, in which people stay in their allotted spot regardless of whether they want to or not. On the other

---

[8] I am here glossing over the distinction Kant draws between two kinds of contradictions: a logical contradiction, which arises when we try and think of the maxim as a universal law of nature, and a practical contradiction, which arises when we try and will the maxims as a universal law of nature (see Gr. 4:424).

338 IMAGINATIVE SIGHT AND THE FACULTY OF DESIRE

hand, were this maxim a universal law of nature, then everyone would cut in line whenever they were short on time, and the practice of line formation would fall apart. Now consider a world in which the maxim, I will express gratitude to honor those who have benefitted me, were a universal law of nature.[9] Were everyone to act on the basis of this maxim, a contradiction would not arise the way it does with the line maxim. For Kant, the categorical imperative thus directs us to act only on the basis of maxims that could hold as a universal law of nature, for it is these maxims alone that have the universalizable form that is the mark of moral worth.

According to Kant, it is thus the moral law, in the form of the categorical imperative, that serves as the principle that is the determining ground of the higher faculty of desire. And this law, he claims, is one that we autonomously legislate to ourselves through our practical reason (see Gr. 4:446–7; KpV 5:33).

With this sketch of the faculty of desire in place, let's turn to how our imagination, as a capacity that enables us to see more than we are immediately given, can interface with this faculty on Kant's view.

12.3 Seeing More and the Faculty of Desire

In order to begin drawing out the relevance of our imagination to the faculty of desire, I begin in this section by offering a reconstruction of three basic ways in which imaginatively seeing more can aid us in exercising the faculty of desire, which cut across the lower-higher divide. To be clear, in exploring the different ways our imagination can contribute to these ends, I am teasing out a position that Kant does not explicitly defend, but one that I nevertheless take him to be committed to in light of his general characterization of imagination as a capacity that enables us to see more.

Let me start, then, by saying a bit more about which three basic ways in which we exercise the faculty of desire that I have in mind. The first concerns the specification of practical principles. As I just discussed, on Kant's view, the lower and higher parts of the faculty of desire are each governed by a basic principle: the

---

[9] Kant describes gratitude as follows, "The feeling connected with the judgment is respect for the benefactor (who puts one under obligations), whereas the benefactor is viewed only in relation of love toward the recipient. The feeling connected with this judgment is respect for the benefactor..., whereas the benefactor is viewed as only in a relation of love toward the recipient" (MS 6:454). The context suggests that the "love" at issue here is "practical" love or "benevolence," defined in terms of "making the well-being and happiness of others my *end*" (MS 6:449, 452). He also claims that practical love involves a benefactor "making" themselves "deserving" of a response like gratitude from others (MS 6:450). I take these qualifications to be significant for how we should understand this maxim of gratitude: it involves showing gratitude to those who help us from a place of love, but does not require showing gratitude to those who help us from a place of, say, manipulation, denigration, or other problematic motives.

principle of happiness and moral law, respectively. However, according to Kant, exercises of the faculty of desire are also guided by more specific principles, "maxims," that reflect specific ways of being happy (e.g. through wealth, intelligence, or flowers), or adhering to the moral law (e.g. by being grateful or not cutting in line). Arriving at more specific principles that orient us toward bringing about specific objects or states of affairs is thus one basic way in which we exercise the faculty of desire on Kant's view.

For Kant, another basic way of exercising the faculty of desire involves being able to assess a concrete situation in light of which specific practical principle we should act on in it.[10] Sometimes it will be clear to us which principle is relevant. For example, for someone who is committed to buying flowers and being grateful, it might not be mysterious which practical principles to act on at a florist: they should act on the maxim to buy flowers for happiness and the maxim of expressing gratitude to those who have benefited them. But sometimes it will not be clear to us what practical principles are relevant. For example, for someone who enjoys both flowers and plants, at a garden center, they might feel torn between whether they should act on the flowers-for-happiness or plants-for-happiness principle. Or to take a moral example, suppose on an airplane a man looks at a woman he does not know and hoists her luggage into the overhead bin. On the one hand, this seems helpful. On the other hand, this action might have been motivated by certain gendered assumptions that the woman does not endorse. The woman in this situation might thus find herself unsure about whether she should act on the maxim of gratitude or a maxim of self-respect that concerns resisting such gendered assumptions. In practical situations such as these that are more ambiguous or otherwise not straightforward, though we still need to exercise our faculty of desire in assessing the situation and determining which specific principle to act on, this will require more careful deliberation.

Finally, even if we have determined what specific principle is relevant in our current situation, there may still be a question of how we should actually proceed, and this sort of deliberation about the best course of action is a third basic way we exercise the faculty of desire in Kant's framework. For example, in the flower shop, even if someone has decided to act on the flowers-for-happiness principle, they are faced with the question of what kind of flowers, how many, cut or potted, etc. And if they are also appreciative and have determined the maxim of gratitude is applicable, they still have to decide how to express that gratitude to the florist, e.g. monetarily, verbally, or through some other means.

---

[10] The sort of assessment I have in mind is what O'Neill (drawing on David Wiggins) describes as "situational appraisals" (1990, 182), and Hermann describes in terms of determining "moral salience" (1993, chap. 4).

340 IMAGINATIVE SIGHT AND THE FACULTY OF DESIRE

Though Kant does not explicitly argue for this, what I would now like to propose is that the imaginative capacity for seeing more is something that has a distinctive contribution to make with respect to all three of these ways of exercising the faculty of desire. As I noted in Chapter 11, given Kant's commitment to imagination being a sensible capacity, what we imaginatively do in these scenarios will not turn on non-sensory activities, which some contemporary theorists describe as "imaginative," such as coming up with a creative solution to a practical problem or deploying a thought experiment without the aid of sensory representations. Instead, by describing what our imagination does in terms of seeing more, I mean to stress the sensory nature of what it contributes on Kant's picture. And though the exact sensory activities our imagination enacts in these three practical activities will differ, I take it that they all share a common sensory core: they involve us generating intuitions of imagination (intuitions$_i$) that make a practical difference to us. More specifically, drawing on the idea that I introduced in Chapter 11, I take it that these intuitions$_i$ help us by providing us with sensory representations of the "human guise" of these practical issues (see Rel. 6:64–5n). That is to say, the distinctive contribution that our sensory imagining makes to these activities turns on the ways in which it enables us to intuitively envision what is practically actual and possible for us not just as rational beings, but as human beings.

Turning to the details, beginning with principle specification in Kant's framework, imaginatively projecting different possible ways in which human beings might be happy or act morally can aid us in arriving at the specific practical principles we, in fact, want to commit ourselves to. This imaginative projection will proceed by way of us generating intuitions$_i$ that enable us to visualize different possible models of happiness and moral action, which reflect specific practical principles and the difference they can make in human lives, including externally in our actions and interactions and internally in our thoughts, feelings, and desires.

But more than just iterating possibilities, by making specific practical principles concrete in these human ways, our imaginative projections can serve us in sorting through which specific practical commitments we, ourselves, want to endorse. For example, envisioning more personalized models of happiness that reflect the prioritization of, say, wealth or intelligence, externally and internally, can help us try and determine for ourselves which specific principles of happiness are best suited to who we are as individuals (more on this in §12.4). Likewise, if we take the formulation of the categorical imperative, "*So act that you use humanity, in your own person as well as in the person of any other, always at the same time as an end, never merely as a means*," generating intuitions$_i$ of how someone might adhere to this in relation to, say, strangers, friends, or colleagues, can help us arrive at principles we want to endorse that articulate more specific ways to treat human beings as ends (Gr. 4:429).

SEEING MORE AND THE FACULTY OF DESIRE   341

With respect to situation assessment on Kant's view, the imaginative act of seeing more can contribute in both more straightforward situations and situations that require more careful deliberation about which specific principle to act on. In the former case, we need to be able to see the situation as one in which the principle is salient. To see why, recall once more Kant's physician from the first *Critique*, who understands disease concepts in the abstract but fails to identify cases of them in the concrete (see Chapters 4 and 5). Though part of the physician's problem is an intellectual one, he cannot judge that a patient has, say, cholera, I have argued that, on Kant's view, part of the physician's problem is an imaginative one: he does not have the imaginative art, i.e. the skill or know-how, that enables him to identify when a disease concept is manifesting *in concreto*. And I take it that a similar issue arises in the practical case: in order to practically proceed, it is not enough for us to grasp practical principles in the abstract. We need to be able to see scenarios we find ourselves in as ones that call for us to act on those principles.[11] For example, in the flower shop scenario, in order to respond to this situation as one that calls for me to act on the maxim of gratitude, I need to see the florist's activities as ones that benefit me.

However, on my interpretation of Kant, this sort of sight is not just a matter of passively sensing the situation. I have argued that, on his view, sensing is a receptive process in which we are immediately affected by a situation through our senses and it does not involve concepts (see Chapters 3 and 5). But if we are to see a situation as one in which a practical principle is applicable, then we need a more active and conceptually laden mode of sight: we need the sort of perception that Kant claims imagination is a "necessary ingredient of" (A120n).[12] In his framework, a key component of this perception will be us imaginatively taking up what we sense and generating intuitions$_i$ that represent the scenario as one that calls for us to act on a particular practical principle. For example, in the flower shop, my perception of the florist's actions as ones that call for my gratitude, *per* Kant, will involve me imaginatively generating an intuition$_i$ through which I see the florist in this light.

As for concrete situations in which we need to more carefully deliberate about what practical principle we should act on, it seems the imaginative activity of seeing more again has a role to play on Kant's view. As we deliberate about the situation, our imagination can help us attempt to see it in different lights, by generating intuitions$_i$ that represent the situation in different ways, and on the basis of which

[11] See, e.g. Herman's emphasis on sight and perception in her discussion of rules of moral salience: "What I have argued here is that the Kantian moral agent must have a characteristic way of seeing if he is to judge at all. To be a moral agent one must be trained to perceive situations in terms of their morally significant features" (1993, 83).

[12] I return to the topic of how our imagination contributes to perception in the moral domain in Chapter 13, §13.5.

we can consider which imagined possibility is most fitting to the reality in which we find ourselves. In the airplane scenario, in order to sort through which practical principle is relevant the woman might attempt to imaginatively replay the scenario as one that is helpful or biased by generating intuitions$_i$ that highlight different details and represent the man's actions as motivated in different ways. And as she considers how the situation she, in fact, lived through resonates, or not, with these possible scenarios, she might determine, for herself, which principle the scenario calls for her to act on. Or in the garden center scenario, in order to decide whether the situation calls for buying a flower or plant, the person might try and imaginatively generate an intuition$_i$ that represents either at their home, and through this envisioning of possibilities realize that one or the other of those scenarios is what their own pursuit of happiness calls for. In this case as in the airplane case, it seems we proceed by imaginatively seeing more to a situation in light of alternative possibilities that we project in intuitions$_i$, and then determining what principle is appropriate on the basis of which imagined possibility is most apt to the reality in which we find ourselves.

Finally, with respect to scenarios in which we have determined what principle is relevant, but we need to deliberate about what course of action to pursue, here too we can draw on the imaginative capacity to see more. As we deliberate, we can attempt to imaginatively see different possible courses of action that we, as the human beings that we are, might pursue. In so doing, we might imaginatively project intuitions$_i$ that represent courses of action, including their external and internal profile, on the basis of similar scenarios in the past. In imaginatively projecting a new flower or plant at home, someone might generate an intuition$_i$ that draws on their past domestic experiences with flowers or plants, which reflect not only how flowers look, but also how they felt in response to them. However, these activities might proceed in more creative and inventive ways, as we envision human courses of action that are unlike ones we ourselves have enacted in the past.[13] For example, in deciding how to express gratitude to a florist, even if they have never done this before, someone might generate an intuition$_i$ of sending a postcard or pastries as a way of expressing their gratitude, which represents not just this action, but the possible interpersonal effect of this action.[14] In this sort of imaginative act, they open up new possibilities of action for themselves. But whether through more familiar or creative paths, the imaginative projection of possible human courses of action in intuitions$_i$ can play a helpful role in our deliberating about how exactly we, as the human beings that we are, should act in a situation we find ourselves in.

---

[13] See Biss (2014) for discussion of the moral imagination involved in creatively generating new possibilities of moral action as important and distinct from the moral imagination involved in moral perception and moral judgment.

[14] As I noted earlier, Kant mentions the role imagination plays in sympathy at MS 6:457. See Vilhauer (2021; 2022) for discussion.

Piecing this together, when we consider what is involved in these exercises of the faculty of desire, as we navigate abstract principles and concrete particulars, the imaginative activity of seeing more contributes in valuable ways in Kant's framework. Through intuitions₁ in which we try and concretely work out the external and internal contours of practical possibilities and actualities from a human perspective, we see more than we are immediately given in a way that contributes to our pursuit of happiness and morality in specific situations and in light of specific practical principles.

With this more general reconstruction of how imaginatively seeing more can productively interact with the faculty of desire on Kant's view in place, I now want to take a closer look at two more specific ways in which this imaginative sight interacts with the lower and higher faculty of desire: the first concerns his description of happiness as a so-called "ideal of imagination" and the second concerns the assessment of maxims in light of the categorical imperative.

12.4 Imagination and the Pursuit of Happiness

As I discussed in Chapter 10, in the *Groundwork*, Kant claims that happiness is "not an ideal of reason, but of the imagination, which rests merely on empirical grounds" (Gr. 4:418; see also KU 5:430, MS 6:452, KpV 5:61).[15] It might be tempting to read this claim as shorthand for the claim that, given its indeterminate status, the concept of happiness is, in some sense, "unrealizable."[16] However, in this section, I argue that by describing happiness as an ideal of imagination, Kant has something more substantive in mind: as human beings, part of how we try and solve the problem of happiness is by imaginatively envisioning concrete models of human happiness in the form of ideals. And through these imaginative projections, we come to see more to happiness than our indeterminate concept of it provides. To develop this argument, I first lay out what it means for happiness to be an ideal of imagination and what sort of imaginative sight this involves, before considering the role that this ideal plays in relation to the lower and higher faculties of desire, respectively.

In order to unpack Kant's notion of what happiness is as an ideal of imagination, let's begin with Kant's notion of an ideal. As I discussed in Chapter 10, Kant

---

[15] Commentators who discuss Kant's theory of happiness often neglect his description of it as an "ideal of imagination" in the *Groundwork*. For example, in their commentaries on the *Groundwork*, Timmermann (2007, §II), Hills (2009), and Allison (2011, chap. 6) do not mention this claim. See, however, brief discussions in Reath (2006, 46); Clewis (2009, 79–80); Varden (2020, 56–7); Timmermann (2022, 16, 19–20).

[16] See, e.g., Barney's gloss of happiness, *qua* an ideal of imagination, as the "essentially unrealizable," "infantile fantasy" of "the condition of a being for whom 'everything goes according to wish and will'" (2015, 162), and Kohl's gloss of happiness as "an unrealizable idea of imagination" that amounts to a "mere wish" that "does not represent any determinate state of affairs" (2017, 526).

344 IMAGINATIVE SIGHT AND THE FACULTY OF DESIRE

describes an ideal in general as a representation of "an individual being as adequate to an idea," where an idea is a concept of reason that represents some sort of perfection or maximum (KU 5:232; see also A568/B596).[17] As he sometimes puts it, the ideal involves a representation of an individual as an "Urbild," an "archetype," who perfectly realizes an idea (see A569–70/B598–7; KU 5:232; BL 24:47; ML2 25:577). For example, Kant cites a "sage" as an ideal that represents an archetypal individual who perfectly embodies the idea of wisdom (A569/B597). This said, Kant also insists that an ideal does not involve a representation of any actual human individual: our "natural limits" make is "impossible" for us to achieve such perfection (A570/B598). The archetypal individual is, instead, a personified standard of perfection that we can strive to approximate, but never hope to attain.[18]

In the case of the ideal of happiness, the idea at issue is the idea of happiness, which, to repeat, Kant glosses in terms of "a maximum of well-being, in my present and every future condition" (Gr. 4:418).[19] The ideal of happiness, for Kant, thus involves a representation of an archetypal individual who perfectly realizes maximal well-being. More specifically, given my suggestion in Chapter 11 that Kant thinks we need to represent practical concepts to ourselves in human guise, the ideal of happiness will involve a representation of an archetypal human or human-like figure who embodies maximal well-being. And given that Kant claims that happiness is something that "rests merely on empirical grounds," the ideal of happiness will also involve a representation of an archetypal anthropomorphic figure whose maximal well-being rests on taking pleasure and satisfaction in empirical things, such as wealth, intelligence, and health (Gr. 4:418).

However, by describing the ideal of happiness as an ideal of imagination, Kant takes on a further commitment: insofar as the ideal is a product of imagination, it will involve some kind of intuition$_i$ in which we imaginatively project a happy human archetype. To repeat some examples from Chapter 10, if we think happiness turns on prioritizing wealth, then we might generate an intuition$_i$ that represents a Gatsby-style individual (who comes to a happy end). Or if we think it turns on privileging intelligence, then we might project a George Eliot-style individual. I take it that in projecting these intuitions$_i$, we do not just imaginatively represent the external events and relationships in a human life, but also what it is like from the inside to lead a life organized around such a pursuit.

But why exactly does Kant ascribe the ideal of happiness to imagination? To answer this question, I think we need to return to Kant's claim that happiness is an indeterminate concept. As I discussed above, on his view, the indeterminacy of

---

[17] I address the relationship between ideals of reason and ideals of imagination in Chapter 13.
[18] Kant, in fact, warns of expecting that archetypes can be realized in the sensible world as something that gives rise to "enthusiasm" (see AF 25:529).
[19] See also KU 5:430; MS 6:452; KpV 5:61.

happiness poses a problem for us: though we can "never say determinately" what the happiness is that we "actually wish and want," given that we are subject to the demand to be happy, each of us must nevertheless try and determine what it means for us, as the individuals that we are (Gr. 4:418). And though we will never achieve "complete certainty" in this, we must nevertheless make the attempt (Gr. 4:418).

In analyzing Kant's account of how we attempt to determine what happiness involves, interpreters often appeal to his account of prudential reason and so-called "imperatives of prudence" or "empirical counsels, e.g., of diet, of thrift, of politeness, of restraint, and so on, which experience teaches on average advance well-being most" (Gr. 4:417–18).[20] Though no doubt an important part of Kant's picture, I shall make the case that our imaginative sighting of happiness in the form of an ideal also has a distinctive role to play in this regard.[21] More specifically, given how indeterminate the concept of happiness is, the basic idea I want to develop is that having an imaginative vision of happiness as embodied in a human archetype serves us in clarifying how happiness can manifest in a human guise. For example, a Gatsby- or George Eliot-style ideal of happiness provides us with a concrete way to envision personalized courses of human happiness that turn on prioritizing wealth or intelligence respectively. And in projecting these ideals, we can explore how these models of happiness manifest externally in one's actions and interactions with others, as well as internally in one's thoughts, feelings, character, and ways of ordering hedonic preferences and desires in a human life.

By my lights, there are a couple of different ways in which we can productively think of this imaginative effort to determine the concept of happiness for ourselves as involving seeing more on Kant's view. As I noted above, the individual that we imaginatively represent is not any actual human being; it is an intuitive representation of an archetype who perfectly embodies well-being. Insofar as this is the case, generating an imaginative ideal of happiness involves a kind of seeing more: it involves envisioning a human figure who, in their perfect happiness, outstrips anyone we have ever come across.

However, I would like to suggest a second way in which our imagination, as the capacity to see more, can contribute to our grasp of happiness in Kant's framework, which turns on a kind of presence-independence. As I am conceiving it, imaginatively projecting happiness in the presence of objects in the relevant sense amounts to

---

[20] See Reath (2006, chap. 2); Wood (2013, 69–76); Kohl (2017); Timmermann (2022, chap. 2).

[21] I am thus sympathetic to Reath's emphasis on the role that imagining has vis-à-vis happiness in helping us determine our preferences by imagining "what it would be like to attain" them and setting a "standard in terms of which individual desires may be assessed or rationally criticized" (2006, 46). Barney (2015), meanwhile, implies a more skeptical attitude toward happiness as an ideal of imagination, as a kind of "infantile fantasy" that we should replace in the course of our moral development with a conception of "happiness-as-rational-system," which is "pursued ... under the guidance of prudence" and which features in Kant's conception of the highest good (2015, 163).

346 IMAGINATIVE SIGHT AND THE FACULTY OF DESIRE

projecting an ideal of happiness in an intuition; that draws on what each of us has experienced, for ourselves, as pleasing or displeasing, satisfying or unsatisfying. Though how we project the ideal of happiness often proceeds in this way, the fact that Kant attributes such projection to imagination opens up the possibility that what we project can extend beyond what has been hedonically realized in our own lived experience. Indeed, given our imaginative capacity to see more than we are, in fact, given, it seems that our imaginative projections of happiness can involve intuitions; that represent hedonic possibilities that have not been actual in our lives. Granted, as I argued in Chapter 3, Kant is committed to our imagination, in all its activities, being constitutively dependent on the material delivered through sensibility, i.e. on representations that have been offered to us through outer and inner sense. Insofar as this is the case, on his view, our imaginative projection of hedonic possibilities will need to take its cue from some material provided by the senses. Nevertheless, it seems that within these confines, our imagination can project visions of happiness that outstrip the pleasures and satisfactions we have personally lived.

Regardless of how these imaginative projections proceed, one thing that they help us do is try and determine the concept of happiness by bringing into sharper relief how different models of happiness can shape a human life. And, as I see it, part of what motivates Kant in describing imagination as an ideal of happiness is the recognition that the imaginative projection of happiness in the form of ideals is a way in which we make this indeterminate concept more intuitively determinate to ourselves by giving it a human texture.

However, I take it that this does not exhaust the practical use of happiness as an ideal of imagination on Kant's view. For in addition to providing us with a concrete vision of what happiness might look like, we can also imaginatively project, and potentially orient, our own lives in light of these ideals, as we explore how they resonate with our own hedonic commitments and desires as the individuals that we are. For example, though pursuing wealth might antecedently seem good, once we imagine our own life in light of the Gatsby-style ideal, we might realize that the arc of such a life is not one we ultimately want for ourselves and abandon this pursuit. Projecting our own lives in light of a variety of different ideals of happiness might also help us strike on what order and balance among our hedonic preferences and desires we want to pursue vis-à-vis the whole of our well-being. And imaginatively exploring hedonic possibilities that have not been actual in our own lived experience can potentially transform our pursuit of happiness by orienting us in unprecedented directions in our lives.

To illustrate, let's consider Patricia Highsmith's novel, *The Price of Salt* (or *Carol*) (1952).[22] *The Price of Salt* is a novel about many things, but one of those things is a love story between Therese Belivet and Carol Aird, which ends more or

---

[22] Originally published pseudonymously under the name "Claire Morgan."

less happily (at least romantically).[23] In penning this ending, Highsmith tells us she took herself to be doing something unprecedented in American literature:

> The appeal of *The Price of Salt* was that it had a happy ending for its two main characters, or at least they were going to try to have a future together. Prior to this book, homosexuals male and female in American novels had had to pay for their deviation by cutting their wrists, drowning themselves in a swimming pool, or by switching to heterosexuality (so it was stated), or by collapsing—alone and miserable and shunned—into a depression equal to hell.   (2004, 292)

Highsmith also includes excerpts from some letters that readers sent her regarding the significance of this romantic vision: "Yours is the first book like this with a happy ending! We don't all commit suicide and lots of us are doing fine," and, "I am eighteen and I live in a small town. I feel lonely because I can't talk to anyone" (2004, 292). For the former reader, the vision of happiness Highsmith presents in *The Price of Salt* resonates with hedonic goods that are present to them. But for the latter reader, this novel presents a kind of happiness that outstrips their own lived experience. And the Kantian idea that I would like to suggest is that for a reader like the second one, engaging with how Therese and Carol find, navigate, and experience romantic happiness, internally and externally, in *The Price of Salt* can provide them with material to draw on in generating an intuition, in which they imaginatively project an ideal of happiness that turns on the attainment of hedonic goods and the satisfaction of desires in a human life that have, as yet, been absent, rather than present in their own.[24] Projecting their own life in light of this vision of happiness, in turn, has the potential to transform their pursuit of happiness: as they project themselves into it, they might realize that this ideal resonates with how they want to pursue happiness in their own lives and they reorient accordingly.[25]

---

[23] "It would be Carol, in a thousand cities, a thousand houses, in foreign lands where they would go together, in heaven and in hell. Therese waited. Then as she was about to go to her, Carol saw her, seemed to stare at her incredulously a moment while Therese watched the slow smile growing, before her arm lifted suddenly, her hand waved a quick, eager greeting that Therese had never seen before. Therese walked toward her" (Highsmith 2004, 287). See Nair (2019) for discussion of how this romantic happy ending, which is accompanied by Carol's loss of custody of her child, calls into question the assumption that a happy ending means a "happy ever after" that involves marriage and motherhood (see also Ahmed 2010, chap. 3, 249n2). See Kelly (2020) for discussion of how the ending of the novel encourages readers to imagine what the happy ending might consist in, which addresses Todd Haynes's film adaptation *Carol* (2015) and fanfiction.

[24] However, see Varden (2020, chap. 3) for criticisms of Kant's own binary, cisist, heterosexist view of sexuality, and a defense of a Kantian view of sexuality that can accommodate polyamorous, polysexual, and LGBTQIA orientations and the importance of non-moralized features of human sexuality as part of human happiness.

[25] This said, Kant cautions against taking ideals in novels too seriously: "to try to realize the ideal in an example, i.e., in appearance, such as that of the sage in a novel, is not feasible, and even has about it something nonsensical and not very edifying, since the natural limits which constantly impair the completeness in the idea render impossible every illusion in such an attempt" (A570/598). However, if

348 IMAGINATIVE SIGHT AND THE FACULTY OF DESIRE

To be clear, I do not mean to imply that in Kant's framework the only way that such imaginative projection proceeds is by way of fiction. We can envision possibilities of happiness when left to our own devices, by exercising our imagination in what Kant describes as "inventive" or "creative" ways, e.g. through visualization. We can also envision possibilities of happiness through a more communal inventive effort, e.g. through conversation or collaboration. And, indeed, this sort of collective imagining can have transformative and even revolutionary effects, orienting us toward a vision of happiness on a larger social scale that calls for dramatic changes in our current social world.[26]

However, regardless of the route we pursue to the imaginative projection of these possibilities, what I hope to have motivated is the idea that Kant's commitment to imagination as a capacity that enables us to see more has an important role to play in our pursuit of happiness. To make this point in terms that I used in §12.2, through ideals of happiness, our imagination, as the capacity to see more, has a significant practical use vis-à-vis the specification of the basic principle of happiness that governs our lower faculty of desire. And by helping us try and solve the problem of determining what our happiness consists in, our imaginative projection of both ideals of happiness and ourselves in light of those ideals, can help us arrive at more specific principles of happiness that we endorse, as the individuals that we are, which orient us toward specific objects or states of affairs to bring about in our lives.

But what about the higher faculty of desire? Is there any reason to think that happiness as an ideal of imagination also bears on our pursuit of morality? As I suggested above, this is a complicated issue. On the one hand, in Kant's framework, it seems we have reason to worry about imaginative projections of happiness as potentially tempting us away from what morality demands of us.[27] For one thing, this imaginative ideal might involve desires that are "*contrary to*" reason (MAM 8:112). We might, for example, project a Don Juan skilled in seduction or a Villanelle skilled in assassination as our ideal of happiness—activities Kant, at least, would regard as immoral.[28] However, even if our vision of happiness is not contrary to morality, Kant warns of the temptation to prioritize happiness over the moral law. In his words, we might make the principle of happiness the "supreme determining ground of choice," rather than the moral law

we treat ideals from novels as personifications of standards that we can only attempt to approximate, then this worry need not arise. See Eldridge (1989) for a defense of a historicized, Hegelian-inflected Kantian ethics that identifies literature and narrative as crucial resources to draw on in our moral efforts.

[26] For discussion of revolutionary uses of imagination in oppressive social structures, see Babbitt (1996); Biss (2013).

[27] Though Kant by no means denies the importance of happiness, he insists that "making someone happy is quite different from making him good" (Gr. 4:442).

[28] Villanelle is the lead character in Luke Jenning's novel *Codename Villanelle* (2017) and its sequels, which was adapted for television in the series *Killing Eve* (2018–22).

(KpV 5:23). It seems that our imaginative projections might contribute to this end, as we find ourselves more moved by an imaginative vision of happiness than the stern call of moral duty. Seen from one perspective, then, our projections of happiness might appear to be an imaginative activity that Kant thinks we must be careful to curb.[29]

On the other hand, it seems that the imaginative ideal of happiness has a positive role to play vis-à-vis the higher faculty of desire for Kant. In particular, it appears to play a role in relation to what Kant describes as our moral duty to happiness.[30] In the second *Critique*, for example, Kant claims that, "It can even in certain respects be a duty to attend to one's happiness, partly because happiness (to which belong skill, health, wealth) contains means for the fulfillment of one's duty and partly because lack of it (e.g. poverty) contains temptations to transgress one's duty" (KpV 5:93; see also Gr. 4:399).[31] Here, Kant suggests that we have an indirect duty to attend to our happiness, in part, as a means to fulfilling other moral duties, and, in part, because a lack thereof can tempt us away from our moral duties. However, if we are to be able to attend to our happiness, then it seems we need to take steps to try and determine what our happiness consists in and specify particular principles of happiness that we want to endorse. This, of course, is especially challenging given the indeterminate nature of the concept of happiness. But for reasons that I just offered, it appears that the imaginative projection of the ideal of happiness in human guise can be especially clarifying toward this end on Kant's view. For Kant, then, though the imaginative ideal of happiness might lead us morally astray, he also thinks that our imaginative capacity to see more with respect to happiness can serve us morally in our efforts to fulfill the duty to happiness.

12.5 Imagination and the Categorical Imperative

The final dimension of the moral use of imaginative seeing more that I want to discuss in this chapter bears on its connection to the categorical imperative. As I emphasized above, on Kant's view, the principle that governs the higher faculty of

---

[29] See, e.g., Barney's discussion of happiness as an ideal of imagination as an "infantile fantasy" (2015, 162).

[30] For discussion, see Cohen (2009, chap. 4.3); Kahn (2022), who also addresses Kant's apparent denial of happiness as a duty at MS 6:451; and Varden (2020, chap. 1), who argues that the indirect duty to happiness involves "non-rational" and "non-moral," though not immoral, dimensions that serves us our in light of our predisposition to animality, which orients us toward self-preservation, sex, and community (Rel. 6:26), and our predisposition to humanity, which orients us in a more reflective and rational way toward self-love and social sense of self.

[31] Though I will not pursue this here, presumably having a more determinate conception of happiness also bears on us discharging the duty of beneficence: "the maxim of making others' happiness one's end" (MS 6:452).

350   IMAGINATIVE SIGHT AND THE FACULTY OF DESIRE

desire is the moral law, which, for us, amounts to the categorical imperative: "So act that the maxim of your will could always hold at the same time as a principle in a giving of universal law." As I also noted, on Kant's view, in order to assess whether a maxim could hold as a universal law, he proposes a test: consider whether your maxim could, without contradiction, hold as a universal law of nature.

It is certainly appealing to think that our imagination, as a capacity to see more, has something valuable to contribute to this universalizability test. In order to figure out whether a maxim holds as a universal law, don't we imaginatively envision a world, other than the one present to us here and now, where this maxim holds as a universal law of nature? Christine Korsgaard, for example, casts this test as follows, "Kant's test may be regarded as a formalization of the familiar moral challenge: 'What if everybody did that?' In order to answer this question, you are to imagine a world where everybody does indeed do that" (Gr. Introduction, xviii–xix).[32]

Attributing to our imagination a role in relation to the universalizability test is also enticing in light of Kant's suggestion that treating maxims "as if they were to hold as universal laws of nature" is a way of "bringing" the moral law "closer to intuition" (Gr. 4:436).[33] And one might think that it is because this process involves imaginatively seeing a world in which the maxim is a law of nature that we bring the moral law "closer to intuition."[34]

On this issue, we must be careful. In the "Typic" chapter of the second *Critique*, Kant claims that the universalizability test proceeds by way of "the understanding (not the imagination)" (KpV 5:69). I shall have more to say about why Kant takes this to be the case in the following chapter. For now, however, the point I want to make is that this passage indicates that, for Kant, although the universalizability test can involve imagination, it does not have to.[35] That is to say, on Kant's view,

---

[32] See also Johnson (1985); Church (2013, 220–3).

[33] In this stretch of text, Kant suggests that all three formulations of the moral law in terms of the universal law of nature, humanity, and kingdom of ends brings the moral law "closer to intuition" (Gr. 4:436–7).

[34] Johnson (1985, 274–5) defends this view not just with respect to the formula of the law of nature, but with respect to the formulae of humanity, autonomy, and the kingdom of ends.

[35] I thus disagree with Johnson's argument to the effect that the universalizability test "must" involve "the imaginative metaphorical process of conceiving a world where what we now do freely is naturally necessitated according to universal laws of nature" (1985, 273). Johnson argues that what makes the process involved in the universalizability test imaginative is not that it involves "images," but rather that it involves a "metaphorical" process of "ordering or structuring representations in a new manner" (1983, 276). However, given my interpretation of Kant's theory of imagination, this metaphorical process cannot count as imaginative unless intuitions are involved. I also disagree with Freydberg's (2005, chap. 2) claim that the Typic must involve imagination because it involves "synthesis" (see, e.g., 82–3). As I discussed in Chapters 5 and 6, though Kant accords certain form of synthesis to imagination, he accords other forms of synthesis to the understanding. I also disagree with Church's claim that unless imagination is involved, the universalizability test "lacks substance" and is "merely verbal—a case of concepts that are empty for lack of the intuition needed to give them content" (2013, 222). I take it that Kant's view in the Typic commits him to the possibility of us running the

although one way we can consider whether a maxim can serve as a universal law of nature is by imagining a world in which this is the case, we can also just think about a world in which this is the case and draw a conclusion without resorting to any such imaginative seeing. For example, in order to assess my maxim to cut in line whenever I am short on time, I could try and imaginatively visualize a world in which everyone did this and detect a contradiction in that way. But I could also detect a contradiction without generating any intuitions; just by thinking about such a world and drawing the conclusion that the practice of line formation would not be viable in it.

Note that here is another juncture at which Kant's commitment to imagining being sensory rather than non-sensory is relevant (see Introduction, §0.2.1). Were Kant to regard as imaginative non-sensory episodes in which we, without the aid of sensory representations, suppose or entertain that some proposition is the case, then it would seem that whether the universalizability test proceeds by way of seeing or supposing, it involves imagining. However, I have argued that on Kant's view, all our imagining is sensible; in which case if we merely suppose that a maxim holds as a universal law of nature, without in some way sensibly representing this to ourselves, then it does not count as an episode of imagining for Kant. This would, instead, amount to an act of "the understanding (not the imagination)."

This said, although Kant does not think that the universalizability test requires that we imagine a maxim as a universal law of nature, it certainly seems useful. And in cases when this imaginative sight is helpful, it seems that we have a moral use of imagination, which serves us in assessing the moral worth of maxims and deciding what objects or states of affairs to bring about through our higher faculty of desire. Caveats in place, then, in addition to its use in relation to the duty of happiness, this use of imagination in relation to the categorical imperative is another morally valuable exercise of imaginative seeing more vis-à-vis the higher faculty of desire.

12.6 Conclusion

In order to begin reconstructing the way in which imagination plays a significant role in our practical lives on Kant's view, I dedicated this chapter to considerations about how our imagination, as a cognitive capacity that enables us to see more than is immediately present to us, can contribute to our exercise of the faculty of desire. To this end, I offered an account of what sort of contributions imaginatively seeing more can make to three basic ways in which we exercise the

---

universalizability test through wholly intellectual acts of judgment, through which we can nevertheless detect substantive contradictions in conception and volition.

faculty of desire in Kant's framework: in the specification of practical principles, the practical assessment of concrete situations, and deliberation about which course of action to pursue in concrete situations. In this discussion, I brought to light various ways in which this seeing more can serve us practically by enabling us to generate intuitions₁ that help us represent in human guise certain possibilities (e.g. personalized models of happiness or moral courses of action) and certain realities (e.g. specific situations or hedonic commitments).

I then explored Kant's account of happiness as an ideal of imagination and the role seeing more plays in our efforts to try and determine what this concept means not only for us as human beings, but also for us as the individuals that we are. I argued that with respect to the lower faculty of desire, imaginatively sighting happiness can orient and potentially transform how we, as individuals or collectively, pursue happiness. With respect to the higher faculty of desire I claimed that although Kant sometimes worries about the potentially morally subversive effects of the imaginative ideal of happiness, he is also committed to the imaginative ideal of happiness having a positive role to play in specifying how we are to fulfill the moral duty to happiness. Finally, I suggested that there is another way in which imaginative seeing more can serve us morally: though not necessary, it can aid us in the moral assessment of maxims when we run the universalizability test by imagining a world in which our maxim is a universal law of nature.

However, this range of ways in which imaginatively seeing more plays a valuable role in our practical lives does not exhaust Kant's vision of the practical use of imagination. For as I shall now argue, when we think through the relevance of Kant's account of imagination as the faculty of exhibition to our practical endeavors, we shall uncover other vital ways in which he thinks imagination shapes our pursuit of morality.

Seeing More: Kant's Theory of Imagination. Samantha Matherne, Oxford University Press.
© Samantha Matherne 2024. DOI: 10.1093/9780191999291.003.0013

13
Imaginative Exhibition in Morality

Such strange illumination
The Possible's slow fuse is lit
By the Imagination

—Emily Dickinson, #1687

13.1 Introduction

In response to Schiller's worries that he offers an overly severe account of moral life in which sensibility has no robust role to play, Kant says, "Professor Schiller... disapproves of this way of representing obligation... Since we are however at one upon the most important principles, I cannot admit disagreement..., the morally oriented reason (through the imagination) calls sensibility into play" (Rel. 6:23n; see Chapter 11). In this chapter, I argue that in Kant's framework one of the main ways in which "reason calls sensibility into play" is through imagination, as the faculty of exhibition. As was the case in my analysis of his account of the theoretical and aesthetic use of imagination, I argue that a central theme in his account of the moral use of imagination is the idea that our imagination functions cognitively well by making concepts, here, moral concepts, sensible to us in a way that facilitates our concrete comprehension of them.

However, I open in §13.2 with a discussion of some initial reasons to worry that Kant can accord imagination, as the faculty of exhibition, a substantive role in our moral lives. I focus, more specifically, on Kant's arguments about why concepts related to the moral law, practical freedom, and the morally good, *qua* ideas of the supersensible, cannot be imaginatively exhibited. Nevertheless, in spite of these concerns, I make the case for why Kant regards imaginative exhibition as something that is morally valuable.

To this end, I canvass various ways in which Kant thinks our imagination morally serves us by making moral ideas sensible through indirect and direct modes of exhibition. In §13.3, I focus on Kant's account of how our imagination indirectly exhibits moral ideas in our aesthetic engagement with beauty, art, and sublimity. Then in §§13.4–13.5, I turn to the question of whether Kant also countenances the possibility of our imagination directly exhibiting moral ideas to us. Though his remarks about the limits of imaginative exhibition might seem to

354　IMAGINATIVE EXHIBITION IN MORALITY

rule out this possibility, I argue that he acknowledges a range of morally beneficial ways our imagination can directly exhibit moral ideas. In §13.4, I examine the direct exhibition involved in the imaginative projection of ideals and I examine Kant's account of how this serves us in morally assessing actions and measuring our moral progress. In §13.5, I turn to the topic of direct exhibition through moral examples. Though Kant's account of moral examples is complicated, I argue that, on his considered view, our imaginative engagement with moral examples, drawn from both fiction and real life, serves us in our on-going moral development by facilitating our comprehension of moral concepts in human guise, and by providing us with proof that, for all our limitations, it is really possible to act morally.

13.2　The Limits of Imaginative Exhibition Worry

So, why might we initially doubt that Kant can ascribe the imaginative exhibition of moral ideas a positive role to play in our moral lives? The particular worry that I shall explore concerns moral ideas related to the moral law, practical freedom, and the morally good.[1] And the core of the worry is this: the supersensible status of ideas, *qua* concepts of reason that "go beyond the possibility of experience," is incompatible with the possibility that they can be sensibly exhibited by our imagination (A320/B377; see also A313/B370, A327/B383).

One way into this worry is through the lens of Kant's characterization of ideas of reason as "indemonstrable" in the third *Critique* (see KU 5:341–4). There, Kant claims that ideas of reason are not "demonstrable...if by demonstrating, as in anatomy, it is...**exhibiting** that is understood" (KU 5:342; transl. modified). By exhibiting in this context, Kant has in mind exhibiting a concept "in intuition" (KU 5:342). And he claims that ideas of reason cannot be exhibited because they "contain a **concept** (of the supersensible) for which no suitable intuition can ever be given" (KU 5:342). More specifically, since exhibiting, as we have seen, involves intuitions of imagination (intuitions$_i$), Kant asserts that when it comes to ideas, "**imagination**, with its intuitions, never attains [*erreicht*] to the given concept" (KU 5:343).

In his moral writings, Kant also seems to affirm the limits of imaginative exhibition specifically with respect to moral ideas. In particular, as we shall now see, he appears to deny the possibility of the imaginative exhibition of foundational moral ideas related to the moral law, practical freedom, and the morally good.

---

[1] I do not mean to suggest that these are the only moral ideas relevant to this discussion. The question of the exhibition of the idea of virtue (see, e.g., his mention of the "exhibition of pure virtue" (KpV 5:151; transl. modified)) and the idea of the highest good (see Gibbons 1994, chap. 5, and Kneller 2007) are also of interest. But for reasons of space I shall primarily restrict my focus to worries surrounding the exhibition of these three moral ideas.

Let's begin with the apparent limits of exhibition when it comes to the moral law.[2] As he describes these limits rather suggestively at the end of the Analytic of the Sublime,

> imagination...finds nothing beyond the sensible to which it can attach itself...Perhaps there is no more sublime passage in the Jewish Book of the Law than the commandment: Thou shalt not make unto thyself any graven image, nor any likeness either of that which is in heaven, or on earth, or yet under the earth...The very same thing also holds of the representation of the moral law...[W]here the senses no longer see anything before them, yet the unmistakable and inextinguishable idea of morality remains, there it would be more necessary to moderate the momentum of an unbounded imagination..., rather than...to look for assistance for them in images.   (KU 5:274)[3]

Here, Kant suggests that it is misguided to look for an imaginative exhibition of the moral law, e.g. in an image, because the moral law involves an idea of something beyond the bounds of the sensible.

Kant also emphasizes the limits of imaginative exhibition with respect to the moral ideas of freedom and the morally good. About freedom, Kant says the following in the course of discussing why ideas of reason are "indemonstrable":

> the rational concept...of that on which our power of choice in relation to moral law must be based, namely the idea of transcendental freedom, is already in terms of its species an indemonstrable concept and idea of reason...because...nothing can be given in experience that corresponds to its quality at all.   (KU 5:343)

The idea of "transcendental freedom" that he references here is the concept of "a causality...through which something happens without its cause being further determined by another previous cause, i.e., an **absolute** causal **spontaneity** beginning **from itself**" (A446/B474; see also A533/B561, KpV 5:56). And he takes practical freedom, i.e. the "power of choice in relation to the moral law," to be "based on" transcendental freedom because it involves a form of absolute causal spontaneity: "determining oneself from oneself, independently of necessitation by sensible impulses" in accordance with the moral law (KpV 5:48; see also A534/B562, KpV 5:55). Insofar as both ideas of transcendental and practical freedom involve

---

[2] Though the moral law is a principle rather than a concept, in the KU 5:274 passage he aligns it with the "idea of morality," and he claims it is something that "lies in the idea as the foundational of all actions of *rational* beings" (Gr. 4:452–3).

[3] In particular, the sort of "unbounded" imagination Kant worries about is an "unreined" (*zügellos*) imagination that contributes to enthusiasm or an "unruled" (*regellos*) imagination that contributes to "visionary rapture" (*Schwämerei*) (KU 5:275).

356 IMAGINATIVE EXHIBITION IN MORALITY

a representation of a supersensible form of causality, Kant claims that they lie beyond the scope of what our imagination, sensibly limited as it is, can represent. As he sometimes frames the issue, "It is...absolutely impossible to give anywhere in experience an example of [the idea of freedom as a faculty of absolute spontaneity], since among the causes of things as appearances no determination of causality that would be absolutely unconditioned can be found" (KpV 5:48).

Finally, regarding the idea of the morally good, Kant defines this idea in terms of the "effect possible through freedom" (KpV 5:57). Here, one might think that the prospects of imaginative exhibition are brighter: for even if Kant denies that we can imaginatively exhibit the idea of freedom as a supersensible cause, couldn't he still allow for us to imaginatively exhibit the morally good as an effect of this cause in the sensible world?[4] For example, suppose that someone's expression of gratitude is an "effect" of an autonomous exercise of their will in accordance with the moral law: since this action is a sensible one, couldn't we represent it as an effect of freedom, hence as exhibiting the idea of the morally good?

In the Typic chapter of the second *Critique*, however, Kant appears to answer this question in the negative. This chapter parallels the Schematism chapter in the first *Critique*, and as we shall now see, part of his argument turns on the claim that unlike with the categories, where it is possible for us to imaginatively exhibit them through schemata, with the morally good, no such imaginative exhibition is possible.[5]

By way of some background, the topic of the Typic chapter is what is involved in judging "an action possible for us in sensibility" to be a "case" of the morally good (KpV 5:67). Kant immediately notes the challenge that such judgments pose: the morally good is the result of,

> the will...determined independently of anything empirical (merely through the representation of a law)...; however, all cases of possible action that occur can be only empirical, that is, belong to experience and nature; hence, it seems absurd to want to find in the sensible world a case which, though as such it stands only under a law of freedom and to which there could be applied the supersensible idea of the morally good, which is to be exhibited in it *in concreto*.
>
> (KpV 5:68)

---

[4] In his discussion of the claim that ideas of reason are "indemonstrable," Kant distinguishes between ideas that are fully indemonstrable, like <freedom> for which "nothing can be given in experience that corresponds to its quality and all," and ideas that are indemonstrable to a "degree," like <virtue>, for which "no experiential product of that causality [of freedom] attains the degree that the idea of reason prescribes as a rule" (KU 5:343).

[5] For discussion of Kant's limitation of imagination in the Typic, see Bielefeldt (2003, 47–53) and Westra (2016).

THE LIMITS OF IMAGINATIVE EXHIBITION WORRY   357

Here, Kant suggests that *prima facie* there is something "absurd" about thinking we can identify a concrete action as exhibiting the idea of the morally good because the former is empirical and sensible, whereas the latter is something supersensible.

For Kant, the challenge of making judgments about something empirical and sensible as a case of something supersensible echoes the problem of homogeneity that he raised in the Schematism chapter of the first *Critique*. Recall from Chapter 7 that in the Schematism Kant raises the question of how it is possible for us to make judgments in the theoretical realm in which we subsume empirical intuitions of appearances under the categories, given that the categories are pure and intellectual, whereas empirical intuitions are empirical and sensible (see A137–8/B176–7). In the Typic chapter, Kant raises another problem of homogeneity, this time in the practical realm: how is it possible for us to make judgments in which we subsume empirical intuitions of sensible actions under the idea of the morally good, since the former pertains to what is sensible while the latter to what is supersensible.

In the Schematism chapter, Kant's solution to the theoretical problem of homogeneity proceeds by way of an appeal to a "procedure of imagination" that "projects" an "intuition...given a priori," a transcendental schema, that is capable of mediating between empirical intuition and appearances, on the one hand, and the categories, on the other (KpV 5:68–9; transl. modified; see Chapters 5 and 7). But when it comes to the practical problem of homogeneity, Kant insists another solution must be found:

> pure theoretical reason...had means at hand of escaping from these difficulties, namely...its theoretical use...depended upon intuitions...given a priori (as *schemata*)...On the other hand, the morally good as an object is something supersensible, so that nothing corresponding to it can be found in any sensible intuition; and judgment under laws of pure practical reason seems, therefore, to be subject to special difficulties.   (KpV 5:68)

He continues, "no intuition can be put under...the concept of the unconditioned good...—and hence no schema on behalf of its application *in concreto*" (KpV 5:69). As we might make the point, on Kant's view, unlike in the case of the categories, where it is possible to imaginatively alight on a temporal pattern that exhibits them in intuition$_i$, in the case of the morally good, there simply is no spatio-temporal pattern, no "look," that all cases of the morally good share that our imagination can project.[6] For Kant, then, it is not possible for our imagination to generate schematic intuitions$_i$ that mediate between the morally good and

---

[6] See Huemer (2007, 86), McBrayer (2010), Werner (2016) for the discussion of the idea that there is no "look" that moral actions share in contemporary debates about moral perception.

358 IMAGINATIVE EXHIBITION IN MORALITY

empirical intuitions of sensible actions in the way that it could in relation to the categories. But without schematic intuitions$_i$ to do this mediating work, how are we able to judge concrete actions as cases of the morally good?

Kant's solution to this question proceeds in two parts. First, Kant argues that recognizing an action as a case of the morally good does not require that we recognize "an event in the sensible world" as a case of the morally good; instead, he argues that we need to recognize that the "determining ground" of the action, i.e. the motive or maxim behind it, is morally good (KpV 5:68–9). For example, in order to judge whether an expression of gratitude is a case of the morally good, we should look not to the spatio-temporal event of this expression, but rather to the maxim that serves as the determining ground of this action.

Second, striking a familiar note, Kant claims that in order to figure out whether the maxim behind the action is morally good or not, we should run the universalizability test: "ask yourself whether, if the action you propose were to take place by a law of nature of which you were yourself a part, you could indeed regard it as possible through your will" (KpV 5:69). But in the Typic chapter Kant makes several new points about the universalizability test. For one thing, he insists that this test is a procedure of "no cognitive faculty other than the understanding (not the imagination)" (KpV 5:69).[7] As I discussed in Chapter 12, this does not preclude the possibility that we exercise our imagination in considering whether a world in which the relevant maxim is a law of nature would involve contradictions or not, but this imaginative exercise is optional. But what is not optional, *per* Kant, is exercising our understanding when we run this test: we must always think about whether such a world would be contradictory or not.

Moreover, in the Typic, Kant introduces the new language of a "type" (*Typus*) to describe the universalizability test:

> what the understanding can put under an idea of reason is not a *schema* of sensibility but a law...and hence a law of nature though only as to its form; this law is what the understanding can put under an idea of reason on behalf of judgment, and we can, accordingly call it the *type* [Typus] of the moral law...Such a law is...a *type* for the appraisal [*Beurteilung*] of maxims in accordance with moral principles. (KpV 5:69)

---

[7] As I noted in Chapter 12, Johnson (1985) and Freydberg (2005, chap. 2) argue that in spite of Kant's claims to the contrary, the procedure Kant describes in the Typic requires imagination. Johnson takes this to be the case because it involves a metaphorical process he attributes to imagination (1983, 273, 276), and Freydberg takes this to be the case because it involves synthesis and he attributes all synthesis to imagination on Kant's view (2005, 82–3). However, on my reading of Kant's theory of imagination, unless intuitions$_i$ are involved, neither a metaphorical nor a synthesizing process can count as imaginative. But for reasons that I explore in this section, the involvement of intuitions$_i$ in the Typic procedure is precisely what Kant appears to be wary of.

THE INDIRECT EXHIBITION OF MORAL CONCEPTS   359

Here, Kant indicates that in order to determine whether the maxim behind an action is a case of the morally good, we rely not on a schema, but on a type. A type, for Kant, represents a law of nature, or, more specifically, the "form" of a law of nature as a universal law that governs the sensible world. And his thought is that in order to determine whether a maxim is a case of the morally good, we "appraise" it in light of this type, by asking whether it could serve as a universal law that governs the sensible world without contradiction. If the answer is "no," then Kant claims that the maxim, and the action it motivates, cannot count as morally good.

In Kant's analysis of the idea of the morally good in the Typic chapter, we thus find him denying that this idea can be imaginatively exhibited in sensible intuition$_i$. Indeed, we find him denying that it can be imaginatively exhibited either in empirical intuition$_i$ or in the sort of *a priori* intuition$_i$ involved in a transcendental schema. And though he argues that we can nevertheless judge a concrete action as a case of the morally good, he indicates that this proceeds not through a process mediated by imagination, but rather through a "procedure of the understanding," a universalizability test, in which we appraise a maxim in light of the type of the law of nature.

Stepping back, we thus have reason to think that, on Kant's view, imaginative exhibition reaches its limits with respect to moral ideas. For when it comes to ideas related to the moral law, practical freedom, and the morally good, Kant claims, to repeat, "**imagination**, with its intuitions, never attains [*erreicht*] to the given concept" (KU 5:343).

However, in what follows, I argue that a closer look at Kant's account of imaginative exhibition in the moral domain reveals that there is more leeway in his view than there initially seems to be. Indeed, I aim to show that there are a wide variety of morally beneficial ways in which Kant allows for our imagination to indirectly and directly exhibit moral ideas to us.

13.3 The Indirect Exhibition of Moral Concepts through Beauty, Art, and Sublimity

Over the course of Parts II and III, I have explored Kant's account of both direct and indirect ways that the imaginative exhibition of concepts proceeds. Recall that, on Kant's view, direct exhibition involves our imagination exhibiting concepts through intuitions$_i$, the sensible content of which maps onto the logical content of concepts in a straightforward way. Think, here, of the intuition$_i$ of a hydrangea I have when I see one in a garden: this intuition$_i$ is a perceptual image that represents blue flowers in large clusters of star-shaped blooms atop a stem that has large serrated green leaves arranged as a whole. As a direct exhibition, the content of this intuition$_i$ maps onto the marks contained in the content of

360 IMAGINATIVE EXHIBITION IN MORALITY

<hydrangea>, such as <having large clusters of star-shaped blooms>, <having large serrated green leaves>, <having a stem>, etc. By contrast, indirect exhibition involves our imagination exhibiting concepts in intuition$_i$ in a more circuitous way, e.g. through symbols or metaphors, which invite patterns of reflection through which we grasp the concept in a more open-ended fashion (see Chapters 9, 10). Think, for example, of Rainer Maria Rilke's "Blue Hydrangea" (*Blaue Hortensie*), in which the blue of a hydrangea "pales like antique writing paper: blues / in yellows, purples, and the greys of dust" ("wie in alten blauen Briefpapieren / ist Gelb in ihnen, Violett und Grau"), "But suddenly, a newborn blue is seen.../ that blue, now stirred, rejoices in the green" ("Doch plötzlich scheint das Blau sich zu verneuen.../ ein rührend Blaues sich vor Grünem freuen") (2015, 96–7). From a Kantian perspective, in this poem Rilke offers us an aesthetic idea that imaginatively represents the concept <rejuvenation> through a hydrangea in which we discover beneath the "paling," "papery" blue with its yellows, purples, and greys "of dust," a blue "rejoicing" in green. Although the concept <rejuvenation> does not contain hydrangeas as part of its logical content, nevertheless this aesthetic idea offers us a creative perspective on it, which "aesthetically enlarges" it and expands our comprehension of it (KU 5:315).

As I also emphasized in my analysis of the sublime in Chapter 10, Kant maintains that indirect exhibition is especially salient with respect to supersensible ideas.[8] As he puts it, in indirect exhibition, "to a concept which only reason can think, and to which no sensible intuition can be adequate, an intuition is attributed" (KU 5:351).[9] Indeed, I argued that attending to indirect exhibition is the key to appreciating Kant's account of the elevated role our imagination plays in relation to the sublime, as we use intuitions$_i$ of very large or very powerful objects in nature to imaginatively exhibit the idea of our rationality as what is properly sublime.

Given my purposes here, I want to now approach the worry about the limits of imaginative exhibition with respect to moral ideas through the lens of indirect exhibition. What I shall argue in the rest of this section is that when we look at the third *Critique*, we find Kant countenancing the possibility of our imagination indirectly exhibiting moral ideas in our aesthetic engagement with the beautiful and sublime.[10] And I hope to show that in these aesthetic activities, we find an

---

[8] See Chignell (2010, 190, 201) for emphasis on the role that indirect exhibition through symbols plays in relation to ideas. See Kraus (2020, chap. 5) for the argument that the regulative use of ideas of reason involves exhibition, with particular emphasis on how this works in the case of the idea of the soul.

[9] See also, "if [the concept] cannot be exhibited immediately, but only in its consequences (*indirecte*), it may be called the symbolization of the concept... [This] is expedient for concepts of the super-sensible" (WF 20:279; transl. modified).

[10] Though I here focus on indirect exhibition through aesthetic means, Kant also points toward religious means to this end, e.g. in his discussion of religious symbols in the *Religion*. For discussion, see Ferrarin (2008, §3); Englander (2011); Palmquist (2015); Guyer (2020, chap. 11); Wood (2020, chaps. 1, 5).

THE INDIRECT EXHIBITION OF MORAL CONCEPTS   361

important moral use of imagination on Kant's view: a use that turns on our imagination creatively engaging in aesthetic activities that serve us morally by facilitating our comprehension of these moral ideas, thus fulfilling our need to have a sensible way to "hold on to" them (Rel. 6:64–5n; see discussion in Chapter 11).[11]

Let's continue on the theme of the sublime. On my interpretation, our imaginative engagement with both the dynamical and mathematical sublime involves the exhibition of moral ideas on Kant's view.[12] This is a bit more straightforward in the case of the dynamical sublime and our aesthetic engagement with very powerful objects, given his explicit presentation of this engagement as something that involves a relation between imagination and "the **faculty of desire**" (KU 5:247). According to Kant, in the context of the dynamical sublime, our imagination exhibits moral ideas related to the sublimity of our practical reason and freedom:

> [the dynamical sublime] calls forth our power (which is not part of nature) to regard those things about which we are concerned (goods, health and life) as trivial, and hence to regard [nature's] power ... as not the sort of dominion over ourselves and our authority to which we would have to bow if it came down to our highest principles and their affirmation or abandonment. Thus nature is here called sublime merely because it raises the imagination to the exhibition of those cases in which the mind can make palpable [*fühlbar*] to itself the sublimity of its own vocation [*Bestimmung*] even over nature.   (KU 5:262; transl. modified)

As I analyzed this line of thought in Chapter 10, for Kant, our imagination is able to indirectly exhibit the moral idea of the sublimity of our practical rationality and freedom vis-à-vis intuitions$_i$ of very powerful objects in nature, such as volcanoes or raging thunderstorms. Indeed, I see this thought as one that at least partially motivates Kant's claim that the dynamical sublime "reveals in us an unfathomable depth of this supersensible faculty" of "inner freedom"—a revelation that happens not just intellectually, but intuitively, as our imagination makes our freedom palpable to us (KU 5:271).[13]

---

[11] Bielefeldt (2003) and Westra (2016, chaps. 6–7) also emphasize the importance of symbolic representation in the context of Kant's moral philosophy; however, they treat these symbolic activities as activities of understanding and judgment, rather than of imagination. By contrast, I regard these symbolic activities as activities in which our imagination "attributes" an "intuition" to a moral idea (KU 5:351).

[12] Insofar as the exhibition at issue here proceeds via intuitions$_i$ of objects in nature, it does not seem to present moral ideas in a human guise the way that other modes of moral exhibition do. However, I take this to be consistent with Kant's emphasis on the indirect nature of this exhibition, which requires not any similarity between the content of the intuition$_i$ and concept, but only similarity in how we reflect on them. This point also applies to Kant's account of beauty as a symbol of the morally good that I discuss below.

[13] See also Kant's claim in this context that the dynamical sublime makes the moral law "aesthetically knowable [*ästhetisch-kenntlich*]" (KU 5:271).

362 IMAGINATIVE EXHIBITION IN MORALITY

As for the mathematical sublime, although Kant argues that in this case our imagination relates to reason not as the faculty of desire (i.e. as practical reason), but rather as a "**faculty of cognition**" (i.e. as theoretical reason), there are nevertheless grounds for thinking it involves our imagination indirectly exhibiting moral ideas through intuitions$_i$ of very large objects.[14] To see this, recall that, on Kant's view, the indirect exhibition of a concept involves an intuiton$_i$ that invites a pattern of reflection that conduces to the pattern of reflection that the concept calls for. As I discussed, when we consider the mathematical sublime in this light, we find Kant characterizing the intuitions$_i$ of very large objects as ones that invite a pattern of reflection that is similar to the pattern of reflection of respect that moral ideas related to the moral law and freedom call for. Given this parallel in reflection, I take it that we can attribute to Kant the view that in the mathematical sublime, the feeling of respect we have in relation to intuitions$_i$ of very large objects can encourage the feeling of respect that the moral law and freedom call for, and hence these intuitions$_i$ can serve as indirect exhibitions of those ideas.

Turning now to Kant's analysis of the beautiful, there too we find him pursuing the idea that moral ideas can be indirectly exhibited through aesthetic means. In one vein, in §59 of the third *Critique*, Kant intimates that our imagination can indirectly exhibit the idea of the morally good through intuitions$_i$ of the beautiful.[15] More specifically, he claims that the beautiful can serve as "the symbol of the morally good," insofar as reflection on the intuition$_i$ of a beautiful object is conducive to reflection on the idea of the morally good (KpV 5:353).[16] In this vein, he claims that the way we reflect on the intuition$_i$ of something beautiful, such as a flower or a poem, is "analogical to the consciousness of a mental state produced by moral judgments" about the <morally good> (KU 5:354). Kant spells out this analogy in terms of the idea that the reflection on both the beautiful and the <morally good> involves "a certain ennoblement and elevation above the mere receptivity for a pleasure from sensible impressions" and "esteems the value of others" (KU 5:353). For example, in Kant's framework, when I judge a hydrangea to be beautiful, my pleasure is not determined through the receptivity of sense, but rather through the free play of my imagination and understanding. And when I lay claim to the agreement of others regarding this aesthetic judgment, *per* Kant, this is motivated by a kind of esteem for them, as appreciators

---

[14] As I noted in Chapter 10, while some commentators deny that the mathematical sublime has a practical orientation (see Gibbons 1994, 142–3, 148; Pillow 2000, 71–3, 107; Guyer 2005, 227–8; Clewis 2009, 7, 17, 66–7; Brady 2013a, 173, 180–1), I am sympathetic to readings, such as Merritt's (2018b), that take it to have a practical orientation.

[15] For discussions of this claim that lay emphasis on the role that our imagination plays, see Guyer (1993, chap. 6); Munzel (1995); Rueger and Evren (2005).

[16] Kant, however, also adduces several important distinctions between the two with regard to the role of concepts, interest, freedom, and universality (KU 5:354).

who share the same capacities I do.[17] So too in the case of the morally good, when I judge, say, the act of expressing gratitude to those who have benefitted us to be morally good, I recognize that this action is one that is determined not hedonically, but rather in accordance with the moral law. And in this judgment, I display esteem for others, as moral agents. For Kant, then, the intuitions$_i$ that our imagination generates in our engagement with the beautiful serve to symbolically exhibit the idea of the morally good when our reflection on the former transports us to reflection on the latter.

In addition to these remarks about beauty being a symbol of the <morally good>, Kant argues that our imagination can exhibit moral ideas in a more open-ended way through other beauty-related routes. As I discussed in Chapter 9, Kant argues that aesthetic ideas can exhibit moral ideas. Recall his example of Frederick the Great's poem that exhibits the moral idea of a cosmopolitan disposition through "everything agreeable in a beautiful summer day, drawn to a close, which a bright evening calls to mind" (KU 5:316). Kant also mentions cases in which our intuitions$_i$ of natural beauty can indirectly exhibit moral ideas: "the white color of the lily seems to dispose the mind to ideas of innocence" (KU 5:302). Here, I take Kant's implicit thought to be that the intuition$_i$ of the white lily indirectly exhibits the moral idea of innocence because the way we reflect on the former is conducive to the way we reflect on the latter.

For Kant, then, far from it being the case that our imagination is unable to exhibit moral ideas, his aesthetic theory points toward a variety of ways in which moral ideas can be indirectly exhibited through our intuitions$_i$ of the sublime and beautiful. Insofar as this is the case, the limits of imaginative exhibition worry is better framed as a worry about the direct exhibition of moral ideas.

However, before turning to this issue of direct exhibition, I want to pause here and highlight the moral use of imagination that has just emerged: the moral use of its aesthetic activities that indirectly exhibits moral ideas to us. As is the case with all imaginative exhibition, on Kant's view, the indirect exhibition of moral ideas in the context of the beautiful and sublime has a cognitive function: it facilitates our comprehension of those ideas. But insofar as this exhibition proceeds in an aesthetic context, on my reading at least, it fulfills this cognitive function in a creative way: our imagination, in its aesthetic freedom, finds creative ways to render these moral ideas, which extend our comprehension of them in new, surprising, and cognitively directions. To elaborate on this point about creativity, I want to consider a couple of examples.

The first is an example of the sublime. Consider the way in which our imagination facilitates our comprehension of our practical freedom through our engagement with a thunderstorm. From a Kantian point of view, though we might have

---

[17] See Matherne (2023a) for emphasis on this line of thought in a defense of a Kantian account of the virtue of aesthetic humility that cuts against aesthetic arrogance.

364 IMAGINATIVE EXHIBITION IN MORALITY

an intellectual grasp of the power of this freedom, by enabling us to intuitively grasp its power through the lens of the power of a thunderstorm, our imagination gives us a new animating perspective on it.

The second is a literary example that I shall discuss at more length: Jane Austen's exploration of the moral idea of friendship in *Emma*. Here, let's take our cue from Kant's gloss of the idea of moral friendship in terms of the "the union of two persons through equal mutual love and respect" (MS 6:469).[18] In contrast with the logically straightforward way Kant analyzes <moral friendship> in the *Metaphysics of Morals*, *Emma* offers us a fictional world that, though not entailed by this idea, illuminates it in human guise.[19] In Kant's technical language, *Emma* offers us an aesthetic idea that indirectly exhibits the idea of friendship through "supplementary representations of the imagination," which do not analytically "lie in" the concept, but which nevertheless "aesthetically enlarge" the concept and "animate the mind by opening up for it the prospect of an immeasurable field of related representations" (KU 5:315). This aesthetic idea turns on a host of "supplementary representations" that illustrate the idea of moral friendship in a "complete" way in the fictional world of Highbury in which Austen carefully juxtaposes the conduct and consciousness of the characters who populate it (KU 5:314).

For example, in order to bring out the need for equal mutual love and respect in moral friendship, Austen chooses to contrast the more asymmetrical friendship between Emma and Harriet with the more symmetrical friendship between Emma and Mr. Knightly as they play out over the course of events in Highbury. Thanks to the omniscient narrator, we are offered descriptions of the external patterns of action and interaction, as well as the internal patterns of thought and feeling, that contour these friendships, for good and ill. For ill, in the Emma-Harriet case, we are given a picture of a friendship that "must sink": a friendship in which Emma's meddling, elitist tendencies and Harriet's naïve, diffident tendencies converge into a dynamic marked by manipulation, miscommunication, and misunderstanding, not to mention near-disastrous romantic consequences (2012, 332).[20] But for good, in the Emma-Knightly case, as we witness them

---

[18] For discussion of Kant's theory of moral friendship, see Langton (1992); Marcucci (1999); Filippaki (2012); Varden (2020, 66–71).

[19] For discussion of friendship in *Emma*, see Thomason (2015; who situates it in the context of friendship in the 18th century); Badhwar and Dadlez (2018; who situate it in the context of Aristotle's notion of friendship). For another Austen-Kant parallel, see Eldridge's (1989, chap. 6). discussion of *Pride and Prejudice* in relation to a Hegelian-inflected Kantian ethics.

[20] Consider, for example, the narration of Emma's internal state as she realizes what a poor friend she has been: "she felt that she had been risking her friend's happiness on most insufficient grounds," and she realizes "How improperly had she been acting by Harriet! How inconsiderate, how indelicate, how irrational, how unfeeling had been her conduct! What blindness, what madness, had led her on!" (2012, 279, 281). The narrator also provides us with a conversation between Emma and Harriet to reinforce the fact of their poor dynamic. Speaking about her romantic affections, Harriet says, "I should not have thought it possible...that you could have misunderstood me," but Emma's refrain of "Harriet!" and "Good God!...this has been a most unfortunate—most deplorable mistake!" reveals that Emma has done nothing but misunderstand (2012, 280).

THE INDIRECT EXHIBITION OF MORAL CONCEPTS   365

playfully and critically engage with one another, and eventually reach "something so like perfect happiness, that it could bear no other name," we are offered a model of friendship that, though not without its own limits, more closely approximates a bond of mutual love and respect (2012, 297).[21]

Emma's curated vision of moral friendship, in turn, offers us, as readers, the opportunity to expand our conceptual horizons on this idea, as we reflect on it in an open-ended way. In Kant's words, as we imaginatively explore these contrasting pairs of friends, an "immeasurable field of related representations" is opened to us, which pertains to the "implications" of <moral friendship>, e.g. how it bears on patterns of human conduct, conversation, and consciousness, and its "affinity" with other concepts, e.g. how we understand others and ourselves.[22] By engaging with this immeasurable field, we can "aesthetically enlarge" our idea of moral friendship in light of the concrete ways in which it can be realized, and fail to be realized, in human lives and human minds, which extend beyond whatever purely logical grasp of this concept we might have (KU 5:315). And though Kant certainly thinks there is much to be gained by working through a "dry" and "abstract" articulation of <moral friendship> in a philosophical text, his theory of aesthetic ideas suggests a commitment to the benefit of working through a "lively" and "concrete" articulation of this concept in a novel like *Emma*, which exhibits this concept in creative, but no less cognitively valuable, way to us (see Axviii, BL 24:126–7; VL 24:835).

All this is to say, Kant's analysis of the more indirect and open-ended way our imagination exhibits moral ideas in the aesthetic context points toward an important moral use of imagination on his view. Through these aesthetic activities, our imagination provides us with a creative grasp of moral concepts that animates them for us in ways that enrich our concrete comprehension of them.

This said, though these aesthetic activities of imagination have moral significance for us, note that these activities are somewhat peripheral to our everyday moral activities. Indeed, this moral use of the imagination occurs in the context of contemplative aesthetic activities in which, *per* Kant, we are to set aside our

---

[21] Consider, for example, the symmetry we find in the communication and interiority of Emma and Knightly in Vol. 3, Chap. XIII. Emma tells Knightly, "if you have any wish to speak openly to me as a friend, or to ask my opinion of any thing that you may have in contemplation—as a friend, indeed, you may command me.—I will hear whatever you like. I will tell you exactly what I think" (2012, 295–6). Knightly responds, "Emma, I accept your offer—Extraordinary as it may seem, I accept it, and refer to you as a friend...You hear nothing but truth from me...But you understand me.—Yes, you see, you understand my feelings" (2012, 296). Internally resonating with these words, the narrator tells us that, "While he spoke, Emma's mind was most busy, and, with all the wonderful velocity of thought, had been able—and yet without losing a word—to catch and comprehend the exact truth of the whole" (2012, 296).

[22] See, e.g., the repetition of language of "understanding" and "misunderstanding" in the passages from *Emma* that I have quoted above.

366 IMAGINATIVE EXHIBITION IN MORALITY

interests in order to reflect on the beauty and sublimity at hand.[23] But paradigmatic moral activities like deliberation, choice, or interaction with others are not of this contemplative aesthetic sort. This raises the question of whether Kant thinks that there is any role for the imaginative exhibition of moral ideas to play internal to these everyday moral activities. And what I shall now argue is that not only does Kant acknowledge such a role, but also that direct imaginative exhibition is crucial to this end.

13.4 The Direct Exhibition of Moral Ideas through Moral Ideals

In spite of Kant's skeptical remarks about the possibility of direct imaginative exhibition in the moral context, in the next two sections, I bring out two ways in which he nevertheless accords it an important role in our moral activities: in this section, I explore how this works in moral ideals of imagination, and in the next, in moral examples.

Kant's commitment to ideals of imagination making a valuable contribution in the practical context is one I began exploring in Chapter 12.[24] There, I focused on Kant's analysis of happiness as an ideal of imagination and its relationship to the faculty of desire. In this section, however, I shall focus on a different set of ideals of imagination: moral ideals that involve the imaginative projection of a human (or human-like) individual that embodies a moral idea. After saying a bit more about what these moral ideals of imagination amount to, I argue that they should be understood as a kind of direct exhibition of moral ideas that serve us in our moral activities.

As a reminder, Kant, in general, defines an ideal as a representation of an archetypal individual that is adequate to an idea (see A568/B596; KU 5:232; AC 25:99). The ideal of happiness, for example, involves an imaginative representation of a human (or human-like) individual that has attained a maximum of well-being in relation to certain hedonic goods, e.g. health, wealth, or intelligence.

According to Kant, ideals have a "regulative" function for us: they serve as standards of perfection that guide our evaluations, actions, and progress (A569/ B597).[25] Take, for example, the ideal of friendship: a representation of an archetypal friend who perfectly embodies the moral idea of being united with others

---

[23] More precisely, on Kant's view, the "**determining ground**" of a judgment of the beautiful and sublimity, i.e. the pleasure at its basis, cannot be interested, although he allows for judgments of the beautiful to subsequently produce an interest in us (see KU §§41–2).

[24] See also Englert (2022) for discussion of the practical role of ideals on Kant's view.

[25] See also the regulative claim that the ideal gives us a "rule...for following or judging [*Beurtheilung*]" (A570/B598). In endorsing this regulative view of ideals Kant suggests that his view parts ways with Plato to an extent. For though Kant cites Plato's account of ideas as of "the most perfect thing of each species of possible beings and the original ground of all its copies in appearance,"

THE DIRECT EXHIBITION OF MORAL IDEAS THROUGH MORAL IDEALS   367

"through equal mutual love and respect" (MS 6:469). From Kant's perspective, we can use this ideal as a standard against which we judge instances of friendship that we encounter, as well as a standard that we hold ourselves accountable to and strive toward in our own activities as a friend.

However, Kant also warns against expecting that any actual human being can ever fully measure up to an ideal given our limitations.[26] In this vein, he says about the sage as the ideal of wisdom,

> to try to realize the ideal in an example, i.e., in appearance, such as that of the sage in a novel, is not feasible, and even has about it something nonsensical and not very edifying, since the natural limits which constantly impair the completeness in the idea render impossible every illusion in such an attempt.
>
> (A570/B598)[27]

Indeed, in the Friedländer lectures on anthropology, we find Kant warning that the "expectation" that these archetypes can be fully realized in the sensible world can give way to "enthusiasm" (see AF 25:529).[28] For example, he suggests that if we enthusiastically expect our actual friends to fully measure up to the archetypal friend, then we will be disappointed to such an extent that we might slip into misanthropy (see AF 25:530). So, instead of expecting any person to fully measure up to an ideal, Kant claims that we should treat an ideal as a standard of perfection that we can "compare ourselves" to, "judging [*beurtheilen*] ourselves and thereby improving ourselves" in light of, "even though we can never reach the standard" (A569/B597). So understood, ideals are not representations of a reality of perfection that we can achieve, but rather standards that we, in the reality of our imperfection, can only "progress" toward and "approximate without end" (KpV 5:32; see also A316–17/B372–4, MS 6:383, DWL 24:697).

With this sketch of ideals in place, let's now turn to Kant's account of the source of ideals. In the first *Critique*, Kant credits reason with such ideals (see A570/B598). Though he also talks of "ideals of sensibility," e.g. a "wavering sketch" a painter has of what they want to paint, he suggests that these are ideals in an

---

Kant rejects what he takes to be Plato's commitment to the "creative power" of these ideas in the "divine understanding" (A568–9/B596–7; see also ID 2:396).

[26] In his discussion of Kant's theory of moral examples, Louden suggests that we can gloss the actual persons involved in examples as "exemplars," defined as "morally exceptional individuals who serve as models of excellence for the rest of us" (1992, 311). McMullin (2020), following Crowell (2017), also explores the Kant-inspired idea that we can hold ourselves up as an "exemplar" not only for others to follow, but for us to follow as we strive to become the self we want to be. However, if by "exemplar" we have in mind an "archetype," then, *per* Kant, the individual at issue cannot be an actual person, but an imaginatively projected perfect person.

[27] See, e.g., "an ideal can serve...for judgment [*Beurtheilung*], but it cannot be actually attained" (AF 25:530).

[28] For discussion of Kant's theory of enthusiasm, see Clewis (2018).

368 IMAGINATIVE EXHIBITION IN MORALITY

"improper" sense because they are not grounded in "an intelligible concept" (A570/B598).

However, in the third *Critique*, Kant appears to acknowledge cases in which our imagination generates ideals in the proper sense.[29] This emerges in §17 where Kant discusses an "ideal of imagination" that he calls "the ideal of beauty" or "archetype of taste" (KU 5:232, 233). In this context, he asserts his familiar refrain that, "**Idea** signifies, strictly speaking, a concept of reason, and **ideal** that representation of an individual being adequate to an idea" (KU 5:232). And he glosses the ideal of beauty as an imaginative representation that "exhibits" the idea of a perfectly beautiful instance of the human species (KU 5:232; transl. modified).[30] Far from being just a wavering sketch without an intelligible concept underwriting it, this ideal is an ideal in the proper sense, underwritten by our intelligible concept of a human being. Granted, in this context, he is concerned with an aesthetic ideal; however, in his discussion of imagination in the *Anthropology* Kant speaks of cases of "exhibiting concepts (called ideas) that belong to morality," which suggests that he also countenances the possibility of moral ideals that involve our imagination (recall: *Einbildungskraft*) projecting an archetype (recall: *Urbild*) that represents moral ideas in human guise (Anthro. 7:192).[31]

Applying his picture of ideals in general to moral ideals of imagination, the latter serve us morally by providing us with standards of perfection that guide our judgments, actions, and progress. However, recall from Chapter 12 that, at least on my reading, part of what it can mean for our imagination to project ideals in human guise is to project ideals that have a rich human texture and that reflect how ideas can be embodied in a human life and mind. Insofar as this is the case, it seems that moral ideals of imagination can provide us with standards of perfection that are, in this sense, more concrete and embodied than the ideals we grasp in an abstract and disembodied way through reason alone, and can thus serve us in a distinctive way.

---

[29] Makkreel (1990, 116) and Gibbons (1994, 100) argue that this marks a significant shift in Kant's view of ideals. However, already in *Anthropology Collins* (1772/3) Kant discusses ideals that belong to sensibility, and he glosses them as "an idea in concreto," hence as a representation of an intelligible concept (AC 25:98; my transl.). And in *Anthropology Friedländer* (1775/6) Kant treats some ideals as products of imagination, *qua* a capacity for "Dichtung" (composition, invention), which represent ideas, hence concepts (AF 25:524; see, e.g., "The perfect concept of a thing is the idea, but if one fabricates [*fingirt*] an image in keeping with this idea, then this is an ideal" (AF 25:529)).

[30] Although Kant says that the ideal of imagination must have as its "basis" "some idea of reason in accordance with determinate concepts," and that it must be "fixed by a concept of objective purposiveness" of "the **human being**," he also says that it "does not rest on concepts" (KU 5:232–3). I take the latter claim, however, to be shorthand for Kant saying that we do not project this ideal through the understanding, but rather through the imagination.

[31] I take it that sometimes these moral ideals of imagination will be more specific, e.g. the ideal of friendship or appreciativeness, and sometimes more general, e.g. the ideal of a good will. I also take it that happiness as an ideal of imagination amounts to a practical ideal of imagination that rests on the indeterminate, but not unintelligible, concept of a maximum of well-being.

At this point, I want to return to the limits of exhibition worry and make the case that moral ideals of imagination, in fact, involve the direct exhibition of moral ideas. At the very least, Kant is committed to these moral ideals being the product of exhibition: they are intuitions$_i$ that our imagination generates to represent moral ideas as embodied in an archetypal human figure. But what kind of exhibition is this?

On the one hand, the fact that what our imagination exhibits is an idea suggests that indirect exhibition is at issue. Recall Kant's claim in the third *Critique* that ideas, as representations of the supersensible, are "indemonstrable," i.e. not capable of direct exhibition. Recall also his implication in the Typic that, as representations of the supersensible, moral ideas are too heterogeneous with sensible intuition to be exhibited. These remarks, which motivated the limits of imaginative exhibition worry in the first place, would seem to preclude the possibility of our imagination directly exhibiting moral ideas; in which case moral ideals would involve indirect exhibition.

On the other hand, Kant's account of direct exhibition might be capacious enough to accommodate moral ideals of imagination. As I emphasized above, the point he tends to emphasize in his discussion of direct exhibition is that the sensible content of the intuition$_i$ involved needs to map onto the logical content of the concept in a straightforward way (see KU §59). But it would seem that moral ideals of imagination do just this: they involve an intuition$_i$ that our imagination projects precisely on the basis of the logical content contained in the moral idea. For example, when projecting the ideal of the perfectly grateful person, our imagination is guided by the moral idea of appreciativeness, and accordingly represents an archetypal individual who is perfectly appreciative. Granted there is no actual person who will ever be perfectly appreciative. But the archetypal human figure that is imaginatively represented seems adequate to the idea of appreciativeness. To the extent that the sensible content of a moral ideal of imagination maps onto the logical content of a moral idea, the former would thus seem to qualify as direct, rather than indirect, exhibition. And what this suggests is that, on Kant's view, direct exhibition of moral ideas is not strictly speaking ruled out; at least in the case of moral ideals of imagination, moral ideas can be directly exhibited in intuitions$_i$ that represent archetypal individuals, in light of which we can judge, and hopefully improve, our moral conduct.

13.5 Direct Exhibition through Moral Examples

Although I have made the case that Kant countenances the possibility of our imagination directly exhibiting moral concepts vis-à-vis moral ideals, as we have just seen, moral ideals do not involve representing actual human beings as measuring up to a moral idea; they represent a perfect individual that, as such,

370 IMAGINATIVE EXHIBITION IN MORALITY

surpasses us. But what about the prospect of direct exhibition when it comes to actual human beings: does Kant think that we can, through our imagination, represent an actual human being's actions as directly exhibiting moral ideas? Suppose I witness someone express gratitude. Can I imaginatively represent their action as directly exhibiting a moral idea? As I discussed in Chapter 5, on Kant's view, an empirical intuition_i that directly exhibits a concept is an "example"; in which case, I think we can frame the question about direct exhibition at hand as one about moral examples. Does Kant think that we can imaginatively generate empirical intuitions_i that represent what actual human beings do as exemplifying moral ideas?[32]

For reasons I rehearsed above, Kant's answer to this question about moral examples appears to be "no." Recall his claim from the Typic, "it seems absurd to want to find in the sensible world a case which, though as such it stands only under a law of freedom and to which there could be applied the supersensible idea of the morally good, which is to be exhibited in it *in concreto*" (KpV 5:68). Recall also his claim about the impossibility of examples of freedom, "It is...absolutely impossible to give anywhere in experience an example of [the idea of freedom as a faculty of absolute spontaneity], since among the causes of things as appearances no determination of causality that would be absolutely unconditioned can be found" (KpV 5:48). In a similar vein, Kant says the following about examples of the moral law: "the moral law is given...as a fact of pure reason of which we are a priori conscious and which is apodictically certain, though it be granted that no example of exact observance of it can be found in experience" (KpV 5:46). In these three passages, Kant thus appears to rule out the possibility of our imagination directly exhibiting the action of an actual human being as exemplifying moral ideas.

These passages might, moreover, seem to echo the following famous passage from the *Groundwork*: "it is absolutely impossible by means of experience to make out with complete certainty a single case in which the maxim of an action that otherwise conforms with duty did rest solely on moral grounds and on the

---

[32] In the *Metaphysics of Morals*, Kant distinguishes between two types of examples, theoretical and moral: "'Instance' [*Beispiel*], a German word, is commonly used as synonymous with 'example' [*Exepel*], but the two words really do not have the same meaning. To take something as an *example* [Exempel] and to bring forward an *instance* [Beispiel] to clarify an expression are altogether different concepts. An example [*Exempel*] is a particular case of a *practical* rule, insofar as this rule represents an action as practicable [*Thunlichkeit*] or impracticable [*Unthunlichkeit*], where an *instance* is only a particular (*concretum*), represented in accordance with concepts as contained under a universal (*abstractum*), and is an exhibition of a concept merely for theory" (MS 6:479n; transl. modified). Here, Kant indicates that a *Beispiel* is a theoretical example of a particular that falls under a concept, and these were the sort of examples that I discussed in the context of Kant's theory of perception in Chapter 5. Meanwhile, he glosses an *Exempel* as a moral example of a particular action that falls under a moral rule and shows that action to be "practicable" or not. But in spite of these differences, I take both a theoretical *Beispiel* and a moral *Exempel* to involve the activity of exhibition: our imagination generates an intuition_i of a particular as exhibiting something conceptual, whether that be a theoretical concept in the case of a *Beispiel* or a moral concept or moral rule in the case of an *Exempel*.

representation of one's duty" (Gr. 4:407). For Kant, an action that "conforms with" duty is "morally correct" in the sense that it does not conflict with the moral law, but it lacks "moral worth" because it is not done "from duty," i.e. it lacks the right moral motivation (KpV 5:159; Gr. 4:398). Think, for example, of Kant's shop-keeper who performs the morally correct action of charging all their customers the same price, but is motivated by interest in "his advantage" (Gr. 4:397). And what Kant appears to be claiming in the above passage is that it is impossible for us to determine whether an action in experience is an example of a merely mor-ally correct action or whether it, in fact, has moral worth.

Though this line of thought resonates in some ways with the passages from the second *Critique* I just cited, the reasons Kant offers for why we cannot find moral examples in experience in the *Groundwork* are rather different,

> even with the keenest self-examination we find nothing besides the moral ground of duty that could have been powerful enough to move us to this or that good action...from this it cannot be inferred with certainty that no covert impulse of self-love, under the mere pretense of that idea, was not actually the real determining cause of the will...we can never...get behind our covert incentives, since, when moral worth is at issue, what counts is not action, which one sees, but those inner principles of actions that one does not see. (Gr. 4:407)

Here, Kant suggests that we can never tell "with certainty" whether an action has a moral motivation or whether it is motivated by a "covert impulse" of the "dear self" (Gr. 4:407). He tethers this uncertainty to the fact that we cannot "see" the "inner principles," i.e. maxims, motivating the action. In the *Groundwork*, then, Kant's reasons for being skeptical about finding examples of moral worth in experience turn on the opacity of motives: finding such examples of morally worthy action would require being able to "see" something we cannot "see": moral motivation.[33]

However, from the point of view of Kant's moral philosophy, the lack of moral examples does not appear to be a problem. Indeed, in the *Groundwork* he insists that, "one could not give morality worse counsel than by seeking to borrow it from examples" (Gr. 4:408). This claim is part and parcel of Kant's overarching argument to the effect that the foundation of morality lies not in experience, but rather *a priori* in reason. As he puts it in his ethics lectures,

> What is apodictically *a priori* needs no example, for there I perceive the neces-sity *a priori*...All cognitions of morality...can be set forth apodictically, *a priori*

---

[33] For more discussions of the opacity worry, see Cohen (2008); Ware (2009); Hakim (2017); Berg (2020); Russell (forthcoming a).

372 IMAGINATIVE EXHIBITION IN MORALITY

through reason. We perceive *a priori* the necessity of behaving so and not otherwise; so no examples are needed in matters of... morality. (EC 27:333)

But Kant's wariness of moral examples is also of a piece with his cautioning words about examples more generally:

as far as the correctness and precision of the insight of the understanding is concerned, examples more usually do it some damage, since they only seldom adequately fulfill the condition of the rule (as *casus in terminis*) and beyond that often weaken the effort of the understanding to gain sufficient insight into rules in the universal and independently of the particular circumstances of experience. (A134/B173)

Here, Kant suggests that in our efforts to understand universals, e.g. rules or principles, examples can do "damage" because we tend to get too focused on the particular and lose sight of the universal. In this cautionary mood, Kant characterizes examples as a kind of "leading string" (*Gängelband*) or "go-cart" (*Gängelwagen*), likening them to devices children use when learning to walk but which should eventually be dispensed with (KpV 5:152; A134/B174).

Yet in spite of Kant's critical remarks about moral examples, we also find passages like this,

before a humble common man in whom I perceive [*wahrnehme*] rightness of character in a higher degree than I am aware of in myself *my spirit bows*, whether I want it to or whether I do not... Why is this? His example holds before me a law that strikes down my self-conceit when I compare it with my conduct, and I see [*sehe*] observance of that law and hence its *practicability* [*Thunlichkeit*] proved before me in fact... [T]he law made intuitive by an example... strikes down my pride. (KpV 5:76–7)

In this passage, far from denying that the moral law can be exemplified, Kant suggests that it is possible for us to feel respect in response to "seeing" or "perceiving" someone's conduct as an "example" in which the moral law is "made intuitive."

Later in the second *Critique*, we also find Kant discussing at length the example of Henry Norris, who refused Henry VIII's demand to lie to condemn the innocent Anne Boleyn and who was executed for this refusal (KpV 5:155–6).[34] After detailing this example, Kant says,

---

[34] I return to this example at more length in my account of Kant's use of examples in moral education below.

DIRECT EXHIBITION THROUGH MORAL EXAMPLES   373

Thus morality must have more power over the human heart the more purely it is exhibited. From this it follows that if the law of morals and the image of...virtue are to exercise any influence at all on our soul, they can do so only insofar as they are laid to heart [*gelegt wird*] in their purity.   (KpV 5:156; transl. modified)

Here, instead of denying that we can find any images that exhibit the moral law, Kant lauds Norris's example as an "image" that "purely exhibits" morality and that has "power over the human heart" and "influence" "on our soul" accordingly.

What these more sympathetic passages suggest is that we need to take a closer look at cases in which Kant countenances the use of moral examples before ruling out the possibility that he thinks our imagination can directly exhibit moral ideas through moral examples drawn from experience. To this end, I shall examine Kant's more positive account of moral examples with an eye to motivating the idea that imaginatively exhibiting moral concepts through examples is something that he thinks is not just possible, but makes a significant contribution to our moral lives.[35] In particular, I consider the sanguine account of moral examples that Kant presents in three contexts: in his own moral writings, in his account of moral education, and in his discussion of the sort of perceptual episode of respect in the second *Critique* that I just cited. By underscoring what our imagination contributes in our engagement with such moral examples, I hope to bring to light Kant's commitment not only to the possibility of the direct imaginative exhibition of moral concepts through examples, but also to why we need this in the course of our moral development and in our on-going moral lives.

13.5.1 Moral Examples in Kant's Writings

Kant's own moral writings are rife with examples. Think of Kant's example of the philanthropist, who helps others in spite of his grief (Gr. 4:398); the other philanthropist, who helps others in spite of his cold and indifferent temperament (Gr. 4:398); the shopkeeper, who does not overcharge inexperienced customers (Gr. 4:397); the four examples of someone contemplating suicide, making a lying promise to gain money, neglecting their natural talents, and refusing to help others (Gr. 4:421–4, 429–30); the person who would give up his "lustful inclination...if a gallows were erected in front of his house" (KpV 5:30); or the person who refuses a prince's demand on pain of execution to "give false testimony

---

[35] I am thus sympathetic to the approach of other commentators who emphasize Kant's positive account of moral examples, such as O'Neill (1990, chap. 9); Louden (1992; 2009); Munzel (1999, chap. 5); Guyer (2016). However, none of these commentators emphasize the imaginative dimension of Kant's account of our engagement with moral examples, which is what I aim to do here.

374 IMAGINATIVE EXHIBITION IN MORALITY

against an honorable man" (an example that clearly has Norris overtones) (KpV 5:30).

For many of his readers, these examples are quite helpful, providing us with something concrete and human to hold on to in the midst of his abstract theorizing. This benefit is not something Kant is oblivious to. As he makes the point at the outset of the first *Critique*, "the reader has a right to demand first **discursive** (logical) **clarity through concepts**, but then also **intuitive** (aesthetic)[36] clarity, through **intuitions**, that is, through examples or other illustrations *in concreto*" (Axvii–xviii).[37] Here, Kant suggests that readers have a "right to demand" that a philosophical text offer them both conceptual clarity "*in abstracto*" and intuitive clarity "in concreto" about the subject matter. Note that this sort of intuitive clarity is what I described in Chapter 4 in terms of the concrete comprehension of concepts facilitated by imaginative exhibition. As I discussed, on Kant's view, by exhibiting concepts to us in intuition$_i$ our imagination gives us a grasp of how concepts, which we understand in the abstract, sensibly manifest in the concrete. So, I take it that in this passage when he claims that examples in philosophical writing give readers intuitive clarity, he is assuming that readers will imaginatively engage with these examples and generate intuitions$_i$ that directly exhibit the relevant concepts.

Applying this to his moral philosophy, Kant uses moral examples to provide readers with the opportunity to gain intuitive clarity and comprehension with respect to the abstract moral concepts he analyzes, like duty, the categorical imperative, moral worth, moral goodness, etc.[38] And, as I proposed in Chapter 11, in this context, he thinks it is especially important for us to have examples of how these moral concepts show up in human guise, i.e. in the actions, interactions, characters, thoughts, and feelings of us as human beings. But in order for moral examples to serve this purpose, on Kant's view, we need to imaginatively engage with them. For example, in the case of the cold-hearted philanthropist, we are not just to think about the case; that would only give us discursive clarity about the concept of moral worth. If we are to have intuitive clarity through this

---

[36] Here "aesthetic" is meant as a synonym with "intuitive," not as something that pertains to phenomena like the beautiful or sublime.

[37] In this context, Kant suggests that, "Examples and illustrations always appeared necessary to me, and hence actually appeared in their proper place in my first draft. But then I looked at the size of my task and the many objects with which I would have to do, and I became aware that this alone, treated in a dry, merely **scholastic** manner, would suffice to fill an extensive work" (Axviii). Kant, of course, does not drop all of his examples: just think of his famous examples of perceiving a house or experiencing freezing water in §26 of the B Deduction (see Chapters 6–7), or perceiving a house versus a ship moving downstream in the Second Analogy (A192–3/B237). By Kant's own lights, one of the reasons that these examples are so effective for readers is that they provide us with some intuitive clarity about the abstract thoughts he is trying to articulate, e.g. about the objective validity of the categories or causality.

[38] This use of examples to intuitively clarify moral concepts that Kant countenances is thus distinct from a use of examples as the basis of morality that he condemns (see Gr. 4:408).

DIRECT EXHIBITION THROUGH MORAL EXAMPLES 375

example, we need to imagine a human being, marked by indifference, choosing to act in beneficent ways. More technically put, we need to imaginatively generate an empirical intuition$_i$ that directly exhibits the concept of moral worth through a representation of the philanthropist as a psychologically complex human being who nevertheless has to choose and to act. And it is through this sort of direct exhibition that we can arrive at intuitive comprehension of the concept of moral worth in Kant's framework.

This said, the moral examples that Kant typically uses in his moral writings are of a particular sort: they are what I shall call "fictional," rather than "real" moral examples.[39] As I am using these terms here, "fictional" moral examples involve actions that have been invented and have not actually occurred, whereas "real" moral examples involve actions of actual human beings that have occurred. The shopkeeper and philanthropist examples count as "fictional," whereas the Henry Norris example counts as "real" in this sense.

By my lights, fictional moral examples have implications for how we think about Kant's concerns about the opacity of motives in relation to moral examples. For in fictional moral examples, we are free to fix the motive of the action as moral and imaginatively represent someone as morally motivated. Think, here, of Kant's philanthropist example. Kant constructs the example in such a way that the philanthropist has a moral, rather than a non-moral motive: "when no longer incited to it by any inclination, he nevertheless tears himself out of this deadly insensibility and does the action without any inclination, simply from duty; not until then does it have its genuine moral worth" (Gr. 4:398). Note that the way Kant presents this example specifies how we are to fill out the motivational nexus of the philanthropist and puts us in a position to imaginatively represent his actions as an example of the idea of moral worth. Insofar as this is the case, I think we can restrict the scope of Kant's worry about opacity of motives in relation to moral examples: if it is a worry, then it is not a worry about fictional moral examples, but about real moral examples. However, even when it comes to real moral examples, as we shall now see, in his theory of moral education and certain perceptual episodes involving respect, he allows for us to imaginatively exhibit actions of actual human beings as examples of moral ideas.

13.5.2 Moral Examples in Education

In order to think through the role that Kant attributes to moral examples in his theory of moral education, I shall focus on his rather extended treatment of this

---

[39] O'Neill (1990, 165–6) refers to these as "ostensive" and "hypothetical" examples; and Guyer (2016) refers to them as "empirical examples" and "thought-experiments."

376 IMAGINATIVE EXHIBITION IN MORALITY

issue in the Doctrine of Method in the second *Critique*.[40] There, he outlines a method for moral education oriented around "founding and cultivating genuine moral dispositions" (KpV 5:153).[41] And he accords real moral examples, especially ones drawn from "the biographies of ancient and modern times," a crucial role in this method (KpV 5:154).[42]

In explicating why real moral examples are needed, Kant claims that part of the purpose of moral education is making the moral law and moral concepts "subjectively practical" to us, which he glosses in terms of them having "*access* to the human mind and *influence* on its maxims" (KpV 5:151, 157). For Kant, then, the point of moral education is not just to provide us with an objective grasp of morality, but to make us subjectively attuned to it in our minds and conduct (see KpV 5:151).

Kant goes on to argue that if the moral law and moral concepts are "to become subjectively practical...the representation of them must be considered in relation to human beings and to the individual human being" (KpV 5:157). I take the emphasis on representing the moral law "in relation to human beings and to the individual human being" to be pivotal for understanding what a subjective grasp of the moral law involves for Kant: it involves grasping what the moral law means, for us, as the limited human beings that we are. This line of thought finds echoes in Kant's claim in the *Religion* that I have cited previously:

> It is plainly a limitation of human reason, one which is ever inseparable from it, that we cannot think of any significant moral worth of the actions of a person without at the same time portraying [*vorstellig zu machen*] this person or his expression in human guise...for we always need a certain analogy with natural being in order to make supersensible characteristics comprehensible [*faßlich*] to us. (Rel. 6:64–5n)

---

[40] Though moral examples also play a role in Kant's account of moral education in the Doctrine of Method in the *Metaphysics of Morals* (MS 6:480–4) and *Lectures on Pedagogy* (see 9:486–93), I focus on the Doctrine of Method in the second *Critique* because it offers a more sustained analysis of moral examples. See Morris (2021) for a discussion of Kant's account of moral "catechism" in MS.

[41] For discussions of Kant's theory of moral education, see Munzel (1999; 2012); Koch (2003); Moran (2009; 2012, chap. 3); Louden (2011, chap. 11); the essays collected in Roth and Surprenant (2012); Sticker (2015); Sweet (2015); Cohen (2016); Golob (2021); Morris (2021); the essays collected in the Special Issue, "Kant on Education and Moral Improvement," ed. Sticker and Bakhurst (2021).

[42] See O'Neill (1990, chap. 9), Louden (1992; 2009), Munzel (1999, chap. 5), Guyer (2016) for discussion of Kant's use of examples in the context of moral education. In addition to examples from biographies, in his discussion of moral catechism in the *Metaphysics of Morals*, Kant suggests that the teacher should serve as a "*good* example" through "exemplary conduct" and that students should be provided with "*cautionary* example[s] in others" (MS 6:479). See Louden (1992, 311–12) and Guyer (2016, §3) for discussion.

Though Kant thinks there are different routes through which moral concepts can be rendered in human guise,[43] in his discussion of moral pedagogy, the route that he emphasizes is through examples drawn from the actual lives of human beings.

While what is ultimately of interest to me is how our imaginative exhibition of concepts can play a role to this end, a few more words are in order about Kant's treatment of real moral examples in the pedagogical context. In addition to emphasizing the importance of examples drawn from actual human lives, Kant maintains that teachers should use examples drawn from ordinary human lives. To this end, he claims that teachers should,

> spare their pupils examples of so-called *noble* (supermeritorious) actions, with which our sentimental writings so abound...for, whatever runs up into empty wishes and longings for inaccessible perfection produces mere heroes of romance who, while they pride themselves on their feeling for extravagant greatness, release themselves in return from the observance of common and everyday obligation, which then seems to them insignificant and petty. (KpV 5:154–5)

Here, Kant warns against the use of examples of "supermeritorious" action, such as someone who "tries with extreme danger to his life to rescue people from a shipwreck, finally losing his own life in the attempt" (KpV 5:158). By Kant's lights, exposure to this sort of example can encourage in students an overly "heroic" conception of morality, as consisting not of "common and everyday obligation," but of "extravagant greatness."[44] Though Kant by no means denies the possibility of morally exceptional deeds, he thinks that the real examples used in moral education should be ones that offer students a grasp of what morality looks like in the everyday.[45]

Kant, in turn, describes two sorts of real moral example in this context: examples of morally correct or incorrect actions, hence ones that conform or fail to

---

[43] In the *Religion* footnote, Kant is primarily interested in indirect exhibition that proceeds through analogies, which he describes in terms of "*schematism of analogy*" (Rel. 6:65n). In this context, he glosses "schematize" in a loose sense to refer to "render[ing] a concept comprehensible through analogy with something of the senses," and thus appears to be using "schematize" as interchangeable with "exhibit" (Rel. 6:65n). However, when he is being more careful, he contrasts schematism as a "direct" mode of exhibition with analogical or symbolic exhibition as an "indirect" mode of exhibition (see KU §59; WF 20:279–80).

[44] In the *Religion*, Kant also argues that, "To teach only *admiration* for virtuous actions, however great a sacrifice these may have cost, falls short of the right spirit that ought to support the apprentice's feeling for the moral good. For, however, virtuous someone is, all the good that he can ever perform still is merely duty; to do one's duty, however, is no more than to do what lies in the common moral order and is not, therefore deserving of wonder. This admiration is, on the contrary, a dulling of our feeling for duty, as if to give obedience to it were something extraordinary and meritorious" (Rel. 6:48–9).

[45] One might recall *Emma* here (see §13.3) or Lyman Cabot's *Everyday Ethics*.

378 IMAGINATIVE EXHIBITION IN MORALITY

conform to the moral law, and examples of morally worthy or unworthy actions, hence ones that have a moral motivation or lack moral motivation (see KpV 5:159–60). The fact that Kant includes real examples of moral worth comes as something of a surprise given his claims in the *Groundwork* to the effect that it is "absolutely impossible by means of experience to make out with complete certainty" a case of morally worthy, rather than merely morally correct action. And though it is, indeed, "absolutely impossible" to ever have "complete certainty" in these matters, Kant nevertheless suggests that students can gain enough insight into the motives behind someone's action to be able to regard it as a real example of moral worth. To see how, consider Kant's suggestion for how teachers should frame the example of Henry Norris:

> [Norris] is offered gain, that is great gifts or high rank; he rejects them... Now threats of loss begin. Among these calumniators are his best friends, who now refuse him their friendship; closer relatives, who threaten to disinherit him... But, so that the measuring of suffering may be full... his family, threatened with extreme distress and poverty... *implor[e] him to yield* and himself though upright... he wishes that he had never lived to see that day that exposed him to such unutterable pain and yet remains firm in his resolution to be truthful. (KpV 5:155–6)

Presenting the example in this way "draw[s] attention" to Norris's "purity of will" by showing that in spite of the powerful non-moral motives that he had to struggle with (e.g. desire for personal gain, peer pressure, concern for the happiness of his family, or concern for his own happiness and his own life),[46] it was "respect for the [moral] law" that ultimately motivated him to act as he did (KpV 5:157). For Kant, then, even though a student can never be absolutely certain that Norris's action was morally motivated, by articulating Norris's motivational nexus in this way, a teacher can put a student in a position to regard Norris's action as a real example of moral worth.

According to Kant, engaging with real moral examples makes the moral law and moral concepts "subjectively practical" to students in a couple of ways. For one thing, he claims that examples help students "sharpen" their "judgment" (*Beurteilung*) concerning specific cases of human action that are morally correct/incorrect or morally worthy/unworthy (KpV 5:159).[47] The Norris episode, for example, gives students the opportunity to sharpen their judgment by reflecting on cases of morally incorrect actions, such as demanding someone lie to

---

[46] See Guyer (2016, §5) for emphasis on the role moral examples play for Kant in illustrating the struggle involved in being morally virtuous.
[47] See O'Neill (1990, 168–9), Louden (1992, 308, 311–12) for emphasis on the role that moral examples play in "sharpening" judgment on Kant's view. See Guyer (2016, §4) for discussion of the role examples play particularly with respect to teaching students about imperfect duties.

condemn an innocent person and killing an innocent person, as well as morally correct actions, such as refusing to lie to condemn an innocent person.

For another, Kant maintains that examples of morally worthy actions are particularly effective in subjectively attuning students to the importance of morality in their own conduct and character. To this end, he claims that although when students engage with examples of morally correct actions, they might "admire" them, they can adopt a more "contemplative" attitude toward them, which does involve any "interest" to "seek" out morally correct actions (KpV 5:160).[48] But when students engage with examples of morally worthy actions, Kant claims that this awakens a feeling of respect that orients them toward acting morally. As he puts it, "[the moral] law..., through the positive worth that observance of it lets us feel, finds easier access through the *respect for ourselves* in the consciousness of our freedom" (KpV 5:161). As he spells this feeling out, when a student engages with an example of morally worthy conduct, they will have "an initial feeling of pain," as they recognize that the moral law is to be prioritized over the happiness and pleasure that they sensibly value (KpV 5:161). But this feeling of pain gives way to a positive feeling of elevation in their "consciousness" of the moral law and their freedom, as a capacity to act on the basis of the moral law (KpV 5:159, 161).

To be clear, on Kant's view, the pedagogical purpose of such examples is not to encourage students to just imitate them:

> Imitation [*Nachahmung*] has no place at all in moral matters, and examples serve for encouragement only, i.e., they put beyond doubt the feasibility [*Thunlichkeit*][49] of what the law commands..., but they can never entitle us to set aside their true original, which lies in reason, and to go by examples.
>
> (Gr. 4:409; see also EC 27:334)

Instead of imitation, Kant thinks engaging with examples of morally worthy actions should "encourage" students to act in an autonomous way on the basis of the moral law.[50]

With this sketch of the pedagogical use of real moral examples in place, let's return to the imaginative dimension of this process. According to Kant, part of what is involved in engaging with real moral examples is the student treating them as a "lively exhibition" of moral concepts (KpV 5:161; transl. modified).

---

[48] Kant, indeed, suggests that the students can find in such examples "a form of beauty," but this, for Kant, would be a paradigmatically "disinterested" way of relating to them (KpV 5:160).

[49] I return to the issue of the relationship between examples and encouragement concerning the "feasibility" of the moral law in §13.5.3.

[50] For discussions of the worry that imitating moral examples threatens autonomy in the Kantian framework, see Munzel (1999, chap. 5); Warnick (2008, 21–2); Louden (2009, 65, 79); Zagzebski (2017, 150–3); McMullin (2019, 121–5). See Saunders and Sticker (2020) for discussion of the apparent tension between Kant's account of moral education and his account of freedom in his theory of transcendental idealism.

380 IMAGINATIVE EXHIBITION IN MORALITY

As I have argued, on Kant's view, the cognitive capacity through which we entertain such "lively exhibition" is the imagination. For Kant, then, when students interact with real moral examples, they do not just think about these scenarios without the aid of intuitive representations. They imaginatively bring these scenarios to life, generating intuitions$_i$ of the persons and actions involved as exemplifying the relevant moral concepts. In the Norris case, for example, the student uses their imagination to not only envision the interactions between Norris, Henry VIII, and Anne Boleyn, but also to project Norris's inner state, including his motivations, suffering, and resolution. By giving students something to "sensibly hold onto," something in a human guise, their imaginative engagement with real moral examples facilitates their comprehension of moral concepts in a way that makes them "subjectively practical," giving them "access to the human mind" and "influence on" maxims of the student.

In his moral pedagogy, instead of dismissing the possibility of the imaginative exhibition of real moral examples, we thus find Kant embracing this possibility. Indeed, he commits himself to the importance of students' imaginatively engaging with the actions of actual human beings as examples not only of morally correct or incorrect action, but also of morally worthy action. And on his view, such imaginative engagement is needed for students to develop a subjective grasp of the moral law and moral concepts as they bear on who we are, as human beings.

This said, though, one might concede that Kant acknowledges the importance of real moral examples as a kind of pedagogical tool to be utilized with children, one might think that he regards them as something that should eventually be dispensed with. After all, as I noted above, Kant likens examples to the "leading-strings" or "go-carts" that children rely on when they are learning to walk.

While Kant is certainly wary of us relying too much on examples in our moral endeavors, the cognitive function that he ascribes to imaginative exhibition in this context, of facilitating our concrete, human comprehension of moral ideas, has purchase in our on-going moral lives. As we saw above, Kant suggests that the need for comprehension through exhibition is tethered to a "limitation of human reason, one which is ever inseparable from it": as creatures who are at once sensible and rational, we need concepts to be "made sensible" to us through exhibition (Rel. 6:64n). Insofar as this is the case, we all have a need, regardless of how developed we are, to have moral ideas made comprehensible to us through imaginative exhibition.

What is more, as I have highlighted, according to Kant, the comprehension of concepts through exhibition is a kind of "aesthetic perfection" of cognition, which turns on us developing an ever-richer grasp of how concepts manifest *in concreto* (see Chapters 4 and 8). And we can realize this aesthetic perfection as much in a practical context as in a theoretical or aesthetic context. However, when we realize it in the moral context, it has practical import: for the more we comprehend of moral concepts, the more "subjectively practical" they become. Think, for example, of our comprehension of the general idea of the <morally good> or more specific moral ideas of <friendship> or <gratitude>: at no point is our comprehension of these moral ideas fully settled. Instead, our comprehension of them develops over time, as we discover new ways in which they manifest, and relate to one another, in the external and internal course of a human life.

For Kant, then, even if there are ways in which moral examples serve children that do not serve adults, imaginatively engaging with examples is something that has on-going value in our moral lives, facilitating and enriching our comprehension of moral concepts. Indeed, this imaginative engagement appears to be part of a learning process in our moral lives we never reach the end of. And though such examples need not be of the real variety, as we saw above, Kant thinks that real moral examples have a particularly forceful grip on us insofar as they show us what it is like for moral ideas to be embodied in the lives and minds of actual human beings.[51]

In the end, in spite of Kant's apparent claims to the contrary, his account of real moral examples in the context of moral education reveals a commitment to the value of direct imaginative exhibition of moral ideas in our moral lives. However, as we shall now see, it is not just in a pedagogical context that Kant countenances the possibility of the direct exhibition of moral ideas vis-à-vis real examples; it is one he countenances in perception as well.

13.5.3 Moral Examples in Perception

While many of Kant's moral examples are at some perceptual remove from us, if we return to the following passage in the second *Critique*, we find him pointing toward the possibility of finding moral examples face to face:

---

[51] It is perhaps also worth noting that Kant prefaces his pedagogical discussion of examples with the remark that adults also enjoy reflecting on real moral examples: "of all arguments there are none that excite the participation of persons who are otherwise soon bored with subtle reasoning and that bring a certain liveliness into the company than arguments about the *moral worth* of this or that action. Those for whom anything subtle and refined in theoretical questions is dry and irksome soon join in when the question of how to make out the moral import or a good or evil action that has been related" (KpV 5:153). This said, he also notes that we have a tendency to want to deny that actions from experience are, indeed, real examples of moral worth for less than admirable reasons. In this vein, Kant notes that this tendency can be revealing of "a character" "prone to contest this worth by accusations and fault-finding" or perhaps of an "enemy of virtue" (KpV 5:153; Gr. 4:407). However, in another vein, he claims that, all of us "give way to [respect] only reluctantly with regard to a human being. We try to discover something that could lighten the burden of it for us, some fault in him to compensate us for the humiliation that comes upon us through such an example" (KpV 5:77). What these remarks suggest is that, from Kant's perspective, we should be wary of a tendency in ourselves to dismiss every potential real moral example of moral worth, as a tendency that is reflective of something less than admirable in us.

before a humble common man in whom I perceive [*wahrnehme*] rightness of character in a higher degree than I am aware of in myself *my spirit bows*, whether I want it to or whether I do not...Why is this? His example holds before me a law that strikes down my self-conceit when I compare it with my conduct, and I see [*sehe*] observance of that law and hence its *practicability* [*Thunlichkeit*] proved before me in fact...[T]he law made intuitive by an example...strikes down my pride.   (KpV 5:76–7)

In this passage, which I shall refer to as the "respect in perception passage," Kant describes a scenario in which we "see" or "perceive" someone's action as a real moral example, and feel respect as a result.[52] All too briefly, on Kant's view, the feeling of respect is a complex feeling that involves, on the one hand, a negative feeling of "displeasure" at the recognition that the moral law has priority over what we care about "as sensible beings," and, on the other hand, a positive feeling of "esteem" for the moral law and "elevation" on account of our freedom (KpV 5:73–4, 79).[53] So, in the respect in perception passage, Kant suggests that certain perceptual encounters with other people can occasion a feeling of respect in us, when we "see" or "perceive" their action as an "example" of the observance of the moral law.[54] For example, suppose I have been running around all day in a rather mean-spirited mood, feeling hostile toward everyone I encounter.[55] I then witness someone express gratitude to someone else in a heartfelt and humble way. What the respect in perception passage suggests is that it is possible that I perceive this act in such a way that it "strikes down" my self-conceit, as I see their appreciative act as an example of the "moral law made intuitive," and feel respect for the moral law accordingly.

Though Kant does not explicitly claim that this sort of perceptual episode involves imagination, when we consider it in light of his theory of imagination as the faculty of exhibition, there is reason to think imagining is involved. For one

---

[52] My focus, here, is perceiving a person's conduct as a moral example, rather than perceiving a person as a person. For a Murdoch-inspired discussion of what is involved in perceiving a person as a person on Kant's view, see Merritt (2017; she cites Murdoch's emphasis on imagination, but does not explore this topic at length). For an account of perceiving persons as persons that draws loosely on Kant's notion of productive imagination, see Church (2013, chap. 5; 2016). I also focus primarily on the claim that someone's action can invite a feeling of respect in the moral law, rather than on how we show respect for persons through loving attention that serves as an incentive for morally engaging with them, which Bagnoli (2003) and Merritt (2017) discuss as part of their analysis of the relationship between Kant's and Murdoch's moral theories.

[53] Kant also treats respect as something that has a motivational component: "This feeling...serve[s] as an incentive to make this law its maxim" (KpV 5:76). I also touched on respect in my discussion of the dynamical sublime in Chapter 10.

[54] Kant is clear that in such a scenario, it is "strictly speaking...the law that his example holds before us" that we respect (KpV 5:78).

[55] In the respect in perception passage, Kant suggests that in these episodes, we do not necessarily need to be behaving poorly ourselves. Instead, he says, "I may even be aware of a like degree of uprightness in myself, and yet the respect remains" (KpV 5:77).

thing, Kant's language of "examples" in this passage, at least on my interpretation, alerts us to the fact that the cognitive activity of exhibition has a role to play here, as we imaginatively generate an empirical intuition$_i$ that represents the person's action as an example of an observance of the moral law. For instance, in order to regard someone saying "thank you" as an example of an observance of the moral law, we need to imaginatively generate an empirical intuition$_i$ that represents that verbal act as an expression of gratitude.

I also take Kant's language of treating the person's action as "making the moral law intuitive" to point toward the involvement of imaginative exhibition. As I have argued, on Kant's view, making concepts "sensible" or "intuitive" is the cognitive function of imagination in general and exhibition in particular (see Chapter 4).[56]

However, his language of "perceiving" someone's action as an example also points toward the involvement of imagination. Though Kant uses "perception" in different ways in different contexts,[57] when we think about the sort of perception involved in the respect in perception passage, there are some good reasons to think it is the sort of perception that Kant says imagination is a "necessary ingredient of" (A120n). As I discussed in Chapter 5, on Kant's view, perception is not a merely receptive affair of the senses; it is an active affair of imagination. More specifically, Kant claims that perception involves our imagination taking up what we sense and organizing it into a perceptual image, which represents a particular as exemplifying a concept. And it seems that this sort of imaginative activity is required for the sort of perceptual episode involved in the respect in perception passage. At the very least, this episode requires something more than just sensing someone's action; it involves actively taking this action to be an example of the moral law "made intuitive." And the fact that Kant describes this episode in terms of "perceiving" suggests that this "active taking" is not just an intellectual matter, but has a sensible dimension. Since this sort of active sensible taking is precisely what Kant credits imagination with in perception, then we have good reason to think that the perception involved in the respect in perception involves imagination as a "necessary ingredient."

This said, there are also reasons to be wary of over-drawing the similarities between this kind of moral perception and the experiential perception Kant targets in the first *Critique*.[58] One crucial asymmetry between the two turns on the

---

[56] Granted the moral law is not a concept, but a principle, on Kant's view; nevertheless, his language suggests that it can be "made intuitive" in some way.

[57] See Chapter 5, §5.3.

[58] As I noted in Chapter 12, it seems that there is another way in which imagination serves as a necessary ingredient of perception in the moral context: assessing a situation as one in which we should act on a specific moral principle. I take it that, on Kant's view, this involves perceiving a situation as one in which the concepts operative in the principle are salient (see Herman (1993, ch. 4)), and for this we need to imaginatively represent the situation as one in which those concepts are exemplified. For example, in order to respond to a situation as one in which I should act on the principle of

384 IMAGINATIVE EXHIBITION IN MORALITY

role of schemata. As I argued in Chapter 5, according to Kant, the perception at stake in ordinary experience is something that involves imaginative activities that are guided by schemata. Recall that a schema is an intuition$_i$ generated by imagination, which represent how the marks contained in a concept show up as a whole in space and time. And according to Kant, in perception such schemata guide us in imaginatively synthesizing the manifold delivered through sense in accordance with a concept and generating a perceptual image that represents a particular as exemplifying a concept.

But as emerged in my analysis of the Typic, Kant denies that our imagination can generate schemata for moral ideas related to the moral law, freedom, and the morally good. For, on Kant's view, there is no spatio-temporal pattern that our imagination can project that represents how these ideas manifest sensibly. As I put it, there is no general "look" that all cases of the moral law, freedom, and the morally good share in common which our imagination could schematically capture. However, if no schemata are possible for moral ideas, then how could we, in perception, imaginatively exhibit a particular action as exemplifying a moral idea?

What I would like to propose is that there is an alternative imaginative activity of direct exhibition possible in such moral perception: direct exhibition that is guided by moral judgments.[59] More specifically, I take the moral judgments at issue to be what Kant calls "determining" judgments: judgments in which we subsume a particular under a "given" universal, the particular here being the action we see and the universal here being the concept of moral worth (KU 5:317).[60] After detailing what exactly this judgment-guided imaginative exhibition amounts to, I shall make the case that this imaginative activity nevertheless provides moral benefits to us that judgment alone cannot provide.

Let me preface this discussion by noting that, on my interpretation of Kant, the role that judgment plays here is another significant asymmetry between moral perception and theoretical perception. In Part II, I made the case that Kant distinguishes the perception our imagination is responsible for in experience from the activity of judgment that our understanding is responsible for. As I put it in

---

expressing gratitude to honor those who have benefitted me, I must be able to perceive another person as a benefactor. And according to the view of perception I developed in Part II, in order to perceive someone as a benefactor Kant thinks I must engage in imaginative synthesis and perceptual image formation that is guided by a schema for the concept <benefactor>. However, I take this account of perception in the moral context to just be an instance of our imagination engaging in the activity it does in any context in which it enables us to perceive a particular as exemplifying a concept—it just so happens that in this context, the relevant concepts are ones that appear in a moral maxim.

[59] For discussion of the broader relationship between imagination and moral judgment, see Johnson (1985); Freydberg (2005; 2013); Ferrarin (2008); and Biss (2014).

[60] I thus, here, set aside questions about the role imagination might play vis-à-vis moral judgments of the "reflecting" type in which "only the particular is given, for which the universal is to be found" (KU 5:179). See O'Neill (1990, 180–6), Munzel (1999), and Bremner (2023) for emphasis on the importance of reflecting moral judgments for Kant; and see Johnson (1985), Arendt (1982, 68–9), Ferrarin (2008), and Dunn (ms) for discussion of the role imagination plays vis-à-vis reflecting moral judgments.

Chapter 5, we should distinguish the perception involved in the imagination stage of experience from the recognitional judgment at issue in the understanding stage of experience. I distinguished the two stages, in part, in terms of the idea that the perception involved in the imagination stage of experience does not involve making judgments in which we recognize that there are existing objects that our representations correspond to and are necessitated by, as the understanding of experience does. I could, for example, perceive a hydrangea without making the judgment that there exists a hydrangea in front of me that my representations correspond to and are necessitated by. All that this perception requires is the imaginative generation of a perceptual image that represents what subjectively appears to me as exemplifying the concept <hydrangea>.

However, in the respect in perception passage, we have reason to regard the perception at stake not as a perception that precedes judgment, but rather as guided by it in some sense.[61] I say "in some sense" because I take it that the judgment and perception can temporally coincide; however, the judgment will nevertheless have a kind of logical priority, as something our imaginative activities depend upon. As I see it, we have reason to attribute to Kant a judgment-guided model of this moral perception because, in these episodes, we are not just perceptually representing how things subjectively appear to us, as we do in the imagination stage of experience. Kant tells us that we are observing something "in fact." This suggests that in these episodes we are perceptually representing how things objectively are. However, on Kant's view, our grasp of how things objectively are depends on us making judgments; indeed, he claims that this objective determination is, "the aim of the copula is in them" (B141–2). Insofar as this is the case, it seems that a judgment of some sort needs to guide the perception at stake in the respect in perception passage. And I take it that a judgment of this sort is what guides our imaginative activities in moral perception in lieu of a schema.

In order to work through these details, let's return to Kant's distinction between two different types of moral examples: examples of morally correct/incorrect actions and morally worthy/unworthy actions. If we are to perceive someone's action as "in fact" a real example of either type, my suggestion is that we must make a moral judgment in which we determine that their action meets the relevant criteria. In the case of morally correct or incorrect action, we need to judge that their action conforms or conflicts with the moral law. And in the case of morally worthy or unworthy action, we need to judge that their action is or is not morally motivated. Bringing this to bear on the respect in perception passage, if we are to be able to regard someone's action as "in fact" an example of the

---

[61] Insofar as I take this imagination-dependent perception to be guided by judgment, I take it to be distinct from the sort of imaginative perception that someone like Nussbaum claims is involved in "the primacy of intuitive perception" in the practical domain (1990, 141).

observance of the moral law, then we need to not only judge that their action is morally correct, but also that they have a moral, rather than a non-moral, motive.

However, in the respect in perception passage Kant does not say that we "judge" someone's conduct as an example of the observance of the moral law; he says that we "see" or "perceive" that this is the case. I take this to mean that Kant conceives of such scenarios as having a perceptual dimension. And, for reasons I offered earlier, I take imagination to be a "necessary ingredient" of this kind of moral perception. As I would reconstruct his position, in such an episode we, through our senses, are causally affected by someone's action, and this gives rise to an empirical intuition of sense (intuition$_s$) that contains a manifold. Our imagination is, in turn, responsible for synthesizing this manifold in such a way that results in an intuition$_i$ that represents the action as an example of the observance of the moral law. This synthesis, I take it, is guided not by schemata for moral ideas, but rather by a judgment to the effect that the action is morally correct and worthy. Under the guidance of a moral judgment, then, we are able to imaginatively generate an intuition$_i$ (a perceptual image) in which we represent not only the external action as conforming to the moral law, but also the agent as motivated in the right way. And by representing the moral law as "made intuitive" in this fashion, our imagination contributes to the perception in which a feeling of respect for the moral law is occasioned in us. For Kant, then, our imagination is, indeed, a necessary ingredient of moral perception, but in this case, our imagination is oriented by our moral judgment.

But if moral perception involves imaginative activities that are guided by moral judgment in this way, one might wonder whether these activities are morally significant, or whether they are just biproducts of something morally significant. Otherwise put, is there reason to think that they do any moral work for us over and above the work already done by the judgment?[62]

What I would now like to argue is that there are, indeed, distinctive moral benefits that these imaginative activities have that contribute to our moral lives in ways that extend beyond what is accomplished by the attendant activity of moral judgment on Kant's view. For one thing, as I have argued, for Kant, as human beings, we subjectively need concepts and ideas to be made intuitive to us in human guise if we are to concretely comprehend them. And I take this to be part of what Kant has in mind when he emphasizes the importance of the moral law being "made intuitive" to us in the example of someone's action. According to Kant, then, it is important that the episode involved has a perceptual dimension because it serves us subjectively by "making" the moral law "intuitive" to us, as embodied in the mind and action of an actual human being.

---

[62] For contemporary discussions of this worry in the context of moral perception and cognitive penetration, see Werner (2017; 2018).

DIRECT EXHIBITION THROUGH MORAL EXAMPLES   387

However, in the respect in perception passage, Kant also says that in this epi-sode, "I see [*sehe*] observance of that law and hence its *practicability* [*Thunlichkeit*] proved before me in fact" (KpV 5:77). Here, Kant indicates that seeing someone's conduct as an example of observance of the moral law "proves" something to me "in fact": it proves the "practicability" of the moral law. For Kant the "practicabil-ity" of the moral law amounts to the possibility that we, as human beings, can indeed act morally. And what I would like to suggest is that an important dimen-sion of this proof of practicability turns on a general theme in his theory of imag-ination: imaginative exhibition facilitates proof of real possibility.

Recall from Chapter 1 that, on Kant's view, an object is really possible if it can be given and that the concept of such objects are not empty, but rather have "objective reality," i.e. they relate to objects that can be given. In Chapter 4, I made the case that, for Kant, part of why imaginative exhibition cognitively matters is on account of the role that it plays to this end in furnishing us with a literal demonstration of the objective reality of a concept. And in Chapter 5, I argued that Kant accords our imagination an important role to play vis-à-vis the proof of real possibility of objects in the context of experience. Extending this line of thought into the moral context, what I am here proposing is that Kant again accords our imagination a crucial role to play in the proof of real possibility. But in this context, the really possible objects at issue are moral human actions, the concepts at issue are moral ones, and the proof is of the "practicability" of these concepts, as ones that can make a difference in our lives.[63]

In order to explicate the sort of proof of real possibility at issue here, it is help-ful to recognize a distinction between what I shall refer to as an "objective" and "subjective" proof of the practicability of the moral law on Kant's view.[64] By an "objective" proof of the practicability of the moral law, I have in mind the sort of proof Kant describes in the second *Critique* that proceeds by way of "rational" or "a priori" cognition (KpV 5:12). He argues that this sort of objective proof is pro-vided *a priori* by way of the so-called "fact of reason," through which we are con-scious that the moral law is binding on us and that we have the freedom required to act on the basis of it (see KpV 5:31, 47).

However, as I anticipated in my discussion of moral pedagogy, in addition to this objective grasp, Kant claims that we have a subjective grasp of the practicabil-ity of the moral law and freedom, as having "*access* to the human mind" and

---

[63] Relevant here is the distinction that Kant draws between concepts having "objective theoretical reality" and "practical reality" (KpV 5:56). According to Kant, a concept has "objective theoretical reality" when it refers to a really possible object, paradigmatically one that can be given through intu-ition (see A239/B298; KU 5:351). By contrast, Kant claims that a concept has "practical reality" when it refers to something volitional, viz. "dispositions" or "maxims."

[64] Louden (1992, 315; 2009, 74) refers to these as "formal" or "logical" and "informal" or "anthro-pological" proofs, but I think that this "objective"-"subjective" language tracks Kant's contrast between an "objective" grasp of something via concepts and a "subjective grasp" that proceeds via intuitions and exhibition.

388 IMAGINATIVE EXHIBITION IN MORALITY

"*influence* on its maxims" (KpV 5:151, 157). As I understand the difference, whereas the objective grasp of practicability involves intellectually recognizing that we, as rational beings, are bound by the moral law and autonomously capable of acting on it, the subjective grasp of practicability involves some sort of conviction that we, as limited human beings, can actually act morally.

According to Kant, moral examples have a vital role to play in proving to us the real possibility of morality, *qua* subjectively practicable.[65] In this vein in the *Metaphysics of Morals*, he says, "A good example [*Exempel*] (exemplary conduct) should...serve...as proof that it is really possible to act in conformity with duty" (MS 6:479).[66] Or as he puts it in the *Groundwork*, "examples serve for encouragement only, i.e., they put beyond doubt the practicability [*Thunlichkeit*] of what the law commands" (Gr. 4:409; transl. modified). Indeed, on Kant's view, by providing proof of the subjective practicability of morality, examples not only give us "encouragement" that morality can be "effective," but also help ward off the worry that morality is "a mere phantom" or "vain affectation and delusive self-conceit" (KpV 5:159, 154).

When Kant thus says in the respect in perception passage that perceiving someone's moral example provides us with proof of the practicability of the moral law, I understand him to mean that moral examples prove the subjective practicability of the moral law to us. However, notice once again that in the respect in perception passage Kant insists that this subjective proof of practicability proceeds by way of the moral law being "made intuitive" for us in an example. By my lights, what this reveals is that, on Kant's view, this subjective proof does not just proceed by way of an intellectual judgment. Though judgment is relevant for Kant, given our needs as human beings, this subjective proof also requires that the moral law is made intuitive to us in human guise. And this latter work, I have been arguing, is the work of imaginative exhibition in moral perception: perception that allows us to see human actions as morally correct and worthy.

Notice, moreover, that the sort of moral example involved in the respect in perception passage is not a fictional example, nor is it a real moral example that is some temporal distance from us; it is a real moral example of someone's action, present to us. And it seems that on Kant's view, there is a particular kind of force that the proof of the real possibility of morality has when we see it made intuitive, here and now. For though presumably all real moral examples can promise us proof of real possibility, it seems that being perceptually confronted with such examples can be particularly effective in giving us encouragement that we, limited beings that we are, can actually act morally.

---

[65] See Louden (1992, 314–15; 2009, 72–7) and Guyer (2016, §5) for discussion of the role Kant accords examples in establishing the real possibility of us acting morally. However, neither Louden nor Guyer consider the role imagination plays here.

[66] See also his claim that the concept of freedom "has...a real application which is exhibited *in concreto* in dispositions or maxims" (KpV 5:56).

CONCLUSION   389

For Kant, then, the generation of intuitions$_i$ that exhibit how the moral law can actually make a difference in our lives as human beings has an important role to play vis-à-vis the subjective proof of the practicability of the moral law. And according to my interpretation, this thought is precisely what we would expect from Kant given his theory of imagination more generally: for, as I have urged, on his view, part of what the proof of real possibility requires is that our imagination generate intuitions$_i$ that literally demonstrate the reality of the concept at stake. So just as in the theoretical context Kant argues that the imagination's activity of exhibition provides us with intuitions$_i$ that help put us in a position to prove the reality of concepts of experience, in the moral domain we find he is committed to the imagination's activity of exhibition providing us with intuitions$_i$ that help put us in a position to prove the reality, i.e. practicability, of concepts of morality.

13.6 Conclusion

In spite of the skeptical worry that when it comes to imagination, Kant thinks the only morally responsible way to proceed is by suppressing it,[67] in this chapter I have brought to light his positive vision of a morally oriented imagination, *qua* the faculty of exhibition. Indeed, I have argued that, on Kant's view, as is the case in the theoretical and aesthetic domain, in the moral domain our imagination functions cognitively well by making moral concepts sensible to us.

I opened with a discussion of some reasons we might initially worry that Kant can accord imaginative exhibition a substantive role in the moral domain given the apparent limitations of exhibition with respect to moral ideas. However, I went on to show that we nevertheless find Kant acknowledging a wide variety of ways in which our imagination can exhibit moral ideas, through indirect and direct means.

To this end, I argued that Kant countenances the indirect exhibition of moral ideas in an aesthetic context through our imaginative engagement with beauty and sublimity, and I underscored his commitment to this facilitating a creative comprehension of our moral ideas, which expands our grasp of them in rich and open-ended directions. I also claimed that, on Kant's view, our imagination can directly exhibit moral ideas through both moral ideals and moral examples. In the case of moral ideals, I explored Kant's commitment to the imaginative projection of archetypal individuals providing us with concrete standards of perfection that guide our moral judgments, actions, and progress. Meanwhile, in the case of moral examples, I mounted an argument to the effect that, for Kant, the sort of imaginative activities of exhibition that we enact in relation to moral examples,

---

[67] See Chapter 11.

fictional and real, contributes to our moral development and on-going moral lives by facilitating our comprehension of how those ideas are manifest in human minds and actions, and by contributing to the proof that it is really possible for us, as human beings, to act morally.

All told, I hope to have shown that if we approach Kant's practical philosophy through the lens of his theory of imagination, then we find that rather than ignoring imagination or treating it as something that is morally subversive, his view allows for our imagination to play a robust role in our practical lives. In particular, I have explored the ways in which the cognitive activities we are capable of through imagination of seeing more than is immediately present and of making concepts sensible through exhibition contribute to our practical activities at a great many levels: to our specification of practical principles, our appraisal of concrete situations in light of specific practical principles, our deliberation about what sorts of actions to pursue in concrete situations, our pursuit of happiness, our assessment of moral motives in light of the categorical imperative, our morally salient aesthetic activities, our projection of moral ideals, and our engagement with moral examples, fictional and real. Though not all of these activities are moral, many of them are. And in those that are, we find a variety of ways in which our imagination serves us morally: in seeing moral possibilities and moral realities, in comprehending moral concepts and forging moral commitments, and in providing moral proof and moral encouragement. It is ultimately in these activities that we find a Kantian vision of moral imagination—the imagination of an integrated moral agent in whom reason has called sensibility into play.

Far from imagination reaching its limits in the practical domain, we thus find in Kant a picture of imagination as something that contributes in a pervasive way in our practical pursuits, just as it does in ordinary experience and aesthetic engagement. Indeed, what we find is confirmation that in the Kantian framework, the way we see is imaginative through and through.

Seeing More: Kant's Theory of Imagination. Samantha Matherne, Oxford University Press.
© Samantha Matherne 2024. DOI: 10.1093/9780191999291.003.0014

Conclusion

> it absolutely cannot do without the imagination
>
> —DWL 24:710

Kant has been received as a champion of many things: a champion of reason, of enlightenment, of the bounds of experience. What I have argued is that he is no less a champion of imagination. On this point, I am in agreement with readers like Hegel and Heidegger who see in Kant's theory of imagination some of his most important philosophical insights. However, whereas Hegel and Heidegger pursued the metaphysical import of this theory, I have pursued its import for understanding just how imaginative we are. In sharp contrast with a traditional conception of imagination as a kind of fantasy we only enact in relation to what is not real or absent, I have shown that Kant is committed to imagination being something we exercise just as much in relation to what is real and present. Indeed, I have made the case that, in Kant, we find a vision of imagining as something that suffuses our lives.

In an effort to clarify this Kantian vision of imagination, I took on two, related, tasks. My first task was to think through Kant's answer to the question "what is it to imagine." I approached this issue in light of Kant's account of what imagination is in general in Part I. In sum, I argued that, on Kant's view, to imagine is to exercise a cognitive capacity that belongs to sensibility and that is tasked with mediating between sensibility and understanding. More specifically, I claimed that, for Kant, to imagine is to spontaneously generate a distinctive kind of intuition, represent objects even without their presence, and exhibit concepts in a way that makes those concepts sensible to us and, thereby, facilitates our concrete comprehension of them. And in clarifying what Kant understands imagination to be in general, I attributed to him a unified account of imagination as a single cognitive capacity that we can exercise in a variety of ways.

My second task was to explore Kant's answer to the question "what use is it to imagine." To this end, I examined Kant's account of the use our imagination has in three contexts: in the theoretical (or epistemic) context of ordinary perception and experience; in the aesthetic context of our engagement with beauty, art, and sublimity; and in the practical context of our pursuit of happiness and morality. Though I canvassed a wide array of theoretical, aesthetic, and practical phenomena in the course of this discussion, I have insisted that they are all, indeed, imaginative phenomena: the result of an exercise of "the imagination"—a remarkably flexible, yet unified cognitive capacity. And in order to bring out this unity and flexibility, I laid particular emphasis on Kant's commitment to the variety of constrained and creative, playful and serious ways, in which our imagination helps us see more and functions cognitively well through acts of exhibition in which it renders our concepts sensible and expands our conceptual horizons.

Though in discharging these two tasks, I have advanced a systematic interpretation of Kant's position, I have also aspired to put forward a Kantian theory of imagination that speaks to us still today. Indeed, as interest in the use imagining has not just in transcending the world, but in helping us engage with it is on the rise, I have offered the Kantian model of imagination as a resource to draw on. And though skepticism about the unity of imagination may also be on the rise, I have presented a model of what a unified theory of imagination can look like, which situates an analysis of imaginative phenomena in an account of what kind of capacity imagination is in general. More basically still, as we continue to wonder about what imagining is and how imaginative we are, I hope to have shown that the Kantian approach promises to elucidate our imagination, in all its force, as that which enables us to see more.

Seeing More: Kant's Theory of Imagination. Samantha Matherne, Oxford University Press.
© Samantha Matherne 2024. DOI: 10.1093/9780191999291.003.0015

Bibliography

Abaci, Uygar. 2008. "Kant's Justified Dismissal of Artistic Sublimity." *The Journal of Aesthetics and Art Criticism* 66 (3): 237–51.

Abaci, Uygar. 2010. "Artistic Sublime Revisited: Reply to Robert Clewis." *The Journal of Aesthetics and Art Criticism* 68 (2): 170–3.

Abaci, Uygar. 2022. "Kant's Enigmatic Transition: Practical Cognition of the Supersensible." In *The Sensible and Intelligible Worlds: New Essays on Kant's Metaphysics and Epistemology*, edited by Karl Schafer and Nicholas F. Stang, 360–81. Oxford: Oxford University Press.

Ahmed, Sara. 2010. *The Promise of Happiness*. Durham, NC: Duke University Press.

Albers, Josef. 1963. "Introduction." *Interaction of Color*. New Haven and London: Yale University Press.

Aldea, Andreea Smaranda. 2013. "Husserl's Struggle with Mental Images: Imaging and Imagining Reconsidered." *Continental Philosophy Review* 46 (3): 371–94.

Aldea, Andreea Smaranda, and Julia Jansen. 2020. "We Have Only Just Begun: On the Reach of the Imagination and the Depths of Conscious Life." *Husserl Studies* 36 (3): 205–11.

Allais, Lucy. 2009. "Kant, Non-Conceptual Content and the Representation of Space." *Journal of the History of Philosophy* 47 (3): 383–413.

Allais, Lucy. 2010. "Kant's Argument for Transcendental Idealism in the Transcendental Aesthetic." *Proceedings of the Aristotelian Society* 110 (1): 47–75.

Allais, Lucy. 2011. "Idealism Enough: Response to Roche." *Kantian Review* 16 (3): 375–98.

Allais, Lucy. 2015. *Manifest Reality: Kant's Idealism and His Realism*. Oxford: Oxford University Press.

Allais, Lucy. 2017. "Synthesis and Binding." In *Kant and the Philosophy of Mind*, edited by Anil Gomes and Andrew Stephenson, 25–45. Oxford: Oxford University Press.

Allen, Keith. 2015. "Hallucination and Imagination." *Australasian Journal of Philosophy* 93 (2): 287–302.

Allison, Henry. 1973. *The Kant-Eberhard Controversy*. Baltimore: Johns Hopkins Press.

Allison, Henry. 1990. *Kant's Theory of Freedom*. Cambridge: Harvard University Press.

Allison, Henry. 2001. *Kant's Theory of Taste: A Reading of the Critique of Aesthetic Judgment*. Cambridge: Cambridge University Press.

Allison, Henry. 2004. *Kant's Transcendental Idealism*. New Haven: Yale University Press.

Allison, Henry. 2011. *Kant's Groundwork for the Metaphysics of Morals: A Commentary*. Oxford: Oxford University Press.

Allison, Henry. 2012. *Kant's Theory of Freedom*. Cambridge: Cambridge University Press.

Allison, Henry. 2015. *Kant's Transcendental Deduction: An Analytical-Historical Commentary*. Oxford: Oxford University Press.

Altorf, Marije. 2008. *Iris Murdoch and the Art of Imagining*. London: Continuum.

Anderson, R. Lanier. 2015. *The Poverty of Conceptual Truth: Kant's Analytic/Synthetic Distinction and the Limits of Metaphysics*. New York: Oxford University Press.

Apter, Emily, Barbara Cassin, Jacques Lezra, and Michael Wood, eds. 2014. *Dictionary of Untranslatables: A Philosophical Lexicon*. Princeton, NJ: Princeton University Press.

BIBLIOGRAPHY

Aquila, Richard E. 1983. *Representational Mind: A Study of Kant's Theory of Knowledge*. Bloomington, IN: Indiana University Press.

Arana, Andrew. 2016. "Imagination in Mathematics." In *The Routledge Handbook of Philosophy of Imagination*, edited by Amy Kind, 463–77. London: Routledge.

Arcangeli, Margherita. 2019. *Supposition and the Imaginative Realm: A Philosophical Inquiry*. Abingdon: Routledge.

Arcangeli, Margherita. 2020. "The Conceptual Nature of Imaginative Content." *Synthese* 199 (1–2): 3189–205.

Arcangeli, Margherita. 2021. "Narratives and Thought Experiments: Restoring the Role of Imagination." In *Epistemic Uses of Imagination*, edited by Christopher Badura and Amy Kind, 183–201. New York: Routledge.

Arendt, Hannah. 1981. *The Life of the Mind*. San Diego: Harcourt.

Arendt, Hannah. 1982. *Lectures on Kant's Political Philosophy*. Chicago: University of Chicago Press.

Aristotle. 2016. *Clarendon Aristotle Series: De Anima*. Translated by Christopher Shields. Oxford: Oxford University Press.

Austen, Jane. 2012. *Emma*. Edited by George Justice. New York: W.W. Norton & Co.

Babbitt, Susan E. 1996. *Impossible Dreams: Rationality, Integrity, and Moral Imagination*. Boulder, CO: Westview Press.

Bäck, Allan. 2005. "Imagination in Avicenna and Kant." *Tópicos* 29 (29): 101–30.

Badura, Christopher, and Amy Kind, eds. 2021. *Epistemic Uses of Imagination*. New York: Routledge.

Badhwar, Neera, and E.M. Dadlez. 2018. "Love and Friendship: Achieving Happiness in Jane Austen's *Emma*." In *Jane Austen's* Emma: *Philosophical Perspectives*, edited by E.M. Dadlez, 25–53. Oxford: Oxford University Press.

Bagnoli, Carla. 2011. "Respect and Loving Attention." *Canadian Journal of Philosophy* 33 (4): 483–516.

Bailey, Olivia. 2017. "Empathy, Concern, and Understanding in The Theory of Moral Sentiments." *The Adam Smith Review* 9: 273–92.

Bailey, Olivia. 2021. "Empathy with Vicious Perspectives? A Puzzle about the Moral Limits of Empathetic Imagination." *Synthese* 199: 9621–47.

Bailey, Olivia. 2022. "Empathy and the Value of Humane Understanding." *Philosophy and Phenomenological Research* 104 (1): 50–65.

Bakhurst, David. 2021. "Human Nature, Reason and Morality." *Journal of Philosophy of Education* 55 (6): 1029–44.

Bakker, Nienke, and Riopelle, Christopher. 2019. "The *Sunflowers* in Perspective." In *Van Gogh's Sunflowers Illuminated: Art Meets Science*, edited by Ella Hendriks and Marije Vellekoop, 21–47. Amsterdam: Amsterdam University Press.

Banham, Gary. 2005. *Kant's Transcendental Imagination*. New York: Palgrave Macmillan.

Banham, Gary. 2013. "The Transcendental Synthesis of Imagination." In *Imagination in Kant's Critical Philosophy*, edited by Michael L. Thompson, 68–96. Berlin: De Gruyter.

Barney, Rachel. 2015. "The Inner Voice: Kant on Conditionality and God as Cause." In *The Highest Good in Aristotle and Kant*, edited by Joachim Aufderheide and Ralf Bader, 158–82. Oxford: Oxford University Press.

Bates, Jennifer Ann. 2004. *Hegel's Theory of Imagination*. Albany: State University of New York Press.

Bauer, Nathan. 2012. "A Peculiar Intuition: Kant's Conceptualist Account of Perception." *Inquiry* 55 (3): 215–37.

Baumgarten, Alexander. 2014. *Metaphysics*. Translated by Courtney Fugate and John Hymers. London: Bloomsbury.

BIBLIOGRAPHY 395

Baxley, Anne Margaret. 2008. "Pleasure, Freedom and Grace: Schiller's "Completion" of Kant's Ethics." *Inquiry* 51 (1): 1–15.

Baxley, Anne Margaret. 2010. "The Aesthetics of Morality: Schiller's Critique of Kantian Rationalism." *Philosophy Compass* 5 (12): 1084–95.

Beiner, Ronald, and Jennifer Nedelsky. 2001. *Judgment, Imagination, and Politics: Themes from Kant and Arendt.* Lanham, MD: Rowman & Littlefield.

Beiser, Frederick. 2005. *Schiller as Philosopher.* Oxford: Oxford University Press.

Bell, David. 1987. "The Art of Judgement." *Mind* 96 (382): 221–44.

Bennett, Jonathan. 1966. *Kant's Analytic.* Cambridge: Cambridge University Press.

Benovsky, Jiri. 2015. "Aesthetic Appreciation of Landscapes." *The Journal of Value Inquiry* 50 (2): 325–40.

Benovsky, Jiri. 2020. "Depiction, Imagination, and Photography." In *Imagination and Art: Explorations in Contemporary Theory*, edited by Keith Moser and Ananta Sukla, 559–81. Leiden: Brill.

Berg, Anastasia. 2020. "Kant on Moral Self-opacity." *European Journal of Philosophy* 28 (3): 567–85.

Berninger, Anja, and Íngrid Vendrell Ferran, eds. 2023. *Philosophical Perspectives on Memory and Imagination.* New York: Routledge.

Bielefeldt, Heiner. 2003. *Symbolic Representation in Kant's Practical Philosophy.* Cambridge: Cambridge University Press.

Birrer, Mathias. 2017. *Kant und die Heterogenität der Erkenntnisquellen.* Kantstudien-Ergänzungshefte. Berlin: De Gruyter.

Biss, Mavis. 2013. "Radical Moral Imagination: Courage, Hope, and Articulation." *Hypatia* 28 (4): 937–954.

Biss, Mavis. 2014. "Moral Imagination, Perception, and Judgment." *The Southern Journal of Philosophy* 52 (1): 1–21.

Biss, Mavis. 2021. "On Trying Too Hard: A Kantian Interpretation of Misguided Moral Striving." *Journal of Philosophy of Education* 55 (6): 966–76.

Blake, William. 2005. *Selected Poems.* New York: Penguin Books.

Bloch, David. 2007. *Aristotle on Memory and Recollection: Text, Translation, Interpretation, and Reception in Western Scholasticism.* Boston: Brill.

Blomme, Henry. 2017. "Die Rolle der Anschauungsformen in der B-Deduktion." In *Immanuel Kant. Die Einheit des Bewusstseins*, edited by Udo Thiel and Giuseppe Motta, 75–88. Berlin: De Gruyter.

Boden, Margaret A. 2004. *The Creative Mind: Myths and Mechanisms.* London: Routledge.

Böhme, Hartmut, and Gernot Böhme. 1996. *Das Andere der Vernunft. Zur Entwicklung von Rationalitätsstrukturen am Beispiel Kants.* Frankfurt am Main: Suhrkamp.

Borges, Maria. 2008. "Physiology and the Controlling of Affects in Kant's Philosophy." *Kantian Review* 13 (2): 46–66.

Boswell, Terry. 1988. "On the Textual Authenticity of Kant's Logic." *History and Philosophy of Logic* 9 (2): 193–203.

Bowman, Brady. 2011. "A Conceptualist Reply to Hanna's Kantian Non-Conceptualism." *International Journal of Philosophical Studies* 19 (3): 417–46.

Brady, Emily. 1998. "Imagination and the Aesthetic Appreciation of Nature." *The Journal of Aesthetics and Art Criticism* 56 (2): 139–47.

Brady, Emily. 2012. "Reassessing Aesthetic Appreciation of Nature in the Kantian Sublime." *The Journal of Aesthetic Education* 46 (1): 91–109.

Brady, Emily. 2013a. "Imagination and Freedom in the Kantian Sublime." In *Imagination in Kant's Critical Philosophy*, edited by Michael L. Thompson, 163–82. Berlin: De Gruyter.

BIBLIOGRAPHY

Brady, Emily. 2013b. *The Sublime in Modern Philosophy: Aesthetics, Ethics, and Nature.* Cambridge: Cambridge University Press.

Brady, Emily. 2019. "The Kantian Sublime and Greatness of Mind." In *The Measure of Greatness*, edited by Sophia Vasalou, 197–214. Oxford: Oxford University Press.

Breitenbach, Angela. 2015. "Beauty in Proofs: Kant on Aesthetics in Mathematics." *European Journal of Philosophy* 23 (4): 955–77.

Breitenbach, Angela. 2018. "The Beauty of Science without the Science of Beauty: Kant and the Rationalists on the Aesthetics of Cognition." *Journal of the History of Philosophy* 56 (2): 281–304.

Breitenbach, Angela. 2020. "One Imagination in Experiences of Beauty and Achievements of Understanding." *The British Journal of Aesthetics* 60 (1): 71–88.

Breitenbach, Angela. 2021. "Imaginative Reflection in Aesthetic Judgment and Cognition. In *The Court of Reason*, edited by Beatrix Himmelmann and Camilla Serck-Hanssen, 1009–16. Berlin: De Gruyter.

Bremner, Sabina Vaccarino. 2023. "Practical Judgment as Reflective Judgment: On Moral Salience and Kantian Particularist Universalism." *European Journal of Philosophy* 31 (3): 600–21.

Burch, Matthew, and Irene McMullin, eds. 2020. *Transcending Reason: Heidegger on Rationality.* New York: Rowman & Littlefield Publishers.

Burch-Brown, Joanna. 2021. "Reflection and Synthesis: How Moral Agents Learn and Moral Cultures Evolve." *Journal of Philosophy of Education* 55 (6): 935–48.

Burwick, Frederick. 1989. *Coleridge's Biographia Literaria: Text and Meaning.* Columbus: Ohio State University Press.

Byrne, Ruth M. J. 2005. *The Rational Imagination: How People Create Alternatives to Reality.* Cambridge, MA: MIT Press.

Caimi, Mario. 2012. "The Logical Structure of Time According to the Chapter on the Schematism." *Kant-Studien* 103 (4): 415–28.

Callanan, John. 2014. "Kant on the Acquisition of Geometrical Concepts." *Canadian Journal of Philosophy* 44 (5/6): 580–604.

Callanan, John. 2020. "The Comparison of Animals." In *Kant and Animals*, edited by John Callanan and Lucy Allais, 19–41. Oxford: Oxford University Press.

Callanan, John, and Lucy Allais, eds. 2020. *Kant and Animals.* Oxford: Oxford University Press.

Camp, Elisabeth. 2007. "Showing, Telling and Seeing. Metaphor and 'Poetic' Language." *Baltic International Yearbook of Cognition, Logic and Communication* 3 (1): 1–24.

Camp, Elisabeth. 2009. "Two Varieties of Literary Imagination: Metaphor, Fiction, and Thought Experiments." *Midwest Studies in Philosophy* 33 (1): 107–30.

Camp, Elisabeth. 2017. "Why Metaphors Make Good Insults: Perspectives, Presupposition, and Pragmatics." *Philosophical Studies* 174 (1): 47–64.

Carpenter, Alexander. 2012. "The 'Ground Zero' of Goth: Bauhaus, 'Bela Lugosi's Dead' and the Origins of Gothic Rock." *Popular Music and Society* 35 (1): 25–52.

Carroll, Noël. 2002. "The Wheel of Virtue: Art, Literature, and Moral Knowledge." *The Journal of Aesthetics and Art Criticism* 60 (1): 3–26.

Carroll, Noël. 2014. "The Creative Audience." In *The Philosophy of Creativity*, edited by Elliot Samuel Paul and Scott Barry Kaufman, 62–81. New York: Oxford University Press.

Carruthers, Peter. 2002. "Human Creativity: Its Cognitive Basis, Its Evolution, and Its Connections with Childhood Pretence." *The British Journal for the Philosophy of Science* 53 (2): 225–49.

Carruthers, Peter. 2006. *The Architecture of the Mind: Massive Modularity and the Flexibility of Thought.* Oxford: Oxford University Press.

Carruthers, Peter. 2011. "Creative Action in Mind." *Philosophical Psychology* 24 (4): 437–61.
Carruthers, Peter, and Peter K. Smith. 1996. *Theories of Theories of Mind*. Cambridge: Cambridge University Press.
Carson, Emily. 1997. "Kant on Intuition in Geometry." *Canadian Journal of Philosophy* 27 (4): 489–512.
Carston, Robyn. 2010. "XIII-Metaphor: Ad Hoc Concepts, Literal Meaning and Mental Images." *Proceedings of the Aristotelian Society* 110 (3): 295–321.
Carston, Robyn. 2018. "Figurative Language, Mental Imagery, and Pragmatics." *Metaphor and Symbol* 33 (3): 198–217.
Casey, Edward. 2003. "Imagination, Fantasy, Hallucination, and Memory." In *Imagination and its Pathologies*, edited by J. Philips & James Morley, 65–91. Cambridge: MIT Press.
Cassirer, Ernst. 1951. *The Philosophy of the Enlightenment*. Translated by Fritz Koelln and J. Pettegrove. Princeton, NJ: Princeton University Press.
Cassirer, Ernst. 2021. *The Philosophy of Symbolic Forms*, Volume 3: *The Phenomenology of Cognition*. Translated by Steve G. Lofts. London: Routledge.
Chalmers, David. 2002. "Does Conceivability Entail Possibility?" In *Conceivability and Possibility*, edited by Tamar Gendler and John Hawthorne, 145–200. Oxford: Oxford University Press.
Chang, Jeff. 2005. *Can't Stop, Won't Stop: A History of the Hip-Hop Generation*. New York: Picador.
Chaplin, Rosalind. 2022. "Kant on the Givenness of Space and Time." *European Journal of Philosophy* 30: 877–98.
Chaouli, Michel. 2017. *Thinking with Kant's* Critique of Judgment. Cambridge: Harvard University Press.
Chignell, Andrew. 2007a. "Belief in Kant." *The Philosophical Review* 116 (3): 323–60.
Chignell, Andrew. 2007b. "Kant on the Normativity of Taste: The Role of Aesthetic Ideas." *Australasian Journal of Philosophy* 85 (3): 415–33.
Chignell, Andrew. 2009a. "Are Supersensibles Really Possible? The Evidential Role of Symbols." In *Proceedings of 10th Kant-Congress*, 99–109. Berlin: De Gruyter.
Chignell, Andrew. 2009b. "Kant, Modality, and the Most Real Being." *Archiv für Geschichte der Philosophie* 92 (2): 157–92.
Chignell, Andrew. 2010. "Real Repugnance and Belief and Things-in-Themselves: A Problem and Kant's Three Solutions." In *Kant's Moral Metaphysics*, edited by James Krueger and Benjamin Lipscomb, 177–210. Berlin: De Gruyter.
Chignell, Andrew. 2011. "Real Repugnance and Our Ignorance of Things-in-Themselves: A Lockean Problem in Kant and Hegel." *Internationales Jahrbuch des Deutschen Idealismus* 7: 135–59.
Chignell, Andrew. 2012. "Kant, Real Possibility, and the Threat of Spinoza." *Mind* 121 (483): 635–75.
Chignell, Andrew. 2014. "Modal Motivations for Noumenal Ignorance: Knowledge, Cognition, and Coherence." *Kant-Studien* 105 (4): 573–97.
Chignell, Andrew. 2017. "Kant on Cognition, Givenness, and Ignorance." *Journal of the History of Philosophy* 55 (1): 131–42.
Chipman, Lauchlan. 1972. "Kant's Categories and Their Schematism." *Kant-Studien* 63 (1–4): 36–50.
Choi, Yoon. 2019. "Spontaneity and Self-Consciousness in the Groundwork and the B-Critique." *Canadian Journal of Philosophy* 49 (7): 936–55.
Church, Jennifer. 2013. *Possibilities of Perception*. Oxford: Oxford University Press.
Church, Jennifer. 2016. "Perceiving People as People." In *Knowledge Through Imagination*, edited by Amy Kind and Peter Kung, 160–84. Oxford: Oxford University Press.

398 BIBLIOGRAPHY

Clarke, Bridget. 2006. "Imagination and Politics in Iris Murdoch's Moral Philosophy: Politics and the Imagination." *Philosophical Papers* 35 (3): 387–411.

Clewis, Robert. 2009. *The Kantian Sublime and the Revelation of Freedom*. Cambridge: Cambridge University Press.

Clewis, Robert. 2010. "A Case for Kantian Artistic Sublimity: A Response to Abaci." *The Journal of Aesthetics and Art Criticism* 68 (2): 167–70.

Clewis, Robert. 2015. *Reading Kant's Lectures*. Berlin : De Gruyter.

Clewis, Robert. 2018. "The Feeling of Enthusiasm." In *Kant and the Faculty of Feeling*, edited by Kelly Sorensen and Diane Williamson, 184–207. Cambridge: Cambridge University Press.

Cohen, Alix. 2008. "Kant on Anthropology and Alienology: The Opacity of Human Motivation and Its Anthropological Implications." *Kantian Review* 13 (2): 85–106.

Cohen, Alix. 2009. *Kant and the Human Science: Biology, Anthropology, and History*. London: Palgrave Macmillan.

Cohen, Alix. 2014. "Kant on the Ethics of Belief." *Proceedings of the Aristotelian Society* 114: 317–34.

Cohen, Alix. 2016. "The Role of Feelings in Kant's Account of Moral Education." *Journal of Philosophy of Education* 50 (4): 511–23.

Cohen, Alix. 2018. "Kant on Beauty and Cognition." In *Thinking about Science and Reflecting on Art: Bringing Aesthetics and the Philosophy of Science Together*, edited by Otávio Bueno, George Darby, Steven French, and Dean Rickles, 140–54. London: Routledge.

Cohen, Alix. 2020. "A Kantian Account of Emotions as Feelings." *Mind* 129 (514): 429–60.

Cohen, Ted. 1982. "Why Beauty is a Symbol of Morality." In *Essays in Kant's Aesthetics*, edited by Ted Cohen and Paul Guyer, 221–36. Chicago: University of Chicago Press.

Coleridge, Samuel Taylor. 2015. *Biographia Literaria*. Cambridge: Cambridge University Press.

Collier, Mark. 2010. "Hume's Theory of Moral Imagination." *History of Philosophy Quarterly* 27 (3): 255–73.

Conant, James. 2016. "Why Kant Is Not a Kantian." *Philosophical Topics* 44 (1): 75–125.

Conant, James. 2017. "Kant's Critique of the Layer-Cake Conception of Human Mindedness in the B Deduction." In *Kant's Critique of Pure Reason*, edited by Jim O'Shea, 120–39. Cambridge: Cambridge University Press.

Costelloe, Timothy. 2018. *The Imagination in Hume's Philosophy: The Canvas of the Mind*. Edinburgh: Edinburgh University Press.

Cottrell, Jonathan. 2015. "David Hume: Imagination." In *Internet Encyclopedia of Philosophy*, edited by J. Fieser and B. Dowden. https://iep.utm.edu/hume-ima/

Craik, Dinah. 1859. *A Life for a Life, Volume II*. London: Hurst and Blackett.

Crawford, Donald. 1974. *Kant's Aesthetic Theory*. Madison: University of Wisconsin Press.

Crawford, Donald. 1982. "Kant's Theory of Creative Imagination." In *Essays in Kant's Aesthetics*, edited by Ted Cohen and Paul Guyer, 151–78. Chicago: University of Chicago Press.

Crowell, Steven. 2017. "Exemplary Necessity: Heidegger, Pragmatism and Reason." In *Pragmatic Perspectives in Phenomenology*, edited by Ondrej Svec and Jakub Capek, 242–56. New York: Routledge.

Crowther, Paul. 1991. *The Kantian Sublime: From Morality to Art*. Oxford: Oxford University Press.

Currie, Gregory. 2010. "Tragedy." *Analysis (Oxford)* 70 (4): 632–8.

Currie, Gregory. 2013. "Imagination and Make-Believe." In *The Routledge Companion to Aesthetics*, edited by Dominic Lopes and Berys Gaut, 342–51. London: Routledge.

Currie, Gregory. 2020. *Imagining and Knowing: The Shape of Fiction*. Oxford: Oxford University Press.

Currie, Gregory, and Ian Ravenscroft. 2002. *Recreative Minds: Imagination in Philosophy and Psychology*. New York: Oxford University Press.

Dahlstrom, Daniel. 2010. "The Critique of Pure Reason and Continental Philosophy: Heidegger's Interpretation of Transcendental Imagination." In *The Cambridge Companion to Kant's Critique of Pure Reason*, 380–400. Cambridge: Cambridge University Press.

Dahlstrom, Daniel. 2018. "'Knowing How' and Kant's Theory of Schematism." In *The Philosophy of Immanuel Kant*, edited by Richard Kennington, 71–85. D.C.: Catholic University Press of America.

Davies, Martin, and Tony Stone. 1995. *Folk Psychology: The Theory of Mind Debate*. Oxford: Blackwell.

de Boer, Karin. 2016. "Categories versus Schemata: Kant's Two-Aspect Theory of Pure Concepts and His Critique of Wolffian Metaphysics." *Journal of the History of Philosophy* 54 (3): 441–68.

de Boer, Karin. 2020. *Kant's Reform of Metaphysics: The Critique of Pure Reason Reconsidered*. Cambridge: Cambridge University Press.

Debus, Dorothea. 2014. "'Mental Time Travel': Remembering the Past, Imagining the Future, and the Particularity of Events." *Review of Philosophy and Psychology* 5 (3): 333–50.

Debus, Dorothea. 2016. "Imagination and Memory." In *The Routledge Handbook of Philosophy of Imagination*, edited by Amy Kind, 135–48. London: Routledge.

Deimling, Wiebke. 2014. "Kant's Pragmatic Concept of Emotions." In *Kant on Emotion and Value*, edited by Alix Cohen, 108–25. London: Palgrave Macmillan.

Deligiorgi, Katerina. 2006. "Grace as Guide to Morals? Schiller's Aesthetic Turn in Ethics. *History of Philosophy Quarterly* 23 (1): 1–20.

Deligiorgi, Katerina. 2020. "Kant, Schiller, and the Idea of a Moral Self." *Kant-Studien* 111 (2): 303–22.

Detel, Wolfgang. 1978. "Zur Funktion des Schematismuskapitels in Kants Kritik der reinen Vernunft." *Kant-Studien* 69 (1–4): 17–45.

Dewey, John. 1922. *Human Nature and Conduct*. New York: H. Holt.

Dickinson, Emily. 1960. *The Complete Poems of Emily Dickinson*. Edited by Thomas Herbert Johnson. Boston: Little, Brown.

Dmitrieva, Nina A. 2021. "The Kantian Origins of Sergei Rubinstein's Theory of Moral Improvement." *Journal of Philosophy of Education* 55 (6): 1126–41.

Doggett, Tyler, and Andy Egan. 2007. "Wanting Things You Don't Want: The Case for an Imaginative Analogue of Desire." *Philosophers' Imprint* 7: 1–17.

Doggett, Tyler, and Andy Egan. 2012. "How We Feel about Terrible, Non-Existent Mafiosi." *Philosophy and Phenomenological Research* 84 (2): 277–306.

Domski, Mary. 2010. "Kant on the Imagination and Geometrical Certainty." *Perspectives on Science* 18 (4): 409–31.

Doran, Robert. 2015. *The Theory of the Sublime from Longinus to Kant*. New York: Cambridge University Press.

Dorsch, Fabian. 2012. *The Unity of Imagining*. Frankfurt: Ontos Verlag.

Dorsch, Fabian. 2016. "Hume." In *The Routledge Handbook of Philosophy of Imagination*, edited by Amy Kind, 40–54. New York: Routledge.

Dorsch, Fabian, and Fiona Macpherson, eds. 2018. *Phenomenal Presence*. Oxford University Press.

400 BIBLIOGRAPHY

Dreyfus, Hubert L. 2006. "Overcoming the Myth of the Mental." *Topoi* 25 (1–2): 43–9.

Dufour, Éric, 2003. "Remarques sur la note du paragraphe 26 de l'Analytique transcendantale. Les interpretations de Cohen et de Heidegger." *Kant-Studien* 94 (1): 69–79.

Dunlop, Katherine. 2009. "'The Unity of Time's Measure': Kant's Reply to Locke." *Philosophers' Imprint* 9: 1–31.

Dunlop, Katherine. 2012. "Kant and Strawson on the Content of Geometrical Concepts." *Noûs* 46 (1): 86–126.

Dunn, Nicholas. 2021. "Subsuming 'Determining' under 'Reflecting': Kant's Power of Judgment, Reconsidered." *Inquiry* (ahead-of-print): 1–27.

Dunn, Nicholas. n.d. "Hidden Art, Special Talent: Kant on Imagination and Judgment." Manuscript.

Dyck, Corey W. 2014. *Kant and Rational Psychology. Kant and Rational Psychology*. Oxford: Oxford University Press.

Dyck, Corey W. 2019. "Imagination and Association in Kant's Theory of Cognition." In *Konzepte der Einbildungskraft in der Philosophie, den Wissenschaften und den Künsten des 18. Jahrhunderts*, edited by Rudolf Meer, Giuseppe Motta and Gideon Stiening, 351–370. Berlin: De Gruyter.

Eldridge, Richard. 1989. *On Moral Personhood: Philosophy, Literature, Criticism, and Self-Understanding*. Chicago: University of Chicago Press.

Elgin, Catherine Z. 2014. "Fiction as Thought Experiment." *Perspectives on Science* 22 (2): 221–41.

Elliott, R. K. 1972. "Imagination in the Experience of Art." *Royal Institute of Philosophy Supplement* 6: 88–105.

Ellis, Addison. 2017. "The Case for Absolute Spontaneity in Kant's Critique of Pure Reason." *Con-Textos Kantianos: International Journal of Philosophy* 1 (6): 138–64.

Ellison, Ralph. 1995. *Invisible Man*. New York: Vintage International.

Engell, James. 1981. *The Creative Imagination: Enlightenment to Romanticism*. Cambridge, MA: Harvard University Press.

Englander, Alex. 2011. "Kant's Aesthetic Theology: Revelation as Symbolisation in the Critical Philosophy." *Neue Zeitschrift für Systematische Theologie und Religionsphilosophie* 53: 303–17.

Englert, Alexander T. 2022. "How a Kantian Ideal Can Be Practical." *Inquiry* (ahead-of-print): 1–28.

Engstrom, Stephen. 2006. "Understanding and Sensibility." *Inquiry* 49 (1): 2–25.

Engstrom, Stephen. 2010. "Reason, Desire, and the Will." In *Kant's Metaphysics of Morals: A Critical Guide*, edited by Lara Denis, 28–50. Cambridge: Cambridge University Press.

Espagne, Michel. 2014. "Bildung." In *Dictionary of Untranslatables: A Philosophical Lexicon*, edited by Barbara Cassin, Michael Wood, Jacques Lezra, and Emily Apter, 111–19. Princeton, NJ: Princeton University Press.

Euclid. 1847. *The First Six Books of the Elements of Euclid*, ed. Oliver Byrne. London: William Pickering.

Fahmy, Melissa Seymour. 2021. "Shadow Students in Georgia: A Kantian Condemnation." *Journal of Philosophy of Education* 55 (6): 1057–71.

Falduto, Antonino. 2020. "Introduction: Schiller's Challenge to Moral Philosophy— Schillers Herausforderung für die Moralphilosophie." *Kant-Studien* 111 (2): 224–6.

Falkenstein, Lorne. 1995. *Kant's Intuitionism: A Commentary on the Transcendental Aesthetic*. Toronto: University of Toronto Press.

Ferrara, Alessandro. 2008. *The Force of the Example: Explorations in the Paradigm of Judgment*. New York: Columbia University Press.

BIBLIOGRAPHY 401

Ferrarin, Alfredo. 1995a. "Construction and Mathematical Schematism Kant on the Exhibition of a Concept in Intuition." *Kant-Studien* 86 (2): 131–74.

Ferrarin, Alfredo. 1995b. "Kant's Productive Imagination and Its Alleged Antecedents." *Graduate Faculty Philosophy Journal* 18 (1): 65–92.

Ferrarin, Alfredo. 2008. "Imagination and Judgment in Kant's Practical Philosophy." *Philosophy & Social Criticism* 34 (1–2): 101–21.

Fesmire, Steven. 2003. *John Dewey and Moral Imagination: Pragmatism in Ethics.* Bloomington, IN: Indiana University Press.

Fichant, Michel. 2004. "Espace esthétique et espace géométrique chez Kant." *Revue de Métaphysique et de Morale* 44 (4): 530–50.

Filieri, Luigi. 2021. "Concept-Less Schemata: The Reciprocity of Imagination and Understanding in Kant's Aesthetics." *Kantian Review* 26 (4): 511–29.

Filippaki, Eleni. 2012. "Kant on Love, Respect and Friendship." *Kant Yearbook* 4 (1): 23–48.

Fisher, Naomi. 2017. "Kant on Animal Minds." *Ergo* 4: 441–62.

Fleischacker, Samuel, and Vivienne Brown, eds. 2010. *Essays on the Philosophy of Adam Smith: Essays Commemorating the 250th Anniversary of the Theory of Moral Sentiments.* New York: Taylor and Francis.

Fletcher, Natalie M. 2016. "Imagination and the Capabilities Approach." In *The Routledge Handbook of Philosophy of Imagination*, edited by Amy Kind, 392–404. New York: Routledge.

Flynn, Thomas. 2006. "Sartre as Philosopher of the Imagination." *Philosophy Today* 50: 106–12.

Formosa, Paul. 2021. "A Kantian Approach to Education for Moral Sensitivity." *Journal of Philosophy of Education* 55 (6): 1017–28.

Franzwa, Gregg. 1978. "Space and Schematism." *Kant-Studien* 69 (2): 149–59.

Frede, Dorothea. 1995. "The Cognitive Role of Phantasia in Aristotle." In *Essays on Aristotle's De Anima*, edited by Martha C. Nussbaum and Amélie Oksenberg Rorty, 279–96. Oxford: Oxford University Press.

Frederick II. 2020. *Frederick the Great's Philosophical Writings.* Edited by Avi Lifschitz. Translated by Angela Scholar. Princeton, NJ: Princeton University Press.

French, Steven. 2020. "Imagination in Scientific Practice." *European Journal for Philosophy of Science* 10 (3): 1–19.

French, Steven, and Milena Ivanova. 2020. *The Aesthetics of Science: Beauty, Imagination and Understanding.* New York: Routledge.

Freydberg, Bernard. 2005. *Imagination in Kant's Critique of Practical Reason.* Bloomington, IN: Indiana University Press.

Freydberg, Bernard. 2013. "Functions of Imagination in Kant's Moral Philosophy."?" In *Imagination in Kant's Critical Philosophy*, edited by Michael L. Thompson, 105–22. Berlin: De Gruyter.

Fricke, Christel. 1990. "Explaining the Inexplicable. The Hypotheses of the Faculty of Reflective Judgement in Kant's Third Critique." *Noûs* 24 (1): 45–62.

Friedlander, Eli. 2015. *Expressions of Judgment: An Essay on Kant's Aesthetics.* Cambridge: Harvard University Press.

Friedman, Michael. 1990. "Kant on Concepts and Intuitions in the Mathematical Sciences." *Synthese* 84 (2): 213–57.

Friedman, Michael. 2000. "Geometry, Construction, and Intuition in Kant and His Successors." In *Between Logic and Intuition: Essays in Honor of Charles Parsons*, edited by Gila Sher and Richard Tieszen, 186–218. Cambridge: Cambridge University Press.

Friedman, Michael. 2012. "Kant on Geometry and Spatial Intuition." *Synthese* 186 (1): 231–55.

BIBLIOGRAPHY

Friedman, Michael. 2015. "Kant on Geometry and Experience." In *Mathematizing Space*, edited by Vincenzo Risi, 275–309. Cham: Springer.

Friend, Stacie. 2022. "Emotion in Fiction: State of the Art." *The British Journal of Aesthetics* 62 (2): 257–71.

Frierson, Patrick R. 2014a. "Affective Normativity." In *Kant on Emotion and Value*, edited by Alix Cohen, 166–90. London: Palgrave Macmillan.

Frierson, Patrick R. 2014b. *Kant's Empirical Psychology*. Cambridge: Cambridge University Press.

Frierson, Patrick R. 2021. "Discipline and the Cultivation of Autonomy in Immanuel Kant and Maria Montessori." *Journal of Philosophy of Education* 55 (6): 1097–111.

Fugate, Courtney D. 2014. *The Teleology of Reason: A Study of the Structure of Kant's Critical Philosophy*. Berlin: De Gruyter.

Funkhouser, Eric, and Shannon Spaulding. 2009. "Imagination and Other Scripts." *Philosophical Studies* 143 (3): 291–314.

Gabbert, Elisa. 2022. "A Poem (and a Painting) about the Suffering That Hides in Plain Sight." *The New York Times*, March 6, sec. Books. https://www.nytimes.com/interactive/2022/03/06/books/auden-musee-des-beaux-arts.html.

Gaiger, Jason. 2020. "Projective and Ampliative Imagining." In *Philosophy of Sculpture*, edited by Kristin Gjesdal, Fred Rush, and Ingvild Torsen, 17–32. New York: Routledge.

Gammon, Martin. 1997. "'Exemplary Originality': Kant on Genius and Imitation." *Journal of the History of Philosophy* 35 (4): 563–92.

Garrett, Don. 2008. "Hume's Theory of Ideas." In *A Companion to Hume*, edited by Elizabeth Radcliffe, 41–57. Oxford: Wiley-Blackwell.

Gasché, Rodolphe. 2003. *The Idea of Form: Rethinking Kant's Aesthetics*. Stanford: Stanford University Press.

Gaut, Berys. 1998. "Imagination, Interpretation, and Film." *Philosophical Studies* 89 (2/3): 331–41.

Gaut, Berys. 2003. "Creativity and Imagination." In *The Creation of Art: New Essays in Philosophical Aesthetics*, edited by Berys Gaut and Paisley Livingston, 148–73. Cambridge: Cambridge University Press.

Gaut, Berys. 2014. "Mixed Motivations: Creativity as a Virtue." *Royal Institute of Philosophy Supplement* 75: 183–202.

Gaut, Berys, and Paisley Livingston, eds. 2003. *The Creation of Art: New Essays in Philosophical Aesthetics*. Cambridge: Cambridge University Press.

Geiger, Ido. 2021. "Kant on Aesthetic Ideas, Rational Ideas and the Subject-Matter of Art." *The Journal of Aesthetics and Art Criticism* 79 (2): 186–99.

Geiger, Ido. 2022. *Kant and the Claims of the Empirical World*. Cambridge: Cambridge University Press.

Gendler, Tamar, and John Hawthorne. 2002. *Conceivability and Possibility*. Oxford: Oxford University Press.

Gendler, Tamar Szabó. 2003. "On the Relation between Pretense and Belief." In *Imagination, Philosophy, and the Arts*, edited by Matthew Kieran and Dominic Lopes, 125–41. London: Routledge.

Gendler, Tamar Szabó, and Shen-yi Liao. 2016. "The Problem of Imaginative Resistance." In *The Routledge Companion to Philosophy of Literature*, 405–18. London: Routledge.

Giaquinto, Marcus. 2007. *Visual Thinking in Mathematics*. Oxford: Oxford University Press.

Gibbons, Sarah L. 1994. *Kant's Theory of Imagination: Bridging Gaps in Judgement and Experience*. Oxford: Oxford University Press.

Gilmore, Jonathan. 2019. "Imagination and Film." In *The Palgrave Handbook of the Philosophy of Film and Motion Pictures*, 845–63. Cham: Springer International Publishing.

Gilmore, Jonathan. 2020. *Apt Imaginings: Feelings for Fictions and Other Creatures of the Mind.* Oxford: Oxford University Press.

Ginsborg, Hannah. 2008. "Was Kant a Nonconceptualist?" *Philosophical Studies* 137 (1): 65–77.

Ginsborg, Hannah. 2015. *The Normativity of Nature: Essays on Kant's Critique of Judgement.* Oxford: Oxford University Press.

Goldman, Alvin I. 2006. *Simulating Minds: The Philosophy, Psychology, and Neuroscience of Mindreading.* Oxford: Oxford University Press.

Golob, Sacha. 2014. "Kant on Intentionality, Magnitude, and the Unity of Perception." *European Journal of Philosophy* 22 (4): 505–28.

Golob, Sacha. 2016a. "Kant as Both Conceptualist and Nonconceptualist." *Kantian Review* 21 (3): 367–91.

Golob, Sacha. 2016b. "Why the Transcendental Deduction Is Compatible with Nonconceptualism." In *Kantian Nonconceptualism*, edited by Dennis Schulting, 27–52. London: Palgrave Macmillan.

Golob, Sacha. 2020. "What Do Animals See? Intentionality, Objects, and Kantian Non-Conceptualism." In *Kant and Animals*, edited by John Callanan and Lucy Allais, 66–88. Oxford: Oxford University Press.

Golob, Sacha. 2021. "Kant on Revolution as a Sign of Moral Progress." *Journal of Philosophy of Education* 55 (6): 977–89.

Gomes, Anil. 2010. "Is Kant's Transcendental Deduction of the Categories Fit for Purpose?" *Kantian Review* 15 (2): 118–37.

Gomes, Anil. 2014. "Kant on Perception: Naïve Realism, Non-Conceptualism, and the B-Deduction." *The Philosophical Quarterly* 64 (254): 1–19.

Gomes, Anil. 2017. "Naïve Realism in Kantian Phrase." *Mind* 126 (501): 529–78.

Gomes, Anil. 2022. "Moral Vision." In *The Murdochian Mind*, edited by Silvia Caprioglio Panizza, Mark Hopwood, 142–55. London: Routledge.

Gomes, Anil, and Andrew Stephenson. 2016. "On the Relation of Intuition to Cognition." In *Kantian Nonconceptualism*, ed. Dennis Schulting, 53–79. London: Palgrave Macmillan.

Gomes, Anil, and Andrew Stephenson, eds. 2017. *Kant and the Philosophy of Mind.* Oxford: Oxford University Press.

Gorodeisky, Keren. 2011. "A Tale of Two Faculties." *The British Journal of Aesthetics* 51 (4): 415–36.

Gorodeisky, Keren. 2013. "Schematizing without a Concept? Imagine That!" In *Kant und die Philosophie in weltbürgerlicher Absicht*, edited by Stefano Bacin, Alfredo Ferrarin, Claudio La Rocca, and Margit Ruffing, 59–70. Berlin: De Gruyter.

Goy, Ina. 2012. "Kant on Formative Power." *Lebenswelt* 2 (2): 26–49.

Gregor, Mary J. 1985. "Essays in Kant's Aesthetics." *International Studies in Philosophy* 17 (3): 94–6.

Gregory, Dominic. 2016. "Imagination and Mental Imagery." In *The Routledge Handbook of Philosophy of Imagination*, edited by Amy Kind, 97–110. London: Routledge.

Griffith, Aaron M. 2012. "Perception and the Categories: A Conceptualist Reading of Kant's Critique of Pure Reason: Perception and the Categories." *European Journal of Philosophy* 20 (2): 193–222.

Grüne, Stefanie. 2009. *Blinde Anschauung. Die Rolle von Begriffen in Kants Theorie sinnlicher Synthesis.* Philosophische Abhandlungen; Bd. 96. Frankfurt am Main: Klostermann.

Grüne, Stefanie. 2011. "Is There a Gap in Kants B Deduction." *International Journal of Philosophical Studies* 19 (3): 465–490.

Grüne, Stefanie. 2016. "Allais on Intuitions and the Objective Reality of the Categories: Intuitions and Objective Reality." *European Journal of Philosophy* 24 (1): 241–52.

Grüne, Stefanie. 2017a. "Are Kantian Intuitions Object-Dependent?" In *Kant and the Philosophy of Mind*, edited by Anil Gomes and Andrew Stephenson, 67–85. Oxford: Oxford University Press.

Grüne, Stefanie. 2017b. "Givenness, Objective Reality, and A Priori Intuitions." *Journal of the History of Philosophy* 55 (1): 113–30.

Grüne, Stefanie. 2022. "Kant on Concepts, Intuitions, and Sensible Synthesis." In *The Sensible and Intelligible Worlds: New Essays on Kant's Metaphysics and Epistemology*, edited by Karl Schafer and Nicholas Stang, 90–115. Oxford: Oxford University Press.

Guyer, Paul. 1977. "Formalism and the Theory of Expression in Kant's Aesthetics." *Kant-Studien* 68 (1): 46–70.

Guyer, Paul. 1987. *Kant and the Claims of Knowledge*. Cambridge: Cambridge University Press.

Guyer, Paul. 1993. *Kant and the Experience of Freedom: Essays on Aesthetics and Morality*. Cambridge: Cambridge University Press.

Guyer, Paul. 1997. *Kant and the Claims of Taste*. 2nd ed. Cambridge: Cambridge University Press.

Guyer, Paul. 2005. *Values of Beauty: Historical Essays in Aesthetics*. Cambridge: Cambridge University Press.

Guyer, Paul. 2006. "Is There a Transcendental Imagination." In *Kreativität. Deutscher Kongreß für Philosophie*, edited by Abel Günter, 462–83. Hamburg: Felix Meiner Verlag.

Guyer, Paul. 2009. "The Harmony of the Faculties in Recent Books on the *Critique of the Power of Judgment*." *The Journal of Aesthetics and Art Criticism* 67 (2): 201–21.

Guyer, Paul. 2010. "The Deduction of the Categories: The Metaphysical and Transcendental Deductions." In *The Cambridge Companion to Kant's* Critique of Pure Reason, edited by Paul Guyer, 118–50. Cambridge: Cambridge University Press.

Guyer, Paul. 2014. *A History of Modern Aesthetics*. Cambridge: Cambridge University Press.

Guyer, Paul. 2016. "Examples of Moral Possibility." In *The Virtues of Freedom*, 260–72. Oxford: Oxford University Press.

Guyer, Paul. 2020. *Reason and Experience in Mendelssohn and Kant*. New York: Oxford University Press.

Haag, Johannes. 2007. *Erfahrung und Gegenstand: das Verhältnis von Sinnlichkeit und Verstand*. Philosophische Abhandlungen; Bd. 95. Frankfurt am Main: V. Klostermann.

Haag, Johannes. 2013. "Kant on Imagination and the Natural Sources of the Conceptual." In *Contemporary Perspectives on Early Modern Philosophy*, edited by Martin Lenz and Anik Waldow, 65–85. Dordrecht: Springer.

Hakim, David. 2017. "Kant on Moral Illusion and Appraisal of Others." *Kantian Review* 22 (3): 421–40.

Hamawaki, Arata. 2006. "Kant on Beauty and the Normative Force of Feeling." *Philosophical Topics* 34 (1–2): 107–44.

Hanna, Robert. 2001. *Kant and the Foundations of Analytic Philosophy*. Oxford: Oxford University Press.

Hanna, Robert. 2005. "Kant and Nonconceptual Content." *European Journal of Philosophy* 13 (2): 247–90.

Hanna, Robert. 2008. "Kantian Non-Conceptualism." *Philosophical Studies* 137 (1): 41–64.

Hegel, G.W.F. 1997. *Faith and Knowledge*. Translated by Walter Cerf and H.S. Harris. Albany: State University of New York Press.

Heidegger, Martin. 1990. *Kant and the Problem of Metaphysics*. 4th ed. Translated by Richard Taft. Bloomington, IN: Indiana University Press.

Heidegger, Martin. 1997. *Phenomenological Interpretation of Kant's Critique of Pure Reason*. Translated by Parvis Emad and Kenneth Maly. Bloomington, IN: Indiana University Press.

Heidemann, Dietmar. 2016. "Kant's Aesthetic Nonconceptualism." In *Kantian Nonconceptualism*, edited by Dennis Schulting, 117–44. London: Palgrave Macmillan.

Helfer, Martha. 1996. *The Retreat of Representation*. Albany: State University of New York Press.

Henrich, Dieter. 1969. "The Proof-Structure of Kant's Transcendental Deduction." *The Review of Metaphysics* 22 (4): 640–59.

Henrich, Dieter. 1992. *Aesthetic Judgment and the Moral Image of the World: Studies in Kant*. Stanford: Stanford University Press.

Henrich, Dieter. 1994. *The Unity of Reason: Essays on Kant's Philosophy*. Cambridge, MA: Harvard University Press.

Herman, Barbara. 1993. *The Practice of Moral Judgment*. Cambridge, MA: Harvard University Press.

Herman, Barbara. 2007. *Moral Literacy*. Cambridge: Harvard University Press.

Highsmith, Patricia. 2004. *The Price of Salt*. New York: W.W. Norton.

Hill, Thomas. E. 1999. "Happiness and Human Flourishing in Kant's Ethics." *Social Philosophy and Policy* 16: 43–75.

Hills, Alison. 2006. "Kant on Happiness and Reason." *History of Philosophy Quarterly* 23 (3): 243–61.

Hills, Alison. 2009. "Happiness in the *Groundwork*." In *Kant's Groundwork of the Metaphysics of Morals: A Critical Guide*, edited by Jens Timmermann, 29–44. Cambridge: Cambridge University Press.

Hills, Alison, and Alexander Bird. 2018. "Creativity without Value." In *Creativity and Philosophy*, edited by Berys Gaut and Matthew Kieran, 95–107. New York: Routledge.

Hills, Alison, and Alexander Bird. 2019. "Against Creativity." *Philosophy and Phenomenological Research* 99 (3): 694–713.

Hills, David. 1997. "Aptness and Truth in Verbal Metaphor." *Philosophical Topics* 25 (1): 117–53.

Hills, David. 2017. "The What and the How of Metaphorical Imagining, Part One." *Philosophical Studies* 174 (1): 13–31.

Hobbes, Thomas. 1996. *Leviathan*. Cambridge: Cambridge University Press.

Hoerth, Jackson. 2020. "Schematism and Free Play: The Imagination's Formal Power as a Unifying Feature in Kant's Doctrine of the Faculties." *Con-Textos Kantianos* 12: 314–37.

Hopkins, Robert. 2016. "Sartre." In *The Routledge Handbook of Philosophy of Imagination*, edited by Amy Kind, 102–14. London: Routledge.

Horstmann, Rolf-Peter. 2018. *Kant's Power of Imagination*. Cambridge: Cambridge University Press.

Huemer, Michael. 2007. "Compassionate Phenomenal Conservatism." *Philosophy and Phenomenological Research* 74 (1): 30–55.

Hughes, Fiona. 2007. *Kant's Aesthetic Epistemology: Form and World*. Edinburgh: Edinburgh University Press.

Humberstone, I. Lloyd. 1992. "Direction of Fit." *Mind* 101 (401): 59–84.

Hume, David. 2007. *A Treatise of Human Nature, Vol. 1*. Edited by David Fate Norton and Mary J. Norton. Oxford: Clarendon Press.

406 BIBLIOGRAPHY

Husserl, Edmund. 2005. "Phantasy and Image Consciousness." In *Phantasy, Image Consciousness, and Memory (1898–1925)*, 1–116. Dordrecht: Springer.

Ichikawa, Jonathan. 2009. "Dreaming and Imagination." *Mind & Language* 24 (1): 103–21.

Ilyes, Imola. 2017. "Empathy in Hume and Smith." In *The Routledge Handbook of Philosophy of Empathy*, edited by Heidi Maibom, 98–109. London: Routledge.

Indregard, Jonas Jervell. 2017. "Self-Affection and Pure Intuition in Kant." *Australasian Journal of Philosophy* 95 (4): 627–43.

Indregard, Jonas Jervell. 2021. "Kant and the Pre-Conceptual Use of the Understanding." *Archiv für Geschichte der Philosophie* 103 (1): 93–119.

Jankowiak, Tim. 2014. "Sensations as Representations in Kant." *British Journal for the History of Philosophy* 22 (3): 492–513.

Jansen, Julia. 2016. "Husserl." In *The Routledge Handbook of Philosophy of Imagination*, edited by Amy Kind, 89–101. London: Routledge.

Jauernig, Anja. 2021. *The World According to Kant*. Oxford: Oxford University Press.

Johnson, Andrew. 2005. "Kant's Empirical Hedonism." *Pacific Philosophical Quarterly* 86 (1): 50–63.

Johnson, Mark. 1985. "Imagination in Moral Judgment." *Philosophy and Phenomenological Research* 46 (2): 265–80.

Johnson, Mark. 2016. "Moral Imagination." In *The Routledge Handbook of Philosophy of Imagination*, edited by Amy Kind, 355–67. London: Routledge.

Kaag, John. 2011. *Idealism, Pragmatism, and Feminism: The Philosophy of Ella Lyman Cabot*. Lanham, MD: Lexington.

Kahn, Samuel. 2022. "Kant and the Duty to Promote One's Own Happiness." *Inquiry* 65 (3): 327–38.

Kain, Patrick. 2010. "Practical Cognition, Intuition, and Fact of Reason." In *Kant's Moral Metaphysics: God, Freedom, and Immortality*, edited by Benjamin J. Bruxvoort Lipscomb and James Krueger, 211–30. Berlin: De Gruyter.

Kania, Andrew. 2015. "An Imaginative Theory of Musical Space and Movement." *The British Journal of Aesthetics* 55 (2): 157–72.

Kant, Immanuel. 1900–. *Gesammelte Schriften*. Berlin: De Gruyter and predecessors.

Kant, Immanuel. 1968. "Metaphysik v. Schön." In *Gesammelte Schriften* Bd. 28, Hft. 1, 461–524.

Kant, Immanuel. 1992a. *Lectures on Logic*. Translated and edited by J. Michael Young. Cambridge: Cambridge University Press.

Kant, Immanuel. 1992b. *Theoretical Philosophy, 1755–1770*. Translated and edited by David Walford and Ralf Meerbote. Cambridge: Cambridge University Press.

Kant, Immanuel. 1993. *Opus Postumum*. Translated and edited by Eckart Förster and Michael Rosen. Cambridge: Cambridge University Press.

Kant, Immanuel. 1996a. *Practical Philosophy*. Translated and edited by Mary Gregor. Cambridge: Cambridge University Press.

Kant, Immanuel. 1996b. *Religion and Rational Theology*. Translated and edited by Allen Wood and George di Giovanni. Cambridge: Cambridge University Press.

Kant, Immanuel. 1997a. *Critique of Practical Reason*. Translated and edited by Mary Gregor. Cambridge: Cambridge University Press.

Kant, Immanuel. 1997b. *Lectures on Ethics*. Edited by Peter Heath. Translated by J.B. Schneewind and Peter Heath. Cambridge: Cambridge University Press.

Kant, Immanuel. 1997c. *Lectures on Metaphysics*. Translated and edited by Karl Ameriks and Steve Naragon. Cambridge: Cambridge University Press.

Kant, Immanuel. 1997d. *Prolegomena to Any Future Metaphysics That Will Be Able to Come Forward as Science: With Selections from the Critique of Pure Reason*. Translated and edited by Gary Hatfield. Cambridge: Cambridge University Press.

Kant, Immanuel. 1998a. *Critique of Pure Reason*. Translated and edited by Allen W. Wood and Paul Guyer. Cambridge: Cambridge University Press.

Kant, Immanuel. 1998b. *Religion within the Boundaries of Mere Reason and Other Writings*. Translated and edited by Allen Wood and George di Giovanni. Cambridge: Cambridge University Press.

Kant, Immanuel. 1999. *Correspondence*. Translated and edited by Arnulf Zweig. Cambridge: Cambridge University Press.

Kant, Immanuel. 2000. *Critique of the Power of Judgment*. Edited by Paul Guyer. Translated by Paul Guyer and Eric Matthews. Cambridge: Cambridge University Press.

Kant, Immanuel. 2002. *Theoretical Philosophy after 1781*. Edited by Henry Allison and Peter Heath. Translated by Gary Hatfield, Michael Friedman, Henry Allison, and Peter Heath. Cambridge: Cambridge University Press.

Kant, Immanuel. 2005. *Notes and Fragments*. Edited by Paul Guyer. Translated by Curtis Bowman, Paul Guyer, and Frederick Rauscher. Cambridge: Cambridge University Press.

Kant, Immanuel. 2007. *Anthropology, History, and Education*. Edited by Günter Zöller and Robert Louden. Translated by Mary Gregor, Paul Guyer, Robert Louden, Holly Wilson, Allen Wood, Günter Zöller, and Arnulf Zweig. Cambridge: Cambridge University Press.

Kant, Immanuel. 2012a. *Groundwork of the Metaphysics of Morals*. Revised ed. Translated and edited by Mary Gregor and Jens Timmermann. Cambridge: Cambridge University Press.

Kant, Immanuel. 2012b. *Lectures on Anthropology*. Edited by Allen Wood and Robert Louden. Translated by Robert Clewis, Robert Louden, G. Felicitas Munzel, and Allen Wood. Cambridge: Cambridge University Press.

Kant, Immanuel. 2014. "On Kästner's Treatises." Translated by Christian Onof and Dennis Schulting. *Kantian Review* 19 (2): 305–13.

Keats, John. 2001. *Complete Poems and Selected Letters*. New York: Modern Library.

Keller, Pierre. 1998. *Kant and the Demands of Self-Consciousness*. Cambridge: Cambridge University Press.

Kelly, Alice M. 2020. "'Lots of Us Are Doing Fine': Femslash Fan Fiction, Happy Endings, and the Archontic Expansions of the *Price of Salt* Archive." *Lit: Literature Interpretation Theory* 31 (1): 42–59.

Kemal, Salim. 1992. *Kant's Aesthetic Theory: An Introduction*. London: Palgrave Macmillan.

Kemp Smith, Norman. 1962. *A Commentary to Kant's Critique of Pure Reason*. New York: Humanities Press.

Kern, Andrea. 2000. *Schöne Lust. Eine Theorie der ästhetischen Erfahrung nach Kant*. Frankfurt am Main: Suhrkamp.

Kern, Andrea. 2017. *Sources of Knowledge: On the Concept of a Rational Capacity for Knowledge*. Cambridge, MA: Harvard University Press.

Kieran, Matthew, and Dominic Lopes, eds. 2003. *Imagination, Philosophy, and the Arts*. London: Routledge.

Kind, Amy. 2001. "Putting the Image Back in Imagination." *Philosophy and Phenomenological Research* 62 (1): 85–109.

Kind, Amy. 2011. "The Puzzle of Imaginative Desire." *Australasian Journal of Philosophy* 89 (3): 421–39.

Kind, Amy. 2013. "The Heterogeneity of the Imagination." *Erkenntnis* 78 (1): 141–59.

408 BIBLIOGRAPHY

Kind, Amy. 2016a. "Imagining under Constraints." In *Knowledge Through Imagination*, edited by Amy Kind and Peter Kung, 145–59. Oxford: Oxford University Press.

Kind, Amy, ed. 2016b. *The Routledge Handbook of Philosophy of Imagination*. London: Routledge.

Kind, Amy. 2018. "Imaginative Presence." In *Phenomenal Presence*, edited by Fabian Dorsch and Fiona Macpherson, 165–80. Oxford: Oxford University Press.

Kind, Amy, and Peter Kung, eds. 2016. *Knowledge through Imagination*. Oxford: Oxford University Press.

Kirwan, James. 2005. *Sublimity: The Non-Rational and the Irrational in the History of Aesthetics*. New York: Routledge.

Kitcher, Patricia. 1990. *Kant's Transcendental Psychology*. New York: Oxford University Press.

Kitcher, Patricia. 2011. *Kant's Thinker*. Oxford: Oxford University Press.

Kneller, Jane. 1993. "Discipline and Silence: Women and Imagination in Kant's Theory of Taste." In *Aesthetics in Feminist Perspective*, edited by Hilde Hein and Carolyn Korsmeyer, 179–92. Bloomington, IN: Indiana University Press.

Kneller, Jane. 2007. *Kant and the Power of Imagination*. Cambridge: Cambridge University Press.

Kneller, Jane. 2013. "Imagining Our World." In *Imagination in Kant's Critical Philosophy*, edited by Michael Thompson, 141–62. Berlin: De Gruyter.

Koch, Lutz. 2003. *Kants ethische Didaktik*. Würzburg: Ergon-Verl.

Kohl, Markus. 2017. "The Normativity of Prudence." *Kant Studien* 108 (4): 517–42.

Kohl, Markus. 2020. "Kant on Cognizing Oneself as a Spontaneous Cognizer." *Canadian Journal of Philosophy* 50 (3): 395–412.

Kornilaev, Leonid. 2021. "Kant's Doctrine of Education and the Problem of Artificial Intelligence." *Journal of Philosophy of Education* 55 (6): 1072–80.

Kosch, Michelle. 2006. *Freedom and Reason in Kant, Schelling, and Kierkegaard*. Oxford: Oxford University Press.

Kozak, Piotr. 2023. *Thinking in Images*. London: Bloomsbury.

Kraus, Katharina. 2019. "The Parity and Disparity between Inner and Outer Experience in Kant." *Kantian Review* 24 (2): 171–95.

Kraus, Katharina. 2020. *Kant on Self-Knowledge and Self-Formation: The Nature of Inner Experience*. Cambridge: Cambridge University Press.

Kravanja, Aljoša. 2023. "Two Models of Kantian Construction." *Journal of Transcendental Philosophy* (ahead-of-print). https://doi.org/10.1515/jtph-2022-0013.

Kumar, Apaar. 2018. "Kant and the Harmony of the Faculties: A Non-Cognitive Interpretation." *Kantian Review* 23 (1): 1–26.

Kung, Peter. 2010. "Imagining as a Guide to Possibility." *Philosophy and Phenomenological Research* 81 (3): 620–63.

Kung, Peter. 2016a. "Imagination and Modal Epistemology." In *The Routledge Handbook of Philosophy of Imagination*, edited by Amy Kind, 437–50. London: Routledge.

Kung, Peter. 2016b. "Thought Experiments in Ethics." In *Knowledge Through Imagination*, edited by Amy Kind and Peter Kung, 227–46. Oxford: Oxford University Press.

Küplen, Mojca. 2015. *Beauty, Ugliness and the Free Play of Imagination: An Approach to Kant's Aesthetics*. Cham: Springer.

Lambeth, Morganna. 2021. "A Case for Heidegger's Interpretation of the Kantian Imagination, Vo. 3." In *The Court of Reason*, edited by Camilla Serck-Hanssen and Beatrix Himmelmann, 1287–96. Berlin: De Gruyter.

Lambeth, Morganna. 2022. "Resisting Tiny Heroes: Kant on the Mechanism and Scope of Imaginative Resistance." *The Journal of Aesthetics and Art Criticism* 80 (2): 164–76.

Lambeth, Morganna. 2023. *Heidegger's Interpretation of Kant*. Cambridge: Cambridge University Press.

Land, Thomas. 2011. "Kantian Conceptualism." In *Rethinking Epistemology*, edited by Guenther Abel and James Conant, 197–239. Berlin: De Gruyter.

Land, Thomas. 2014. "Spatial Representation, Magnitude and the Two Stems of Cognition." *Canadian Journal of Philosophy* 44 (5–6): 524–50.

Land, Thomas. 2015a. "No Other Use Than in Judgment? Kant on Concepts and Sensible Synthesis." *Journal of the History of Philosophy* 53 (3): 461–84.

Land, Thomas. 2015b. "Nonconceptualist Readings of Kant and the Transcendental Deduction." *Kantian Review* 20 (1): 25–51.

Land, Thomas. 2016. "Moderate Conceptualism and Spatial Representation." In *Kantian Nonconceptualism*, edited by Dennis Schulting, 145–70. London: Palgrave Macmillan.

Landy, David. 2015. *Kant's Inferentialism: The Case against Hume*. New York: Routledge.

Landy, David. 2020. "Kant's Better-than-Terrible Argument in the Anticipations of Perception." *Kantian Review* 25 (1): 77–101.

Langkau, Julia. 2021. "On Imagining Being Someone Else." In *Epistemic Uses of Imagination*, edited by Christopher Badura and Amy Kind, 260–78. New York: Routledge.

Langland-Hassan, Peter. 2012. "Pretense, Imagination, and Belief: The Single Attitude Theory." *Philosophical Studies* 159 (2): 155–79.

Langland-Hassan, Peter. 2016. "On Choosing What to Imagination." In *Knowledge Through Imagination*, edited by Amy Kind and Peter Kung, 61–84. Oxford: Oxford University Press.

Langland-Hassan, Peter. 2020. *Explaining Imagination*. Oxford: Oxford University Press.

Langton, Rae. 1992. "Duty and Desolation." *Philosophy* 67 (262): 481–505.

Langton, Rae. 1998. *Kantian Humility*. New York: Oxford University Press.

Langton, Rae. 2019. "IV—Empathy and First-Personal Imagining." *Proceedings of the Aristotelian Society* 119 (1): 77–104.

Leech, Jessica. 2017. "Kant's Material Condition of Real Possibility." In *The Actual and the Possible*, edited by Mark Sinclair, 94–116. Oxford: Oxford University Press.

Lennon, Kathleen. 2015. *Imagination and the Imaginary*. Abingdon: Routledge.

Lessing, Gotthold Ephraim. 2012. "*Laocoön: An Essay on the Limits of Painting and Poetry*." In *Classic and Romantic German Aesthetics*, edited by Jay Bernstein, 25–130. Cambridge: Cambridge University Press.

Levy, Arnon, and Peter Godfrey-Smith, eds. 2020. *The Scientific Imagination: Philosophical and Psychological Perspectives*. New York: Oxford University Press.

Liang, Yibin. 2020. "Kant on Inner Sensations and the Parity Between Inner and Outer Sense." *Ergo* 7: 307–38.

Liang, Yibin. 2021. *Bewusstsein und Selbstbewusstsein bei Kant. Eine neue Rekonstruktion*. Kantstudien. Ergänzungshefte. Berlin: De Gruyter.

Liao, Shen-yi. 2013. "Moral Persuasion and the Diversity of Fictions." *Pacific Philosophical Quarterly* 94 (3): 269–89.

Liao, Shen-yi, and Tamar Szabó Gendler. 2011. "Pretense and Imagination." *Cognitive Science* 2 (1): 79–94.

Long, Christopher P. 1998. "Two Powers, One Ability: The Understanding and Imagination in Kant's Critical Philosophy." *The Southern Journal of Philosophy* 36 (2): 233–53.

Longuenesse, Béatrice. 1998. *Kant and the Capacity to Judge*. Translated by Charles T. Wolfe. Princeton, NJ: Princeton University Press.

410 BIBLIOGRAPHY

Longuenesse, Béatrice. 2005. *Kant on the Human Standpoint*. Cambridge: Cambridge University Press.

Longuenesse. Béatrice. 2008. "Kant's Theory of Judgment, and Judgments of Taste: On Henry Allison's Kant's Theory of Taste." *Inquiry* 46: 143–63.

Lopes, Dominic McIver. 1998. "Imagination, Illusion and Experience in Film." *Philosophical Studies* 89 (2/3): 343–53.

Lopes, Dominic McIver. 2021. "Beyond the Pleasure Principle: A Kantian Aesthetics of Autonomy." *Estetika* LVIII/XIV (1): 1–18.

Louden, Robert. 1992. "Go-Carts of Judgment, Exemplars in Kantian Moral Education." *Archiv für Geschichte der Philosophie* 74 (3): 303–22.

Louden, Robert. 2009. "Making the Law Visible: The Role of Examples in Kant's Ethics." In *Kant's* Groundwork of the Metaphysics of Morals: *A Critical Guide*, edited by Jens Timmermann, 63–81. Cambridge: Cambridge University Press.

Louden, Robert. 2011. *Kant's Human Being: Essays on His Theory of Human Nature*. New York: Oxford University Press.

Lu-Adler, Huaping. 2015. "Constructing a Demonstration of Logical Rules, or How to Use Kant's Logic Corpus." In *Reading Kant's Lectures*, edited by Robert Clewis, 137–58. Berlin: De Gruyter.

Lukac de Stier, María. 2011. "Hobbes on the Passions and Imagination: Tradition and Modernity." *Hobbes Studies* 24 (1): 78–90.

Lyman Cabot, Ella. 1906. *Everyday Ethics*. New York: H. Holt and Company.

Lyotard, Jean François. 1994. *Lessons on the Analytic of the Sublime: Kant's Critique of Judgment*. Stanford: Stanford University Press.

Macpherson, Fiona, and Fabian Dorsch, eds. 2018. *Perceptual Imagination and Perceptual Memory*. Oxford: Oxford University Press.

Macpherson, Fiona, and Dimitris Platchias, eds. 2013. *Hallucination: Philosophy and Psychology*. Cambridge, MA: MIT Press.

Magri, Tito. 2023. *Hume's Imagination*. Oxford: Oxford University Press.

Maibom, Heidi. 2020. *Empathy*. London: Routledge.

Makkai, Katalin. 2021. *Kant's Critique of Taste: The Feeling of Life*. Cambridge: Cambridge University Press.

Makkreel, Rudolf A. 1984. "Imagination and Temporality in Kant's Theory of the Sublime." *The Journal of Aesthetics and Art Criticism* 42 (3): 303–15.

Makkreel, Rudolf A. 1990. *Imagination and Interpretation in Kant: The Hermeneutical Import of the Critique of Judgment*. Chicago: University of Chicago Press.

Maly, Sebastian. 2012. *Kant über die symbolische Erkenntnis Gottes*. Kantstudien-Ergänzungshefte. Berlin: De Gruyter.

Mancosu, Paolo. 2005. *Visualization, Explanation and Reasoning Styles in Mathematics*. Dordrecht: Springer.

Marcucci, Silvestro. 1998. " "Moral Friendship" in Kant." *Kant-Studien* 90: 434–41.

Marshall, Colin. 2017. "Kant on Impenetrability, Touch, and the Causal Content of Perception." *European Journal of Philosophy* 25 (4): 1411–33.

Marshall, Colin and Barker Aaron. forthcoming. "Kant on Modality." In *Oxford Handbook of Kant*, edited by Anil Gomes and Andrew Stephenson. Oxford: Oxford University Press.

Matherne, Samantha. 2013. "The Inclusive Interpretation of Kant's Aesthetic Ideas." *The British Journal of Aesthetics* 53 (1): 21–39.

Matherne, Samantha. 2014a. "Kant and the Art of Schematism." *Kantian Review* 19 (2): 181–205.

Matherne, Samantha. 2014b. "Kant's Expressive Theory of Music." *The Journal of Aesthetics and Art Criticism* 72 (2): 129–45.

BIBLIOGRAPHY 411

Matherne, Samantha. 2015. "Images and Kant's Theory of Perception." *Ergo* 2 (29): 737–77.

Matherne, Samantha. 2016. "Kantian Themes in Merleau-Ponty's Theory of Perception." *Archiv für Geschichte der Philosophie* 98 (2): 193–230.

Matherne, Samantha. 2018. "Merleau-Ponty on Abstract Thought in Mathematics and Natural Science." *European Journal of Philosophy* 26 (2): 780–97.

Matherne, Samantha. 2019. "Kant on Aesthetic Autonomy and Common Sense." *Philosophers' Imprint* 19 (24): 1–22.

Matherne, Samantha. 2021a. *Cassirer*. London: Routledge.

Matherne, Samantha. 2021b. "Cognition by Analogy and the Possibility of Metaphysics." In *The Cambridge Critical Guide to the* Prolegomena, edited by Peter Thielke, 215–234. Cambridge: Cambridge University Press.

Matherne, Samantha. 2023a. "Aesthetic Humility: A Kantian Model." *Mind* 132 (526): 452–78.

Matherne, Samantha. 2023b. "Ella Lyman Cabot's Everyday Ethics." In *The Oxford Handbook of American and British Women Philosophers in the Nineteenth Century*, edited by Lydia Moland and Alison Stone. Oxford: Oxford University Press.

Matherne, Samantha. 2023c. "Imagining Freedom: Kant on Symbols of Sublimity." In *The Idea of Freedom: New Essays on Kant's Theory of Freedom*, edited by Dai Heide and Evan Tiffany, 217–244. Oxford: Oxford University Press.

Matherne, Samantha. forthcoming. "Kant on the Aesthetic Normativity of Colors and Tones." In *Normative Realism*, edited by Paul Boghossian and Christopher Peacocke. Oxford: Oxford University Press.

Matthews, Patricia M. 1996. "Kant's Sublime: A Form of Pure Aesthetic Reflective Judgment." *The Journal of Aesthetics and Art Criticism* 54 (2): 165–80.

Mattos, Fernando Costa. 2013. "The Postulates of Pure Practical Reason: A Possible Place for Imagination in Kant's Moral Philosophy?" In *Imagination in Kant's Critical Philosophy*, edited by Michael L. Thompson, 123–40. Berlin: De Gruyter.

McBrayer, Justin P. 2010. "A Limited Defense of Moral Perception." *Philosophical Studies* 149 (3): 305–20.

McDowell, John. 1996. *Mind and World*. Cambridge, MA: Harvard University Press.

McDowell, John. 2009. *Having the World in View: Essays on Kant, Hegel, and Sellars*. Cambridge, MA: Harvard University Press.

McGinn, Colin. 2004. *Mindsight: Image, Dream, Meaning*. Cambridge, MA: Harvard University Press.

McLear, Colin. 2011. "Kant on Animal Consciousness." *Philosophers' Imprint* 11 (15): 1–16.

McLear, Colin. 2014. "The Kantian (Non)-Conceptualism Debate." *Philosophy Compass* 9 (11): 769–90.

McLear, Colin. 2015. "Two Kinds of Unity in the Critique of Pure Reason." *Journal of the History of Philosophy* 53 (1): 79–110.

McLear, Colin. 2016a. "Getting Acquainted with Kant." In *Kantian Nonconceptualism*, edited by Dennis Schulting, 171–97. London: Palgrave Macmillan.

McLear, Colin. 2016b. "Kant on Perceptual Content." *Mind* 125 (497): 95–144.

McLear, Colin. 2017. "Intuition and Presence." In *Kant and the Philosophy of Mind*, edited by Anil Gomes and Andrew Stephenson, 86–103. Oxford: Oxford University Press.

McLear, Colin. 2020a. "Animals and Objectivity." In *Kant and Animals*, edited by John J. Callanan and Lucy Allais, 42–65. Oxford: Oxford University Press.

McLear, Colin. 2020b. "On the Transcendental Freedom of the Intellect." *Ergo* 7 (2): 35–104.

McLear, Colin. 2021. "Kantian Conceptualism/Nonconceptualism." In *The Stanford Encyclopedia of Philosophy*, edited by Edward N. Zalta. Fall ed. Metaphysics

412 BIBLIOGRAPHY

Research Lab, Stanford University. https://plato.stanford.edu/archives/fall2021/entries/kant-conceptualism/.

McLear, Colin. forthcoming. *Kant's Order of Reason: On Rational Agency and Control.* Oxford: Oxford University Press.

McMahon, Jennifer A. 2014. *Art and Ethics in a Material World: Kant's Pragmatist Legacy.* New York: Routledge.

McMullin, Irene. 2019. *Existential Flourishing: A Phenomenology of Virtues.* Cambridge: Cambridge University Press.

McQuillan, J. Colin. 2018. "Baumgarten, Meier, and Kant on Aesthetic Perfection." In *Kant and His German Contemporaries, Volume II: Aesthetics, History, Politics, and Religion,* edited by Daniel O. Dahlstrom, 13–27. Cambridge: Cambridge University Press.

Meerbote, Ralf. 1972. "Kant's Use of the Notions 'Objective Reality' and 'Objective Validity.'" *Kant-Studien* 63 (1–4): 51–8.

Meerbote, Ralf. 1982. "Reflection on Beauty." In *Essays in Kant's Aesthetics,* edited by Ted Cohen and Paul Guyer, 55–86. Chicago: University of Chicago Press.

Melnick, A. 2001. "Categories, Logical Functions, and Schemata in Kant." *The Review of Metaphysics* 54 (3): 615–39.

Merleau-Ponty, Maurice. 2012. *Phenomenology of Perception.* Translated by Donald Landes. Abingdon: Routledge.

Merritt, Melissa. 2012. "The Moral Source of the Kantian Sublime." In *The Sublime: From Antiquity to the Present,* edited by Timothy Costelloe, 37–49. Cambridge: Cambridge University Press.

Merritt, Melissa. 2017. "Love, Respect, and Individuals: Murdoch as a Guide to Kantian Ethics." *European Journal of Philosophy* 25 (4): 1844–63.

Merritt, Melissa. 2018a. *Kant on Reflection and Virtue.* Cambridge: Cambridge University Press.

Merritt, Melissa. 2018b. *The Sublime.* Cambridge: Cambridge University Press.

Merritt, Melissa, and Markos Valaris. 2017. "Attention and Synthesis in Kant's Conception of Experience." *The Philosophical Quarterly* 67 (268): 571–92.

Messina, James. 2014. "Kant on the Unity of Space and the Synthetic Unity of Apperception." *Kant-Studien* 105 (1): 5–40.

Meynell, Letitia. 2014. "Imagination and Insight: A New Account of the Content of Thought Experiments." *Synthese* 191 (17): 4149–68.

Michaelian, Kourken. 2016. *Mental Time Travel: Episodic Memory and Our Knowledge of the Personal Past.* Cambridge, MA: MIT Press.

Michaelian, Kourken, Denis Perrin, and André Sant'Anna. 2020. *Memory as Mental Time Travel.* Dordrecht: Springer.

Modrak, Deborah. 2016. "Aristotle on Phantasia." In *The Routledge Handbook of Philosophy of Imagination,* edited by Amy Kind, 15–26. London: Routledge.

Moore, Thomas. 2018. "Kant's Deduction of the Sublime." *Kantian Review* 23 (3): 349–72.

Moran, Kate. 2009. "Can Kant Have an Account of Moral Education?" *Journal of Philosophy of Education* 43 (4): 471–84.

Moran, Kate. 2012. *Community and Progress in Kant's Moral Philosophy.* Washington, DC: Catholic University of America Press.

Moran, Richard. 1989. "Seeing and Believing: Metaphor, Image, and Force." *Critical Inquiry* 16 (1): 87–112.

Moran, Richard. 1994. "The Expression of Feeling in Imagination." *The Philosophical Review* 103 (1): 75–106.

Mörchen, Hermann. 1970. *Die Einbildungskraft Bei Kant*. Berlin: De Gruyter.

Morris, Courtney. 2021. "Kant's Moral Catechism Revisited." *Journal of Philosophy of Education* 55 (6): 990–1002.

Mudd, Sasha. 2017. "The Demand for Systematicity and the Authority of Theoretical Reason in Kant." *Kantian Review* 22 (1): 81–106.

Munzel, Felicitas. 1995. "'The Beautiful Is the Symbol of the Morally-Good': Kant's Philosophical Basis of Proof for the Idea of the Morally-Good." *Journal of the History of Philosophy* 33 (2): 301–30.

Munzel, Felicitas. 1999. *Kant's Conception of Moral Character: The "Critical" Link of Morality, Anthropology, and Reflective Judgment*. Chicago: University of Chicago Press.

Munzel, Felicitas. 2012. *Kant's Conception of Pedagogy: Toward Education for Freedom*. Evanston: Northwestern University Press.

Murdoch, Iris. 2001. *The Sovereignty of Good*. London: Routledge.

Murphy, Alice. 2022. "Imagination in Science." *Philosophy Compass* 17 (6): n/a.

Myskja, Bjø K. 2001. *The Sublime in Kant and Beckett: Aesthetic Judgement, Ethics and Literature*. Berlin: De Gruyter.

Nair, Sashi. 2019. "Loss, Motherhood and the Queer 'Happy Ending'." *Journal of Language, Literature and Culture* 66 (1): 46–58.

Nanay, Bence. 2010. "Perception and Imagination: Amodal Perception as Mental Imagery." *Philosophical Studies* 150 (2): 239–54.

Nanay, Bence. 2015. "Perceptual Content and the Content of Mental Imagery." *Philosophical Studies* 172 (7): 1723–36.

Nanay, Bence. 2016. "Hallucination as Mental Imagery." *Journal of Consciousness Studies* 23 (7–8): 65–81.

Nanay, Bence. 2017. "Sensory Substitution and Multimodal Mental Imagery." *Perception* 46 (9): 1014–26.

Nanay, Bence. 2018a. "Multimodal Mental Imagery." *Cortex* 105: 125–34.

Nanay, Bence. 2018b. "The Importance of Amodal Completion in Everyday Perception." *I-Perception* 9 (4): 1–16.

Naragon, Steven. 1990. "Kant on Descartes and the Brutes." *Kant-Studien* 81 (1): 1–23.

Newton, Alexandra. 2015. "Kant on the Logical Origin of Concepts." *European Journal of Philosophy* 23 (3): 456–84.

Nichols, Shaun, ed. 2006. *The Architecture of the Imagination*. Oxford: Oxford University Press.

Nichols, Shaun. 2020. "The Propositional Imagination." In *The Routledge Companion to Philosophy of Psychology*, edited by Sarah Robins, John Symons, and Paco Calvo, 360–9. London: Routledge.

Nichols, Shaun, and Stephen Stich. 2000. "A Cognitive Theory of Pretense." *Cognition* 74 (2): 115–47.

Nichols, Shaun, and Stephen Stich. 2003. *Mindreading: An Integrated Account of Pretence, Self-Awareness, and Understanding Other Minds*. Oxford: Oxford University Press.

Ninan, Dilip. 2009. "Persistence and the First-Person Perspective." *The Philosophical Review* 118 (4): 425–64.

Ninan, Dilip. 2016. "Imagination and the Self." In *The Routledge Handbook of Philosophy of Imagination*, edited by Amy Kind, 274–85. London: Routledge.

Noë, Alva. 2004. *Action in Perception*. Cambridge, MA: MIT Press.

Novitz, David. 1999. "Creativity and Constraint." *Australasian Journal of Philosophy* 77 (1): 67–82.

414 BIBLIOGRAPHY

Nussbaum, Martha C. 1990. *Love's Knowledge: Essays on Philosophy and Literature.* New York: Oxford University Press.

Nussbaum, Martha C. 2001. *Upheavals of Thought: The Intelligence of Emotions.* Cambridge: Cambridge University Press.

Nuyen, A.T. 1989. "The Kantian Theory of Metaphor." *Philosophy & Rhetoric* 22 (2): 95–109.

Nuzzo, Angelica. 2008. *Ideal Embodiment: Kant's Theory of Sensibility.* Bloomington, IN: Indiana University Press.

Nuzzo, Angelica. 2013. "Imaginative Sensibility Understanding, Sensibility, and Imagination in the Critique of Pure Reason." In *Imagination in Kant's Critical Philosophy*, edited by Michael L. Thompson, 19–48. Berlin: De Gruyter.

O'Brien. Lucy. "Imagination and the Motivational View of Belief." *Analysis* 65 (1): 55–62.

O'Neill, Onora. 1990. *Constructions of Reason: Explorations of Kant's Practical Philosophy.* Cambridge: Cambridge University Press.

Onof, Christian, and Dennis Schulting. 2014. "Kant, Kästner and the Distinction between Metaphysical and Geometric Space." *Kantian Review* 19 (2): 285–304.

Onof, Christian, and Dennis Schulting. 2015. "Space as Form of Intuition and as Formal Intuition: On the Note to B160 in Kant's Critique of Pure Reason." *The Philosophical Review* 124 (1): 1–58.

O'Shaughnessy, Brian. 2000. *Consciousness and the World.* Oxford: Oxford University Press.

Ostaric, Lara. 2017. "The Free Harmony of the Faculties and the Primacy of Imagination in Kant's Aesthetic Judgment." *European Journal of Philosophy* 25 (4): 1376–410.

Palmquist, Steven. 2015. *Comprehensive Commentary on Kant's* Religion Within the Bounds of Bare Reason. West Sussex: Wiley Blackwell.

Parsons, Charles. 1964. "Infinity and Kant's Conception of the 'Possibility of Experience'." *The Philosophical Review* 73 (2): 182–197.

Parsons, Charles. 1982. "Kant's Philosophy of Arithmetic." In *Philosophy, Science, and Method*, edited by Sidney Morganbesser, Patrick Suppes, and Morgan White, 568–94. New York: St. Martin's Press.

Parsons, Charles. 1992. "The Transcendental Aesthetic." In *The Cambridge Companion to Kant*, edited by Paul Guyer, 62–100. Cambridge: Cambridge University Press.

Paton, H. J. 1936. *Kant's Metaphysic of Experience: A Commentary on the First Half of the Kritik Der Reinen Vernunft.* London: G. Allen & Unwin.

Pendlebury, Michael. 1995. "Making Sense of Kant's Schematism." *Philosophy and Phenomenological Research* 55 (4): 777–97.

Pendlebury, Michael. 1996. "The Role of Imagination in Perception." *South African Journal of Philosophy* 15 (4): 133–8.

Pendlebury, Michael. 2017. "A Kantian Account of Animal Cognition." *The Philosophical Forum* 48 (4): 369–93.

Pereboom, Derk. 1988. "Kant on Intentionality." *Synthese* 77 (3): 321–52.

Peters, Julia. 2018. "Kant's Gesinnung." *Journal of the History of Philosophy* 56 (3): 497–518.

Phillips, James, and James Morley, eds. 2003. *Imagination and Its Pathologies.* Cambridge, MA: MIT Press.

Pillow, Kirk. 2000. *Sublime Understanding: Aesthetic Reflection in Kant and Hegel.* Cambridge, MA: MIT Press.

Pillow, Kirk. 2001. "Jupiter's Eagle and the Despot's Hand Mill: Two Views on Metaphor in Kant." *The Journal of Aesthetics and Art Criticism* 59 (2): 193–209.

Pippin, Robert. 1976. "The Schematism and Empirical Concepts." *Kant-Studien* 67 (2): 156–71.

Pippin, Robert. 1982. *Kant's Theory of Form: An Essay on the Critique of Pure Reason*. New Haven: Yale University Press.

Pippin, Robert. 1987. "Kant on the Spontaneity of Mind." *Canadian Journal of Philosophy* 17 (2): 449–75.

Plato. 2008. *The Dialogues of Plato*, Volume 3: *Ion, Hippias Minor, Laches, Protagoras*. Translated by R. Allen. New Haven: Yale University Press.

Pollok, Konstantin. 2017. *Kant's Theory of Normativity: Exploring the Space of Reason*. Cambridge: Cambridge University Press.

Posy, Carl J. 1992. *Kant's Philosophy of Mathematics: Modern Essays*. Dordrecht: Kluwer Academic Publishers.

Prauss, Gerold. 1971. *Erscheinung bei Kant*. Berlin: De Gruyter.

Prichard, H. A. 1909. *Kant's Theory of Knowledge*. England: Clarendon Press.

Reath, Andrews. 2006. *Agency and Autonomy in Kant's Moral Theory*. Oxford: Oxford University Press.

Reiter, Aviv. 2021. "Kant on the Aesthetic Ideas of Beautiful Nature." *British Journal of Aesthetics* 61 (4): 403–19.

Reiter, Aviv, and Ido Geiger. 2018. "Natural Beauty, Fine Art and the Relation between Them." *Kant-Studien* 109 (1): 72–100.

Reiter, Aviv, and Ido Geiger. 2021. "Batteux, Kant and Schiller on Fine Art and Moral Education." *Journal of Philosophy of Education* 55 (6): 1142–58.

Richardson, Alan. 2003. "Conceiving, Experiencing, and Conceiving Experiencing: Neo-Kantianism and the History of the Concept of Experience: Topoi: Logic and Human Experience." *Topoi* 22 (1): 55–67.

Rilke, Rainer Maria. 2015. *New Poems*. Translated by Len Krisak. Rochester: Camden House.

Rind, M. 2002. "Can Kant's Deduction of Judgments of Taste Be Saved?" *Archiv für Geschichte der Philosophie* 84 (1): 20–45.

Risi, Vincenzo. 2015. *Mathematizing Space: The Objects of Geometry from Antiquity to the Early Modern Age*. Cham: Springer.

Robins, Michael H. 2002. "The Possibility of Practical Reason, J. David Velleman. Oxford University Press, 2000." *Economics and Philosophy* 18 (2): 351–85.

Robins, Sarah, John Symons, and Paco Calvo, eds. 2020. *The Routledge Companion to Philosophy of Psychology*. Abingdon: Routledge.

Robinson, Andrew. 2011. *Genius: A Very Short Introduction*. Oxford: Oxford University Press.

Roche, Andrew F. 2011. "Allais on Transcendental Idealism." *Kantian Review* 16 (3): 351–74.

Roche, Andrew F. 2018. "Kant's Transcendental Deduction and the Unity of Space and Time." *Kantian Review* 23 (1): 41–64.

Rogerson, Kenneth F. 2008. *The Problem of Free Harmony in Kant's Aesthetics*. Albany: State University of New York Press.

Rohs, Peter. 2001. "Bezieht sich nach Kant die Anschauung unmittelbar auf Gegenstände?" In *Kant und die Berliner Aufklärung*, edited by Volker Gerhardt, Rolf-Peter Horstmann, and Ralph Schumacher, 214–28. Berlin: De Gruyter.

Rosefeldt, Tobias. 2019. "Kant on Imagination and the Intuition of Time." In *The Imagination in German Idealism and Romanticism*, edited by Gerad Gentry and Konstantin Pollok, 48–65. Cambridge: Cambridge University Press.

Rosefeldt, Tobias. 2021. "Kant on the Epistemic Role of the Imagination." *Synthese* 198 (13): 3171–92.

416 BIBLIOGRAPHY

Rosefeldt, Tobias. 2022. "Kant on Decomposing Synthesis and the Intuition of Infinite Space." *Philosophers' Imprint* 22 (1): 1–23.

Rosen, Michael. 2022. *The Shadow of God: Kant, Hegel, and the Passage from Heaven to History*. Cambridge, MA: Harvard University Press.

Roth, Klas, and Chris W. Surprenant, eds. 2012. *Kant and Education: Interpretations and Commentary*. New York: Routledge.

Rueger, Alexander. 2008. "The Free Play of the Faculties and the Status of Natural Beauty in Kant's Theory of Taste." *Archiv für Geschichte der Philosophie* 90: 298–322.

Rueger, Alexander, and Şahan Evren. 2005. "The Role of Symbolic Presentation in Kant's Theory of Taste." *The British Journal of Aesthetics* 45 (3): 229–47.

Rush, Fred. 2001. "The Harmony of the Faculties." *Kant-Studien* 92 (1): 38–61.

Russell, Francey. forthcoming a. "The Opacity of Human Action." In *Kant's Fundamental Assumptions*, edited by Colin Marshall and Colin McLear. Oxford: Oxford University Press.

Russell, Francey. forthcoming b. "Kant's Fantasy." *Mind*.

Ryle, Gilbert. 1984. *The Concept of Mind*. Chicago: University of Chicago Pres.

Sá Pereira, Roberto Horácio de. 2013. "What Is Nonconceptualism in Kant's Philosophy?" *Philosophical Studies* 164 (1): 233–54.

Sá Pereira, Roberto Horácio de. 2017. "A Nonconceptualist Reading of the B-Deduction." *Philosophical Studies* 174 (2): 425–42.

Sartre, Jean-Paul. 2004. *The Imaginary: A Phenomenological Psychology of the Imagination*. Revised by Arlette Elkaim-Sartre. London: Routledge.

Sassen, Brigitte. 2003. "Artistic Genius and the Question of Creativity." In *Kant's* Critique of the Power of Judgment: *Critical Essays*, edited by Paul Guyer, 171–9. Lanham, MD: Rowman & Littlefield.

Saunders, Joe, and Martin Sticker. 2020. "Moral Education and Transcendental Idealism." *Archiv für Geschichte der Philosophie* 102 (4): 646–73.

Savile, Anthony. 1987. *Aesthetic Reconstructions: The Seminal Writings of Lessing, Kant and Schiller*. Oxford: Blackwell.

Savile, Anthony. 1993. *Kantian Aesthetics Pursued*. Edinburgh: Edinburgh University Press.

Schafer, Karl. 2021. "A System of Rational Faculties: Additive or Transformative?" *European Journal of Philosophy* 29 (4): 918–36.

Schafer, Karl. 2022a. "Kant's Conception of Cognition and Our Knowledge of Things-in-Themselves." In *The Sensible and Intelligible Worlds: New Essays on Kant's Metaphysics and Epistemology*, edited by Karl Schafer and Nicholas Stang, 248–78. Oxford: Oxford University Press.

Schafer, Karl. 2022b. "Kant on Reason as the Capacity for Comprehension." *Australasian Journal of Philosophy* (ahead-of-print): 1–19.

Schafer, Karl. 2023. "Practical Cognition and Knowledge of Things-in-Themselves." In *The Idea of Freedom: New Essays on the Kantian Theory of Freedom Kantian Freedom*, edited by Dai Heide and Evan Tiffany, 83–109. Oxford: Oxford University Press.

Schafer, Karl, and Nicholas F. Stang, eds. 2022. *The Sensible and Intelligible Worlds: New Essays on Kant's Metaphysics and Epistemology*. Oxford: Oxford University Press.

Schaper, Eva. 1964. "Kant's Schematism Reconsidered." *Review of Metaphysics* 18 (2): 267–292.

Schellenberg, Susanna. 2013. "Belief and Desire in Imagination and Immersion." *The Journal of Philosophy* 110 (9): 497–517.

Schmitz, Friederike. 2015. "On Kant's Conception of Inner Sense: Self-Affection by the Understanding: On Kant's Conception of Inner Sense." *European Journal of Philosophy* 23 (4): 1044–63.

Schofield, Malcolm. 1995. "Aristotle on Imagination." In *Essays on Aristotle's De Anima*, edited by Martha C. Nussbaum and Amélie Oksenberg Rorty, 249–78. Oxford: Oxford University Press.

Schuessler, Rudolf. 2021. "Kant, Casuistry and Casuistical Questions." *Journal of Philosophy of Education* 55 (6): 1003–16.

Schulting, Denis, ed. 2016. *Kant's Non-Conceptualism*. London: Palgrave Macmillan.

Schulting, Denis. 2017. *Kant's Radical Subjectivism*. London: Palgrave Macmillan.

Sedgwick, Sally. 2001. "Productive Imagination as Original Identity: Kant's 'Transcendental Deduction' in Hegel's Glauben und Wissen." In *Kant und die Berliner Aufklärung*, edited by Volker Gerhardt, Rolf-Peter Horstmann, and Ralph Schumacher, 343–52. Berlin: De Gruyter.

Seel, Gerhard. 1988. "Über den Grund der Lust an schönen Gegenständen: Kritische Fragen an die Ästhetik Kants." In *Kant: Analysen—Probleme—Kritik*, edited by H. Oberer and Gerhard Seel, 317–56. Würzburg: Königshausen & Neumann.

Sellars, Wilfrid. 1967. "Kant's View on Sensibility and Understanding." *The Monist* 51 (3): 463–91.

Sellars, Wilfrid. 1968. *Science and Metaphysics: Variations on Kantian Themes*. London: Routledge.

Sellars, Wilfrid. 1978. "The Role of Imagination in Kant's Theory of Experience." In *Categories: A Colloquium*, edited by Henry W. Johnstone Jr., 231–45. Pennsylvania: The Pennsylvania State University Press.

Sethi, Janum. 2019. "Two Feelings in the Beautiful: Kant on the Structure of Judgments of Beautiful." *Philosophers' Imprint* 19 (34): 1–17.

Sethi, Janum. 2020. "'For Me, In My Present State': Kant on Judgments of Perception and Mere Subjective Validity." *Journal of Modern Philosophy* 2 (9): 1–20.

Sethi, Janum. 2021. "Kant on Empirical Self-Consciousness." *Australasian Journal of Philosophy* (ahead-of-print): 1–21.

Sethi, Janum. 2022. "Kant on Common Sense and Empirical Concepts." *Kantian Review* 27 (2): 257–77.

Setton, Dirk. 2020. *Autonomie und Willkür. Kant und die Zweideutigkeit der Freiheit*. Berlin: De Gruyter.

Shabel, Lisa. 1998. "Kant on the 'Symbolic Construction' of Mathematical Concepts." *Studies in History and Philosophy of Science: Part A* 29 (4): 589–621.

Shabel, Lisa. 2007. "Kant's Philosophy of Mathematics." In *The Cambridge Companion to Kant and Modern Philosophy*, edited by Paul Guyer, 94–128. Cambridge: Cambridge University Press.

Shaddock, Justin. 2015. "Kant's Transcendental Idealism and His Transcendental Deduction." *Kantian Review* 20 (2): 265–88.

Shaddock, Justin. 2018. "Kant's Conceptualism: A New Reading of the Transcendental Deduction." *Pacific Philosophical Quarterly* 99: 464–88.

Shah, Nishi, and J. David Velleman. 2005. "Doxastic Deliberation." *The Philosophical Review* 114 (4): 497–534.

Shakespeare, William. 2013. *A Midsummer Night's Dream*. Edited by R.A. Foakes. Cambridge: Cambridge University Press.

Sherman, Nancy. 1998. "Empathy and Imagination." *Midwest Studies in Philosophy* 22 (1): 82–119.

Shockey, R. Matthew. 2021. *The Bounds of Self: An Essay on Heidegger's Being and Time*. New York: Routledge.

Siegel, Susanna. 2010. *The Contents of Visual Experience*. Oxford: Oxford University Press.

418 BIBLIOGRAPHY

Siegel, Susanna. 2021. "The Contents of Perception." In *The Stanford Encyclopedia of Philosophy*, edited by Edward N. Zalta. Fall ed. Metaphysics Research Lab, Stanford University. https://plato.stanford.edu/archives/fall2021/entries/perception-contents/.

Sinclair, Mark. 2017. *The Actual and the Possible: Modality and Metaphysics in Modern Philosophy*. Oxford: Oxford University Press.

Sinhababu, Neil. 2013. "Distinguishing Belief and Imagination." *Pacific Philosophical Quarterly* 94 (2): 152–65.

Sinhababu, Neil. 2016. "Imagination and Belief." In *The Routledge Handbook of Philosophy of Imagination*, edited by Amy Kind, 111–23. London: Routledge.

Smit, Houston. 2000. "Kant on Marks and the Immediacy of Intuition." *The Philosophical Review* 109 (2): 235–66.

Smit, Houston. 2009. "Kant on Apriority and the Spontaneity of Cognition." In *Metaphysics and the Good: Themes from the Philosophy of Robert Merrihew Adams*, edited by Samuel Newlands and Larry M. Jorgensen, 188–251. Oxford: Oxford University Press.

Smith, Adam. 2002. *The Theory of Moral Sentiments*. Cambridge: Cambridge University Press.

Smyth, Daniel. 2014. "Infinity and Givenness: Kant on the Intuitive Origin of Spatial Representation." *Canadian Journal of Philosophy* 44 (5–6): 551–79.

Sommerlatte, Curtis. 2016. "Empirical Cognition in the Transcendental Deduction: Kant's Starting Point and His Humean Problem." *Kantian Review* 21 (3): 437–63.

Sontag, Susan. 1961. *Against Interpretation and Other Essays*. New York: The Noonday Press.

Sorensen, Kelly, and Diane Williamson, eds. 2018. *Kant and the Faculty of Feeling*. Cambridge: Cambridge University Press.

Sorenson, Roy. 2016. "Thought Experiment and Imagination." In *The Routledge Handbook of Philosophy of Imagination*, edited by Amy Kind, 407–19. London: Routledge.

Standish, Paul. 2021. "Preface." *Journal of Philosophy of Education* 55 (6): 907–8.

Stang, Nicholas F. 2016. *Kant's Modal Metaphysics*. Oxford: Oxford University Press.

Stang, Nicholas F. 2023. "Kant's Schematism of the Categories: An Interpretation and Defence." *European Journal of Philosophy* 31 (1): 30–64.

Stephenson, Andrew. 2011. "Kant on Non-Veridical Experience." *Kant Yearbook* 3 (1): 1–22.

Stephenson, Andrew. 2015. "Kant on the Object-Dependence of Intuition and Hallucination." *The Philosophical Quarterly* 65 (260): 486–508.

Stephenson, Andrew. 2017. "Imagination and Inner Intuition." In *Kant and the Philosophy of Mind*, edited by Anil Gomes and Andrew Stephenson, 104–23. Oxford: Oxford University Press.

Sticker, Martin. 2015. "Educating the Common Agent: Kant on the Varieties of Moral Education." *Archiv für Geschichte der Philosophie* 97 (3): 358–87.

Sticker, Martin. 2021. "Kant on Thinking for Oneself and with Others—the Ethical a Priori, Openness and Diversity." *Journal of Philosophy of Education* 55 (6): 949–65.

Sticker, Martin, and David Bakhurst, eds.. 2021. "Kant on Education and Improvement: Themes and Problems." *Journal of Philosophy of Education* 55 (6): 909–20.

Stock, Kathleen. 2017. *Only Imagine: Fiction, Interpretation and Imagination*. Oxford: Oxford University Press.

Stokes, Dustin. 2014. "The Role of Imagination in Creativity." In *The Philosophy of Creativity*, edited by Elliot Samuel Paul and Scott Barry Kaufman, 157–84. New York: Oxford University Press.

Stokes, Dustin. 2016. "Imagination and Creativity." In *The Routledge Handbook of Philosophy of Imagination*, edited by Amy Kind, 247–62. London: Routledge

Stokes, Dustin. 2019a. "Memory, Imagery, and Self-Knowledge." *Avant* 10 (2): 1–18.

Stokes, Dustin. 2019b. "Mental Imagery and Fiction." *Canadian Journal of Philosophy* 49 (6): 731–54.

Stone, Tony, and Martin Davies, eds. 1995. *Mental Simulation: Evaluations and Applications.* Oxford: Blackwell.

Strawson, P.F. 1966. *The Bounds of Sense: An Essay on Kant's "Critique of Pure Reason."* London: Methuen.

Strawson, P.F. 1974. "Imagination in Perception." In *Freedom and Resentment, and Other Essays*, 45–65. London: Methuen.

Strohminger, Margot, and Juhani Yli-Vakkuri. 2017. "The Epistemology of Modality." *Analysis (Oxford)* 77 (4): 825–38.

Stroud, Scott R. 2014. *Kant and the Promise of Rhetoric*. University Park, PA: The Pennsylvania State University Press.

Stueber, Karsten. 2011. "Imagination, Empathy, and Moral Deliberation." *The Southern Journal of Philosophy* 49: 156–80.

Summa, Michela. 2022. "On the Functions of Examples in Critical Philosophy—Kant and Husserl." In *Phenomenology as Critique: Why Method Matters*, edited by Andreea Smaranda Aldea, David Carr, and Sara Heinämaa, 25–43. London: Routledge.

Summa, Michela, Thomas Fuchs, and Luca Vanzago, eds. 2017. *Imagination and Social Perspectives: Approaches from Phenomenology and Psychopathology*. London: Routledge.

Sutherland, Daniel. 2004. "The Role of Magnitude in Kant's Critical Philosophy." *Canadian Journal of Philosophy* 34 (3): 411–41.

Sutherland, Daniel. 2017. "Kant's Conception of Number." *The Philosophical Review* 126 (2): 147–90.

Sutherland, Daniel. 2022. *Kant's Mathematical World: Mathematics, Cognition, and Experience*. Cambridge: Cambridge University Press.

Sweet, Kristi. 2015. "Kant and the Liberal Arts: A Defense." *The Journal of Aesthetic Education* 49 (3): 1–14.

Sweet, Kristi. 2023. *Kant on Freedom, Nature, and Judgment: The Territory of the third Critique*. Cambridge: Cambridge University Press.

Symington, Paul. 2011. "Metaphysics Renewed: Kant's Schematized Categories and the Possibility of Metaphysics." *International Philosophical Quarterly* 51 (3): 285–301.

Tang, Yingying. 2018. "Imagination in the Appreciation of Nature: A Comparative Approach." *Philosophy East & West* 68 (3): 929–43.

Tetens, Johann Nicolas. 1913. *Über die allgemeine speculativische Philosophie. Philosophische Versuche über die menschliche Natur und ihre Entwickelung, erster Band*. Berlin: Reuther & Reichard.

Thomas, Alan. 2009. "Perceptual Presence and the Productive Imagination." *Philosophical Topics* 37 (1): 153–73.

Thomason, Laura E. 2015. "The Dilemma of Friendship in Austen's Emma." *The Eighteenth Century* 56 (2): 227–41.

Thompson, Michael L. 2013. *Imagination in Kant's Critical Philosophy*. Berlin: De Gruyter.

Timmermann, Jens. 2007. *Kant's Groundwork of the Metaphysics of Morals: A Commentary*. Cambridge: Cambridge University Press.

Timmermann, Jens. 2009. *Kant's* Groundwork of the Metaphysics of Morals: *A Critical Guide*. Cambridge Critical Guides. Cambridge: Cambridge University Press.

Timmermann, Jens. 2022. *Kant's Will at the Crossroads*. Oxford: Oxford University Press.

Tolley, Clinton. 2013. "The Non-Conceptuality of the Content of Intuitions: A New Approach." *Kantian Review* 18: 107–36.

420 BIBLIOGRAPHY

Tolley, Clinton. 2016. "The Difference Between Original, Metaphysical and Geometrical Representations of Space." In *Kantian Nonconceptualism*, edited by Dennis Schulting, 257–85. London: Palgrave Macmillan.

Tolley, Clinton. 2017. "Between 'Perception' and Understanding, From Leibniz to Kant." *Estudos Kantianos* 4 (2): 71–98.

Tolley, Clinton. 2019. "Kant on the Role of the Imagination (and Images) in the Transition from Intuition to Experience." In *The Imagination in German Idealism and Romanticism*, edited by Gerad Gentry and Konstantin Pollok, 27–47. Cambridge: Cambridge University Press.

Tolley, Clinton. 2020. "Kant on the Place of Cognition in the Progression of Our Representations." *Synthese* 197 (8): 3215–44.

Toon, Adam. 2012. *Models as Make-Believe: Imagination, Fiction and Scientific Representation*. London: Palgrave Macmillan.

Tracz, Brian. 2020. "Imagination and the Distinction Between Image and Intuition in Kant." *Ergo* 6: 1087–120.

Trivedi, Saam. 2017. *Imagination, Music, and the Emotions: A Philosophical Study*. Albany: State University of New York Press.

Tropper, Sarah. 2019. "The Importance of Imagination in Leibniz." In *Konzepte der Einbildungskraft in der Philosophie, den Wissenschaften und den Künsten des 18. Jahrhunderts*, edited by Rudolf Meer , Giuseppe Motta, und Gideon Stiening, 25–38. Berlin: De Gruyter.

Tuna, Emine Hande. 2020. "Imaginative Resistance." In *The Stanford Encyclopedia of Philosophy*, edited by Edward N. Zalta. Summer ed. Metaphysics Research Lab, Stanford University. https://plato.stanford.edu/archives/sum2020/entries/imaginative-resistance/.

Valaris, Markos. 2008. "Inner Sense, Self-Affection, and Temporal Consciousness in Kant's Critique of Pure Reason." *Philosophers' Imprint* 8: 1–18.

Van Leeuwen, Neil. 2011. "Imagination Is Where the Action Is." *The Journal of Philosophy* 108 (2): 55–77.

Van Leeuwen, Neil. 2013. "The Meanings of 'Imagine' Part I: Constructive Imagination." *Philosophy Compass* 8 (3): 220–30.

Van Leeuwen, Neil. 2014. "The Meanings of 'Imagine' Part II: Attitude and Action." *Philosophy Compass* 9 (11): 791–802.

Van Leeuwen, Neil. 2016. "Imagination and Action." In *The Routledge Handbook of Philosophy of Imagination*, edited by Amy Kind, 286–99. London: Routledge.

Varden, Helga. 2020. *Sex, Love, and Gender: A Kantian Theory*. Oxford: Oxford University Press.

Varden, Helga. 2021. "Towards a Kantian Theory of Philosophical Education and Wisdom: With the Help of Hannah Arendt." *Journal of Philosophy of Education* 55 (6): 1081–96.

Veal, Michael E. 2007. *Dub: Soundscapes and Shattered Songs in Jamaican Reggae*. Middletown, CT: Wesleyan University Press.

Velleman, J. David. 2000. *The Possibility of Practical Reason*. New York: Oxford University Press.

Vendrell Ferran, Íngrid. 2023. "Fictional Empathy, Imagination, and Knowledge of Value." In *Ethics and Empathy*, edited by Magnus Englander and Susi Ferrarello, 375–97. Lanham, MD: Rowan and Littlefield.

Vilhauer, Benjamin. 2021. "'Reason's Sympathy' and its Foundations in Productive Imagination." *Kantian Review* 26: 455–474.

Vilhauer, Benjamin. 2022. "'Reason's sympathy' and Others' Ends in Kant." *European Journal of Philosophy* 30: 96–112.

Villinger, Rahel. 2018. *Kant und die Imagination der Tiere*. Konstanz: Konstanz University Press.

Virgil. 2005. *Aeneid*. Translated by Stanley Lombardo. Indianapolis: Hackett.

Vogelmann, Rafael Graebin. 2018. "Can We Make Sense of Free Harmony?" *Studi Kantiani* 16 (1): 53–74.

Walden, Kenneth. n.d. *The Imperative of Genius*. Manuscript.

Walsh, W.H. 1957/8. "Schematism." *Kant-Studien* 49 (1–4): 95–106.

Walton, Kendall L. 1990. *Mimesis as Make-Believe: On the Foundations of the Representational Arts*. Cambridge, MA: Harvard University Press.

Wang, Weijia. 2020. "Kant's Mathematical Sublime: The Absolutely Great in Aesthetic Estimation." *Kantian Review* 25 (3): 465–85.

Ware, Owen. 2009. "The Duty of Self-Knowledge." *Philosophy and Phenomenological Research* 79 (3): 671–98.

Warnick, Bryan. 2008. *Imitation and Education: A Philosophical Inquiry into Learning By Example*. Stony Brook: State University of New York Press.

Warnock, G.J. 1949. "Concepts and Schematism." *Analysis* 9 (5): 77–82.

Watkins, Eric. 2017. "Kant on the Distinction between Sensibility and Understanding." In *Kant's Critique of Pure Reason*, edited by Jim O'Shea, 9–27. Cambridge: Cambridge University Press.

Watkins, Eric. forthcoming. "Kant's Criticism of Metaphysics." In *The Oxford Handbook of Kant*, edited by Anil Gomes and Andrew Stephenson. Oxford: Oxford University Press.

Watkins, Eric, and Marcus Willaschek. 2017a. "Givenness and Cognition: Reply to Grüne and Chignell." *Journal of the History of Philosophy* 55 (1): 143–52.

Watkins, Eric, and Marcus Willaschek. 2017b. "Kant's Account of Cognition." *Journal of the History of Philosophy* 55 (1): 83–112.

Waxman, Wayne. 1991. *Kant's Model of the Mind: A New Interpretation of Transcendental Idealism*. New York: Oxford University Press.

Waxman, Wayne. 2014. *Kant's Anatomy of the Intelligent Mind*. New York: Oxford University Press.

Weatherston, Martin. 2002. *Heidegger's Interpretation of Kant: Categories, Imagination and Temporality*. London: Palgrave Macmillan.

Wedin, Michael V. 1988. *Mind and Imagination in Aristotle*. New Haven: Yale University Press.

Weinberg, Jonathan M., and Aaron Meskin. 2006. "Puzzling over the Imagination: Philosophical Problems, Architectural Solutions." In *The Architecture of the Imagination*, edited by Shaun Nichols, 175–202. Oxford: Oxford University Press.

Weinberg, Jonathan M., and Aaron Meskin. 2011. "Imagination Unblocked." In *The Aesthetic Mind*, edited by Elisabeth Schellekens and Peter Goldie, 239–53. Oxford: Oxford University Press.

Wenzel, Christian Helmut. 2005. "Spielen nach Kant die Kategorien schon bei der Wahrnehmung eine Rolle? Peter Rohs und John McDowell." *Kant-Studien* 96 (4): 407–26.

Werner, Preston J. 2016. "Moral Perception and the Contents of Experience." *Journal of Moral Philosophy* 13 (3): 294–317.

Werner, Preston J. 2017. "A Posteriori Ethical Intuitionism and the Problem of Cognitive Penetrability." *European Journal of Philosophy* 25 (4): 1791–809.

Werner, Preston J. 2018. "Moral Perception without (Prior) Moral Knowledge." *Journal of Moral Philosophy* 15 (2): 164–81.

Westra, Adam. 2016. *The Typic in Kant's Critique of Practical Reason: Moral Judgment and Symbolic Representation*. Kantstudien-Ergänzungshefte. Berlin: De Gruyter.

Wheatley, Phillis. 2001. *Complete Writings*. New York: Penguin Books.

Wiesing, Lambert. 1996. "Phänomenologie des Bildes nach Husserl und Sartre." *Phänomenologische Forschungen* 30: 255–81.

Willaschek, Marcus, and Eric Watkins. 2020. "Kant on Cognition and Knowledge." *Synthese* 197 (8): 3195–213.

Williams, Jessica. 2012. "How Conceptually Guided Are Kantian Intuitions?" *History of Philosophy Quarterly* 29 (1): 57–78.

Williams, Jessica. 2018. "Kant on the Original Synthesis of Understanding and Sensibility." *British Journal for the History of Philosophy* 26 (1): 66–86.

Williams, Jessica. 2020. "'The Shape of a Four-Footed Animal in General': Kant on Empirical Schemata and the System of Nature." *HOPOS* 10 (1): 1–23.

Williams, Jessica. 2021. "Kant on Aesthetic Attention." *The British Journal of Aesthetics* 61 (4): 421–35.

Williams, Jessica. 2022. "Attention and the Free Play of the Faculties." *Kantian Review* 27 (1): 43–59.

Williamson, Diane. 2015. *Kant's Theory of Emotion: Emotional Universalism*. New York: Palgrave Macmillan.

Williamson, Timothy. 2007. "Philosophical Knowledge and Knowledge of Counterfactuals." *Grazer Philosophische Studien* 74 (1): 89–123.

Williamson, Timothy. 2016. "Knowing by Imagining." In *Knowledge Through Imagination*, edited by Amy Kind and Peter Kung, 113–23. Oxford: Oxford University Press.

Wiltsher, Nick. 2016. "Against the Additive View of Imagination." *Australasian Journal of Philosophy* 94 (2): 266–82.

Wiltsher, Nick and Aaron Meskin. 2016. "Art and Imagination." In *The Routledge Handbook of Philosophy of Imagination*, edited by Amy Kind, 179–91. London: Routledge.

Winegar, Reed. 2013. "An Unfamiliar and Positive Law: On Kant and Schiller."*Archiv für Geschichte der Philosophie* 95 (3): 275–97.

Winegar, Reed. 2021. "Kant's Antinomy of Taste and the Supersensible." In *The Court of Reason*, edited by Beatrix Himmelmann and Camilla Serck-Hanssen, 1095–102. Berlin: De Gruyter.

Winegar, Reed. 2022. "Kant's Three Conceptions of Infinite Space." *Journal of the History of Philosophy* 60(4): 635–59.

Wolff, Christian. 1968. *Christiani Wolffii Psychologia empirica*. Hildesheim: Olms.

Wood, Allen. 2013. "Kant on Practical Reason." *Kant on Practical Justification: Interpretive Essays*, edited by Mark Timmons and Sorin Baiasu, 58–86. Oxford: Oxford University Press.

Wood, Allen. 2018. "Feeling and Desire in the Human Animal." In *Kant and the Faculty of Feeling*, edited by Kelly Sorensen and Diane Williamson, 88–106. Cambridge: Cambridge University Press.

Wood, Allen. 2020. *Kant and Religion*. Cambridge: Cambridge University Press.

Wretzel, Joshua. 2018. "Organic Imagination as Intuitive Intellect: Self-knowledge and Self-constitution in Hegel's Early Critique of Kant." *European Journal of Philosophy* 26 (3): 958–73.

Wuerth, Julian. 2014. *Kant on Mind, Action, and Ethics*. Oxford: Oxford University Press.

Wyrębska-Đermanović, Ewa. 2021. "Kantian Moral Education for the Future of Humanity: The Climate Change Challenge." *Journal of Philosophy of Education* 55 (6): 1045–56.

Yablo, Stephen. 1993. "Is Conceivability a Guide to Possibility?" *Philosophy and Phenomenological Research* 53 (1): 1–42.

Young, J.M. 1982. "Kant on the Construction of Arithmetical Concepts." *Kant-Studien* 73 (1): 17–46.

Young, J.M. 1984. "Construction, Schematism, and Imagination." *Topoi* 3 (2): 123–31.

Young, J.M. 1988. "Kant's View of Imagination." *Kant-Studien* 79 (2): 140–64.

Zagirnyak, Mikhail. 2021. "Sociability and Education in Kant and Hessen." *Journal of Philosophy of Education* 55 (6): 1112–25.

Zagzebski, Linda. 2017. *Exemplarist Moral Theory*. Oxford: Oxford University Press.

Zinkin, Melissa. 2003. "Film and the Transcendental Imagination: Kant and Hitchcock's The Lady Vanishes." In *Imagination, Philosophy and the Arts*, edited by Matthew Kieran and Dominic Lopes, 254–67. London: Routledge.

Zinkin, Melissa. 2006. "Intensive Magnitudes and the Normativity of Taste." In *Aesthetics and Cognition in Kant's Critical Philosophy*, edited by Rebecca Kukla, 138–61. Cambridge: Cambridge University Press.

Zinkin, Melissa. 2021. "Kant on Wonder as the Motive to Learn." *Journal of Philosophy of Education* 55 (6): 921–34.

Zöller, Gunther. 2019. "The Faculty of Intuitions A Priori: Kant on the Productive Power of the Imagination." In *The Imagination in German Idealism and Romanticism*, edited by Gerad Gentry and Konstantin Pollok, 66–85. Cambridge: Cambridge University Press.

Zuckert, Rachel. 2005. "Boring Beauty and Universal Morality: Kant on the Ideal of Beauty." *Inquiry* 48 (2): 107–30.

Zuckert, Rachel. 2006. "The Purposiveness of Form: A Reading of Kant's Aesthetic Formalism." *Journal of the History of Philosophy* XLIV (4): 599–622.

Zuckert, Rachel. 2007. *Kant on Beauty and Biology: An Interpretation of the "Critique of Judgment."* Cambridge: Cambridge University Press.

Index

Because the index has been created to work across multiple formats, indexed terms for which a page range is given (e.g. 52–53, 66–70, etc.) may occasionally appear only on some, but not all, of the pages within the range.

Aeneid 109
aesthetic ideas 23, 73–4, 251 n.4, 283–4, 288–98, 314, 360, 363–5, 368
   see also genius
aesthetic perfection 47 n.56, 96 n.68, 117, 263–4, 330 n.13, 380–1
affection 1, 41–2, 59 n.27, 70, 77–80, 82, 84–6, 89 n.55, 91, 93–5, 97
affinity 59 n.28, 291, 294–5, 314, 365
agreeable 253–5, 259, 262–3
analogies 43–4, 118–19, 126–7, 313–14, 362–3, 376
Analogies of Experience 165, 231–3, 241
anatomist example 113–17, 119–20, 354
animals 6, 154
anticipation 6, 10, 12, 76, 103, 143 n.32, 146
Anticipations of Perception 80 n.31, 140, 228–31, 238 n.46, 239–40
appearances 75–6, 83 n.40, 85, 91–2, 140, 142–3, 158–60, 165, 171, 174–5, 179, 202–3, 205–9, 214–16, 226–33, 235–6, 238–40, 355–7, 370
apperception 52, 64 n.40, 133 n.11, 140 n.27, 163 n.81, 167, 184 n.24, 194–5, 198, 204, 205 nn.53, 54, 227 n.25
archetype 308, 343–5, 367–8
Arendt, Hannah 23–4, 106 n.17, 153 n.61, 384 n.60
Aristotle 1, 106–7, 364 n.19
arithmetic 181–2, 188, 199 n.47
association 6 n.16, 21–2, 55–61, 124–5, 144, 166, 274–7, 290, 308–9, 319
attention 275–6, 382 n.52
attributes
   aesthetic 291–2, 314
   logical 289, 291
Austen, Jane 364–5
Axioms of Intuition 228–30

Baumgarten, Alexander 2, 106–8, 117 n.42
beauty
   artistic 251–2, 262–3, 280, 282–3;
      see also aesthetic ideas; free play; genius
   judgments of 252–5, 257, 301–3
   natural 251–2, 262–3, 280

belief 1 n.2, 7 n.18, 9 n.24, 12–17
Blake, William 251, 254–5, 261, 264–6, 272, 276–8
boredom 273, 277, 381 n.51

Cabot, Ella Lyman 23–4, 334, 377 n.45
Carey, Mariah 60–1, 104, 108, 144, 171, 228–9, 235–6
categorical imperative 330 n.11, 337–8, 340, 349–51, 374–5, 390
categories
   dynamical 209, 233, 240–2, 271–2
   and empirical intuition 147–8, 179–80, 202–10, 214, 226–33, 235–7
   and figurative synthesis 194–202, 217–18
   logical content of 220–1, 223–7, 234, 237–8, 240–1
   mathematical 209, 233–40, 242, 271–2, 279
   see also schematism
causality
   category of 208–9, 232–3, 240–2, 272
   and freedom 355–6, 370
   and imagination 86–7
   and sensibility 41–2
   and understanding 41–2
cognition
   broad versus narrow 35–40, 49, 52, 93, 119–21, 125–6, 136–7, 158, 160–1, 172–4, 268–9
   faculty of 13–14, 33–5, 41, 48–9, 53–4, 306–7, 329–30, 335–6
   practical 46
   symbolic 46
   theoretical 18, 45–8, 321–2
   versus belief and knowledge 14–15
   versus thought 44, 93
cognitive function
   of imagination 26–7, 52, 66–7, 69, 95–100, 102, 111–12, 115–19, 125–6, 133, 135–6, 157–8, 170, 174–5, 179, 184–5, 193, 196–7, 201–2, 210, 215–21, 243–6, 258–9, 268–9, 271, 280–1, 297–8, 317, 321, 330–1, 363, 380, 383

426 INDEX

cognitive function (*cont.*)
  object-facing versus subject-facing aspect
    46–9, 70–1, 96–7, 115, 258–9, 268–9, 274,
    278, 280–1, 297–8, 321, 330–1
  object-facing versus subject-facing
    end 258–9, 268–9, 274, 278, 280–1,
    297–8
  of sensibility 42–9, 70–1, 94–5, 97–8
  of sense 69–71, 95, 97–8, 157, 174–5
  of understanding 42–9, 165, 169–70, 174–5
common root 3, 17–18, 41, 50, 52–3
community 240–2
composition 26, 40, 55, 65, 74, 81–3, 87, 105,
  138, 140–1, 227–31, 233, 235–6, 238–40,
  242, 265–8, 270–5, 277–80, 304–6, 320–1
comprehension 47–8, 69, 96–8, 100, 102,
  113–19, 123–8, 133, 196, 213, 219–20,
  225–6, 245, 263, 267–9, 271, 294–5, 297–8,
  300, 304, 308, 311–14, 318, 321, 330–2, 353,
  359–61, 363–5, 374–5, 379–81, 389–91
concepts 42
  empirical 27, 133–8, 147, 152–7, 160–2,
    168–9, 173–6, 179–80, 211, 220–1, 239–40,
    271–2, 279, 286–7, 292–3
  formation 29–30
  generality 42, 148–9
  indeterminate 257, 260–1, 269, 271, 277–8,
    336, 343–6, 349
  undetermined 257, 260–1, 269, 271, 277–8
  pure *see* categories
  supersensible 118–19, 306, 315–16, 321–2,
    353–7, 360, 369–70; *see also* reason, ideas of
  see also conceptualism; free play,
    conceptualization; understanding
conceptualism 8, 20, 23, 27–8, 97, 133–6, 156,
  164–5, 175, 179–80, 183 n.22, 205, 207–8,
  211, 213–14, 239–40, 243, 250, 280
connection 171, 227–8, 231–3, 241–2
conscious representation of objects 7, 15, 17–18,
  36–7, 40, 49, 85, 119, 127–8, 137, 158–60,
  163–5, 168, 172, 174–5, 205, 207–8
constraint
  architectural 17–20, 245
  conceptual 127, 150–2, 154, 175, 213,
    219–21, 225–6, 234, 237–8, 240–1,
    245, 249, 255–6, 260–1, 273–4, 282,
    288–9, 317
  epistemic 16–17, 20, 132
  formal 87–8, 94, 97–100
  imaginative 290
  material 87–94, 97–100, 108–9, 185
  volitional 16–20
contemplation 251–3, 262, 301, 379

creativity
  in aesthetics *see* aesthetic ideas; free play,
    creativity in; genius, creativity in; sublime,
    creativity in
  in practical agency and morality 342,
    348, 360–6

Deduction
  A Deduction 52, 58–9, 64–5, 84–5,
    92, 135–62
  aim and strategy of B Deduction 202–4,
    208–9
  B Deduction 57, 59, 61–4, 87–8, 92, 99, 105,
    140–1, 143–4, 166–7, 178, 182–3, 188–211,
    213–14, 217–19, 225–6, 229–31, 234–5, 243
  A versus B Deduction 61–2, 143 n.34, 178 n.2
  Metaphysical 58 n.26, 92, 144 n.36, 182,
    222 n.19, 224
definitions 101–2
deliberation 331–2, 339, 341, 390
delusion 19 n.82, 76, 325 n.3
demonstration 39–40, 113, 116, 119, 121, 126–7,
  161–2, 173–4, 312, 318–19, 354–5, 369,
  387, 389
desire
  faculty of 13–14, 34–5, 306–7, 329–30, 335–9,
    343, 348–9, 351–2, 361–2
  like imagining 13
  satisfaction 336
determinacy
  determinacy achievement 37–8, 137,
    158–61, 172–3
  spatio-temporal 38, 82–6, 97–8, 100, 104–6,
    111, 127–8, 137, 145–6, 158–61, 165, 170,
    172–5, 179, 187–8, 191–2, 196–7, 200,
    206–11, 214, 225–31, 233, 236–42, 244,
    265–7, 271, 275
Dewey, John 23–4
Dickinson, Emily 353
disinterest 253, 259, 301, 379 n.48
dreams 9–12, 17–20, 48, 68–9, 76, 90–1, 274 n.61
dub 117–18, 120–1, 123–5, 139

Eliot, George 309, 344–5
Eliot, T.S. 55–6, 59
Ellison, Ralph 287–91, 287 n.11, 293–4, 296–7
empirical concept formation 29–30, 160 n.74,
  263 n.36
entertainment 274–6, 279–80, 293
enthusiasm 326 n.4, 344 n.18, 355 n.3, 367
ens imaginarium 178, 181–3, 210
estimation 303–4, 306
Euclid 188

even-without-presence definition of
imagination 7, 26–7, 54, 71, 74, 87–8,
106–11, 126–8, 133, 146, 156, 176, 195–6,
244–5, 265–6, 332–4, 391
examples
in education 372, 375–81
fictional versus real 375
in Kant's writing 373–5
moral 369–89
in perception 118, 153–6, 160–2, 381–9
exhibition 114–21
definition of imagination 26–7, 111–14,
121–7, 146, 244–5, 265–6, 332–3
direct 29, 127, 150–1, 219–22, 225–6, 269,
312, 317, 320–1, 353–4, 363, 366–89
indirect 28–9, 127, 291–2, 300–1, 312–22,
359–66
experience 18, 137–9, 206, 231, 241
see also stages of experience

fantasy 1–2, 10–11, 16, 18–20, 26–7, 102, 106–8,
111, 131, 136, 275, 334, 343 n.16, 345 n.21,
349 n.29, 391
feeling of pleasure and displeasure 79–81, 89–90
and aesthetic judgments 252–5, 263
faculty of 13–14, 34–5, 53–4, 244,
329–30, 335
and happiness 325–6, 336–7, 345–7, 351–2, 366
and the sublime 299, 301–3
fiction 22, 24, 90 n.58, 276 n.65, 294, 309, 348,
364, 375, 389–90
see also novels
formal constraint on imagining *see* constraint
formation 55, 81–2, 87
concept 29–30, 155 n.67, 198–201, 212–13,
222–3, 263 n.36
definition of imagination 26–7, 102–6, 111,
126–7, 244–5, 265–6
faculty of 7, 103–5, 142, 176
in perception, *see* images, perceptual
Frederick the Great 291–2, 363
free play
apprehension in 265–8, 270, 274–80
composition in 265–8, 270–5, 277–80
conceptualization in 260–2, 269, 271, 276–8
creativity in 259–65, 270–80
exhibition in 250, 256–7, 260–1, 265–73,
277–80
freedom of 255–9, 274–80
multicognitive interpretation 28, 250–1, 257,
265, 280
precognitive interpretation 28, 250–1,
256–7, 269–70

and subject- and object-facing cognitive
ends 258–9, 268–9, 274, 278, 280–1
freedom
idea of freedom 353, 355–6, 370
and the sublime 299–300, 310–11, 317–21
see also causality, and freedom; creativity; free
play, freedom; genius, freedom;
spontaneity, and freedom
freezing water example 105, 206–7, 209, 214,
226, 232–5, 241–2, 374 n.37
friendship 308, 364–7, 380–1
function *see* cognitive function

genius 21–3, 28, 66, 282–7, 297–8
creativity in 288–9, 291–8
freedom of 282–4, 286–97
see also aesthetic ideas; Ellison, Ralph
geometry *see* mathematics
Gibbons, Sarah 3
good
aesthetic judgments of the 253, 256–7,
260 n.27, 263, 301
morally 315–16, 356–9, 362–3, 370,
380–1, 384
God 44–6, 48, 93, 118–19, 325–6
gratitude 262–3, 337–9, 341–2, 356, 358, 362–3,
369–70, 380–2

hallucination 10–11, 17–20, 72, 107–8, 113,
124–5, 173, 246
happiness
concept of 336–7, 343, 345–6, 349
and duty 348–9
as ideal of imagination 308–10, 319, 325–6,
329, 334–5, 343–9
principle of 335–9, 348
see also desire, faculty of
Hegel, G.W. F. 3, 37 n.19, 52–3, 391
Heidegger, Martin 3, 39 n.26, 50, 51 n.2, 53 n.6,
62 n.34, 75 n.18, 84 n.46, 92 n.64, 144 n.35,
178 n.2, 178 n.3, 181, 183–4, 212–13,
222–3, 391
highest good 29–30
Highsmith, Patricia 90–1, 346–7
Hobbes, Thomas 1–2, 106–7
house examples 18–20, 44–5, 76–7, 90–1, 103,
105, 110–11, 206–7, 209, 214, 226, 229–31,
266–7, 275–6, 278, 374 n.37
Hughes, Fiona 3
Hume, David 1 n.2, 4 n.10, 13 n.56, 18–20, 23–4,
107 n.20, 132 n.7, 202–3, 276–7
Husserl, Edmund 2, 106–7
hypochondria 17, 19

428 INDEX

ideas
 moral ideas 353–63, 365–6, 368–70, 373, 375, 380–1, 384, 386, 389–90
 see also aesthetic ideas; freedom, idea of; reason, ideas of
ideals 308, 343–4, 366
 of happiness 29, 308–10, 319, 326–7, 329, 335, 343–9, 352
 of imagination 29, 308–10, 319, 326–7, 329, 335, 343–9, 352
 moral 25, 29, 366–70, 389–90
 of reason 367–8
 of sensibility 367–8
illusion 173, 367
 see also delusion; hallucination; hypochondria
illustration 82, 110 n.27, 116, 123–4, 142–3, 374
images 1–2, 22, 40, 48, 72–3, 103–4, 173, 261, 277–8, 291–2, 294–5, 355, 373
 perceptual 141–9, 152–62, 168–75, 206, 226–31, 233, 235–40, 242, 244, 246, 265–7, 270–1, 273, 277, 292–3, 304–5, 314, 359–60, 383–6
 pure 191–3, 234–5
imitation 82, 103, 285–6, 379
intention 286–7
intuition
 blind 44–5, 94–5
 formal 177, 180–4, 188–94, 196–8, 201–2, 206–11, 213–14, 217–20, 225–6, 233–5, 239–40, 243–4, 246
 form of 180, 182–5, 188–9, 192–3, 204, 208–9
 given versus made 78–82, 104, 180, 185–93
 and immediacy 42, 52, 70–2, 74–7, 79, 81–2, 87–8, 94–5, 97–8, 110
 intuitive representation 54, 69–73
 of imagination 26, 71–4
 manifold of 55, 62, 65, 74, 79–80, 82–3, 140–1, 143–6, 149, 154, 157–8, 160, 168–9, 190, 194–5, 228, 231, 244, 266–7, 277
 pure 27–8, 91–2, 132–4, 177–80, 182–93, 197, 199, 201–4, 208–11, 213–14, 216–21, 225–7, 234–5, 243–4
 singularity 42, 52, 147–8
invention 11–12, 55–6, 74, 76, 90–1, 113, 274–5, 277, 342, 348, 375
involuntary imagining 18–20

Johnson, Mark 24–5, 326–7
judgment
 aesthetic 252–5, 262, 301–3, 362–3
 cognitive 252, 301–2
 determining 252, 255–9, 268–9, 272–3, 278, 297–8, 301, 384
 power of 112–13, 116 n.41, 122–4, 147

of recognition 162–75, 227–8, 232–3, 241–2, 259–60, 264–5, 275, 384–5
reflecting 252, 301, 384
 see also stages of experience, understanding; subsumption

Keats, John 260
Kind, Amy 16–17, 245
know-how 116, 118, 150–2, 155, 175, 220–1, 245, 284–5, 341
knowledge 14–21, 35, 116, 150–2, 220, 284–5, 308
Kung, Peter 16–17, 245

Langland-Hassan, Peter 13
limitation 237–8
logical content 220–1, 223–7, 234, 237–8, 240–1
logical functions 196–7, 222–4
logical possibility 39, 137
Longuenesse, Béatrice 181–5, 189–90, 202, 204, 212–13, 223

magnitude 181–7, 189, 192–3, 201–2, 204, 228 n.26, 229 n.28, 234–7, 239 n.48, 271 n.53, 303–6
make-believe 11, 22
material constraint on imagining *see* constraint
mathematics 6, 17–18
 arithmetic 181–2
 and beauty 273, 279
 concepts 198–201
 construction 12, 73–4, 91, 108, 124, 147 n.44, 186–8, 190–1, 199–200
 geometry 91, 108, 181–2, 186–8, 190–1, 193, 200–1, 273, 278
 and perception 236–7
 and schematism 147 n.44
matter 80, 92–3, 185–6, 228–31, 233, 238–40, 266 n.43, 266–7, 271, 304–5
maxims 64–5, 334–5, 337–9, 341, 349–51, 358–9, 370–1, 376, 379–80, 387–8
McDowell, John 3–4
mechanics 181–2, 188, 199 n.47
memory 10–12, 18–20, 29–30, 76, 107–8, 146
Merleau-Ponty, Maurice 168 n.89, 239 n.49
metaphor 22, 35 n.7, 42 n.35, 291–5, 314, 330, 350 n.35, 358 n.7, 359–60
modality 215, 233
 knowledge of 17
 see also modal achievement of cognition; practicability of morality; real possibility
modal achievement of cognition 37–40, 119–21, 137, 160–2, 173–4
moral action
 correct/incorrect 371, 377–80, 385–6, 388
 worthy/unworthy 371, 377–80, 385–6

moral imagination 24–5, 326–7, 390
moral law *see* categorical imperative
moral progress 366–8, 389–90
moral salience 339 n.10
motives 358, 371, 375, 377–8, 386, 390
Murdoch, Iris 23–4, 382

negation 237–40
non-conceptualism *see* conceptualism
non-sensory imagining 6–7, 9–11, 68–9, 100,
    127–8, 330–1, 340, 351
Norris, Henry 372–5, 377–80
novels 294, 346–8, 367
    see also Austen, Jane; Ellison, Ralph; fiction;
    Highsmith, Patricia; Woolf, Virginia

objective reality 39–40, 119–21, 125–6, 137,
    161–2, 173–4, 387
"On Kästner's Treatises" 186–8
originality 285–6

perception
    amodal perception 14, 110, 132, 146
    perceptual images, *see* images, perceptual
    perceptual presence 14
    and schematism 147–57, 160, 168–9, 173–5
    and synthesis 143–6, 149, 152, 154–8,
        168–73, 175
    see also stages of experience, imagination
perfection 117, 263–4, 308, 327, 343–4, 366–8,
    377, 380–1, 389–90
perspective shifting 11
perspective taking 22
physician example 116, 118, 123–4, 151,
    155–6, 341
Plato 283 n.2, 366 n.25
poetry 113, 124, 253, 262–4, 266, 274 n.60,
    283 n.2, 284, 291–2, 294, 362–3
    see also *Aeneid*; Blake, William; Dickinson,
    Emily; Eliot, T.S.; Frederick the
    Great; Keats, John; Rilke, Rainer Maria
practicability of morality 372, 382, 387–9
pre-Critical 54–5, 64, 66, 99, 102–6, 143–4
problem-solving 11, 21
productive imagination 11–12, 21, 56–61,
    61 n.32, 73–4, 90–2, 191, 194–5,
    217–18, 228, 244, 274–7, 282, 286–7,
    290, 293–5
propositional imagining 9

reality 9, 11, 16–17, 21–2, 237–40
    see also objective reality
real possibility 38–40, 119–21, 125–6,
    161, 387
    practical versus theoretical 387–9

reason 1, 3, 17, 52–3, 316–17, 320–2, 348–9, 368
    and artistic production 284, 286–7
    fact of reason 387
    faculty of 299–300, 302–3, 307
    human 118–19, 331, 376, 380
    ideas of 121, 126–7, 260 n.29, 261 n.30,
        292–3, 308, 311, 315, 317–18, 344, 360, 368
    ideals of 367–8
    imagination as instrument of, *see* sublime
    practical 25, 300, 302–3, 311, 326–9, 335–8,
        353–9, 361, 370–2, 390
    prudential 345
    theoretical 300, 302–3, 305–8, 311,
        318–20, 362
receptivity
    and beauty 253, 362–3
    and the faculty of desire 335–6
    and imagination 53–61, 69, 77–8, 81, 84–94,
        97–8, 100, 108–9, 126–8, 140–2, 180, 185,
        193, 210, 245
    and sense 70, 77–81, 95–8, 104, 123, 157–60,
        165, 174–5, 195–6, 341, 383
    of sensibility 41–2, 52, 55, 62, 70, 77–8, 98–9,
        106, 109, 125–6, 182–4, 189–90,
        210–11, 215
recognition, *see* judgment, of
    recognition; synthesis, of recognition
reflection 172, 312–14, 316, 378–9
    see also judgment, reflecting
regulative use 29–30, 366–7
reproductive imagination 6, 11–12, 56–61,
    89–90, 144–6, 154–6, 162–3, 166–7,
    169–72, 229–31, 235–6, 246, 274–5, 290
    see also association
respect 316–19, 325–6, 338 n.9, 339, 362, 364–7,
    372–3, 378–9, 382–8
revolution 24, 348
Rilke, Rainer Maria 359–60

Sartre, Jean Paul 2
Schellenberg, Susanna 13
schematism 147–52
    art of 20, 150–1, 212
    of mathematical categories 234–40
    of dynamical categories 240–2
    and time 218–21, 225–6, 234, 240–1
    transcendental schemata 217–21, 225–7, 233
    without concepts 269
    see also exhibition, direct; perception, and
    schematism
Schiller, Friedrich 327–9, 353
science 17–18, 21, 116 n.40, 150–1, 199 n.47,
    263 n.36, 274 n.61, 279 n.67, 284–5
self-knowledge 17
self-opacity 371, 375

430 INDEX

sense 97–8, 100
  cognitive function of 95, 97, 123–4
  inner versus outer 75–6, 79, 89–90
  intuitions of 71–2, 74, 108, 133–4, 204, 214
  process of 77–81, 104, 110, 123
  sensing 14, 16, 69, 341, 383
  see also stages of experience, sense
sensation 36, 59, 79–81, 88–91, 108–9, 140,
  185–6, 228–31, 238–9, 253, 262, 266–7
  merely subjective 80–1, 89–90
  objective 80–1, 85, 89–90, 158–9
sensibility
  bipartite account 7, 14, 26, 68–71, 93–100,
    104, 134–5, 157, 204
  functional profile, *see* cognitive function, of
    sensibility
  imagination as greatest faculty of 68
  as faculty of intuition 49, 54, 70–1, 74
  see also intuition; receptivity, of sensibility;
    space; time; Transcendental Aesthetic
sensibility view of imagination 26, 51, 54–61,
  68–9, 98–100, 195–6
sensible qualities 229–31, 238
sensory imagining 9–11, 68–9, 100, 127–8,
  330–1, 340, 351
Shakespeare, William 283 n.2
Smith, Adam 23–4
space
  concepts of 198–202
  as infinite 181–2, 184–7, 189, 192–3,
    201–2, 204
  mereology of 181–7, 189, 192–3, 204
  as singular 181–7, 189, 192–3
  shapes 82–3, 100, 104, 145–6, 154, 191–2,
    273, 275
  see also determinacy, spatio-temporal;
    intuition, formal intuition; intuition, form
    of intuition; intuition, given versus
    made; mathematics, geometry
spontaneity
  absolute versus relative 86–7, 94–5,
    97–8, 100
  and freedom 355–6, 370
  of imagination 7–8, 26, 55–62, 66–7, 69–70,
    77–8, 81, 86–100, 104–6, 111, 127–8, 133,
    142–4, 157, 174–5, 180, 185, 195–6,
    254, 391
  of practical reason 335–6
  of understanding 41–2, 49, 52–4, 61–3, 95–6,
    195, 254
stages of experience
  imagination stage 27, 135–6, 138–40, 156–65,
    168–75, 179, 204, 206–8, 210–11, 227–8,
    233, 242, 384–5

  sense stage 27, 135–6, 138–9, 157–62, 165,
    170, 172, 174–5, 179, 204–11, 226
  three 27, 135, 137–9, 175, 179
  understanding stage 27, 135–6, 138–9, 156–8,
    162–75, 179, 206–7, 210–11, 226, 232–3,
    240–3, 384–5
Strawson, P.F. 3–4
sublime
  creativity in 300–1, 312, 315, 317–18, 321
  dynamical 301–3, 306–11, 319–20, 361
  judgments of 301–3
  mathematical 301–7, 310, 318–19, 361–2
substance 45, 137–8, 223–5, 227, 231, 240–2,
  271–2, 290
subsumption 92–3, 123, 138, 147–8, 152, 166–9,
  172–5, 215–16, 252, 255–8, 260, 264–5,
  272–3, 301, 357, 384
supposition 22
symbols 46, 48, 73, 126–7, 291–3, 295, 313–16,
  359–60, 362–3
sympathy 23–4, 325 n.1, 326 n.5, 327–8, 331–2,
  342 n.14
synopsis 84 n.45
synthesis
  of apprehension 58–9, 87 n.51, 92, 112 n.29,
    140–1, 143–6, 154–6, 162–3, 169–72,
    205–8, 227 n.25, 229–31, 235–6, 246,
    265–8, 270, 274–80, 304–5
  figurative 62–3, 92, 177–8, 180–4, 191,
    194–202, 204–9, 213–14, 216–20, 225–7,
    233–4, 239–40, 243, 246
  and imaginative activity 26, 40, 55, 58–61,
    81–2, 84–7, 92, 105–6, 266–7, 386
  intellectual 172, 174–5, 195, 197–8, 233, 242
  in perception 143–7, 149, 151–8, 168–75,
    205–9, 229–31, 235–8, 242, 246
  of recognition 162–75
  of reproduction 144–6, 154–6, 162–3,
    169–72, 229–31, 246
  threefold 59, 143–4, 162–3
  and understanding 62–3
  see also composition, connection

taxonomy question 8–9
  external 12–16, 50–1, 69, 100, 135, 139, 175
  internal 9–12, 56–7
third thing view of imagination 26, 51–4,
  67–8, 98–100
thought experiments 17, 330, 340, 375 n.39
time
  concepts of 198–202
  determination 218–21, 225–6, 234, 240–1
  as infinite 181–2, 184–5, 189, 192–3,
    201–2, 204

mereology 181–5, 192–3, 204
sequence, series, and play 83, 100, 104–5,
  159–60, 171, 188, 192, 206–7, 214,
  232–3, 266–7
as singular 181–5, 188, 192–3, 204
see also determinacy, spatio-temporal;
  intuition, formal; intuition, form of;
  intuition, pure; schematism, and time
totality 234–5, 306, 315
Transcendental Aesthetic 85, 178, 181–4, 186–9,
  193–4, 202–4, 212–13
transformation
  and creativity 21, 293
  in experience 138–9, 141, 157
  practical 24, 334, 346–7, 352
Typic 350–1, 356–9, 369–70, 384

understanding
  as faculty of concepts 49, 64–6, 194, 256–7,
    267–8, 270, 301
  in free play 254–9, 262, 270, 273–5, 278, 280
  in genius 282–3, 286–90, 297–8, 302–3
  see also apperception; categories; cognitive
    function, of understanding; concepts;

judgment; spontaneity, of understanding;
  stages of experience, understanding;
  synthesis, intellectual
understanding view of imagination 26, 51, 61–6,
  68, 98–100, 195
unity question 5–8, 127–8, 246, 280–1, 391–2
universalizability test 349–52, 358–9
use question 16
  aesthetic 21–3
  epistemic 16–21
  practical 23–6

van Gogh, Vincent 262–3
visualization 9–11, 18–20, 55–6, 68–9, 76, 340,
  348, 350–1
vocation 28–9, 300–1, 311, 316–20, 361
voluntary imagining 18–20, 30, 245,
  274–5, 277

Walton, Kendall 5–6, 8, 33 n.1
Waxman, Wayne 181, 183–5
will 335
Wolff, Christian 106–8
Woolf, Virginia 23, 108, 112

The manufacturer's authorised representative in the EU for product safety is
Oxford University Press España S.A. of el Parque Empresarial San Fernando de
Henares, Avenida de Castilla, 2 – 28830 Madrid (www.oup.es/en or product.
safety@oup.com). OUP España S.A. also acts as importer into Spain of products
made by the manufacturer.

www.ingramcontent.com/pod-product-compliance
Lightning Source LLC
Chambersburg PA
CBHW072052290825
31867CB00004B/343